Energy Policy in Perspective

CRAUFURD D. GOODWIN, EDITOR

Energy Policy in Perspective: Today's Problems, Yesterday's Solutions

CRAUFURD D. GOODWIN
WILLIAM J. BARBER
JAMES L. COCHRANE
NEIL DE MARCHI
JOSEPH A. YAGER

THE BROOKINGS INSTITUTION
Washington, D.C.

HD
9502
U52
E51795

Copyright © 1981 by
THE BROOKINGS INSTITUTION
1775 Massachusetts Avenue, N.W., Washington, D.C. 20036

Library of Congress Cataloging in Publication Data:

Main entry under title:

Energy policy in perspective.

   Includes index.

   1. Energy policy—United States—History—Addresses,
essays, lectures.   I. Goodwin, Craufurd, D. W.
HD9502.U52E51795   333.79′0973   80-22859
ISBN 0-8157-3202-3
ISBN 0-8157-3201-5 (pbk.)

9 8 7 6 5 4 3 2 1

THE BROOKINGS INSTITUTION is an independent organization devoted to nonpartisan research, education, and publication in economics, government, foreign policy, and the social sciences generally. Its principal purposes are to aid in the development of sound public policies and to promote public understanding of issues of national importance.

The Institution was founded on December 8, 1927, to merge the activities of the Institute for Government Research, founded in 1916, the Institute of Economics, founded in 1922, and the Robert Brookings Graduate School of Economics and Government, founded in 1924.

The Board of Trustees is responsible for the general administration of the Institution, while the immediate direction of the policies, program, and staff is vested in the President, assisted by an advisory committee of the officers and staff. The by-laws of the Institution state: "It is the function of the Trustees to make possible the conduct of scientific research, and publication, under the most favorable conditions, and to safeguard the independence of the research staff in the pursuit of their studies and in the publication of the results of such studies. It is not a part of their function to determine, control, or influence the conduct of particular investigations or the conclusions reached."

The President bears final responsibility for the decision to publish a manuscript as a Brookings book. In reaching his judgment on the competence, accuracy, and objectivity of each study, the President is advised by the director of the appropriate research program and weighs the views of a panel of expert outside readers who report to him in confidence on the quality of the work. Publication of a work signifies that it is deemed a competent treatment worthy of public consideration but does not imply endorsement of conclusions or recommendations.

The Institution maintains its position of neutrality on issues of public policy in order to safeguard the intellectual freedom of the staff. Hence interpretations or conclusions in Brookings publications should be understood to be solely those of the authors and should not be attributed to the Institution, to its trustees, officers, or other staff members, or to the organizations that support its research.

Foreword

FOR AT LEAST the past half-century U.S. energy policy has been strongly influenced by vigorous debate over the costs and benefits of alternative courses of action—a debate to which various Brookings studies have contributed. But extremely complex problems often defy analytical probing, and past experience may represent the best or most reliable source of evidence about the effects of current policy alternatives. History may thus compensate partially for the social scientist's well-known shortage of laboratory evidence.

This volume is the result of a second Brookings effort to cast light on an important public policy issue by focusing on the history of the subject. The first such effort, a study of the search for a wage-price policy during the period 1945–71, led to the publication of *Exhortation and Controls* (Brookings, 1975), also edited by Craufurd D. Goodwin. The present study examines the formulation of energy policy from the end of World War II through 1979. As in the earlier book, chapters on each administration explore how problems of policy were perceived, what measures were proposed for their solution, what segments of the economy and society were involved in the policymaking process, what governmental machinery was created, and what impeded successful pursuit of policy goals.

This study clearly reveals that although Americans may perceive them to be of recent origin, energy problems actually have a long history, as do many of the policy responses proposed or adopted in the past few years. This book is thus intended to enable the reader to judge the nation's present energy problems and the policies advocated for their solution in historical perspective.

Each contributor to this volume is an economist with a long-standing interest in the history of economic policy: Craufurd D. Goodwin of Duke University, William J. Barber of Wesleyan University, James L. Cochrane of the University of South Carolina, Neil de Marchi of Duke University, and Joseph A. Yager of the Brookings Institution. Cochrane and Gary L. Griepentrog of the University of South Carolina prepared the quantitative review that constitutes the appendix.

Research for this project was made possible by grants from the Ford and Rockefeller foundations. Its successful completion depended on the cooperation and assistance of the directors and staffs of the presidential libraries; the National Archives and its various repositories; and the historians and staffs of the Department of Energy, Congress, and other parts of government. A study of this kind is in a valid sense a public audit of the political process. That it can be completed at all outside government affirms the nation's faith in its political process.

The manuscript was edited by Tadd Fisher. It was checked for accuracy by Judith L. Cameron, Penelope Harpold, and Ellen W. Smith. Florence Robinson prepared the index.

The views expressed in this book are those of the contributors and should not be ascribed to the Ford Foundation, to the Rockefeller Foundation, or to the staff members, officers, or trustees of the Brookings Institution.

BRUCE K. MAC LAURY
President

October 1980
Washington, D.C.

Contents

Text Tables

Appendix Tables

Editor's Preface

WHEN the energy crises of the 1970s struck, Americans tended to believe that by and large both the problems and the proposed solutions were new under the sun. In fact, as this volume shows, both had substantial histories. The American perception of energy problems grew out of difficulties with the production and distribution of energy from particular sources: petroleum, natural gas, coal, falling water, and nuclear fission. A comprehensive view was often obscured by conflicts among the protagonists of individual fuels and the complexities of their arguments. Nevertheless, the cacophony of controversy over "fuels policies" failed to deflect the attention of those persons whose concern throughout the years anticipated the larger energy issues that plague Americans today.

This book is an examination of the emerging American recognition of important energy issues and the attempts to construct public policy to deal with them. It focuses mainly on those parts of the federal government most closely involved, although it also touches on state governments and the private sector. The tale is as old as the nation, but the first developments that seem particularly important now occurred early in this century in connection with the conservation movement and the beginnings of hydroelectric development. The story in this volume begins with a discussion of energy policy during the Truman administration and continues with accounts of policy in each administration since then, ending with the difficulties faced by Jimmy Carter in 1979. For their source material, the authors followed the "paper trail" left by government, especially the collections in presidential libraries and in the National Archives in Washington, D.C. They also examined published works and records held by private individuals and interviewed or corresponded with many of the principals engaged in developing energy policy. This volume is scarcely the last word on the evolution of American energy policy, but it is the first attempt to trace the history of this policy in depth, and it should help to reveal where important questions remain unanswered and where opportunities for further research lie.

The reader will find himself being led along a path with many peculiar jogs and turns. Learning to understand and deal with energy issues has not been a matter of proceeding along a straight line from darkness to light. The path often doubles back, and the nation has repeatedly failed in its search for accurate diagnoses and sensible approaches to energy problems. Much of the story is about the explorations of committees and commissions, about the intervention of special interests, and—in a heartening number of cases—about how farsighted persons comprehended the situation and recommended constructive public policy, which at times was accepted and implemented.

From the mass of detail in these chapters certain underlying questions and patterns of events emerge. The paramount question during the past four decades has been how this huge federal democracy could mobilize itself to wrestle with the large issues of energy. The history reviewed by the authors begins with a period when primary responsibility lay in one multipurpose federal department (Interior) and its collateral congressional committees, but with secondary responsibility diffused elsewhere throughout the federal system. A later period witnessed much direct involvement by the Executive Office of the President, and most recently innumerable special offices, agencies, and finally a single executive branch department devoted entirely to energy problems have been created. Throughout all the periods task forces, working groups, special committees, and commissions have abounded. Practically all found they were addressing a range of issues that could not be ignored indefinitely, but amazingly little coherent policy was formulated.

What would be the best way for government and industry to cooperate and to accommodate both public and private interests? How could policymakers decide and act upon the most appropriate trade-off between independence from foreign supplies and efficiency (meaning the purchase of energy wherever in the world it might be cheapest)? How could the nation best prepare to substitute one predominant fuel for another? Should the production of synthetic fuels from domestic sources be encouraged? If so, how? Many energy problems resemble those encountered elsewhere in the economy, though at the moment they are more acute. For example, energy industries are prone to oligopoly and undesirable side effects such as environmental degradation. Energy policy on these and other questions has been formulated as part of a larger debate about the most suitable role for government in a free economy—whether as planner, producer, intermediary, constrainer, controller, or stimulator. The debate has often been complicated by circumstances: market participants, for example, like the southwestern producers of hydrocarbons or the northeastern consumers of energy, have been exceptionally powerful forces in national politics, and Appalachian bituminous coal miners have been among the most disadvantaged members of American society.

Despite the remarkable continuity of many of the problems faced by energy policymakers, stark changes have occurred—reversals so dramatic that it has often been difficult for the nation's leaders or its people to grasp the magnitude of the changes. Above all, the postwar period witnessed a shift from abundant energy and concern about falling prices for producers to desperate shortage and sharply rising prices for consumers. Complicating matters on the world scene generally, the United States moved from a dominant position among its allies to a situation in which power and authority were widely dispersed and in which small and militarily insignificant states could destroy the international and interdependent systems that America had come to count on.

The response to such recurring questions as whether, how much, and how best to restrict imports of foreign energy, and whether and in what fashion to encourage the production of synthetic fuels from domestic sources was often more sophisticated and enlightened in the earlier administrations than in some of the later ones under review. Although the authors' purpose has not been to present cost-benefit analyses of particular policies, the reader may well take away a sense of the ineffectiveness of measures to cope with energy problems—regulation, subsidies, penalties, and direct public ownership of producing facilities. Indeed this chronicle points to the effectiveness of the free market as a mechanism for achieving economic ends if for no other reason than that nothing else seems to work any better. At the same time, the authors paint a depressing picture of how almost all participants in energy markets, despite their rhetoric to the contrary, have been perfectly willing, nay eager, to sacrifice freedom of trade if regulation or control promised some short-run gain. The promise of capturing monopoly or monopsony rents was enough time and again to mobilize buyers and sellers to reject market-clearing prices. Cries of "inequity" or "exploitation" were often the beginning of the downfall of free market mechanisms and the start of a search for alternative allocative structures, such as government agencies, public corporations, or regulatory commissions, all of which are now entrenched in the energy landscape.

Perhaps the most important message of this book is that the issue of energy demands serious and continuing national attention grounded in a better understanding of the choices and their implications. So often the account that follows prompts one to ask "Why in the world did we do *that*?" and the answer must be that national leaders simply did not foresee the full effects of what they were doing. Either they were misled by special interests or lacked dispassionate analyses as guides to action. Although clear thought and full understanding do not guarantee reasoned action in human affairs, surely they foster it. This book, then, reflects the authors' belief that knowledge of where the United States has been in energy policy is essential to determining where it should go.

C.D.G.

List of Abbreviations

AEC   Atomic Energy Commission
API   American Petroleum Institute

BCOA   Bituminous Coal Operators Association
BPA   Bonneville Power Administration
Btu   British thermal unit

CBO   Congressional Budget Office
CCF   Central Classified Files of the Secretary
CEA   Council of Economic Advisers
CIA   Central Intelligence Agency
COLC   Cost of Living Council
CPA   Civilian Production Administration
CVA   Columbia Valley Administration

DDEL   Dwight David Eisenhower Library (Abilene, Kansas)
DOE   Department of Energy

ECPA   Energy Conservation and Production Act (1976)
EMB   Energy Mobilization Board
EPCA   Energy Policy and Conservation Act (1975)
ERDA   Energy Research and Development Administration
ERFCO   Energy Resources Finance Corporation

FEA   Federal Energy Administration
FEO   Federal Energy Office
FPC   Federal Power Commission
FTC   Federal Trade Commission

GAO   General Accounting Office
GATT   General Agreement on Tariffs and Trade
GDP   gross domestic product
GNP   gross national product
GRFL   Gerald R. Ford Library (Ann Arbor, Michigan)
GTAC   General Technical Advisory Committee

HSTL   Harry S. Truman Library (Independence, Missouri)

IEA   International Energy Agency
INFCE   International Nuclear Fuel Cycle Evaluation

JFKL   John F. Kennedy Library (Waltham, Massachusetts)

LBJL   Lyndon B. Johnson Library (Austin, Texas)
LWR   light-water reactor

mcf   thousand cubic feet
MIT   Massachusetts Institute of Technology
MOIP   Mandatory Oil Import Program
MOPPS   Market Orientation Program Planning Study
mpg   miles per gallon

NA   National Archives (Washington, D.C.)
NATO   North Atlantic Treaty Organization
NIRA   National Industrial Recovery Act
NPC   National Petroleum Council
NSC   National Security Council
NSRB   National Security Resources Board

OAPEC   Organization of Arab Petroleum Exporting Countries
OCDM   Office of Civil and Defense Mobilization
OCR   Office of Coal Research
OCS   outer continental shelf
ODM   Office of Defense Mobilization
OECD   Organisation for Economic Co-operation and Development
OEP   Office of Emergency Planning; Office of Emergency Preparedness
OF   Official File(s)
OGD   Oil and Gas Division (Interior Department)
OMB   Office of Management and Budget
OPA   Office of Price Administration
OPEC   Organization of Petroleum Exporting Countries
OPS   Office of Price Stabilization
OST   Office of Science and Technology

PAD   Petroleum Administration for Defense
PAW   Petroleum Administration for War
PIES   Project Independence Evaluation System
PMPC   President's Materials Policy Commission (Paley Commission)
PRC   Petroleum Reserves Corporation
PSAC   President's Science Advisory Committee
PSC   Petroleum Study Committee
PSF   President's Secretary's Files
PWRPC   President's Water Resources Policy Commission

R&D   research and development
REA   Rural Electrification Authority
RFF   Resources for the Future, Inc.
RG   Record Group

SEC   Securities and Exchange Commission
Sohio   Standard Oil of Ohio

TNEC   Temporary National Economic Committee
TOSCO   [The] Oil Shale Corporation
TVA   Tennessee Valley Authority

UMW   United Mine Workers

Energy Policy in Perspective

CHAPTER ONE

The Truman Administration: Toward a National Energy Policy

CRAUFURD D. GOODWIN

HARRY S. TRUMAN became President of the United States on April 12, 1945, facing a host of urgent problems, among which the energy needs of the nation did not rank high. He had yet to win a two-front war, convert a wartime economy to peace, construct a new world order out of the chaos of collapsing empires, constrain a growing socialist bloc, and make certain that the tragedy of the Great Depression did not happen again. As it turned out, adequate energy supplies were a precondition for the solution of all these problems, and President Truman was forced repeatedly to confront the subject of energy during his eight-year administration. Truman did not set out self-consciously to forge a "national energy policy," as might be done today. Rather he was led to policy formation by the sheer power and momentum of events. Energy questions emerged in two interrelated forms: first, through the need to understand and provide for all crucial elements of the economic system, and second, from the particular problems of individual fuels. These two approaches to the subject of energy are discussed in this chapter and the next.

RESEARCH for this and the following chapter was carried out in the National Archives in Washington, D.C., and in the Harry S. Truman Library in Independence, Missouri. I deeply appreciated the assistance of the staffs of these institutions, persons who unfortunately are too numerous to mention by name. Several participants in events I have reported read early drafts. While absolving them from errors that may remain and apologizing for interpretations with which they may differ, I wish to thank especially David E. Bell, Alfred C. Wolf, C. Girard Davidson, Samuel Moment, Ivan Bloch, Henry Caulfield, J. Ed Warren, and Maynard Hufschmidt.
  The following abbreviations are used in the footnotes in this chapter: Central Classified Files of the Secretary (CCF), Harry S. Truman Library (HSTL), National Archives (NA), Official Files (OF), President's Materials Policy Commission (PMPC), President's Secretary's Files (PSF), and Record Group (RG).

Truman's Inheritance

The Truman administration was heir to three relatively distinct bodies of thought about energy. The first, which grew out of the depression and the intellectual tradition of the New Deal, held that if the free market economy threatened to produce unemployment and suffering comparable to that of the 1930s, the economy must be reconstructed and reorganized. New Deal theorists were seldom unanimous about specific principles on which to proceed, but they did agree that certain key sectors of the economy should be planned and regulated more than others so as to achieve desired social results. Energy was one such sector. In fact, such projects as the Tennessee Valley Authority (TVA), rural electrification, and the applications to petroleum of the National Industrial Recovery Act came virtually to epitomize the economics of the New Deal.

The second body of thought concerning energy arose out of the national emergency of war. It recognized that energy is peculiarly essential to mobilization and requires special government effort to assure its adequate production and distribution. Whereas those who called for national energy policies during the New Deal could do so with a measure of detachment and resort to principle, full-scale war forced the administrators of energy policies and the institutions of mobilization to develop plans with urgency and authority. The production of adequate energy had to be their sole objective toward the ultimate goal of military victory. In the face of a threat to national survival all other criteria could be neglected.

The third body of thinking belonged to those who interpreted the energy sector of the economists' model of the free market economic system. This body of thought showed that only a regime of relatively small-scale, competitive buyers and sellers could guarantee minimum costs, equity, and income distribution in accordance with productivity. In addition, only under competition could great concentrations and abuses of social and political power be avoided. Democracy and social justice, as well as efficiency, required preservation of the free market whenever possible. Where this was impossible, public utility status and regulation were the only alternatives. These principles of industrial organization, which of course predated the New Deal, were enshrined in such legislation as the Sherman Anti-Trust Act of 1890 and the Clayton Anti-Trust Act of 1914, as well as such government institutions as the Federal Trade Commission, the Antitrust Division of the Justice Department, and the Federal Power Commission. Defenders of the free market identified the energy sector as a problem area at an early date and were always on their guard to detect abuses of monopoly in it and to prescribe the necessary remedial action—either fragmentation or control of the market participants.

When President Truman assumed office in 1945 all three of these bodies of thought concerning energy were thriving and had adherents both inside and outside government. The story of energy in his administration is largely one of competition and interaction among these three against a backdrop of the cold war, the Korean emergency, pressures from special interests, and macroeconomic challenges of recession and inflation.

The Memory of Depression

The terrible suffering of the 1930s became a powerful liberating force on American thinking about economic affairs. During the depression virtually all economic policies and institutions were subjected to close scrutiny, and even the wildest reform proposals received a decent hearing. No one could deny that the free market system as it was then constituted must be defective or that some remedial actions were called for. The issue was not whether there was a problem but rather what to do about it and how to do it. The energy sector of the economy received a lot of attention on both counts.

Before the advent of Keynesian macroeconomics in the late 1930s and early 1940s many professional and amateur economists suspected that inflexibility in the economic system had caused the depression. Somehow the system had lost so much of its competitive character that it could no longer respond effectively to sudden change, especially to the kind of market crisis that had occurred in the late 1920s. No matter whether an economist subscribed to a theory that attributed the depression to secular declines in effective demand, to instabilities in the banking system, or to any other factor, the absence of competition in markets helped to explain the incapacity of the system to adjust to change of all kinds. Shifts in demand or supply in imperfect markets might lead, not to new market-clearing prices, but to unsold stocks of merchandise and unemployed productive factors. Moreover, monopolized sectors did not respond constructively to public programs to deal with recession, such as those of the early New Deal. The more traditional complaints against monopoly also were present during the depression. It was appreciated that monopolies might not produce with the most efficient scale of operations at minimum average cost. In addition, from a distributional perspective imperfection might shift income flows toward the relatively more monopolized sectors, through concentrated power both in the product and factor markets. But for obvious reasons these considerations received less attention than did the charge that monopolies caused recession and impeded recovery. The various approaches to monopoly—regulation, manipulation, nationalization, and breakup—all received attention during the administration of Franklin Roosevelt.

Energy-related industries, especially petroleum and electric power, had been among the prime targets for antimonopoly activity from the earliest days. The breakup of the Standard Oil trust in 1911 was one of the first triumphs under the Sherman Act, and in the 1930s the focus of attention in the Justice Department was still sharply on petroleum. The growth of mergers in the electric power industry and the obvious potential for monopoly of this rapidly growing sector led to the creation of the Federal Power Commission in 1930. Massive federal waterpower developments under such administrative structures as the TVA and the Bonneville Power Administration were designed to achieve electrification and also irrigation, land reclamation, industrialization, and other goals—not quite national economic planning but a big step in that direction.

Federal government activities designed to expose and remedy market imperfections during the 1930s were extensive; probably the most influential single inquiry was conducted between 1938 and 1941 by the Temporary National Economic Committee (TNEC), created by a joint resolution of Congress to study monopoly and concentration of power and to make recommendations for remedial legislation. President Roosevelt emphasized in his message to Congress at the creation of the TNEC that the committee should view its task as the rescue, not the execution, of the free market system: ". . . over the field of industry and finance we must revive and strengthen competition if we wish to preserve and make workable our traditional system of free private enterprise."[1] The TNEC was an interdepartmental effort, with the Justice Department taking a leading role. Questions suggested at the outset for investigation were

(1) to what extent in any given area it can be said that prices are determined competitively; (2) in what areas has price competition disappeared or begun to disappear so that it may be extremely difficult or perhaps impossible to

1. *Investigation of Concentration of Economic Power: Final Report and Recommendations of the Temporary National Economic Committee*, S. Doc. 35, 77 Cong. 1 sess. (Government Printing Office, 1941), p. 15.

restore; (3) in what areas has price competition disappeared or begun to disappear as a result of practices which are susceptible of social control; (4) in what areas have non-competitive price policies created barriers against the production of goods in a quantity and at a price which will help maintain and improve the American standard of living; (5) are there any areas in which monopolistically determined prices and industrial efficiency go hand in hand; (6) are there any areas in which an attempt to restore price competition would interfere with the methods of mass production.[2]

The onset of World War II drew attention away from the TNEC final report and impeded implementation of its recommendations. However, as an investigative activity lasting over three years and resulting in more than 20,000 pages of direct testimony and 3,300 technical exhibits, it served to strengthen the awareness of monopoly among broad segments of the American people, especially Congress. The essential TNEC message was that "the basic solution of curtailed production for selfish ends is to be found . . . in the development of competing industries and firms." It was the responsibility of government "to insure an adequate supply at competitive prices, so that, furthermore, competition may develop which will prove effective in the peacetime period following the defense effort."[3]

The petroleum industry was a prime target of the TNEC. No fewer than seven volumes of testimony about it were collected by the committee and then published and distributed widely. Among other topics these volumes dealt with market interpenetration, pricing practices, growth of the industry's assets, and institutions created to assist in the restraint of competition. One of the special TNEC monographs prepared by Roy C. Cook of the Antitrust Division of the Department of Justice presented explicit conclusions that were implicit in the open hearings: "Today the petroleum industry is controlled by 20 major oil companies which have developed from some of the Standard Oil units as well as non-Standard competitors, all of them being fully integrated and acting as a group monopoly on identical policies." Cook claimed that the oil "majors" had effective control over all levels of the industry from wells through refineries to transportation; the smaller "independents" were not an effective source of competitive pressures. He concluded with a suggestion that alarmed leaders of the industry: "In many respects the characteristics of

2. "Memorandum with Respect to the Role of the Department of Justice in the Investigation of the Temporary National Economic Committee," August 5, 1938, Attorney General, Monopoly Study, Leon Henderson File, Milton Katz Papers, HSTL.

3. *Investigation of Concentration of Economic Power*, p. 24.

the petroleum industry resemble those of a public utility, and because of the public interest involved in the problems of the consumer and national defense, it is conceivable that the continuance of present practices and conditions may lead to regulation of the industry by the State and Federal Governments on public utility principles."[4]

Other approaches to dealing with monopoly in the energy industries were in a sense the obverse of the negative critiques of the TNEC and the trustbusters. Some antimonopolists saw the solution of the monopoly problem in vigorous enforcement of the antitrust laws; at a minimum this would make the industry behave more as if it were competitive. Others saw monopoly as a challenge to which government should respond creatively and imaginatively; in the energy sector government could begin experiments with new mechanisms that would replace the competitive market. This line of thought was the inspiration for a succession of groups charged specifically with the planning of natural resources: the National Resources Board (1934–35), the National Resources Committee (1935–39), and the National Resources Planning Board (1939–43). The several broad objectives of these groups were not always spelled out clearly, but above all the committee and the boards were absorbed by the problems of the depression; the sense of crisis inspired them to seek alternative mechanisms to the market system for the allocation of resources. In addition these early resource planning groups responded to the rather ill-defined cry for conservation that went back at least to the days of President Theodore Roosevelt. To economists "conservation" simply means economic efficiency, or the exploitation of resources to yield the largest possible consumer satisfaction at a rate determined by the time preferences of resource owners and consumers. But to others conservation means a slowing down of resource use in the interest of future generations. This vaguer notion of conservation had been perpetuated by such enthusiasts as Gifford Pinchot, former governor of Pennsylvania and professional forester.

In 1939 a major report from a special Energy Resources Committee to the National Resources Committee was a high point of achievement by resource planning and conservation groups. The theme of this document was that all energy resources (coal, oil, natural gas, and waterpower) are

4. Roy C. Cook, *Control of the Petroleum Industry by Major Oil Companies,* Temporary National Economic Committee, Monograph 39, 76 Cong. 3 sess. (GPO, 1941), pp. 51–52. See also Ellis W. Hawley, *The New Deal and the Problem of Monopoly: A Study in Economic Ambivalence* (Princeton University Press, 1966).

closely interrelated and require the systematic attention of government. "It is time now to take a larger view, to recognize more fully than has been possible in the past that each of these energy resources affects the others, and that the diversity of problems affecting them and their interlocking relationships require the careful weighing of conflicting interests and points of view." The broad rationale for resource planning was the need for "conservation." The fundamental principle of public policy that the Committee took as the basis for its recommendations was that "government intervenes with control measures when the economic organization of a segment of the economy is such as not to yield socially desirable results." The committee reviewed the contemporary circumstances of the four energy sources and recommended public policy for each of them. Coal was seen to be suffering from "surplus of capacity." The committee had little faith in the effectiveness of market mechanisms to generate the appropriate supply response to discourage submarginal coal producers; it called instead for "public supervision" and "some means . . . for effectively balancing production against requirements, whether by control of prices, by control of distribution, or by both." It was necessary "to control the opening of new mines and retard expansion of capacity beyond reasonable requirements."[5]

Whereas abundance was the problem with coal, impending exhaustion of resources was the issue with oil and gas. In this case "we must consider whether to use more wisely our available supply, to manufacture high-cost substitutes, or to depend on foreign oil for our motor cars and airplanes, our tractors, and our battleships." Without providing its own answers to these questions the committee proposed that "a Federal oil conservation board or commission should be created within the appropriate Government department to administer the Federal interest in the oil-and-gas industry and to make necessary rules and regulations concerning the production of and commerce in oil and gas."[6]

The committee found the fewest policy enigmas in the area of waterpower. Unlike other fuels, the hydroelectric source was "not reduced by use"; in fact, its nonuse constituted waste. It was noted that, unfortunately, the capacity of waterpower to fill America's energy needs was strictly limited but should be exploited quickly and fully. The committee believed that only the federal government was capable of developing this

5. *Energy Resources and National Policy,* Report of the Energy Resources Committee to the Natural Resources Committee (GPO, 1939), pp. 1, 3, 5.
6. Ibid., pp. 2, 3.

industry so as to take into account potentially conflicting interests in "flood control, public water supply, stream pollution, irrigation, and navigation." The committee endorsed the "multiple-purpose plans for stream development . . . for whole drainage basins" represented by the TVA and saw only a limited role for the private sector. In fact, "Federal policy should, in general, embrace eventual merging of private waterpower plants into the system covered by any basin plan."[7]

For the more distant future the committee recommended government support of research to promote "efficiency," "economy," and shifts in demand to "lower grade fuels." It also recommended the organization of "an advisory planning group for the energy resources" to be one component of an overall planning agency concerned with national resources. A "national energy resources policy" should be prepared that would amount to more than "a simple sum" of policies toward particular fuels. The committee concluded its report with an ironic prophesy. "It is not likely that backward steps will be taken; it is not likely that we shall retreat from the social and economic advances made in the domain of the energy resources. Rather, it is likely that we shall press on toward the objective of the general welfare."[8]

The importance of the investigations into energy policy during the 1930s, especially those of the TNEC and the National Resources Committee, is not merely that they raised and publicized many of the issues that would become important again after the war; they served also to educate and sensitize many persons in the legislative and executive branches who would be crucial figures in the discussion of the later period —to mention but a few: Senator Joseph C. O'Mahoney, chairman of the TNEC and of energy-related congressional committees during and after the war; Sumner T. Pike, a TNEC member and one of the first commissioners of the Atomic Energy Commission; Harold L. Ickes, chairman of the National Resources Committee and secretary of the interior under Roosevelt and briefly under Truman.

Energy Goes to War

Policies for mobilizing the various energy sources during World War II will be discussed in the next chapter. It is important to note here, how-

7. Ibid., pp. 2, 3, 4.
8. Ibid., pp. 3, 4, 5.

ever, that the overall posture toward energy problems changed drastically in wartime both because the goals of the economic system shifted and because many of the constraints on policy were lifted dramatically. The relatively vague and often conflicting and controversial objectives of consumer satisfaction, free choice, and full employment all became subservient to winning the war. Peacetime perceptions of the dangers of monopoly, concentration of power, and other than optimum exploitation of finite resources were all put in abeyance for the duration. Moreover, former adversaries were brought together to work in harness, as it were, under a flag of truce. Through such devices as the Petroleum Administration for War, business and government forgot or repressed their differences temporarily and worked for a common goal. In the federal government, responsibility for energy matters moved outward from the Department of the Interior to the Department of State, the Military Establishment, the War Production Board, the Office of Price Administration, the Foreign Economic Administration, and myriad other agencies established to mobilize the economy for war. In all of these, representatives of the energy industries took vital parts and at the end of the war enjoyed a strong sense of gratitude throughout government for their participation. In many respects energy policy was easier to construct for war than for peace. But the old questions and dilemmas of peace were never far beneath the surface.

Peace and the Cold War

As the end of the war drew near it became clear that one important background condition that would be changed for all American domestic and foreign policy was the new role of the United States in the world. Issues that could be viewed in the 1930s from a merely national perspective now had to be seen globally. This change was especially marked in the case of natural resources. During the war the United States discovered that on the one hand its own resource independence was fast disappearing and that on the other hand resource scarcities lay at the root of much world conflict. Both Germany and Japan, after all, had been bent on acquiring new territories and the resources they contained.

In the yeasty period of discussion that preceded the end of the war the development of a sound postwar energy policy was given considerable priority. One of the major natural resource questions facing the nation, as discerned by Stephen Raushenbush, an influential staff member of the Interior Department, was "Can a sensible fuel policy be devised?" He concluded that "neither Congress nor the Administration are presently organized to consider this and similar questions either on a broad national level or on a level of disinterested weighing of economic costs and advantages. Every measure comes up as a special commodity interest measure, is handled by a special interest agency, and goes before special interest committees of Congress." He called for a "rethinking and restatement of our resource problems" that "should be very specific and be put in terms of dollars and cents" in contrast to the "over generalized approach which the NRPB [recently terminated National Resources Planning Board] felt constrained to take."[9] Others in the Interior Department also speculated about how such broad objectives could be achieved. In January 1943 William E. Warne of the Bureau of Reclamation floated a scheme both to equip "several of the bureaus [of the department] with facilities for economic study and planning within their subject matter" and to create a central Coordination Council reporting to the secretary "to present a rounded analysis of multiple problems without distortions arising from jealousies or the pride of high-morale bureaus, and equally without interference with the administrative channels direct from the Secretary's office to the bureau heads."[10]

Harold Ickes, wily old bureaucratic infighter and veteran of the New Deal, moved quickly with the new President to establish the Interior Department's responsibility for the international as well as the domestic dimensions of resource problems. On May 31, 1945, he wrote to Truman proposing "a world conservation conference following the end of the war." He explained that "the war has taken a heavy toll of the forests, the oil, the coal, and the iron and other metals" and that demands could not be expected to decline in peacetime. A world conference, he suggested, could prepare an inventory of natural resources, explore the extent of resource depletion, and discuss techniques for conservation, including "development of synthetic fuels" and "prevention of private monopolization of natural resources." The underlying theme of the conference would be "the place of conservation and wise use of resources

9. Stephen Raushenbush, "Natural Resource Problems and Programs," n.d., Mineral Policy, 1944 File, Branch of Economics and Statistics Files, Records of the Department of the Interior, RG 48, NA.

10. "Memorandum Regarding a Centralized Research, Planning and Coordinating Agency in the Department of the Interior," attached to memorandum, William E. Warne to Michael W. Straus, January 7, 1943, Planning and Coordinating Division File, Branch of Economics and Statistics Files, RG 48, NA.

in the preservation of world peace." In essence, he implied, the New
Deal could be extended around the globe. Ickes emphasized that the late
President Roosevelt had been "favorable to the idea" of such a con-
ference.[11]

Ickes' proposal was reviewed for Truman by an equally old New
Dealer, Samuel I. Rosenman, former judge and special counsel to Roosevelt, who recommended that no action be taken for several months until
decisions were made "about the personnel in the Department of Interior."
This advice was accepted, and the proposed conference was in fact post-
poned for a full four years.[12]

Perhaps as a substitute for the proposed worldwide conservation conference, Ickes held a Post-War Resources Institute in the Interior Department, November 5–9, 1945. The idea for the institute came from several
of his most imaginative staff members, and the meeting was organized
by Assistant Secretary Oscar L. Chapman. A key problem listed for
consideration was "What regional or national solutions are possible for
the problems of coal, oil, natural gas and hydroelectric power competition?"[13] One of the institute's seven sessions was devoted to "fuels and

11. Ickes to the President, May 31, 1945, Subject File: Cabinet, Secretary of the
Interior, PSF, Harry S. Truman Papers, HSTL. On April 17 the old conservationist
Gifford Pinchot also wrote to White House aide William D. Hassett reporting on
Roosevelt's enthusiasm for such a conference up until his death. (Pinchot to Hassett,
April 17, 1945, ibid.) Hassett sent a copy of Pinchot's letter to Matthew J. Connelly
with a cover note on April 28, 1945 (ibid.). Assistant Secretary Oscar L. Chapman
prepared the conference proposal for Ickes. Staff suggestions to Chapman emphasized the need to understand the resource implications of the new U.S. world role.
Stephen Raushenbush, director of economics and statistics in the Division of Power,
stressed in particular the importance of comprehending the implications of technological change such as nuclear power—"a cheap source of energy that will change
the old requirements of industrial location." (Memorandum, John B. Bennett, "Proposed World Conservation Conference: Summaries of Suggestions by Ward Shep-
ard, Stephen Rauschenbush, Wesley C. Clark, and John B. Bennett," April 12, 1945,
Department of Interior Files, Subject File: World Conservation Conference, Dale E.
Doty Papers, HSTL.) The academic world was interested as well in focusing greater
public attention on conservation. For example, in 1944 Myron W. Watkins of New
York University had proposed the formation of a U.S. Conservation Commission to
arrange for "a supplementation of market criteria of profitability in directing the
allocation and use of resources." "Scarce Raw Materials: An Analysis and a Proposal," *American Economic Review*, vol. 34 (June 1944), p. 243.
12. Rosenman to the President, June 4, 1945; and Truman to Ickes, June 6,
1945; both in Subject File: Cabinet, Secretary of Interior, PSF, HSTL.
13. William E. Warne, Joel D. Wolfsohn, and Stephen Raushenbush to Secretary Ickes, March 24, 1945; and Oscar Chapman to the staff, May 10, 1945; both in
Department of Interior Files, Subject File: Post-War Resources Institute, Doty Papers, HSTL.

energy." A report suggested that the "general level of discussion was exceptionally high, with prevailing regard for democratic concepts, for the general welfare and for a well-rounded, expanding economy; with only faint undertones of jurisdictional thinking."[14]

Two features of this gathering are especially noteworthy from the vantage point of thirty-five years. First, the particular mix of Interior Department responsibilities seemed to dictate that energy questions be viewed from a wide perspective. A whole range of what would now be called environmental concerns about the social costs of development was raised by representatives of nonenergy parts of the department: the Fish and Wildlife Service, the Division of Territories, the Office of Land Utilization, and the National Park Service.[15] Second, the entire meeting was suffused with awareness of the new and wider international stage on which resource dramas would be played in the future. In the case of minerals the institute concluded: "Department needs an international point of view; should concern itself with foreign as well as domestic sources."[16] It called for leadership by the Interior Department in the recently formed interdepartmental Executive Committee on Economic Foreign Policy and similar bodies.

Most of the department's staff at the institute who dealt specifically with energy questions began by doing so from the perspective of the particular source for which they had responsibility (electricity in the Bureau of Reclamation, Division of Power, and Bonneville Power Administration; coal in the Bureau of Mines and the Solid Fuels Administration for War; oil and gas in the Petroleum Administration for War). But quickly they attempted to move to a wider plain. Obviously the staff who were present at the Post-War Resources Institute had had four years of war in

14. Evelyn N. Cooper to C. Girard Davidson, "Postwar Resources Institute," April 30, 1946, ibid. A verbatim transcript of discussions at the institute is in the Branch of Economics and Statistics Files, RG 48, NA.

15. This tension between "environmentalists" and "developers" remained strong in the department. For example, a vigorous controversy emerged during the discussion of how to conduct a conservation conference proposed for 1947. In connection with the use of public property, such as Jackson Hole, Howard Zahniser, the executive secretary of the Wilderness Society, advised Secretary of the Interior Julius A. Krug to devise an "accepted basis for comparing the value of the area in its natural state with its money-profit possibilities if exploited." (An environmental impact statement?) Reclamation Commissioner Michael W. Straus, on the other hand, warned of the danger of defining conservation too narrowly to mean environmental preservation at the expense of ignoring development. Zahniser to Krug, October 4, 1947; and Straus to Under Secretary Chapman, September 26, 1947, CCF, 1-70, RG 48, NA.

16. Cooper to Davidson, "Postwar Resources Institute."

which to reflect and were prepared for some brave new postwar thought and action.

A general question considered in most of the sessions was whether the sacred notion of a region, especially a region as small as a river valley, any longer made sense analytically when most important issues had become national or international. The conclusion was that regional planning not only might lead to duplication of effort but also to inconsistencies of policy (as in the development of synthetic fuels in one region while fuel surpluses plagued others).

The interrelationships among fuels and their problems constituted the dominant theme of the energy panels. For example, natural gas was presented as a special challenge for the immediate future. A speaker estimated that there would be only ten to twenty years during which gas could be consumed without restriction; during that time its unrestricted use might "seriously affect the coal industry."[17] Moreover, some sectors might be led to convert to gas only to face the costs of reconversion in a short time. Participants were uncertain about whether regulation was the answer to this problem, but a proposed Texas-Louisiana policy of selling gas locally at preferential rates appeared to achieve two purposes: developing the South and protecting coal. Similar uncertainties about the desirability of moving ahead rapidly with synthetic fuels were related to the future price of natural gas and the unpredictable direction of technological development. Questions were raised about the proper role for government in the development of synthetics (perhaps to cover the costs of obsolescence in the synthetics industry if technology changed rapidly?) and whether from a conservation viewpoint to go first with coal or shale. The growing dependence of the United States on foreign natural resources of all kinds loomed large in the discussion, but participants differed about whether to import freely and conserve domestic supplies, whether to protect domestic industries so as to enable them to advance the margin of exploitation beyond levels reached worldwide, and whether to accumulate stockpiles.

The Interior Department staff labored hard to produce "principles" on which to base a national energy policy and came up with the following:

1. Most economic sources of energy should be used to minimize cost.
2. Plentiful and depletionless resources should be used whenever possible in place of scarce and depleting resources.

17. Ibid.

3. Source of energy with special characteristics should not be used for purposes for which other less specialized energy sources are available.
4. Best and most efficient technologies should be used without hindrance.
5. Elements of stability should be considered in marketing energy.
6. The less labor and capital required to energize our economy is best for the economy; high levels of employment are promoted by efficiency.[18]

It is clear that in 1945 the Department of the Interior, with the powerful team of Secretary Ickes and Under Secretary Abe Fortas at its head, was prepared and anxious to take on a central role in the development of a national, and if need be international, energy policy. It already had responsibility for various aspects of policy related to the individual energy sources—oil, gas, coal, and hydroelectric installations—and it looked forward to the transfer of more authority from the various temporary wartime agencies. A whole series of developments prevented this evolution from taking place, however.

First of all, the transformation of the Interior Department into what in effect would be a Department of Energy, Resources, and the Environment did not appeal to the President. The problem was partly a personality conflict. Harold Ickes was a complicated and difficult man whom President Roosevelt in his supreme self-confidence had been willing to tolerate and manage. But to Truman, Ickes was an insufferable and irresponsible relic of a previous administration who seemed to delight in reading lectures to the new chief executive. More profoundly, the enlargement of the authority of the Interior Department smacked of the planning philosophy of the New Deal with which Truman was never comfortable. Matters came to a head in February 1946 when Ickes resigned (or was fired) over a matter of principle, which in fact was energy-related. He refused to testify positively in support of a faithful party worker, Edwin Pauley, who wished to become under secretary of the navy, intimating that Pauley's long association with the oil industry should disqualify him from gaining authority over the valuable naval petroleum reserves.[19] Ickes' replacement, Julius A. Krug, former chairman of the War Production Board and chief engineer of the TVA, did not have the flamboyant personality of Ickes—a necessary attribute to lead the department quickly into a new activist role.

Evelyn N. Cooper, one of the staff holdovers in the secretary's office, reported sourly to Assistant Secretary C. Girard Davidson in May 1946,

18. Ibid.
19. Ickes to the President, February 12, 1946, OF 6, HSTL.

after Ickes' departure, that little progress was being made to implement the plans of the 1945 institute. "The 1947 programs," she said, "represent merely extensions of previous programs, adjusted to peacetime conditions. They reflect little of the far-seeing and enlightened thinking manifested at the Institute. . . . the Department cannot hope for widespread public support of its 1947 program because it does not represent general issues but only myriad budget items." The energy programs were a particular disappointment: ". . . no work appears to be scheduled on the basic problems of what to do about an over-expanded coal industry, about the shortage of special purpose coals and about competition from other fuels. As to the development of synthetic liquid fuels and the conservation and production of petroleum, natural gas and helium, there is room for question whether the programs reflect well-developed and defined policy. Again, the problem of competitive fuel appears to be overlooked."[20] Such comments support the evident impression in the White House for some time after Ickes' departure that the Interior Department remained a nest of his advocates and a hotbed of advanced New Deal thought.[21]

The second factor that helped loosen the department's grip on energy policy in the years immediately after World War II was a new set of national goals that began to emerge from fast-moving world affairs. Just as in the 1930s the depression had often submerged the objectives of efficiency, equity, and dispersion of economic and social power, so in the

20. Cooper to Davidson, May 15, 1946, Department of Interior Files, Subject File: Post-War Resources Institute, Doty Papers, HSTL.

21. An unusually candid and unsigned memo in the White House files from this period provides unflattering thumbnail sketches of the senior personnel at the Interior Department, many of whom would remain active in the energy field for years to come. For example, Michael Straus, head of the Bureau of Reclamation, was described as "the master mind in all the extra-curricular activities that Ickes indulged in." Joel Wolfsohn, assistant commissioner of the General Land Office, was "a member of the Ickes inner circle," Arthur "Tex" Goldschmidt, director of the Division of Power, "became a public power expert when Fortas wanted a fellow in the job whom he could handle . . . he is known to have pronounced leftist views not only on public power but on other questions. Stephen Raushenbush—a minister without portfolio, but really Ickes' chief economic adviser, is on Division of Power payroll. A deep thinker, Steve is known to have furnished much of the research for several of Ickes' 'best' ideas in the last 5 years. He is married to a daughter of the late Justice Brandeis." The memo concluded: "There is no dearth of good smart brains in Interior. Under the Ickes-Straus-Fortas triumvirate however a fellow had to be a political shyster, a glib talker and a little leftist to get any place. Interior is ready for a great improvement, but it cannot be done unless a good many changes are made promptly." OF 6 (1945–48), Truman Papers, HSTL.

1940s consciousness of a worldwide struggle with communism also led to new priorities. It appeared that resources had become too important to entrust entirely to one executive department, especially one whose experience and very title signaled a primarily domestic orientation. In effect the postwar period was an awkward halfway point between war and peace during which considerations related to both had to be taken into account. The Interior Department continued to play a part with respect to the various fuels for which it had been assigned some responsibility (everything but nuclear power), but it remained generally domestic in orientation. A search began throughout government for new organs, institutions, and units of executive departments that would have a broader perspective than that of the Interior Department, that might coordinate the various offices concerned, or that might have as a single focus the mobilization of the resources of the United States and the free world in the struggle against communism.

One proposal was presented to President Truman on December 6, 1946, by John D. Small, administrator of the Civilian Production Administration (CPA), successor to the War Production Board, for the establishment of a permanent peacetime National Security Resources Board (NSRB). Such a board, he suggested, would prepare "plans for rapid and effective mobilization" and to this end would maintain "accurate current information on our resources of materials and facilities, but also well informed estimates of essential requirements."[22] A skeletal staff and a network of industry advisory committees would be transferred from the CPA to work closely with the regular cabinet departments. The proposal in essence was for a new institution that would keep up the nation's guard in peacetime and make sure it was never again as unprepared as at Pearl Harbor.

After President Truman expressed interest in Small's proposal, the details were submitted for consideration to John R. Steelman, the assistant to the president, by Philip F. Maguire, deputy administrator of the CPA. An important element of the proposal was for continuing market analysis of strategic areas and the preparation of plans to intervene in the event of crisis:

. . . it should be entirely feasible to develop a master coordination of demand and supply for various strategic materials at different levels of emergency requirements. This would be one of the most important functions of this Board.

22. "Proposal for Establishment of a Permanent Peacetime National Security Resources Board," attached to memorandum, Maguire to Steelman, January 27, 1947, OF 1295, Truman Papers, HSTL.

In addition to the compilation of a budget of resources and demands, methods should be developed, ready for use, whereby the two sides of the equation could be brought into balance. Such a balance sheet, or budget of resources, complete in quantities and in all the operating details needed in wartime, would be a monumental accomplishment. It would serve as the base for all other industrial mobilization planning.[23]

The NSRB was created by the National Security Act of 1947, which recognized that in effect the United States was not yet fully at peace, or that it at least should be ready for the outbreak of renewed hostilities at any time. The NSRB was composed of a chairman and all members of the President's cabinet except the attorney general and the postmaster general. One of its statutory functions was to develop "programs for the effective use in time of war of the Nation's natural and industrial resources for military and civilian needs."[24] Initially it was organized as an independent agency, but in June 1949 it was transferred to the Executive Office of the President. One of its eleven offices was dubbed Energy and Utilities. For energy-policy planning, the establishment of the NSRB meant a partial return to the circumstances of World War II when the civilian aspects of energy were separated from the actual and potential needs of mobilization.

Just how valuable and effective the NSRB was depends on one's point of view. It was a creature of the early cold war. When the Korean emergency occurred it withered with the progress of mobilization, and its functions were assumed by the Office of Defense Mobilization and other agencies. The NSRB directed a good deal of its efforts to energy policy. Four of the eight major studies completed as early as the end of 1948 dealt with energy policy, three on electric power and one on liquid fuels.[25] By the end of 1949 the NSRB had no less than seventeen separate studies on energy problems planned or in progress, dealing with all the major fuels and requiring the cooperation of a variety of other agencies in addition to the Department of the Interior.[26]

23. Ibid. See also J. D. Small to Truman, December 5, 1946, and February 18, 1947; and Truman to Small, December 13, 1946; all in National Military Establishment–Security Resources Board File, Clark M. Clifford Papers, HSTL.

24. 61 Stat. 495.

25. "Summary of Special Presentation to the President and Members of the Board, by the Staff of NSRB," December 10, 1948, NSRB Doc. 97, Subject File: Agencies, NSRB, PSF, HSTL.

26. "Materials for Use in NSRB Program Development," NSRB Doc. 116/2, NSRB Folder, White House Confidential Files, Truman Papers, HSTL. NSRB activities up to 1951 are described in the unusually full *Report of the Chairman* (GPO, 1951).

During its short life span the NSRB revealed clearly the great difficulty in a democracy of planning for crisis while relative normalcy prevails. First of all, during peacetime it was hard for anyone to take the planning process seriously; so many other considerations seemed to take precedence over remote future eventualities. In wartime the need was not for planning but to get on with the job. Moreover, with the return of peace, resource questions moved back to the regular departments and agencies, and a new planning unit found an abundance of toes to step on. One observer told presidential assistant Steelman that by 1951 the agency had become "a laughing-stock around town."[27] In that year a White House task force headed by David H. Stowe, an administrative assistant to the President, examined the past and future of the NSRB and found the following five "general failings":

1. Lack of Guides to the Scope and Nature of the NSRB job.
2. Failure to understand essential characteristics of a Presidential staff role.
3. Failure to see the total job.
4. Tendency to approach NSRB job as if war were always six weeks away.
5. Lack of leadership.[28]

The task force heard from Charles E. Odegaard, executive director of the American Council of Learned Societies, that the need for resource planning was as great in 1951 as it had been in 1947 when the board was created, for example, to help the United States "develop patterns of use of its own resources in relation to possible use of those of other nations in such a way as to take account of security considerations."[29]

27. "R.P.A." to Steelman, April 25, 1951, NSRB Projects File, Harold L. Enarson Papers, HSTL. Sooner or later the NSRB seems to have offended every department on whose traditional authority it impinged—for example, the Justice Department for recommending a broad waiver of antitrust laws during an emergency, the Defense Department for prescribing techniques of mobilization, the Commerce Department for suggesting the allocation of scarce minerals, and the Interior Department for duplicating resource planning. In 1948 the President found it necessary to remind NSRB Chairman Arthur M. Hill that his "statutory duty" was "to advise the President," not to exercise "directive or coordinating authority." Truman to Hill, May 24, 1948. See also memorandum, James E. Webb, Director of the Bureau of the Budget, to the President, "Waiver of Anti-trust Laws during War or National Emergency," May 25, 1948; and Secretary of Commerce Charles Sawyer to Secretary of Defense James Forrestal, September 23, 1948; all in Office Files of the Director, Records of the Bureau of the Budget, RG 51, NA.
28. "Notes on Stowe Task Force Report on NSRB," NSRB File, Correspondence Files of Lyle Craine, RG 48, NA.
29. Charles E. Odegaard, "Planning for National Security," NSRB Projects File, Enarson Papers, HSTL.

The task force agreed with Odegaard and suggested the following objectives for an invigorated board:

(a) identify current key deficits about which something should be done in peacetime

(b) anticipate alternative wartime deficit situations as bases for planning alternative wartime measures

(c) anticipate a technique of resources and requirements data collecting and analysis in time of war as a basis for controlling flow of resources to war effort.[30]

W. Stuart Symington, the chairman of the NSRB at that time, agreed with the conclusion that the board had an important role to play in developing the strategy of U.S. foreign policy as it related to dependence on imported raw materials. Using the cold war rhetoric of the time, he suggested that instead of the scattershot efforts of the past the NSRB should concentrate on preparing the necessary national strategy for materials acquisition to take into account both quantity and price; then the units of the free enterprise system and the military should be left to work out the tactics for implementing this strategy. He wrote to the President as follows:

If the United States wins in this world struggle against communism, all other freedom-loving nations also win; but if we lose, freedom will perish from the earth. . . .

As we continue to use up our diminishing natural resources, the resources of other countries become more than desirable—they become essential, to the maintenance of our economy. . . .

Either we fully believe in the capitalistic system, or we do not. Of course we do, and therefore enlightened free enterprise must be sold to the world as the right answer to the evils of communism.

Free enterprise cannot be sold by doling out our resources indiscriminately, however. Our policy should be a two-way street. If that is not so, then in the long run it will be difficult, if not impossible to obtain the resources necessary to sustain our economy; and those materials we do obtain will come in at such exorbitant prices as to seriously affect that economy.

The base of any efficient future planning of our national resources, therefore, must be a purposeful foreign policy, one which is clear to our military leaders so they in turn can plan efficiently; and one which insures this country obtaining, on a mutually fair basis, those raw materials essential to the preservation of free governments.[31]

It would have been extremely interesting to see if, as Symington proposed, a reinvigorated, redirected NSRB might have been able to serve

30. "Notes on Stowe Task Force Report on NSRB."
31. NSRB, *Report of the Chairman*, pp. 38–39.

as the broad national strategic planning unit for resource disposal and acquisition during peacetime complementary to, rather than competitive with, the operating departments. But the hour was late and the Truman administration had run out of peacetime.

A source of inspiration for the NSRB, mentioned in the initial plan submitted to Truman in late 1946, was the venerable World War I and II mobilizer Bernard M. Baruch. Baruch was never entirely satisfied with the National Security Act, however, and repeatedly advised greater vigilance, especially with respect to such crucial commodities as fuels. In 1949 in response to a letter from Baruch, Interior Secretary Krug wrote that his department had joined the NSRB in preparing for every eventuality, and he insisted that he himself shared Baruch's sense of emergency. "I am certain that you must know that I have no feeling of false security and that we in this Department are alive to the situation. . . . In fighting a war, even if it is 'cold,' there are always critical and dangerous areas. I hope that this Nation realizes that we are, in essence, still fighting for our political existence and must relentlessly attack whenever the opportunity presents itself."[32] At least with his old "Chief," Krug was not prepared to swim against the stream of security consciousness.

Other circumstances of the postwar world beyond the loss of Ickes and the crises of the cold war combined to block the dreams of Interior Department staff of becoming the central planning agency for all energy matters—indeed for all resource affairs. To begin with, there were the familiar jealousies of rival departments. For example, an unsigned and undated memorandum "prepared for the information of U.S. Department of Agriculture officials" apparently in 1946 but sent to the White House as well described "A New Threat to a Functional Executive Branch: The Campaign to Establish the Department of the Interior as the Resource Development Agency of the Federal Government." The author of this memorandum described with alarm the growing "aspirations" of the department and its "quiet maneuvers" such as the proposed extension of valley authorities and the creation of regional offices. But

32. Krug to Baruch, October 20, 1949, Subject File: Cabinet, Secretary of the Interior, PSF, HSTL. There is a substantial literature dealing with the development of American foreign and security policy after World War II. See especially John Lewis Gaddis, *The United States and the Origins of the Cold War, 1941–1947* (Columbia University Press, 1972); and Charles S. Maier, "The Politics of Productivity: Foundations of American International Economic Policy after World War II," in Peter J. Katzenstein, ed., *Between Power and Plenty: Foreign Economic Policies of Advanced Industrial States* (University of Wisconsin Press, 1978), pp. 23–49.

worst of all, he found that an examination of internal documents "indicates that the Department of the Interior is actually operating *as though it had already been made responsible for all resource development activities of the Federal government.*"[33] The author deplored this development for two reasons: first, because it would involve one government agency "coordinating" the activities of others at the same administrative level, and second, because it would bestow inferior status on mere "servicing" agencies (such as the Agriculture Department) even while it left some servicing units in the Interior Department intact. The Commerce Department was no less concerned. The head of the Bureau of Foreign and Domestic Commerce wrote: "If Interior carries out these plans, I seriously question whether it would be possible for Commerce to establish an industry division or divisions concerned with petroleum, fuels and metals without extensive duplication of effort with Interior."[34]

The author of the Agriculture Department memorandum called for restraints on the ambitions of the Interior Department and the establishment of "coordinating machinery in the office of the President to deal with resource development." As it turned out, others had similar ideas. J. Donald Kingsley of the White House staff suggested to John Steelman an interagency committee "to plan and operate a program for Natural Resources Conservation and Development." He complained: "There are approximately twelve federal agencies concerned with natural resource matters. There is no coherent statement of national policy to serve as a guideline for private and public interests. Every year, in the presidential messages, some mention is made of the problem of conservation and development of natural resources—but rarely is anything concrete accomplished."[35] Kingsley, of course, was concerned with natural resources in a large sense, but energy resources were included thereunder.

Undoubtedly some people expected the planning of energy resources in the executive branch, as called for by Kingsley, to be one of the tasks assumed by the new Council of Economic Advisers (CEA), appointed in 1946 under the terms of the Employment Act of that year. Indeed, the House Special Committee on Postwar Economic Policy and Planning, which reported in December 1946, envisioned the CEA's main function

33. The unsigned memorandum is in OF 6 (1945–48), Truman Papers, HSTL (emphasis in the original).

34. H. B. McCoy to Bernard L. Gladieux, April 23, 1946, Oils-Mineral, General File 312, RG 151, NA.

35. Kingsley to Steelman, January 16, 1947, General Classified Files, Conservation, Records of John R. Steelman, Office of War Mobilization, HSTL.

to be the preparation of "long-run studies of the national economy."[36] In fact, however, the seeming intractability of inflation and the constant threat of returning recession kept the CEA's time horizon very short during its first few years.[37] Moreover, only one of the first council members, John D. Clark, had had experience with the energy field (he had been vice-president of Standard Oil of Indiana), and he was overshadowed by the chairman, Edwin G. Nourse, an agricultural economist, and the other member, Leon H. Keyserling, a New Deal theorist of wide interests who was preoccupied with large questions of economic growth. The first extensive council discussion of long-run resource issues appeared in the second annual report in 1947, but this was merely a summary of the Interior Department's position paper presented to the CEA, and it did little more than repeat long-standing policies and standard doctrine about the need for conservation, research, planning, and government participation in sectors where unrestrained private investment did not perform satisfactorily, such as electric power.[38]

John Clark's explanation for the CEA's neglect of basic resource questions was that by accepting full employment and price stability as objectives it implicitly rejected the use of what the French called "indicative planning." For the council's purposes the long-term composition of output was relatively unimportant and, in fact, barely even its business. The aggregate volume of production and the prices at which it was transacted in the short run were matters of immediate concern, and willy-nilly "the long-range objective is also the short-term goal."[39] By this reasoning resources became important mainly to the extent that they might create bottlenecks and thereby generate unemployment and inflation. But even in such cases the CEA was reluctant to sanction intervention, both because of the sanctity of the free price system and because it could not predict the effects of actions. It is significant that to illustrate

36. *Postwar Economic Policy and Planning,* H. Rept. 2729, 79 Cong. 2 sess. (GPO, 1946), p. 22.

37. A discussion of the tensions between the long run and the short in the CEA's early days appears in an unpublished manuscript by John D. Clark, one of the first council members: Clark Papers, HSTL. See especially chap. 11, "Long-Range Programs," and chap. 12, "The Problem of Planning."

38. Council of Economic Advisers, *Second Annual Report to the President, December 1947,* pp. 8–9. The Interior Department's "Proposals for Inclusion in the Economic Report to Congress" can be found in Economic Report File, Office Files of Evelyn Cooper, RG 48, NA. Secretary Krug's testimony on the report is in Joint Economic Report Committee File, Office Files of Oscar Chapman, RG 48, NA.

39. Clark, manuscript, chap. 11, p. 16.

this point in 1948 Clark selected an example from the industry he knew best, petroleum.

The governing factor in the economic machine is price. It is through changes in price that economic forces are shifted and economic conditions are modified. The mandate of the Employment Act does not permit the government to take charge of the determination of prices, that being an essential function of private management in a free economy. How serious is this limitation upon the economic planner is disclosed in innumerable incidents, such as the increase in crude oil prices late in 1947. The market price had been raised high enough to develop a production of about 5 million barrels per day, to induce widespread exploration, and to cause the drilling of new wells to reach the limit set by the availability of steel pipe and other materials. There was need for more oil, but there was no need for a higher price in order to continue the production of 5 million barrels per day and to induce the drilling of new wells and the search for new fields. The current price was entirely adequate for those purposes, and it was clear that it was only the shortage of steel pipe and other materials which prevented much greater activity.

If there was any way to bring more crude oil into the market by raising the price, the sensible procedure would have been to offer the higher price for the additional supply. If no more oil could be found, it would have been far more reasonable for the government to reduce the demand to the available supply at the current price by cutting of the less essential uses than to permit the over-demand to push up a price which was already high enough to induce maximum production. The government could take neither of these prudent actions because the government does not fix prices by direct action in a free economy.

There was no indirect action available to the government, and the free market was permitted to determine the price. The demand brought about an increase of 35 cents per barrel which the public has been paying ever since upon 5 million barrels of oil per day which would have been produced at the old price. There was an increase in production of about 150,000 barrels per day within a few weeks, and this was expanded somewhat in a few months, but this could hardly be attributed to the impact of price rises when the old price had induced drilling operations as extensive as the material situation permitted. Assuming, however, that the higher prices were responsible for some addition to the production above the level it would have reached at the former price, the fact remains that the public paid 35 cents per barrel more than was necessary for several million barrels of oil in order to bring into the market a very small addition to the supply. It is simple arithmetic to compute what would have been saved if the same result could have been reached by the payment of a government subsidy for the additional oil, but it would be anything but simple to devise a practicable method to determine who should get the subsidy. The production of some commodities proceeds under such conditions, however, that the subsidy policy with respect to high-cost production was applied successfully during the war, as in the case of some mine products.[40]

In October 1947 Chairman Nourse informed Secretary Krug: "After some delay, we have recently added a very competent full-time man to our staff in the area of resources development—Mr. Joseph L. Fisher."[41] Nevertheless, throughout the Truman years the council remained resolutely macroeconomic in its basic orientation. At times council members seemed almost to rejoice in their ignorance of the microeconomic details of specific energy markets. For example, in 1951 Leon Keyserling, by then CEA chairman, replied angrily to a published report that he was part of a new "brain trust" discoursing in secret on all manner of economic subjects.

I do not know much about water supply systems, and cannot recall having engaged in discussion of them with anybody. I have on appropriate occasion expressed interest in a few power and water projects essential to resource development and to building our defenses. . . . I cannot recall having discussed rural electrification programs with anybody since the advent of the defense program. . . . While every citizen must hope that industrial and other peaceful uses for atomic energy will be found, I do not know much about the subject and have discussed it with no one.[42]

It was clear from testimony such as this that if advice on energy policy was coming from anywhere it was not coming from the CEA.

But if the CEA eschewed responsibility for energy policy, such was not the case with the State Department, exhilarated by America's new world role and under the vigorous leadership of such powerful figures as Secretary Dean Acheson, and in economic areas, Under Secretary William L. Clayton and Assistant Secretary Willard L. Thorp. Even before the war ended Under Secretary of the Interior Abe Fortas wrote to his opposite number at the State Department complaining that "certain actions taken by the Department of State during the past few years create the impression that it does not fully appreciate or recognize the responsi-

40. Ibid., chap. 12, pp. 6–8.

41. Nourse to Krug, October 22, 1947, Economic Council (Dr. Nourse) File, Chapman Office Files, RG 48, NA. Evelyn Cooper informed Assistant Secretary Davidson that Bertram M. Gross, administrative assistant to Chairman Nourse, had assured her that the council endorsed the regional development goals of the Interior Department and waited only for Fisher's arrival to work on the subject. Cooper to Davidson, June 11, 1947, Memoranda and Notes for Mr. Davidson File, Cooper Office Files, RG 48, NA.

42. Keyserling to Prentice-Hall, Inc., October 24, 1951, CEA, Leon Keyserling File, Roy Blough Papers, HSTL.

bilities of the Department of the Interior in problems relating to certain foreign natural resources." He asked for the return of the Minerals Attaché Service, which had been transferred to the State Department in 1942, and for representation on all appropriate interagency committees. Equally strong appeals by Assistant Secretary Michael W. Straus and by Ickes himself received replies in the negative from Secretary of State Edward R. Stettinius, Jr., and Assistant Secretary Clayton.[43] As under secretary of the interior, Chapman wrote to Secretary Krug in 1946 about the alarming way in which the State Department was then trespassing on the Interior Department's traditional territory. In particular he complained that the latter had repeatedly been denied membership on the important interagency Executive Committee on Economic Foreign Policy, which reviewed such questions as oil imports. This committee had established a Subcommittee on Conservation of Natural Resources and had permitted the Interior Department to become a member of this lower body. But now, as reported by Chapman, this subcommittee had identified as its first order of business "urgent problems of domestic conservation and its relation to foreign trade," a subject traditionally the concern exclusively of the Interior Department. The Executive Committee had another Subcommittee on International Commodity Problems and proposed to create a petroleum committee to forecast levels of supply and demand. All reports from the Executive Committee and its subcommittees were "submitted to the Secretary of State for approval or disapproval by him. The effect of this is to place in the hands of the Secretary of State the final approval on matters of conservation and security, which to a large extent deal with domestic problems."[44]

Perhaps the greatest indignity for the Interior Department was the proposed takeover by the State Department of responsibility for a World Conservation Conference (renamed the Scientific Conference on the Conservation and Utilization of Resources, under United Nations auspices), which had originally been proposed by Harold Ickes and Gifford Pinchot. An interdepartmental working committee chaired by Stephen Raushenbush of the Interior Department with representatives from the Agriculture, State, and Commerce departments, drew up plans for the

43. Clayton to Ickes, January 24, 1945; Abe Fortas to Joseph C. Grew, January 17, 1945; Michael Straus to Robert A. Taft, February 5, 1945; Ickes to Stettinius, February 9, 1945; and Stettinius to Ickes, March 16, 1945; all in CCF 11-6, RG 48, NA.

44. Chapman to Krug, April 26, 1946, CCF 1-70, RG 48, NA.

conference. All the while, however, the State Department seemed to resist the principle of leadership resting in the Interior Department.[45] The conference was ultimately held at Lake Success, New York, in August and September 1949 with Secretary Krug at the head of the U.S. delegation. The themes Krug stressed in his welcoming address were relatively noncontroversial ones—the need to assist the poor countries of the world and the hope held out by scientific advance. It is significant, however, that the first three "opportunities" he noted for the years ahead were all in the energy area: "1. The peacetime application of atomic energy. 2. More effective utilization of solar energy. 3. Development of synthetic fuels, particularly from oil shales."[46]

U.S. foreign economic responsibilities, most of which had energy implications, grew dramatically after World War II: to build a new world trading system, facilitate recovery from destruction, undertake a massive assistance program to poor countries, and mobilize a coordinated defense of the free world. Moreover, the proper balance among those activities had to be found, as well as between unilateral and multinational efforts and between public and private enterprise as the vehicle for their achievement. Innumerable particular questions persisted such as how the federal government should act toward its large corporations operating abroad and what steps should be taken to assure supplies of such crucial commodities as petroleum. The Interior Department was not the only place in government that doubted the competence of the State Department to guide the foreign economic policy of the United States adequately. But as there was no agreement on an alternative, the question remained open, dispersion of authority persisted, and in many aspects

45. Raushenbush to Francis Biddle, February 14, 1947; and Ivan Bloch to Under Secretary Chapman, "Conference with Mr. Dean Rusk, Director, Office of Special Political Affairs, Department of State," April 11, 1947, both in CCF 1-70, RG 48, NA.

46. "Welcoming Address by Secretary of the Interior J. A. Krug to United Nations Scientific Conference on the Conservation and Utilization of Resources, Lake Success, New York, August 17, 1949," CCF 1-70, ibid. See also memorandum, Krug to Acheson, "United Nations Scientific Conference on the Conservation and Utilization of Resources," November 30, 1949, ibid. The ten sessions of the conference on "fuels and energy" must have been the most extensive general discussion on this set of topics up to that time. Planning documents are in CCF 1-43, RG 48, NA. It is significant, however, that these sessions were not organized by the Interior Department but by "Mr. [John A.] Loftus of the State Department." See memorandum, Evelyn Cooper to Under Secretary Chapman, October 7, 1947, International Resource Conference File, Oscar L. Chapman Papers, HSTL.

of foreign affairs the Interior Department remained largely on the outside looking in.[47]

Undoubtedly one of the most serious obstacles to the formation and implementation of a national energy policy after World War II, by the Interior Department or by any other unit in the executive branch, was the peculiar relationship that came to exist between government and industry. This relationship remained in a state of flux and ambiguity and was often so fraught with inconsistencies that it seemed to induce near-schizophrenia in government leaders charged to implement it. It is not possible to examine the relevant corporate records to get both sides of the story, but the government records lend little support to any simple conspiracy explanation of corporations attempting to gain control of government so as to increase their profits and of officials acquiescing so as to feather their own personal nests. Rather, there appears to have been genuine uncertainty on all sides about what the correct relationship should be between the public and private sectors. The structural models for a free market system were simply not very helpful on the subject. The simple competitive model suggested that the proper relationship between government and corporations should be mainly supervisory or, if necessary, adversarial. Government should break up concentrations of economic power, prevent combinations from coming into existence, and if necessary, regulate concentrated industries. As discussed above, this tradition was well developed during the 1930s in the work of the TNEC, the Federal Trade Commission, and the Antitrust Division of the Justice Department.

The message of the government's antimonopoly responsibilities was played like an obligato throughout the Truman years, even though the issue was politically a very divisive one. "Liberal" or "progressive" elements of the Democratic party, such as the trade unions and Americans for Democratic Action, were ever-conscious of the opportunity for "profiteering" and for "theft" from the poor people of America by "monopoly-capitalists," and nowhere did they think this was more likely than in the energy area. The liberals lobbied for the budgets of the antimonopoly programs of government, and they cried out at what they

47. Examples of correspondence in the White House files critical of foreign economic policymaking in the State Department are Joseph M. Jones to Clark M. Clifford, November 23, 1949; memorandum for discussion, David D. Lloyd, January 14, 1950; memorandum of conversation, George M. Elsey, January 17, 1950; all in H.S.T. Admin–Foreign Economic Policy Planning File, George M. Elsey Papers, HSTL.

claimed was the unsavory presence of businessmen in government.[48] On the other side conservative congressmen and businessmen repeatedly questioned the competence and even the loyalty of any public servants who were especially assiduous in attacks on concentrated industries. In a rare and clever attempt to draw support for antimonopoly programs from conservative elements the CEA suggested that the best way to forestall steadily increasing government control of industry was to stamp out monopolies before they had a chance to grow.[49]

Businessmen might be pardoned for some confusion over government intentions with respect to monopoly. In the 1930s and during the war they were invited into the innermost councils of government to search for "cooperative" solutions to the two major national challenges of depression and mobilization. Experiments with attacks on the former were terminated by the arrival of the latter. From then on, at least, the experience of government with the private sector seemed generally to be very positive. Testimony at the end of the war was plentiful about the contribution of businessmen who had been lent to government for the duration. Undoubtedly the experience for many bureaucrats was exhilarating. Businessmen brought a fresh, new "take charge" attitude to their jobs. And typically they got their work done efficiently and with dispatch.

When the war ended it was only natural for government to search for some type of relationship that would preserve the efficiency of the business-government partnership that had worked so well in war. At the same time, it was necessary to make peace with the principles of antitrust, which cautioned against all industry-government relationships likely to create market imperfections. Two institutions emerged from this search for a middle ground: first, councils of businessmen "advisory" to relevant parts of government, and second, jobs within government more or less reserved for businessmen formally or informally on leave from

48. In 1947 members of the White House staff discussed the political significance of antimonopoly efforts for the election one year away. A memorandum, "Points Regarding the Antitrust Program," prepared by an "anonymous source" was distributed by Charles Murphy in October to George Elsey, Charles Stauffacher, and David Bell. It recommended among other things: "Public attacks by Government officials on the antitrust laws, and the economic philosophy which they represent should be halted." Monopolies File, Files of Charles S. Murphy, Truman Papers, HSTL.

49. Memorandum, Paul T. Homan to John Clark, "Antitrust Message," January 26, 1949, CEA Files, Paul T. Homan, Edwin G. Nourse Papers, HSTL.

the private sector. The businessmen who became involved in these institutions often found them puzzling and frustrating because of the change of style and mixture of objectives they entailed. At the same time they provided an ear and a voice in government for the leaders of business and perhaps above all an opportunity to resist the imposition of policies perceived to be inimical to business interest. Guardians of antitrust, such as the Justice Department, also found these institutions worrisome; after all they exhibited the disturbing phenomenon of the lion lying down with the lamb.[50] Government was actually bringing together participants in potential cartels, commodity agreements, and other iniquities government had sworn to oppose. And yet as a halfway house between wartime mobilization and peace these institutions did seem peculiarly appropriate for the cold war economy.[51]

Deepening worries about the seeming ambivalence of government toward control of monopoly and relations with the private sector can be seen generally throughout those parts of government inhabited by economists in the years right after the war.[52] In the Interior Department, where advisory committees were unusually vigorous, concern about their role came to a head in 1949. Assistant Secretary C. Girard Davidson led the demands for reform. Discussion was precipitated by the publication

50. The cooperation of advisory committees in the control of inflation was solicited specifically under a joint resolution enacted December 30, 1947 (61 Stat. 945), and an executive order (9919) of January 3, 1948, was required to exempt these committees from the antitrust laws in the performance of this task. Nevertheless, Interior Department staff remained nervous about the extent of this exemption. See Alfred C. Wolf to Walton Seymour, December 29, 1947; James Boyd to Seymour, January 26, 1948; and Evelyn Cooper to Seymour, January 28, 1948, all in Anti-Inflation Program File, Office Files of Walton Seymour, RG 48, NA. The legal issues raised by advisory committees were discussed by Assistant Attorney General Wendell Berge in "Industry Advisory Committees and the Antitrust Laws," an address to the Annual Convention of the National Oil Marketers Association, September 27, 1946, Oil and Gas Matters File, Chapman Office Files, RG 48, NA.

51. As the organ of government most reminiscent of wartime, the NSRB made use of a plethora of advisory committees, both those set up by other agencies and those created specially. A list of these committees in 1948 and their meetings is in NSRB, "Roster of Advisory Committees, September 15, 1948," OF 1295, Truman Papers, HSTL.

52. Examples are the Bureau of the Budget (see memorandum, J. Weldon Jones to the director, "Economic Questions Raised by the 1948 Budget," March 7, 1947, Council of Economic Advisers File, James E. Webb Papers, HSTL) and the CEA (see Clark, manuscript, chap. 11, p. 9, where he noted in 1948, "anti-trust policy . . . has been studied by the Council for two years with no satisfactory result"; Clark Papers, HSTL).

of *A National Oil Policy for the United States* by the National Petroleum
Council, an advisory committee created in 1946. This report, which
seemed to imply it had government sanction, caused Davidson to prepare
a blistering memorandum to Secretary Krug; after reflection, he never
sent it. What he had to say is instructive all the same.

As you know, I have consistently questioned the network of special interest
advisory committees which have been established in the Department. Perhaps
more than any other Department, we, because of our custodianship of the
natural resources of the Nation, are subject to extreme pressures by groups
who stand to gain from exploitation of those resources. It goes without saying
that we must work with such groups. It is, however, detrimental to the public
interest to let such groups set our policies for us or to affiliate themselves with
us in such a fashion that they seem to be setting our policies. I am not prepared at the moment to recommend a specific plan for revision of our advisory committee setup, which possibly might call for an over-all commission
representing all groups to act as a holding company for the present special interest committees. I do feel, however, that we must find a new system which
balances the pressures of the different special interest groups and which gives
us freedom to make our decisions in terms of the public interest.

I have also stated before that those portions of the Department which
work very closely with industry cannot abdicate their responsibility for setting national policies in which the public interest dominates, even though at
times it may adversely affect the industry concerned. I do not see how we can
properly expect an industry with so much at stake to be able to make a guiding policy for us which might seriously affect the industry's interests, if these
interests conflict with the larger public interest as is certain to happen from
time to time.[53]

Although Davidson did not send this memorandum to Krug, he obviously made his feelings known to the secretary and did succeed in
scotching a proposal from James Boyd, director of the Bureau of Mines,
that a similar policy statement be prepared by the National Minerals
Advisory Council. In this case he wrote to the secretary as follows:

I would like to suggest that a proper policy statement should do the following:
(1) Cover separately each important mineral and its special problems.
(2) Consider on an equal plane the interests of the mining industry, the
    mineral processing and consuming industries, the ultimate consumers,
    and national requirements for civilian needs and security.
(3) Present the various recommendations in the interests of each of the
    foregoing factors and show which are consistent and which are in

53. Davidson to Krug (marked "not sent"), May 3, 1949, Oil (Policy) File,
Minerals and Fuels Division Files, RG 48, NA.

conflict. In the cases of conflict, the report should attempt an objective appraisal in the maximum national interest—not in the maximum interest of any segment of the industry.[54]

Moreover, Davidson did not give up on the subject. In 1950 he undertook a departmental inquiry into the whole question of advisory groups. In an interim report in July he described the results of conversations with "members of the Secretary's office who are not directly concerned in advisory committee operations" (that is, not the businessmen in government). One suggestion from these persons was that the committees simply be abolished: "While the present type of advisory committees served admirably for war and immediate postwar situations, other methods of consultation with outside groups, such as ad hoc committees and public hearings, might be more useful under present conditions." But if the present system were retained committees should not continue to "represent a single special interest, industry or otherwise." Committees should reflect the ever present "conflict between special interests." Moreover, committees should be organized more broadly on a functional base. For example, "a Committee on Energy might replace the present National Petroleum Council and the Bituminous Coal Advisory Council, with electric power representation added." Finally, the staff of all advisory committees should be firmly rooted in the secretary's immediate office and should essentially run them. Above all "policy questions should not be submitted to advisory committees for discussion and advice until this Department itself has formed its own views in regard to policies or proposed policies."[55]

What Davidson was suggesting in this report would have amounted to the first real change in the relationship of the Interior Department to the business community since World War II. It was perhaps only one of many comparable tragedies of public policy that his suggestions coincided with the invasion of South Korea from the North. His argument that wartime conditions no longer prevailed and that new peacetime links between government and industry had to be constructed thereby lost its force. In fact, the system of advisory councils lasted throughout the Truman years more or less unscathed.

54. Memorandum, Davidson to Krug, "Advisory Councils and a National Minerals Policy," April 18, 1949, Bureau of Mines 1948–49 File, Chapman Office Files, RG 48, NA. Krug rejected Boyd's request in Krug to Boyd, April 22, 1949, ibid.
55. Memorandum, C. Girard Davidson, "Advisory Groups: Interim Report," July 10, 1950, attachment to Davidson to Assistant Secretary Warne and others, September 18, 1950, Advisory Councils File, Joel D. Wolfsohn Papers, HSTL.

Interior Department Progress toward Policy

Despite the impediments thrown in its way the Interior Department made considerable progress toward acting as the national energy policy planner. The reason why lies in a combination of external events and stirrings in the department itself. Two developments in particular created a public demand for discussion of energy policy, a demand that only the department could supply in any large measure. First of all, in the years right after the war, shortages of all the major fuels appeared at different times, especially in the winter months. In retrospect it can be seen that these shortages were temporary and usually related to episodic bottlenecks in steel, transportation, refinery capacity, or other parts of the delivery system. But the shortages often were accompanied by substantial price rises and by uncertainty about whether the phenomena were manipulated and short or long run. The second development was the decision by President Truman to assist massively the economic recovery of Europe through what became known as the Marshall Plan. An immediate question for most Americans about this decision was what would it mean at home, especially what strains it would place on the resource base of the American economy.

The Interior Department's first response to these two concerns took place in June 1947 in accordance with a request from the President to study quickly the effect of foreign aid on national resources. The so-called Krug Report, *National Resources and Foreign Aid,* published in October 1947, was a companion to a broader CEA study of the overall economic effect of foreign aid.[56] These two reports became basic source material for study by a citizens' committee under the chairmanship of Commerce Secretary W. Averell Harriman. In cooperation with all the resource-related departments and agencies a team of Interior Department staff headed by Assistant Secretary Warne prepared a series of studies of commodities and the prospects for their growth in supply under the stimulus of rapidly increasing aggregate demand. (The Interior Department handled all the fuel studies in cooperation with the Commerce and State departments.) The conclusion of the Krug Report was on the whole rather optimistic. Bottlenecks and shortages could indeed be ex-

56. U.S. Department of the Interior, *National Resources and Foreign Aid* (GPO, 1947); and "The Impact of Foreign Aid upon the Domestic Economy: A Report to the President by the Council of Economic Advisers" (October 1947).

pected to occur, for example in coal, but with careful management (including "government-industry cooperation") these could be overcome, and the final result of strengthening the world economic system would be worth the cost. Interior Department staff even worried that one cost of the aid program might be the generation of overcapacity, which could not be sustained by demand when normalcy returned.[57]

One of the purposes of the Krug Report was to reduce public fears about resource scarcities. Congress in particular, that sensitive barometer of public opinion, reported widespread worry and confusion. But the Krug Report did not succeed entirely in this objective, mainly because shortages and price increases did persist in certain areas during the following year. The House Committee on Interstate and Foreign Commerce was in the forefront of the clamor for more information and action. This committee had long been concerned about the petroleum market, and with the prospect of a new shortage ahead, it held hearings during the second half of 1947. During the hearings the committee was "uniformly assured by representatives of government and the petroleum industry that there was no cause for alarm." Accordingly when shortages did appear in the early winter of 1948 the committee set out on a sustained "general study into fuel supply and demand . . . or, using another term, an energy-resources study, and not a series of four separate studies into petroleum, natural gas, coal and electric power." The committee insisted in its preliminary report that "it is imperative, in the interest of the Nation's prosperity and security, for the Congress to think, and, if necessary, to act, in terms of a national fuel policy rather than a national petroleum policy, a national coal policy, a national electric-power policy, and a national natural-gas policy."[58] The committee emphasized that both short-run and long-run forebodings prompted its inquiries; among the former was the prospect of a cold winter, among the latter the chance that "the public in a few years may have to return generally to a four-cylinder small horsepower automobile." The committee set forth an

57. Assistant Secretary Warne summarized for the Senate Foreign Relations Committee on November 13, 1947, the "purpose and scope" of the Krug Report as well as "the way in which it was prepared and generally about its conclusions." His statement is in *Interim Aid for Europe*, Hearings before the Senate Committee on Foreign Relations, 80 Cong. 1 sess. (GPO, 1947), pp. 178–236. The minutes of the Krug Committee and various pertinent documents are in Departmental Committees File, Chapman Office Files, RG 48, NA.

58. *Fuel Investigation*, Preliminary Report from the House Committee on Interstate and Foreign Commerce, H. Rept. 1270, 80 Cong. 2 sess. (GPO, 1948), p. 2.

extraordinarily ambitious "outline of fuel investigation," which it was never able to follow.[59] Although it was able only to call for a national energy policy and not to produce one, it did act as a catalyst for those in the Interior Department who sought any excuse to resume leadership in energy policy.

An important development in the department that affected its capacity to respond to the demands for a national energy policy and to overcome obstacles to this goal was a fundamental administrative reorganization that began soon after the arrival of Secretary Krug. Ickes had given style and drama to the department, but an effective manager he was not. Although the department's responsibilities and authority grew enormously during his tenure, he left it more a collection of loosely connected baronies than a well-integrated department, and it was without a set of coordinated department policies. Krug was an experienced executive who quickly saw that major changes had to be made. The most important changes for purposes of energy were a strengthening of the Office of the Secretary and the creation in this office of a coordinating Program Committee and Program Staff. The moving forces behind the reorganization under Krug were two assistant secretaries, both lawyers, Warner W. Gardner and C. Girard Davidson, the first the former solicitor of the department and the latter former chief counsel of the Bonneville Power Administration.[60] Apparently Secretary Krug's unhappy experience with the hurried preparation of the Krug Report convinced him of the need

59. Further progress reports on the fuel investigation study during 1948, which dealt mainly with aspects of specific current petroleum problems, were *Fuel Investigation,* H. Rept. 1321, 80 Cong. 2 sess. (GPO, 1948); *Fuel Investigation: Petroleum and the European Recovery,* H. Rept. 1438, 80 Cong. 2 sess. (GPO, 1948); *Fuel Investigation: Petroleum Prices and Profits,* H. Rept. 2342, 80 Cong. 2 sess. (GPO, 1948); and *Fuel Investigation,* H. Rept. 2468, 80 Cong. 2 sess. (GPO, 1948).

60. Discussion of a reorganization was as old as the department itself. Gardner made his first detailed proposals as solicitor in "Memorandum for the Secretary," May 27, 1946, Regionalization (Special Assignment) File, Branch of Economics and Statistics Files, RG 48, NA. The weakness of the analytical capacity of the department, especially when compared with the new CEA, was pointed out to Krug by George A. Lamb, assistant director of the Bureau of Mines, together with a suggestion that the bureau establish a new Economics and Statistics Branch. (Lamb to Krug, October 14, 1946, CCF 11-6, RG 48, NA.) In 1950 an administrative history of the Department of the Interior was prepared by a team from the Woodrow Wilson School of Princeton University, supervised by George A. Graham, professor of politics. As far as I can tell the history was never published. A draft chapter, "The Program Staff, Program Committee, and Field Committees," by James W. Clark, is a helpful guide to the postwar reorganization. A copy is in Princeton Survey File, Minerals and Fuels Division Files, RG 48, NA.

for some central analytic unit in the department. In 1947 he created the Program Staff substantially out of the team that prepared the report, and he named an old associate from TVA, Walton Seymour, as director.

The Program Staff and the Program Committee created in 1948 with representatives from the department's main operating units was charged to examine "all policies and programs of the Department with the objective of ascertaining that (a) they are integrated and internally consistent; (b) they constitute a full utilization of the Department's powers for carrying out the responsibilities of the Department; (c) they are appropriately related to the programs and policies of other agencies of government; and (d) they are in proper context with the current and prospective needs of the national economy."[61] One sympathetic observer asked to comment on the new Program Staff compared them to "a group of 'shock troops' . . . if these move fast enough, the red tape artists can't catch up with them, and neither can Bureau chiefs."[62] Predictably there was some opposition to the idea of the Program Staff from the operating bureaus and from some congressmen who feared the interposition of a new layer in their relations with these bureaus. Nevertheless, by 1950 there were twelve professional members of the staff, four assigned to field committees around the country that were charged with the internal consistency of department programs within a region. One of the initial goals of the staff was improvement of the analytical capacity of the operating bureaus as well, and one of the first achievements in this direction was the creation of the office of chief economist in the Bureau of Mines.[63]

Inevitably the Program Staff tackled energy policy early on because of the insistent pressures on the secretary, whose instinctive response was to ask for facts. In October 1947 the Geological Survey produced for him a report on the fuel and energy situation in the United States that offered detailed estimates of supplies (based substantially on industry data) and repeated the familiar conclusion that the short-run

61. Clark, "The Program Staff, Program Committee, and Field Committees," p. 16.

62. Ivan Bloch to Walton Seymour, November 17, 1948, Minerals Program File, Craine Correspondence Files, RG 48, NA.

63. During 1949 the Program Staff drew up plans for a new economic unit in the bureau and for a "statistical audit" of the bureau's publications by the National Bureau of Economic Research. One of the tasks of the unit would be "Projection of Future Energy Requirements—by finished energy commodities, by primary energy sources, by function (e.g., heat, power, etc.), by class of consumer." Walton Seymour to James Boyd, July 29, 1949. This and other planning documents are in Organization Bureau of Mines File, Craine Correspondence Files, RG 48, NA.

problems were really with steel and transportation and not with energy. In the long run, although domestic petroleum supplies might decline (with Alaska offering the one bright question mark) mineral fuels in the aggregate should be adequate "to meet probable demands for generations to come."[64]

Krug was not satisfied with this study alone, and in April 1948 he complained to Seymour that for several months he had been requesting "a general study of the Nation's energy and fuel requirements . . . and our best guess as to how these needs would be met . . . even some 'guesstimates' would be better than nothing. I don't think any of the past projections by the principal industries involved reflect a realistic appraisal of the total needs of our expanding fully employed economy operating at a tempo which can meet our domestic needs and our increasing commitments abroad."[65] With an election coming up the White House was worried about energy as well. As chairman of the Fuel and Power Task Committee, Seymour advised White House economic consultant Robert C. Turner that although these markets were in a "very delicate balance between supply and demand . . . the imposition of Government controls will probably not be necessary except in the event of serious production breakdowns."[66]

In November 1947 Under Secretary Chapman testified before the House Committee on Banking and Currency about the inflationary potential in the energy sector, a situation he found "explosive," although he could not provide many details. He complained that "the Department's present authority and appropriation for statistical and economic work on coal and oil are totally inadequate in the present emergency situation."[67] Answers to the Congressmen's questions awaited more research.

64. Acting Director, Geological Survey, to the Secretary of the Interior, October 21, 1947, Geological Survey File, Minerals and Fuels Division Files, RG 48, NA. Lyle Craine, consultant, explained the "minerals job" of the Program Staff as he saw it in 1949. It would have a large energy component, especially for the study of the entire synthetic fuels program. Craine to Alfred C. Wolf, March 23, 1949, General File, Craine Correspondence Files, RG 48, NA.

65. Krug to Seymour, April 22, 1948, Oscar Chapman File, Files of the Program Staff, RG 48, NA.

66. Seymour to Turner, May 17, 1948, Seymour Office Files, RG 48, NA.

67. Statement of Oscar L. Chapman, Acting Secretary of the Department of the Interior, before the House Committee on Banking and Currency, November 25, 1947, E.R.P. [European Recovery Program] Krug Report, St. of Union Messages, etc. File, Chapman Office Files, RG 48, NA.

In October 1948 the Interior Department was invited to join an Energy Resources Survey Group of the NSRB and to update the Krug Report. Seymour was the department's main representative in these efforts. The new NSRB study was to be "concerned with the drain on our resources of the national security and related programs in the aggregate rather than merely the foreign aid program."[68] In fact this particular energy study was prompted mainly by the Defense Department's nervousness about petroleum and would not lead to quick results. (See the discussion of petroleum in chapter 2.)

In December 1948 Secretary Krug submitted to the President material proposed for inclusion in the economic report, with a thirty-two page section on energy, which called above all for more study and policy formation in addition to programs to stimulate production and reduce waste. He wrote: "We should be doing much more in determining our energy reserves, in producing and using our fuels less wastefully, and in developing power from inexhaustible hydroelectric sources instead of exhaustible coal, oil and gas."[69]

Finally, in May 1949 Seymour submitted to Secretary Krug the long-awaited report, "Energy Uses and Supplies, 1939, 1947, 1965." It had been prepared by Harold J. Barnett, an economist and member of the Program Staff, and embodied the most sophisticated treatment of energy statistics at least since the report of the National Resources Committee in 1939. The report became the basis for most public statements about energy policy from the Interior Department for several years to come.

Barnett argued that four features of energy resources justified the careful study and planning of such resources: most fuels were finite in quantity, could not be increased in production or substituted for each other without substantial lead time, were developed only with very large investments, and were produced frequently in noncompetitive industries. Using a modification of Wassily Leontief's pioneering input-output techniques, which were relatively novel at that time, he made rough projections for both supplies of and demands for all the major fuels. He acted on a range of heroic assumptions, some of which today seem very shrewd (for example, the continued unprofitability of synthetic fuels)

68. Arthur M. Hill to Krug, September 22, 1948, and October 4, 1948; and Chapman to Hill, October 8, 1948; all in Director of Program Staff–Krug Report File, Seymour Office Files, RG 48, NA.

69. U.S. Department of the Interior, "Proposals for Inclusion in the Economic Report to the Congress," December 1, 1948, attached to memorandum, Krug to the President, December 3, 1948, Personal Files of Samuel Moment.

and others naive (for example, the progressive fuel efficiency of the automobile engine). Barnett concluded that if national output increased by 70 percent between 1947 and 1965, as expected, the increase in fuel required for heat would be slightly more than 20 percent, for motion only 10 percent, and for power (electric and direct drive) 70 percent. This meant that the total fuel requirements in 1965 would be only 30 percent over 1947, a projection explained by "technical advances in combustion, use of more efficient temperatures and pressures, extension of insulation practices, and other technical advances." Barnett was less confident on the supply side but predicted "conspicuous relative increases . . . in hydropower, natural gas, and crude oil" and absolute declines for "other energy commodities" (that is, mainly coal). He also estimated "a substantial increase in crude imports on combined grounds of cost and American company ownership of important foreign reserves." He assumed that solar, nuclear, and synthetic fuels would not be factors because of cost, conceding that in the case of synfuels people might say, " 'Eventually oil must come from coal; why not start now when this would serve security in addition.' Against the view are, among other arguments, large domestic shale deposits, and the rich tidal shelf to supplement limited inland petroleum reserves; and American free-trade policy." In the long run Barnett's main contribution may have been to show the complexities, limitations, and opportunities of aggregate energy projection, an art that was not to progress much beyond his accomplishments for some years.[70]

The Barnett study quickly began to have a discernible effect on Interior Department statements. Whereas Under Secretary Chapman had been uncertain about the energy future in 1947, and a year later

70. The first draft of Barnett's paper is in Power Division File, Chapman Office Files, RG 48, NA. The study was subsequently revised and published. See Harold J. Barnett, *Energy Uses and Supplies, 1939, 1947, 1965,* Bureau of Mines Information Circular 7582 (Department of the Interior, 1950). As background for his report, Barnett prepared "distillations of all the recent energy forecasts of which I have knowledge," both private and public—some thirteen in all from 1938 to 1949. If nothing else, this exercise produced a valuable historical document. See Barnett to Seymour, Memorandum Number 4—Staff use only, November 30, 1948, Harold J. Barnett File, Seymour Office Files, RG 48, NA. Barnett recalled that his report "resulted from discussion between Adm. Lewis Strauss (AEC) and J. A. Krug (Interior Secretary), who thought they needed a view of energy in future (related to their respective energy responsibilities)." The report became part of Barnett's Harvard Ph.D. dissertation (1953), "Atomic Energy in the United States Economy: A Consideration of Certain Industrial, Regional, and Economic Development Aspects." Letter to Joseph A. Pechman, November 30, 1978.

material prepared for his address to the League of Women Voters predicted that "total energy needs will increase at least 50 percent within next ten years,"[71] with Barnett behind him he could take a more confident and less alarmist position. In addition Barnett's work seems to have thrown up as by-products several large issues of energy policy that continued to rattle around in the department and the nation for some time to come. One issue was whether energy supplies were liable to be the limiting factor on American economic growth. Barnett had shown that there tended to be a short-run fixed relationship between gross national product and energy use. This implied clearly that energy might be the effective constraint of the future on growth. As Barnett wrote to Seymour, "If during the next decade GNP were to increase by a third, as the President's Economic Report suggests, then energy requirements would increase about proportionately. This is a neutral phrasing. Put another way, GNP is not likely to increase by a third unless energy is forthcoming in adequate volume, at low enough prices, *and* in the forms which the economy requires."[72] A related issue developed by another Interior Department staff member, Ivan Bloch, was whether concentration in the energy industries had led to the development of big-unit technology and thereby to the continuation of such concentration and the neglect of energy sources suitable for small-scale production.[73]

Two events in 1949 gave a substantial fillip to the energy policy activities of the Interior Department staff. First, to almost everyone's surprise Harry Truman began a second term as president, and opportunities opened up for four more years of bold and innovative policies.[74] The

71. "Material for Secretary Chapman's Address before the League of Women Voters of the District of Columbia, December 14, 1948," Public Addresses, vol. 5, Chapman Papers, HSTL. "The Outlook for Energy Resources," a section of a large document entitled "Program Requirements for the National Resources Responsibilities of the Department of the Interior, December, 1951," prepared by the Program Staff, depended heavily on Barnett's 1949 study. Department of Interior Program Staff File, Doty Papers, HSTL.

72. Barnett to Seymour, December 21, 1948, Harold J. Barnett File, Seymour Office Files, RG 48, NA.

73. Bloch to Davidson, December 27, 1948; and Barnett to Seymour, December 29, 1948; both in Barnett File, ibid.

74. Shortly after the election Secretary Krug distributed to his senior staff a collection of the President's statements made before and during the campaign that were relevant to the department's responsibilities, especially commitments by Truman to public power projects and the concept of regional development. "Presidential Policy Statements for Guidance in Future Policy Formulation," November 30, 1948, White House, the President File, Chapman Papers, HSTL.

second event was the replacement in December 1949 of Secretary Krug
by Oscar Chapman, long a senior man in the department with roots well
back in the New Deal. Chapman was no Ickes, but he was a certified
liberal with an appreciation of competent subordinates and openness to
imaginative ideas.[75]

Chapman quickly took a number of actions relevant to energy policy.
He directed the Program Committee and the Program Staff to follow up
the Barnett study so that the department might at last have a blueprint
by which to assert its proper "role in national energy affairs." Certain
important features of the energy situation had been identified by this
study, but the committee agreed that they had not been fully explored.
Large questions remained concerning the extent of substitutability among
the uses of final energy products and among fuels as primary sources;
the supply trends of individual energy products; energy requirements per
unit of output (Barnett had detected a downward trend); influential
variables in energy markets such as the growth and changing product
mix of national output, productivity advances, and relative cost movements of various inputs.[76]

The Program Committee concluded that what was needed was a full-
fledged National Energy Resources Policy Commission. An eloquent
appeal was made for such a commission to do in 1949 what the National
Resources Committee had done a decade before. As one of the most
powerful statements to date of the case for a national energy policy this
Interior Department document is worth citing at some length.

. . . we are still considering energy policies separately through particularized
agencies, committees, advisory groups, and working parties, usually attempting to work out a specific problem. Among the Federal Departments, for
instance, there are about ten inter-agency groups dealing with coal, petroleum, energy, fuel, power and related matters from the standpoint of security, foreign policy, foreign trade, or other aspects of the over-all energy
problem. Similarly, there are a number of advisory groups dealing with different energy matters. The National Petroleum Council and the National
Bituminous Coal Advisory Council are two such committees representing
energy supplying industries.

This piecemeal attack on our inter-related energy resources problems
makes for inadequate consideration of the national interest and failure fully

75. For details of Chapman's career at the Interior Department, see Clayton R.
Koppes, "Oscar L. Chapman: A Liberal at the Interior Department, 1933–1953"
(Ph.D. dissertation, University of Kansas, 1974).

76. Agenda, Twelfth Meeting of the Program Committee, December 5, 1949,
Oscar Chapman File, Program Staff Files, RG 48, NA.

to know where we are heading with respect to our crucial energy supplies. Over-all considerations are lost in attempts to find easy solutions to particular problems. Special interests naturally have greater weight in such handling of isolated problems.

A broad and integrated attack on our energy problems would minimize the effectiveness of special pleading and would put our overriding concern for national welfare and security in proper perspective in considering special problems of specific segments of the energy supply components of our economy. It is difficult to fend off such recurring attacks of special interests as the efforts to avoid regulation of gas pipelines, to take the Tidelands out of Federal jurisdiction and to reverse our policy with respect to supplying transmission lines for public power projects, without a public awareness of the relationship of these matters to a national energy policy directed to our welfare and security. It is even more difficult to take essential affirmative action, such as measures for solving the problems of the coal industry, for developing a synthetic liquid fuels industry, or for protecting our interests in foreign oil supplies, without a comprehensive national energy policy.[77]

The document noted that the House Committee on Interstate and Foreign Commerce had set out to conduct a study comparable to that proposed by the Program Committee, but to be effective the study had to be an executive, not a congressional, one.

Chapman submitted a proposal for an Energy Policy Commission to President Truman on February 24, 1950, inexplicably with a memorandum of justification that was far weaker than the Program Committee document that had initiated the idea. Presidential assistant Charles S. Murphy in his cover note to the President reported that "the file does not appear to me to contain anywhere an adequate explanation of the reasons why the Commission is thought to be necessary," and he recommended that the matter be referred to the Bureau of the Budget for study.[78] The file copy bears the word "Drop," and this in fact seems to have been the fate of the proposal.[79]

One argument for a national energy policy not appearing directly in the case presented to President Truman but circulating in the Interior Department at the time was that if full employment and price stability were really to be obtained and maintained, specific goals and production targets in the energy industries had to be specified in advance. If the market—where imperfections were so great—were left to do the job,

77. "Memorandum on the Need for an Energy Resources Policy Commission," n.d. Subject File: Cabinet, Secretary of Interior Miscellaneous, PSF, HSTL.

78. Memorandum, Murphy to the President, February 24, 1950, OF 6, Truman Papers, HSTL.

79. Memorandum, Chapman to the President, n.d., OF 6, ibid.

physical shortages and inflation followed by glut and deflation were bound to result.[80] This was essentially a short-run variant of the concern for the relationship between energy supplies and growth expressed by Barnett a little earlier. Discussion of this point took place in detail in connection with House bill 2756, the so-called Spence Bill, or Economic Stabilization Act of 1949, introduced by Brent Spence, chairman of the House Committee on Banking and Currency. Various high officials of the department offered support for the bill, noting usually that Interior Department programs, such as those in public power and synthetic fuels, were consistent with it.[81] But one economist, Samuel Moment, expressed most clearly to a staff member of the Joint Committee on the Economic Report the implications for natural resource markets of this proposed legislation and of the national commitment to full employment and price stability generally.

To me the Employment Act of 1946 is meaningful only to the extent that specific production, employment and purchasing power goals are set, consistent with the terms "full" and "maximum." But business leaders and journalists and many government men have avoided talking about how to measure such goals. The reasons for avoidance: either they don't accept the purposes of the Act, or else they think the purposes are attainable through general measures.

When the Council of Economic Advisers early this year asked the government agencies to prepare statements on critical commodity areas and requirements by 1954 in order to lay the groundwork for the Spence Bill, the statements generally displayed economic illiteracy. Only the work on Steel (Ed Hoover and Louis Bean) and my job on Power made some effort to estimate requirements in terms of full employment and maximum production. The Bureau of Mines' statements in initial form carried the Elmer Pherson fatalism and disregarded requirements in this sense partly by assuming the country couldn't meet them out of decreasing ore reserves, and partly because the mineral economists don't know how to estimate requirements to meet the purposes of the Act. The Department of Commerce statements were drawn under Sawyer's edict to confine themselves to innocuous facts.[82]

80. Temporary shortages of fuels and inflation in costs were regular concerns of Interior Department spokesmen. In a press release in January 1948 Secretary Krug called for a voluntary 15 percent reduction in consumption to permit continued equitable distribution. Articles 1 File, Max W. Ball Papers, HSTL.

81. For example, Krug to Elmer B. Staats, January 10, 1949; and Davidson to Congressman Hugh B. Mitchell, April 7, 1949, both in Economic Stabilization Act of 1949, Spence Act File, Davidson Office Files, RG 48, NA.

82. Moment to Theodore J. Kreps, November 14, 1949, Economic Report File, Cooper Office Files, RG 48, NA.

Moment urged that the Joint Committee hold hearings to show the American people how the current structure of the economic system could not in fact attain the goals that had been set for it under the Employment Act of 1946. On a lower philosophical plane a member of the Program Staff noted that if the Interior Department were not better supplied with capacity for economic analysis, it would be unable to pull its weight with the CEA and the Budget Bureau in these continuing discussions of how to achieve full employment and growth.[83]

The second action taken by new Interior Secretary Chapman with respect to energy policy, in addition to encouraging broad national inquiries into the subject, was further reorganization of the department, in part to provide for a continuing focus on the whole energy field. One stimulus for the reorganization was undoubtedly a report of the Hoover Commission in 1949 and the pressure for greater efficiency and accountability in government the report represented.[84] Senior staff members of the Interior Department were disappointed with the Hoover Commission report because it did not accept their wish to become the Department of Natural Resources—probably for the same reason the idea had been rejected several years before. Program Staff complained that the Hoover Commission had recommended that the Interior Department continue with "a miscellany of construction activities and subsoil and water resources activities" but without "coherence" or "orientation of purpose"; the department's response to this recommendation was a counterproposal once again that the broad responsibility for natural resources be assigned to the Interior Department and that the secretary "have the freedom to organize the Department" as he "saw fit."[85] Senator O'Mahoney, chairman of the Interior and Insular Affairs Committee, actually prepared a bill in 1949 that would have created a Department of Natural Resources. This move pleased the Interior Department leadership but got nowhere in Congress.[86]

83. Unsigned memorandum, "Economic Analysis Relating to Minerals," February 21, 1949, General File, Craine Correspondence Files, RG 48, NA.

84. See Commission on Organization of the Executive Branch of Government, *Department of the Interior: A Report to the Congress* (GPO, 1949). The commission, established July 7, 1947, was chaired by Herbert Hoover.

85. Walton Seymour to Secretary Chapman, "Policy Decisions to Be Made on the Hoover Commission Report," April 26, 1949, Program Staff File, Chapman Office Files, RG 48, NA.

86. Seymour to Chapman, August 12, 1949; and Chapman to Krug, n.d., Proposed Legislation File, Craine Correspondence Files, RG 48, NA.

As a preliminary move toward a less dramatic reorganization, the Program Staff envisaged the creation of two administrative units in the department concerned, respectively, with water resources and minerals.[87] Assistant Secretary Davidson had proposed the preparation of a distinct "minerals program" for the department by the Geological Survey and the Bureau of Mines as early as August 1947 but with little immediate success.[88] The Program Staff responded to Davidson's cries of frustration by observing sadly that while "the responsibility of government for promoting economic stability has now become generally accepted . . . the minerals agencies of the Department still generally limit their activities to technological research and service to industry."[89] Finally, on December 1, 1950, Department of the Interior Order 2602 established the Office of Assistant Secretary for Mineral Resources with three divisions —Minerals and Fuels, Geography, and Oil and Gas. In the energy area the new assistant secretary had supervisory responsibility over the Bureau of Mines and the Geological Survey as well as over the Oil and Gas Division. The first of the new divisions was created as a planning unit to advise the assistant secretary "on the development, coordination, and management of programs for his area"; its purpose was to "review, evaluate, and make recommendations on the development and utilization of minerals and fuels" and to "assist the Assistant Secretary in supervising and coordinating the execution of these programs by the bureaus and other agencies."[90] In essence this order provided for the first perma-

87. Memorandum, Walton Seymour to the Secretary and Under Secretary, "Policy Decisions To Be Made on the Hoover Commission Report," April 26, 1949, Oscar Chapman File, Program Staff Files, RG 48, NA. Some of the detailed discussion of organization in the field of resources considered by the Hoover Commission was in *Organization and Policy in the Field of Natural Resources: A Report with Recommendations* (GPO, 1949), submitted to the Commission on Organization of the Executive Branch of the Government by the Task Force on Natural Resources. Lyle Craine of the Program Staff discussed the reasons for department criticism of the Hoover Commission recommendations, which included the need to manage natural resources in a coherent fashion, given the national commitment to full employment and security of the West. Craine to Julian W. Feiss, June 8, 1949, General File, Craine Correspondence Files, RG 48, NA.

88. A chronology of unsuccessful efforts to generate a minerals policy between August 1947 and March 1948 is contained in Minerals Program File, Craine Correspondence Files, ibid.

89. Walton Seymour to Secretary Chapman through Assistant Secretary Davidson, n.d., Program Statements File, Craine Correspondence Files, ibid.

90. Department of the Interior Order 2602, "Assistant Secretary for Mineral Resources," December 1, 1950, Bureaus and Offices, Minerals and Fuels Division File, Wolfsohn Papers, HSTL.

nent planning unit concerned broadly and exclusively with resources and energy in the federal government.

By the time the order was issued in December 1950 an extensive search had already been conducted for staff. The type and caliber of candidates for director of the Division of Minerals and Fuels give a clear indication of the functions and status intended for it. The first choice was George W. Stocking, chairman of the Economics Department at Vanderbilt University, director for a time of the fuels division of the Office of Price Administration during World War II and one of the country's most distinguished resource economists. He declined. The other three candidates on the short list were Philip H. Coombs, then with the Economic Cooperation Administration; Joseph P. Loftus, on the Agriculture Department staff; and Donald H. Wallace, a professor of economics at Princeton.[91]

To complement the new analytical strength proposed for the Minerals and Fuels Division, increased analytical capacity was created in the Bureau of Mines. From its beginning the Program Staff had been concerned about the absence in the department of a strong economic research unit. Staff members Ivan Bloch and Lyle E. Craine made a number of studies of the question and concluded that the Bureau of Mines was the appropriate location for such a unit; it would be necessary only to "amplify and clarify the functions and activities of the Economics and Statistics Service . . . so that they will go beyond the compilation of statistics" and into "the fields of economic analyses and planning." One of the charges to such a unit would be to "study the production, costs, distribution, transportation, prices and marketing phases of the minerals industries in order to develop plans for meeting future mineral requirements as affected by depletions, import and export conditions, and other factors which may change the availability of supply."[92] Director James Boyd submitted his reorganization plan for the Bureau of Mines to Secretary Krug in July 1949; major justification for the plan was the need to improve and coordinate analysis for the formulation of

91. Memorandum, "Minerals and Fuels Division: Candidates for Positions," n.d., ibid.

92. Ivan Bloch, "Economics and Statistics in the Bureau of Mines," circa early 1949. This and documents concerning improvement of economic analysis in the bureau and the department are contained in the Lyle Craine Papers and in the Bureau of Mines Reorganization File, Branch of Economics and Statistics Files, RG 48, NA.

national policy.[93] The analytical capacity of the first chief economist in the bureau, Sam H. Schurr, could be seen in his "Proposed Material for Inclusion in President's Economic Report" in November 1950. In this material Schurr looked forward to substantial progress in the formation of a national fuels policy and to the illumination of some issues long shrouded in confusion, notably the desirability of oil imports and of favored tax treatment for domestic fuels production.[94]

Korea, Mobilization, and Switched Policy Priorities

It was ironic and in no small degree tragic that just as the Interior Department, after five years, was pulling itself together in the energy field and was proposing both the formulation of a broad national policy and an administrative structure capable of giving the subject sustained professional attention, hostilities involving the United States in Korea broke out once again. Priorities returned to the simple provision of the fuels necessary for mobilization, and Interior Department planning units lost much of their authority. The secretary of the interior was given substantial defense responsibilities in the resources area, but through a range of new mobilization units. The very order that created the new assistant secretary for minerals transferred many of the functions of his Oil and Gas Division to a new Petroleum Administration for Defense, patterned after the World War II Petroleum Administration for War. Comparable bodies created for other energy sources were the Defense Solid Fuels Administration and the Defense Power Administration. A Defense Program Staff, headed by Alfred C. Wolf of the department's Program Staff, was established to provide analysis and advice for the secretary of the interior. But mobilization was not a situation in which a unit of this kind could be widely influential. One of the problems faced by the Interior Department in constructing energy policy at the end of World War II had been the diffusion of authority among innumerable agencies. Now, after a period of gradual coalescing this dispersion began once again, not only to the "temporary" mobilization units in the department but to such agencies as the Defense Production Administration, and the always ambitious and voracious State and Defense departments.

93. Boyd to Krug, "Organization of the Bureau of Mines," July 22, 1949, CCF 11-6, RG 48, NA.
94. *Economic Report* File, Davidson Office Files, RG 48, NA.

Even though defined as only an "emergency," developments in Korea produced many of the problems and the responses characteristic of full-scale war. In particular, industry advisory councils and businessmen employed by government resumed their former roles with little acknowledgment of the doubts and reservations expressed by Girard Davidson only a few months before. In addition to the National Petroleum Council, which had existed since 1946, and the National Bituminous Coal Advisory Council, created in 1948, an Electric Utility Defense Advisory Council was organized in October 1950, a Coke Advisory Committee in February 1951, and a Gas Industry Advisory Council in March 1951. These groups met frequently in Washington to "provide advice and data" and "for discussions of matters of mutual interest." All the advisory councils met jointly on May 9, 1951, when they were addressed by the President and other high officials. Among the declared purposes of this meeting was "to bring home to industry the necessity for carrying out its mobilization responsibilities while at the same time sustaining the civilian economy and its needs for materials and goods, and attaining both objectives in the uncomfortable atmosphere of controls, regulations, and meager supplies of raw materials and construction materials." For the time being, once again, the bywords were "teamwork and cooperation" rather than "conflict of interest" or "restraint of trade."[95]

With the nation's attention turned elsewhere, planning for the new Division of Minerals and Fuels continued all the same. In March 1951 Ivan Bloch, a longtime consultant to the secretary's office, originally from the Bonneville Power Administration, recommended a work program. In his view this should center on the preparation of a "national minerals policy." The first task was to raise public awareness of the need for such a policy: "the public has only a faint consciousness of the magnitude and the seriousness of the problem, and of its world-wide implications." The second task was to define and represent "the public interest" in the field, "leading to the enunciation of a consistent and homogeneous public policy." An overriding difficulty, he noted, was the absence of reliable information. "Basic" facts were unavailable, partly because no one set out to collect them, partly because of the weak federal authority to gather data, and partly because of the tax laws that "inhibit the free flow of important information." He complained: "We may not be a 'have not' Nation, but we are certainly a 'know-not what we have' Nation." Personnel were also a problem; government employees in the

95. Materials related to this meeting are contained in Speech File, PSF, HSTL.

minerals field were mainly technicians with narrow fields of specialization. "By training, by disposition, and probably most by force of circumstance, these technicians seem to have preferred to confine themselves officially to the abstractions of their fields of specialization without too much continuous reference to the social, economic and political effects of their work."[96]

Bloch argued that the "Departmental Opportunity" was to "bear the key responsibility for stimulating, developing and maintaining a national minerals [which would subsume fuels] policy. It can no longer afford to carry out this responsibility merely by 'riding herd' over a discontinuous aggregation of dispersed programs—no matter how excellent they may be individually." To this end the staff of the new division "must be considered as a contemplative and facilitating arm of the Secretariat in the field of minerals and fuels." The staff of the division should be grouped along commodity lines with one "field" designated "fuels." Moreover, the staff should not accept any limitation of focus imposed by other government units; it should undertake "the evaluation of actions taking place in defense production, and also with regard to problems involving international matters." He recommended that the division staff select several important mineral industry groups, of which one would be "oil, gas and coal," and discover

where special attention and effort will be required to sustain or improve the availability of raw materials, or where it may be desirable to develop substitutes. They are the areas in which the public interest is directly involved, and where Departmental programs will be necessary to prevent or remedy critical deficiencies. The description of these critical areas will facilitate the examination of basic policy in the development or modification of regulatory devices, the development of public incentives, the stimulation of both public and private exploratory and research programs, and the betterment of cooperative relations between public and private segments of the minerals and fuels division.[97]

96. Memorandum, Ivan Bloch to Assistant Secretary Dale Doty, "An Appraisal of Mineral Policy and the Functions of the Minerals and Fuels Division," March 19, 1951, Bureaus and Offices, Minerals and Fuels Division File, Wolfsohn Papers, HSTL.

97. Ibid. The Division of Management Research in the department approved the substance of Bloch's proposal except for the recommendation that the division be organized by broad commodity groups. This was seen as duplicating (or threatening) the commodity experts in the operating units. Memorandum, Director, Division of Management Research to Assistant Secretary Doty, "Mineral Policy—Functions of Minerals and Fuels Division," March 29, 1951, CCF 11-6, RG 48, NA.

Meanwhile even though the eyes of the nation were turned toward the emergency, the members of the Program Staff were not idle. In a substantial planning document completed in December 1951, a document that in the circumstances may not have left the department, they suggested elements of a peacetime national energy policy. Above all, they urged that substitutability of energy resources both "in *use* and in source" should be maximized so as both to minimize the impact of bottlenecks that might occur in any one resource and to increase the effective degree of competition. Such interchangeability among services could be improved by more research on synthetic fuels and such new processes as underground coal gasification. The main problem with hydroelectricity was the long lead time needed for supply to respond to changes in demand; therefore the nation should move ahead with more construction now. In the case of gas it could be expected that its decline "would be preceded by warning signs of sufficient clarity and duration to enable the economy to make the corrective adjustments." Petroleum afforded the big dilemma. The most important question was "What insurance in the way of fostering substitutes should the United States Government undertake now and in the future? The answer to this question depends partly on trends in oil consumption and discovery, and partly on such factors as the size of military requirements in case of war, the contractability of civilian demand, and the extent to which the extraction of oil from known reserves could be speeded up." National policy here required serious and sustained attention to this situation. "Continuing appraisal of all the relevant factors is required so that the warning signs can be heeded early enough and appropriate action taken."[98]

A Senate Committee and a Presidential Commission Tackle Energy Matters

So long as the Korean conflict persisted, which was beyond the end of the Truman administration, it was impossible for the new Minerals and Fuels Division or the Program Staff to gain center stage with a discussion of energy or any other subject. But by joining ranks with two other bodies more in the public eye—the Senate Committee on Interior and

98. "Program Requirements for the Natural Resources Responsibilities of the Department of the Interior, December 1951," Department of Interior Program Staff File, Doty Papers, HSTL.

Insular Affairs and the Paley Commission—the Interior Department was able to have considerable effect during the remaining two years.

Via the Senate Committee on Interior and Insular Affairs Secretary Chapman in effect accomplished much of what we hoped to gain from a National Energy Commission. With the cooperation of Committee Chairman O'Mahoney, who had been chairman of the TNEC many years before, Chapman obtained at least some of the national inquiry into energy policy that President Truman had denied him. In July 1950, taking advantage of the profound public concern about the capacity of the American economy to withstand another prolonged conflict, Chapman used arguments reminiscent of his letter to the President a few months before to call for a full-scale study of energy, past, present, and future. "The lesson of the past is that, because of substitution among fuels, the problems of any energy industry cannot be studied in isolation, but only in conjunction with all other energy industries. However, the past does not tell us what the future trends in the energy industries will be. . . . To appraise the future and to provide guideposts for the development of sound energy programs and policies an investigation of the scope proposed . . . is required."[99] In contrast to the cool reception he received for his ideas in the White House, several senators, notably Wayne Morse, warmly endorsed Chapman's suggestions. Among a number of proposals about how the committee should operate, Chapman's carried the day.[100] The committee proceeded to carry out the stipulations of Senate Resolution 239, passed March 15, 1950, to (1) make a full and complete investigation and study of the available fuel reserves in the United States and the present and probable future rates of consumption thereof; (2) to formulate a national fuel policy to meet the needs of the United States in times of peace and war, such policy to include the use of all fuels and energy resources except atomic energy; (3) to study and recommend methods of encouraging development to assure the availability of fuels adequate for an expanding economy and the security of the United States; and (4) to report to the Senate at the earliest practicable date. In a press release announcing the fuels study Senator O'Mahoney

99. Statement of Secretary of the Interior Oscar L. Chapman in *Fuel Study Proposals*, Hearing before the Senate Committee on Interior and Insular Affairs, 81 Cong. 2 sess. (GPO, 1950), p. 32.

100. *Fuel Study Proposals*, Hearing, especially pp. 94–99. The committee faced three proposals: S. 3215 and S.J. Res. 157 would have set up commissions aimed primarily at the problems of coal and S. Res. 239 by Senator Francis J. Myers called for a study of all fuel reserves and present and future rates of consumption.

explained clearly the two motives that prompted him, first, to assess the danger that inadequate energy might constrain the growth of the American economy—a point of crucial importance in the "war of ideologies" —and second, to examine "the problems of competition not only within the respective fuel industries but among them."[101]

The Interior Department provided most of the staff services for the Senate fuels study. The first installment of input was the Barnett report, issued in 1949 and revised in 1950, but this was followed shortly by a stream of materials from Ivan Bloch, who as chairman of a special department Energy Committee, was assigned responsibility to assist the senators.[102] The department's position on energy policy in general, along lines expressed in the Program Staff statement, was given to the committee by Director of the Division of Power Joel D. Wolfsohn in an address entitled "Enough Is Not Enough."[103]

The two principal tasks the Interior Department undertook for the committee during its investigation were the preparation of a very valuable volume, *Basic Data Relating to Energy Resources*,[104] containing information gathered from throughout the department, and the organization of a series of round table discussions with experts from the energy industries.[105] The round table illustrated both the opportunities and the weakness of congressional inquiry on this topic. On the one hand the discussion captured some public attention for the issue, especially the attention of lawmakers. On the other hand it often degenerated into rather

101. Senate Committee on Interior and Insular Affairs, "Can Energy Resources Pay the National Debt of the U.S.?" press release, October 15, 1950, pp. 2, 4.

102. W. E. Warne to Senator Joseph C. O'Mahoney, October 23, 1950; and memorandum, Ivan Bloch to Assistant Secretary Davidson, "Status of Work for Senate Interior and Insular Affairs Committee re Senate Resolution 239: 'Fuels Study,' " October 30, 1950; both in Fuels Survey Departmental Energy Subcommittee File, Minerals and Fuels Division Files, RG 48, NA. Robert Heilbroner asked Bloch for copies of as many committee records as possible so that he might "present the problem to the public at large" through "Harper's Magazine (as well as other publications)." Heilbroner to Bloch, December 3, 1950, ibid.

103. Minerals and Fuels Division File, Wolfsohn Papers, HSTL.

104. *Basic Data Relating to Energy Resources*, S. Doc. 8, 82 Cong. 1 sess. (GPO, 1951).

105. *National Fuel Reserves and Fuel Policy*, Hearings before the Senate Committee on Interior and Insular Affairs, 82 Cong. 1 sess. (GPO, 1951). Discussion of Interior Department assistance to the committee is in a memorandum, Inge Kaiser, Executive Secretary, Energy Committee, to Assistant Secretary Davidson, December 14, 1950; and Kaiser to Assistant Secretary Doty, February 15, 1951; both in Fuels Survey Departmental Energy Subcommittee File, Minerals and Fuels Division Files, RG 48, NA.

breathless and unsophisticated expressions of concern over declining reserves and the visible clashes between special interests. The oil and gas people asserted that energy problems simply did not exist and that there was no need for such a thing as a "fuels policy." The coal people responded that only in coal lay the long-term energy salvation of America; if the nation allowed the coal industry to languish because of a temporary abundance of oil and gas it would live to rue such neglect. To observers of the round table it must have appeared that the term "fuels policy" had in fact come to mean restraints on petroleum development, assistance to coal, and almost symbolically, full-scale commercial development of synthetic fuel from coal.[106]

The second external means by which the Interior Department contributed to consideration of national energy policy during the last two years of the Truman presidency, in addition to the Senate Committee inquiry, was the President's Materials Policy Commission (known as the Paley Commission after its chairman, William S. Paley). To some degree Secretary Chapman may have helped to persuade the President of the need for this inquiry through his appeal in early 1950 for a national energy policy commission. But it is more likely that Chapman's proposal and the impetus for the Paley Commission both come out of the same climate of concern about the depletion of nonrenewable raw materials, accentuated after mid-1950 by the Korean emergency. The formal proposal to create the commission came from Stuart Symington, chairman of the National Security Resources Board, and the rationale was explicitly the relationship of materials to national defense. Symington wrote to the President in December 1950 that "there is nothing more important to the future security of the United States than obtaining, now and in the future, an adequate supply of those raw materials necessary to build up our defenses and maintain our economy. Already in many cases short-

---

106. Memorandum, Ivan Bloch to Secretary Chapman, March 13, 1951, CCF 1-188, RG 48, NA. Interior Department staff continued to assist the Senate committee through its counsel, Arthur Sandusky, with subsequent hearings on the fuel question. See memorandum, Inge Kaiser to Larry E. Imhoff, May 24, 1951, Bureaus and Offices, Minerals and Fuels Division File, Wolfsohn Papers, HSTL. The enthusiastic support given to the inquiry by the coal industry is described in a memorandum, Bloch to Assistant Secretary Davidson, "Senate Resolution 239, Fuels Survey: Meetings with Anthracite Group," October 24, 1950, ibid. Congressman Daniel J. Flood in the interest of the Pennsylvania anthracite miners recommended to President Truman a variant on the theme of a fuels policy; he wanted a "Natural Energy Resources Commission to investigate the quantity, distribution, utilization and conservation of natural energy resources in the United States, as distinct from atomic energy." Flood to President Truman, May 4, 1951, OF 174, Truman Papers, HSTL.

ages of such materials are serious, and in some cases critical."[107] Earlier in 1950 Symington had asked Paley, chairman of the Board of the Columbia Broadcasting System, to serve as chairman of a special NSRB committee on natural resources; now he asked Truman to convert the committee into a presidential commission, and the President agreed.[108]

Energy was only one part of the subject assigned to Paley and his fellow commissioners, including Edward S. Mason, a Harvard economist; George R. Brown and Arthur R. Bunker, two businessmen; and Eric Hodgins, a journalist long associated with *Fortune*.[109] But it was an important part. The commission decided to identify certain commodity groups for special attention, and "energy and fuels" was one of these; then it examined these commodities with respect to domestic and foreign resources, technology, and security. It assembled a full-time staff of about fifty, with Philip Coombs, an economist experienced in government, as director of research. A work schedule of only about a year required the staff to depend heavily on the analytical resources of the principal government departments and agencies. In addition research contracts were made with private groups and conferences were held with representatives of industry.[110]

The Paley Commission is unusually important in the history of energy policy formulation for several reasons. First of all, it provided contrast to the two main sources of attention to the subject within government up to that point—congressional committees and the Interior Department staff. In this sense its closest lineal predecessor was the Natural Resources Committee of the late 1930s. Second, it brought together energy economists and related specialists from all the relevant parts of the government as well as from industry and the universities to explore the topic and either agree or point up differences of perspective. Third, it expressed clearly and succinctly the constraints on worldwide growth and prosperity implicit in dependence on finite energy sources. "It took nature over 500 million years to store in the ground these stockpiles of

107. Symington to Truman, December 27, 1950, OF 3035, Truman Papers, HSTL.
108. Truman to Paley, January 2, 1951; and Paley to Truman, January 8, 1951, ibid.
109. William Clayton, formerly assistant secretary of state but now in private life in Houston, was invited to join the commission but declined. Telegram, Clayton to the President, January 19, 1951, ibid.
110. Paley to the President, June 7, 1951, OF 3035, HSTL. White House staff members who commented on this preliminary communication from Paley feared that the commission and its subject might get out of hand and that the study might take too long to complete and be too diffuse to have effect. Memorandum, Marjorie B. Belcher and John C. Houston for John R. Steelman, June 13, 1951, ibid.

'fossil fuels' which civilization is now consuming in a flash of geologic time." It was inevitable that "the time will come . . . and perhaps well beyond 1975, when civilization's energy needs will outrun nature's declining store of fossil fuels available for economic use. Before this happens, ways must be found to harness economically such unconventional sources as solar and atomic energy."[111]

The Paley Commission conclusions were by and large upbeat. The commission saw an approximate doubling of energy requirements by the year 1975.[112] But it saw nothing to fear so long as energy resources could be "found, processed, and delivered at real costs close to present levels." To achieve this result it proposed the rapid development of the resources of the poorer nations of the world and encouragement to technological advancement both to improve substitutability among fuels and to increase the efficiency of recovery methods for coal, oil, and gas. It predicted an increase in oil imports, a gradual shift back to coal from oil and gas, and commercial production of "synthetic oil, probably first from shale and later from coal . . . within a decade or so—perhaps sooner." Imports and synthetics would "keep the price of domestic crude from rising more than 25 to 30 percent (relative to the Nation's general price level) over the next 25 years, and the rise may be far less." The commission could not see a very large role for government in making sure that the future unfolded smoothly. Its principal recommendation was for an "underground stockpile" of petroleum in the form of unused capacity on the continental shelf and "reserve capacity" in refining and transportation. "It will cost money—a great deal perhaps—but the price of this insurance would be cheap if war should come." The commission was nervous about the potential cost of synthetic fuel and recommended only that government give limited financial assistance to the construction of a few small-scale commercial plants and continue to study the matter. It supported the long-standing Interior Department policies of coal re-

111. President's Materials Policy Commission, *Resources for Freedom*, vol. 1: *Foundations for Growth and Security* (GPO, 1952), pp. 104, 106.

112. This projection, based on a population increase to 195 million in 1975, was substantially below the mark. By August 1951 some of the commission staff and consultants, notably Palmer Putnam and Arnold C. Harberger, had concluded that the 195 million projection was implausibly low, but "what to do about it now is another problem." Coombs response was: "Public policy should be formulated on a prudent basis—which does not mean buying *complete* insurance against the *worst possible* contingencies," and the projection stood. Memorandums, Palmer Putnam to Robert Blum, August 10, 1951; and Putnam for the files, August 10, 1951 (with handwritten note by Philip Coombs on the latter), General File, Energy, PMPC, HSTL.

search and hydroelectric development and the Atomic Energy Commission's first tentative steps toward commercial nuclear power.[113]

Despite the limited role it proposed for government in energy markets the Paley Commission called loudly for "a comprehensive energy policy" on the ground that "so numerous and vital are the interrelations among all sectors of the energy field, that problems in any one sector must be dealt with always in full consideration of the side effects on all other sectors." Moreover, those dealing with all aspects of energy policy must have an awareness of "the broader problems of materials, economic growth, and national security."[114]

The commission did not attempt to spell out the administrative implications of its conclusions except to insist that the "hydra heads of energy policy must be reined together" in "one central agency of the Government."[115] It recommended also that the Department of the Interior "strengthen its program analysis staffs and intensify its fact-gathering and analytical activities."[116] The best way to deal with the security problems of the postwar era, it argued, was to import energy resources freely so as to conserve domestic sources, and to maintain large ready reserves in the event these external sources were temporarily closed off. In particular, a commission staff member observed, "the Free World . . . cannot be allowed to become over dependent on Middle East oil because of the lack of assurance that those supplies would be available in time of war."[117]

It is noteworthy that the Paley commissioners, like so many other contemporary analysts, saw the energy problems of the future and their solutions mainly from the supply side of the market. Evidently they believed that energy consumption bore a fixed relationship to the gross national product, mutable only through technological improvements in the conversion mechanisms, and they judged the determination of individual tastes for energy as opposed to other goods to be beyond the legitimate purview of government. Indeed, consumers were enjoined to avoid "physical waste," and the automobile industry was urged to "lead

113. The information and quotations in this paragraph are from PMPC, *Resources for Freedom,* vol. 1, pp. 107, 108, 110.
114. Ibid., p. 129.
115. Ibid., p. 130.
116. Ibid., p. 26.
117. Charles Schwarz, "First Draft—Energy Resources," January 31, 1952, and "Report—First Draft," September 4, 1951, Policy Recommendations, Energy Memoranda File, PMPC, HSTL.

the nation toward a more efficient use of its liquid fuel supplies."[118] But clearly there was more hope for conservation in production than in consumption.

Naturally in the Paley Commission's final report, controversy was substantially eliminated. In the commission's records, however, disputes among staff and commissioners are readily visible. It is worth reviewing briefly what these differences were so as to gain a picture of the state of the discussion about energy policy among serious, informed persons during the final two years of the Truman presidency.

The question of taxation, in the wider context of the tax treatment of mineral production generally, received a great deal of attention. First of all, Sam Schurr, chief economist of the Bureau of Mines, and members of his staff explained the issues in this complex subject for the commission.[119] It seemed that the questions fell into three categories related to (1) equity in the tax system, (2) the overall integrity of the tax structure ("one exception leads to another"), and (3) the efficiency of a tax measure in achieving the goals it set out to achieve. Coombs explained to the commission that the first category of issues might best be left to a President's Commission on Metaphysics. The second was important to government but not central to the Paley Commission's work. The third was relevant particularly to problem cases of minerals when markets did not achieve the results desired by society. Here the tax system could be called on to "(1) intensify the technological search for more abundant substitutes, (2) encourage development of foreign reserves and output, (3) make more efficient use of available reserves (i.e., conservation) at every stage from mining through end use and recycling, and (4) *maintain an intensive search for additional reserves within our own borders.*"[120]

But when it came down to cases—whether a particular goal was appropriate, whether the existing tax system achieved this goal, and whether another device might not achieve the goal more efficiently—the staff and the commissioners were often divided. For example, on the question of percentage depletion one staff group recommended its elimination; others, however, favored its reform, while several believed that the subject was still too murky for them to make a recommendation and

118. PMPC, *Resources for Freedom,* vol. 1, p. 109.

119. Sam Schurr to Philip Coombs, with attachment, May 2, 1951, Taxation and Incentives File, PMPC, HSTL.

120. Memorandum, Philip Coombs to commissioners, "Observations on the Minerals Tax Question," November 14, 1951, Taxation and Incentives File, ibid. (emphasis in the original).

that it needed further study.[121] A specific proposition by the staff that the "receipt of percentage depletion allowance be made conditional upon the expenditure of equivalent funds for exploration" was not accepted by the commission.[122]

In some rough degree commissioners and staff appear to have opposed percentage depletion to the extent that they had professional economics training. Their compromise recommendation was that the allowance be retained but not increased or extended to other materials. Even with this compromise Edward Mason insisted that the following footnote be inserted in the report: "Commissioner Mason concurs in this recommendation but not for the reasons set forth in the preceding pages. He is content to 'let well enough' alone because he believes that an elimination of the percentage depletion privilege would produce disastrous and undesirable reductions in asset values in the mineral industries and because he has been unable to discover any practical way of shifting from the present basis to an alternative method of treating depletion without involving a disruption to the production of minerals that, at this stage, we can ill afford."[123]

Other issues that either puzzled the Paley Commission staff and commissioners or generated controversy among them included reform of the mineral leasing laws; whether to acquire buffer stocks to stabilize markets; when government rather than private enterprise should engage in direct exploration for minerals; how to discourage the use of natural gas for such purposes as boiler fuel; and just how to carry out effective policies to create petroleum reserves, develop synthetic fuels, and encourage technological advance in all energy areas. The question of the appropriate role for the large corporation throughout the energy field lurked in many of the Paley Commission discussions. Company spokesmen offered persuasive arguments both that only the large oil majors enjoying depletion allowances could provide the capital necessary for high-risk exploration and that large oligopolistic companies are required to operate effectively overseas.[124]

121. Eugene E. Oakes to C. R. Peterson, September 14, 1951; Mary E. McDermott to C. J. Dwyer, September 20, 1951; and Cornelius J. Dwyer to Robert Blum, September 20, 1951; all in ibid.

122. Oakes to Peterson, September 14, 1951.

123. Mason to Paley, February 18, 1952, General Records, Finance, PMPC, HSTL.

124. Memorandum, Eugene E. Oakes to Philip Coombs and Wilbert G. Fritz, "Interview with Mr. Joseph E. Pogue, September 19, 1951, Concerning the Financ-

At a special meeting of the full commission (a relatively rare occurrence) representatives of the business community, including Emilio G. Collado, assistant treasurer of Standard Oil of New Jersey, explained what policies would be most helpful to corporations acquiring materials abroad. These included creating a new trade assistance agency outside the State Department.[125]

The Paley Commission was intended only partly to improve understanding of materials problems and to generate alternative policies for consideration by policymakers; such achievements on a full scale could not have been expected in only a year of work. But it was expected to prepare a synthesis of current thinking and to acquaint the public with the limitations imposed on action of all kinds by finite resources. The commission's style and work program were affected by this complex of objectives. It was no coincidence that one commissioner was a distinguished economist—a choice that would assure quality control and bridges to the scholarly world—while the chairman and the other most active member were prominent leaders of the media. The latter, Eric Hodgins, was designated editor in chief of the report.

The commission set out to reach its audience in the process of its deliberations as well as with its final product. It began with a series of hearings on the various parts of its subject. Energy resources received special attention because they were "a major limiting factor in shifting from scarce to abundant sources of production materials." In its hearings on this topic the commission set out to cast light on the following subjects: "the special regulatory problems of oil and gas and coal; the limited known reserves of oil; the abundance of coal and its substitutability for oil via hydrocarbon synthesis; the expansibility of hydropower; the competitive interrelations of all three etc."[126]

The commissioners and the staff paid a great deal of attention to the packaging and "merchandising" of their results. The audience for the report was defined as "everybody who ought to be interested in it." Hodgins suggested that the most a "conscientious citizen" could be ex-

---

ing of the Oil and Gas Industries," September 21, 1951, Taxation and Incentives File, PMPC, HSTL; and "Report of Interview with an 'Experienced Counsel of Oil Company,'" Administrative File, Paley Report Interviews, PMPC, HSTL.

125. See William C. Ackerman, minutes of a meeting on March 13, 1951, Administrative File, Committee Meetings, PMPC, HSTL.

126. Max Isenbergh, "Preliminary Proposals on Plans and Arrangements for Hearings for Discussion and Development," March 26, 1951, General Records, PMPC, HSTL.

pected to read was about three hours' worth, or somewhat less than an issue of *Time* magazine. Special studies should be published separately. William C. Ackerman, executive secretary of the commission, suggested that the "effectiveness" of the report could be achieved in two ways: "(a) in increasing public information and understanding of the materials problem, . . . (b) in building necessary interest at this time for the adoption of policy recommendations." This meant that a major assault had to be launched on the media as well as direct publication. "Policy-forming officials will be directly impressed if they see an impressive display of the Report and its recommendations in our major media."[127] In fact, the commission was quite successful in achieving its goals. Considering the fact that by design the report was far from spectacular or alarmist and that it appeared after the emergency that prompted its creation had passed, it received impressively wide attention from a variety of media, from commercial television to learned journals.[128] In the opinion of one commissioner, by showing that "over the next decade or as far as one could see ahead, there wasn't a serious materials problem confronting the United States," the commission "had a good deal of influence."[129] It can be argued also that if the public was not

127. Eric Hodgins to Paley, Coombs, and Ackerman, "The Report Itself," July 16, 1951, General Records, Preparation, PMPC, HSTL. See also memorandum, Ackerman to the file, "The PMPC Audience," August 23, 1951, Administrative File, Press Plans, PMPC, HSTL; Ackerman to Paley and others, "An Information Program for the PMPC Report," May 30, 1952, ibid.; Hymen E. Cohen to Eric Hodgins, "Possible Volume III Materials," October 20, 1951, General Records, Preparation, PMPC, HSTL; and Ackerman to Paley, "Press Information and Distribution," March 29, 1952, ibid.

128. See, for example, "The Crisis in Raw Materials," *Fortune,* August 1952, pp. 114–17, 160, 163–64, 166–68, 170; "Meeting the Threat of Creeping Scarcities," *Commercial and Financial Chronicle,* September 18, 1952; "What Is Our Materials Future? Policy Body Says 'Ominous,' " *Newsweek,* June 30, 1952, p. 75; "Prospect for the U.S.: Permanent Shortages," *Business Week,* June 28, 1952, pp. 160–62; Edward S. Mason, "Raw Materials, Rearmament, and Economic Development," *Quarterly Journal of Economics,* vol. 66 (August 1952), pp. 327–41; and "Not Enough Materials for U.S.: Interview with William S. Paley," *U.S. News and World Report,* August 15, 1952, pp. 44–50. The conclusions of the Paley Commission were explored by Edward R. Murrow of CBS in a classic television documentary.

129. Edward S. Mason, Oral History Interview, July 17, 1973, HSTL. In fact, some readers reached far more pessimistic conclusions than those of the commissioners. At a round table on the Paley Report held by the Conference Board, Eugene Ayres of the Gulf Research and Development Company said that when he put all the pieces of demand and supply together as presented by the commission he did not find an easily manageable situation but an "explosive mixture" that would ignite a critical worldwide shortage of liquid fuels by 1975, plus or minus a few years. (Conference Board, *Resources: A Conference Board Report* [New York: Conference

made aware of a coming energy crisis, the Paley Commission at least exposed the roots of the problem.

The Paley Report, *Resources for Freedom,* was delivered to the President late in June 1952. His response was to charge the relevant government departments to determine how best to implement the recommendations.[130]

The NSRB was given the task of reviewing the Paley recommendations and suggesting steps to be taken for their accomplishment. In a report on December 10, 1952, Chairman Jack Gorrie reported that the board agreed with the commission in most of its recommendations about energy. It supported more coal research, subsidies to a few synthetic fuel plants, more hydroelectric power (including the St. Lawrence Seaway), atomic energy development, conservation of petroleum, and more analysis and data on all resource subjects, although it did note dissent among government agencies over whether to use industries themselves rather than government units to collect data. The NSRB endorsed strategic petroleum reserves but left open whether unused capacity offshore or special well-spacing on shore would serve this purpose.[131] For its part the Interior Department reacted to the NSRB response by suggesting that these objectives might be accomplished most effectively by establishing, if not a Department of Natural Resources, at least a new Min-

---

Board, 1953], pp. 30–33.) Yet some other readers were more optimistic: Colin Clark in one of the principal critiques of the report claimed that the commission's statistical techniques had led to excessively gloomy conclusions. "We may find the world demand for fuel only a little increased in twenty-five years' time, even assuming that atomic power has not yet begun to displace it." "Afterthoughts on Paley," *Review of Economics and Statistics,* vol. 36 (August 1954), p. 270.

130. "Statement by the President on the President's Materials Policy Commission, July 1, 1952," *Public Papers of the Presidents of the United States: Harry S. Truman, 1952–53* (GPO, 1966), pp. 454–55. (Hereinafter *Public Papers.*) An official of the Federal Trade Commission, commenting on an "interagency conference" to plan a response to the President, reported that an official of the Defense Materials Procurement Agency, presumably a businessman on loan to government, "suggested that in as much as industry has a big stake and responsibility in the development of resources for future use, that concerns, especially those with world-wide connections in the materials supplies business, should have an opportunity to look over the reports of the various agencies and offer comments before the report is sent to the President." Memorandum for John M. Blair, July 21, 1952, Recommendations of the PMPC-FTC File, Stephen S. Spingarn Papers, HSTL.

131. National Security Resources Board, *The Objectives of United States Materials Resources Policy and Suggested Initial Steps in Their Accomplishment* (GPO, 1952). Memorandums containing reactions by the Federal Power Commission to both the Paley Commission Report and the NSRB commentary on it are in Federal Power Commission File, Doty Papers, HSTL. The raw responses used in drawing up the NSRB report are in File 41-11, Records of NSRB, RG 304, NA.

erals Resources Service within the department.[132] The hour was late, however, and implementation had to be left for the next administration.

Conclusion

Was there in fact any energy policy during the Truman administration? The answer must depend on the definition of "policy." A moderately liberal definition, such as a "set of decisions designed to carry out a chosen course of action," permits a fairly confident "yes." Above all, during these eight years there was a growing appreciation that a sector of the economy concerned with the production and distribution of energy deserved national attention; and increasingly this attention was given by analytical units in the Interior Department and the NSRB, to a lesser extent by other executive departments, in congressional committees, and by the Paley Commission. Although the term "energy policy" was widely used in these years, there was no explicit national debate on the subject and therefore no clear consensus or aggregate decision on what such a policy should contain. However, a certain set of principles, which by the end of the period had become almost a common denominator, may be inferred from the most important discussions. These principles, the result of inquiry and debate, might be stated as follows:

1. The energy sector has peculiar features that dictate public attention to it and intervention in it. At a minimum this implies the need for collecting reliable data and training competent analysts in the public sector. The rationale for this is that energy problems could lead to short-term fluctuations, constraints on long-term growth, and suffering by energy-producing regions. All may follow mistaken actions related to energy.

2. Certain peculiar features of energy markets, notably complex technology and economies of scale, require the development of new and imaginative modes of industry and government cooperation and control. The challenge is to preserve efficiency while avoiding the costs of monopoly and conflicts between public and private interest.

3. Major discontinuities are liable to be the source of serious problems in energy markets, either when finite reserves, such as natural gas, decline sharply or when technology changes dramatically, as in the case of nuclear power. Government has a responsibility to anticipate and if

132. Program Staff, "Status of Materials Resources Policy and Highlights of Major Issues, January 10, 1953," Reports and Recommendations on Departmental Programs File, Program Staff Office Files, RG 48, NA.

possible to minimize the painfulness of these discontinuities. An approach to this problem suggested repeatedly during the Truman years was to increase the substitutability of fuels both at the source and in use. The best hope to achieve this goal was through research and development. For example, if natural gas could be expected to decline suddenly in a few years, scientists should concentrate both on alternative sources of gas (coal gasification, for one) and on devices to facilitate the conversion from gas to other fuels. Debate revolved around the question of how much the market could be counted on to arrange for this substitution. Government planners worried that if left to itself, private enterprise might have motives that would conflict with the public good (for example, in consequence of ownership of two potentially competing fuels) or would wait until too late in conversion because of a short profit horizon. Leaders in the private sector, on the other hand, complained of bureaucratic myopia and waste of public funds. Few questioned the wisdom of some government activity to facilitate substitution, but many questioned the degree.

4. With the memory of World War II still sharp, the Korean emergency at hand, and the increasing consciousness of a long cold war ahead, special provision must be made to guarantee sufficient energy in the event of renewed international conflict. There was genuine uncertainty about the tactical implications of this strategic principle. On the one hand it might be best to import as much foreign energy as possible so as to conserve domestic supplies for emergencies; this tactic, however, might cause domestic industries to atrophy from neglect and to be unavailable when needed. On the other hand the nation might insist on energy independence and eschew imports through the protected development of synthetic fuels and accelerated exploitation of reserves. The danger here was that the cost might lead to a sharp deceleration of growth in national output and loss of the "race with communism" through national anemia if not from foreign dependence. The policy conclusion reached by most thoughtful people on this subject was that some sensible balance had to be found between dependence and costly autarchy. Exactly where this balance should lie had to remain a matter of judgment.

Although one can argue about the existence of an energy policy in the aggregate during the Truman administration, it is undeniable that there was policy aplenty concerning individual fuels. These policies are discussed in the next chapter.

CHAPTER TWO

Truman Administration Policies toward Particular Energy Sources

CRAUFURD D. GOODWIN

EVEN THOUGH noticeable stirrings occurred during the Truman administration, and before, toward a coherent national energy policy, most policy issues continued to be limited to individual fuels and forms of energy generation. In this chapter the evolution of these narrower bodies of policy is examined, beginning with the most important, petroleum, and concluding with the most promising yet puzzling, nuclear power.

Petroleum

To a striking degree policy questions about petroleum facing President Truman had all appeared before World War II, even if only vestigially. In most cases answers to these questions were left for a later administration to discover. The questions were roughly as follows:

1. Could the free market system be left to determine the proper rate of production of, and especially exploration for, a commodity of such paramount importance to the nation as oil? As early as World War I some policymakers answered "no" to this question and provided favored tax treatment for producers as an incentive, including percentage depletion.

2. Was it necessary for the federal government to cooperate with the oil producers and the oil-producing states in marketing their product? The answer was usually "yes," but the reasoning behind this response

THE FOLLOWING abbreviations are used in the footnotes of this chapter: Central Classified Files of the Secretary (CCF), Harry S. Truman Library (HSTL), National Archives (NA), Official Files (OF), President's Secretary's Files (PSF), President's Water Resources Policy Commission (PWRPC), and Record Group (RG).

was clouded and often confused. The main argument presented to the public was that uniquely in petroleum production unrestrained competition led to less than optimum rates of extraction and therefore to "waste." Much truth unquestionably lay in this argument when it was applied to a single pool of petroleum where, under the applicable "rule of capture," each well owner found it in his interest to extract as much as possible of this free good before his competitor could do so. The result in this case was sometimes loss of pressure and recoverable oil. But the argument was extended to suggest that government, by permitting and assisting cooperative (noncompetitive) marketing among oil producers, could offer relief to this industrial sector at the same time as it encouraged conservation. The confusion between the two elements of this argument obscured discussion of it. It was difficult for everyone to appreciate that waste in an economic sense occurs just as much with too slow a rate of exploitation of a resource as with too rapid a one; that monopolistic activities produced such a wastefully slow rate; and that although petroleum resources were indeed finite, other fuels were substitutable with petroleum and it was the long-run supply of *energy,* not of petroleum, that was relevant to the calculations of an optimum long-run price.

The federal government was asked to enter the market for petroleum to restrain competition among states, that is, to police an oligopolistic agreement at the national level. During the 1930s the producers developed a complicated system for output limitation whereby states and their producers were given quotas known as "allowables" so that the total national output would in theory add up to an amount corresponding to a desired price on the consumers' demand curve. To maintain this system the federal government had to perform two functions: (a) enforce the quotas, which was accomplished by the so-called Connally Hot Oil Act of 1935 that prohibited the interstate movement of oil produced contrary to state laws (that is, above quota);[1] and (b) collect nationwide statistics on demand (expressed as refinery demand at specified prices) so that the quota-making body, the Interstate Oil Compact Commission, could adjust its allocations to stabilize or adjust price. This statistical task was assigned to the Bureau of Mines.

3. Was there a case for bigness in the petroleum industry on the grounds that size stimulated technological development, that risks of exploration needed to be widely distributed, or for other reasons? In the

---

1. The act (15 U.S.C. 715) was known informally by the name of the senator who introduced it, Democrat Thomas T. Connally of Texas.

view of the Justice Department's Antitrust Division and the Federal Trade Commission (FTC) the answer to this question was resoundingly "no." But to others the answer remained in doubt.

4. Did the growing dependence of the United States on foreign supplies require a new national policy on imports, the role of U.S. corporations abroad, and organization of the government to deal with oil producers in the rest of the world?

5. What should be the relationship between government and the oilmen? On the one hand too close a relationship opened opportunities for conflict of interest, and even corruption. The memory of Teapot Dome remained vivid. But on the other hand petroleum was an unusually complex industry, and it was extremely difficult for an amateur in government to understand it, let alone manipulate it. In general this question usually was submerged during periods of crisis, whether of war or depression, but reappeared with the return of normalcy.

The incidents that brought attention to petroleum policy during the Truman administration all led to struggles with one or more of these basic questions. These struggles were carried out against the background of the search for a wider national energy policy described in chapter 1.

The Perspective of Sumner Pike

One person who gave sustained and informed attention to some of the big questions of petroleum policy in the years just before the Truman presidency was Sumner T. Pike. Pike had a long career in and around the oil business before entering public service in the 1930s, first selling equipment, then managing oil investments for an insurance company, and finally as vice-president of the successful domestic and international development firm of Case, Pomeroy and Company from 1928 to 1938. He was the Commerce Department's representative on the Temporary National Economic Committee (TNEC), and he became a member of the Securities and Exchange Commission in 1939. While keeping his post on the SEC, Pike in 1942 succeeded George W. Stocking as director of the fuel price division of the Office of Price Administration (OPA). After the war President Truman appointed him one of the first members of the Atomic Energy Commission.[2] By following some of Pike's writings

2. A brief biographical sketch of Pike, "Sumner T. Pike: New OPA Oil Price Chief," appeared in *National Petroleum News,* December 30, 1942, p. 2. This paper reported delightedly on Pike's appointment at OPA. "He has the tact to get along

during part of his public career it is possible to gain an unusual perspective of the petroleum issues that were awaiting President Truman in 1945.

Despite a lifetime of immersion in the hurly-burly of the oil world Pike usually stood back to see the big picture. His first exposure to large questions of policy came as a member of the TNEC and led him to write what he referred to as "a sort of semi-hysterical report" entitled "Semantics of the Oil Hearings," which was never published. In this work his main point was that in discussions of petroleum policy, confusion ran high in no small part because of problems of communication. Oilmen, economists, and lawyers all took different approaches to issues and all used words that had arbitrary coded meanings rather than obvious ones; for example, "majors" and "independents"; "waste," "conservation," and "proration"; "competition" and "monopoly"; and "well-potential."[3]

Full exposure to the TNEC hearings on the oil industry, which ran from September 25 to October 25, 1939, led Pike to draft a long article, or short book, which he shared with colleagues such as Willard Thorp and G. S. Guthrie but never revised or carried further. In it he argued that growth and change had occurred very rapidly in the oil industry and that the national interest dictated serious and detached attention to this industry. But this seemed not to be taking place. Pike was concerned particularly about less than optimum utilization of both domestic and foreign resources, including natural gas. He emphasized that no estimate of "discoverable oil" in the United States was "much good," but he guessed that between 50 billion and 60 billion barrels remained. This would not last very long. He recommended that prices of oil be allowed to rise gradually so as to encourage exploration and gradual conversion to alternative fuels. "Eventually we shall have to go into a basis high enough to fill our production deficit by imports, secondary recovery methods, shale extraction, synthesis of substitutes or some combination of two or more of them." He recommended "the creation by Congress of a Board for the purpose of coordinating the interests of the Federal

---

with Mr. Ickes, the entree to the White House and the 'inner circle,' and his oil background assures him something better than a 'give-him-a-trial' reception from the industry." A native of Maine, Pike received his B.A. degree from Bowdoin College in 1913 magna cum laude with straight A's in economics. His college transcript is in Personal File, Sumner T. Pike Papers, HSTL. An interesting account of a trip made by Pike and Everette L. DeGolyer in 1938 to estimate the oil potential of Venezuela is in the Petroleum Reserves Corporation File, Pike Papers, HSTL.

3. Pike to Theodore J. Kreps, July 31, 1940, with attachment dated December 2, 1939, TNEC–Draft of Report on the Oil Industry File, Pike Papers, HSTL.

Government, the Interstate Oil Compact, the States and the petroleum industry in the better conservation of our oil and gas resources."[4]

Pike's experience in the OPA during the war seems to have altered his views about oil policy in two respects. First, although he was himself a well-known oilman, he came to regard with alarm the extent to which the industry's interest could conflict with the national interest and the way in which the industry seemed willing to reject the latter for the former. The particular incident that sensitized Pike was a request from the industry, and from Harold Ickes, in 1943 for an increase in the price of oil by 35 cents a barrel and a corresponding increase in product prices. Pike and his staff examined the industry's case with impressive care and rejected it, admitting only that some incentive payments for additional exploration might be justified.[5] The problem would become a familiar one: with a very large market and an inelastic supply in the short run, a major transfer of wealth to the oil producers was required to bring about a small increase in production. Given the choice, Pike and the OPA were unwilling to sanction such a transfer. The reaction from Ickes and from the industry was furious, and a vigorous campaign was waged against the decision, including pressures on congressmen to intervene. Pike was horrified and obviously disillusioned with his former colleagues in the industry. He wrote to the OPA administrator:

I am sure that you see, much more than I, the unsavory spectacle of elements of both industry and government which regard these Acts not as the law of the land which mean what they say, but merely as another hurdle to be topped in reaching an objective. It seems a queer anomaly that after Congress has passed its legislation the very members who voted for the Act continue to put pressure on us to do things for their constituents which are clearly illegal, or else call for the widest relaxation of the safeguards set up to prevent inflation.[6]

The other effect of wartime experience on Pike was to make him even more aware than he had been in 1939 of the impending U.S. dependence on foreign petroleum. Wartime demands made the future deficit seem

4. "TNEC Hearings on the Oil Industry" (1939), pp. 25, 55, 64, ibid.
5. The reasons for Pike's rejection of the price increase are summarized in a memorandum, Pike to Prentiss M. Brown, "Proposed Increase in Crude Oil Prices," April 7, 1943, OPA Personal File, Pike Papers, HSTL. A more complete statement of the case is in a letter (presumably drafted by Pike), Chester Bowles to Fred M. Vinson, n.d., with attachment, "Crude Oil Prices: A Statement of the Case for and against a General Increase," and in a press release, October 29, 1943, both in ibid.
6. Pike to Prentiss Brown, April 29, 1943, ibid.

closer and he became concerned about how to adjust to it. In a remarkably prescient letter to Leon Henderson in 1942 he said:

. . . instead of stimulating discoveries in this country by incentive prices, we should, as a long-range policy, be not only willing but happy to get into the foreign oil market and purchase substantial quantities of our domestic needs as long as they can be had cheaply. Otherwise, I visualize with a good deal of horror our sudden necessitous entrance in some not far distant day into the foreign markets, and boy at that time will we be held up! We might just as well get started in those markets as early as possible and while we can do those countries some good, and effect the transition from an exporting to an importing nation gradually, in the meantime not trying to find all our domestic oil at once. Actually, this sort of a course means complete removal of the tariff and I suppose that's a political impossibility at the present. But its just common sense and some day will perhaps be done.[7]

By 1943 Pike was even more convinced than he had been a year earlier that America's oil future lay abroad, especially in the Middle East. He described to one correspondent in glowing detail the potential of this area for oil production, and he complained that the United States was not equipped to take advantage of it.

The American Government and the American oil companies have got to take an extremely lively interest in the preservation and maintenance of American rights in these areas if we are to have any confidence in our ability to get plenty of oil at a reasonable price for the next generation. . . . the proper handling of our interests in the Persian Gulf district requires a severe wrench from the present thinking of both the State Department and the interested American oil companies. I fondly hope that we are beginning to see a realization of this problem in the formation of the Petroleum Reserves Corporation.[8]

Perhaps because of his mounting disillusionment both with the efficiency and the patriotism of the large U.S. oil corporations, Pike continued to press for the development of the Petroleum Reserves Corporation (PRC), a public body founded in July 1943 that fell under the general supervision of the Foreign Economic Administration. In suggested testimony he wrote for the head of the FEA in March 1944, he said: "The Government has . . . no definite continuous policy for aid to American interests in their exploration and exploitation of foreign oil fields. I view the Petroleum Reserves Corporation as a vehicle through which such a policy will be developed. . . ."[9]

Pike worked closely with Lauchlin Currie and others in the FEA to

7. Pike to Henderson, November 24, 1942, ibid.
8. Pike to Daniel Bertrand, September 8, 1943, Oil Personal File, Pike Papers, HSTL.
9. Pike to Leo T. Crowley, March 25, 1944, with attachment, Petroleum Reserves Corporation Personal File, Pike Papers, HSTL.

specify just what this agency's petroleum responsibilities should be. But as the end of the war drew near he clearly had a sense of foreboding as he watched the Interior Department—through its wartime agency, the Petroleum Administration for War (PAW)—and the State Department jockeying for position in the field. He wrote worriedly to Currie in July 1944:

FEA has been consistently given the run-around by PAW and in recent months has been the subject of strangely chilly treatment from the State Department. PAW with its close industry connections and announced intention of dissolution shortly after the war is of all agencies the least fitted to determine the long term foreign petroleum policy of the Government. State is, of course, responsible for such policies but is ill-equipped in manpower and experience for their detailed formulation and certainly for their administration.[10]

Pike left the OPA in May 1946 to turn his attention to the problems and possibilities of an emerging new energy source, atomic power.

Oil for Peace and War

The depression left the oil industry surrounded by a maze of regulations and institutions contrived mainly by the industry itself: the Interstate Oil Compact, the Connally Hot Oil Act, and an oil tariff. In the middle of the controversies attending the creation of such regulations stood the unpredictable Secretary of the Interior Harold Ickes. On the one hand Ickes gave some comfort to the oil interests because he favored public intervention to help with their problems. But on the other hand he generated consternation and concern because often he seemed to go too far and to favor regulation unwanted by the industry and even, God forbid, the treatment of oil as a public utility—especially if he, Ickes, were to be the regulator.

World War II changed the situation dramatically. Instead of coping with oversupply, government and the industry were faced with the need to increase production drastically, control prices, institute rationing in the short run, and worry about supplies for the long run if the war were protracted. As early as 1939 Roosevelt conferred limited emergency powers on Ickes and in May 1941 designated him petroleum coordinator for national defense. Ickes' approach was to work closely with the oil companies and to gain them favors, such as temporary exemption from antitrust proceedings, in return for their cooperation with government. As the storm clouds grew darker Ickes pressed for greater authority,

10. Pike to Currie, July 14, 1944; also Pike to Currie, July 17, 1944, and A. E. Ernst to Pike, July 12, 1944; all in ibid.

particularly over the export of oil and the behavior of companies abroad. On the day after Pearl Harbor he advised Roosevelt that the only way for government to make corporate interest coincide with national interest was to formulate and enforce a "national policy."

The fact is that we have no adequate national policy with respect to petroleum, and no international policy that I know of except to protect the interests of our nationals . . . it may be against the national interest to sell oil outside of the United States or to sell it as fast as it can be produced.[11]

But it was not until a year later that Roosevelt gave Ickes the power he wanted, to make and to enforce national policy as petroleum administrator for war.

Throughout the war Ickes continued to work with the oil industry, rather than to attempt to preside over it, and to act as its voice in return for full cooperation. His deputy was a prominent oilman, Ralph K. Davies, and he depended heavily on a Petroleum Industry War Council for advice. Not only did Ickes hold the trustbusters and miscellaneous reformers off the oil companies, but he also fought repeatedly for price increases, tax concessions, materials allocation, and pipeline construction.[12] The industry was pleasantly surprised and puzzled by his perfor-

11. Ickes to Roosevelt, December 8, 1941, CCF 1-188, RG 48, NA.
12. Ickes outlined his philosophy in two books during the war: *The Autobiography of a Curmudgeon* (Reynal, 1943), and *Fightin' Oil* (Knopf, 1943). He was always forceful and forthright in his advocacy. Upon being rebuffed by OPA Administrator Chester Bowles after an appeal for a price increase at the end of the control period in 1946, he replied: "You endeavor to make the point that the supply deficiencies in question might be averted through a continued exercise of war power directives by this Office. Your reasoning on this score only shows, however, that you do not understand the petroleum economics involved." (Ickes to Bowles, January 22, 1946, CCF 1-188, RG 48, NA.) A protracted dispute occurred during 1944 over a Treasury Department decision to require that geological and geophysical expenditures in connection with petroleum exploration be treated for tax purposes as capital investment rather than expenses. Ickes supported the industry's objections but evidently with some misgivings. He wrote to Stephen Raushenbush in the department: "I would like to have your independent judgment on this question of taxes on the oil and gas industry. As Administrator I would want to do what I legitimately may to give proper representation to the viewpoint of the oil industry, but I do not want to get out of bounds. I believe that the oil industry, along with others, should pay its just taxes. For years there has been a specific exemption for 'depletion' the propriety of which I question, but with respect to which I have raised no question because of my relationship to the industry." (Ickes to Raushenbush, August 16, 1944, Oil Depletion and Exploration (Personal) File, Branch of Economics and Statistics Files, RG 48, NA.) Ickes responded with remarkable acerbity even to implicit criticsm, or faint praise, of PAW and the industry during the war. For example, see Ickes to Senator Francis Maloney, March 19, 1943, Harold L. Ickes File, General Subject File Box 3, Records of the Senate Special Committee on the Gas and Oil Shortage, RG 46, NA.

mance, but its suspicions remained. After all was this not still the vintage New Dealer who favored public utility status?

The responsibility for petroleum production and distribution during the war rested with PAW, but the task of controlling its price and allocation lay with the OPA. Some remarkable feats of rationing were accomplished, especially in 1943 when tanker losses reduced deliveries dramatically to the East Coast.[13]

The oil industry concluded that its continuing fears about Ickes had been justified by his handling of the petroleum reserves issue. The Petroleum Reserves Corporation was created in July 1943 with Ickes as president and chairman as a device to purchase crude petroleum outside the United States for the allies and the occupied areas, and according to Ickes "by its very existence to persuade the British to negotiate with us with respect to Mideastern oil."[14] Ickes and his staff, however, soon developed the concept of national petroleum reserves at home and abroad as a device to enforce oil policy. Their first project was to acquire full or part ownership of the California Arabian Standard Oil Company. But the company resisted, the entire industry became agitated by the implied precedent, and Ickes withdrew.[15] In March 1944 Ickes proposed to Roosevelt a new tack—creating a Federal Petroleum Reserves Board to be made up of the secretaries of the army, navy, and interior and charged to estimate and administer all the national reserves of petroleum. "I believe that a Board of this sort will make it possible to establish an oil policy to meet this country's future needs."[16] Ickes continued to press for such a board with Truman, emphasizing Roosevelt's interest in it. It is impossible to ascertain Ickes' real intentions for the petroleum reserves program— whether it was intended merely to be a bargaining chip for negotiations with other producers abroad, as Ickes sometimes suggested; a mechanism

13. The distinguished economist, Joel Dean, chief of the OPA Fuel Rationing Division, produced for his staff a succession of twenty-five remarkable "educational memoranda" setting forth alternative forms of rationing and their respective costs and benefits. Copies are in OPA Fuel Form File, General Subject File Box 6, Records of the Senate Special Committee on the Gas and Oil Shortage, RG 46, NA. As gasoline and fuel rationing began to cause increasing hardships, pressures for relief mounted on Congress. Letters and memorandums from Dean and others explaining OPA's programs are in OPA File, General Subject File Box 6, ibid.

14. The solicitor of the Interior Department prepared a history of the PRC for Ickes in a memorandum, November 19, 1945, CCF 1-188, RG 48, NA. See also Ickes to Truman, November 6, 1945, ibid.

15. George W. Stocking, *Middle East Oil: A Study in Political and Economic Controversy* (Vanderbilt University Press, 1970), pp. 98–101.

16. Ickes to Roosevelt, March 4, 1944, Oil Reserves Program (Domestic) File, Office Files of Abe Fortas, RG 48, NA.

to accomplish a few limited wartime objectives; or indeed a trial balloon on the road to a petroleum public utility. The second overt act to implement the reserves idea was a negotiation for the construction of a pipeline across Arabia. This, too, was enough to frighten the oilmen; the industry portrayed the PRC as Ickes' diabolical device to nationalize their foreign operations.[17] In November 1945 Ickes wrote to the chairman of the board of the Reconstruction Finance Corporation, the bureaucratic parent of the PRC, saying that in return for oil industry support of the Anglo-American Petroleum Agreement, then before the Senate, "I have committed myself to the oil industry to recommend the dissolution of this Corporation as quickly as that objective is reached." He explained further:

The American Petroleum Industry has developed a strong antagonism toward the Petroleum Reserves Corporation because it believes that it sees in such a Government corporation a threat to the continued independence of the industry. The charter of P.R.C. embraces the field of oil operations and the Industry reads into this all manner of sinister meaning. These fears are, of course, not well grounded but they exist nevertheless and, if the Corporation were continued with an expanded charter, it would continue to stir up controversy and bad feeling from which, in this situation, there is nothing to be gained.[18]

But the dissolution of the PRC did not allay the fears of the industry, which retained a deep suspicion that Ickes and his associates harbored some dark plot to regulate or even to nationalize the industry. The suspicion was strengthened by a discussion in the Interior Department in 1944 about a "consolidation or regrouping of all the oil and gas functions of the Department." Apparently Assistant Secretary Michael Straus began the discussion by recommending the "creation of a consultative policy body in the office of the Petroleum Conservation Division" composed "entirely of representatives of Department oil agencies." Mean-

17. Ickes to Truman, May 7, 1945, Subject File: Cabinet, PSF, HSTL. The Petroleum Industry War Council expressed its opposition to the pipeline in a letter to Senator Francis Maloney. "Why is it necessary that this project, (unlike other projects undertaken by the United States Government in wartime), calls for *continued Government ownership*, contrary to the traditional American policy of noncompetition with private enterprise? The proposal, too, gives the Government the right to decide where any of this oil shall be sold, and to whom!" (William R. Boyd to Maloney, March 27, 1944, W. R. Boyd File, Correspondence File Box 2, Records of the Senate Special Committee Investigating Petroleum Resources, RG 46, NA.) Ickes reacted with characteristic intemperance to Senate questioning of the purposes of the PRC. See correspondence between Ickes and Senator Maloney in Harold L. Ickes File, Correspondence File Box 6, ibid.

18. Ickes to Charles B. Henderson, November 6, 1945, CCF 1-188, RG 48, NA.

while the department's solicitor prepared an opinion that the secretary had in fact the authority to "transfer, consolidate, or regroup all the oil and gas functions of the Department," including those lodged in the General Land Office, the Geological Survey, the Office of Indian Affairs, the Bureau of Mines, and Federal Petroleum Board, and the Petroleum Conservation Division that enforced the Connally Act. It was word that such a "violent measure" might be in the wind that, according to Straus, led "assailants and critics" to detect "a move toward the Government taking over the oil industry."[19] The Departmental Petroleum Committee, proposed by Straus, was created in December 1944.[20]

As the war became more intense in 1943 and 1944, and as more and more congressmen felt the ire of their constituents about shortages of fuel oil and gasoline, an increasing number of congressional committees undertook investigations into the problem. The result was much confusion and diffusion of effort. Secretary Ickes reported in 1945 that since the creation of PAW either he or his staff had appeared more than one hundred times before twenty different committees and subcommittees of the House and Senate on the subject of oil. To help remedy this situation the Senate in 1944 focused its efforts by establishing a single Special Committee to Investigate Petroleum Resources, chaired first by Senator Francis Maloney of Connecticut and after his death in 1945 by Senator Joseph C. O'Mahoney of Wyoming. An extremely ambitious plan for the committee's work was drawn up by management consultant Milo R. Perkins covering almost every imaginable topic related to petroleum, domestic and international, including whether the postwar oil trade should be conducted on principles of freedom or under a "world oil compact" and "what steps should be taken to increase U.S. reserves abroad."[21] Without significant analytical capacity of its own, however, the committee soon found what its successors were to discover: that it

19. Memorandum, Straus to the Under Secretary, March 2, 1944, with opinion of the Solicitor attached, CCF 1-094a, RG 48, NA.
20. Department of the Interior Order 2012, December 1, 1944, Secretary of the Interior 1942–1946 File, Oscar L. Chapman Papers, HSTL.
21. The Perkins outline is attached to memorandum, Richard Joyce Smith to Senator Francis Maloney, June 17, 1944, Milo Perkins (outline) File, Correspondence File Box 9, Records of the Senate Special Committee Investigating Petroleum Resources, RG 46, NA. The committee's chief counsel, Henry S. Fraser, proposed a much more modest agenda than did Perkins to deal with two topics only: "diplomatic support" to U.S. oil interests abroad and "post-war disposal of refineries, pipelines, and tankers." "Proposed Agenda," February 27, 1945, Henry S. Fraser File, Correspondence File Box 4, ibid.

was substantially at the mercy of events, and that through its hearings it
could do little more than provide data and a forum for the expression of
well-known positions by the major actors in the situation, in this case the
industry, the Interior Department, and the OPA. During the first year of
the committee's work attention was addressed mainly to the proposed
trans-Arabia pipeline and the Anglo-American Petroleum Agreement.
But by the time the work of the committee was completed in 1946, hearings had also been held on cartels, sources of supply, operations abroad,
postwar requirements, disposal of wartime facilities, the history of PAW,
special problems of the independents, and the creation of the Oil and Gas
Division in the Interior Department.[22]

As the war ended, many expressed doubts about how the nation
formed and implemented petroleum policy, and various schemes for new
units to do the job better were suggested. Among other pressures PAW
came under attack from trade unions as "being operated for and by the
major oil companies, and to the disadvantage of the workers."[23] The
Bureau of the Budget, which in 1945 was still the main source of economic advice to the President, was deeply concerned that PAW skewed
petroleum policy in favor of the large companies. William Pincus, a
Budget Bureau staff member, wrote in October 1945:

> The significant thing is that at the present critical juncture, in the absence
> of a national petroleum policy, the industry people in PAW are going to in-
> form the Congress concerning the extent and use of our petroleum resources.
> Who will represent the public? The answer is no one directly. Some balance

22. The American Petroleum Institute took the unusual step of publishing as a
pamphlet a "summarization of testimony before the Special Senate Committee" by
fifty-seven industry witnesses, prepared by Alfred Jacobsen, president of the Amerada Petroleum Corporation: *Petroleum: Recommendations for a National Oil
Policy* (Washington, D.C.: API, 1946). Committee opposition both to the trans-
Arabia pipeline and to the Anglo-American Petroleum Agreement appear to have
led to abandonment of both projects and the bitter enmity of Secretary Ickes. See
Cordell Hull File, Correspondence File Box 5, and Harold L. Ickes File, Correspondence File Box 6, Records of the Senate Special Committee Investigating Petroleum Resources, RG 46, NA. The committee's final report might almost have been
written by the industry. It recommended promotion of interstate compacts at home
and abroad, opening the public lands to drilling, limitation of work on synthetics
to research only, "encouragement" of secondary recovery, continuation of favorable tax provisions to industry, and policies "to promote full development of the
petroleum resources of the whole world for the benefit of all peoples of the world."
Investigation of Petroleum Resources in Relation to the National Welfare, S. Rept. 9,
80 Cong. 1 sess. (Government Printing Office, 1947), p. 55.

23. Harold Ickes to O. A. Knight, president, Oil Workers International Union,
July 16, 1945, CCF 1-188, RG 48, NA.

may be added by the appearance of independent oil producers but this, of course, is not sufficient. The organized power of the big oil companies has been recently demonstrated by their ability to force a revision of the International Oil Treaty which, in itself, was innocuous enough but which the industry interpreted as the beginning of a small degree of Government intervention and control. The sad part of this whole picture is that we don't have a national petroleum policy and certainly the PAW is not the kind of agency which can be depended upon to evolve the beginnings of such a policy. Its character and the kind of job it was intended to do make it unsuitable for such a task.[24]

It was clear to Pincus that PAW should soon be terminated, but he could not see clearly what should rise in its place.

Ralph Davies expressed deep concern to Secretary of the Interior Julius Krug in April 1946 about a rumor of "an interdepartmental oil board of some kind."[25] Apparently he and other leading oilmen realized that change was in the wind and concluded that the only sensible approach was to direct it. They proposed that a pale peacetime equivalent of PAW be created with an oilman at its head and an industry advisory council looking over his shoulder. Davies spoke to Secretary Krug in April 1946 about this idea and evidently convinced him easily. Truman, too was won over quickly. On May 3, 1946, Truman wrote to Krug announcing the termination of PAW, adding, "I am in agreement with your views that steps should now be taken to assure coordination in peacetime of the Federal Government's many interests in petroleum, petroleum products and associated hydrocarbons. . . . I have been impressed with the great contribution of government-industry cooperation to the success of the war petroleum program, and feel that the values of such close and harmonious relations between Government and industry should be continued. I, therefore, suggest that you establish an industry organization to consult and advise with you." The President asked that Davies "remain on for a brief period to assist in organizing and launching these activities."[26]

The proposal by Davies to create what became the Oil and Gas Division (OGD) of the Department of the Interior aroused at least some

24. Memorandum, William Pincus to "Mr. Miles," "The Role of PAW as an Industry Lobby in the Determination of National and International Petroleum Policy," October 24, 1945, Petroleum Administration for War–General File, Office Files of the Director 1939–1946, Records of the Bureau of the Budget, RG 51, NA.
25. Davies to Krug, April 10, 1946, CCF 1-188, RG 48, NA.
26. "Letter to Secretary Krug Concerning Termination of the Petroleum Administration for War, May 3, 1946," *Public Papers: Harry S. Truman, 1946* (GPO, 1961), pp. 232–33.

controversy. Mid-1946 was not the best time for serious reflection on important institutional change, however: the administration still had not found its feet and was faced with its first congressional elections; the Interior Department was in disarray from the loss of its longtime leader, Ickes. But there was some interesting comment all the same. Worried noises came from such departmental units as the Geological Survey, which missed the point of the proposal and thought Davies had in mind a large, complex, and powerful structure bent on devouring their own oil operations.[27] The Commerce Department, which regretted its steady loss of responsibility for petroleum during the 1930s and in World War II, thought that the OGD would deliver the coup de grace to its continuing involvement.[28] A more serious question came from Warner W. Gardner, former Interior Department solicitor and now assistant secretary. He remained "unconvinced that the Connally Act, at least in its criminal enforcement aspects, has any relation to the economy of this decade," and he worried that the new OGD would perpetuate and enshrine this restrictionist device left over from the depression.[29]

Oil Abroad

By the middle of World War II it had become unequivocally clear that America's oil future lay abroad. The war itself gave a foretaste of vastly increased energy consumption levels, and rates of discovery in the United States seemed to be leveling off or slowing down. But most important of all, opportunities for development in other parts of the world appeared to be enormous. A technical mission to the Middle East for PAW, led by petroleum consultant Everette DeGolyer, reported unequivocally on February 1, 1944: "The center of gravity of world oil production is shifting from the Gulf-Caribbean area to the Middle East—to the Persian Gulf area—and is likely to continue to shift until it is firmly established

27. W. E. Wrather to Under Secretary Chapman, April 24, 1946, Oil and Gas Matters File, Office Files of Oscar Chapman, RG 48, NA.

28. Henry A. Wallace to the President, June 10, 1946; and Wallace to Joseph C. O'Mahoney; both in Oils-Mineral-General File 312, RG 151, NA.

29. Memorandum, Gardner to "Mr. Myer," Executive Director, Coordination Committee, July 22, 1946, Coordination, General: Committee Memoranda File, Records of the Coordination Committee, 1946–47, RG 48, NA. Gardner also commissioned a staff paper, "Organization and Functions of the Oil and Gas Division," during the OGD's early months in 1946. The staff writer of this paper was clearly puzzled by the division's role. The paper is in Oil and Gas Division File, Minerals and Fuels Division Files, RG 48, NA.

in that area."[30] Professional opinion flowing to policymakers suggested that the United States had no choice but to rethink carefully its oil policy abroad and to act quickly. For example, William E. Wrather, director of the Geological Survey and a member of the DeGolyer mission, wrote to Secretary Ickes in 1944:

Adequate military security can best be assured by promptly supplementing our domestic reserves in the most promising foreign areas. The foreign situation is inextricably involved with the domestic. If (as seems probable) we face a declining discovery rate at home, we must make good the deficit by seeking reserves abroad. . . . Geological evidence indicates that the Near East can become, with only a limited campaign of drilling, the rival of the United States. Transportation, refining facilities and market outlet must be supplied before this prolific source can be integrated into the world-wide oil economy. It would therefore be inexcusable national folly for us not to adopt an aggressive oil policy in that area.[31]

The issue then became, not whether the United States should pursue its petroleum interests abroad, but how much and through what means. Wrather thought "this could probably best be accomplished by lending prompt and continuing diplomatic support to American nationals, supplementing such support with Government funds to meet the costs of transportation and refining facilities, with ample provision for amortizing in a reasonable time the Government funds so invested."[32] One industry expert wrote to Secretary Ickes in 1944 with the novel suggestion, which he termed "dynamite," that America conserve its dwindling reserves for emergencies and rather than maintaining tariffs impose "taxes on domestic production while permitting tax free imports."[33]

The oil industry was able to express itself through a Foreign Operations Committee of oilmen advisory to the PAW administrator. In November 1943 the committee issued *A Foreign Oil Policy for the United States,* which noted that petroleum was becoming steadily more important worldwide and that the United States was about to become a net importer. In order to make the best of a bad situation the nation must assist its private oil companies to get their share of the world's reserves

30. "Preliminary Report of the Technical Oil Mission to the Middle East," February 1, 1944, Petroleum Reserves Corporation File, Correspondence File Box 9, Records of the Senate Special Committee Investigating Petroleum Resources, RG 46, NA.

31. Wrather to Ickes, February 22, 1944, CCF 1-094a, RG 48, NA.

32. Ibid.

33. Eugene Ayres to Ickes, March 29, 1944, Oil (Foreign) PRC File, Fortas Office Files, RG 48, NA.

and become "a powerful force for world reconstruction." The five principles of "an immediate foreign oil policy" should be a guarantee of no government oil enterprise, exemption from "the risk of violating American laws" overseas (antitrust), cooperation and support from the government abroad, ultimate disposition of government facilities and supplies to private industry, and provision for the return of properties and compensation from the enemy. To implement such a policy it was desirable that "the American petroleum industry should be admitted more fully into the policy councils of the Government of the United States" and that an "International Oil Compact" be negotiated comparable to the domestic Interstate Oil Compact.[34]

The notion of American industry becoming active in the Middle East to ensure the nation's future lifeblood was mixed at this time with a sense that one of the great commercial opportunities of the postwar world lay in Mideast oil and that the most powerful country in the world naturally deserved a large piece of this action. The so-called As-Is Agreement signed by Standard Oil of New Jersey, the Royal Dutch Shell Group, and the Anglo-Persian Oil Company at Achnacarry, Scotland, in 1928 had guaranteed American firms some Middle East access, but the sense now was that events justified a redistribution of the cake. This position was taken by Raymond L. Buell of Time, Inc., in a "foreign policy memorandum" entitled "An American Policy toward the Middle East," which was especially well received by persons to whom he sent it in Congress.[35]

The State Department's position on foreign oil was set forth by its adviser on petroleum policy, Charles B. Rayner, before the Senate Special Committee Investigating Petroleum Resources in June 1945. Rayner

34. Foreign Operations Committee, *A Foreign Oil Policy for the United States* (Washington, D.C.: Petroleum Administration for War, 1943), pp. 11–12. Another group, the Petroleum Industry War Council, endorsed the "substance" of this document in January 1944. In March it issued its own report, *A National Oil Policy for the United States* (Washington, D.C.: PIWC, 1944), in which the council reiterated the principles of government nonintervention and "conservation" but specifically rejected stockpiling and "strategic reserves for security purposes." It favored "adequate world oil developments, under the leadership of United States nationals" with "diplomatic support and machinery for international consultation." But it also urged that imports be handled in "an orderly and flexible manner" and not be permitted "in excess of economic needs and not required in the national interest" (pp. 4–5).

35. R. L. Buell, "Foreign Policy Memorandum No. 3: An American Policy toward the Middle East," August 6, 1944, Raymond Buell File, Correspondence File Box 2, Records of the Senate Special Committee Investigating Petroleum Resources, RG 46, NA. See also Francis Maloney to Buell, August 18, 1944, and Henry S. Fraser to Maloney, September 13, 1944, both in ibid.; John M. Blair, *The Control of Oil* (Pantheon Books, 1976), p. 337; and Stocking, *Middle East Oil*.

portrayed petroleum as the most important element in World War II. The United States won because it had petroleum in abundance; both Germany and Japan fought for it and lost because they were unsuccessful in capturing it in time. Worldwide demand for it might confidently be predicted to rise dramatically and U.S. production to decline as a proportion of world production. It was essential, therefore, for the Department of State to render "active, energetic, and consistent support . . . to the United States petroleum industry in its foreign operations and problems."[36]

A contrary position on how to deal with foreign oil was presented in detail in a report on Near East oil by another State Department official, John H. Leavell, petroleum attaché in the Division of Near Eastern Affairs. Leavell thought that the issues were much larger than merely filling the U.S. oil deficit and making money. On the one hand the Near East was a political tinderbox that the United States could leave to private enterprise only at its peril, and on the other hand cheap and abundant oil was the secret both to the development of the poor countries of the world and to full employment in the United States.

No foreign policy of our country is of more importance to its security and welfare and to the future peace of the world than a fair and proper solution of the development and distribution of the oil in this area. There is no conceivable method by which the standard of living throughout the world can be as quickly raised as to furnish cheap oil in abundant quantities. There is no comparable method to employ our labor and our war factories as to supply the equipment to use this oil.[37]

Leavell was not persuaded that American oil companies could safely be left to pursue their own interests in the Near East. The stakes were far too high ("the greatest single prize in all history") and the dangers too great. He feared above all that competition from the British and the Russians, both of whom operated through government agencies, would be overwhelming. Accordingly he favored

purchase by our Government at a liberal figure of controlling interests in American-owned companies in this area. . . . The writer has listened to nu-

36. *American Petroleum Interests in Foreign Countries,* Hearings before the Senate Special Committee Investigating Petroleum Resources, 79 Cong. 1 sess. (GPO, 1946), p. 19. Worries about the antitrust implications of the sort of policy favored by Rayner were expressed by Allen C. Phelps of the Federal Trade Commission in his statement, "Post-War Policy as to Cartels," Subject File Box 10, Records of the Senate Special Committee Investigating Petroleum Resources, RG 46, NA.

37. John H. Leavell, "Summary of Report on Near East Oil," n.d., Petroleum Reserves Corporation Personal File, Pike Papers, HSTL.

merous reasons as to why this plan is fatally dangerous. All of the reasons
when boiled down to their essence become one: namely, the objection to
"Government in Business." . . . The writer believes this is a special and different case, in which true competition between many units will not exist;
the money and attendant risks involved are too great for private enterprise;
the economic and military security of our country is involved; the peace of the
world is placed in private hands without authority of the Government to
enact regulations over them, but with the responsibility of the Government to
protect the industry against all comers.

The alleged dangers of "Government in Business" must be carefully
weighed against the very grave dangers attendant upon the failure of this Department [State] to have direct and immediate power to guide the exploitation
of this controlling world resource.[38]

Leavell's voice was barely heard, and Rayner's proposal for a close
working relationship between the State Department and the large oil
companies prevailed.[39]

Secretary of the Interior Ickes remained characteristically ambivalent
about the strategy of U.S. oil operations overseas. He made repeated
public declarations of his enthusiasm for the free market abroad as well
as at home, but he was careful always to offer qualifications. For example, he told the Economics Club of New York in 1944:

In both the foreign and domestic sectors I believe that the job should be done
by private enterprise to the fullest extent that this may be possible. I see nothing inconsistent in declaring that I also believe that there must be recognition
of a national interest in our oil resources, irreplaceable as they are. By "national interest," I do not mean nationalization of the oil industry, or Government competition with industry, or Government domination of industry. I
mean that the Government must make certain that, for whatever needs the
future may bring, it will have all of the oil that it requires, where it is required,
and when it is required. How this is to be done, involves the whole broad and
complex problem of what our national oil policy should be.[40]

How it was done, in fact, was pretty much as Wrather had suggested
and the large companies wished. After the brief and abortive scheme of
the PRC to construct a publicly owned trans-Arabia pipeline, U.S. oil
operations abroad were conducted exclusively by the industry with the
close cooperation and encouragement of government. The nature of this

38. Ibid.
39. Assistant Secretary of State to Henry Wallace, August 23, 1945, with attachment, "Organization of Petroleum Facilities Coordinating Committee," Oils-
Mineral-General File 312, RG 151, NA.
40. Harold L. Ickes, "The Role of the U.S. Government in Domestic and Foreign Oil Reserves: Address before the Economics Club, New York City, May 9,
1944," Statements and Addresses of Administrator Ickes File, Ralph K. Davies
Papers, HSTL.

public-private partnership was illustrated clearly in the negotiation of an Anglo-American Petroleum Agreement as the war came to an end. This treaty in part was intended to replace the old "red line" market division worked out by Britain and France after World War I to monopolize the petroleum resources of the Middle East. The proposed new arrangement would minimize conflict between American and British oil interests while recognizing the increasing world power of the former and the relative decline of the latter. As Ralph K. Davies, deputy petroleum administrator for war and one of the negotiators, reported to the industry, this was also an attempt to set up abroad a means to achieve "order and decency" in the international oil trade comparable to that enjoyed at home. (Even the administrative instrument proposed in the agreement, an International Petroleum Commission, had a familiar ring.) In defense of this potentially restrictionist device Davies warned: "Enormous volumes of oil are available today in foreign parts and how this oil moves in international trade will surely set domestic values in the end. The pressure of supplies may arise abroad but the effect thereof cannot help but be felt at home." The question faced by the negotiators, he said, was "will the intensified international competition be sane and orderly or will it be along those destructive lines that can only operate to produce chaos and bring about a deterioration of oil values the world over?" For those skeptics in the industry who worried about the intentions of bureaucrats in favoring such a treaty, Davies said: "Remember that the government officials who negotiated the Agreement had throughout the counsel and advice of six industry consultants."[41]

The cozy relationship that grew up among the oil companies, the State Department, and PAW caused some people in government concern. William Pincus in the Budget Bureau worried in October 1945 "that the State Department might, through its international activities relating to petroleum, begin to determine the broad outlines of our total petroleum policy in the absence of a domestic policy and considering that the national and international petroleum pictures are interrelated. This is a very significant problem." Pincus was puzzled by the posture of the Interior Department toward foreign oil.

Where does Interior and particularly Ickes stand? Is Ickes in a position to take a stand at present since the Government has maintained a "hands-off" policy up to the present? Should Interior be the one to take the lead in devel-

41. Ralph K. Davies, "International Oil: An Address before the San Joaquin Valley Oil Producers Association, January 30, 1946," Addresses and Statements File, Davies Papers, HSTL.

oping our policy? What should be its relations to Navy and War and State? Finally, why has Ickes apparently followed the industry line, relying upon Davies, and not acted with respect to petroleum as he has with respect to other matters, i.e., taking a strong independent stand?[42]

In the Interior Department there was at least some uneasiness about the course of foreign developments. For example, when he was the department's solicitor, Warner Gardner took strong issue with PAW about the form of the proposed Anglo-American agreement. He conceded that it might "serve to offset the traditional advantages of the British companies," but he wrote to Krug and Chapman, "My first concern with the agreement is that it contains the possibility of being administered in such a fashion as to promote the growth of international petroleum cartels." Gardner was suspicious of the superficially innocuous statistical functions of the International Commission and its charge to search for "means by which such demands and supplies may be correlated so as to further the efficient and orderly conduct of the international petroleum trade." He warned that "this provision could be so administered as to justify the allocation of international markets and international price-fixing. Any such cartel arrangement would be thoroughly undesirable. The general flavor of the Agreement, with its emphasis upon the orderly conduct of international trade and the solicitude for the oil operators, serves somewhat to strengthen my apprehensions as to the purpose of this clause."[43]

As it turned out, the Senate failed to ratify the Anglo-American Petroleum agreement. The monopolistic potential was too blatant, and despite the renegotiation carried out by Davies with industry representatives present, the industry as a whole failed to give its full support. The main reason it did not pass was not because it threatened to injure the ultimate consumers of petroleum products who by and large were unorganized and inarticulate; their welfare seems to have been remembered by only a few public servants, such as Solicitor Gardner, who pointed out that it was sensible to buy in the cheapest markets and take advantage of low-cost foreign supplies so long as they were available. Rather, the rejection grew out of a fear of import growth, a fear experienced by three groups: (1) persons concerned about the security implications of na-

---

42. William Pincus to "Mr. Miles," October 24, 1945, Petroleum Administration for War–General File, Office Files of the Director 1939–1946, Records of the Bureau of the Budget, RG 51, NA.

43. Gardner to Chapman, March 1, 1946, Oil and Gas Matters–1945 File, Chapman Office Files, RG 48, NA; and Gardner to Krug, April 12, 1946, CCF 1-188, RG 48, NA.

tional dependence on a critical good produced abroad, (2) suppliers of other fuels,[44] and (3) independent petroleum producers and refiners who feared the loss of markets in the first case and sources of supply in the second.

The failure of the Anglo-American treaty can be traced substantially to pressure on Congress from independent producers, refiners, and dealers. The independents dreaded competition from what they saw as a potential tidal wave of Middle East oil. Their arguments, which continued for several decades after the war, were that America could be self-sufficient into the indefinite future, if only it would take care of its domestic producers. J. Howard Pew of Sun Oil Company said in August 1946: "We discover more oil every day and shall continue to do so as long as Americans remain free men and our competitive enterprise system provides incentives for them to put forth the necessary effort."[45] The National Oil Policy Committee of the Independent Petroleum Association of America declared in October 1946: "The abundance of oil and gas for this Nation depends not upon static measures—upon locking up reserves, or turning in panic to un-needed imports, or to any other artificial, negative measures. It depends upon *dynamic* policies—upon the continued, vigorous search for oil and gas by a strong, healthy, experienced, competitive industry operating in accordance with sound conservation practices, and encouraged by prices sufficient to provide incentive for the high risks involved."[46] Over the next few years all parts of government concerned with petroleum heard regularly from the independents.[47]

44. On this point, of course, positions could vary. On the interagency Committee on Conservation of Natural Resources in 1946 the representative of the Navy Department was the principal advocate of tariff reductions, presumably on the ground that the use of imports would conserve domestic supplies for emergencies. Minutes of Meeting of Committee on Conservation of Natural Resources, August 22, 1946, Conservation of Natural Resources File, Chapman Office Files, RG 48, NA.

45. Pew cited by Helen A. Grickis in a letter to Joseph C. O'Mahoney, August 30, 1946, O'Mahoney File, Correspondence File Box 9, Records of the Senate Special Committee Investigating Petroleum Resources, RG 46, NA.

46. "A National Oil and Gas Policy," adopted at the Seventeenth Annual Meeting of the Independent Petroleum Association of America at Fort Worth, Texas, October 29, 1946, Policy re Petroleum Resources File, Administrative File Box 25, ibid.

47. For example, memorandum, Senator Kenneth S. Wherry to Secretary Krug, October 13, 1947, concerning "the effectiveness of Public Law No. 506, 79th Congress . . . to encourage and protect oil refineries not having their own source of supply," Geological Survey File, Chapman Office Files, RG 48, NA; and memorandum, John A. Loftus, "Middle East Oil Deals, Conversation with Lester A.

In fact, it became routine to anticipate pressure from this direction and, if possible, to head it off. For example, in supporting special project and export licenses to enable the Anglo-Iranian Oil Company to expand its pipeline system in 1948, Max W. Ball, director of the Oil and Gas Division, emphasized that a portion of the increased output would go to three independent refineries.[48]

Understandably a sizable increase in petroleum imports was bound to be the signal for intensified attention to the import question. This occurred for the first time in 1948 when total imports rose from around 160 million barrels in 1947 to almost 190 million, and imports exceeded exports for the first time since the early 1920s. In addition the Middle East emerged as a major source, moving from less than 20 percent of imports to about one-third. This growth in imports was associated with

Webb, Atlantic Refining Company," January 14, 1947, Subject File: Memoranda of Conversation, Office Files of the Assistant Secretary of State for Economic Affairs, 1946–47, HSTL. The position of the Interior Department in support of "small oil refineries" is expressed well in a letter from the Secretary to Senator Carl A. Hatch, circa 1945, Oils-Mineral-General File 312, RG 151, NA. An account of testimony from independents critical of the oil majors, cartels, and PAW (which was described as their servant), is contained in Margeurite Richardson to the Secretary, March 28, 1946, CCF 1-290, RG 48, NA. An example of the highly emotional mail received by the President from independents is Delmo J. Ciucci, President, Independent Fuel Oil Dealer Association of Chicago, to President Truman, December 18, 1948, Oils-Mineral-General File 312, RG 151, NA. An example of pressure on Congress from the independents is a letter from Russell B. Brown, General Counsel of the Independent Petroleum Association of America, to Senator Joseph C. O'Mahoney, January 31, 1946, with attached resolution recommending that "a proper policy with relation to the importation of petroleum into the United States be developed." Russell B. Brown File, Correspondence File Box 2, Records of the Senate Special Committee Investigating Petroleum Resources, RG 46, NA.

48. Memorandum, Max W. Ball to Secretary Krug, "Anglo-Iranian Pipeline," June 14, 1948, Oil and Gas Division File, Minerals and Fuels Division Files, RG 48, NA. The State Department, which typically had close relationships with the majors, also had a "policy of encouraging wider company participation in the development of Middle Eastern oil reserves," and it seems to have tried repeatedly to increase the number of opportunities for independent companies abroad. See "Memorandum, by the Assistant Chief of the Petroleum Division (Moline), August 6, 1948: Saudi Arabia's Offshore Oil," *Foreign Relations of the United States, 1948*, vol. 5: *The Near East, South Asia, and Africa* (GPO, 1975), pt. 1, p. 29. In 1947 greater competition in the Middle East was described as a "desirable long range objective" but not "a goal to be attained within a specified time period of one or two years, nor as a policy of which the petroleum companies necessarily would be informed." "Memorandum, by the Assistant Chief of the Petroleum Division (Eakens) to Mr. George C. McGhee, Special Assistant to the Under Secretary of State for Economic Affairs (Clayton), March 4, 1947," ibid., *1947*, vol. 5: *The Near East and Africa*, p. 650.

a distinct softening of the price for domestic crude. A letter of concern to the President in February 1949 about this situation from former Governor Alfred Landon of Kansas, an oil-producing state, was the occasion for the first relatively wide discussion of the import question in the federal government. Governor Landon suggested the imposition of quotas or other emergency measures. The Budget Bureau drafted a memorandum to be sent in reply that argued against any further trade barriers on the ground that the import problem was not all that serious and would probably be short-lived. Moreover, with remarkable candor the memo assured Governor Landon that the major importers of oil also were significant participants in the internal market: "It would not be in their interest to dump foreign oil on the domestic market in view of their stake in a strong domestic industry."[49] Robert E. Friedman, acting director of the OGD, advised the White House merely to answer Governor Landon's inquiry in a "general" way. The question had been "under consideration" before the letter arrived, he wrote, and "the matter is so complex that it would require far more intensive analysis and study than has yet been completed."[50]

As international tensions mounted in 1949 it was the National Security Resources Board that expressed most concern about imports. In the short and medium run, C. Griffith Johnson of the NSRB wrote to presidential assistant John Steelman, there seemed little cause for worry. The major importer, Jersey Standard, was already moving to cut its imports as the Budget Bureau had predicted. This should maintain "the health of the domestic crude industry, in particular the independents." Beyond the near horizon, however, the future was more obscure:

There is undoubtedly a long-run problem with respect to petroleum imports and the proper Government policies in this area. From a security as well as domestic welfare angle, it is important to maintain an adequate rate of development in domestic fields and yet also a volume of imports which will prevent undue exhaustion of those fields. Conceivably the lower production costs of foreign oil could lead, over a period of years, to a level of imports and a de-

49. "Staff Memorandum for the President on Governor Landon's Letter of February 2 on Petroleum Imports and Domestic Petroleum Development," attached to draft by W. G. Fritz, Truman to Landon, May 6, 1949, OF 56, Harry S. Truman Papers, HSTL. Other oil states voiced similar expressions of concern to those of Kansas; for example, D. W. Hovey, President of the Gulf Coast Refiners Association, to Charles Sawyer, September 9, 1949, General Products of the Department of Commerce–Petroleum Industry Box 336, RG 40, NA.

50. Friedman to Marjorie B. Belcher, May 24, 1949, OF 56, Truman Papers, HSTL.

pression of the domestic crude price which might impair the efficiency and progress of domestic producers. A few large companies control the important foreign sources and their interests may not be in line with the interests of the country. Thus this is a proper subject for analysis and surveillance by appropriate Government agencies."[51]

The clamor about oil imports increased in 1950 rather than lessened. The explanation lay in the size of the flow, which rose from 188 million barrels in 1948 to 310 in 1950.[52] The independents kept up their pressures on Congress, and in January Congressman Wright Patman, chairman of the House Select Committee on Small Business, submitted a report calling for emergency restraints.[53] But the major change came with the entry of the coal industry into the discussion; it began to see its future severely affected by this new source of oil. The coal industry case was presented by the National Bituminous Coal Advisory Council, a consultative group to the Bureau of Mines. The Petroleum Imports Committee of the council submitted a report to Secretary Chapman in March 1950 that was a thorough and surprisingly dispassionate analysis of recent events and their implications. The committee observed that oil imports for the first time had risen fast enough to cut into rather than merely supplement the markets both for domestic petroleum and other fuels. There was every prospect that with the enormous potential of the Middle East this pattern would continue. The committee speculated that much lower foreign production and exploration costs, the need of American oil companies to show a return on heavy investments, and pressure from the producing countries were reasons for the development. The import that had hurt coal the most was residual fuel oil. As some of the older demands for this product had dried up, especially with the spread of the diesel engine, the price had fallen and it had attracted new markets in areas traditionally served by coal, especially heating. In a covering letter to Chapman the chairman of the council pointed out some of the implications of this rise in imports. In addition to domestic oil and coal production, transportation also was affected. "Traffic declines because of the displacement of railroad-handled coal by ocean-transported oil have shrunk carrier capacity." In the short run the main costs were losses to

51. Johnson to Steelman, February 14, 1949, ibid.

52. Douglas R. Bohi and Milton Russell, *Limiting Oil Imports: An Economic History and Analysis* (Johns Hopkins University Press for Resources for the Future, 1978), pp. 22–23.

53. *The Effects of Foreign Oil Imports on Independent Domestic Producers,* H. Rept. 2344, 81 Cong. 2 sess. (GPO, 1950).

domestic coal, oil, and railroad operators and transitional unemployment for their workers. In the long run, however, the American economy would have to pay other costs of dependence on foreigners, in particular a slowdown in research on substitutes ("interest is rapidly lost in the advancement of synthetic output") and the danger that the supplies could be cut off at any time. "Continuation of the import trend followed by an interruption of foreign oil supply would find the country short of fuel such as its economy would require for peacetime and especially wartime operations. In effect, oil imports are weakening instead of bolstering the country's fuel position."[54]

By the spring of 1950 the oil import question had become hot politics. The Subcommittee on Unemployment of the Senate Labor and Public Welfare Committee, chaired by Senator Matthew M. Neely, considered recommending an increase in the crude oil tariff from 10.5 cents to $1.05 a barrel, and the idea received support from employers and trade unions in both the domestic oil and coal industries. Without any government policy yet in place, Secretary Chapman was ambivalent in dealing with the question. In April he wrote to Congressman Robert L. Doughton, chairman of the House Ways and Means Committee, that a cost-benefit appraisal of the tariff proposal would be complex. The main cost would be a higher price for oil to consumers. The benefits would come in protecting various parts of the domestic energy industries. "Exploration for new domestic reserves of petroleum, the further development of secondary recovery, continuation of the large expenditures for the development of the oil reserves of the continental shelf, and the production of synthetic liquid fuels from the Nation's ample reserves of coal and oil shale, are all dependent to a greater or lesser degree on the price of petroleum in the United States."[55] Chapman doubted that an oil tariff could do much to help coal because the competition was with oil generally, domestic and foreign, rather than specifically with imported oil. On April 4, 1950, the Interior Department provided the White House with a four-page memorandum on oil imports, which summarized the issues in all their complexity. After describing the history of imports it explained the inherently conflicting interests involved and pointed out the need for choice among alternatives at the highest level. Because this was one of

54. L. E. Tierney to Oscar Chapman, March 9, 1950, with "Report of Petroleum Imports Committee to National Bituminous Coal Advisory Council," March 1, 1950, CCF 11-34, RG 48, NA.

55. Chapman to Doughton, n.d., Oil Imports File, Joel D. Wolfsohn Papers, HSTL.

the principal documents the president used in reaching a conclusion it is worth reproducing its concluding presentation of the main issues.

The conflict of interests is about as follows (note that some of the companies in (a), (b), and (c) are identical:

(a) American companies producing abroad (as well as in the U.S.) want to import to realize on their substantial overseas investments. But they tend to exercise restraint to prevent fall in the price of crude and *absolute* displacement of domestic production, in which they share.

(b) American oil distributors want the imports to continue and, in fact, increase, because the greater the imports the lower the price of fuel oil, the better are the distributors able to compete with gas and coal, and the greater their business volumes and profits.

(c) American companies not producing abroad, and their state governments, want to increase their own production, without breaking price, i.e., through displacing imported oil.

(d) Coal operators and labor are against oil imports which, by depressing the price of fuel oils, compete with and displace coal markets.

(e) Energy consumers are in favor of oil imports because these mean lower fuel oil prices, and continued pressure on the domestic companies and their state governments to reduce the price of crude. The imports also represent an offset to future ability of these companies and state governments to sponsor a rise in oil prices.

(f) The Federal Government, representing all of the above groups, has all of their interests. In terms of policy issues:

(i) *International trade policy:* The Federal Government favors the oil imports.

(ii) *Competitive market policy:* The Federal Government favors the oil imports.

(iii) *Conservation* (i.e., saving domestic oil resources): The Federal Government might favor the oil imports.

(iv) *Profitable private business:* Oil industry profit rates are high now, and have been during at least the past decade. So the Federal Government would have no reason to intervene on this ground. But coal profits are now low. The Federal Government could intervene to reduce oil imports if it decided that it wanted to help the coal industry and that this was the efficient way to do it.

(v) *National security policy:* This argues neither for or against Federal Government intervention. See Energy Subcommittee Report, March 13, 1950.

(vi) *Favoring small business policy:* The average size of domestic producer (against imports) is smaller than the average size of U.S. oil importer (favors imports). The average size of oil consumer (favors imports) is smaller than the average size of domestic oil distributor (favors imports) is smaller than the average size of domestic oil producer (against imports).

(vii) *Long term national growth policy:* If long term economic growth is enhanced by low cost energy supplies, the Federal Government would favor the imports.[56]

President Truman replied to Secretary Chapman on May 2: "Your memorandum on oil imports is most interesting." He seemed to come down on the side of some protection for the independent refiners and even to oppose any net importation of crude.

I wish you would make a survey of the situation and inform these oil gentlemen that their efforts to put the independent refineries out of business is not going to be a thing that the people will stand for. I can't see anything wrong with the importation of crude oil in equal amounts as our exports of the products, but when they begin flooding the markets with fuel oil, diesel oil, greases and things of that sort, that is evidently a concerted effort on the part of the big companies to put the little refineries out of business. Please take a look at it.[57]

This presidential directive stirred up a good deal of activity at the Interior Department. First of all, on May 6 Secretary Chapman directed the OGD to undertake a "thorough study" of the import question, including consideration of "the possible alternatives for controlling the import situation, should that be desirable. This should, of course, cover voluntary agreements without legislation, and possible legislative approaches."[58] Joel Wolfsohn reported to Chapman on May 25 and at a meeting on June 8 that preliminary study had shown the question to be "much larger and more grave than it would seem to be at first glance." In addition to the trade-offs already set forth in the April memorandum conflicts among regions were involved. The Southwest would be the gainer from a tariff and the eastern seaboard the loser. The international implications also were complex: "The importation of oil is one of the principal factors in maintaining dollar balances." Wolfsohn concluded: "A long range, rather than a quickie study is essential if the coal industry is really to be benefitted and if the other resources are put in their proper perspective. This Department should be the one charged with such an over-all study."[59] As was the case with so many other national

56. "Memorandum Concerning Oil Imports," April 14, 1950, ibid.
57. Truman to Chapman, May 2, 1950, ibid.
58. Chapman to OGD Director Hugh A. Stewart, May 6, 1950, Department of Interior Files–Oil and Gas, Dale E. Doty Papers, HSTL.
59. Memorandum, Wolfsohn to Chapman, "Oil Imports," May 25, 1950, Oil Imports File, Wolfsohn Papers, HSTL; memorandum, Wolfsohn to Chapman, "Meeting on Oil Imports," June 9, 1950, Oil and Gas Division File, Chapman Office Files, RG 48, NA. The Petroleum, Fuels and Energy Division, Office of In-

issues, the Korean emergency during the summer of 1950 terminated the deliberate search for a solution of the import problem. It stood in the way of the study Wolfsohn sought and put the whole issue on hold for the remainder of the Truman administration. The exceptional petroleum demands created by mobilization removed the issue of how to cope with excess supply and turned attention instead to the possibility of a deficit.[60] It was left to the next president to face the import question anew.

Oiling the Wheels of Government

The Oil and Gas Division was established by order of the secretary of the interior on May 6, 1946. Nominally it had the following functions: to help coordinate the government's oil and gas policies and to advise the secretary about them, to analyze and present data on petroleum supply and demand, to provide a communications link with the states and the oil industry, and to administer the Connally Act.[61] The value of the OGD differed for its various constituencies. It got the oilmen and their friends

---

dustry and Commerce, Department of Commerce, prepared its own study of the effects of oil imports and concluded that oil tariffs were an inefficient way to help coal and "would conflict with our established national commercial policy of freeing and expanding trade." H. B. McCoy to Assistant Secretary Thomas C. Blaisdell, August 28, 1950. See also H. B. McCoy to the Solicitor, April 28, 1950; Lester M. Carson to Thomas C. Blaisdell, Jr., June 9, 1950; and McCoy to Senator Scott W. Lucas, June 20, 1950; all in Oils-Mineral-General File 312, RG 151, NA.

60. On July 25, only one month after the invasion from the north in Korea, Chapman could write to the President that "the independent refiners generally speaking, are now operating at a profit for the first time in a number of months." (Chapman to Truman, July 25, 1950, Oil Imports File, Wolfsohn Papers, HSTL.) Chapman's information was based on a report to him from Hugh A. Stewart, director of the OGD. (Stewart to Chapman, July 19, 1950, Oil and Gas Division File, Minerals and Fuels Division Files, RG 48, NA.) The detailed report on imports requested by the President in May and assigned by Chapman to the OGD finally reached the White House on July 19. It turned out to be an elaborate rebuttal of the charges by the independents and the coal industry. The conclusion was "that no curtailment of oil imports is necessary or desirable; that the national economy and national interest will be better served by a continuance of oil imports at no less than current rates; and that production controlled by American companies at home and abroad be maintained in its present vigorous and healthy condition." Stewart to Raymond F. Mikesell, July 19, 1950, with attachment, "Paper Dealing with Petroleum Imports and Exports (Prepared for the White House)," ibid.

61. The chapter of the Princeton administrative history of the Interior Department (see note 60, chapter 1) on the Oil and Gas Division by H. H. Strode is in Princeton Survey File, Minerals and Fuels Division Files, RG 48, NA. The chapter tells a rather different story from what follows here.

in Congress off the secretary's back. It allowed the oil industry and the oil states virtual self-administration of the Connally Act, gave them a voice and an ear at the very heart of government, and perhaps most important of all served as a blocking mechanism in the way of other structural change. As soon as the OGD came into existence those who were calling for some central petroleum policymaking body could be told "there it is." In a confidential memorandum to the secretary setting forth a blueprint for the OGD, Ralph Davies, the OGD's real father, observed that at the outset some industry people might perceive even this body as a threat. However, "as against a threat to the industry's independence, I am convinced this is the move that, in fact, best protects the industry's continued independence."[62]

Max Ball, first full-time director of OGD, was a petroleum geologist and private consultant who had served at different times with the U.S. Geological Survey, at the Bureau of Mines, and on the staff of several major oil companies. He was just what the industry leaders wanted, and they were not disappointed in his performance.[63] Over the two years of his directorship Ball did almost exactly what might have been expected from him in the circumstances. Above all he vigorously presented the industry position within government and without, sometimes with considerable subtlety.

Some of the issues Ball and his staff faced called for a straightforward response. For example, he took a firm position in the department that public lands should be opened up as quickly as possible and on the most generous terms to the oil industry: "The Department should in each case go as far as the [Federal Mineral Leasing] Acts reasonably permit to encourage and promote exploration and development, and . . . where the Acts are subject to more than one interpretation the Department should

62. Ralph K. Davies, "Recommendation to the Secretary of the Interior that There Be Created in Interior a 'Division of Oil and Gas' with Supporting Inter-Agency and Industry Advisory Committees," April 5, 1946, Oil and Gas Matters File, Chapman Office Files, RG 48, NA.

63. See the *Washington Evening Star,* August 30, 1954, for an obituary of Ball. The *Oil Reporter* exclaimed happily when Ball was appointed that "he hasn't the slightest desire to make OGD other than a small, compact service unit" (December 31, 1946). Throughout his two-year directorship Ball himself emphasized repeatedly the very limited role he saw for the OGD. See also Max Ball, "Five Percent Make Fifty," *Mines Magazine,* April 1947, pp. 12–14. The press release announcing the appointment of Ball and the resignation of Davies, together with a parting letter from the latter, are in Correspondence and Clippings File 1-3, Max W. Ball Papers, HSTL.

adopt the interpretation most likely to result in discovery of new reserves and productive capacity."[64] He defended oil price increases with all the arguments available, some quite sophisticated—for example, that high prices for oil would shift demand to coal. In light of the oligopoly he helped to administer, some of his arguments for price rises were quite disingenuous. For example, when urging the secretary not to speak out against a price increase in 1948 he concluded: "If we believe in a competitive economy, as we all say we do, then we must subscribe to its motivating force, the law of supply and demand, and recognize price as its controlling factor. To the extent that we interfere with the function of price we negative [sic] the benefits of competition and move toward a planned economy."[65]

One of the proposals to government by the large oil majors, voiced as early as 1943, was that it collect worldwide "demand" statistics in the way it did at home through the Bureau of Mines. Such collection was defended on grounds of international security, but incidentally it provided data essential for the operation of a worldwide oligopoly. The OGD accomplished this statistical task from 1946 through the Interdepartmental Committee on Petroleum Requirements. The assumption of this responsibility by the OGD in the Interior Department, where the industry could influence the collection process directly, rather than by the Commerce Department, where the relationship might be more tenuous, became a source of continuing "conflict between the two Departments in dealing with the petroleum industry on such subjects as foreign and domestic trade promotion, the collection and dissemination of statistics on petroleum at home and abroad, and other general economic matters pertaining to the petroleum industry."[66]

64. Ball to Joel Wolfsohn, January 29, 1947, Oil and Gas Division 1946–47 File, Chapman Office Files, RG 48, NA.

65. Memorandum, Ball to Secretary Krug, "Departmental Expressions about Petroleum Prices," January 7, 1948, Oil and Gas Division 1948–49 File, Chapman Office Files, RG 48, NA. When Krug failed to accept Ball's advice and called instead for government controls over price and allocation of crude oil, it was reported in the press that Ball submitted his resignation. Correspondence and Clippings File 3, Ball Papers, HSTL.

66. H. B. McCoy to I. M. P. Stokes, April 30, 1948, Oils-Mineral-General File 312, RG 151, NA. See also Oscar Chapman to Secretary of Commerce Henry Wallace, March 21, 1946; and J. A. Krug to Wallace, August 9, 1946; both in General Products of the Department of Commerce–Petroleum Industry, Box 336, RG 40, NA.

Miscellaneous OGD policy recommendations during Ball's tenure included the sale of the government-owned Big Inch and Little Big Inch pipelines for gas rather than petroleum transmission (which brought charges from small independents that the monopoly power of the large companies would be increased thereby, through cutting off the independents' access to a potential common carrier), governmental support of petroleum research, and prior consultation by the Treasury Department with the OGD on all tax changes affecting the industry.[67]

The greatest challenges to Ball came during the petroleum shortages that appeared episodically in the postwar years. These raised two questions for the public and for Congress. First, were they contrived by the oil industry to accomplish the price increases that accompanied them? And second, why should the federal government maintain an oligopolistic instrument such as the Connally Act if pressures on prices had now moved from downward to upward? The responses of Ball and the industry to these questions were very clever. For the long run, they argued, the situation had not changed substantially from the 1930s—abundance and low prices were just over the horizon. In the inspiring words of Max Ball: "I envision a greater oil industry, domestic and overseas, than we have ever had or dreamed; I envision for the public a more abundant supply of better petroleum products at lower relative costs than it has ever known."[68] The danger for America, he said, lay in confusing the short run with the long run. In the short run the need was for prices to drift upward, thereby stimulating supply and cutting back demand, two processes that had been retarded by price control during the war.

In 1947 Ball advised that all that was needed to deal with a temporary shortage was a "vigorous campaign for conservation and equitable distribution of petroleum products." He insisted that "allocation, rationing, and price control are more likely to counteract than to supplement the necessary counter measures."[69] The White House was very cool to the notion of a "conservation" campaign to deal with the shortage, but the

67. "Typical Major Policy Recommendations of the Oil and Gas Division during the Period May 1946–December 1948," Oil and Gas File, Minerals and Fuels Division Files, RG 48, NA.

68. Max W. Ball, "Looking Ahead with the Petroleum Industry," address before Marketing Division, American Petroleum Institute, May 6, 1948, Articles File 1, Ball Papers, HSTL.

69. Ball to Chapman, November 23, 1947, Price Control and Anti-inflation File, Chapman Office Files, RG 48, NA.

industry, led by the American Petroleum Institute, went ahead vigorously anyway.[70] Like so many other voluntary conservation programs before and after it, this one too did not seem to work. The pressure on and from Congress increased to probe the source of the shortage further. Numerous high-level meetings were held throughout government and there was even talk of an embargo on exports. Concern about the shortage grew in the military as well as in the civilian sector.[71] In January 1948 Secretary Krug instructed Ball to prepare "a projection of the United States petroleum outlook for the next ten years in general, and the next five years in whatever detail you consider practical."[72]

The oil industry's response to this mounting agitation was the familiar technique of a blocking action. To head off the widespread demands for some sort of controls, it agreed through the National Petroleum Council to formulate under Public Law 395 a voluntary allocation scheme through which the current shortages would be shared among consumers. Ball argued that this scheme would solve the shortage more effectively than would controls. Moreover, he said, "It is also my belief that the carrying out of the program will not restrain trade or weaken the competitive mechanism of the petroleum industry. Its effect is more likely to be, on the contrary, to help retain as part of the competitive mechanism independent dealers and distributors who may otherwise be forced out of business."[73] Skepticism of this device was considerable, especially in Congress, and officials of the Interior Department found themselves repeatedly on

70. Ball held a meeting of industry leaders at the Interior Department in December 1947 to coordinate the campaign and reported to Krug: "During the meeting Bob Turner of the White House handed me a note saying 'Steelman takes a very dim view of the President's and probably of the Government's sponsoring the appeal for fuel conservation.' (quoted from memory)." Memorandum, Ball to Krug, "Industry Campaign for Fuel Conservation," December 13, 1947, Oil and Gas Division 1946–47 File, Chapman Office Files, RG 48, NA.

71. J. A. Krug to William Averell Harriman, May 28, 1947; William C. Foster to Wallace M. White, July 23, 1947; Thomas C. Blaisdell, Jr., to Harriman, June 20, 1947; and Dewey Short to David K. Bruce, January 8, 1948; all in General Products of the Department of Commerce–Petroleum Industry, Box 336, RG 40, NA. James H. Mayes of the Office of International Trade, Department of Commerce, reported that in fact some of the current exports of oils and greases were supplies declared "surplus" by the armed forces and sold to the Russians! Mayes to William C. Foster, June 20, 1947, ibid.

72. Krug to Ball, January 20, 1948, Oil and Gas Division 1948–49 File, Chapman Office Files, RG 48, NA.

73. Ball to Robert E. Friedman, January 25, 1948, ibid.

the defensive.[74] Ball himself was often before Congress, especially the House Committee on Interstate and Foreign Commerce, chaired by Charles A. Wolverton, and the Subcommittee on Oil of the House Armed Services Committee, chaired by Dewey Short. His message continued to be the same, that the petroleum industry faced a long-run challenge that it could meet on its own if given the money, the materials, and breathing space through temporary voluntary conservation.[75] When Congressman Short suggested that what the nation needed was a National Oil Commission Ball replied that in the OGD the nation already had "a live, effective, and coordinated organism in being to handle oil problems."[76]

In the Interior Department itself the spectacle of Max Ball, who amounted to an industry representative, taking the lead in discussions of national policy during a time of intense public agitation galvanized the critics of the current administrative structure. Clearly the suspicion was widespread that the department was being used to restrain the supply responsiveness of the petroleum market and thereby to permit the postwar increases in demand to raise prices more than would have been necessary under more competitive conditions. Assistant Secretary C. Girard Davidson argued that the oligopolistic bottlenecks were at least twofold. In addition to its own supply limitation the petroleum industry was restrained in any expansion of capacity it might wish to make by an oligopolistic steel industry that preferred higher prices and stagnant production to in-

74. For example, Krug to Congressman J. Parnell Thomas, January 10, 1948, Control Program (P.L. 395) Voluntary Agreement File, Office Files of Walton Seymour; and Krug to Senator Kenneth S. Wherry, June 17, 1948, Oil and Gas Division File, Minerals and Fuels Division Files, RG 48, NA. The secretary's own assistant expressed the legal opinion that the voluntary plan went beyond P.L. 395 and might violate antitrust laws. She reported that the OGD, however, "was not disposed to treat [her objections] seriously." (Evelyn N. Cooper to Secretary Krug, June 28, 1948, Oil and Gas Division 1948–49 File, Chapman Office Files, RG 48, NA.) Secretary Krug had written to Ball only a few weeks before: "I have had to go to bat on at least three separate occasions to obtain Justice Department approval for interim agreements concerning oil and petroleum products. . . . I am completely unwilling to impose on the good nature of the Attorney General again." Krug to Ball, May 5, 1948, ibid.

75. Ball prepared a sixty-page "digest" ("Report on the Oil Situation," February 15, 1948) of testimony before these committees. Committees and Conferences—Petroleum File, Office Files of N. H. Collisson, RG 48, NA.

76. Memorandum, Ball to Secretary Krug, "Draft of a Letter to Dewey Short," June 28, 1948, Oil and Gas Division 1948–49 File, Chapman Office Files, RG 48, NA.

creased capacity and the uncertain effects this might generate.[77] Secretary
Krug himself seems to have joined the ranks of the critics. In July 1948 he
complained to Ball of the "further delay in completion of the 'white paper'
on the petroleum situation" he had requested months before and observed:
"The continued rise in petroleum prices provides heavy evidence that the
marginal demand for petroleum is being squeezed out in a manner which
is exceedingly harsh to the real interest of many people of this country."[78]

The most vociferous critic of Ball and the whole concept of the OGD
was Assistant Secretary Davidson. In June 1948 just after Ball had resigned his position he and Davidson exchanged a series of memorandums
for the record that apparently had grown out of a controversy conducted
in private. Davidson complained that inasmuch as Ball

held strongly a set of views which were at variance with those of the President
and the Department, such views slipped into letters and speeches prepared by
you or your office. In most instances, policy statements at variance with, or
which did not adequately reflect the views, of the President and the Department have been caught in time—witness the letter [to Senator Wherry] which
was the occasion for our discussion. On the other hand, it has also been true
that there have been some instances in which letters have been sent out or
speeches have been made by members of the Secretariat in which such items
were not caught in time.

The difficulty, as I see it, is that the conviction with which you maintain
your position requires what amounts to policing of the work prepared in your
division. . . .[79]

Ball responded indignantly to this memorandum challenging Davidson
to find specific cases of public utterances at variance with department doctrine. He admitted that he was personally more opposed to controls than
others in the department, but added: "This is clearly my right, to have
such personal views and to contend for them within the official family."[80]
It appeared that Ball did not realize that the real issue was whether, as
representative of one single interest group, he should be "within the official family" at all.[81] If anyone doubted that the director of the OGD was in

77. Davidson called repeatedly for increased steel capacity, through the construction of government plants if need be, from 1948 until his departure in 1950.
His speeches on the subject and reactions to them are contained in Steel Clippings
(mentioning CGD) File, C. Girard Davidson Papers, HSTL.

78. Krug to Ball, July 17, 1948, Oil and Gas Division File, Minerals and Fuels
Division Files, RG 48, NA.

79. Davidson to Ball, June 21, 1948, ibid.

80. Ball to Davidson, July 14, 1948, ibid.

81. Evidently Ball felt so harassed by his critics that on June 28, 1948, he wrote
to Secretary Chapman formally outlining his "personal relationships with major oil
companies," Oil and Gas Division 1948–49 File, Chapman Office Files, RG 48, NA.

fact a special interest pleader, it could be pointed out that when announcing his resignation Ball explained to a congressional committee that "with
the approval of Secretary Krug I have asked the National Petroleum Council if it would appoint a Committee to find a man to recommend to him."[82]

With the departure of Ball from the OGD in mid-1948 several parts of
government turned more seriously to the possibility of developing a "national petroleum policy." A problem in formulating such a policy lay in
the wide diffusion of authority with respect to petroleum by this time. The
following agencies all had some degree of responsibility for the commodity: the Petroleum Division of the Department of State, the Office of
International Trade of the Department of Commerce, the Armed Services
Petroleum Board, the Petroleum Division of the NSRB, and the Petroleum
Economics Branch of the Bureau of Mines. The presidential directive that
set up the OGD charged it to "coordinate" these various agencies, and an
Interdepartmental Petroleum Committee was in fact created to this end
on July 8, 1946. But Ball's views and those of the industry were that effective coordination was not necessarily a good thing. It was not a very long
step from coordination to control. Ball explained to the first meeting of
the National Petroleum Council (NPC) that government was organized
"functionally" and that any government-wide oil planning would contra-
vene this principle. "To attempt to cut across this functional organization
by an agency exercising supervision over all activities with relation to a
single commodity would set up organizational strains and stresses that to
my way of thinking would be wholly impractical."[83] At the time of Ball's
departure the Interdepartmental Petroleum Committee was still at work
on the White Paper that was to be the basis of a national oil policy. At
last, in May 1949 a report from the OGD said, "A final version of a proposed document of petroleum policy for the U.S. was considered on May
16 by an Interagency Staff Group, selected by the National Security Resources Board to deal with this subject. It was finally determined that no
such policy paper is necessary or particularly desirable at this time. The
document will be circulated to the interested agencies for whatever use
it might be to them."[84]

Perhaps frustration at the failure of any sort of national oil policy was
behind a bill introduced in Congress in 1949 (House bill 6047) "to estab-

82. "Obituary from Wolverton Committee," Correspondence and Clippings File
4, Ball Papers, HSTL.

83. Remarks delivered at a meeting of the National Petroleum Council, January
21, 1947, Oil and Gas Division 1946–47 File, Chapman Office Files, RG 48, NA.

84. Report, May 1949, Oil and Gas Division 1948–49 File, ibid.

lish a Petroleum Policy Council for the purpose of developing, clarifying, and coordinating national policies relating to petroleum, and for other purposes." However, faced with opposition from the executive departments that were to be coordinated and from the industry that might be regulated, this initiative too got nowhere.[85]

As in the past when the petroleum industry had sensed a strong ground swell of opinion and had responded to it with a blocking device, so it reacted protectively once again. But this time the blocking tactic may have gone too far. In April 1949 the ninety-member NPC, an industry advisory group to the OGD, issued *A National Oil Policy for the United States,* a twenty-three-page document that could easily have been mistaken for an official report. It can only be described as outrageously self-serving, however. It was merely a list of policies concerning oil that were perceived as beneficial to the industry. These included encouragement of "industry efforts" toward "conservation," development of synthetic fuels by private industry rather than government and on the industry's timetable, continuation of percentage depletion and expense provisions of the tax code, relaxation of lease restrictions on public lands, turnover of offshore lands to the states (and thereby to the industry), and in all respects favorable treatment of the industry so that it could continue to generate capital internally. The report favored the protection of "independents" but declared: "The oil industry is opposed to monopoly and believes that competition contributes to the public good." It did not, of course, explain how this principle squared with the Interstate Oil Compact or operations of the majors abroad.[86]

The Interior Department secretariat was horrified by the NPC report, and the controversy surrounding the report precipitated a broad inquiry into industry advisory committees. Secretary Krug responded to the report in detail in a remarkably forthright address to the American Petroleum

85. Walton Seymour to Assistant Secretary Davidson, October 12, 1949, General File, Correspondence Files of Lyle Craine, RG 48, NA; and Charles Sawyer to the Director, Bureau of the Budget, December 5, 1949, Petroleum Industry File, Box 336, RG 40, NA. Program Staff member Harold J. Barnett attended the NPC meeting of January 26, 1950, and provided an amusing and critical account of the discussion of manpower, reserves, imports, leasing, and other matters. He reported that chairman Walter B. Hallanan opened the meeting by describing the council as "a buffer to encroachment by Government officials." Barnett to Seymour, February 2, 1950, National Petroleum Council File, Minerals and Fuels Division Files, RG 48, NA.

86. National Petroleum Council, *A National Oil Policy for the United States* (Washington, D.C.: NPC, 1949), p. 14.

Institute at Pittsburgh on April 28, 1949. This address, which may have been drafted by Assistant Secretary Davidson, marked the most open break between government and industry over petroleum policy since the end of World War II. The main theme of the address was that the roles that competitive market forces and government did and should play regarding petroleum were not dealt with fairly in the report. Moreover, the proper formulation and casting of these roles had to be at the heart of a national policy. Because Krug's address was so important as a watershed in government policies, it is useful to quote it at length.

. . . it [the report] does not mention as desirable elements of national oil policy (1) those measures necessary to assure prices to the public no higher than will provide profits for sustaining new investment in exploration and production in the industry, nor (2) any measures to protect the independent and small petroleum producer and refiner. These elements obviously belong to an oil policy that serves equitably all interested groups in the country. . . . By asserting a devotion to principles of free competition and by avoiding discussion of widespread restraints on competition, the report pays only lip service to free competition. By failing to discuss the weaknesses of free competition that have led to waste in unrecovered oil and gas, the report supports uncritically a continuation of past wastes except as they can be gradually eliminated by actions of individual states. . . . The report calls for price determination through free markets in oil and gas and coal. This is an unrealistic recommendation. Government regulation of gas prices exists and is desirable to protect consumers in the same way that regulation of electric rates is necessary. Oil prices have been controlled by the industry, aided by state regulation of production and by concentration in the hands of a few companies of American controlled oil fields in foreign countries. There has been no standard of proper price levels in oil except the decisions of the oil people to produce, and the control by the oil people of the price of imported oil. This gives the public no assurance of continued protection. The government must view with suspicion the prices and profits of recent years in the petroleum industry and cannot trust the industry to determine prices because free markets do not exist continuously.[87]

In a memorandum to Secretary Krug that he never sent, Assistant Secretary Davidson argued that the NPC report was in fact just what the department deserved for its dereliction concerning oil policy:

. . . although we have an Oil and Gas Division charged with the responsibility for developing policy and program in the field, we, in effect, transferred that responsibility to the National Petroleum Council, our industry advisory com-

87. "Comments on Report of the National Petroleum Council—A National Oil Policy for the United States," attached to draft of a letter, Krug to Horace M. Albright, May 3, 1949, Oil (Policy) File, Minerals and Fuels Division Files, RG 48, NA.

mittee. The report which the council wrote was no more than one would expect under the circumstances. It defended the long-time policies of the industry. There were places where it obviously disagreed with established policies of this Department, particularly in the case of tidelands and synthetic liquid fuels. On the whole, however, it gave us little guidance on the matter of oil policy except for the restatement of certain vague general principles which are now almost too trite to need repetition.[88]

Davidson complained that to compound the injury an unfortunate impression was gained by the press that this report was the department's authorized position; this had required the strong denunciation by Secretary Krug in Pittsburgh. "We were put in the public position of offending the industry with which we wanted to maintain good relations in order to clarify our own position."[89]

The debacle surrounding the NPC report and the issues it raised precipitated a good deal of discussion in the Interior Department about the council, the OGD, and the treatment of oil generally in the department and throughout the government. Some of the concerns and suggested reforms were quite specific. For example, following hearings on the oil supply and distribution problem by the Senate Small Business Committee at least one Interior Department staff member, Samuel Moment, an economist with the Division of Power, urged that the Bureau of Mines "discontinue compilation and publication of estimates of crude oil demand." It was clear to him that the statistics were being used to maintain an oligopolistic device that was inimical to the public interest. In March, before the NPC report had been issued, Moment urged not only that publication of these statistics cease but that the Bureau of Mines be "directed not even to make estimates for internal use because even if they are not published, there are ways for the figures to leak out and be put to use in controlling production."[90] Assistant Secretary Davidson endorsed Moment's concern and asked for a discussion of the matter with James Boyd, director of the Bureau of Mines.[91] In November, after no action had been

88. Unsent memorandum, Davidson to Krug, May 3, 1949, ibid.

89. Ibid.

90. Memorandum, Moment to Evelyn Cooper, "Discontinuance of Crude Oil Demand Forecasts, Bureau of Mines," May 24, 1949, Bureau of Mines File, Craine Correspondence Files, RG 48, NA. Unsigned critical comments on Moment's memorandum are attached to this copy of it.

91. Memorandum, Evelyn Cooper to Davidson, "Forecasts of Petroleum Demand," May 19, 1949; and memorandum, Davidson to Boyd, "Monthly Petroleum Forecasts," May 31, 1949; both in Commodities–Petroleum File, Minerals and Fuels Division Files, RG 48, NA.

taken, Moment returned to the subject with a carefully documented statement of the case. He concluded in part:

I have pointed out that it is improper for the Department to contribute to production and price control through the device of making these forecasts under the guise of a conservation measure. I have stated that no legislative authority exists for this purpose, and that if it is to be sought, it should be accompanied by provisions that protect the public interest against the petroleum industry charging prices according to what the traffic will bear. I have asserted that under present law, the Department ought to confine its conservation program to technical measures taken with the States and the petroleum industry to insure maximum recovery of the oil in the ground. . . .

I believe the Department should cease making these forecasts, should call for a program with the States and the industry dealing only with technical measures to assure maximum recovery of oil in the ground, and should advise the President and the Congress that the oil demand forecasts made by the Government in order to control production and prices is contrary to the public interest unless the Government is also permitted to participate with the industry in price determination in order to protect the public. I think that if the Department is to serve the public interest it should take these actions. Apathy constitutes one-sided aid to the petroleum industry.[92]

Apparently Moment still did not carry the day.

When Oscar Chapman succeeded Krug as secretary of the interior late in 1949 one of his high priorities was to formulate a national oil policy. In December 1949, prompted by John Steelman, he held a meeting on the subject with representatives of the Departments of State, Defense, and Commerce; the NSRB; and the Bureau of Mines. Under Secretary of Defense Stephen Early was especially vehement about the need for a national petroleum policy "on which they could base strategic plans." The recent failure of the NSRB interagency group to achieve "a firm policy statement" was blamed variously on "the rapid shifting of the economic, military, and political scene" and the fact that "the discussions were not held at a sufficiently high level," or "properly staffed." Those attending Chapman's meeting reached no firm conclusion about what to do with the problem, except to make the suggestion that the secretary of the interior become a member of the National Security Council.[93]

92. Moment to Evelyn Cooper, November 1, 1949, ibid.
93. "Summary of the Petroleum Policy Meeting Held in the Office of the Secretary of the Interior, December 28, 1949," Petroleum Policy File, Chapman Office Files, RG 48, NA. In a briefing memorandum for this meeting James Boyd suggested to Chapman why the other government agencies had not taken full advantage of the Interior Department's own Interdepartmental Petroleum Committee to achieve the coordination they desired: "(1) they feel that they have sole jurisdiction over

In 1950 consideration of a new structure to deal with oil and gas became part of the reorganization studies of the department. It was proposed that a new assistant secretary for mineral resources would have responsibility for overall policy and program direction, for representing the Department on oil and gas matters before other agencies or outside of Government; and for actual operating coordination of the operating bureaus under his jurisdiction. A study, "Program and Organization for the Administration of the Oil and Gas Responsibilities of the Department of the Interior," was completed in August 1950 by Ivan Bloch and Lyle E. Craine of the Program Staff. A draft of this report, apparently by Craine, recommended the creation of a new commodity division of the Bureau of Mines to be called Oil and Gas, which would incorporate all the functions and personnel of the existing OGD plus the Petroleum and Natural Gas Branch and the Synthetic Liquid Fuels Branch of the bureau. The Interior Department's principal oil responsibilities that would remain outside the new division under this plan were in the Geological Survey. Of special significance was the emphasis in the report on the status of the new OGD as an "operating" division or an "action shop." The "policy framework" for the commodity programs would be set "by the Assistant Secretary and his staff in association with the staff of the Secretary and other Assistant Secretaries." Moreover, the assistant secretary and staff would conduct all contacts outside the department with other government agencies and with the industry. Clearly the intent of this document was to achieve a coherent policy toward petroleum and to minimize in every way opportunities for possible conflict of interest.[94] The Korean emergency and the passage of the Defense Production Act of 1950 influenced Bloch to transmit a less radical version of this report to Assistant Secretary Davidson than that proposed by Craine. He did recommend a clearer distinction between policy and operations, but the writing was on the wall that the old OGD would not now under any condition be abolished. Instead it

---

certain problems and (2) insistence that interagency petroleum committees established by other departments have jurisdiction. This is particularly true in the case of the Department of State and its International Petroleum Policy Committee (a subcommittee of the Executive Committee on Economic Foreign Policy)." Boyd to Chapman, December 27, 1949, ibid.

94. "Program and Organization for the Administration of the Oil and Gas Responsibilities of the Department of the Interior," August 31, 1950, attached to memorandum, Lyle Craine to Paul Unger, "Notes on the Oil and Gas Activities in the Department," September 14, 1950, with attachments, Project File, Minerals and Fuels Division Files, RG 48, NA.

would be given new life and vigor by being transformed into the Petroleum Administration for Defense.[95]

Oil for Defense

When World War II ended numerous agencies believed that they had, or should have, inherited responsibility for the security of petroleum. The Interior Department, of course, saw this as part of the broad mandate it coveted.[96] The State Department, on the other hand, argued that the petroleum market had become so concentrated and worldwide in operation that decisions by the participating companies were "in fact decisions in the field of foreign policy" and therefore their responsibility.[97] The International Petroleum Policy Committee, a subcommittee of the interagency Executive Committee on Economic Foreign Policy was a main means through which the State Department took leadership among government departments.[98] Even the Commerce Department, however, dreamed of increasing its role and perhaps acquiring the petroleum attachés from the State Department.[99]

By 1948 fundamental differences in attitude toward foreign petroleum policy had emerged between the Interior Department on one side, led by the OGD, and the State Department and the military services on the other.

95. Memorandum, Bloch to Davidson, "Functions and Organization Dealing with Oil and Gas Matters," September 2, 1950, ibid. Apparently the reform movement went no further because in January 1951 Paul Unger could recommend to Assistant Secretary Dale E. Doty a "review of the present oil and gas operations of the Department" as if the Craine-Bloch work of a few months before had not taken place. He recommended appointing a consultant (Ralph S. Brown or Hollis B. Chenery) for three months to do the job. Memorandum, Unger to Doty, "Project for Consultant: Study with Recommendations on Governmental Responsibility and Public Policy in Regard to Oil and Gas," January 24, 1951, ibid.

96. A special cabinet-level meeting on petroleum supply, held June 17, 1947, by Secretary Krug symbolized the Interior Department's efforts to take the lead on security questions. The agenda and supporting documents are in Petroleum Requirements File, Chapman Office Files, RG 48, NA.

97. Memorandum, "Mr. Wilcox" to W. L. Clayton, "Testimony on Anglo-American Petroleum Agreement," January 29, 1946, Subject File: Petroleum, Office Files of the Assistant Secretary of State for Economic Affairs, HSTL.

98. For example, in late 1948 and early 1949 this committee considered whether the United States should use its influence through the Marshall Plan to acquire secure access to oil produced by British and Dutch companies abroad. Agenda documents concerning this issue are in Committees and Conferences Miscellaneous File, Collisson Office Files, RG 48, NA.

99. James H. Mayes to H. P. van Blaroom, April 26, 1946, Oils-Mineral-General File 312, RG 151, NA.

The Interior Department position, reflecting the views of the independents as well as the majors, was that for the immediate future America would be able to supply almost all its own needs from its own domestic sources, in peace or war. As Edward B. Swanson, assistant director of the OGD, told Arthur E. Goldschmidt, the department's representative on the Executive Committee on Economic Foreign Policy, "when the time of significant dependence on foreign sources will arrive is not now a matter which requires immediate definition."[100] In consequence the government policy should be "particularly to retain or re-establish the opportunities for private enterprise in oil. We should do this because oil history shows that the necessary development can be achieved only by private enterprise, which can assume the risks involved in oil exploration." The danger in the sort of gloomy talk that was coming from the State Department, said Swanson, was that it might lead foreign countries to place U.S companies "over the barrel" in fixing terms for what imports were necessary.[101]

The position of the State and Defense departments that emerged after the war was that in the event of renewed hostilities the situation would be much more serious than that predicted by Swanson. They estimated that perhaps one-quarter of domestic requirements could not be provided from domestic sources. For the allies the problem would be even greater. In light of this likely deficit they raised the possibility of pursuing all means of increasing the free world oil output, including perhaps even U.S. government loans to nations that insisted on development by their own nationals rather than by the multinationals.[102] In 1946 the Army-Navy Petroleum Board told the O'Mahoney Committee of the Senate that America must recognize its worldwide military responsibilities and make cer-

100. Swanson to Goldschmidt, January 20, 1948, Harold J. Barnett File, Seymour Office Files, RG 48, NA.

101. Ibid. Harold J. Barnett, the energy economist on the Program Staff, commented to Goldschmidt on Swanson's memo that he could not see where the oil would come from domestically to fight another war. "The mobilization addition to production capacity, in short, will not be available unless this government sponsors it in some way." Barnett also objected to Swanson's assumptions that all foreign oil nationalizations were "objectionable solely because they are national (i.e. socialization) programs." Barnett to Walton Seymour, January 3, 1949, Barnett File, ibid.

102. "Petroleum: World Supply and Demand Situation, Special Background Paper for Use in Discussion of Petroleum at the [State Department] Rio de Janeiro Conference of Economic Officers," ibid. In 1949 the State Department issued a balance sheet of production of various materials in East and West, including "Estimated Petroleum Consumption in the Hypothetical War Year 1953," *Comparison of Eastern and Western Productive Capabilities for Peace and War*, OIR Report 5104 (December 9, 1949), marked "Secret." A copy is in Secretary of State File, PSF, HSTL.

tain that the aggregate petroleum production of the free world was adequate, not simply that of the United States. This would require close cooperation between the government and the large oil companies. Specifically:

There are three fundamental principles involved in the support of the foreign oil holdings of the United States nationals if they are to be of real value in times of emergency:
(1) They should be owned or controlled by nationals of the United States.
(2) The United States government should maintain friendly international relationships in their support.
(3) The military strength of the United States should be sufficient to protect the lines of communication to the countries in which they are located.[103]

Another military spokesman in April 1948 described a proper policy as one encouraging both domestic and foreign production, "development of a synthetic industry of 'appropriate' size," "stockpiling to the extent necessary in natural reservoirs when a method that is profitable and technically sound has been discovered," and "substitution of other energy sources for oil."[104]

The defense establishment remained concerned about the need to defend far-flung petroleum suppliers in the event of war, and it wished to know how crucial these suppliers really were and how the nation might cope in an emergency without them. The secretary of defense submitted a report, "Proposed National Petroleum Program," dealing with this problem to the NSRB in December 1948. This proposal came at a time when the State Department was working on a statement, "Foreign Petroleum Policy," and the NPC was working on its own report.[105] Perhaps most im-

103. "Statement of the Navy's Position with Relation to a National Oil Policy," Oil and Gas Division, Interior Department File, Correspondence File Box 5, Records of the Senate Special Committee Investigating Petroleum Resources, RG 46, NA. Secretary of the Navy James Forrestal had urged Senator O'Mahoney to pay particular attention to the "vital relationship of petroleum to the military and naval services of the United States." Forrestal to O'Mahoney, May 2, 1945, Postwar Petroleum Requirements File, Subject File Box 19, Records of the Senate Special Committee, ibid.

104. "Report of Statement of Colonel G. H. Vogel to the San Joaquin Oil Producers Association," enclosed with memorandum, H. B. McCoy to I. M. P. Stokes, May 6, 1948, Oils-Mineral-General File 312, RG 151, NA.

105. The Defense Department report and the State Department inquiry are mentioned in a letter, Robert A. Lovett, Acting Secretary of Defense, to James Lay, Executive Secretary of the National Security Council, December 27, 1950, NSC 97, NSC Meeting No. 100 File, PSF, HSTL. The NPC report is discussed earlier in this chapter.

portant of all, the NSRB was completing its own staff study, "A National Liquid Fuels Policy," prepared by Wallace E. Pratt, petroleum consultant to the board and formerly vice-president and director of Standard Oil of New Jersey. This formerly classified thirty-four-page document deserves special attention because it contained the first full development of the national security implications of petroleum policy as perceived especially by the oil majors, the State Department, and the NSRB. It recommended that the bulk of the world should be required to obtain its oil from the Middle East rather than from the western hemisphere, with American firms playing a role as middlemen. For U.S. needs, the capacity of North American and northern South American resources (the "minimum strategic defense area") should be developed quickly to equal "total anticipated requirements for combined military and essential civilian purposes." Then:

> In normal times we should restrict our withdrawals from sources within this minimum strategic defense area, under the administration of the established conservation authorities, to a rate lower than the most efficient rate (M.E.R.). By this procedure we would create a military stockpile in the ground, the ideal storage place for petroleum. The potential surplus producing capacity so created—that is, the margin between the actual peacetime producing rate and the aggregate M.E.R. of the oil fields within the limits of our minimum strategic defense area—should easily exceed 1 million barrels daily. It must at all times be sufficient, when added to the amount which can be saved out of our normal peacetime consumption by wartime rationing to essential civilian demand, to meet our anticipated requirements for military purposes in wartime.[106]

The theory behind this proposed policy was simple even if the actual application of it might be complex. The domestic petroleum industry should be encouraged to develop excess capacity by permitting it to retain those prewar price support and supply-restricting devices that had grown up at a time of abundance. Imports should be permitted, indeed encouraged, in an amount equal to this excess capacity plus the amount that aggregate petroleum use could be restrained by rationing in an emergency. In 1948 this implied an appropriate level of imports of several million barrels a day. There is no evidence that the Pratt report became a formal blueprint

106. National Security Resources Board, "A National Liquid Fuels Policy: A Preliminary Staff Study of Liquid Fuels for National Security" (August 1948). Some of Pratt's ideas were anticipated in "Petroleum Resources," an address he delivered to the American Institute of Mining and Metallurgical Engineers on February 22, 1944. Wallace E. Pratt File, Subject File Box 10, Records of the Senate Special Committee Investigating Petroleum Resources, RG 46, NA.

for subsequent petroleum policy, but the practice of imposing only modest restraints on imports through tariffs and quotas is consistent with it. Moreover, its silence on both synthetic fuel development and aboveground storage as major factors in strategic planning was characteristic of later thinking.

In May 1949 an interagency staff group reported that it was unable to reconcile all the various documents but in any event was not persuaded of the need for a single national petroleum policy.[107] In December 1949 Secretary Chapman held one more meeting on the subject, but no further action was taken before the outbreak of hostilities in Korea the next summer.[108] Chapman did appoint a Military Petroleum Advisory Board of industry persons "to provide the National Military Establishment and the Department of the Interior with expert industry counsel, advice, and information on oil and gas matters relating to national security and defense," and this seems in some degree to have satisfied the secretary of defense in his attempts at strategic planning.[109]

The Korean emergency brought a sudden reversal in petroleum policy and an almost eerie return to the conditions of World War II. Before war broke out a campaign had been waged successfully in the Department of the Interior and in Congress against the lopsided industry-oriented character of the OGD and the NPC, and preparations were being made to eliminate or severely reform both through the reorganization of the Interior Department secretariat and the assignment of responsibility for mineral resources to Assistant Secretary Davidson.[110] But now most of these plans were forgotten almost overnight. The government again went on a war footing. Under the Defense Production Act of 1950 the president delegated defense responsibilities to the heads of existing government agencies, and the OGD was rescued by what was in effect conversion into the Petroleum Administration for Defense (the OGD continued to exist

107. Untitled OGD report on various matters, dated May 1949, Oil and Gas Division 1948–49 File, Chapman Office Files, RG 48, NA.

108. "A Report to the National Security Council by the Executive Secretary on A National Petroleum Program," NSC 97 (December 28, 1949), NSC Meeting No. 100 File, PSF, HSTL.

109. Louis A. Johnson to the Secretary of the Interior, July 20, 1949, Oil and Gas Division 1948–49 File, Chapman Office Files, RG 48, NA.

110. Davidson reported that just as hostilities broke out "we were considering how best to implement the recommendations in the report of the House Appropriations Committee that the Oil and Gas Division be dissolved or substantially reduced." Davidson to Secretary Chapman, October 2, 1950, Petroleum Administration for Defense File, Minerals and Fuels Division Files, RG 48, NA.

in name to administer the Connally Act). A powerful oilman and veteran of the Petroleum Administration for War, Bruce K. Brown, was brought in as head (nominally deputy administrator under Secretary Chapman as administrator), and with him came many former PAW colleagues (referred to by Brown as "re-treads"). Many, including Brown, served without compensation from government and continued to receive their corporate salaries. In Brown's words the old principles of "a maximum degree of cooperation between all of the parties concerned" and adherence to "the free enterprise *competitive* system that prevails in the petroleum industry" (meaning no direct government operations) were revived. The NPC was retained intact.[111] The old understanding accepted implicitly during World War II was reaffirmed that in return for voluntary cooperation from the industry the Interior Department, through the Petroleum Administration for Defense (PAD) or other agencies would extend its assistance in obtaining materials, price increases, incentive payments, and favored treatment on oil leases. If someone like Assistant Secretary Davidson could still see the public interest as broader than this generous treatment of the oil industry, he could be dismissed as a sorehead or even as disloyal.[112] The NPC seemed invigorated by Korea and continued to issue

111. Address by Bruce K. Brown before the Interstate Oil Compact Commission, Houston, Texas, December 13, 1950, CCF 1-188, RG 48, NA. See also Clayton R. Koppes, "Oscar Chapman, A Liberal at the Interior Department, 1933–1955" (Ph.D. dissertation, University of Kansas, 1974), p. 448. The staff of the Commerce Department at this time suggested that "the conflicting interests of the N.P.C. membership as regards foreign oil" provided a sound reason for that department to get back heavily into the petroleum field. (Lester M. Carson to Thomas C. Blaisdell, Jr., August 11, 1950, Oils-Mineral-General File 312, RG 151, NA.) At the same time, the department named from industry its own Foreign Petroleum Advisory Committee. Lester M. Carson to Dean O. Bowman, July 21, 1950, ibid.

112. In December 1950 Davidson objected to the negotiation of "special" noncompetitive oil and gas leases as a war measure. (Davidson to Dale Doty, November 13, 1950, Oil and Gas Leasing File, Minerals and Fuels Division Files, RG 48, NA.) In February 1951 Brown presented the case to Chapman for the introduction of World War II-type "financial" incentives, mainly certificates of necessity providing for accelerated amortization for tax purposes, and in a few cases three-year supply contracts. (Brown to Chapman, February 5, 1951, CCF 1-188, RG 48, NA.) In a letter on January 22, 1952, Brown appealed to the Office of Price Stabilization (OPS) for a price increase on middle distillates and made a case to Chapman that in its phraseology could have come from Ralph K. Davies or Ickes in World War II— only a price increase would guarantee warm homes on the East Coast. (Brown to Chapman, January 23, 1952, ibid.) Brown's appeal was rejected by OPS Director Michael V. DiSalle, with language that might have come from Sumner Pike ten years before, that is, "the price increase which you propose is both an inefficient and costly

self-serving statements, an attack on the Treasury Department, for example, for questioning the wisdom of the percentage depletion allowance.[113]

A remarkable feature of this period was what appeared to be a conversion in the attitude of Secretary Chapman comparable to that of Secretary Ickes during World War II when he changed from a New Deal liberal to a died-in-the-wool defender of big business. Whether the conversion was real or simply an exigency of war is unclear, but intermittently throughout the emergency Chapman issued paeans of praise for the NPC together with denials that it and PAD were in any way partial to the large corporations over smaller ones or the consumers.[114] Davidson's concerns about conflict of interest expressed so eloquently in 1949 and 1950 seem to have disappeared without a trace. In fact, the conflict of interest question and the expectations of dollar-a-year men about their proper reward for government service seem to have become something of a joke in the department. With a covering note stating that he was "familiar with this situation," Brown sent to Chapman the following news report in April 1952: "Circulating rapidly through the oil industry now is a story, substantiated in full by the Petroleum Administration for Defense, of how a long-time company official returned to his job earlier this year after serving a long hitch at PAD and was fired almost immediately. PAD swears that company heads told this man to his face that he was being discharged because he did not do enough for the company while with the government."[115]

At the end of his period in office Chapman wrote a long explanation for his behavior during the war to Congressman Emanuel Celler, chairman

---

way of solving whatever shortage problem may develop." (DiSalle to Brown, n.d., ibid.) Chapman continued the pleas for higher prices for the oil industry. Chapman to Roger L. Putnam, administrator, Economic Stabilization Agency, June 10, 1952, ibid.

113. "Interim Report of the National Petroleum Council's Committee on Capital and Materials Requirements for Increasing Availability of Petroleum Products (Million Barrel Committee)," February 26, 1951, National Petroleum Council File, Chapman Papers, HSTL.

114. Memorandum, Chapman, "National Petroleum Council," July 14, 1952, National Petroleum Council File, Chapman Papers, and also the President's copy in OF, loose, Truman Papers, HSTL; and Chapman to J. H. Valentine, a "small" refiner, April 23, 1951, CCF 1-188, RG 48, NA. PAD's denial of favoritism to the large companies was contained in memorandum, J. Ed Warren to Secretary Chapman, "PAD and Small Business," August 5, 1952, ibid.

115. Brown to Chapman, April 22, 1952, CCF 1-188, RG 48, NA.

of the House Judiciary Committee. This was a most revealing statement
of what a cold, or even a lukewarm, war could do for the policy stance of
this liberal administrator.

. . . the free world is today engaged in an ideological struggle on the outcome
of which may depend the future of freedom and liberty as we know it. . . .
Mindful of the great responsibility thus imposed upon me and knowing the
gigantic task which Secretary Ickes accomplished so successfully during
World War II in supplying the petroleum needs of this country and its allies,
I have naturally sought to follow the pattern he established whenever it is
possible to do so. . . . If the current cold war or even a hot war should be lost
because of inadequate petroleum supplies, those who sat in judgment upon my
stewardship of this agency would not forgive me because I had rigidly adhered, not only to the statutory requirements of the antitrust laws and their
judicial construction, but also to the many other interpretations placed upon
them by individuals and committees.[116]

The Department of Defense, and especially the Joint Chiefs of Staff,
had been insisting since 1948 that a national petroleum policy or an
agreed upon emergency plan was absolutely essential for the effective defense of America. The response of the OGD had been that there would be
no serious problem in an emergency and that therefore there was no need
for a plan. With the outbreak of hostilities in Korea, however, the Defense
Department became much more insistent and estimated for the National
Security Council (NSC) that if full-scale war were to begin in 1954 "in
the geographic areas which would be available to such power, a deficit in
refining capacity of 1½ million barrels per day, as well as ½ million barrels per day of crude production, will exist at the outbreak of war."[117] In
response to this expression of concern President Truman acted decisively
and instructed the director of defense mobilization "to develop a national
petroleum program leading to the complete supply of Allied requirements, for consideration by the National Security Council."[118]

The Office of Defense Mobilization (ODM) turned to PAD for assistance in preparing the requested national petroleum policy, and in the
circumstances there were strong new reasons for PAD to cooperate enthusiastically. Above all, Bruce Brown had become alarmed at the position taken by Defense Mobilization Director Charles E. Wilson in a paper,

116. Chapman to Celler, January 2, 1953, ibid.
117. "A Report to the National Security Council by the Executive Secretary on
A National Petroleum Program," December 28, 1950, NSC 97, NSC Meeting No.
100 File, PSF, HSTL.
118. James S. Lay, Jr., "Note by the Executive Secretary to the National Security
Council on a National Petroleum Program," December 28, 1950, ibid.

"Defense Production Policy" (ODM Document 4), that petroleum programs should have a secondary priority in the defense effort and "await the meeting of present needs."[119] Such a "secondary" designation would, of course, mean for the industry delayed access to scarce materials and fewer incentive payments, licenses, and other favors. At issue, in particular, was the issuance of accelerated amortization certificates under the Defense Production Act for new construction deemed essential to the war effort. Whereas the industry had perceived correctly that a sense of crisis surrounding the availability of its product in peacetime was liable to lead to government interference and control, in an emergency where controls were already in place such a sense of crisis was necessary to obtain preferential treatment from government.

So the strategy changed. In the spring of 1951 PAD submitted "a secret report [still classified in 1980] analyzing supply and demand factors for petroleum in the event of war," which the NSC entered in its "97" series.[120] The petroleum picture was found to be much darker than anticipated earlier and might require maximum national sacrifice. Evidently the report did the trick, for John D. Small, chairman of the Munitions Board, wrote to Wilson on May 9 observing that NSC 97 was now "in conflict with" ODM Document 4, and he concluded: "I hope this possible interpretation of ODM Document #4 is not allowed to interfere with the important program being developed under NSC Document #97."[121] Wilson seems to have taken Small's advice, and he asked PAD to take the lead immediately in planning for all eventualities, including the need for rationing in full-scale war or loss of the Middle East.[122] The NSC asked PAD to sup-

119. Brown discussed and quoted from ODM 4 in a memorandum to Secretary Chapman, "ODM Document #4—'Defense Production Policy,'" May 16, 1951, CCF 1-188, RG 48, NA.

120. The conclusions of this document appeared in "A Brief Summary of the Petroleum Situation," an unclassified two-page memorandum for Secretary Chapman, which said "the analysis indicates that, during the last year of a major war even with the most severe rationing believed possible, the demand for petroleum by the U.S. and her allies would reach 12,225,000 b/d or almost 25% over the year 1950." To fill this demand the industry would have to increase its drilling and construction of refinery and transportation facilities. The naval oil reserves would have to be invaded. "The tidelands question should be settled so that maximum exploration and development of those areas can proceed. In general, the incentives for investment in petroleum facilities should be maintained." Attachment to memorandum, Bruce Brown to Secretary Chapman, April 25, 1951, ibid.

121. Reported in Bruce Brown to Secretary Chapman, May 16, 1951, ibid.

122. Office Memorandum, Bruce Brown, "PAD Conference with Mr. Eric Johnston on Monday, July 23, 1951," July 24, 1951, ibid.

plement NSC 97 in various ways. One action taken was to request the National Petroleum Council to estimate the alternative costs of producing 1 million extra barrels of oil a day (1) by an increase in conventional domestic production, (2) through synthesis from coal, or (3) from oil shale.[123]

Throughout the rest of the Truman administration PAD's voice could be heard in most discussions of security quietly making the point that in the future if the fragile oil sufficiency were to be preserved, American foreign policy had to keep petroleum needs clearly in view not only when dealing with the Middle East but in the case of Latin American and Canadian producers as well.[124] PAD publicly presented the position that the supplies were still adequate and could be expected to remain so as long as the nation took full advantage of "its vast area of yet untested potential oil land, its vigorous technology for finding oil, and its climate of free economic enterprise that stimulates the search for oil."[125] The NPC presented the same message in a report, "Oil and Gas Availability," in January 1952: "In short, the United States and the world can count upon increasing supplies of oil and gas not only for the next few years but for the foreseeable future provided that reasonable economic incentives, ade-

123. In its calculations the NPC took account of possible increases in foreign oil in adjacent friendly countries. This angered some Mexicans who thought it inappropriate for Americans to be counting their assets as part of U.S. reserves. Chapman apologized in a letter to the managing director of Petroleos Mexicanos. Chapman to Senator Antonio J. Bermudez, May 18, 1951, CCF 1-188, RG 48, NA.

124. For example, "Statement of Policy Proposed by the National Security Council on United States Objectives and Policies with Respect to the Arab States and Israel," April 24, 1952, NSC 129/1, p. 12, NSC Meeting No. 115 File, PSF, HSTL; Louis A. Johnson and Cary R. Wagner to the President, August 8, 1951, concerning arrangements with Canada for exploiting the Alberta tar sands, Subject File: Agencies, Oil Reserves, PSF, HSTL; and "The National Security Interest in Successful Trade Agreement Negotiations with Venezuela," attached to memorandum, Dean Acheson to James S. Lay, Jr., February 29, 1952, NSC Meeting No. 113 File, PSF, HSTL. Chapman wrote to Congressman John W. Heselton in March 1951 that he considered "the further development of the oil resources of Mexico" as "a matter of prime importance . . . during the present emergency." Chapman also favored "a loan to Mexico for the purposes of oil development." (Chapman to Heselton, March 9, 1951, CCF 1-188, RG 48, NA.) The importance cannot be determined of PAD's voice in allowing large payments to Middle East governments in 1951 to be classified as taxes to foreign governments rather than as royalties, with very substantial savings to the companies in consequence. See Blair, *The Control of Oil*, pp. 200–02.

125. Petroleum Administration for Defense, *A Graphic Review of U.S. Oil Reserves from 1920 to 1951* (PAD, 1952).

quate materials, and a favorable climate for private investment prevail."[126] The Paley Commission expressed an identical opinion at this time with the only additional caveat that synthetic fuels should be permitted to grow so as to provide an effective price ceiling for natural crude. "Private business can be counted on to bring about the bulk of necessary adjustments at an appropriate pace if no uneconomic impediments to domestic crude oil exploration and production are allowed to develop, if imports are permitted to flow freely in whatever amount the price situation dictates, and if synthetic production is not discouraged by shortages of capital, monopolistic restraints, or the like."[127]

An exchange that took place in the fall of 1951 between Ralph S. Trigg, a deputy administrator of the Defense Production Administration, and Bruce Brown illustrates nicely the effect that mobilization had had on fuels policy in general and petroleum policy in particular. Trigg sent a low-key letter to Brown expressing concern about the difficulty of "apportioning scarce materials," especially steel, among producers of "the three common fuels: oil, gas and coal." A problem in deciding whether steel should be allocated to oil grew out of uncertainty about whether "regulations on expansion" might be implemented under "the conservation laws of some States, notably, Texas." Information was difficult to obtain, he noted, because "the petroleum industry is not classed as a public utility."[128] It is not clear whether Trigg recognized the number of raw nerves he was touching in one short letter. In any event he received from Brown, the senior government official concerned with petroleum policy, a five-page blast responding to his questions and observations one by one. In general, Brown objected strongly to the notion of a need for an overall fuels policy; the potential substitution among fuels was more illusion than real. Concerning the implication that excess capacity arising out of market imperfection should be a concern in policymaking, Brown wrote:

. . . the petroleum industry quite understandably is not classed as a public utility, and I know of no reason why it should be. It is my understanding that

126. National Petroleum Council, "Summary of the Report of the Committee on Oil and Gas Availability," January 29, 1952, CCF 1-188, RG 48, NA. The report was made available to the Paley Commission on a confidential basis in June 1951. John R. Suman to William S. Paley, June 15, 1951, General Records–Energy, PMPC, HSTL.

127. President's Materials Policy Commission, *Resources for Freedom*, vol. 1: *Foundations for Growth and Security* (GPO, 1952), p. 109.

128. Trigg to Brown, September 24, 1951, CCF 1-188, RG 48, NA.

such classification properly is applied only to industries serving the general public under conditions of or approaching monopoly or exclusive franchise to operate in certain areas or over certain routes. Quite a different condition obtains as regards the oil industry, in which no monopoly or domination in any areas is enjoyed by any single company or limited group of companies. On the contrary, it is an industry marked by keen competition among those presently engaged in it, and is an industry open to any newcomers who desire to enter the business.

The conservation laws and related State administrative agencies do not either in theory or fact constitute a source of "regulations on expansion in times of increasing demand." The purpose and function is the regulation of oil and gas consumption practices in order to prevent or minimize physical waste of oil and gas at the source. They do not attempt to suppress or stimulate demand but rather to meet actual demand efficiently.[129]

Clearly the exigencies of war had served to sweep from the highest levels of the Interior Department those concerns about market conditions in the petroleum industry that grew in 1949–50.

The Voluntary Agreement

During the last two years of the Truman presidency two series of events drew attention to the question of whether competition did in fact prevail in the petroleum industry: first, the so-called Iranian crisis of 1951 and its handling by the government and the industry, and second, the publication of the FTC report on the international petroleum cartel a year later.[130] Coming in sequence as they did, the two incidents built up momentum in the growth of public interest, which produced a legacy of questions and suspicion for the presidents who were to follow.

The superficial facts of the Iranian case are straightforward.[131] In mid-April 1951 after political turmoil in Iran, a strike threatened the Abadan refinery, the largest in the Middle East. This followed a decision by the Iranian government a month earlier to nationalize the oil industry. To deal with the situation PAD called a meeting of all American oil companies having business abroad and all government agencies having con-

129. Brown to Trigg, October 15, 1951, ibid.

130. Federal Trade Commission, *The International Petroleum Cartel*, Committee Print 6, Subcommittee on Monopoly of the Senate Select Committee on Small Business, 83 Cong. 2 sess. (GPO, 1952).

131. Two detailed reports on the crisis and the actions taken to deal with it, one on the substance of the issues and the other on the legal questions involved, were prepared for Secretary Chapman in June 1952 by the deputy administrator and the general counsel of PAD. They are dated June 13, 1952, and June 25, 1952, and are in CCF 1-188, RG 48, NA.

cern for security and foreign affairs. Subsequently the decision was made to take action under section 708 of the Defense Production Act of 1950, which authorized the President "to consult with representatives of industry, business . . . with a view to encouraging the making by such persons with the approval by the President of voluntary agreements and programs to further objectives of this Act."[132] A Foreign Petroleum Supply Committee composed entirely of participating companies was created and granted immunity from prosecution under the federal antitrust laws and the Federal Trade Commission Act of 1914 for actions taken within the scope of the voluntary agreement. The committee was empowered to investigate problems and make recommendations to the petroleum administrator for defense.

In fact, the Abadan refinery was owned by the British Anglo-Iranian Oil Company and served mainly customers in the Eastern Hemisphere. American security was hardly threatened directly. The voluntary agreement was explained to the American people both as an action to assist "friendly foreign nations" who depended on this refinery and in recognition "that petroleum supply is a world-wide matter and that shortages in one location necessarily involve adjustments in remotely distant areas."[133] The necessary government officials approved the agreement and a "Plan of Action No. 1" prepared by the companies and setting forth "cooperative actions" designed "to offset the deficit of supplies of crude oil and refined products resulting from the interruption of Iranian petroleum operations."[134] In the words of the PAD general counsel, the Foreign Petroleum Supply Committee and its subcommittees "determined the supplies of petroleum products in free friendly nations in order to anticipate supply shortages which it would be necessary to meet. They considered the most efficient means of moving the products necessary to meet these probable demands with a maximum use of available tankers and terminal facilities."[135]

One did not have to be very cynical to suspect that the voluntary agree-

132. A. P. Frame to Secretary Chapman, April 25, 1951, ibid. Bruce Brown complained to Chapman that even at the early stage of discussions about Iran PAD experienced difficulties "with Graham Morison's staff" (antitrust) in the Justice Department. "They will not budge one inch about their position on committees." Brown to Chapman, April 25, 1951, ibid.
133. Petroleum Administration for Defense, press release, June 28, 1951, Petroleum Administration for Defense File, Chapman Papers, HSTL.
134. Elmer E. Batzell to Secretary Chapman, June 13, 1952, p. 9, CCF 1-188, RG 48, NA.
135. Ibid.

ment had objectives beyond that of meeting the needs of free world allies at a time of crisis. The agreement clearly gave the international oil companies collectively a new weapon in their worldwide operations. Above all, it permitted them to discipline a would-be breakaway seller from a monopsony arrangement for the sale of crude oil. The Iranians, it turned out, needed discipline on a second count because of the nationalization. Clearly the most effective device for bringing the breakaway back in line was to fill from other sources the needs of all its potential customers—which is just what the voluntary agreement did.[136]

A second suspicion about the intention of the voluntary agreement concerned interests much closer to home. It seemed possible either that PAD and the industry had welcomed the temporary shortage created by the Iranian crisis to explain a price movement upward or that at least the mechanism created by the voluntary agreement provided the arrangements and the information necessary to control the worldwide market, and thereby the home market, through a global oligopoly.[137] By the end of 1951 Chapman and PAD were being attacked from several sides by critics as diverse as the Michigan attorney general and a subcommittee of the House Judiciary Committee for being the tool of the oil oligopoly.[138] Other executive branch agencies also were becoming nervous about continuation of the agreement. The assistant attorney general for antitrust

136. That discipline of a recalcitrant supplier was a primary motive in the voluntary agreement is clear from various statements of observers at the time. For example, Walter Levy, a petroleum consultant, told a Paley Commission interviewer in July 1951 that nationalization would be "more and more frequent" and oil company profits much lower "if the Iranians are successful in operating their industry." (Raymond Mikesell, "Memorandum of Meeting with Walter Levy," July 6, 1951, File I B4 (a) Petroleum, PMPC, HSTL.) One PAD expert thought the Iranian problem might be solved merely by getting the British out through the sale of the Anglo-Iranian Oil Company to U.S. and other interests. Charles Rayner to S. C. Snodgrass, October 22, 1951, PAD File, Chapman Papers, HSTL.

137. A hint that this might be the case was given very early when PAD's plan to cope with the Iranian shortage, developed in July 1951, warned that the country must be prepared for "an extremely tight position in regard to residual fuel oil on the East Coast this winter" with "many pricing problems for OPS." Memorandum, "Supplying Petroleum to Free World without Iran," July 12, 1951, PAD File, ibid.

138. Bruce Brown replied to the charge from Michigan in a letter to William S. Broomfield, chairman of the Michigan Interim Legislative Committee, December 7, 1951, CCF 1-188, RG 48, NA. Charles E. Gately, assistant general counsel of PAD, prepared defensive "Comments on Report of the Subcommittee on Study of Monopoly Power (Celler Committee) Regarding the Foreign Voluntary Aid Program" in a seventeen-page memorandum, December 15, 1951, sent to Congressman Celler on April 9, 1952, ibid.

called for a review of the agreement in December 1951, and members of his staff informed PAD in February 1952 that they had recommended it be terminated.

Plan of Action No. 1 was in fact brought to an end by Secretary Chapman on July 8, 1952, to general sounds of approval from outside the department.[139] But controversy continued over whether the voluntary agreement itself should stay in place. The staffs of the Antitrust Division and the FTC said absolutely not, and the attorney general recommended that immunity from prosecution pursuant to section 709 of the Defense Production Act be withdrawn.[140] But Chapman received more varied reactions from within his department. A report in July, presumably prepared in PAD, expressed concern that the United States was becoming increasingly dependent on supplies of foreign oil just at the time when the companies were losing a firm grip on their foreign sources. A number of developments lay at the root of the problem: above all the decline of British power and "the growing desire of the various oil-producing countries to subject their oil resources—even though they could have never developed them themselves—to direct national control and to formulate and carry out their own oil policies in line with what they consider to be their sovereign rights." The current East-West struggle made the issue more than merely a philosophical one.

The question arises, therefore, whether in a situation where a vital power position of the United States is at stake it can afford to apply fully the normal and traditional laws of sovereign self-determination to the control of under developed countries over the oil in their soil. . . . How far does the dependence

139. For example, Corwin D. Edwards, director of the Bureau of Industrial Economics in the FTC, wrote to the chairman: "This termination is most welcome. As you know, the Bureau of Industrial Economics had doubts of the desirability of Plan of Action No. 1 when it was instituted." (Edwards to the Chairman, July 10, 1952, FTC International Petroleum Report File 1952-3, Stephen S. Spingarn Papers, HSTL.) Undoubtedly influenced by the controversy surrounding the voluntary agreement, the Justice Department proposed a general "survey to investigate the operation of industry advisory committees under the Defense Production Act" in cooperation with the FTC. (See H. Graham Morison to James M. Mead, March 25, 1952, Department of Justice Antitrust Division Memoranda 1951–52 File, Morison Papers, HSTL.) Philip B. Perlman gave carefully qualified approval for a PAD Instruction No. 2 "to establish committees and appoint supply directors in various parts of the country" in May. Perlman to Secretary Chapman, May 13, 1952, Department of Justice, Antitrust Division File, Morison Papers, HSTL.

140. Henry Miller, an FTC assistant general counsel, recommended to Chairman Mead that the commission support the attorney general's action. Miller to Mead, September 12, 1952, FTC International Petroleum Report File 1952–3, Spingarn Papers, HSTL.

of the world on this resource overrule the traditional concepts of sovereign rights of these nations to produce, supply or withhold oil in line with their own desires? To what extent are they free, if they so desire, to nationalize and displace the present operating companies?[141]

The conclusion was inescapable: "the companies face most difficult odds" and "on whatever legal, economic or political grounds a case against some of the activities of foreign oil operators might be made at home or abroad, one principle appears to be overriding, and that is that it is essential to the national interest of the United States to retain American control over foreign oil in such a manner that the oil continues to be available to the United States and other members of the free world without undue interference from any side."[142]

The argument that Chapman ultimately used for keeping the voluntary agreement alive was that if anything happened to "dislocate the commercial channels of supply" there would "be a mechanism in existence which could be utilized promptly to correct the situation."[143] The strongest possible case for continuation of the Foreign Petroleum Supply Committee, which existed under protection of the voluntary agreement, was made in a seventeen-page, single-spaced memorandum in August by J. Edward Brantly, assistant deputy administrator of PAD's Foreign Petroleum Operations. He noted that "Congress has determined that the national defense is paramount whenever its necessary requirements may conflict with the requirements of the Antitrust Laws," and then he proceeded to argue that the statistics gathered by the committee, said by some to be the basis for oligopoly, were essential for defense. The military had grown to depend on the data when preparing contingency plans, and because the source was often sovereign foreign nations, information could not be acquired by the government by compulsion. To bring the subject close to home Brantly predicted that "there will be a world-wide shortage of heating oils and distillates in the last quarter of 1952 and the first quarter of 1953" (a prospect always calculated to bring a chill to any legislator or senior bureaucrat even in the heat of summer) and that only careful planning based on accurate information such as that gathered by the committee could avert a crisis.[144]

141. "The Progressive Threat to the U.S. Position in Foreign Oil," July 25, 1952, p. 8, Petroleum Cartel 1952 File, Chapman Papers, HSTL.

142. Ibid., p. 11.

143. Chapman to John R. Steelman, Acting Director of Defense Mobilization, July 11, 1952, CCF 1-188, RG 48, NA.

144. Brantley to J. Ed Warren, August 19, 1952, ibid.

Brantly's arguments were not sufficient to persuade everyone in government. Secretary of Defense Robert A. Lovett concurred in Chapman's judgment that the agreement continued to be necessary, but the attorney general did not, and on September 2 he requested Administrator Henry H. Fowler of the Defense Production Administration to withdraw the agency's request for the voluntary agreement. Chapman forwarded Brantly's memorandum of August 19 to Fowler, but to no avail: the agreement was terminated.[145]

Doubtless there were two sides to the issue of whether to preserve the voluntary agreement and in effect to sacrifice competition in the interest of national security. What is significant is that in the Korean emergency, as in World War II, spokesmen for competition, and thus for the energy consumer, disappeared from the main energy planning body, the Department of the Interior. Such spokesmen did remain elsewhere in government, however, most prominently in the Justice Department and the FTC, where soon they were to become unusually vocal.

The FTC Report

Both the Justice Department and the FTC had over the years perceived the large integrated oil companies as primary targets for antitrust investigation. At least as early as April 1948 the FTC was pointing out to the White House that worldwide cartels might be inimical to U.S. foreign policy by raising the costs of materials for such programs as the Marshall Plan above what they might have been under competition; and it very likely had the oil companies in mind.[146] In December 1949 Corwin D. Edwards, director of the Bureau of Industrial Economics of the FTC, recommended that an investigation of antitrust violations in petroleum be undertaken. The study began in January 1950 and was completed in the autumn of 1951.[147] Over this period, of course, the world situation

145. Lovett to Secretary Chapman, September 13, 1952; and Chapman to Fowler, September 26, 1952; ibid.

146. Robert E. Freer, FTC Chairman, to the President, April 29, 1948, Federal Trade Commission File, Murphy Papers, HSTL. Charles S. Murphy, presidential assistant, recommended that the matter be referred to the Executive Committee on Economic Foreign Policy. (Murphy to the President, April 29, 1948, ibid.) The Commerce Department took an ambiguous position on oil company integration, concluding "that there are logical arguments on both sides of this question." H. B. McCoy to the Solicitor, April 13, 1949, Oils-Mineral-General File 312, RG 151, NA.

147. Memorandum, Edwards to Commissioner Spingarn, May 23, 1952, FTC International Petroleum Report File, Spingarn Papers, HSTL. The history of the FTC report can be well documented because Spingarn wrote full and descriptive

changed dramatically. From a time of high sensitivity to conflicts of interest and a constructive searching for new institutional relationships between government and business the country moved to a war footing. Consequently when the report was finished it was stamped "secret" and distributed only "to a selected list of government officials who make day to day decisions about petroleum matters."[148] But as might have been predicted, news of its existence and conclusions soon leaked to Congress and to the press. Attorney General J. Howard McGrath informed Manly Fleischmann, the administrator of the Defense Production Administration, of assertions in "the public press . . . that certain of the companies to whom you issued directives are engaged in a world-wide cartel arrangement."[149] This communicaton was passed along to Chapman for comment. Oil industry and PAD sensitivity to such broad charges of monopolistic behavior was heightened by controversy over the voluntary agreement, and Chapman replied sharply and—in light of what had gone before and the FTC report, which he had already received—hypocritically.

Regarding the cartel charges in the public press to which the Attorney General's letter refers, I have this to say: I have no knowledge as to the truth or falsity of any charge that certain of the companies, which, in response to my plea voluntarily participated in the foreign aid program, are engaged in a world-wide cartel arrangement. I have no material, documentary or otherwise, to substantiate that charge. Any investigation which should be made of the subject matter does not come within my jurisdiction.[150]

The Justice Department made use of the FTC report, together with its own investigations and those of several congressional committees, to prepare a recommendation to the president that he present the facts to a grand jury "and, if these facts are established and the grand jury so directs, that

---

memorandums and collected relevant documents for his files. H. B. McCoy of the Commerce Department opposed the FTC study at its start because it would simply cover old ground, bring the FTC into "areas which are properly those of other departments," and constitute "still another specialized and independent approach to the general monopoly problem and will result in still more confusion as to government policy and administration." (McCoy to the Solicitor, March 17, 1950, Oils-Mineral-General File 312, RG 151, NA.) The FTC report is discussed in Burton I. Kaufman, "Mideast Multinational Oil, U.S. Foreign Policy, and Antitrust: The 1950s," *Journal of American History*, vol. 63 (March 1977), pp. 937–59.

148. Edwards to Spingarn, May 27, 1952.
149. McGrath quoted in Chapman to Fleischmann, February 15, 1952, CCF 1-188, RG 48, NA.
150. Ibid.

a criminal indictment be returned against the American oil companies and either the foreign companies or their subsidiaries found in the United States; and that a cvil suit be filed contemporaneously to dissolve the cartel, to dissipate the allocation and price-fixing arrangements as illegal, and to enjoin any possible future agreements, arrangements or actions designed to recreate or to result in any activities eliminating competition in the petroleum industry."[151] What both the FTC and the attorney general reported was far from surprising to anyone close to the oil industry. They charged that dominance of the world oil market had been achieved by the seven principal companies, and they set forth the history and operation of the cartel, explaining the As Is, or "Red Line," Agreement of 1928 and subsequent monopolistic instruments and practices that provided for division of the market, price supports, and punishment for competitors from outside the group. The FTC and the Justice Department found that the effect in general of the cartel's activities was to maintain prices above competitive levels, and in particular to require the U.S. government to pay exorbitant prices for the oil required for the military and for such special programs as the Marshall Plan.[152]

Pressures from Congress both for the release of the FTC report and for action against the alleged cartel became intense. With memories of cold winters still fresh in the voters' minds, punishment of greedy oil companies was an attractive campaign plank in the election year of 1952.[153] The State Department, through Assistant Secretary Willard Thorp, continued to insist that release of the report would be inimical to U.S. security interests. On June 23 President Truman announced that he had "requested the Attorney General to institute appropriate legal proceedings with respect to the operations of the international oil cartel" while continuing to keep the report confidential.[154] Finally, in July agreement was reached to pub-

151. "The World Oil Cartel," Petroleum Cartel File, Chapman Papers, HSTL.
152. An account by the Petroleum Branch, Industry Division of the Mutual Security Agency, August 15, 1952, of the agency's struggles with the oil industry over purchases for the European Recovery Program is in Oil Personal File, Pike Papers, HSTL.
153. Senator Thomas C. Hennings recounted his two-month effort to obtain action on the oil report in a press release, June 22, 1952, FTC International Petroleum Report File, Spingarn Papers, HSTL.
154. Truman to the Secretaries of State, Defense, Interior, and Commerce, and the FTC, June 23, 1952, ibid. It appears that the attorney general and Assistant Attorney General H. Graham Morison may have met with the President on the subject of prosecution soon after May 19. See Morison to J. Howard McGrath, May 19, 1952, Department of Justice, Antitrust Division Memoranda File, Morison Papers, HSTL.

lish the report with the most sensitive parts removed, and it appeared on August 2, 1952, as a publication of the Senate Small Business Committee whose chairman, John Sparkman, was Democratic candidate for vice-president in the upcoming November election.[155]

The FTC report raised strong emotions on all sides, not simply because of the importance of the antitrust suits that followed, but because of the issues of principle involved. The oil companies believed that they had become victims of anachronistic ideologues who were out of touch with reality, closeted and protected in the inner reaches of the Justice Department and the FTC. The industry contended that it was locked in a fierce struggle around the world with the power of international communism, the highly centralized oil operations of competitor nations such as the Dutch and the British, and the nationalistic governments of new countries that threatened to nationalize property or even cut off supplies. To expect the oil companies to operate in such a world according to a model and a set of principles contrived for an ideal state by some ivory-towered intellectuals was like asking them to fight a major war with both hands tied behind their backs. To add insult to injury, the companies found themselves charged with misbehavior just at the time when in their view they had responded with maximum cooperation and self-sacrifice to the second national emergency in ten years. James Terry Duce, vice-president of Aramco, expressed succinctly the views of the petroleum community in a letter to Secretary Chapman:

In the cartel proceedings and in the staff report of the Federal Trade Commission, I feel we are walking with a flaming torch in a powder magazine. We are giving aid to the enemy. . . . we should not take the risk of jeopardizing the very existence of so potent a source of American power. Like it or not, the American oil industry abroad is in effect an arm of our government or, perhaps I should say, of the American body politic. . . . No industry has developed such advanced social and economic policies. Its very success in these things is one of the great triumphs of the American system and this makes it the great target for the Communists. My plea is to stop, look and listen.[156]

Karl Ettinger, oil consultant, brought the criticism to a more personal level. He said that the FTC report was "the product of lawyers and economists, and no greater experience in handling petroleum problems went

155. See FTC, *The International Petroleum Cartel*. Aspects of the cartel case are discussed by one of the report's authors, John Blair, in his book *The Control of Oil*, pp. 71–73.

156. Duce to Chapman, October 23, 1952, Petroleum Cartel File, Chapman Papers, HSTL.

into the making of this book than that of an occasional purchase of gaso-line from a filling station." He attributed the report to pressure from one FTC commissioner, John Carson, and the influence of the International Cooperative League.[157] One industry publication speculated: "We know how Alger Hiss was able to influence Government policies in favor of Russia. So one is justified in wondering if there were any Communist-inclined officials in the Federal Trade Commission responsible for the secret international oil industry report."[158]

The antitrusters, on the other hand, believed they were engaged in combat with one of the ultimate monopolies. Not only were the restric-tions they attacked domestic, they were worldwide as well. Moreover, the commodity the monopolists controlled was the very lifeblood of modern society. But what seems to have angered the FTC and the Justice Depart-ment staffs the most was that their enemy refused to fight on the issues fair and square. Both agencies found that pressure on their budgets in congressional appropriations committees and even in the Budget Bureau seemed to increase with the vigor of their antitrust activities.[159] But more important than this, the companies attacked the very principles on which antitrust operated, "to shake the faith of the American people in our laws against illegal monopolies and restraints of trade."[160] This technique raised the question of whether a free society could in fact endure with the concentrations of economic power that some monopolies and oligopolies represented.

More than any other single person FTC Commissioner Stephen J. Spin-

157. Karl E. Ettinger, "What Does the Federal Trade Commission Cartel Report Mean?" speech at the Fall Meeting of the Empire State Petroleum Association, Lake Placid, N.Y., September 29, 1952, FTC Attacks on the Oil Report File, Spingarn Papers, HSTL. Because Ettinger was such a persistent critic of the report Spingarn checked him out with a friend identified only as "M." The informant told him that Ettinger was a part-time consultant for the State Department and was "employed by the Humble Oil Company." Memorandum for the File, "Dr. Karl E. Ettinger," Janu-ary 14, 1953, ibid.

158. Cited by Stephen Spingarn on the radio program "Longine Chronoscope," December 12, 1952, transcription, ibid.

159. See H. Graham Morison to the President, December 12, 1951 (complaining of a cut by the Budget Bureau in funds for the Antitrust Division); and Morison to Clapp, Hodges, and McCauley, January 3, 1952 (urging careful preparations for the appropriations hearing); both in Department of Justice, Antitrust Division File, Morison Papers, HSTL. On the FTC budget problems see James M. Mead and Stephen Spingarn to the President, November 5, 1952, Subject File: Agencies, PSF, HSTL.

160. H. Graham Morison to President Truman, June 25, 1952, Department of Justice, Antitrust Division Memoranda File, Morison Papers, HSTL.

garn rallied in defense of the petroleum cartel report and responded hip and thigh to attacks on it from the industry. As a former White House aide, he had unusual access to the president, and during the remaining months of the Truman presidency he kept up a steady flow of materials to the White House, to his fellow commissioners, and to the public describing and denouncing what he found to be a "world-wide bitter propaganda attack."[161] One of the charges made repeatedly by the oilmen was that both the oil-producing nations and the Soviet Union were using the FTC report to defame the United States. Spingarn told Charles Murphy, special counsel to the President: "It is my distinct impression that the oil companies are kicking the Soviet bear in the rump and then saying, 'see how mad he is.' "[162] Spingarn suspected that oil companies were in fact the main publicists of the report abroad. (He reported that Caltex had distributed pamphlets about it to "molders of public opinion in 67 countries.") Their purpose was to use the clamor generated in this way abroad as an argument against the legal proceedings growing out of the report at home.[163] He tried repeatedly and unsuccessfully to have the President direct the Central Intelligence Agency to explore the matter, and to permit him to discuss the charges at a meeting of the NSC.[164]

Understandably Spingarn was deeply troubled by the personal and highly vituperative character of many of the attacks on the report. He reported to Senator Sparkman in December that at least 188 editorials, news stories, articles, and the like, had appeared dealing with the report: "the great majority are nothing more than vicious and intemperate attacks of the type usually employed by those who cannot document their charges and who do not wish to discuss a subject on its merits."[165] He soon generalized the question of the report's reception into a consideration of the broad subject of ethics in government. In Spingarn the oil companies and

161. Spingarn to the President, November 7, 1952, with various examples of the "propaganda" attached, FTC Attacks on the Oil Report File, Spingarn Papers, HSTL.

162. Spingarn to Murphy, November 13, 1952, Federal Trade Commission File, Murphy Papers, HSTL. On November 4 Spingarn asked the NSC to explore the oil company claims. Spingarn to James Lay, November 4, 1952, ibid.

163. Spingarn documented the propaganda campaign in a lengthy memorandum for the record, December 24, 1952, Anti-Monopoly Conferences File, Spingarn Papers, HSTL.

164. Spingarn, Memorandum for the Oil Report File, December 30, 1952, FTC Attacks on Oil Report File, Spingarn Papers, HSTL.

165. He remarked that the attacks had turned up only one error of fact in the report. Spingarn to Sparkman, December 24, 1952, ibid.

all monopolists faced a remarkably energetic and dedicated opponent. He held press conferences, issued press releases, appeared on radio programs, appealed to all the government agencies he could think of, and on December 10 convened a bipartisan luncheon with representatives from most of the regulatory agencies, members of Congress, and others, to discuss ways of dealing with "unethical pressures on independent quasi-judicial Commissions." At the luncheon it was asserted that "unethical pressures on the independent Commissions and unfair attacks (such as imputations of disloyalty) indicate a breakdown of democratic government and for that reason must be countered with the greatest firmness."[166] The chairman of the Interstate Commerce Commission suggested that federal regulatory commissions might be given contempt powers to protect them from such unfair attacks.[167]

As the Truman administration approached its last days Spingarn began to feel the ground falling away beneath him, less because the Eisenhower administration was visible just ahead than because it seemed that his old Democratic colleagues were losing backbone in their final moments. In particular he got word that oil company pressures were now concentrated on the President and on the NSC to discontinue the antitrust suits. He found out early in January 1953 that the security significance of the lawsuits would be discussed at an NSC meeting on January 9, and he worked hard to have his position represented there.[168] At the NSC meeting the

166. "E. W. K.," "Memorandum for the Files Re. S. J. S. Luncheon at the Willard Hotel, December 10, 1952," ibid. Spingarn replied on the radio program "Longine Chronoscope" (December 12, 1952) to an earlier interview (December 10, 1952) with Bruce Brown, former deputy administrator of PAD. Transcripts of both programs are in ibid. Spingarn held two lengthy press conferences to set the record straight on December 5 and December 17. Transcripts are in FTC Attacks on Oil Report File and FTC Press Conference File, Spingarn Papers, HSTL. A press release on December 24, 1952, is in Anti-Monopoly Conference File, Spingarn Papers. Two especially eloquent statements of the problems of guarding the public interest in the face of unethical pressures from special interests are in a letter to Brown from Corwin D. Edwards, January 9, 1953, and a memorandum for the record by Spingarn, "An Ethics-in-Government Issue," December 24, 1952, in FTC Attacks on Oil Report File and Anti-Monopoly Conferences File, Spingarn Papers. Spingarn's account of a meeting with Senator Sparkman and others to consider how to deal with the propaganda is in Memorandum for the Files, November 19, 1952, Stephen J. Spingarn FTC File, Murphy Papers, HSTL.

167. Spingarn to Robert Engler, January 6, 1953, FTC Attacks on Oil Report File, Spingarn Papers, HSTL.

168. Spingarn described as follows his unsuccessful attempts to penetrate the State Department for this purpose: "Secretary Acheson disqualified himself because his firm—the Covington firm—has oil clients; Undersecretary Bruce disqualified

members had before them two documents on national security problems concerning free world petroleum demands and potential supplies: (1) NSC 138, by the secretary of the interior, December 8, 1952; and (2) NSC 138/1 in three parts by the departments of State, Defense, Interior, and Justice. In essence the material from the first three departments was consistent in stressing the probable threat to U.S. vital interests from the publicity of a criminal trial. The State and Defense departments recommended that the criminal proceedings be terminated. Only the Justice Department made the case that in the widest sense the security of freedom depended on proceeding swiftly with the grand jury investigation. "Free private enterprise can be preserved only by safeguarding it from excess of power, governmental and private. . . . National security considerations dictate that the most expeditious method be employed to uncover the cartel's acts and effects and put an end to them. . . . We cannot promote free private enterprise and productivity abroad unless we are seen to conscientiously enforce our laws designed to preserve them for our own economy and our own domestic and foreign commerce."[169] Reportedly the advice of General Omar Bradley was most influential with President Truman on this occasion and the President ordered that the criminal proceedings be dropped and the much less important civil suit be kept alive.[170]

The issue of the oil cartel report really ended on January 12, 1953, when President Truman announced his decision regarding the symbolic choice he had to make between two positions that had been in conflict throughout much of his administration: security considerations and the

---

himself because his former wife was an oil heiress; Paul Nitze disqualified himself because his present wife was a Pratt of Standard Oil; Harold Linder disqualified himself for some reason or other. . . . Charles Bohlen, the State Department counsellor, was thrown into the breech at the last moment. . . . Apparently Bohlen does not have a drop of oil in his veins." (Spingarn, Memorandum for the Files, January 23, 1953, ibid.) After the incident Spingarn raised much more serious questions about conflict of interest among State Department officials, especially concerning Under Secretary David Bruce and Legal Adviser Adrian Fisher. Memorandum, Spingarn, "Some Facts Pertinent to the Oil Cartel Case," February 12, 1953, Anti-Monopoly Conferences File, Spingarn Papers, HSTL.

169. NSC 138/1, NSC Meeting No. 128 File, PSF, HSTL.

170. Spingarn wrote on January 23: "On Saturday, January 17, I had lunch with Charlie Murphy. He told me that the President had told him on Monday (January 12) that he regretted his decision, that he thought the NSC had sold him a bill of goods. (Of course, to my way of thinking, this was true because the NSC had themselves been sold a bill of goods and were just passing it along.)" Memorandum for the Oil Report File, January 23, 1953, FTC Attacks on Oil Report File, Spingarn Papers, HSTL.

emergency requirements for energy on the one side, and the need to develop a balanced, just, and workable economic system on the other. By making the choice he did and by essentially suppressing the principles of antitrust on security grounds, he left the challenge of resolving the two positions for the long run for his successors.

On January 12, 1953, Spingarn wrote a final plea to the President, fully documented, making the argument that rather than harming the security of the nation, antitrust prosecution of the oil companies would accomplish just the reverse. The danger to America was not that its critics would learn of imperfections in its system but rather that failure to prosecute would prove the nation was unwilling and unable to correct these faults. "Perhaps no theme is more insistent in Soviet propaganda than this alleged subservience of democratic governments to financial and industrial interests. The antitrust laws of this country are looked upon as nothing more than a sham and pretext, to be trotted out occasionally in order to delude the people into thinking that monopoly is going to be effectively dealt with."[171] Finding that in fact he was too late, Spingarn released his memo, with a few portions deleted, to the press the same day. The full FTC voted three to two to disavow Spingarn's action.[172] But matters were winding down and the inauguration was only days away.

The Tidelands Oil Controversy

When people who lived through the Truman years are asked about their memory of petroleum policy they are likely to recall the tidelands controversy. Although this issue was politically important and dragged on throughout Truman's two terms, it involved more questions of fiscal federalism and simple politics than it did fundamental issues of energy policy.

The matters in dispute were relatively straightforward. When President Truman came to office it was still uncertain whether mineral rights to submerged coastal lands rested with the states or with the federal government. The oil companies favored the former presumably because they hoped for lower royalties and easier access by playing one state off against another. The stakes were high and the companies and the states pressed their case

171. Spingarn to the President, January 12, 1953, Subject File: FTC, PSF, HSTL.
172. Federal Trade Commission, press release, January 15, 1953, FTC Attacks on Oil Report File, Spingarn Papers, HSTL. Spingarn tells about the commission meeting in a memorandum for the Oil Report File, January 23, 1953, ibid. He held a press conference to defend himself and make public his position on January 16. A transcript is in FTC Press Conference File, Spingarn Papers, HSTL.

hard. A main reason why Harold Ickes refused to testify in behalf of Edwin Pauley, when the oilman hoped to become under secretary of the navy, was because of an offer he said Pauley made to him at the Chicago convention to "raise $300,000 from the oil men in California, who have interests in offshore oil, if they could be assured that the Federal Government would not try to assert title to these oil lands."[173] Ickes' position was that the bulk of future oil supplies might well lie under the ocean, and therefore it was desirable to press "a suit so that the courts might say whether or not the Federal Government has any title in or to any part of this oil."[174]

Despite President Truman's well-publicized differences with Ickes, they were not far apart on the tidelands matter. In 1947 the President vetoed an act of Congress to settle the matter in favor of the states by quit-claim. Shortly thereafter the Supreme Court ruled that the federal government did indeed have dominion and paramount rights in offshore land and resources. Throughout, the companies and the oil states fought vigorously for their interests, and they were joined by some nonoil states that perceived this to be a fundamental states' rights issue.[175] Even though the title question was effectively settled by the courts, other questions of leasing provisions remained, in particular whether the Mineral Leasing Act of 1920, which governed actions on dry land, applied under water as well.[176] Moreover, Congress kept proposing that the oil lands be returned to the states, while Truman vowed to make sure "that these assets are kept for the benefit of the whole United States and not allowed to get into the hands of special privileged promoters."[177] From his uncomfortable retirement Ickes kept fulminating against the corruption he perceived surrounding the demands for states' rights. For example:

The Capitol today is swarming with greasy-fingered oil lobbyists who, as usual, have crackling greenbacks to spend *ad lib* in quarters where they will do the most good. What they dearly want, at whatever price, is another quit-

173. Extract from memorandum by Ickes, September 6, 1944, in Subject File: Cabinet, PSF, HSTL.

174. Ickes to the President, February 12, 1946, OF 6, HSTL.

175. In 1947 Max Ball advised Secretary Krug that in the interest of increasing oil production the Interior Department should simply give federal leases to those who had obtained invalid state leases in good faith. Ball to Krug, July 12, 1947, Oil and Gas Matters File, Chapman Office Files, RG 48, NA.

176. Memorandum for the Files, Mastin G. White, "Oil and Gas Operations in the Submerged Coastal Lands of the Gulf of Mexico," June 6, 1950, Bureau of Reclamation File, Chapman Office Files, ibid.

177. Truman to Secretary Chapman, May 23, 1951, Subject File: Cabinet, PSF, HSTL.

claim bill which would convey ownership of the offshore oil lands away from all of the people, thereby losing the taxpayer literally billions of dollars that might be used on the education of their children. Slick operators want to enrich themselves at the expense of the children. They are not willing even to set these publicly owned undersea lands up as a reserve for our armed forces or to dedicate them to the payment of the public debt. Ruthless greed has never paraded so wantonly in hideous nakedness. Human nature can be seen at its worst in Washington today where devoted Senators and Representatives are supposed to be working for the public welfare in deference to their oaths of office. Mammon is in the saddle while civic virtue runs to cover. Oil continues to befoul the pure stream of our democratic power.[178]

Ironically, it was their congruity of opinion on the tidelands question that helped to bring Truman and Ickes together again, just as it had once divided them. They kept up a warm correspondence about what, together, they called the "big steal."[179]

The Korean War showed that the tidelands controversy, like so many other issues, could be affected several ways by what was perceived to be a challenge to national security. On the one hand it was possible to argue that the tidelands were an obvious component in a natural system of national strategic reserves. On the other hand it could be argued equally well that the emergency required exploitation of all available resources no matter where they were located. It was advice of the latter kind that the President received from the Interior Department and the industry-dominated Petroleum Administration for Defense. In October 1952 Interior Department Solicitor Mastin White drew up a memorandum for Secretary Chapman to send to the President setting forth "the urgent need of the nation for a rapid and substantial expansion in the domestic production of oil" through "the development of the oil and gas deposits in the submerged lands of the continental shelf."[180] Again in January 1952 Bruce Brown, PAD deputy administrator, argued that security considerations pointed unequivocally "toward freeing for testing and development the largest known, undeveloped oil province in the Western Hemisphere— that is, the tidelands and submerged areas off our coasts."[181]

The pressure on the President to open up the tidelands was unremitting, but he resisted to the end. Perhaps in an attempt to balance his decision

178. "Oil Befouls Our Public Life," *New Republic,* March 26, 1951, p. 17.
179. Ickes to Truman, July 9, 1951; Truman to Ickes, July 10, 1951; Ickes to Truman, August 23, 1951; and Truman to Ickes, August 25, 1951; all in General File Ickes, PSF, HSTL.
180. Mastin G. White to Secretary Chapman, with attachments, October 25, 1951, Tidelands Oil Controversy File, Chapman Papers, HSTL.
181. Brown to Secretary Chapman, January 21, 1952, CCF 1-188, RG 48, NA.

to drop the criminal suit against the oil cartel, in January 1953 just before his departure from office he issued an executive order establishing the tidelands as a national oil reserve. Despite a warning from Senator Lyndon B. Johnson that this action would "burden us with a needless division at a time when our unity is needed" and that it "would be interpreted as a spiteful act,"[182] President Truman presumably was signaling to his successor and to the American people as a whole that they had best be on their guard against those who would exploit for purely selfish purposes this crucial but diminishing element of the national energy supply.

Gas

The full potential of natural gas to become a major fuel emerged only during World War II. The consulting firm of DeGolyer and MacNaughton showed in a detailed study in 1945 that larger and larger proportions of gas to oil were being discovered in the United States, apparently because of the increasing number of wells being drilled at greater and greater depths. Because of an inadequate distribution system, however, much of the gas was either capped or wasted. Many new uses for the gas could be found if the market structure were developed and the price raised. DeGolyer advised a Senate committee: "Increase in price is the greatest conservation agent in the world. When the price of any commodity is so low that the cost of conserving it is equal to or greater than the value of the commodity, it is hardly worth conserving."[183] At the end of the war, however, the Interior Department was still "without a formulated program toward gas."[184] Whether to intervene to encourage conservation and "efficient" use was the first issue the government had to face. This question was pushed forward in 1945–46 by the need to dispose of two major pipelines (the Big Inch and the Little Big Inch) that had been constructed during the war as an emergency measure to carry oil from the Southwest

182. Johnson to Truman, January 13, 1953, Natural Resources File, Murphy Files, HSTL.

183. DeGolyer reported the results of his firm's natural gas study to the O'Mahoney Committee of the Senate in 1945. See *Investigation of Petroleum Resources,* Hearings before the Senate Special Committee Investigating Petroleum Resources, 79 Cong. 1 sess. (GPO, 1946), p. 57.

184. Michael W. Straus to Edward B. Swanson, March 20, 1945, CCF 1-290, RG 48, NA. During the war Sumner Pike, then a member of the Securities and Exchange Commission, told a meeting of financiers that natural gas was the big sleeper of the energy field likely to be limited in its development only by restraints introduced by the coal and gas interests. "Financial Opportunities in the Fuel Industries," speech to Financial Analysts of Philadelphia, July 26, 1944, Pike Papers, HSTL.

to the populous Northeast. One argument for maintaining these lines to carry oil was that if operated as common carriers, they might open competitive opportunities for small oil producers cut off from transport facilities by the large integrated companies. But Under Secretary Abe Fortas found that all the bids to purchase the pipelines for oil use were from the "major oil interests" (which favored their use for gas but evidently were prepared to keep them from competitors if used for oil), and so this argument was discounted heavily. Another argument pointed out by representatives of the armed forces was that reconversion to military use would be easier if the lines remained filled with oil rather than gas. Finally, the National Coal Association, the coal-carrying railroads, and the United Mine Workers all favored use for oil because they perceived petroleum to be less competitive with coal than with gas. Senator W. Lee O'Daniel of Texas, who sought to settle the issue by legislation (Senate bill 368), favored oil so that gas would remain in the Southwest as an attraction to new industry.[185]

The Interior Department secretariat examined the arguments and, despite its limited ability to make precise estimates of effects, concluded that none had much weight compared with the conservation opportunities in the use of the lines for gas.[186] The options considered were whether to sell the lines to the "gas people" or the "oil people." Since most influential oil people came to favor sale to the gas people, there was not much real ground for controversy.[187] A case for a third option came from Assistant

185. Amos E. Taylor, Director of the Bureau of Foreign and Domestic Commerce, presented all sides of the question and concluded that the old lines should continue to carry oil and that new lines should be built for gas. Taylor to Secretary of Commerce Henry Wallace, February 2, 1945, Oils-Mineral-General File 312, RG 151, NA.

186. Evelyn N. Cooper to C. Girard Davidson, October 9, 1946, Pipeline-Gas File, Minerals and Fuels Division Files, RG 48, NA. The Bureau of Mines, the Geological Survey, and the Oil and Gas Division submitted a fifteen-page joint "Memorandum Report on the Post-War Use of the Big Inch and Little Big Inch Pipelines," agreeing unanimously that the lines should carry gas rather than oil. Pipeline-Gas File, ibid.

187. W. Alton Jones, president of the Cities Service Company, wrote to Senator O'Mahoney in January 1946 that the combination of the requirement that the lines be used as common carriers and the skeptical "attitude of the Department of Justice" were enough to keep the majors from operating the lines for oil. "Those to whom I have talked feel reluctant to join in the creation of another vehicle through which charges of wrong-doing might be aimed at them unless the economic advantages accruing were sufficiently compelling to justify the risk and trouble of defending themselves against improper accusation." Jones to O'Mahoney, January 3, 1946, Anti-Trust Aspect of the Acquisition of Pipelines File, Subject File Box 16, Records of the Senate Special Committee Investigating Petroleum Resources, RG 46, NA.

Secretary C. Girard Davidson and Stephen Raushenbush of the Division of Power, who argued that the lines should be used exclusively for the transportation of gas that currently was being flared or wasted.[188] A fourth proposal, explored by Under Secretary Chapman, was to repressurize depleted oil fields in New York, Pennsylvania, West Virginia, Kentucky, Ohio, and other eastern and midwestern states. C. L. Moore of the Bureau of Mines reminded Chapman that such a scheme, although technically feasible, "has the basic disadvantage that it requires a new and extensive intrusion of the Federal Government into the economic life of the country."[189]

By turning the wartime pipelines over to gas in 1946 the government created a new set of problems for itself, perhaps without realizing it. The single issue that came to dominate public discussion, at least by 1947, was whether the rapidly growing industry should be regulated by the federal government and specifically by the Federal Power Commission. The Natural Gas Act of 1938 provided that the FPC must issue certificates of public convenience and necessity before the construction of pipelines, but it was unclear concerning the commission's other responsibilities toward gas, notably the extent to which it should regulate sales in interstate trade. Under the provisions of sections 11 and 14 of the act, which authorized special inquiries, and recognizing the likely growth of the industry, the FPC in September 1944 began a large investigation into all aspects of the interstate regulation of natural gas. It produced a record that was 15,000 pages long, with some 500 exhibits. In February 1947 the FPC warned the President that although its report was still not complete, its critics had decided not to wait for recommendations and probably would push soon for amendment and weakening of the Natural Gas Act.[190] Indeed, starting in 1948 a variety of bills was presented in Congress to exempt the industry from the jurisdiction of the commission. The issue was complex, the stakes were very high for the producers, and the FPC itself was divided over whether it wished to have responsibility for gas price regulation. But Presi-

188. Draft of a letter from the Secretary of the Interior to the President, n.d., marked "not sent," Pipelines-Gas File, Minerals and Fuels Division Files, RG 48, NA.

189. C. L. Moore, "Preliminary Statement on the Technical and Economic Aspects for Conversion of Big Inch and Little Big Inch Pipe Lines to Transportation of Natural Gas," attached to memorandum, R. R. Sayers to Oscar Chapman, April 15, 1946, Oil and Gas Division 1946–47 File, Chapman Office Files, RG 48, NA.

190. Truman to Charles Murphy, February 20, 1947, transmitting FPC Memorandum for the President, "Probable Effort to Amend the Natural Gas Act," Natural Gas File, Murphy Files, HSTL.

dent Truman steadfastly opposed any relaxation of federal control. He and the White House staff seem to have viewed this matter as a straightforward case of attempted monopolistic exploitation of the people by big business, and they could not see any redeeming security arguments for special treatment of the companies such as they found later for the oil majors.[191] Nor did they look ahead to problems of excess demand if prices were controlled below market-clearing levels.

The issue of gas regulation became extremely heated and personal on both sides. One FPC commissioner, Leland Olds, a veteran of the National Resources Committee of the 1930s, was singled out for vigorous vituperation by the gas interests, and his reappointment to the commission was strongly opposed. The White House even found it necessary to conduct a presidential check of charges that Olds was "disloyal" and issued a statement that they were false.[192] Olds, in turn, submitted a long memorandum to the president listing the alleged sins of his tormentors, notably those of Senator Robert S. Kerr of Oklahoma. Phillips Petroleum and the Kerr-McGee Oil Company, of which Kerr was president, he said, stood to "make tens of millions of dollars" from a weakening of the FPC control over gas. He charged Kerr with serious conflict of interest. "The real lobbying has been an 'inside job,' with Senator Kerr carrying on his regular profession of lobbying for oil and gas interests, under cloak of congressional immunity."[193] After a bitter fight in Congress Olds was not confirmed.

The issue of gas regulation was very divisive both ideologically and geographically. Conservatives from the Southwest argued that regulation of gas was designed to rob them of one of their few resources at prices that were far below market value. Liberals and labor spokesmen, who were concentrated in the Northeast, Midwest, and California, argued to the contrary that absence of regulation would result in a "ten billion dollar gift to Senator Kerr and his oil friends." A bill (Senate bill 1498) presented by Senators Kerr and Elmer Thomas in 1950 was described as a welfare program for "Dixiecrats and Republicrats" to be viewed with "disgust" by all Fair Deal Democrats. Even racial prejudice was asserted to be an element in the situation. "The colored people are particularly

191. Critical comments on bills to exempt the gas industry from regulation can be found in memorandums for the President from Charles Murphy, March 1 and July 25, 1949, ibid.

192. Clark M. Clifford to Donald S. Dawson, December 29, 1948, Federal Power Commission File, Clifford Files, HSTL.

193. Olds to the President, October 10, 1949, ibid.

incensed because they regard this measure as a reward to the chief foes of civil right legislation."[194]

The economic arguments used on both sides of the gas regulation question were not impressive. Advocates of deregulation argued that the market was already competitive with about 2,300 producers. They ignored the fact that about seventy-five producers accounted for more than 70 percent of the sales and that peculiarities of the market, like pipeline transmission, opened up all sorts of opportunities for monopolistic behavior. Advocates of regulation, on the other hand, seemed to think of the supply of gas as fixed, with rising prices merely rewarding asset holders with higher values for their ownership of finite resources, rather than leading to an increase in production and reserves. (Was this mode of thought a legacy of Henry George?) They argued also that unregulated gas prices would take "between two hundred and fifty and five hundred millions of dollars" out of the pockets of consumers, thus reducing purchasing power and increasing unemployment.[195]

The case that most agitated the gas interests and their supporters in Congress was a protracted dispute that began in 1946 when the city of Detroit filed a motion requesting the FPC to assert its jurisdiction over the Phillips Petroleum Company, the local suppliers of gas. After lengthy hearings the commission finally held in 1951 that it did not have such jurisdiction. Interests in Wisconsin, Missouri, and Michigan, however, appealed this decision to the United States Court of Appeals, which reversed the FPC ruling. Ultimately the Supreme Court affirmed the judgment of the court of appeals that the FPC did have jurisdiction over "producers and gatherers" of natural gas.[196] The so-called Kerr bill submitted to Congress by Senators Kerr and Thomas in 1950 was an attempt to protect the gas industry from an unsatisfactory outcome in the Phillips case. Because this was an election year emotions ran high during consideration of the

194. Charles M. La Follette, National Director of Americans for Democratic Action, to Gray Leslie, Democratic National Committee, March 6, 1950, Natural Gas File, Murphy Files, HSTL.

195. Charles M. La Follette to the President, April 6, 1950, ibid. A sharp exchange between Dudley F. Pegrum, a defender of the market price as the most efficient means of conserving and allocating natural gas, and Horace M. Gray on behalf of regulation occurred at the 1952 annual meeting of the American Economic Association. See abstracts of papers in "Distribution and Utilization of Natural Gas," *American Economic Review*, vol. 43 (May 1953, *Papers and Proceedings, 1952*), pp. 544–47.

196. "Background Information on History of the Natural Gas Act and Attempts to Amend It," n.d., Natural Gas Source Material File, Sidney R. Yates Papers, HSTL.

bill. The gas-state senators, such as Kerr of Oklahoma and Lyndon Johnson of Texas overstated the evils of regulation, while supporters of controls informed the White House that the presidential position on the issue could be crucial in the election.[197]

With such powerful backers for the Kerr Bill as Lyndon Johnson in the Senate and Speaker Sam Rayburn in the House it was not surprising the bill passed Congress. But Charles Murphy informed the President: "After considerable study and reflection . . . it seems to me that the bill has no merit whatever." Murphy argued that in fact the importance of the bill had been blown out of proportion by its proponents and critics. "For the immediate future, there appears to be no great need for regulation of the price at which natural gas is sold to interstate pipelines. While the trend in prices is almost certain to be upward, it is also likely to be slow and not of important general economic significance in the next few years."[198] But Murphy conceded that the bill had taken on symbolic significance to the protagonists and that a veto would have high political costs, most seriously involving impairment of "relations between the President and the Speaker." It was clear that Murphy himself favored a veto. "I do feel that the enactment of this bill would take some of the shine off of the Fair Deal and confuse to some extent our effort to draw a clear distinction between measures that are in the public interest and those which are for the special interests." The President accepted Murphy's advice and that of the Interior Department and vetoed the bill.

The veto of the Kerr Bill in 1950 did not by any means end the pressures for and against deregulation. In particular, the proponents of regulation remained suspicious that the FPC, by its inaction, was prepared to give what had been denied through legislation.[199]

When the Korean War began, the natural gas industry was informed through the American Gas Association that during the emergency its interests would be handled through PAD. Hugh Stewart of PAD pointed out

197. FPC Commissioner Thomas C. Buchanan prepared for Charles Murphy a list of "misstatements of fact and of law" by Senators Johnson and Kerr during the debate in the Senate on H.R. 1758 (the Kerr Bill). (Buchanan to Murphy, April 13 and 14, 1950, Natural Gas File, Murphy Files, HSTL.) David Bell informed Murphy that "an informal check among the Truman Democrats" had shown that it would "be advantageous to them if the President were to veto" the pending gas bills. Memorandum of telephone message for Murphy, March 31, 1950, ibid.

198. Murphy to the President, April 13, 1950, ibid.

199. Memorandum, Richard E. Neustadt to Charles Murphy, January 15, 1951, ibid.; and Paul H. Douglas and others to Monrad C. Wallgren, FPC Chairman, January 8, 1951, Federal Power Commission File, Murphy Files, HSTL.

that natural gas was merely a gaseous form of the same hydrocarbon as petroleum, the two fuels were produced through similar processes, and they were largely substitutable. The gas people were furious. They pointed out that a major difference between gas and oil was that the former had been placed under tight federal control while the latter had escaped. Therefore, gas required a specific measure of protection from further government infringements.[200] On October 6, 1950, the American Gas Association formally requested the Interior Department to set up a separate gas administration and a Gas Industry Advisory Council. This request was denied in November by Secretary Chapman, but it was repeated in January 1951 on the specific ground, as perceived by Bruce Brown, that it was necessary "to have a gas man instead of an oil man representing them in the coming 'fight for their steel.' " During this period of controversy the gas industry refused to cooperate with PAD, causing Deputy Administrator Brown to worry that the public would suffer.[201] Secretary Chapman achieved a sort of compromise by agreeing to appoint a Gas Industry Advisory Council to PAD separate from the National Petroleum Council, and a special assistant deputy administrator responsible for gas. But the relations between these two vested interests—oil and gas—which were lodged uncomfortably within one government agency, remained tense. The complications for PAD of dealing with the peacetime regulators, the FPC, as well as with the edgy gas industry, were minimized by a sort of territorial treaty signed between the FPC and the Interior Department in 1951.[202]

One of the results for those senior gasmen who took part in PAD was that they experienced for the first time the heady sensation, by now familiar to the oilmen, of participation in the affairs of government rather than merely regulation by it. In October 1951 C. Pratt Rather, the assistant deputy administrator for gas, reported to the American Gas Association on his first six months in office and candidly explained his conversion to the system, concluding, "As you all know there is criticism, from some sources, of industry men in Government, but I am prepared to stand or fall on this statement: God help Government, and industry too, if this

200. Stewart to J. French Robinson, October 18, 1950; and Edward Falck to Robinson, October 24, 1950, Commodities–Gas File, Minerals and Fuels Division Files, RG 48, NA.
201. Bruce Brown to Oscar Chapman, February 13, 1951, CCF 1-188, RG 48, NA.
202. C. Pratt Rather to Deputy Administrator Brown, May 14, 1951; and Brown to Secretary Chapman, May 14, 1951; both in ibid.

sensible alliance is not maintained."[203] Gasmen such as Rather also were exposed directly for the first time to the problems government faced with gas, some of which were accentuated by the emergency. In particular, problems of excess demand at prevailing regulated prices became critical, on occasion requiring resort to informal rationing.[204] Shortages also heightened the tension between users of natural gas, who demanded more production and suspected industry conspiracies, and competitors, such as the coal industry, which insisted on maintaining the production status quo.[205]

One way in which the Interior Department attempted to increase opportunities for competition in the gas industry during the last two years of the Truman administration was through enforcement of the common carrier provision of the Mineral Leasing Act, which stipulated that all pipelines crossing public lands would be required to act as common carriers at reasonable rates, in this case serving small independent gas producers as well as the company that owned the line. The dispute dragged on through the courts, centered on a suit involving the El Paso Natural Gas Company. The issues raised were argued mainly in legal rather than economic terms, however.[206]

The Paley Commission, which reported in 1952, argued that competitive market forces and steadily rising prices could be expected to encourage maximum recovery, minimum waste through flaring, allocation to "highest" uses, and preparation for the day when gas was no longer plentiful. Public intervention was not necessary or desirable except perhaps to encourage conservation in the field.[207] But the commission's conclusions seem not to have been given much weight in policy formation.

Natural gas assumed major importance as a fuel for the first time dur-

203. C. Pratt Rather, "Six Months in the Petroleum Administration for Defense," speech delivered to the American Gas Association, St. Louis, Mo., October 15, 1951, ibid.

204. Memorandum, Bruce Brown to Secretary Chapman, "Limitation of the Use of Natural Gas," June 25, 1951, ibid.

205. Oscar Chapman to Charles Wilson, Director of Defense Mobilization, June 20, 1951 (discussing whether a gas pipeline should be built to Alberta, Canada), ibid.; and Bruce Brown to Secretary Chapman, July 23, 1951 (on the same subject), Pipelines File, Office Files of Richard Searles, RG 48, NA.

206. The common carrier question is discussed in Dale E. Doty to Monrad C. Wallgren, March 19, 1951, and two undated memorandums prepared in the Interior Department, all in Department of Interior File—Bureau of Land Management General, Doty Papers, HSTL.

207. PMPC, *Resources for Freedom*, vol. 2: *The Outlook for Energy Sources*, pp. 15–23.

ing the Truman administration. Because of the opportunities for monopolistic pricing created by transportation through noncompetitive pipelines, the gas industry cried out for public intervention of various kinds. By and large, however, public policy regarding gas seems to have been determined less by economic analysis of the implications of alternative courses of action than by political pressures and a suspicion of concentrations of economic power. In a sense the policies toward gas sown by President Truman and Congress in the early 1950s required their successors to reap problems almost three decades later.

Coal

The period between the two world wars was especially difficult for the American coal industry. The bituminous industry operated in the red in every year from 1924 to 1939 (with the possible exception of 1926). The problem seems to have been that World War I stimulated an increase in capacity that subsequently kept prices unprofitably low. At the end of World War I coal absorbed almost the total reduction in energy demand, in sharp contrast to petroleum and natural gas, both of which continued to grow modestly. The structure of the industry, with many small mines located mainly in depressed parts of the country, meant that the low prices did not lead quickly to the withdrawal of submarginal firms. Fixed costs were so high and alternative uses for resources (especially labor) were so few that unprofitable firms remained in production for long periods even though not covering total costs, and the automatic corrective of shifts in supply to raise prices to the break-even point did not operate. While the difficulties for gas and oil during the depression arose at least as much from the discovery of large new supplies as from depressed aggregate demand, long-term growth always loomed on the horizon. For coal there was only unremitting gloom. In 1932 the production of bituminous coal stood 26 percent below that of 1914, while natural gas showed an increase of 163 percent and crude petroleum 195 percent.[208]

Both mine owners and the miners themselves exerted pressure during the 1920s and 1930s for some sort of government program to ease the industry's agony, and several public investigations were undertaken. Be-

208. Charles H. Hayes, "Regulations Limiting the Industrial Use of Competitive Sources of Energy Are Desirable in the Public Interest," November 1945, p. 1, Post-War Resources Institute File, Wolfsohn Papers, HSTL.

ginning in 1928 a succession of bills was proposed to authorize collective action. Under the National Industrial Recovery Act of 1933 minimum prices and a variety of other regulations were actually implemented. Following the declaration in 1935 that the NIRA was unconstitutional, more specific bills set out to realize the same objectives for coal alone, notably the Bituminous Coal Act of 1937. This act provided for minimum prices based on weighted average costs to be determined by a National Bituminous Coal Commission and for supporting marketing rules and regulations. In 1939 the Department of the Interior assumed the functions of the commission under the act, but in 1943 the act ran out with the onset of mobilization and the need for price ceilings rather than floors. The effect of the 1937 act was, of course, to transform temporarily what had been a relatively free market delivering results that were unsatisfactory from the sellers' standpoint into a market of administered prices that allowed the industry to emerge from the red into the black in 1940 for the first time in more than a decade.[209]

At the end of World War II, when the component parts of the Interior Department still spoke very much as the representatives of the fuels for which they had responsibility, Charles H. Hayes of the Solid Fuels Administration for War (the coal equivalent of the Petroleum Administration for War) expressed the foreboding felt generally throughout government about the postwar outlook for coal. In a paper for the department's Post-War Resources Institute he argued that the long-term prospects were bright but the short term was somber. He estimated that reserves of petroleum might last as short a time as two decades and natural gas no more than half a century. Moreover, the potential for hydroelectric development in America was practically exhausted. The challenge to government, then, was to keep the coal industry intact during the difficult few years while its comparative advantage was low. He called for government protection of coal from what he termed internal and external "dumping" of energy sources that were competitive with coal. In particular he argued that through price differentiation, and especially low prices to large industrial consumers of energy for heat, suppliers of hydroelectric power, natural gas, and residual fuel oil were depleting their own resources at undesirably rapid rates and destroying the coal industry in the bargain.[210]

209. The history of coal price control is set forth in an unsigned memorandum, "Government Price Control: 1935 Act; 1937 Act; Stabilization of Industry; Union Support," in Coal File, Office Files of Evelyn Cooper, RG 48, NA.

210. Hayes, "Regulations Limiting the Industrial Use of Competitive Sources of Energy Are Desirable in the Public Interest."

In November 1946 a member of the Interior Department secretariat, Evelyn Cooper, reviewed for Assistant Secretary Davidson the postwar problems facing coal as they seemed to be emerging. She confirmed that in contrast to the interwar years when contraction of aggregate demand was the challenge, the difficulty now was with competing fuels, especially natural gas. For the indefinite future America would have to depend substantially on oil, gas, and coal for increments to its energy supply. Hydroelectric and atomic energy were not likely to be in the race. The peculiarity of gas was that while it was relatively abundant at the moment, it would be in short supply again in twenty to twenty-five years. By that time it was possible "that coal may have regained all markets lost to these competing fuels and, in addition, may supply an increasing part of the markets previously supplied by oil and gas and will itself be an important raw material for the manufacture of gasoline." She repeated the question put by Charles Hayes the year before: what policies should be implemented during this troublesome quarter-century while oil and gas were on top and coal was on the bottom struggling to survive? Evelyn Cooper concluded that minimum-price legislation was no solution because it failed to deal with the excess supply that would be stimulated. She proposed, instead, a three-part policy consisting of (1) the government's withdrawal of certain marginal mines from production through exercises of the right of eminent domain, a license system, or some other device; (2) public assistance to productivity increases; and (3) rehabilitation of miners replaced by mechanization.[211]

A major complication in developing postwar policy toward coal was the intense labor conflict that broke out in the mines. Some of President Truman's most difficult moments occurred during coal strikes, and his personal relations with John L. Lewis, president of the United Mine Workers, were as strained as with almost any leader, domestic or foreign. The first major bituminous coal strike began to develop early in 1946 and continued intermittently throughout the year. It was conducted with a strong sense prevailing among the mine owners, stated repeatedly to the President, that substantially increased labor costs could not be absorbed by the industry at existing prices for coal, and higher prices would choke off demand by

211. Cooper to Davidson, November 19, 1946, Special Coal Study File, Cooper Office Files, RG 48, NA. Cooper attached extracts from her November 1946 memorandum to a later memorandum to Davidson on the same subject, April 2, 1947, Commodities–Coal File, Minerals and Fuels Division Files, RG 48, NA.

encouraging further shifts to gas, oil, and hydroelectricity.[212] In general the short-run exigencies of keeping the economy operating overwhelmed longer-run energy policy considerations in developing responses to labor problems in coal and led to such actions as temporary government possession of the mines in May 1946.[213] It even may be that in consequence of the intense and repeated headaches generated for leaders of government by industrial relations in the coal industry, these leaders breathed a silent sigh of relief as the nation's dependence on coal gradually declined.

There was never any doubt in the Interior Department that labor troubles in the coal industry were merely a symptom of the more fundamental economic difficulties outlined by Hayes, Cooper, and other staff members. All devices such as temporary government operation of the mines were perceived merely as palliatives. For example, the chief of the Coal Economics Division of the Bureau of Mines, Thomas W. Hunter, advised that despite the seemingly unending strife, labor relations in the coal industry were essentially "healthy." Recent events were merely what could be expected in any declining industry. "The nature of the coal problem is an economic one. If it could be simplified into one word it would be 'prices.' "[214] This consensus led to a decision in February 1947 to prepare a special coal study drawing on the wisdom of all the parts of the Interior Department concerned in any way with the fuel. Staff member Edward Falck prepared the study, and he received some exceptionally thoughtful contributions from various colleagues. N. H. Collisson, a naval captain completing service as administrator of the Coal Mines Administration under the emergency seizure in 1946, provided a series of memorandums in which he argued eloquently that the coal "problem far exceeds the ability of the industry to effect a solution." The results of the coal problem in recent years had been not only that the industry had barely been prevented "from committing suicide as a result of ruinous competition between the various producers" but also that because of economic pressures a miner's life was

212. J. D. Battle, Executive Secretary, National Coal Association, to the President, April 23 and July 16, 1947, OF 175, HSTL. A detailed chronology of the strike, prepared in the White House, is in Coal Case File, Clifford Papers, HSTL.

213. For a president still attempting to get a grip on foreign affairs, a memorandum from Dean Acheson that said "in the foreign field also the coal stoppage strikes at our most vital interests" must have increased the sense of emergency. The undated memo is in Coal Case File, ibid.

214, Hunter to Evelyn Cooper, July 3, 1947, Proposed Coal Report File, Cooper Office Files, RG 48, NA.

more like that of a medieval vassal than that of a citizen of a modern state. "The conditions under which he does live are indescribable and are better fitted for animals." Collisson concluded that "heroic measures are required and that these measures [should] come only after mature study." He looked to the new Atomic Energy Commission as a possible model for coal but hoped also for a major national inquiry on the subject using "the best brains in the country along the lines of economics, medicine, sanitation, housing, engineering, and industrial management."[215]

Early in 1948 Secretary Krug decided to appoint the National Bituminous Coal Advisory Council, perhaps partly to balance the National Petroleum Council, which had existed since 1946, and perhaps also to help in the search for solutions to the seemingly insoluble problems of the industry. There was always the chance that working together the coal operators would find a way out of their apparent dead end.[216] The coal council did not have an auspicious beginning. First of all, it was roundly denounced by John L. Lewis as the first step toward controls. He wrote to Secretary Krug: "I can conceive of nothing more anemic or futile than a Coal Industry Advisory Council attempting to give private advice to you. You have had such a committee to advise you on oil, and it is to be fervently hoped that the consumers of coal will be spared the present unhappy fate of the consumers of oil."[217] In fact, the coal council did exactly what might have been expected of it. Working closely with the Bureau of Mines, just as the NPC worked with the Oil and Gas Division, it formulated the industry's position on issues as they emerged. The coal council took the position, which was accepted widely in the Interior Department, that the energy future of the nation lay inevitably with coal, either directly or through synthetic fuels. The present depression was an aberration of a long-run upward trend, but government policy had to be concerned, nevertheless, with this short-run crisis. The council further argued that the problems were partly of the government's own making. Above all, the internal revenue code (and especially percentage depletion—5 percent

215. Memorandum, Collisson to Edward Falck, "Future of Bituminous Coal," February 10, 1947; and four other memorandums of February 7 and 8 dealing with welfare and retirement, medical and sanitary facilities, mine safety, and workman's compensation; all in Special Coal Study File, Cooper Office Files, ibid.

216. The goals of the council were described by Secretary Chapman in introductory remarks to it, December 14, 1949, CCF 11-34, RG 48, NA.

217. Lewis to Krug, January 22, 1948, Bureau of Mines File, Chapman Office Files, RG 48, NA.

for coal, 27 percent for crude petroleum and gas) as well as transportation charges (publicly subsidized pipelines in contrast to high rail freight rates) were stacked against coal and in favor of its main competitors, oil and gas.

To a striking degree discussion of policy toward coal during the second four years of the Truman presidency was similar to that of the first four years. There was no dearth of appreciation in the executive branch and in Congress of the continuing crisis, but there was little agreement on what to do about it, except search for some technical breakthrough that would open up alternative uses. The years 1947 through 1949 saw an unusually high rate of substitution of oil and gas for coal and led to a great deal of agitation in Congress. Yet the only remedial measure that received general approval was, once again, further study, through some sort of coal commission "to assure a healthy and progressive coal industry prepared to contribute to the maximum to our national well-being." As proposed in Congress, such a commission would deal specifically with coal; in the Interior Department view the focus should be on energy resources of all kinds.[218]

A report by the National Bituminous Coal Advisory Council in April 1951 put the industry's case succinctly and impressively, describing how it had matured over six years since the war's end. The council unanimously agreed that the day of coal's dominance among fuels would certainly return within 50 to 100 years at the latest and perhaps as soon as 15 to 20 years. In the meantime the severe depression of the market for this fuel was caused less by uncompetitiveness than by monopolistic pricing by its principal competitors and suppliers as well as by discrimination from government. In particular, monopolistic petroleum producers priced residual fuel oil artificially low so as to outbid coal while loading costs in unreasonable proportion onto the purchasers of gasoline and other distillates who had access to few competitive fuels. The railroads, on the other hand, charged exorbitant rates for the carriage of coal relative to other freight precisely because there were few alternative methods of transport open to coal producers. The main complaint against government policy was that the depletion allowance for petroleum, coal's main competitor, was more than five times the size of coal's own. It was ironic,

---

218. See statement of Secretary of the Interior Oscar L. Chapman in *Fuel Study Proposals,* Hearing before the Senate Committee on Interior and Insular Affairs, 81 Cong. 2 sess. (GPO, 1950), pp. 28–49; quotation is on p. 29.

the coal producers noted, that they were in trouble substantially because they were an extremely competitive industry dealing with monopolists in the markets for both their inputs and outputs. "All that coal asks is that it be given a fair chance to compete in the fuel market. With competition on an equitable level, coal . . . has and will continue to have a substantial market." Surely if the public were aware of the facts, the report argued, as had its predecessors, the American people would insist on greater equity of treatment among the fuels. "The more that is known about fuels present and prospective, the more chance that each fuel industry will be strong and able to meet its responsibilities as a private enterprise."[219]

It is especially noteworthy that by 1951 the coal industry, unlike oil and gas, did not appeal for government assistance to lessen competition nor did it follow the lead of agriculture and seek either price supports or supply restraints. Instead, it called for fair competition in the markets in which it operated; ironically, this was perhaps the hardest bounty of all for government to bestow. Coal producers sustained an almost pathetic faith that if only government and the American people could understand fully both the nation's long-term dependence on coal and the industry's short-term plight, dispassionate analysis would then reveal "what government should do."[220]

Lest interest flag in the problems of coal, as the years moved on the political pressure was steady from the congressmen most directly concerned, from citizens in the coal-producing regions, and of course from the industry itself. As noted above, oil imports and especially "dumped" imports of residual fuel oil, were presented by the coal people as one cause of their product's decline. The Interior Department's response, which was cold comfort, was to point out that "U.S. crude oil output is legally dictated by the State regulatory commissions, not by free competition," and if imports were reduced through tariffs or quotas, domestic output could simply be increased by the commissions to make up the difference.[221] As concerns about defense and the desirability of energy independence grew during the second Truman administration, the security arguments for special treatment of coal grew in weight. For example, just before the be-

---

219. "Bituminous Coal and Fuels Policy," Report of National Bituminous Coal Policy Committee, April 27, 1951, as amended and adopted by the National Bituminous Coal Advisory Council, May 9, 1951, National Bituminous Coal Advisory Council File, Searles Office Files, RG 48, NA.

220. Ibid.

221. "Memorandum Concerning Oil Imports," April 4, 1950 (unsigned), Oil Imports File, Wolfsohn Papers, HSTL.

ginning of the Korean War a memorandum prepared by the National Security Resources Board pointed out:

The expanded use of oil and natural gas adversely affects the productive capacity and the economic life and financial stability of the solid fuels industry. As a result, productive capacity is lowered, recoverable reserves are lost, valuable dock, port and storage facilities are threatened with financial ruin and eventual dismantlement, our transportation system is being weakened and unemployment is resulting in the solid fuels and railroad industries.

These trends have created a constantly shifting pattern of capability to produce and accentuate the difficulty which will be experienced by the solid fuels industries in playing their allotted role during an emergency.[222]

As soon as the Korean emergency began, some friends of coal firmly contended that security arguments were now strong enough to justify significant protectionist measures, including a cutoff of supplies of steel pipe to the natural gas companies.[223] But an industry that suffered from a chronic surplus had a hard time making persuasive security arguments for favored treatment. It was significant that in contrast to its treatment of the National Petroleum Council, the Interior Department did not recognize the National Bituminous Coal Advisory Council under the Defense Production Act of 1950. There seemed little prospect of a shortage that would require industry-wide cooperation under a "voluntary agreement."[224]

Congressman Daniel J. Flood of Pennsylvania was especially fertile with ideas to help the industry. At different times he suggested the appointment of a "fuel coordinator," the stockpiling of anthracite coal, and the creation of a Natural Energy Resources Commission comparable to the Atomic Energy Commission.[225]

Beginning in mid-1949 the Bureau of Mines set out to improve its economic analytical capacity, partly no doubt in hopes of finding some solutions to the coal problem.[226] The Office of Chief Economist, which grew

222. Memorandum, W. H. Hahman to Edward Falck, "Activities in the Solid Fuels Area," April 21, 1950, NSRB Files 54-23, RG 304, NA.

223. Senators Harley M. Kilgore and Matthew M. Neely and six Congressmen from West Virginia to the President, July 26, 1950, OF 175, HSTL.

224. Charles W. Connor to Secretary Chapman, August 17, 1951; and W. E. Wrather and James Boyd to Chapman, August 9, 1951; both in Office Files of Robert R. Rose, RG 48, NA; and Charles W. Connor to Director of Management Research, Office of the Secretary, December 31, 1952, Advisory Committee File, Chapman Papers, HSTL.

225. Flood to the President, May 4 and 23, 1951, OF 175, HSTL.

226. Materials describing the "organization of economic research and statistics" in the Bureau of Mines are contained in Organization Bureau of Mines File, Craine Correspondence Files, RG 48, NA.

out of this reorganization, appears to have focused mainly on the question of federal mineral taxation and the differential impact of taxes on various fuels.[227] This work did not point clearly to creative new policy. The only hope in that direction seemed to lie with decisive technical change and the conversion of the fuel into some product in greater demand.

Synthetic Fuels

The development of synthetic liquid fuels during the Truman presidency was one of the most controversial energy programs in government and one of the least known outside. "Synfuels" meant very different things to different groups. To the coal industry and the coal-producing states they meant a potential new demand for a product experiencing increasing depression over the period. To the defense establishment they promised a move back toward energy independence at a time when oil imports were steadily growing. To the oil industry they raised the specter of a new competitor—one that adding insult to injury had come to life through federal tax dollars. Finally, to some senior officials in the Interior Department the process of producing synfuels seemed almost fortuitous alchemy, a philosopher's stone capable of turning the black dross of coal and shale into the gold of liquid fuels. These sharp differences in perception help to explain the intense controversy that surrounded the subject; they also explain the high levels of uncertainty and confusion it helped to create.

Uncertain Goals, A Surfeit of Means

In the years immediately before World War II the Bureau of Mines performed a limited amount of research on the conversion of coal and oil shale into liquids but only in the laboratory with bench-scale models.[228]

227. This work initially was aimed in part to inform and later to answer the Paley Commission. The main written product was a report by Chief Economist Sam Schurr that was submitted in draft to the Paley Commission on May 2, 1951, and was distributed more widely during 1952. The report is appended to memorandum, Sam H. Schurr to Philip H. Coombs, May 2, 1951, Taxation and Incentives File, PMPC, HSTL. For commentary see memorandum, Lawrence E. Imhoff to Assistant Secretary of the Interior Wolfsohn, "Federal Minerals Taxation Report," December 4, 1952, CCF 11-6, RG 48, NA.

228. "Commercial Production of Synthetic Liquid Fuels," January 12, 1953, presumably a briefing paper for the new Eisenhower administration, provides a useful overview of synfuel programs during the Truman years. Synthetic Liquid Fuels File, Reports and Recommendations on Departmental Programs 1951–1953, RG 48, NA.

The rationale for the bureau's experiments was complex even at this early stage. As the likelihood of worldwide conflict increased during 1942, R. R. Sayers, director of the bureau, urged a substantial acceleration of activities "to advance the art of oil shale mining and crushing, and shale-oil refining including hydrogenation, as well as to increase our knowledge of oil-shale retorting." His case seemed to rest on the probable need for larger energy supplies in wartime, and he submitted a modest program with an annual cost of only $225,000.[229] However, Stephen Raushenbush, a departmental policy planner close to Secretary Ickes, provided an argument for increased synfuels that went far beyond security. He told Ickes that "the work of the Bureau of Mines on the conversion of coal and oil-bearing shale to oil needs more energetic stimulation than it has been receiving. The probabilities are that these processes will be perfected and then monopolized by the larger companies. It would be highly desirable to have sufficient inventive ability turned loose on the processes by the Government so that the post-war oil production from coal and shale can be carried on competitively by many small companies."[230]

Toward the end of World War II the spectacle of the German armies fighting mainly with synthetic oil from coal, together with fear that America's own petroleum supplies were running out, combined to create an urgent demand for more action by Congress and by the executive. In March 1944 Eugene Ayres, in charge of research and development for Gulf Oil, privately sent a paper he had written, "Oil for the Next War," to Secretary Ickes. It was clear, he said, both that the United States was certain to become increasingly dependent on imported oil and that synthetic processes would not be developed so long as imports remained cheap. From a security perspective this situation would be intolerable. Accordingly, he thought it appropriate

for the Government to place an extra tax on all liquid fuels which do not include some small percentage of an approved substitute. Approved substitutes would be those whose eventual development were regarded as essential to national security. In this way each refiner would have an incentive either to manufacture substitutes or to purchase them for resale, and the manufacturers would have an incentive to bring costs of substitutes as low as possible.

229. Sayers to Secretary Ickes, May 15, 1942, Oil Shales File, Branch of Economics and Statistics, Bureau of Mines Files, RG 48, NA. Sayers may have had his eye on New Brunswick as a source of oil shale. See memorandums, R. A. Cattell to Sayers, May 23 and May 25, 1942, Aviation Gasoline from New Brunswick Shales File, Branch of Economics and Statistics Files, RG 48, NA.

230. Raushenbush to Ickes, November 6, 1942, Oil Royalties and Prices File, Branch of Economics and Statistics, Bureau of Mines Files, RG 48, NA.

The Government could gradually raise the required proportion of substitute until some figure were reached consistent with national security. In the meantime, the profit possibilities would inspire reductions in cost through competitive enterprise, so that increased production of substitute fuels might not place an increasing burden of overall cost on domestic consumption.[231]

In a similar vein Reginald S. Dean, assistant director of the Bureau of Mines, wrote to Raushenbush in March 1944 suggesting "the desirability of insisting on a complete revelation of German technical methods [of coal hydrogenation], and the surrender of their right to use them in the United States should be made a definite part of the peace treaty, otherwise we shall simply find that much of the technologic advance, which has been born out of necessity during the war years in Germany, will be reserved as the quid pro quo for entering into extensive cartels with American firms and, of course, the Imperial Chemical Industries."[232]

The nation decided not to follow the route of directed free enterprise proposed by Ayres; instead, in April 1944 Congress passed the Synthetic Liquid Fuels Act (Public Law 290) under which appropriations for public programs of $85 million had been authorized by the end of the Truman years. The act provided broad authority for the Interior Department to conduct laboratory research and to construct and operate demonstration plants that would illustrate technology yet, in aggregate, not produce a commercially significant quantity of outputs. Even in the throes of war, leaders of the oil industry were ever vigilant lest the Interior Department with its talk of "public utility status" find in synthetics a new way of getting into the oil business.

The department made the decision immediately to move on all known fronts in the synthetics program: coal hydrogenation, gas synthesis from coal, gasoline from natural gas, and oil from shale. The War Department provided the Missouri Ordinance Works as a demonstration site, and the navy gave land for a shale oil plant in Rifle, Colorado. Understandably, attention focused initially on the techniques employed so successfully by the enemy (especially the Fischer-Tropsch method used in Germany), and at the end of the war efforts were undertaken quickly to remove equip-

231. Eugene Ayres, "Oil for the Next War," pp. 5–6, attached to memorandum, Ayres to Ickes, April 5, 1944, Oil (Foreign) PRC File, Fortas Office Files, RG 48, NA.

232. "Comments on 'A National Resources Program for the United States,'" p. 17, attached to memorandum, R. S. Dean to Stephen Raushenbush, March 22, 1944, Mineral Policy, 1944 File, Branch of Economics and Statistics Files, RG 48, NA.

ment and scientists to the United States.[233] Wilburn C. Schroeder, chief of the Synthetic Fuels Section of the Bureau of Mines, was said to have "made a successful investigation of German synthetic fuel development but a few hours behind our victorious armies," and by September 1946 work was being carried on at five locations in the United States with 800 employees.[234] In particular, a major laboratory concerned with the production of oil and gasoline from coal was operating in Pittsburgh. Michael Straus, assistant secretary of the interior, declared optimistically to the O'Mahoney Committee as early as June 1945 that "the unknowns are falling away one by one." After its current program of research the department would "be ready for a United States declaration of oil independence at any time that our dwindling domestic natural petroleum reserves make it necessary to turn to synthetic sources of gasoline. . . . It may be sooner than we realize."[235]

Within a remarkably short time after World War II a pattern began to characterize synfuels development and remained substantially unchanged throughout the Truman presidency. First of all, the program came to support a substantial establishment in the Bureau of Mines that understandably began to provide justification for its own existence and to issue uniformly optimistic pronouncements about its achievements, past and prospective. Schroeder was the principal spokesman for the program. He told the FPC in June 1946 that within three years his office would have "much of the basic information for the production of oil from coal or oil shale on a commercial scale. It is also evident," he said, "that for certain of these processes, sufficient improvement can be made to put them in the range where they may be nearly competitive with petroleum."[236] A year later Schroeder seemed less certain of the economic practicality of synfuels, and with the prospect of rapidly rising oil imports before him, he

233. Harold Ickes to Robert P. Patterson, December 10, 1945; and Julius Krug to Francis J. O'Hara, February 5, 1948 (describing use of German scientists); both in CCF 11-34, RG 48, NA. Government agents removed equipment and plans from both the I. G. Farben and the Krupp companies. See Clarence G. Lasby, *Project Paperclip: German Scientists and the Cold War* (Atheneum, 1971), pp. 26, 49, 107, 164, 186.

234. Memorandum, R. R. Sayers to Under Secretary Chapman, "Synthetic Liquid Fuels Program," September 27, 1946, Bureau of Mines File, Chapman Office Files, RG 48, NA.

235. Statement of Michael W. Straus, Assistant Secretary of the Interior, in *Investigation of Petroleum Resources,* Hearings, pp. 319–20.

236. Statement of W. C. Schroeder before the Federal Power Commission, June 1946, Bureau of Mines File, Chapman Office Files, RG 48, NA.

shifted the weight of his arguments to security. "If the assumption is made that the American petroleum industry can operate freely in the foreign fields and will not have to pay exorbitantly for concessions, taxes, or oil," he said "it is the author's belief that oil can be imported at a lower cost than it can be produced synthetically in this country at this time." He estimated that the current differential was 3 to 5 cents per gallon of products from petroleum in favor of imports over synfuels but warned: "It is the author's belief that the United States, whose economic health and protection are so greatly dependent on oil, should never allow the security of a large proportion of its supply to rest in distant foreign lands."[237]

Most of the relevant internal documents that would reveal the position of the military establishment toward the synthetic fuels question in the years immediately after World War II remain classified. A careful discussion of the security issues was published in 1947, however, by the distinguished strategist Bernard Brodie, and this may reflect some of the thinking that was going on behind closed doors.[238]

Brodie began by accepting the indisputable fact that a steadily declining proportion of American liquid fuels was bound to come in the future from domestic petroleum exploration. Economically the natural evolution would be for American dependence on foreign sources to increase steadily, especially those in the Middle East. The danger in this course was that in wartime the nation could be cut off suddenly from this most crucial resource. (Brodie did not consider the possibility of peacetime interruption.) Moreover, "As our Army becomes increasingly airborne and air-supplied, and as firepower of individual weapons increases, fuel consumption per combatant soldier is bound to rise dramatically—and indeed to become the limiting factor in further mechanization." An obvious answer to this problem lay in synthetics, the raw materials for which lay within the national boundaries. This would come along in due course in any event as the worldwide supply of oil ran out. The issue was whether to give it an added boost now. An obvious device to do so would be a tariff on imported oil, which in proportion to its size, would stimulate the introduction of synthetics in advance of the economically justified time. The consequent higher domestic prices would encourage greater "conservation" on the supply side through more efficient methods of use, and on the

237. W. C. Schroeder, "Synthetic Liquid Fuels in the United States," *Mechanical Engineering,* vol. 69 (December 1947), pp. 989–95.
238. Bernard Brodie, *Foreign Oil and American Security,* Yale Institute of International Studies Memorandum 23 (Yale Institute of International Studies, 1947).

demand side in less automobile driving and the development of more efficient automobile engines. It was not unreasonable to think of using such price manipulation as a means of achieving strategic goals. "If that means that the ordinary motorist's gasoline will cost him five cents more per gallon, then he must accept that additional cost in the same way and for the same purpose that he accepts the financial burden of his army, navy, and air force." But a major strategic cost of tariff-induced higher prices would be a "rapid diminution in our fund of proved reserves." Just as synthetic production was growing, the higher prices would stimulate premature depletion of natural sources. Such a policy would be "like trying to lengthen a rod by adding to one end while rapidly whittling away the other."[239]

In consequence, Brodie concluded, the nation was on the horns of an economic-strategic dilemma. There might be five years of grace before major policy decisions would have to be made, and then it would be necessary to make balanced choices among strategic and economic objectives. He himself favored some mix of restraint on consumption, imports at low tariff rates, and subsidies to the beginnings of a synthetic fuels industry.

Director Sayers of the Bureau of Mines and his successor in 1947, James Boyd, as well as Secretary Krug, repeated the points made by Schroeder, that synfuels were desirable for both economic and security reasons. Depending on the audience, they also observed that developing synfuels might still be the best way to assist the ailing coal industry.[240]

Almost from the beginning of the synfuels program the oil industry's opposition was expressed vociferously and the Interior Department was placed on the defensive. As early as April 1946 the department found it necessary to hold a meeting of reassurance with an "advisory group" from the petroleum producers, and in July 1946 Secretary Krug explained to the president of Phillips Petroleum that while it might be necessary to construct a demonstration plant with output as high as 50 to 200 barrels a day, "we do not wish to compete with the petroleum industry through the operation of demonstration plants, and I can assure you that the production of synthetic liquid fuel at such plants will be held to the lowest possible minimum consistent with attainment of the research and development objectives of the Bureau of Mines."[241]

Although the synthetic fuel program was mainly addressed to two long-

239. Ibid., pp. 4, 22, 23.
240. Examples of statements by Boyd in various forums can be found in Speeches and Statements File, James Boyd Papers, HSTL.
241. Krug to Kenneth S. Adams, July 15, 1946, CCF 11-34, RG 48, NA.

run problems, the need to have energy independence in wartime and the desirability of arranging for a smooth transition sooner or later from petroleum and gas back to products of coal and shale, short-term shortages of petroleum repeatedly gave the program a fillip. The cold winter of 1947–48 and attendant oil shortages caused Congress to feel sharp pressure from constituents and led Secretary Krug in January to urge a step-up in synthetic fuels research as an emergency measure.[242] In a special press release on the crisis Krug coupled an appeal for a voluntary "15 per cent reduction in consumption by all users of gasoline, fuel oil and gas" with a call for "intensification of the development of hydrogenation of oil shales and coal to produce synthetic oils."[243] Both Krug and Boyd testified to Congress that the economic security of the country dictated creation of a synthetic liquid fuel industry, and they recommended immediate construction of three commercial-size prototype plants to employ the three known processes: shale oil recovery, hydrogenation of coal, and gas synthesis. Secretary of Defense James Forrestal also testified in support of such a move on security grounds, so Krug emphasized the wider economic implications. But Krug did note that "the establishment of such an industry would be far too large an operation and would require too much time to be undertaken only after a national emergency had arisen. To attempt it then inevitably would result in a repetition of the oft-told tale of 'too little, too late.' "[244]

Secretary Krug was very careful always to stress that it was his "intent to promote the production of synthetic liquid fuels by industry rather than by Government."[245] Nevertheless, it was not difficult to pick up hints of a contrary position. A department memorandum in December 1947 argued that a program by government to develop synthetic fuels on a crash basis comparable to the Manhattan Project could yield a production of 2 million barrels a day within four to five years at a cost of about $10 billion.

242. "Report of Meeting on Synthetic Fuels, Secretary's Office, January 8, 1948," Oil and Gas Division File, Minerals and Fuels Division Files, RG 48, NA.

243. U.S. Department of the Interior, press release, January 15, 1948, Articles File, Ball Papers, HSTL.

244. Statements of J. A. Krug and James Boyd before the Committee on Public Lands of the House of Representatives, February 5, 1948, Synthetic Liquid Fuels File, Cooper Office Files, RG 48, NA.

245. Krug to Congressman Charles A. Wolverton, Chairman of the House Committee on Interstate and Foreign Commerce, March 12, 1948 (commenting on draft legislation to stimulate synfuel development), Synthetic Liquid Fuels File, Minerals and Fuels Division Files, RG 48, NA.

Another scheme, discussed in February 1948, was for the Reconstruction Finance Corporation to assume "all authority and responsibility for promoting a synthetic liquid fuels industry, . . . construction, ownership, and operation of the plants shall be private, if this can be satisfactorily achieved; otherwise public."[246] In any event the petroleum industry, which had sensitive ears in government, quickly became alarmed. *The National Petroleum News,* a trade weekly, complained that the Interior Department had set out "to frighten; to propagandize Congress into taking action now on the grounds that tomorrow may be too late." Inexplicably, it said, the department seemed to be ignoring the Middle East, "the potentialities of the 'tidelands,' " "the Alaskan frontier," probable reserves elsewhere in the western hemisphere, and even the advice of its own Oil and Gas Division director, Max Ball. The paper belittled the security argument for energy independence and implied that synthetic fuels were merely a subtle tactic to enable government to realize the presumed objectives of Harold Ickes years before to develop public presence in the oil market comparable to that in the electric power market.[247] It is difficult to assess the extent to which oil industry pressure affected the subsequent course of events. But the NPC was asked officially for its view on the subject in February 1948,[248] and after the industry criticisms became intense the process of redrafting bills in the Wolverton Committee of the House of Representatives moved distinctly away from major government involvement in the development of the synfuels industry.[249]

In May 1948 the magazine *Modern Industry* invited Secretary Krug to contribute to its "Debate in Print" section on the question "Should the federal government build a synthetic oil industry?" with the negative position to be taken by A. L. Solliday, executive vice-president of Stanolind Oil and Gas Company of Tulsa, Oklahoma, one of the most vigorous critics of the government program.[250] This presented the department with

246. John L. Hofflund to James Boyd, February 17, 1948; see also unsigned memorandum, "Synthetic Liquid Fuels," December 9, 1947; both in ibid.

247. Herbert A. Yocum, "Interior 'Scare' May Put U.S. into Oil Business in Big Way," *National Petroleum News,* January 28, 1948.

248. Max Ball to Walter Hallanan, February 20, 1948, CCF 11-34, RG 48, NA.

249. Memorandum, Evelyn Cooper to Assistant Secretary Davidson, "Synthetic Liquid Fuels Bill," April 7, 1948, Memoranda and Notes for Mr. Davidson File, Cooper Office Files, RG 48, NA.

250. Stanolind and Hydrocol, Inc., were two firms constructing plants in 1948 to make synthetic gasoline from natural gas. H. B. McCoy to the Solicitor, January 24, 1949, Oils-Mineral-General File 312, RG 151, NA.

an enigma. The very topic for the debate, which was akin to "Have you stopped beating your wife?" promised certain defeat. Moreover, any widespread public controversy seemed likely to increase opposition, which Homer Stewart of the Bureau of Mines said consisted currently of only "a relatively small segment of the petroleum industry."[251] One attempted solution was to submit to the magazine a bland article "The Necessity and Urgency for the Production of Synthetic Liquid Fuels in the United States," by James Boyd that minimized the prospective role of government. The debate in print did take place, however.[252]

The vigor of attacks on the synthetics program in the petroleum trade journals and other places led at least a few persons in the private sector to recoil in disgust. In March 1950 a vice-president of the Union Oil Company (which participated with government in the shale program) was so affronted by what he considered unfair criticisms that he offered gallantly to come to the aid of the bureau. "I do know that the work you and your associates have done is something that Industry has not done and would not have done during this period and that, despite the criticism which has been leveled, we are as far ahead in the synthetic field as a result of your work and not from the Industry at large. If you can give me some ammunition, I will be glad to take some of these thin-skinned boys on."[253] Another sympathetic correspondent wrote to Secretary Chapman in June 1950, "From connections with the oil industry I hear the following talk: that the oil industry does actually fear that shale oil can more than compete with higher cost pool oil, that the industry definitely does not want to see such production started, and that it has indeed engaged in a propaganda campaign to prevent any such action by the Federal Government. This has too many earmarks of the truth."[254] Perhaps under pressure from the oilmen to be given an opportunity to express themselves in a public forum, or perhaps with a desire to let the Bureau of Mines face its tormentors fairly and squarely, Secretary Chapman requested the NPC to "create a committee to: (1) review the estimates made by the Bureau of Mines for the cost of producing synthetic liquid fuels and its estimates of comparative costs of producing liquid fuels from crude oil, (2) prepare independent cost estimates, and (3) make recommendations as to ways

251. Stewart to W. C. Schroeder, n.d.; and Harwood F. Merill, Editor of *Modern Industry*, to Julius Krug, May 5, 1948; both in CCF 11-34, RG 48, NA.

252. "Should the Government Build a Synthetic Oil Industry?" "Yes," J. Boyd; "No," A. L. Solliday, *Modern Industry*, July 1948, pp. 100–02, 104, 106, 108.

253. A. C. Rubel to W. C. Schroeder, March 28, 1950, CCF 11-34, RG 48, NA.

254. H. G. Slusser to Oscar Chapman, June 26, 1950, ibid.

and means, if any, for improvement of future cost estimates by the Bureau of Mines."[255]

A growing complication for the Interior Department in presenting arguments for synthetics was that its program continued to have three main processes that were competing for funds: oil recovery from shale, coal hydrogenation, and gas synthesis. All three had accumulated their own constituencies and loyalties within and without the department, and more and more pressures from these constituencies seemed to transcend mere efficiency considerations. In addition some Interior Department staff favored a fourth process—direct conversion of natural gas to liquid fuel, which would help to neutralize the main competitor of coal. Finally, the prospects of public subsidies attracted a variety of inventors to the department who usually went away disgruntled (often via their congressmen) when their ideas were not supported.[256]

The mounting level of petroleum industry complaints about any extension of synfuels research into commercial production, the gradual elimination of shortages, plus a rising level of world tensions by the beginning of President Truman's second term, led the advocates of synfuels to direct their arguments less and less to long-run economic concerns (including relief to the coal industry) and more and more to security.[257] In January

255. Chapman to Walter B. Hallanan, April 21, 1950, ibid.

256. Examples of controversy surrounding synthetic processes not pursued by the Interior Department are discussed in C. Girard Davidson to John Sherman Bagg, February 24, 1948, ibid.; and Davidson to James Boyd, March 12, 1948 (mainly concerning the "Karrick Process," a technique for using coal to produce synfuels), Synthetic Liquid Fuels File, Minerals and Fuels Division Files, RG 48, NA. An appeal by R. R. Sayers to Secretary Krug for a worldwide conference on shale oil in 1948 gives a sense of how this particular process had acquired its own fraternity. Sayers to Krug, February 28, 1947, CCF 11-34, RG 48, NA.

257. Of course, when speaking directly to their coal constituency, Interior Department officials continued to stress the promise of synthetic processes. In December 1949 Secretary Chapman predicted to the coal producers "that tonnage lost in competition with other forms of energy may be regained in the new outlets for your production." (Address to the Meeting of the National Bituminous Coal Council, December 1949, Public Addresses File, Chapman Papers, HSTL.) The conversion of the Commerce Department from proposals to proceed with commercial production of synthetics between 1948 and 1949 probably reflects the change in thinking of the business community. In 1948 in the face of spot shortages of petroleum the department supported legislation to authorize the construction of commercial facilities to produce synthetics on the grounds that demand for petroleum was "expected to increase at a rate more rapid than the discovery and development of crude producing properties" and that the United States needed "to minimize our dependence on foreign sources upon which we might not be able to rely in any period of emergency." (Attachment to memorandum, David Bruce to the Director of the Bureau

1949 Schroeder informed Boyd that the Armed Services Petroleum Board, the Munitions Board, and the NSRB were all in favor of moving into commercial production of synthetics. The armed services were even prepared to enter into long-term contracts for the purchase of outputs at prices above current market levels if this would be a necessary inducement and legislation were introduced to make it possible.[258] In a letter to the NSRB chairman drafted by Schroeder, Secretary Krug pointed out that "reserves of recoverable oil from shale are estimated in excess of 200 billion barrels or about eight times the proved petroleum reserves," and he noted that "the President and Secretary Forrestal will appreciate your opinion regarding both the desirability of an oil shale plant and the existence of legislative authority that will allow the Government to enter into a long term contract to purchase part or all of the output of the plant at the cost of production."[259] Krug was undoubtedly encouraged in his solicitations by a report from Assistant Secretary William Warne that costs of producing shale oil at the Rifle, Colorado, plant had been reduced to $2.50 a barrel and that the time had arrived for "quite forceful action." He may not have given sufficient attention, however, to a "problem" Warne had just discovered—the large amount of water required for the shale process. Warne noted: "In the Colorado River Basin large water demands

---

of the Budget, March 16, 1948, General Correspondence File 104057, Office of the Secretary of Commerce, General Correspondence Files, RG 40, NA.) Only one year later, however, H. B. McCoy, director of Domestic Commerce, wrote: "In the light of the leveling off of the demand for petroleum products and the rapid development of additional supply sources both at home and abroad, particularly in the Middle East, the urgency of such a development has waned considerably. . . . This lesser urgency, even with a recognition of a longer term supply deficit, would seem to warrant a greater faith in the willingness and ability of the petroleum industry to extend its operations into the synthetics field with a minimum of government prodding." Like the petroleum industry itself, he was opposed to government going beyond the "laboratory research and pilot plant operation" stage. McCoy to the Solicitor, June 21, 1949, Oils-Mineral-General File 312, RG 151, NA.

258. Schroeder to James Boyd, January 14, 1949, CCF 11-34, RG 48, NA. Herbert Yocum disputed this conclusion in "Interpreting the Oil News: Military Leaves Krug Holding the Bag on Synthetic Proposal," *National Petroleum News,* April 14, 1948, p. 7. "While at first it [the Defense Department] appeared to think well of the Krug proposal, by mid-March Defense Secretary Forrestal was indicating a less positive attitude. Now, in mid-April, there is quotable evidence that the military mind is definitely made up that the bridging with synthetics of a gap of that size [2,000,000 b/d] between available supply and the peak requirements of a war emergency just isn't in the cards. In other words, implying Mr. Krug has been talking about something impossible of achievement, like building a tower to the moon."

259. Krug to Monrad Wallgren, February 10, 1949, CCF 11-34, RG 48, NA.

could be extremely complicating factors in any development program unless adequate preparations were made. These preparations may include educational work with the State officials and the other prospective water users."[260]

Answers to letters that came into the Interior Department during 1949 asking about progress on synthetic fuels give a good sense of the state of thinking and policy conclusions in the secretary's office as Truman's second term began. To Bernard Baruch, Krug wrote that on the strictest basis none of the processes yet were economical unless costs, such as transportation, were excluded or uncertain revenues from by-products were included.[261] To Congressman Clarence Cannon, Krug wrote that through its research on technology the department was doing its best to create the basis for a competitive industry for this product "to remove the technical barrier which limits the activities of the independent operator in this field."[262] But his statement to an engineering professor with a technical interest in the subject reflected the weight now being placed on the security argument.

In my opinion, a sound national policy will require substantial synthetic oil production within relatively few years. An established synthetic oil industry that could expand as rapidly as needed would be an excellent insurance against wartime shortages and also against excessive peacetime dependence on foreign sources. Ample domestic supplies might also reduce the enormous cost of protecting distant overseas sources and might help prevent future wars.[263]

Upon his appointment as secretary late in 1949 Oscar Chapman reached the same conclusion as Krug that synfuels were not yet commercially viable; hence a move from experimental to commercial stage was not yet practical. James Boyd brought this sad word to the synthetic fuels program:

I have discussed the question of our approach to synthetic fuels with Mr. Chapman. He feels that unless we can definitely demonstrate, beyond all shadow of doubt, that the immediate development of a commercial-sized synthetic fuels industry is needed in the interest of national defense we should not at this moment even discuss the question of that phase of the program. I told him that I could not demonstrate this at the present state of our knowledge. . . . Mr. Chapman very definitely feels that with the present tenor of

260. Warne to Krug, August 9 and 11, 1949, ibid.
261. Krug to Baruch, October 20, 1949, and Baruch to Krug, October 10, 1949, Subject File Cabinet, Secretary of Interior, PSF, HSTL.
262. Krug to Cannon, October 3, 1949, CCF 11-34, RG 48, NA.
263. Krug to Walter G. Whitman, ibid.

Congress, faced with a five and a half billion dollar deficit in an election year, our efforts would be futile and we would not get the support of the White House.[264]

The Korean War Focuses the Debate

The Korean War had contradictory effects on the synfuels program. In positive terms the conflict brought home the dangers of foreign dependence, accentuated by the increase in net dependence on imports after 1948 and the Iranian crisis. In addition the war effort created an increased demand for some by-products of synthetic processes, notably aromatics such as benzene and toluene, and tilted the economic balance slightly forward. Negatively, the conflict made the opportunity costs of expansion of any experimental program much higher. The alternative to building a synthetic plant of unpredictable result now became the construction of some other facility demonstrably valuable to the mobilization for war or even greater exploration for petroleum.

What is most disillusioning about the debate over synthetic fuels that raged within government during the Korean War is that more and more it was conducted by determined special interests making exaggerated claims on all sides. On one side stood the Bureau of Mines, which by 1949 had more than half of its total budget dedicated to the synthetics program.[265] Allies of the bureau were the coal industry, which continued to hope for a shift in comparative advantage toward its product through the development of synfuels technology, and the security and military establishments, which sought both greater energy independence and a reduction in responsibilities to defend the Middle East at a time when crises were welling up all over the globe.[266] Opposing synthetics, the petroleum

264. Boyd to Arno C. Fieldner, November 29, 1949, Department of the Interior, Bureau of Mines File, Doty Papers, HSTL. Soon after becoming secretary Chapman approved a statement embodying his position on synthetics to be used in response to all letters of inquiry to the department. Memorandum, Chapman to Boyd, "Department's Approach to the Development of a Synthetic Fuels Industry," December 19, 1949, Bureau of Mines File, Minerals and Fuels Division Files, RG 48, NA.

265. Bureau of Mines, "Budget Program—1950 Summarized," Bureau of Mines Budget File, Craine Correspondence Files, RG 48, NA.

266. Because most of the Defense Department documents remain classified for the Korean War the military position must be presumed from various general comments. For example, Rear Admiral Burton B. Biggs, chief of the Petroleum Division of the Department of Defense, testified to the Paley Commission: "From a direct military standpoint, I think the more you can develop these techniques and get the

industry grew more agitated and implacable as the years went on. The industry's voice, the National Petroleum Council, was given increased status after 1950 by its participation in the war effort. In addition the Petroleum Administration for Defense was a government platform from which oilmen could express themselves directly on synthetics.[267] What the situation lacked was a strong and effective third party able to judge among the competing claims and to make firm policy recommendations with the broad public interest at heart.

The Bureau of Mines moved quickly to make its case that the Korean emergency at last provided the trigger for the experimental program to "go commercial." Boyd wrote to Chapman in January 1951 recommending construction of two 15,000-barrel-a-day coal hydrogenation plants, which would cost $326 million and point the way to "ultimate self-sufficiency in liquid fuels." He observed that the Defense Production Act of 1950 authorized such construction and noted candidly "we have awaited a timely moment to push this development. In view of the national emergency, that time appears at hand." He predicted optimistically that "guaranteed loans for the two coal-hydrogenation plants could be repaid, including 3 percent interest in 11½ years with an annual gross profit thereafter of $36 million."[268]

---

bugs out the better it is. But the timing is something else again. It will not help the military over the short period. For the long period, we should find out all we can. Our feeling in the Defense Department is that shale is the most interesting because it can be used for energy in no other form. Coal and gas can be used in their existing form and shale cannot. Our general feeling is that the shale business is more nearly economic, it is not usable otherwise and we have 100 billion barrels more or less." (Minutes, Liquid Fuels Meeting, November 2, 1951, p. 19, Liquid Fuels Meeting File, PMPC, HSTL.) The NSRB records indicate that the board favored moving forward both with the hydrogenation process because of the "chemical by-product possibilities," and shale because of the "indicated supply requirements" and evidence that it could become "a vital complement to the nation's underground oil reserves." Memorandum, Jack O. Gorrie to C. A. Moe, "Appraisal of the Synthetic Liquid Fuels Program and the Need for Extension of Synthetic Liquid Fuels Act," August 9, 1950; and Charles Rayner to Thomas R. Baldwin, January 18, 1951, File 51-11, Records of the National Security Resources Board, RG 304, NA.

267. Bruce Brown, PAD deputy administrator, attacked the synthetics program just as its expansion was being advocated, in a memorandum to Secretary Chapman in July 1951. He denied that a shortage of petroleum was imminent, but even if it were, he argued, coal hydrogenation was a peculiarly uneconomic alternative. Brown to Chapman, July 30, 1951, CCF 11-34, RG 48, NA.

268. Memorandum, Boyd to Chapman, "Defense Expansion of Productive Capacity for Liquid Fuels," n.d. (cover note to copy to Dale E. Doty, January 15, 1951), Department of Interior, Bureau of Mines File, Doty Papers, HSTL.

In July 1951 the secretary of the interior went even further than Boyd proposed. He requested the Defense Production Administration to allot borrowing power up to $455 million to cover synthetic liquid fuels projects of all kinds, with funds to be used mainly to provide financial incentives to private industry to construct fuel plants. Discussions began at the same time with the investment banking firm of F. Eberstadt and Company about the possibility of a price guarantee by government for the outputs of a proposed coal hydrogenation plant.[269] The prospect of substantial funds becoming available at last for synthetic fuel production drew the attention of those influential members of Congress who hoped for facilities to be constructed in their districts. It also brought one of the few direct interventions from the President into the synthetics program in behalf of "my good friend Harley O. Staggers" and the experimental station in Morgantown, West Virginia.[270]

The Interior Department announcement of its wish to expand dramatically its synthetic activities was to the petroleum industry like a red rag to a bull. In response to an agitated letter, Secretary Chapman wrote to the chairman of the NPC Committee on Synthetic Liquid Fuels Production Costs that in the case of shale, at least, "You may disagree with me as to the timing or as to the details of financing, but I honestly cannot see how you can disagree with the basic philosophy."[271] In this Chapman was very overoptimistic. The whole idea of a government role in commercial production of synthetics was roundly denounced by industry leaders. During Senate hearings on a national fuel policy in March 1951 Robert E. Wilson, chairman of the Board of Standard Oil of Indiana, was asked if the nation should encourage the development of a "supplementary supply of fuel." He replied: "If you mean by 'encouragement' doing research, by all means we should and are. If you mean building plants prematurely before this discovery curve turns down, taking steel, manpower, mining labor, and other things that are desperately needed in time of emergency

269. Robert R. Rose to Senator Robert S. Kerr, August 29, 1951; and Rose to Manly Fleischmann, September 8, 1951; both in CCF 11-34, RG 48, NA.
270. The President to Director of the Budget Frederick J. Lawton, April 14, 1951, Office Files of the Director, Bureau of the Budget, RG 51, NA. Examples of communications between prominent legislators concerning the interests of their constituents in synthetics are Paul H. Douglas to Oscar L. Chapman, August 5, 1952, and Chapman to Mike Mansfield, August 21, 1952, both in CCF 11-34, RG 48, NA; and Henry M. Jackson to Frederick J. Lawton, February 18, 1952, Office Files of the Director, Bureau of the Budget, RG 51, NA.
271. Chapman to William S. S. Rodgers, October 30, 1951, CCF 11-34, RG 48, NA.

and diverting them to that, no. If 10 years from now we should find this discovery rate was slowing up, maybe we should then." Paul Kayser, president of the Independent Natural Gas Association said: "There is no point in spending that money displacing sources of supply and retarding the development that is going on."[272]

As time went on the industry position hardened into three main points. Above all, the market should be allowed to handle the transition between fuel sources. Any attempt to interfere with this process would be enormously wasteful of resources. The possibility was not discussed that industries producing different fuels might face different levels of market competition or unequal treatment from government in the form of taxation and direct and indirect subsidies, and that therefore their relative comparative advantages might not be all that real. Second, the industry argued that it could take care of the nation's security needs almost no matter what the crisis. The work of the NPC "million-barrel committee," which set out to show how domestic production could be increased if necessary, was testimony to this capacity. Moreover, it was evident that it would take a decade to build a substantial synthetics industry, and this was a long way over the normal security horizon. Third, the industry argued, the Bureau of Mines had grossly misrepresented the real costs of synthetics and the waste of resources in premature conversion would be much greater than was predicted.

The synthetics question by 1951 boiled down to a dispute over costs. If the costs were too great the issue of government manufacture would become academic. But the estimates were not very satisfactory. The first elaborate set was prepared in 1948 by the Bechtel Corporation under contract from the Bureau of Mines. A revision in 1949 by the bureau led to optimistic claims in 1951 that synthetics were ready to go commercial with a cost of gasoline from hydrogenation and shale of about 11 cents a gallon. Unhappiness with these calculations was not confined to the oil industry. In August 1951 Louis C. McCabe, chief of the Fuels and Explosives Division of the Bureau of Mines and nominally responsible for the Synthetic Fuels Program, drafted a remarkably bitter letter to Secretary Chapman criticizing the program and W. C. Schroeder, its chief. He reported that from its inception "the pilot plant and development program have not followed sound principles and to some extent have ignored the

272. Both the Wilson and the Kayser statements appear in *National Fuel Reserves and Fuel Policy,* Hearings before the Senate Committee on Interior and Insular Affairs Pursuant to S. Res. 239, 82 Cong. 1 sess. (GPO, 1951), p. 36.

advice of the Bureau's research organization. . . . the multimillion dollar programs have not received the critical scrutiny that should be given them." McCabe claimed credit for initiating the NPC study in 1950, and now he called for an impartial outside inquiry by the National Academy of Sciences. This would help to guide the public debate, he argued, as well as the Interior Department's own policy formation. "Since the very start the information released to the public on the synthetic fuels program has been premature and exaggerated. Hardly was a new idea born before the results wished for were released to the country as accomplished fact. Many of these ideas have proved to be very sterile seed under the acid test of the laboratory and demonstration plant. But still there is pre-guessing of research with voodoo, viscera, and voice."[273]

Undoubtedly, with the bitterness of this attack in the background in August 1951, Lawrence E. Imhoff of the secretariat staff submitted to Robert R. Rose, assistant secretary for Mineral Resources, a memorandum calling for a new look at the "objectives, technology, economics, government support, government-industry relationships, specific authority and obstacles" facing the synthetics program.[274] In justifying this proposed research to Under Secretary Richard D. Searles, Rose explained: "Although our various staff members in the Bureau of Mines have the information regarding synthetic liquid fuels in their heads, there is yet no document available containing the information necessary to the actual negotiation of contracts with private industry regarding the erection of synthetic liquid fuel plants both in the oil field and coal-hydrogenation field."[275] This sense of doubt in the Interior Department secretariat, coupled with confidence in the synthetics program that the program could stand any kind of scrutiny in the context of national need, ushered in a period of more external reviews for synthetics.[276] The first appeal from the department for external perspective was made to the Paley Commission, which by the autumn of 1951 was well along with its investigations. Secre-

273. McCabe to Chapman, August 13, 1951, marked "draft," Synthetic Liquid Fuels File, Searles Office Files, RG 48, NA.

274. The substance of the Imhoff memorandum is attached to another memorandum, Rose to Chapman, September 5, 1951, Synthetic Fuels Program File, Rose Office Files, RG 48, NA.

275. Rose to Searles, August 16, 1951, Synthetic Liquid Fuels File, Searles Office Files, RG 48, NA.

276. Schroeder's general sense of optimism was expressed in a memorandum to Assistant Secretary Rose, "Department's Program for Initiating Commercial Synthetic Fuels Plants," September 12, 1951, Synthetic Fuels Program File, Rose Office Files, RG 48, NA.

tary Chapman wrote to William Paley asking for the following information:

An evaluation of the need for a supplement to our domestic liquid fuels supplies. This evaluation should indicate the probable time factor involved if the matter of supplementing liquid fuels supplies is left to the initiative of private industry, based entirely on economic or production cost factors. Further, this evaluation should show whether or not this economic or cost time factor would be adequate to meet security demands.

In view of national security considerations and the cost or economics of the situation, would it be in the best interest of the country for the Government to encourage the establishment of a synthetic liquid fuels industry on an accelerated time table?

The effect of tax exemptions, particularly depletion allowances, on the supplies of the various fuels, and the importance of similar or other tax exemptions on the development of a synthetic liquid fuels industry.[277]

In reply to what were certainly important questions Paley merely suggested that some of the larger issues would be treated in a general way in the commission's report.[278] A memorandum by Paley Commission staff member Cornelius J. Dwyer indicates that the commission was at least as confused as Chapman was by the competing claims. Dwyer speculated about the possible shift in comparative costs that might occur between synthetic and natural oil if such favored treatment to the petroleum industry as percentage depletion were eliminated, and he regretted that the "Domestic Resources" staff of the Commission "did not see fit" to look into this question more carefully.[279]

The long-awaited NPC report on synthetics was submitted in October 1951. The NPC had been asked by the Interior Department secretary to review the Bureau of Mines cost estimates in April 1950 even before the Korean War began. It reported now at a crucial moment for the program, and with devastating results. The NPC calculated that gasoline from the hydrogenation process would cost approximately 41.4 cents a gallon compared with the 11.0 cents estimated by the Bureau of Mines. NPC estimates for shale were between 14 cents and 16 cents, or only a few cents above those of the bureau. The differences in both cases were explained largely by the NPC inclusion of certain costs not mentioned by the bureau,

277. Chapman to Paley, October 1, 1951, CCF 11-34, RG 48, NA.
278. Paley to Chapman, November 28, 1951, ibid.
279. C. J. Dwyer to Robert Blum, October 31, 1951, General File Energy–Oil and Gas, PMPC, HSTL. The Paley Commission's discussion of synthetic fuels and the potential demand for them is in PMPC, *Resources for Freedom*, vol. 4, *The Promise of Technology*, pp. 171–85.

such as the expenses of worker housing, and the exclusion of certain revenues, such as sales of chemical by-products that, the NPC argued, could not be counted on confidently.[280]

The Bureau of Mines had anticipated the NPC report by issuing its own, "Cost Estimates for Coal Hydrogenation," the previous week.[281] This publication was then superseded by another report of November 19, 1951, and various other internal documents attacking the NPC assumptions and methods and arriving invariably at projections of profitability.[282] The industry in turn denounced these new efforts. Wilson of Standard Oil wrote to Assistant Secretary Rose: "It is my opinion that the Bureau of Mines has greatly understated costs, both operating and investment, and overstated the income. Further, the Bureau of Mines does not recognize that a synthetic fuel plant must be financed as a speculative venture and must offer sufficient profits to attract the necessary capital."[283] Bruce Brown told the Paley Commission impatiently that the choice posed by synthetics was simple: "To me, only one of two things can be done. Either you have to go into an enormous government subsidy operation to bring out the oil before it is needed or wait."[284] Eugene Ayres, who had long been involved with Gulf Oil research on synthetics, even offered a timetable for when synfuels would become profitable. "The exploitation of oil shale can be expected to mature by 1965, but since oil shale cannot sup-

280. I have not been able to discover a copy of the NPC report of October 31, 1951. Its conclusions, however, are summarized in "Internal Report of the National Petroleum Council's Committee on Synthetic Liquid Fuels Production Costs," January 29, 1952, CCF 1-188, RG 48, NA.

281. This Bureau of Mines report is summarized in ibid.

282. An eleven-page report, "Synthetic Fuels," December 7, 1951, prepared at the Louisiana, Mo., demonstration plant, concluded that with favorable tax treatment comparable to that of petroleum, a high debt-to-equity ratio, some predictable technical improvements, credit for by-products, sensible location, and sufficient scale, a coal hydrogenation plant could be expected to yield 10 percent profit on investment. (CCF 11-34, RG 48, NA.) For a useful summary of progress and opportunities for the future with coal hydrogenation as seen from the Bureau of Mines in 1952, see L. C. Skinner, "Progress in Coal Hydrogenation," *Gasification and Liquefaction of Coal* (American Institute of Mining and Metallurgical Engineers, 1953). A mission of European scientists that visited American installations in 1952 under the auspices of the Mutual Security Agency recommended close Euro-American cooperation in all further development of coal synthetics. See Organisation for European Co-operation and Development, *The Gasification of Coal, Underground Gasification, Gasification of Mined Coal* (Paris: OECD, 1953).

283. Wilson to Rose, November 30, 1951, CCF 11-34, RG 48, NA.

284. Liquid Fuels Meeting, November 2, 1951, Liquid Fuels Meeting File, PMPC, HSTL.

ply (at reasonable cost) more than a small part of our annual demand for energy, it will be essential to have some sort of utilization of coal well under way by 1970 and operating on a tremendous scale by 1980."[285] In January 1952 the NPC Synthetic Liquid Fuels Production Cost Committee issued another report setting forth in detail what it called the errors of the Bureau of Mines report of November 1951 and analyzing the differences between this report and its own.[286]

Perhaps partly in desperation the Interior Department secretariat decided to appoint an entirely independent third party—a firm called Ebasco Services, Inc., of New York—to "reconcile the more significant differences" between the Bureau of Mines and the NPC. Assistant Secretary Rose conceded to Senator Lester C. Hunt in February 1952: "It is doubtful if complete reconciliation ever can be accomplished, since we are dealing with a problem that is largely hypothetical in nature. . . . my study of the two sets of estimates convinces me that very substantial differences can be attributed to honest differences of opinion. It may be that some of these will remain unresolved until such time as a coal-hydrogenation plant actually is built, although it is my hope that the work done by Ebasco may shed some light upon the matter."[287] In fact, Ebasco arrived at a position about halfway between the NPC and the bureau, predicting that gasoline from hydrogenation could sell at about 28 cents a gallon. Still another private firm, Ford, Bacon and Davis, carried out a study in 1952 on the synthetic liquid fuel potential of the United States under contract with the Army Corps of Engineers. But this report too was inconclusive and raised the wrath of those most closely involved in the Interior Department who by this time objected to all commentaries that did not come out rosy.[288]

The delay caused by the dispute over the real costs of synthetics into 1952 was sufficient to kill the move initiated in 1950 to begin commercial production. By mid-1952 the crisis in Korea seemed to be abating and the petroleum industry seemed to be coping with demands for liquid fuels

285. Ayres to Robert Blum, December 20, 1951, General File–Consumption of Energy, PMPC, HSTL.

286. "Interim Report of the National Petroleum Council's Committee on Synthetic Liquid Fuels Production Costs," January 29, 1952, CCF 1-188, RG 48, NA.

287. Rose to Hunt, February 14, 1952, CCF 11-34, ibid.

288. For example, Bonneville Power Administrator Paul J. Raver to Secretary Chapman, February 18, 1952, Synthetic Fuels Program File, Rose Office Files, RG 48, NA. Summaries of the Ebasco report, "Bureau of Mines Estimates for Synthetic Liquid Fuels Production by the Hydrogenation Process," and the Ford, Bacon, and Davis report, "The Synthetic Liquid Fuel Potential of the United States," are in this file.

very nicely, albeit with increasing dependence on the Middle East. Also, by this date the end of the Truman presidency was drawing near, and the time had clearly passed for the commencement of a large new program that would not bear fruit for many years. The extent to which officials in the White House had lost interest in the subject of synthetic fuels by 1952 may be illustrated by the response to a letter of inquiry about progress with the program. Truman's aide, Matthew J. Connelly, replied to the letter that he had no knowledge of the subject and suggested the inquirer try the Federal Reserve Board!

The Korean War and the years immediately before it illustrated an important feature of the relationship between threats to security and the development of synthetic fuels. During the time of crisis synfuels development would have required a serious commitment of scarce resources for a payoff that was at least five to ten years ahead, by which time the crisis would probably have passed. During the periods of normalcy, on the other hand, the urgency was absent for a resource commitment of any kind.

The debate throughout the Truman presidency over whether to proceed with commercial development of synthetic liquid fuels with some form of government encouragement may be seen in retrospect as enormously important in American history. With the Truman administration, the idea died and the United States continued to increase its dependence on imported petroleum with results that are now well known. It is far from clear whether different actions should have been taken. But it is crystal clear that the process of reaching decisions was far from satisfactory. The dispute was left mainly in the hands of those interests most directly involved—the Interior Department synfuels staff, whose future depended on the continuation of the program, and the petroleum industry, which felt seriously threatened by public encouragement of a potential competitor. The real costs and benefits were never set forth clearly and fairly by either party. Not only were senior staff members of the Interior Department confused and uncertain, but Congress and the public seldom heard more than occasional extravagant, self-interested pronouncements. Even the best calculations that were made seldom contained persuasive analyses of demand and supply elasticities for outputs and inputs, estimates of the effects of technical change, and the external costs of environmental damage in different processes. It would have been far from easy for the Truman administration to present the American people with a good guess about the cost of increasing the country's energy independence through synthetics and anticipating the transition away from the increasingly inadequate domestic petroleum reserves. But it never even came close.

Electric Power

Without doubt electric power was the energy source that presented the new president in 1945 with the most complex history and set of policies and related institutions. The federal government had been in the power business in one way or another for more than half a century at the time he took office—at least from the first Reclamation Act of 1902, by which Congress authorized the construction of multipurpose projects involving the production of hydroelectric power among other goals. A torrent of legislation followed this beginning, with standards set for construction and loans for construction, criteria established for sale of products, and terms laid down for relations among public and private institutions. A high point of legislative specification came with the Federal Water Power Act of 1920.

Power to the People

It has been suggested that electric power development throughout American history has been influenced by three often contradictory "thrusts": for development, for a "progressive" society, and for conservation. The developmental role perceived for electric power was essentially a continuation of that function designated for canals and railways in earlier times. It justified government participation in the industry on the ground that power was an essential prerequisite to economic growth. Progressive doctrine, on the other hand, implied that government must intervene in the production of power so as to protect the consumer and constrain rapacious monopolies. This objective might be accomplished either by public ownership (at the municipal, state, or federal levels and including projects to establish "yardstick" costs) or through regulation of private enterprise. Finally, conservationists proposed a place for government in the power field to help preserve the nation's depleting natural resources. Conservationists such as Gifford Pinchot and Senator George W. Norris favored maximum development of hydroelectric projects because they would reduce the use of exhaustible resources: petroleum, coal, and gas.[289] The production of hydroelectric output from dams was inextricably linked with such related issues as land reclamation, irrigation, flood control, national defense, regional development and cost sharing among levels of government. For example, an important principle, expressed as early as the Reclamation Act of 1906 and repeated in such later legislation as the Raker Act of 1922, the Boulder Canyon Project Act of 1928, and the Tennessee Valley Authority Act of 1933, was that preference in the sale of power from federal projects should be given to municipalities, other public bodies, and cooperatives. In fact, the inclusion of power generation in multiple-purpose projects often reflected more the desires of irrigation interests to reduce their net costs than the need to produce more electricity in the public interest. In consequence decisions about electricity production and distribution frequently reflected objectives and pressures unrelated to the provision of energy.

During the 1930s when many political leaders active in the 1940s and 1950s were getting their start, including President Truman and Interior Secretary Chapman, at least three important elements were present in electric power policy. These survived well into the Truman administration. First, cheap power was perceived as an exceptionally important tool of economic revival in the short run as well as for economic development in the long run. That the best price for energy, at least electric energy, was a low one became a standard piece of dogma within government. Cheap electric power, it was argued, might save the small farmer, the small community, and even American democracy. The apparent inconsistency between this invitation to profligate use and the call for conservation was

289. See Henry P. Caulfield, Jr., "The Living Past in Federal Power Policy," *Resources for the Future Annual Report 1959*, pp. 24–33; and Philip J. Funigiello, *Toward a National Power Policy: The New Deal and the Electric Utility Industry, 1933–1941* (University of Pittsburg Press, 1973). The memorandum prepared at the end of President Truman's second term for the incoming Eisenhower administration, "Development and Marketing of Hydroelectric Power under Multiple-Purpose Projects Authorized by Congress," January 6, 1953, provides a good capsule history of the subject during his presidency and before. A copy is in Reports and Recommendations on Departmental Programs File, Office Files of the Program Staff, RG 48, NA. FPC activities during the Truman administration are discussed in Gale E. Peterson, "President Harry S. Truman and the Independent Regulatory Commissions, 1945–1952" (Ph.D. dissertation, University of Maryland, 1973). For a history and discussion of the Bureau of Reclamation, probably the most important participant in public power development, by one of its former staff members and an assistant secretary in the Truman administration, see William Warne, *The Bureau of Reclamation* (Praeger, 1973). Warne complained that the bureau had been "hounded by theoretical economists who would reduce most political considerations to mathematical formulas" (p. 218).

resolved by an assertion that hydroelectric power went to waste if not consumed, and coal, the customary backup fuel, could be produced with labor that otherwise would be unemployed in such depressed areas as Appalachia. That is, the opportunity cost of public power in resource terms was thought to be very low. Moreover, the attractiveness of the doctrine of low-cost public power as an engine of growth was not confined to such stricken regions as the Tennessee Valley. Increasingly the western and plains states as well as farmers everywhere came to believe that the constraint on their own growth might be the availability of power at reasonable rates. The political coalition of many elements was an important basis of support for Roosevelt's power policies as it would become for those of Truman.

Understandably the main critics of the doctrine of low power rates were private utilities and producers of rival fuels who complained that they were treated unfairly because their competitors were subsidized with tax money. They objected to the creation of what they said was an artificial advantage for one energy source over another. One spokesman for coal estimated in 1945 that "every man employed in hydroelectric power plants displaces over 200 men in the mining industry and an unknown number in transportation and related industries."[290]

The second element in electric energy policy in the 1930s was the concept of regional planning, usually around a river valley system. For this concept TVA was the shining example. In part, adherence to the idea of regional planning came from an appreciation that full-scale national planning was simply not a practical possibility in the late years of the New Deal. The notions of river basin management and regional power develop-

290. Charles H. Hayes, "Regulations Limiting the Industrial Use of Competitive Sources of Energy are Desirable in the Public Interest," paper presented to the Post-War Resources Institute, November 5–9, 1945, Post-War Resources Institute File, Wolfsohn Papers, HSTL. Stephen Spingarn, during the controversy over the FTC oil cartel report in 1952–53, suggested that the nearest equivalent to the oil company activities at that time was the "nation-wide propaganda campaign of the electric and gas utility companies, 1919–1934." The summary of the FTC's report on this subject together with Spingarn's comments on it is in Investigation of Private Power File, Spingarn Papers, HSTL. A news account of an incident when private power and coal spokesmen joined to condemn public power projects just after President Truman took office appeared in the *New York Times,* July 5, 1945. Stephen Raushenbush from the Division of Power replied to the coal industry critics of hydroelectricity in a paper, "Is Any Limitation on the Development of Hydro-Electric Energy in Competition with Coal Desirable in the National Interest and If So How Much?" presented to the Post-War Resources Institute, November 5–9, 1945, Post-War Resources Institute File, Wolfsohn Papers, HSTL.

ment had roots stretching well back before the Roosevelt years, with inspiration from, among other places, the Canadian province of Ontario. But in the 1930s the time was ripe for the idea to flourish. Not only did the president himself lose enthusiasm for bigger planning ideas in his second term, but debates over the notion, with charges of communism and authoritarianism flying in all directions, were bruising and divisive. The concept of planning within small regional units as well as the notion of progress through technology appealed most widely to many American liberal reformers who, with their deep populist origins, believed that true freedom could come only with independence from eastern commercial interests and from Washington.

David E. Lilienthal, TVA chairman, expressed the philosophy of valley development with eloquence and fervor in his book *TVA: Democracy on the March*. In a "statement of faith" at the beginning he explained: "I believe men may learn to work in harmony with the forces of nature, neither despoiling what God has given nor helpless to put them to use. I believe in the great potentialities for well-being of the machine and technology and science; and though they do hold a real threat of enslavement and frustration for the human spirit, I believe those dangers can be averted." In an author's note Lilienthal replied specifically to those who charged that valley authorities were simply a means to increase big government. "TVA is an effective effort to decentralize the functioning of the federal government, to reverse the trend toward centralization of power in Washington, to delegate, dilute, and withdraw federal power *out of Washington* and back into the regions and states and localities, insofar as the development of natural resources is concerned."[291] As Senator from Missouri, Truman had supported the strengthening of the TVA and the idea of extending the principles elsewhere. During the late 1930s the National Resources Planning Board attempted to arrange for some consistency among the various river basin plans, but especially after the board's demise in 1943 this problem of coordination remained unsolved.

291. David E. Lilienthal, *TVA: Democracy on the March* (Harper, 1953), pp. xiv and xxii (emphasis in original). TVA waged an extended battle with the Budget Bureau over the extent to which it should be treated as an independent unit different from other government agencies—a practice with which the bureau had little sympathy. See memorandum, Frederick J. Lawton to Clark M. Clifford, "Tennessee Valley Authority," November 8, 1946; and Lilienthal to Clifford, September 27, 1946 (both in Tennessee Valley Authority File, Files of Clark Clifford, HSTL); and Gordon R. Clapp to Clifford, December 12, 1947, Tennessee Valley Authority File, James E. Webb Papers, HSTL.

The third element in power policy was an old theme that simply became more accentuated in the 1930s: the need for strict regulation of private utilities by strong legislation and effective regulatory authorities. Reformist doctrine on the subject of hydroelectric power had its origin in the ideas of such early writers on resource questions as Henry George and John Stuart Mill. Waterpower, like arable land, was fixed in finite amount by nature. Moreover, it seemed only right and proper both that this resource be used to the full and that increasing rents that would flow to it with economic growth should be shared by all the people. Full use and distributional equity could be achieved either through public ownership or by strict regulation. Roosevelt made utility regulation an important part of his legislative programs while governor of New York State, and he carried this into the presidency. He also brought along from New York Leland Olds who, as FPC chairman, established a strong adversarial relationship with the private power companies.[292] The regulatory thrust of government toward the power companies, of course, went well beyond FPC actions. In addition to forces in the Interior Department that questioned the appropriateness of any hydroelectric construction by private enterprise, the industry came under scrutiny from the FTC, the Justice Department, and above all the SEC under terms of the Public Utility Holding Company Act of 1935, which was designed to reduce large concentrations of power.

It is debatable whether Roosevelt ever hoped to achieve a consistent and comprehensive federal power policy. It is certain he did not succeed. Instead, he left a hodgepodge of policies, some overlapping and others inconsistent, for example, some aimed at conservation and others at increased use, some to promote competition and others to limit it.

In consequence of this complex legacy from earlier administrations President Truman found himself with an extremely confusing situation in electric power. The institutions themselves were bewildering in their complexity. As in the case of other energy sources, the Interior Department had the major responsibility. Three units in the department disposed of substantial amounts of power from various public projects: the Bureau of Reclamation, which built and operated plants in various parts of the country; the Bonneville Power Administration (BPA), which marketed power from Grand Coulee, Bonneville, and other dams; and the South-

292. See, for example, the celebratory memorandum from Olds to Roosevelt describing the long road of regulatory reform they had traveled together, "Victory of Program Outlined in Your 1930 Utility Messages," June 10, 1944, Federal Power Commission File, Clifford Files, HSTL.

western Power Administration, disposing of output in the Missouri, Arkansas, Oklahoma, Texas area. A Southeastern Power Administration was created in the department in 1950. Beyond the Interior Department a variety of other agencies were vitally concerned with electric power: TVA, which reported directly to Congress; the FPC for the approval of construction and rate schedules; the Army Corps of Engineers in the construction of some projects; and the Rural Electrification Administration of the Department of Agriculture for power needs of farmers—to name only the most important.

In 1944, well before the war's end and in anticipation of a return to depression, Congress provided for a large postwar program of new multipurpose projects including power production. The Flood Control Act of 1944 (16 U.S.C. 8253) stated congressional policy in general terms and in the process enunciated two principles that were to be the subject of controversy throughout the Truman presidency. First, "Electric power and energy generated at reservoir projects . . . shall be delivered to the Secretary of the Interior, who shall transmit and dispose of such power and energy in such manner as to encourage the most widespread use thereof at the lowest possible rates to consumers consistent with sound business principles . . . including the amortization of the capital investment allocated to power over a reasonable period of years." And second, "The Secretary of the Interior is authorized, from funds to be appropriated by the Congress, to construct or acquire, by purchase or other agreement, only such transmission lines and related facilities as may be necessary in order to make the power and energy generated at said projects available in wholesale quantities for sale on fair and reasonable terms and conditions to facilities owned by the Federal Government, public bodies, cooperatives, and privately owned companies." The major unanswered issue behind these principles was whether the federal government had a fundamental responsibility to plan for the provision of adequate electric power for the American people or whether it should be merely a wholesale marketer of electric energy produced as a by-product of other activities.

During the Roosevelt administration there had been some attempts to achieve coordination and rationalization among the diverse policies and institutions related to electric power, but not many. It seems that the existence of overlapping, competitive, and even conflicting government units appealed both to Roosevelt and to Secretary of the Interior Ickes. In 1934 Roosevelt did create a National Power Policy Committee, which was "not to be merely a fact-finding body, but rather one for the development and unification of a national power policy."[293] But to the continuing frustration of orderly-minded public servants in the power field this body did no serious work after an initial report on public utility holding companies, even though it remained in existence nominally right into the Truman presidency.[294]

In the absence of wider governmental planning and coordination with respect to electricity the secretary of the interior in 1941 established his own Division of Power charged to cooperate with the Bureau of Reclamation to review contracts for the sale of power and plans for new projects and to make recommendations on these subjects to the secretary, also to make arrangements for distribution and sale of power and to conduct studies of various matters related to power development.[295]

A Branch of Economics and Statistics established in the division became the strongest analytical unit in the department. Among other functions the branch prepared statements of policy and principle on such important issues as river valley development and the related "regionalization" of the staff and administration.[296] By 1943 the success of the Division of Power in helping "to reconcile power policy between the different units of the Department, and between those agencies and other power divisions of the Government" was used to support the case for a wider

293. Wolfsohn to Ickes, March 2, 1936, Memos to Secretary Ickes File, Wolfsohn Papers, HSTL.

294. In Wolfsohn's memorandum to Secretary Ickes of March 2, 1936, he wrote that the following problems cried out for attention by the committee: "unification of the supply of current, the relations between public and private facilities, the feasibility of the common carrier principle in electricity, standardization of the national rate structure, cooperation with State commissions, the extent to which projects for flood control and navigation should provide for power, and rural electrification. Others could be enumerated. Also there is no central clearing house to gather all information relating to power, sort it and draw conclusions to help create an intelligent and continuing national power policy." Wolfsohn estimated that as he wrote, "at least fifteen regular and emergency Federal agencies are directly or indirectly concerned with electric power."

295. A plan of work for the new division was submitted to Secretary Ickes by Acting Director Abe Fortas in an undated memorandum to be found in Department Program—War File, Branch of Economics and Statistics Files, RG 48, NA.

296. In a memorandum for Wolfsohn, April 4, 1946, Stephen Raushenbush provided a chronology of "documents relating to the regionalization idea" going back to 1942. Elsewhere in the Regionalization File, Branch of Economics and Statistics Files, RG 48, NA, are essays with such titles as "Regional Development" and "The Conservation Council." In a memorandum of April 29, 1946, Ivan Bloch summarized for Raushenbush and Ellsworth the arguments "for better planning, programming, and execution of governmental activities within any region." Minerals Program File, Craine Correspondence Files, RG 48, NA.

"Centralized Research, Planning and Coordinating Agency in the Department of the Interior." Indeed "the fact that the Power Division has been used to make economic studies of special problems involving resource use beyond the immediate realm of power demonstrates the existence of a need, so far not clearly articulated, for a similar agency of broader scope."[297] Some concession to wider coordination outside the Interior Department was made by the White House in 1943 with the formation of the Federal Inter-Agency River Basin Committee, whose membership initially included the Corps of Engineers, the Bureau of Reclamation, the Federal Power Commission, and the Department of Agriculture.[298]

One especially interesting proposal for greater coordination of electric power policies that grew out of the Division of Power experience was for a Bureau of Power to take over all the complex power-related activities in the department and thereby "avoid injurious competition between the agencies in the Department charged with the management and disposal of electric power." In proposing this new bureau to Secretary Ickes, Joel Wolfsohn acknowledged that he was "aware of the complexity of the power situation." But he appealed all the same for congressional action that would both achieve unification in the new bureau and establish a Congressional "standing Committee on Power."[299]

The proposed new bureau was not created, nor did the Division of Power continue to develop and grow as a centralizing and coordinating agency as its advocates had hoped. In February 1945 K. S. Wingfield, chief of the division's Branch of Marketing and Operations, proposed a reorganization into separate line and staff units that he believed would increase effectiveness. The former would be called Program Management and the latter Program Development. Both branches would be headed by engineers, but Program Development would have two staff economists "capable of doing original research and planning."[300] In May 1945 Stephen Raushenbush, chief of the Branch of Economics and Statistics, reported that although "theoretically sound," the Wingfield reorganiza-

297. "Memorandum Regarding a Centralized Research, Planning and Coordinating Agency in the Department of the Interior," n.d., attached to memorandum, William Warne to Michael Straus, January 7, 1943, Planning and Coordinating Division File, Branch of Economics and Statistics Files, RG 48, NA.

298. Memorandum, C. D. Curran to the Files, "Federal Inter-Agency River Basin Committee," December 13, 1946, Office Files of the Director, Records of the Bureau of the Budget, RG 51, NA.

299. Memorandum, Wolfsohn to Ickes, January 4, 1945, Power Organization File, Wolfsohn Papers, HSTL.

300. Memorandum, K. S. Wingfield to Arthur Goldschmidt, February 19, 1945, ibid.

tion was not to be and that in fact his own branch was not being given sufficient staff to accomplish even the assignments it already had.[301]

It is difficult to be certain just why the Division of Power failed to evolve as a central planning mechanism; the explanation may simply lie with the personalities. It appears, however, that apart from a few far-sighted persons in or close to the secretary's office, such as Fortas, Wolfsohn, and Raushenbush, the idea of centralization had little appeal. Even for Ickes and Roosevelt tight organization was contrary to their administrative styles of divide and rule. For Congress, centralization was especially threatening. One of the features of decentralized electric power policy and administration was that individual congressmen could easily have direct access to and a close relationship with the administrative units that were of special interest to their constituents.[302] In addition some of Ickes' imperialistic actions concerning power, such as abortive attempts in 1945 and 1946 to take the Rural Electrification Administration away from the Department of Agriculture and analytical functions from the FPC, undoubtedly caused people who otherwise might not have opposed reorganization of his own department to stand in the way of all actions that might increase the Interior Department's potential expansionary power.[303] In any event the analytical functions of the division did not develop. Raushenbush left to take a job with the new United Nations, and other department reformers turned to the Coordination Committee and the idea of a Program Staff as a more promising means to gain perspective and coordinated central direction.[304] In addition, at the suggestion of Joel Wolfsohn the National Power Policy Committee was reactivated; a relic

301. Raushenbush to "Mr. Robertson," May 4, 1945, Division of Power File, Branch of Economics and Statistics Files, RG 48, NA.

302. Soon after the Division of Power was established Congressman Robert F. Jones asked Director Harold D. Smith of the Bureau of the Budget to justify what seemed to him to be duplication of the functions of the FPC. Jones to Harold Smith, April 23, 1943, Office Files of the Director, Records of the Bureau of the Budget, RG 51, NA.

303. Ickes made his case for the transfer of the Rural Electrification Administration to the Interior Department in a letter to Attorney General Francis Biddle, May 3, 1945, CCF 1-1094a, RG 48, NA. A "reorganization plan transferring to the Secretary of the Interior certain functions of the Federal Power Commission" is discussed in a memorandum from Bruce Wright, Assistant Solicitor, to Arthur Goldschmidt, March 12, 1946, Reorganization File, Branch of Economics and Statistics Files, RG 48, NA.

304. A memorandum critical of the weakened Division of Power's guidance to the Coordination Committee in 1946 is that by Assistant Secretary Warner W. Gardner to "Mr. Myer," July 20, 1946, Coordination General: Committee Memoranda File, Coordination Committee Files, RG 48, NA.

of the early Roosevelt years, this committee had been submerged to such a degree that the members had forgotten it existed. When polled, most agencies recommended that the committee be abolished, but President Truman asked that it be revived. It seems to have had no great impact of any kind.[305]

Despite the Interior Department's evident difficulty in achieving very much coordination among the various parts of government concerned with electric power, the department seems to have remained under pressure from Congress to produce some sort of power policy. In particular it became necessary for the department to take a position on such questions as whether government facilities should merely respond to current needs, attempt to anticipate future needs, or perhaps even open up new markets through the aggressive construction of transmission lines and other transportation devices. Related to this set of issues was the question of whether projects should be "operated with a view to developing natural resources and contributing to the economic welfare of the regions in which they operate, rather than merely to secure to the Government a return of its investment."[306]

One solution to this dilemma seems to have been for Secretary Ickes on January 3, 1946, to issue to all his staff an important "Memorandum on Power Policy," which amounted almost to a legal code. In this document principles embodied in the most important acts of Congress dealing with power policy over the previous forty years were synthesized into five "primary objectives" (fully documented) as follows:

1. Federal dams shall where feasible include facilities for generating electrical energy.
2. Preference in power sales shall be given to public agencies and cooperatives.
3. Power disposal shall be for the particular benefit of domestic and rural consumers.
4. Power shall be sold at the lowest possible rates consistent with sound business principles.
5. Power disposal shall be such as to encourage widespread use and to prevent monopolization.[307]

305. The committee records and minutes are in CCF 1-288, RG 48, NA.

306. Bonneville Power Administrator Paul J. Raver to Assistant Secretary Michael Straus, April 24, 1945, General Power Policy File, Division of Power Files, RG 48, NA.

307. Ickes to all staffs of the Department of the Interior, January 3, 1946, Federal Power Policy File, Wolfsohn Papers, HSTL. It appears that this memorandum was drafted by Arthur Goldschmidt, director of the Division of Power, and was not checked in advance with the bureau or agency chiefs. Upon receipt of the

This broad policy statement was then translated into fifteen "operating principles" to be guides for planning, construction, operations, and sales. It was almost as if the department had taken a position in the debate that was taking place at the time in academia over rules versus authorities in economic policy. Having failed to achieve coordination through authority, the Interior Department had decided to try rules. The various power-producing, planning, and selling units might be administratively out of hand, but now at least they would be accountable by a set of standards fixed on high.

Although President Truman himself seems to have been willing by and large merely to endorse and repeat the power policy positions presented to him by the Interior Department staff, during most of his first term the department faced a good deal of criticism from other parts of government.[308] There were two main stimuli for the criticism, the same two in fact that drew attention to other energy sources as well.

The first stimulus was the energy shortage that affected the United States after war's end and was felt in electric power as elsewhere. A serious constraint on public policy in the electricity field in the face of larger-than-expected demands was the difficulty of using price as a major rationing device. "Low" prices had for years been treated as an article of faith and could not now easily be rejected simply because of altered circumstances.[309] The only alternative to price as an allocator of scarce supplies

memorandum the head of the Southwestern Power Administration wrote irritably to Goldschmidt: "In view of the fact that the Secretary has already signed this memorandum and issued it as a basic policy of the Department in power matters, I am reluctant to offer comment on it at this time. . . . I did not have an opportunity to offer my comments on a draft of the memorandum as issued. . . ." Douglas G. Wright to Goldschmidt, January 9, 1946, General Power Policy File, Division of Power Files, RG 48, NA.

308. In a letter to the president of the National Reclamation Association shortly after assuming office, President Truman reaffirmed his enthusiasm for "the underlying common-sense principles of the Tennessee Valley experiment" as a source of "guidance and counsel to the people in other regions, who likewise aspire to put their resources to the greatest use." He reported work in progress on "sixteeen river basins of the west." Truman to Ora Bundy, November 10, 1945, Columbia Valley Authority File, Murphy Files, HSTL.

309. For example, on one occasion when the commissioner of the Bureau of Reclamation asked for permission to modify traditional policy and allow municipal power companies to raise retail power prices substantially above the wholesale rates, Secretary Krug gave him a stern lecture on the relevant doctrine while denying his request. He said in part: "The availability of low-cost power to the ultimate consumer results in many tangible and intangible benefits to the communities which are thereby affected and, through the interrelationships of those communities in the

was an arbitrary system of some kind that would reduce quantities available to consumers; and in fact spot shortages and brownouts became a familiar feature of the postwar world. When these happened the power authorities in government learned that responsibility was a two-edged sword. They had happily taken credit for the increase in generation capacity from projects such as TVA and Bonneville. Now they had to take the blame for supposedly failing to estimate future demand correctly. To a congressman who complained about shortages it was always possible to point to inadequate past appropriations and "false economy" in the legislative branch.[310] But such a position was less persuasive to an agitated public. To complicate matters the Interior Department staff were themselves seldom confident about what the future was likely to hold for electric power and, in this market where the lag between the decision to construct facilities and the receipt of new power was so great, just what policy should be pursued to achieve continuing market equilibrium at low prices.[311] Few attempts were made to relate the future of the electric power market to the future of markets for fossil fuels except to use the occasion of shortages and sudden oil and gas price increases to call for more hydroelectric development.[312] The private utilities and their friends in Congress used the general postwar climate of public disgruntlement with power shortages to press their claims that public projects not only were inefficient and unimaginative in providing for the future but also operated with a variety of concealed subsidies

---

national economy, to the Nation as a whole. These benefits are much more fundamental and widespread than could possibly be the case if they were expressed in terms of reduced local taxes, rather than lowered electric rates." (J. A. Krug to Michael Straus, June 30, 1948, Director of Program Staff Power Policy File, Seymour Office Files, RG 48, NA.) An interesting five-page catechism on public power policy was prepared for Under Secretary Chapman in 1949 incorporating the same received doctrine in the form of answers to possible questions on the subject. Power Division File, Chapman Office Files, RG 48, NA.

310. See, for example, a report, "Significance of Water Power Development," with cover note, December 2, 1947, prepared by Walton Seymour for "Congressman Brown as per his request" to Oscar Chapman, Bureau of Reclamation File, Chapman Office Files, RG 48, NA.

311. A Division of Power statistician in 1947 prepared a forecast for the electric power market that derived supply projections from estimates of generator production and demand from three alternative rates of growth of the U.S. economy from boom to depression. She expected a "continuation of the power shortage" at least into 1951. Memorandum, Bernice Cook to Arthur Goldschmidt, "Power Estimates of Coming Years," April 1, 1947, General Research and Statistics File, Division of Power Files, RG 48, NA.

312. See, for example, U.S. Department of the Interior press release, January 15, 1948, Articles File, Ball Papers, HSTL.

such as unreasonably low depreciation and interest charges, freedom from regulation by the states, and exemption from income taxes.[313]

The second ground for criticism of federal power policy was national security, which seemed to grow in urgency during 1947–48. The NSRB in a series of staff studies of capacity and requirements of electric power systems took strong issue with the priorities over time and among regions established by the Interior Department. A committee of experts from the government and the private sector reported to the NSRB consultant responsible for energy and utilities, Edward Falck, that the situation in many parts of the country was not nearly as bad as that projected by those parts of the department that wished to build additional hydroelectric facilities. Falck assured NSRB chairman Arthur Hill that happily, in the short run at least, some planning was "being tackled aggressively by the electric utility system themselves."[314] Commissioner of the Bureau of Reclamation Michael Straus took strong exception to the NSRB reports, describing them as "a major detriment to the Bureau" used by the Bureau of the Budget "as complete justification for power budget butchery."[315] However, the Commission on Organization of the Executive Branch of the Government (Hoover Commission), which was at work in 1948, heard testimony that supported the NSRB position. Professor Abel Wolman of Johns Hopkins University told the commission that in water resources projects "construction work is becoming an end in itself and that an analysis of the benefits to be derived from this construction work has become a secondary consideration."[316] The Interior Department seemed to have few admirers left for its power policy outside its own ranks and except for those who stood to gain from specific projects.

The Passing of the "Valley Authority"

The Eightieth Congress, with a Republican majority, was predictably critical of those remnants of the New Deal that still loomed large in the

313. Walton Seymour, the director of the Interior Department Program Staff, responded at length to this accumulation of charges, as put to him by the House Appropriations Committee, in a memorandum of January 28, 1948, General Power Policy File, Division of Power Files, RG 48, NA.

314, Falck to Hill, May 11, 1948, with committee reports attached, Power File, Seymour Office Files, RG 48, NA.

315. Straus to Julius Krug, January 7, 1949, ibid.

316. Memorandum, Charles Aikin to Dean Acheson, June 2, 1948, Dean Acheson Papers, HSTL.

administration's program.[317] As a result, in the campaign of 1948 President Truman was able to characterize his opponents as unabashed enemies of power for the masses. In addition he played on regional sensitivities by claiming that "Republican sabotage" of power and irrigation projects was merely part of a continuing strategy "to make the West an economic colony of Wall Street." Moreover, he himself went on the offensive and promised that, if reelected, he would be guided by that "great concept of unified development" represented in TVA and in the stirring rhetoric of David Lilienthal. Indeed, he said that the government was prepared already to move "in other great river basins—such as the Missouri, the Colorado, the Central Valley in California, and the Columbia" as well as to undertake "full development of the St. Lawrence Seaway and Power Project." The Interior Department staff, especially Under Secretary Chapman, who took a major role in the campaign, was naturally overjoyed with the election results and particularly with the president's announced commitment "to effectuate the specific programs and policies to which he has committed himself in his campaign and other speeches." Secretary Krug distributed to all "heads of Bureaus and Offices" a digest of "Presidential Policy Statements for Guidance in Future Policy Formulation."[318]

Only a week after the election Samuel Moment, an economist with the BPA attached to Assistant Secretary Davidson, prepared a very ambitious "program ahead" for the period 1949–52 in the field of electric power. He wrote:

The political reversal in the Presidential election drastically changed the prospects of the BPA program. The outlook for BPA as well as for other Federal hydro plans had been to mark time and defend the principles of (1) Federal responsibility for full power development on river systems, including transmission lines and substations; (2) a rate policy based on cost of power rather than what the traffic will bear; (3) preference to publicly-owned systems in sales of power, and (4) building adequate generation and transmission capacity to meet current power demands. There was little hope in the near future for renewal of a policy of building capacity well in advance of the market and of using power as a lever to foster regional growth.

317. For example, a congressional staff study, "Federal Power Policy," December 20, 1948, repeated all the standard criticisms of public power: inefficiency, waste, market interference, and unfair competition with private utilities. File 401.2, Division of Power Files, RG 48, NA.

318. The quotations in this paragraph are from a memorandum, November 30, 1948, White House—The President File, Chapman Papers, HSTL; and *The Truman Program: Addresses and Messages by Harry S. Truman* (Public Affairs Press, 1948), p. 215.

Now, we have the opportunity to resume a constructive program, and for the first time since 1940 to do it in an atmosphere of peace, with security influences subordinated to regional needs and opportunities.

But at the same time, we ought to do our best to make it unlikely that opponents can ever again put Federal hydro on the defensive, and injure the Northwest and national interests as they did in the past two years. We should have learned that the opponents will not rest and will seek to cripple Federal power movements whenever possible. At best, they may hibernate. Men who think like them are still in Government, notably in the National Security Resources Board and the Munitions Board. . . .

What is lacking is a respected body of facts and analyses on Federal river system engineering-economics that would comprise a bible for Federal power policy. We are constantly subject to controversial sniping against the integrity and value of Federal hydro. We don't have an adequate, well-worked out rebuttal. . . . The Supporters of Federal hydro do not have a consistent, comprehensive and sufficient body of facts and reasons for putting Federal power squarely on its own feet as a new economic institution, as sound and necessary as the petroleum industry.[319]

Obviously much affected by the upbeat mood of the time, Moment outlined no less than eleven types of economic studies that he believed should underlie federal power policy.

Two directions into which the public power people hoped to move in this positive climate were, first, the construction of coal-fired plants to supplement hydroelectricity in Reclamation Bureau projects, and second, the laying of transmission lines widely throughout the country, including areas served predominantly by private utilities. As it turned out, neither of these new directions was accepted by a Congress concerned about the growth of big government and a dreaded "socialism." The election of 1948 did not in fact signal a substantial liberalization either of Congress or of the American people. The Interior Department was repeatedly frustrated during the remainder of the Truman administration by the refusal of Congress to appropriate funds for transmission lines, without which, the department argued, the injunction to plan for required needs and those of preferred customers, such as rural cooperatives, was a mere mockery. In the absence of its own lines the department was forced to resort to the less desirable practice of "wheeling" public power over private lines.[320]

319. S. Moment, "B.P.A. Program—1949–52—Some Proposals," November 12, 1948, attached to memorandum, Moment to William A. Dittmer, November 15, 1948, Bonneville Power Administration File, Seymour Office Files, RG 48, NA.

320. The government's position on "power wheeling contract requirements" was stated in a memorandum by Secretary Chapman, July 14, 1950, Policy on Wheeling Arrangements File, Division of Power Files, RG 48, NA.

A decision was made early in 1949 that the Columbia River valley would contain the first new regional authority. A Columbia Valley Administration bill had been introduced into Congress as early as February 1945, but no action was taken at that time. In 1949 the administration's own CVA bill was developed by a White House group headed by David Bell in consultation with various government agencies and private Northwest groups. Several bills were introduced, notably House bills 4286 and 4287 and Senate bill 1645.[321] The enthusiasts for public power were elated to be on the offensive again. C. Girard Davidson wrote to presidential assistant Charles Murphy in January: "The fight is shaping up in an excellent manner. So far the Republicans and private utilities are against it and the Democrats, labor, and farmers are for it. What more could we ask?"[322] As it turned out, the dispute was by no means as simple as this supposed conflict between the forces of good and evil. Within the federal government itself serious questions and doubts were expressed, and sometimes open opposition, about further application of the valley authority idea. Some of these concerns were simply manifestations of long-standing interagency jealousies and fears of territorial loss. For example, the Department of Agriculture wondered how a CVA would deal with such programs as its own Agricultural Extension Service and the Rural Electrification Administration. Secretary of Agriculture Charles F. Brannan insisted that the proposed CVA, if it were created, should report directly to the President rather than to the rival Department of the Interior. The Department of Commerce repeated many of the worries of the business community that the powers proposed for the CVA were far too wide and that the whole enterprise opened new opportunities for undesirable government intervention in the economy through such devices as "subsidized" power rates.[323] Wilbert G. Fritz of the Budget Bureau pointed out that from a macroeconomic viewpoint a CVA might spend only in periods of prosperity and thereby "aggravate the business cycle." With respect to the longer run, small planning units of this size would not permit government to take ad-

321. An undated memorandum apparently prepared by Kenneth Hechler for the Adlai Stevenson campaign of 1952 describes briefly the history of the CVA bill. Electric Power File, Files of Kenneth Hechler, HSTL.

322. Davidson to Murphy, January 28, 1949, Columbia Valley Authority File, Murphy Files, HSTL. A thirteen-page set of "Questions and Answers on Columbia Valley Administration Bill" was prepared, apparently for the use of senior Interior Department staff in discussing the legislation. Columbia Valley Authority File, Chapman Office Files, RG 48, NA.

323. Ralph R. Will to David E. Bell, February 9, 1949; Charles F. Brannan to the President, February 4, 1949; and William R. Davlin to Bell, February 11, 1949; all in Columbia Valley Authority File, Murphy Files, HSTL.

vantage of the economy's most productive potential nationwide. "That is probably one way to slide inadvertently into a condition of stagnation."[324]

Even at the heart of the Interior Department itself there were nonbelievers, especially those loyal to the old-line power units such as the Bureau of Reclamation. Program staff member Lyle Craine posed thirteen major questions about how the CVA would work, and in particular how it would displace or cooperate with the innumerable interests already in the area. He ended his memorandum significantly with the words "*ad infinitum.*" As early as 1946 some Interior Department staff suggested that regional planning proposals went contrary to the internationalism of the postwar world.[325] It is significant that the two most enthusiastic advocates of new regional authorities, Secretary Krug and Assistant Secretary Davidson, had both come to the department from such units themselves, TVA and BPA, respectively. But by the end of 1950 they had both left Washington.

Congressional hearings on the CVA bill stimulated extensive discussion of the subject. The cause attracted eloquent liberal spokesmen, young and old.[326] Organized opposition came from the Pacific Northwest Development Association, which represented the private utilities and some large business interests. In the end the bill never left committee. In the debate over the issue there were undoubtedly misrepresentations. For example, valley authorities were often pictured as the road to socialism or at least to a federal superstate. The sense one gets from reading the debate today, however, is that by the late 1940s the idea actually had few supporters left and had become something of an anachronism.[327] The TVA was a brilliant

324. Fritz to David Bell, February 16, 1949, CVA File, Files of David E. Bell, HSTL.

325. Memorandum, Craine to A. C. Wolf, "Organization and Administrative Problems Arising in Connection with Valley Authority Legislation," February 10, 1949, General File, Craine Correspondence Files, RG 48, NA. Elmer Pehrson of the Bureau of Mines at the Post-War Resources Institute called for a "broader international point of view" and insisted that "the most important regionalization going on today is that on an international scale." Stenographic Report of Post-War Resources Institute (Third Day), pp. 378, 379, Branch of Economics and Statistics Files, RG 48, NA.

326. See, for example, "Federal Power Policy—Guardian of the Public Interest," statement presented in the Senate by Senator Hubert H. Humphrey, *Congressional Record* (August 24, 1949), pp. 12120–23.

327. Secretary Krug wrote to *Fortune* magazine on May 6, 1949, complaining about the "specific errors" the magazine allegedly printed on the subject. Department of Interior: Power, Northwest File, Seymour Office Files, RG 48, NA. The transcript of a round table chaired by C. Girard Davidson at the American Society for Public Administration meetings in Washington on March 12, 1949, "One Land, Many Agencies," suggests the academic interest in the subject. General File, Craine Correspondence Files, RG 48, NA.

creation of the prewar years designed both to combat depression and to stimulate long-term growth of a depressed region. By 1949 the depression was over and there were no more regions with the relatively homogeneous problems of Appalachia. Moreover, Keynesian economics had shown better ways to combat recession than through public works alone, while more sophisticated understanding of planning pointed toward the maintenance of national flexibility rather than subdivision into small units. By 1949 the valley authority was an idea whose time had passed, even if it lived vigorously in liberal dogma.

Despite the controversy surrounding the CVA bill, both within his own government and without, President Truman did not flag in his support for the principles it contained. Indeed, he worked personally with Secretary Krug to perfect an organizational system that would embody these principles.[328] But he must have had moments of doubt, if for no other reason than that so much of the discussion about power seemed always to be full of contradictions and dispute. Not only was the new authority highly controversial, but even the projections about future needs differed widely. Interior Department spokesmen tended still to paint the bleakest picture for the future, while the NSRB was the most optimistic and the FPC was somewhere in between. And throughout, the public complained bitterly that whoever was responsible for power had not planned sensibly for their current needs. The winter of 1948–49 was the second in a row when power was seriously in short supply, and many people feared it might have a crippling effect on the economy. Davidson reported that the aluminum industry alone had been compelled to reduce production by 50 percent, and he speculated that if adequate energy were not soon available the economy would not be able to sustain an adequate flow of purchasing power and effective demand. "This is the spiral path leading to depression. A shortage of steel or coal or oil or electric power can force us onto that downward path."[329]

328. In a draft memorandum for the President, March 9, 1949, Walton Seymour produced a set of proposals for the organization of federal water resource activities. He argued that the "new comprehensive view" that was required could best be provided by "regional authorities" and as a second choice by a single "water resources development agency." The draft is attached to memorandum, Seymour to the Secretary, March 11, 1949, with attachment, Department of Interior, Bureau of Reclamation File, Doty Papers, HSTL.

329. C. Girard Davidson, "We Need More Electric Power," address before the Economic Action Conference, Washington, D.C., April 11, 1949, Department of the Interior, Power File, Doty Papers, HSTL. Samuel Moment of the BPA repeatedly pointed out the confusing inconsistencies in projections by the different agencies

But the question remained still of how to get a firmer handle on power policy questions. Critics of the CVA and all other drastic legislative innovation suggested that a reinvigorated Federal Inter-Agency River Basin Committee might do the job.[330] But anyone familiar with the unimpressive history of this committee to date could only be skeptical. The President's answer was to appoint a Water Resources Policy Commission (called the Cooke Commission after its chairman, Morris L. Cooke) to consider the issues de novo. David Bell proposed to Charles Murphy in November 1949 that presidential recommendations on a long list of water and power projects be delayed until the report of the commission, expected by December 1950, was released.[331] The only regional project that was not to be held in abeyance until the commission reported was the St. Lawrence Seaway. Planning for this project went back for decades, and relations with Canada were involved. The principal issue raised by the St. Lawrence, however, was also central to the commission's charge, that is, whether this project should be carried out by the state of New York or by the federal government as a regional endeavor applying all the doctrine about rates and preferred customers. The Interior Department argued very hard for the latter approach.[332] The political attractiveness of the federal solution

---

responsible for public power in government. He suggested that one reason why Interior Department projections were higher than the others was because they alone assumed full employment. He urged that a conference of all the forecasters be held to reconcile differences. (Moment to Seymour, May 5, 1949, and May 17, 1949, Power General File, Seymour Office Files, RG 48, NA.) E. Robert de Luccia, chief of the Bureau of Power in the FPC, was the FPC forecaster; he prepared the power section of the Krug Report on the probable impact of the Marshall Plan. In March 1949 de Luccia revised his contribution to the Krug Report for use by the NSRB. Two versions of this later study are in Power File, Seymour Office Files, RG 48, NA. Samuel Moment complained to FPC Commissioner Leland Olds in July 1949 that de Luccia's 1949 report employed "substantially different methods and assumptions" from those he used himself. "It is certainly a handicap to the power generating and distributing agencies in their dealings with the Bureau of the Budget and with Congress to have a number of divergent estimates of power market forecasts coming from federal agencies. Those who want to spend the least money will usually select the lowest power forecasts regardless of the injury resulting to the country." Moment to Olds, July 2, 1949, ibid.

330. Elmer Staats to Charles Murphy, December 8, 1949, and John D. Clark to Murphy, September 16, 1949, Natural Resources File, Murphy Files, HSTL.

331. Bell to Murphy, November 25, 1949, Legislation Relating to Natural Resources File, Spingarn Papers, HSTL.

332. David Bell to Charles Murphy, November 26, 1949, ibid.; and draft memorandum, Walton Seymour to Secretary Chapman, "The Department Power Program: Problems, Policies and Future Trends," December 6, 1949, Power–General File, Seymour Office Files, RG 48, NA.

increased as power rates rose in New England and that region began to complain that it seemed not to benefit from the river basin approach.[333] A compromise solution recommended by the White House was for federal construction with "the final determination of the method by which the power produced at the St. Lawrence project will be disposed of" to be fixed by a "proposed New England–New York Commission."[334]

Water Policy Reconsidered

With the stimulus of a presidential commission, 1950 became a year of inquiry and debate with respect to public power. Adequate representation of New Deal doctrine on the new Cooke Commission was assured by the presence of Leland Olds, whose reappointment to the FPC had been blocked in the Senate. The various units of government concerned with power were pressed into service by the commission to provide information and analysis.[335] One of the commission's most important achievements was to sort out the issues involved and the questions needing answers. In particular the Cooke Commission tried to deal with how benefits and costs could be estimated and allocated for multiple-purpose projects, who in society should receive any "surpluses" that might come through differences between average costs and market prices (electricity users? benefiters from other activities of multipurpose projects? society at large?), trade-offs between national and regional interests, irrigation versus power, what interest rates and payoff periods should be employed, how to use construction policy at power project sites to reduce the business cycle, and so on.[336]

333. Memorandum, Mark Abelson to Paul Unger, "New England Electric Rates," February 27, 1950; and Walton Seymour to Stuart Mann (concerning "the possibility of comprehensive water resource development work by the Federal Government" in New England), March 8, 1950; both in Power Eastern File, Seymour Office Files, RG 48, NA.

334. Memorandum, David Bell to Charles Murphy, "Inter-agency Meeting on St. Lawrence Project," February 9, 1950; and (unsigned) "The Administration's Position on Section 5 of the St. Lawrence Bill," April 12, 1950; both in St. Lawrence Seaway and Power Project File, Bell Files, HSTL.

335. For example, FPC agreed to make estimates of "the actual upper and lower limits of development" for hydroelectricity. Frank L. Weaver to Leland Olds, March 6, 1950, Power File, Records of the PWRPC, HSTL.

336. An initial attempt to specify policy goals was made by Virgil L. Hurlburt of the commission staff in a memorandum to Olds, May 8, 1950, ibid. Detailed replies to a questionnaire raising fundamental issues are in Federal Power Commis-

The various component parts of the public power system seemed especially assiduous in presenting their respective cases during the course of the commission's inquiry. The TVA repeated the oft-told tale of how it had achieved "the development and wider use of electricity in rebuilding an entire region."[337] Secretary Chapman testified before the Cooke Commission that "many of our present difficulties in the field of water resources have arisen because under existing law the basin-wide approach cannot be fully applied." He also called for reaffirmation of the other terms of government policy, including insistence on "the lowest possible rates consistent with sound business principles with preference to be given to public bodies and cooperatives."[338] The FPC chairman argued, above all, for extension of his commission's authority over the TVA and parts of the Interior Department where it did not have responsibility currently, notably the Bureau of Reclamation.[339]

As it turned out, public power had little to fear from the President's Water Resources Policy Commission, although its tilt was distinctly toward valley authorities and away from centralized Interior Department

---

sion Correspondence File, PWRPC, HSTL. An interesting discussion of the constitutional and statutory basis for federal power policy was prepared by Sherman S. Poland, "Memorandum for Mr. Foster," May 23, 1950, Committee on Power Policy Correspondence File, PWRPC, HSTL. It is worth noting that the particular composition of the Interior Department to some extent facilitated the preparation of a document analogous to the present-day environmental impact statement before construction of power projects. For example, in connection with the proposed development of the Rogue River in Oregon, Secretary Chapman insisted on obtaining from his various offices and bureaus "detailed information on the scenic, recreation, and fish and wildlife aspects of the Rogue River Basin, particularly as these are related to proposals for water and power developments in the basin." Memorandum, Chapman to Director, Fish and Wildlife Service, and others, "Rogue River Development," October 4, 1950, Rogue River Development File, Department of Interior Files, Doty Papers, HSTL.

337. Gordon R. Clapp, Chairman of the Board, TVA, "Electricity and the Public Interest," address to the National Rural Electric Cooperative Association, March 7, 1950, Natural Resources File, Hechler Files, HSTL. Greater skepticism could be found among Interior Department economists. In January 1950 Barnett proposed a detailed evaluation of the TVA, which would have decomposed its contributions into at least four "primary effects" and nine "secondary, tertiary, etc. effects." Draft, January 23, 1950, Power Rates File, Division of Power Files, RG 48, NA.

338. Statement of Secretary of the Interior Oscar L. Chapman before the President's Water Resources Policy Commission, May 2, 1950, Public Addresses, vol. 8, Chapman Papers, HSTL.

339. Monrad C. Wallgren to Morris L. Cooke, September 27, 1950, Federal Power Commission Correspondence File, PWRPC, HSTL.

direction. The final report called for continuation of the mixed public-private power system but with government projects still in a favored position: public provision of "hydroelectric power well in advance of power market trends"; licensing (that is, prior approval) of all private facilities "by the responsible river basin commission"; "lowest possible rates to ultimate consumers"; continued preferential sale to certain consumers; and repeal of FPC jurisdiction over any federal project.[340] To the regret of some public servants the commission did not take up the thorny question of how to organize the federal government better to implement the commission's or any other policy.[341] The commission simply could not deal openly with the inescapable fact that water projects were still an important part of American politics, overwhelming in many cases any simple economic logic that might apply.[342] The Interior Department officially "concurred" in all the commission's recommendations. But predictably, some in the department, and Secretary Chapman in particular, rejected the proposed increase in power to valley commissions and the concomitant reduction in departmental responsibilities. Instead, they repeated the venerable proposal for a Department of Natural Resources encompassing the work of the Interior Department and certain functions of other government units such as the Department of Agriculture and the Corps of Engineers.[343]

340. *A Water Policy for the American People: The Report of the President's Water Resources Policy Commission* (GPO, 1950), vol. 1,245–46.

341. Maynard Hufschmidt of the Interior Department Program Staff wrote to Harvey S. Perloff of the commission staff speculating about new organizational modes, including a new "water resources agency" to avoid duplication and achieve unified planning. (Hufschmidt to Perloff, August 19, 1950, President's Water Resources Policy Commission File, General Records of Program Staff, RG 48, NA.) Hufschmidt seems also to have proposed that within the department the Program Staff be given responsibility for giving "clearance" to all river basin developments. "Role of Program Staff in Coordinating Land, Water, Power and Minerals Activities of the Department," August 9, 1950, Program Committee File, Office Files of Maynard Hufschmidt, RG 48, NA.

342. Kenneth Hechler, a White House aide, and Sam Broadbent of the Budget Bureau prepared fascinating memorandums for President Truman in connection with a whistle-stop trip before the 1950 congressional elections in which they recommended that he stress the size of past and prospective local water projects at each stop but endeavor not to "establish policy through precedent which would greatly handicap the President's Water Resource Policy Commission in its operations, and tend to create pressures for larger appropriations." Natural Resources File, Hechler Files, HSTL.

343. "Report of Department of the Interior Task Force Established to Review the Report of the President's Water Resources Policy Commission," May 7, 1951, PWRPC Reports File, General Records of the Program Staff, RG 48, NA. See also Koppes, "Oscar Chapman," p. 331.

Power for War

Soon after the beginning of the Korean War the Interior Department made a strong and successful case for its designation as the chief coordinating unit for electric power under the Defense Production Act of 1950.[344] But the emergency and the distribution of authority among defense agencies in and out of the department did little except reduce congressional appropriations, tip the balance in the debate a little toward private industry, and mute any serious talk of structural reform in the public sector. A Defense Electric Power Administration and an Electric Utility Defense Advisory Council, comparable to the industry committees for petroleum and coal, were created, and suggestions kept arising for revival of the somnolent National Power Policy Committee as an interagency coordinating device.[345] But the time had passed for any such permanent change that might have serious implications for peacetime. One minor result of the emergency was to remove responsibility for analysis and forecasts of power markets from the NSRB, long a thorn in the Interior Department's side.[346]

The various parts of the department dealing with electric power during the Korean War lost no opportunity to point out (1) that the unused capacity in hydroelectric projects that helped to win World War II was no longer present; (2) that waterpower could and should relieve pressure on fossil fuels; (3) "there are hundreds of thousands of horse power wasting to the sea in the Nation's rivers which might be put to work producing electric energy for defense needs"; and (4) that anything approaching full mobilization would bring acute shortages.[347] In particular the emergency

344. Unsigned memorandum, "The Responsibilities of the Department of the Interior for Electric Power under Provisions of the Defense Production Act of 1950," August 11, 1950, Defense Production Act of 1950 File, Wolfsohn Papers, HSTL.

345. "Defense Electric Power Adminis.," Advisory Committees File, Chapman Papers, HSTL; Joel Wolfsohn to the Secretary of the Interior, July 27, 1950, National Power Policy Committee File, Wolfsohn Papers, HSTL; and Murl W. Storms to Wolfsohn, February 8, 1952, ibid.

346. The last NSRB survey was released in April 1950 and was much more satisfactory than its two predecessors from the Interior Department's viewpoint because it depended on data provided by the FPC rather than by the trade association, the Edison Electric Institute. "Project Title: Collection and Tabulation of Data for Third National Electric Power Survey," December 19, 1949; and Dal Hitchcock to William F. McKenna, November 2, 1951; both in NSRB 55-11, RG 304, NA.

347. Memorandum, William Warne to Acting Director, Program Staff, "President's Economic Report," December 20, 1950, General Power Policy File, Division of Power Files, RG 48, NA. Statements of power policy during this period by Secretary Chapman are contained in Records Concerning Electric Power File, Chapman Papers, HSTL.

was used as an argument to push forward the St. Lawrence project, to bring both power to the Northeast and iron ore to the Midwest smelters.[348] A states rights position on this issue continued to be expressed in New York, led by Governor Thomas E. Dewey, with charges that in the St. Lawrence project the Interior Department was bent on nothing less than "socialism."[349] In addition the coal industry claimed that this project was especially threatening to its markets.[350] But the government pressed ahead all the same.

During the Korean War advocates of public power shifted generally back into a defensive mode—into the position they had held in 1947 and 1948. Secretary Chapman reminded the President that federal projects were big revenue earners and Leon Keyserling, chairman of the Council of Economic Advisers, that public investment could be as cost-effective as private.[351] Philip Coombs, research director of the Paley Commission, regretted that this "big fight" over the "private vs. public issue" tended to draw attention away from various fundamental questions such as the extent to which coal must take over from hydro in providing increments of electric power and how the concept of "hydro potential" was relevant only with respect to the prevailing prices of other energy sources.[352] He might have added that the way Secretary Chapman fought the fight drew attention away from the aggregate social costs and benefits of power development, neglecting especially the environmental degradation that would become so controversial two decades later.

348. FPC Chairman Thomas C. Buchanan made the case in detail in a letter to Senator Tom Connally, chairman of the Foreign Relations Committee, February 21, 1952. Federal Power Commission File, Sucher Office Files, RG 48, NA.

349. Leland Olds, appointed director of the department's Northeast Field Staff, described the conflict in a memorandum to the acting director of the Program Staff, May 14, 1951. Leland Olds File, Sucher Office Files, RG 48, NA.

350. The chief of the Coal Branch, Bureau of Mines, responded to this charge in a memorandum for the secretary's office, February 15, 1952, Bureau of Mines File, Sucher Office Files, ibid. It was standard public power doctrine that where hydroelectric energy caused substitution among fuels the regional development generated thereby would ultimately increase the demand for coal in more than equivalent amount. The FPC made this case in detail in "Development of Cheap Water Power in the United States Is Highly Beneficial to the Coal Industry as Indicated by Experience in the Tennessee Valley and the Pacific Northwest," October 18, 1951, Federal Power Commission File, Sucher Office Files, ibid.

351. Chapman to the President, April 12, 1951, Subject File Cabinet, Secretary of the Interior, PSF, HSTL; and Chapman to Keyserling, January 5, 1952, Council of Economic Advisers File, Searles Office Files, RG 48, NA.

352. Coombs to Robert Blum, December 17, 1951, General File Energy–Electric Power, PMPC, HSTL.

Perhaps smelling victory in the presidential elections of 1952, the private electric utilities markedly increased their campaign of criticism of public power that had begun in earnest as early as 1939.[353] Secretary Chapman reported to President Truman in February 1952: "Private power interests have unquestionably mobilized an insidious all-out drive against the Administration's power program . . . directed to take over the control of Federal power projects and our major undeveloped power resources as one of the big stakes in the 1952 elections." He insisted that "the private interests behind this drive are in a most vulnerable position" and urged the President to "take the offensive on behalf of the Administration power program."[354] To the extent that this advice was followed the "offensive" seems to have involved mainly threats of investigation of the private utilities by the FTC, FPC, and congressional committees.[355] In the election campaign the issue was clearly drawn. In a speech at Seattle on October 6 candidate Eisenhower supported the turning over of federal power projects to state or private utility control.[356] Governor Adlai Stevenson replied with just as vociferous support for public power based substantially on arguments and data provided by the Interior Department.[357] In this highly charged political atmosphere of 1952 the development of power

353. H. H. Wilson, a political scientist at Princeton University, prepared a fascinating analysis of this campaign illustrating its subtlety and unscrupulous techniques. ("Campaign of the Electric Utilities," attached to memorandum, Alfred C. Wolf to Reginald Price and others, April 25, 1952, Charles E. Wilson File, Sucher Office Files, RG 48, NA.) The utilities were especially critical of the Paley Commission section on electric energy because of its "over-emphasis" on hydro potential and "under-emphasis" on thermal, including nuclear, possibilities. E. W. Morehouse to William S. Paley, March 27, 1952, General Records–Energy, PMPC, HSTL.

354. Chapman to the President, February 5, 1952, Subject File: Cabinet, Secretary of the Interior, PSF, HSTL.

355. FTC Commissioner Stephen Spingarn complained in August 1952 that plans for investigating the private power companies had been delayed in the White House because presidential assistant David Bell had gone to the Stevenson headquarters in Springfield. (Spingarn to the file, August 25, 1952, Investigation of Private Power File, Spingarn Papers, HSTL.) Other documents, including a draft presidential announcement concerning plans for an investigation, are in this file.

356. An Interior Department document of October 8, 1952, attributed this plan in the first instance to Charles E. Wilson, former president of the General Electric Company, and more generally to the ideas of Thomas E. Dewey. St. Lawrence Plan File, Sucher Office Files, RG 48, NA.

357. For example, a memorandum, "Power Costs: Public vs. Private," evidently prepared by Joel Wolfsohn for the Stevenson campaign, Adlai E. Stevenson 1952 Presidential Campaign File, Wolfsohn Papers, HSTL; and Alfred C. Wolf, Director of the Program Staff, to Charles Murphy, September 26, 1952, together with other campaign material in Natural Resources File, Hechler Files, HSTL.

policy seems to have distinctly taken a back seat to its defense, except for one attempt by the Budget Bureau to implement the recommendations of the Water Resources Policy Commission and bring about greater uniformity in power practices through the establishment of common standards for the construction of new projects, the sale of power, and analysis of outstanding issues.[358]

Electric power had come into the Truman period as a subject in which political, ideological, and bureaucratic considerations counted for more than economic ones. It left the era little changed.

The Promise of the Atom

The possibility that nuclear fission would become an important new source of heat and power was perceived by scientists as early as the 1930s. During the war when scientific effort was devoted overwhelmingly to developing the atomic bomb the realization that this new force might also relieve constraints on postwar economic development was prominent in the minds of America's British partners, for whom energy shortage had been a nemesis stretching back for almost a century. Winston Churchill pressed British rights to the commercial use of atomic energy at Quebec in 1943 and at Hyde Park in 1944. The French were no less interested but had little bargaining power with the principal allies. Many of the scientists and officials of all nations engaged in the wartime research were understandably more attracted to the potential of their work to advance the welfare of humanity than to destroy it. In two ways, however, the continuing tension between the United States and the U.S.S.R. at the end of the war, and then the onset of the cold war, served to retard the development of nuclear power for peacetime uses and the formulation of policy about it: first, the resources of the scientific community had to be devoted substantially to producing bigger and better weapons, and second, security considerations dictated strict secrecy about all aspects of the subject.[359]

358. The draft of the Budget Bureau circular on the subject and reactions from Interior Department staff are in PWRPC File, General Records of Program Staff, RG 48, NA. FPC reactions are in Federal Power Commission, Water Resources Policy File, Doty Papers, HSTL.

359. The unpublished records of the Atomic Energy Commission remain closed to scholars, who, for activities within the nuclear establishment, must depend mainly on the official two-volume *History of the United States Atomic Energy Commission* by Richard G. Hewlett and Oscar E. Anderson, Jr. (Pennsylvania State University Press, 1962 and 1969); especially vol. 1, *The New World, 1939–1946*, pp. 11, 48, 327, 328, 336, 356, 357.

Although at war's end nuclear energy was shrouded in mystery, optimism ran high. Stephen Raushenbush predicted in 1945 "that within twenty years . . . atomic energy will come into major competition with our present energy resources, coal, oil, gas and water, and that the power industry will join the coal industry in shaking in its shoes."[360] But for energy planners the problem remained of just how to get hard data about this new resource. Ivan Bloch of the BPA pointed out to Arthur Goldschmidt of the Division of Power that "the public ownership potentialities of atomic power plants" made the subject of central importance to the Interior Department.[361] Yet Bloch was no better able than members of the general public to obtain the information about costs that would substantiate or disprove this assertion. There was discussion in 1946 of cooperation between the Interior Department and the Cowles Commission for Research in Economics on a study of the economics of atomic energy.[362] But it was clear that both partners would still lack the necessary data to do this job in an informed fashion.[363] In these early postwar years the Interior Department staff must have sympathized with scientists such as William Fowler of the California Institute of Technology who complained bitterly: "Atomic energy means a new economic security. Atomic energy means health and new knowledge. . . . There are many problems, there will be many more, but first of all there must be a start. And that start will only come when books can be read again, when men can speak and hear the truth again, and when scientists and engineers can be free again."[364]

The issue of civilian attention to nonmilitary uses of atomic power came to a head in 1946 with a joint resolution in Congress (House Joint Resolution 326) that the FPC explore the subject of atomic power and report to Congress. FPC Chairman Leland Olds made the arguments for sepa-

360. "Is Any Limitation on the Development of Hydro-Electric Energy in Competition with Coal Desirable in the National Interest and If so How Much?" paper presented to the Post-War Resources Institute, November 5–9, 1945, Post-War Resources Institute File, Wolfsohn Papers, HSTL.

361. Memorandum, Bloch to Goldschmidt, "Atomic Energy and Departmental Interest," September 18, 1946, Atomic Energy File, Chapman Office Files, RG 48, NA. The memorandum was background for a meeting on September 20 on relations with the Atomic Energy Commission wherein the impact of atomic power on other energy sources was a main item for discussion. Atomic Energy File, Records of the Economics and Statistics Branch, RG 48, NA.

362. The Cowles Commission for Research in Economics was a nonprofit corporation founded in 1932 by Alfred Cowles, an economist.

363. Jacob Marschak to Bloch, July 16, 1946, Atomic Energy File, Chapman Office Files, RG 48, NA.

364. Address delivered at Nation Associates Conference, September 1946, ibid.

rating the military and nonmilitary aspects of the subject in a letter to the President on May 22, 1946. President Truman rejected Olds's appeal in the following terms: "The power aspects of atomic energy are so intimately a part of the entire field of atomic energy development that I believe it better to center responsibility in the proposed Atomic Energy Commission."[365] In essence the President's decision determined the pattern of discussion of atomic energy for the course of his presidency. Even though two of the first members of the Atomic Energy Commission were long-time energy men (David Lilienthal and Sumner Pike), during its early years the AEC made few public statements on the subject except for rather bland and general declarations about opportunities in the long run. The AEC recognized that important constraints on its action for some years to come would be limited supplies of scientists and reactor fuel as well as genuine uncertainty about the costs of power generation.[366]

Elsewhere in government, industry, and academe, there was frustration about the difficulty of dealing with the subject with any specificity. For example, J. Weldon Jones of the Budget Bureau pointed out to the director in 1947 that uncertainties about atomic power put the case for all future public power projects in doubt.

It is too early to appraise the potential impact of atomic energy developments on the public power programs of the Government. Nevertheless, some guidelines are needed. The Federal Government is initiating long-range dam and reservoir projects costing hundreds of millions of dollars, which involve hydro-electric power development. Pending more detailed information on the feasibility of general utilization of atomic energy for industrial purposes, how fast should the Government go in developing power from these natural resources? Is it desirable to move at a slower rate until we know more about the utilization of atomic energy? Should we limit the work to fewer projects with greatest economic justification? Should the Government spend large sums on

365. Olds to Truman, May 22, 1946; and Truman to Olds, June 22, 1946; both in OF 692, HSTL.

366. This is clear, for example, in David E. Lilienthal, "Atomic Energy Is Your Business," address in Crawfordsville, Indiana, September 22, 1947, Atomic Energy Speech File, Clifford Papers, HSTL; and Sumner T. Pike, Remarks to the National Industrial Conference Board, March 18, 1948, Speeches File, Pike Papers, HSTL. Background on the creation of the AEC is contained in Hewlett and Anderson, *History of the United States Atomic Energy Commission,* vol. 1; see especially pp. 417–27 and 436–44 for a consideration of peacetime uses. John R. Newman of the Office of War Mobilization and Reconversion was a leader in emphasizing the civilian implications of nuclear power. Debate in the AEC over attention given to nuclear power is discussed in ibid., vol. 2: *Atomic Shield, 1947–1952,* pp. 2, 31, 34, 35, 56, 71, 83, 98–101, 115–17.

facilities which may be obsolete shortly after or even before they are completed?[367]

One White House staff member worried in 1948 that in the absence of public discussion the United States might drift into a policy regarding the public-private mix of rights to "industrial and commercial uses of atomic energy" that "may produce results comparable to those of the industrial revolution."[368] Two academic economists, Joseph E. Loftus and Walter Isard, concluded in 1948 in a paper, "The Impact of Atomic Energy on Economic Studies" (which was discussed in the White House), that "little serious work has been done by economists on the economic aspects of nuclear energy utilization." The reason was not hard to find: "It is the rather widespread persuasion among economists that nothing really serious or substantial can be done in the field until such time as more precise information on the nature and details of nuclear energy applications is available."[369]

Nevertheless, in that brief halcyon period between the Truman reelection of 1948 and the outbreak of the Korean War in 1950 there was a flurry of attention to the possibility of commercial development of nuclear power. An Industrial Advisory Group appointed by the AEC in October 1947 reported in December 1948 that ignorance in the private sector explained the little progress to date on peacetime uses of atomic energy. "The need for Government monopoly in certain important areas, coupled with secrecy, seems to erect an impenetrable barrier to a wish for knowledge." The group called for publication of as much information as possible, an increase of personal contacts between industrial and AEC personnel, and the creation of a General Industrial Advisory Committee.[370] Perhaps in consequence of these recommendations an ad hoc advisory committee on the power industry was created in 1949 by the AEC to develop contacts both

367. Memorandum, Jones to the Director of the Budget Bureau, "Economic Questions Raised by the 1948 Budget," March 7, 1947, Council of Economic Advisers File, Webb Papers, HSTL.

368. Memorandum, R. M. Field to John Steelman, "Industrial and Commercial Uses of Atomic Energy," OF 692, HSTL.

369. J. B. C. Howe to John Steelman, with Isard and Loftus paper attached, October 21, 1948, ibid.

370. "Report of AEC Industrial Advisory Group," *Bulletin of the Atomic Scientists,* vol. 5 (February 1949), pp. 51–56. See also Lawrence R. Hafstad to Sumner Pike, September 13, 1949, as well as speeches by Pike: "Atomic Energy—Fuel of the Future?" April 25, 1949; "Report on Atomic Energy for Peaceful Uses," March 28, 1950; and "Impact of the Atomic Era on the American Economic System," January 16, 1951; all in Speeches File, Pike Papers, HSTL.

with the private sector and with the Interior Department. A consulting engineer, Palmer C. Putnam, was commissioned "to make a study of the maximum plausible world demands for energy over the next 50 to 100 years . . . as background for the Commission's consideration of the economic and public policy problems related to the development and use of machines for deriving electrical power from nuclear fuels."[371] In a statement of policy on the subject Lilienthal acknowledged that public-private cooperation was the "American formula" and that "the faster industry develops our present atomic knowledge the stronger we shall be in a military sense." At the same time, "an atomic furnace or an atomic power plant is virtually an atomic bomb arsenal," and this raised fundamental questions about how profit-motivated private enterprise could be counted on to construct and operate units that would be "foolproof and rascal-proof." Nevertheless, he believed that ways could be found to achieve "gradual de-nationalization of the atom," perhaps initially through private ore-processing, isotope use, and the manufacture of instruments and equipment and only ultimately in power-generation as well.[372] Lilienthal must have been encouraged that material he submitted to presidential aide Clark Clifford on peaceful uses of atomic energy found its way into the 1949 economic report.[373]

These stirrings in the AEC and the industry on the question of nuclear power were reflected in the academic community and in the press. Walter Isard, one of the few acknowledged university experts on the subject, argued that available cost data suggested atomic energy would not have "a revolutionary impact upon world and national economies," and he criticized a report by the Cowles Commission that reached more optimistic conclusions. Evidently the profession as a whole concluded by 1949 that the topic of atomic energy was at least large and important enough to make it the subject of an annual teaching institute held at American University.[374]

371. Palmer C. Putnam, *Energy in the Future* (Van Nostrand, 1953), p. vii, note. *Energy in the Future* was the published version of Putnam's study, in which he did not see great potential in fission because of limited supplies of fuel. He saw most promise in the development of fusion energy.

372. David E. Lilienthal, "Private Industry and the Public Atom," *Bulletin of the Atomic Scientists*, vol. 5 (January 1949), pp. 6–8.

373. George M. Elsey to Bertram M. Gross, January 3, 1950, and Gross to Elsey, January 6, 1950, Atomic Energy Misc. File, Clifford Papers, HSTL.

374. Walter Isard, "Some Economic Implications of Atomic Energy," *Quarterly Journal of Economics*, vol. 62 (February 1948), p. 227. See also Walter Isard and

The press was somewhat more excited than the academics about the promise of atomic energy by 1949. For example, *Business Week* perceived a turnaround in AEC interest and predicted commercial reactor operation by the late fifties.[375]

But not everyone was pleased about this new openness and breadth of attention to atomic energy outside government. President Truman's air force aide, Brigadier General Robert B. Landry, reported to him in April 1949: "I am alarmed about the amount and kind of information concerning atomic energy activities in the United States that appears in public articles. . . . This trend is a dangerous one. . . . It is my considered judgment that a great amount of the information made public to date is detrimental to our future security." A story in the January 1949 *Fortune,* which was the occasion for Landry's report, contained a picture of Oak Ridge facilities that Landry suggested "may offer enemy photo analysts some information concerning plant changes."[376]

Events in the latter half of 1949 and in 1950 combined to guarantee that for the remainder of President Truman's presidency security considerations would overwhelm considerations of the public's right to know and the commercial possibilities of atomic power. First of all, the Soviet Union's detonation of an atomic bomb in August 1949 put the arms race into high gear. AEC priorities shifted unequivocally to military projects, most importantly toward the "super" hydrogen bomb, but also toward a naval reactor for the propulsion of submarines. The fact that technical difficulties plagued the power-breeder reactor program only helped to confirm the shift. The second development was the discovery of a spy, Klaus Fuchs, at the highest level of the British nuclear establishment. A hostile three-month congressional investigation indicated that very tight security had again become the will of the people. Finally, of course, the outbreak of hostilities in Korea assured the return of a wartime atmosphere and the maintenance of a tight veil of security. During the war Lawrence R. Hafstad, director of reactor development at the AEC, argued that power

---

John B. Lansing, "Comparisons of Power Cost for Atomic and Conventional Steam Stations," *Review of Economics and Statistics,* vol. 31 (August 1949), pp. 217–28; and Sam Schurr, "The Cowles Commission Atomic Power Cost Estimates: A Reply," ibid., vol. 32 (February 1950), pp. 100–02. Papers from the teaching institute, in which Isard participated, are in OF 692, HSTL.

375. "Atomic Energy 1949," *Business Week,* April 30, 1949, p. 68.

376. Landry to the President, with attachments, April 6, 1949, Atomic Bomb and Energy File, Confidential File, Truman Papers, HSTL.

reactors might make a crucial contribution to the objective of security by building the country's economic base; but against the advocates of more and bigger weapons his arguments sounded somewhat hollow.[377]

A new element, however, was now firmly in the nuclear energy picture and could not practically be removed even by the crisis—the intense interest of the power industry in exploring the opportunities in atomic power. The ad hoc advisory committee to the AEC, appointed in July 1949 and chaired by Philip Sporn, president of the American Gas and Electric Company, discussed how this might be accomplished. They urged above all that the AEC attempt to develop relationships with the utilities comparable to those of the suppliers of conventional steam and hydroelectric equipment. It was through such a close partnership, they said, that technical progress was made. In addition close cooperation with industry would expose the AEC to that "body of knowledge and experience called utility economics. . . . The issues which are dealt with in this field involve the balancing of all the many factors entering into final cost in an operation in which a great many variables can be introduced, to give an over-all most economical result."[378] One of the proposals noted by the committee as requiring this kind of economic appraisal was that of Charles A. Thomas, president of the Monsanto Chemical Company, in 1950 that AEC reactors producing plutonium for weapons be run "hot" with steam for power generated as a by-product. The first actual generation of electric power from a reactor on December 20, 1951, undoubtedly stimulated further the corporate imagination. A serious power shortage during the war and increased discovery of uranium added to the attractiveness of further explorations.

Reportedly in response to Charles Thomas's proposal for power as a by-product of plutonium production the AEC asked four groups from industry to examine the opportunities for nuclear power on the basis of classified data released to them in the spring of 1951. The four groups reported late in 1951 and 1952. All four were enthusiastic about the possibilities but disagreed about which type of reactor held out the greatest promise for commercial electric power. In the circumstances of the times, with priori-

377. Hewlett and Anderson, *History of the United States Atomic Energy Commission,* vol. 2, pp. 219, 423, 492; and "The Atomic Era—Second Phase," *Business Week,* July 8, 1950, pp. 58–65.

378. "The Electric Power Industry and the AEC," *Bulletin of the Atomic Scientists,* vol. 7 (November 1951), p. 334.

ties still firmly directed toward thermonuclear weapons and naval propulsion, the AEC decision was to do nothing.[379]

It was significant that toward the end of 1951 David Bell, the White House staff member most concerned with electric power policy, had to read in *Business Week* that the AEC had begun to explore commercial opportunities for power development with private companies. He wrote to Charles Murphy:

. . . the story makes no mention of any Federal power agency or personnel being given the opportunity to find out what is going on in the atomic laboratories and to think about how power may be produced and used. It seems to me that this is an unfortunate fact, and that some thought should be going on to see to what extent there is reason to look forward to public power being developed and used from atomic energy. I suggest that a note might be dropped by you to Oscar Chapman making this general point. . . .[380]

Clearly, outside the AEC itself understanding of the relationship between atomic power and the nation's energy needs had still not penetrated the highest levels of policymaking.

The conclusions of the Paley Commission staff members who worked on atomic energy were generally bearish about its prospects, but they used qualifying language very similar to that of Isard and Loftus three years before to state their conclusions. "Since accurate information as to the technological and economic performance of atomic power plants is as uncertain as the future development of the international situation, precise predictions at this time are difficult, if not impossible, to make." The commission's final report noted that the widespread use of nuclear power depended on two developments: low-cost reactor design and the construction of a successful breeder reactor. Even though "it becomes evident that atomic energy will some day become a very important factor in the economy of the world. During the next 25 years its total effect on the energy picture may be limited by military use."[381]

---

379. Hewlett and Anderson, *History of the United States Atomic Energy Commission,* vol. 2, pp. 512, 514, 517. Although the four industry reports were held confidential, their contents were known publicly in some detail. For example, see "Next Steps on Atom Power," *Business Week,* August 9, 1952, pp. 68–70.

380. Bell to Murphy, October 16, 1951, Power File, Murphy Files, HSTL.

381. Memorandum, John R. Thomas to Philip H. Coombs, "Application of Atomic Energy to the Nation's Power Needs," July 12, 1951, with attachment, Administrative File–Atomic Energy, PMPC, HSTL. Comments by the AEC staff, Captain H. G. Rickover, and others on the Paley Commission conclusions are in General File–Atomic Energy, PMPC, HSTL.

In a briefing document prepared for the incoming Eisenhower administration, the Interior Department listed the following three issues of unfinished business requiring "inter-agency study": (1) private vs. public ownership of atomic power facilities and fissionable materials; (2) the allocation of cost between electric power and the fissionable substances produced by the atomic power plants; and (3) the marketing policy to be followed in distributing such power as is developed by public means.[382] Such a list might have been left by every subsequent administration for their successors as well.

Conclusion

What can be said in conclusion about the complex experience with the formulation of policies toward individual energy sources by the end of the Truman administration? Over all hovers the dominant influence of special interests in the policy process: producers, consumers, and even the government bureaucracy. In the case of oil the dominant influence undoubtedly was the industry itself; with gas, it was the consumers of that product, aided by the courts. With hydroelectricity, the various responsible government agencies predominated, while in synthetic fuels the Bureau of Mines dominated the early period, but the threatened petroleum producers prevailed later on.

Another overwhelming impression of the policy process in this period is of the unwillingness of all participants to allow free market forces to operate except in those particular circumstances in which they themselves stood directly to gain. Despite the considerable rhetoric voiced at different times about the importance of free enterprise and capitalism, there were depressingly few serious and thorough discussions of the costs and benefits of the various market interventions that were introduced. It was partly that most of the discussants were deeply self-interested and therefore produced mainly partisan expressions of their case. The wider public interest in some large sense seems to have been the concern of very few, notably some officials of the Interior Department, Justice Department, and the regulatory commissions. But of equal importance, energy issues were seldom able to catch the sustained attention either of the top leaders of the

382. "Status of Materials Resources Policy and Highlights of Major Issues," January 10, 1953, Reports and Recommendations on Departmental Programs File, Office Files of the Program Staff, RG 48, NA.

American government or the public at large. Most important issues of fuels policy were long-range: whether to increase petroleum exports, deregulate gas, construct hydroelectric dams, or develop synthetic fuels. Yet the only issues that could really capture public and presidential attention were short-run events such as winter fuel oil shortages, electricity brownouts, and gasoline price increases. In some cases temporary difficulties were used as an excuse for attention to the long run. But this attention was seldom sustained.

The question of national security affected any discussion of fuels policy in various ways. In one respect it created a sense of urgency that caused such seemingly insignificant questions as the dangers of concentrations of market power to be brushed aside. It also placed a premium on close cooperative relationships between industry and government so that the fuels would indeed be delivered when emergencies appeared. Security considerations also brought industry representatives prominently into government, so as to cope with the emergency but incidentally with a wide effect on how policy was made and executed. In the case of nuclear power, whose peacetime uses were directly in competition with weapon development and military propulsion, security considerations seemed definitely to be a retardant. A complicating effect of security on policies toward particular energy sources was the fluctuating character of this concern. A distinctive feature of most energy policies during this period was their erratic character. Some of this can be attributed to the waves of worry about security and national defense.

The analytical material on which energy policies had to be based in the Truman period was generally unimpressive. But there were exceptions. Some of the work produced by the Program Staff of the Interior Department and by the Office of the Assistant Secretary was of a high order. For example, President Truman had the issues laid out clearly before him on a question as important as whether to permit the growth of oil imports. Similarly the case for valley authorities was presented eloquently, even if to little avail. A weakness in the making of fuels policy, which was well recognized by Interior Department staff, was in the quality of available data, much of it produced by the respective industries. Moreover, little progress was made in bringing about improvement.

It is easy after the fact to suggest what policy should have been constructed to cope with a given issue in the past. One can forget the complexity of the problem as it existed at the time. In the case of fuels policies three prominent sources of complications were, first, that the technological issues often were exceptionally complex, not only because of the ambiguities surrounding such terms as reserves and the mysteries involved in processes like secondary recovery, but also because investments were so large and change so rapid. It was hard enough to be confident about the technical circumstances surrounding a challenge in the present; it was nearly impossible to do so looking very far into the future. Second, most fuel policy questions involved a choice of trade-offs among a myriad of different particular interests: not only between producers and consumers of the product, but also among categories of consumers in different regions, segments of the industry, producers of competing fuels, and foreign countries. In such a situation there was no single "right" policy. Finally, by 1945 the energy markets had become so cluttered with various laws and institutions, many of them concerned with matters far apart from the efficient production and distribution of energy, that practical policies had to take into account a bewildering variety of restraints, from the cheap-power doctrine of the valley authorities to percentage depletion for petroleum.

It is worth noting that during this first presidency after World War II most of the energy market issues appeared and were dealt with that were then rediscovered in the crisis years of the 1970s: the appropriate relationship between industry and government, the proper limit of dependence on foreign sources and how not to exceed it, how to deal with energy sectors that either profited or suffered from change, how much to count on nuclear energy, when to control fuel prices, and whether to attempt to ease the transition among fuels through the sort of public development program undertaken for synthetics. Energy issues that either were not identified clearly or were not dealt with effectively during this period included the environmental implications of most energy production, the possibility of "decoupling" the relationship between energy consumption and growth rates through changes in consumer behavior, and the potential afforded by a wide range of undeveloped energy sources, including nuclear, solar, and geothermal.[383]

383. The Interior Department's interest in solar energy was slight during the Truman years, but it did exist. In February 1949 Secretary Krug asked the Program Staff to prepare "a short survey of solar energy prospects." Walton Seymour reported to Krug, on the basis of a detailed survey paper by Harold Barnett, that "some of the avenues appeared promising," but he observed that "there was virtually no business or government pressure behind the research." Memorandums and reports illustrating Interior Department interest in solar energy can be found especially in Fuels Sources—Energy Subcommittee File, Minerals and Fuels Division Files, RG 48, NA. In August 1949 Secretary Krug announced in a speech at a U.N. conference and

It may be a comment either on the memory of government in America or on the effectiveness of energy policy in the Truman administration that by the late 1970s recollections of these precedents had largely faded from view.

---

in a press conference that he "was looking into solar energy utilization in order to determine whether the Government had a role to play in sponsoring its greater development." This led to conversations with Maria Telkes, a Massachusetts Institute of Technology scientist, about a consulting relationship and to discussions with the National Academy of Sciences about a full-scale study of solar energy. See memorandum, Walton Seymour to the Secretary of the Interior, "Solar Energy," January 4, 1950, Fuels Survey–Energy Subcommittee File, ibid.; and Seymour to Chapman, March 28, 1950, Solar Energy File, Seymour Office Files, RG 48, NA. The Barnett Paper is attached to the January 4 memorandum. Barnett's working papers are in Harold J. Barnett File, Seymour Office Files, RG 48, NA. No funds were made available for the academy study and the matter seems to have been dropped. The issue of solar possibilities kept reemerging in 1951 and 1952, however, with no important result. Joel Wolfsohn asked the Senate Interior Committee for funds for solar research in 1951, to no avail. ("Enough is Not Enough," Minerals and Fuels Division File, Wolfsohn Papers, HSTL.) Palmer Putnam, a consultant to the Paley Commission, was put to work on the subject, but when he took longer than expected to produce results he was "terminated." (Memorandum, Philip Coombs to Robert Blum, "Termination of Palmer Putnam's Solar Energy Study," August 14, 1951, Administrative File–Energy, PMPC, HSTL.) Subsequently Putnam produced one of the earliest published discussions of opportunities afforded by nondepleting energy sources, what he called "income energy" in contrast to "capital energy" provided by fossil fuels. (Putnam, *Energy in the Future*, pp. 97–215.) For reasons that are not clear the White House asked the Interior Department for a full report on solar energy opportunities in January 1952. (Robert E. Day to Kenneth Hechler, January 11, 1952, Solar Energy File, Seymour Office Files, RG 48, NA.) Subsequently a conference on solar energy was held by the Interior Department in May 1952 at which Dr. Telkes was the principal speaker and where various parts of the department expressed an interest in moving into the area. (Memorandum, R. C. Price to Secretary Chapman, "Solar Energy," May 19, 1952, Division of Water and Power File, Searles Office Files, RG 48, NA.) The only pressure for increased use of wood for fuel appears to have come from industry spokesmen. For example, Edgar L. Heermance, Executive Secretary, Northeastern Wood Utilization Council, to W. Stuart Symington, September 5, 1950, Records of the National Security Resources Board, 54-23, RG 304, NA.

CHAPTER THREE

The Eisenhower Energy Policy: Reluctant Intervention

WILLIAM J. BARBER

PART OF the inheritance of the Eisenhower administration was a heightened national consciousness of the prospective supply and demand balances of energy resources and their implications for the nation's longer-term economic outlook. This issue had been highlighted by the Paley Report, submitted to the Truman administration in June 1952 (see chapter 1). The United States, the Paley Commission had insisted, was approaching a fundamental turning point in its economic life. Raw material resources in general and primary energy sources in particular were obviously essential to the nation's continued prosperity, but it could no longer be assumed that domestic supplies would continue to be available on favorable terms. Nature, according to the Paley Report, had "stacked the cards heavily in favor of rising costs by imposing limits on the amounts of highest grade sources easily available."[1]

Evidence of a basic structural shift was already at hand. In the postwar years the United States' historic position as a supplier of energy materials to the rest of the world had been reversed. In terms of British thermal unit (Btu) equivalents the United States had become a net importer of primary fuels. This transformation was notably conspicuous in the nation's increased reliance on foreign sources of oil. In the judgment of the Paley Commission the time was ripe for the formulation of a "comprehensive energy policy" that would approach the problem "in its

THE BULK of the primary material used in this chapter was drawn from the Dwight D. Eisenhower Library in Abilene, Kansas. The author very much appreciated the assistance of the library's able staff, particularly that of David Haight. The following abbreviations are used in the footnotes in this chapter: Dwight D. Eisenhower Library (DDEL), National Archives (NA), and Official Files (OF).

1. President's Materials Policy Commission, *Resources for Freedom,* vol. 1: *Foundations for Growth and Security* (Government Printing Office, 1952), p. 13.

entirety and not as a loose collection of independent pieces involving different sources and forms of energy. . . . The aim must be to achieve a constant pattern of policies and programs throughout the entire energy field."[2]

The Paley Report provided an opportunity for debate about the relationship between the supply constraints imposed by nature and the nation's growth prospects over the longer term. A similar opportunity had arisen more than a century earlier for England, the world's first industrial nation, when sharp rises in agricultural production costs at home after the Napoleonic Wars and major increases in imports of basic foodstuffs had emphasized the natural limits to the domestic supply of the inputs then most essential to sustained economic expansion. The battle lines of policy confrontation had been drawn between those who would shelter a high-cost primary sector at home and those who welcomed cheaper imports. In the disputations of the ensuing decades central policy issues demanding choices had been brought into clear focus: government intervention in support of domestic producers versus freer play for market forces, encouragements to self-sufficiency (justified on national security grounds) versus greater reliance on national specialization and international economic interdependence, and attempts to reduce the costs of the products of nature by investing at home or by investing abroad. The result of this debate owed much to the contributions of the economists of the day who, in the process of diagnosing the linkages between economic growth and nature's "niggardliness," put in place the conceptual apparatus of a new political economy.

In 1952 the ingredients of an analogous intellectual challenge were present. William Paley drew its dimensions to the attention of President-elect Eisenhower on December 14, 1952. When transmitting copies of the report of the President's Materials Policy Commission for the use of the President-elect and his nominees to senior cabinet posts, Paley wrote:

I would like to emphasize that our country has moved into a new era in its economic history, an era in which we can no longer produce enough of many materials at a cost basis to satisfy our expanding economy or security needs. I believe that this trend will continue and increase. I am not an alarmist on this question, but I do like to generate real concern. I feel that if industry and government, principally industry, take appropriate steps to meet our future needs and keep on top of the problem as a continuing matter, this country will not suffer because of the lack of materials. On the other hand, if we trust

2. Ibid., p. 129.

to the accident of the future and fall back on the belief that somehow everything will work out all right, we might find ourselves in serious difficulty.[3]

Nor was Paley alone. A new organization being formed under the name
Resources for the Future had urged candidate Eisenhower to take the
lead in focusing national attention on these matters through the sponsorship of a White House conference to consider them.[4]

Meanwhile a possible agenda for the discussion of energy issues was
being worked out in the bureaucracy. The National Security Resources
Board, which President Truman had asked to coordinate the views of
various departments and agencies on the recommendations of the Paley
Commission, completed this assignment on December 10, 1952. A broad
consensus was reported in support of increased federal funding for the
development of new sources of primary fuels (such as oil from shale)
and for an expanded commitment to major hydroelectric projects. Steps
to accelerate the commercial development of nuclear power were also
called for. Both the federal and state governments were urged to encourage offshore exploration for oil and to promote improved conservation
practices (particularly in connection with the spacing of wells). A
strengthened research program for coal, not only to stimulate productivity in mining but also to develop new product applications, was
recommended.[5]

When the Eisenhower administration took office the Paley Report's
call for a fundamental rethinking of policies toward the energy sector did
not lack advocates. It was to be expected, however, that the reception
their views received would depend on how compatible these views were
with the larger objectives of the new administration. Though many details remained to be worked out, administration leaders who assumed
power on January 20, 1953, had established a reasonably coherent set of
goals for the conduct of both domestic and foreign economic policy. A
comprehensive energy policy per se did not occupy a central position

3. Letter, Paley to Eisenhower, December 15, 1952, OF, Box 922, DDEL.
4. In responding to this suggestion on October 2, 1952, Eisenhower wrote: "If I
am elected I shall be glad to issue or join in an appropriate call of a Conference to
consider the subject of Resources for the Future, and to ask the cooperation of governmental and private agencies in the preparations for and conduct of the conference
meetings." He added that "it is high time that the Conservation Conference of 1908
[which had been called by Theodore Roosevelt] should be reborn in a mid-century
setting!" Eisenhower to Horace M. Albright, October 2, 1952, OF, Box 683, DDEL.
5. U.S. National Security Resources Board, *The Objectives of United States Materials Resources Policy and Suggested Initial Steps in Their Accomplishment* (GPO,
1952), pp. 1–4.

on their agenda. In its application, however, the broader official doctrine
was to affect the structure and performance of various components of the
energy sector in highly significant ways.

Energy Issues and Domestic Economic Policy

Though the Paley Commission had called for a comprehensive, rather
than a piecemeal, approach to the problems of long-run energy supply, it
had not prescribed a specific mix of private and public activities. It stated
the objective of the strategy more generally: the goal was a "program
which embraces all the narrower and more specific policies and programs relating to each type of energy and which welds these pieces
together into a consistent and mutually supporting pattern with unified
direction. This implies no increase in Government activity; it well might
mean less."[6] The Eisenhower administration could be quite comfortable
with the latter proposition. In principle nothing precluded relying on the
market as the coordinating mechanism and allowing the unifying and
directing hand to be invisible. Government, to be sure, was already heavily involved in the energy sector as a producer, as a regulator, and as a
rule-setter. But the nature of that involvement was not immutable. The
new administration's team considered the pattern of federal intervention
in the recent past highly eligible for a searching review.

The administration's basic posture toward the management of the
domestic economy had been amply articulated during the campaign. It
rested on four central premises: (1) that the mix of economic activity
between the private and the public sectors should be redressed in favor
of the private sector; (2) that within the public sector the roles of the
federal government and of state and local governments should be adjusted in favor of the governmental units closest to the people; (3) that
in those cases in which the federal government itself was a supplier of
goods and services, its conduct should conform more closely to standard
business practice; and (4) that in the general development of economic
policies the federal government should attempt to be neutral when confronted with the special claims of producer or consumer groups or of
particular regional interests. In short, the allocative functions of markets
should be reinforced, while direct government participation in the econ-

6. PMPC, *Resources for Freedom*, vol. 1, p. 129.

omy should be retrenched. This was not, however, a doctrine of un-inhibited laissez-faire. A responsibility of the federal government for dampening cyclical disturbances and for correcting market failures was accepted and reaffirmed.

Though these basic premises were articulated in general terms, they had an immediate effect on policies developed toward several of the energy industries. Initially the force of this doctrine fell most heavily where a federal presence had already been established as an energy pro-ducer. The Department of the Interior lost little time in redefining the federal government's posture toward the supply of electric power. The power policy statement of August 1953 asserted that "the primary re-sponsibility for supplying power needs of an area rests with the people locally."[7] The department would remain prepared to be a partner in the construction of sound and necessary projects that were "beyond the means of local, public or private enterprise." It nonetheless hoped that the bulk of this task would be undertaken by others.[8] The Interior De-partment further made clear that it would no longer assume that it had "the exclusive right or responsibility for the construction of dams for the generation, transmission and sale of electric energy in any area, basin, or region."[9] Accordingly it had withdrawn the objection filed by the Truman administration to the proposed construction of a hydroelectric project by a private utility at Hell's Canyon on the Snake River.

Similar considerations informed the administration's treatment of proposals by the directors of the Tennessee Valley Authority for addi-tional budget authorization to build steam-generating plants to meet anticipated load growth in its service area. In May 1953 the Bureau of the Budget insisted that this matter should be handled by requesting the TVA "to submit proposals as to steps that might be taken to encourage non-Federal agencies to participate in meeting the increased load growth in this region thereby reducing the impact of this agency's expansion

7. "Department of Interior Power Policy," August 18, 1953, Bryce Harlow Pa-pers, Box 4, DDEL.

8. In the cabinet's review of the draft of this statement, sentiment favoring a flexible interpretation of this position was expressed. The President and the vice-president—joined by Henry Cabot Lodge, Jr.; Harold E. Stassen; Charles E. Wilson; and Herbert Brownell, Jr.—urged that the public announcement of the Interior De-partment's policy "indicate specifically that the Federal Government planned to undertake certain power projects as soon as budgetary considerations allow." Min-utes of the Cabinet Meeting of July 31, 1953, Ann Whitman Files, Cabinet Series, Box 2, DDEL.

9. "Department of Interior Power Policy."

program on the United States Treasury."[10] The TVA, after all, was the prime exhibit of a government monopoly in the power business. While the administration insisted that it had no wish to "destroy" this enterprise, it was determined that the federal commitment to the TVA should be contained. Moreover, the TVA's budgetary practices should be revised to approximate those of private utilities. But the TVA case was not in harmony with the premises of the official doctrine for an even broader reason. The very existence of the TVA represented a form of regional favoritism that violated the principle of federal neutrality. The nation's taxpayers had subsidized the power bills of a group of geographically favored consumers and had loaded the dice in this group's favor in the competition for new industries. It was recognized that in principle this inequity might be redressed if the federal government were to put comparable facilities in place in all other regions of the country. This possibility, however, could be readily dismissed as being in conflict with the official view of the proper role of federal intervention.[11]

It was also consistent with the basic principles of the official doctrine that the federal government should disengage itself from its monopoly position in the nuclear energy field. In view of the uncertainties surrounding the potential of this new technology, opinions in 1953 diverged widely on its commercial feasibility. The administration, however, had little doubt on one point: that private industry should be the Schumpeterian innovator. The government would be obliged to retain a special role as an inventor and regulator; the security aspects of nuclear energy compelled that. But the scope for private initiative in turning this novel technology to the service of civilian energy needs could still safely and productively be extended. On April 8, 1953, the Atomic Energy Commission indicated that it had drafted a new policy designed to "create a wider opportunity for private investment" in nuclear reactors.[12]

10. Bureau of the Budget memorandum, May 11, 1953, Central Files, Box 234, DDEL. On the same date, Joseph Dodge, director of the Budget Bureau, reported to Sherman Adams that he had arranged to obtain the services of Adolphe H. Wenzell of the First Boston Corporation without compensation "to make a commercial financial appraisal of TVA." (Dodge to Adams, May 11, 1953, ibid.) This apparently innocent arrangement was later to become a focal point of intense controversy.

11. Eisenhower personally subscribed to this position with deep conviction, and it appears as a frequent theme in his private correspondence. An example is his letter to Captain E. E. Hazlitt, July 20, 1954, Whitman Files, Eisenhower Diary Series, Box 3, DDEL.

12. Reported in Draft Memorandum, Bureau of the Budget, "Atomic Power Development and the Need for Amending the Atomic Energy Act at the Present Time," April 20, 1953, OF, Box 523, DDEL.

The aspects of the official doctrine that addressed the appropriate division of labor between state and federal authority contained further implications for the shaping of policy toward some of the energy industries. In particular the doctrine required that regulatory authority over the services of public utilities and over the production of oil and natural gas should be primarily a responsibility of the states. Federal surveillance should be sharply delimited to transactions that were unambiguously interstate in character. A problem loomed, however, over the interpretation of the regulatory jurisdiction assigned by the Natural Gas Act of 1938, and in 1953 this matter was pending in the courts. Nonetheless, the leadership of the executive branch was clear about its reading of the situation: the production and gathering of natural gas in the field was an intrastate affair, but the transmission of gas through interstate pipelines came under federal jurisdiction. The doctrine of "priority to states" was also invoked to justify the assignment of authority over offshore drilling to state governments, up to the "historic boundaries" of the states. Honoring a campaign pledge to constituencies in the Gulf states, the administration pushed passage of legislation in 1953 to effect this allocation of the tidelands.[13] Jurisdiction over the continental shelf beyond the "historic" claims of states remained in federal hands, but the Eisenhower administration changed the rules governing oil development there. In one of his last official acts President Truman had signed an executive order reserving the outer continental shelf to the federal government as a naval petroleum reserve. The Outer Continental Shelf Lands Act of 1953, however, authorized the secretary of the interior to issue leases to private oil promoters.

A common thread ran through the initial applications of the official doctrine to the energy sector: a systematic disengagement of direct federal involvement in the economy. But this did not mean that senior officials of the Eisenhower administration were indifferent to the longer-term problems of energy supply. To the contrary, their view of the world suggested that the best assurance that the nation's long-run needs would be satisfactorily met was to be found in opening more space for private initiative. The task of government was to provide a healthy climate for

13. The Submerged Lands Act of 1953, however, was not a final disposition of this matter. Two states, Texas and Florida, claimed "historic" offshore boundaries of three leagues rather than the three-mile limit recognized in international law. The Departments of State and Justice opposed this departure from accepted international practice, but their objections had been overridden. The definition of offshore boundaries offered in the 1953 act was later challenged in the courts.

private investment; it was distinctly not the government's function to direct the allocation of the economy's resources.

These predispositions were clearly at odds with the view of those who interpreted the Paley Commission's appeal for a comprehensive energy policy as an invitation for more thoroughgoing government planning. In the spring of 1953 the White House was counseled that the President's earlier expressions of active support for a projected conference on resources for the future might be misplaced. The President of the U.S. Chamber of Commerce, for example, reported his view to Eisenhower's first assistant: "To date, the planning of this Conference has been dominated by socialistic thinkers, former government and federal commission employees, and ardent conservationists." The White House was urged to reexamine the plans and objectives of the proposed conference "with a view to insuring that the business viewpoint has an equal chance of being presented."[14]

As events unfolded, a conference was held in Washington, but in December 1953, rather than in March 1953 (as had initially been suggested). It was designated, not a White House conference, but simply the Mid-Century Conference on Resources for the Future. The President appeared for a brief address of welcome, but his remarks were ceremonial.[15]

Energy Issues and International Economic Policy

Both as an importer of oil and as an exporter of coal the American energy sector was linked with world markets. But beyond this the United States was vitally interested in the health of the international energy economy. As the leader of the free world, the United States could not be

14. Laurence F. Lee to Sherman Adams, February 9, 1953, OF, Box 683, DDEL.
15. The apparent disenchantment of the White House with this venture also attracted some critics, among them Paul L. Patterson, governor of Oregon. In response to his criticism a White House staff aide observed that "there has been a slight misunderstanding. The Administration, and more specifically the White House, does not want to give the impression that they have in any way repudiated the forthcoming 'Resources for the Future' meeting. . . . We are helping in three different ways: I understand the President has written a letter endorsing the Conference; I believe he will appear at some time and say a word of greeting to the assembled members; Executive Departments are lending personnel and services to aid in organizing and setting up the meetings." Maxwell M. Rabb to Governor Patterson, September 4, 1953, OF, ibid.

indifferent to the economic fate of its allies and to the adequacy of energy supplies needed to support rebuilding their economies. For its part the Eisenhower administration was determined that the United States would discharge its international leadership role responsibly. A retreat into the isolationism of the interwar years was not entertainable.

In economic terms the fullest expression of the broad vision of America's role in the world economy was found in the study of the Commission on Foreign Economic Policy, which reported to the President on January 23, 1954.[16] This group, under the leadership of Clarence B. Randall, chairman of the Inland Steel Company, had issued a plea for American initiative in the reconstruction of the international economic order. It called for a world in which barriers to trade and to capital movements would be progressively reduced. The model that informed these recommendations was of a piece with the premises of the official doctrine toward the conduct of economic affairs at home. In both cases freer markets were regarded as the primary carriers of progress. In the international arena the opening of greater space for private capital flows would also reduce the claims on the U.S. government to assist friendly nations through special aid programs. But dissenting voices were still to be heard. Long-standing protectionist sentiments were strategically situated in American political life. A majority of the Randall Commission members attempted to deflect one of the protectionist arguments that predictably would be deployed: that freer trade would threaten the national security by weakening industries allegedly vital to the country's defense. The majority position recommended that such pleadings in the future should be adjudicated by the Department of Defense (rather than by the Tariff Commission) and that the incremental costs they occasioned should be charged against the department's budget.

Even before the findings of the Randall Commission were available, the administration had begun to shape positions on two matters affecting the longer-term conditions of international energy supply. The first concerned the problems arising from the continued closure of the Iranian oil fields, which had been shut down since the nationalization of the British-owned Anglo-Iranian Oil Company in 1951. Restoring and expanding oil supplies from this area were regarded as of the highest importance to the strategic security of the North Atlantic Treaty Organization (NATO). In the effort to work out a solution U.S. policymakers

16. Commission on Foreign Economic Policy, *Report to the President and the Congress* (GPO, 1954).

accepted the idea that some form of partnership, which would include substantial participation by the Iranian government, was a political necessity. At the same time, it was hoped that a scheme for compensating the British owners of the Anglo-Iranian Oil Company could be developed, even though it was clear that the Iranian government was not in a position to finance such a transaction. A plan that met these specifications was proposed by the President's special representative, Herbert Hoover, Jr., and it involved the creation of an international consortium organized around a group of oil firms that would in effect buy out at least part of the British interest. Exploratory negotiations along these lines were endorsed by the National Security Council on August 6, 1953, and the President directed the attorney general to "develop a solution which would protect the interests of the free world in the Near East as a vital source of petroleum supplies," including the development of "new or alternative legal relationship(s) between the oil companies of the Western nations and the nations of the Near East."[17]

The participation of American oil companies in the proposed consortium posed a difficulty. The most promising candidates for this undertaking were the five U.S. "majors."[18] They were amply financed and experienced in Middle East operations, though Iran had not formerly been within their sphere of operations. The same five companies, however, were the defendants in a cartel case filed by the Department of Justice.[19]

17. As cited in *The International Petroleum Cartel, the Iranian Consortium and U.S. National Security*, Subcommittee on Multinational Corporations of the Senate Committee on Foreign Relations, 93 Cong. 2 sess. (GPO, 1974) p. vi.

18. In 1953 the U.S. majors were the Standard Oil Company of New Jersey (later Exxon), the Texas Company (later Texaco), Socony-Vacuum Oil Company (later Mobil), the Standard Oil Company of California (later Socal), and the Gulf Oil Corporation.

19. This case had been stimulated by a staff report of the Federal Trade Commission (completed in the fall of 1951), which had concluded that the high degree of concentration in the international petroleum market had facilitated "the development and observance of international agreements regarding price and production policies. Indeed, the concentration of an industry into a few hands may be regarded as the *sine qua non* of effective cartel operations." (*The International Petroleum Cartel*, Committee Print 6, Staff Report to the Federal Trade Commission submitted to the Subcommittee on Monopoly of the Senate Select Committee on Small Business, 82 Cong. 2 sess. [GPO, 1952], p. 33.) Though this report was not formally approved by the Federal Trade Commission, it had provided the basis for a grand jury investigation initiated by the Truman administration. When the Eisenhower administration took office, Attorney General Brownell on January 23, 1953, stated his intention to ask for a delay in the Iranian oil case "because of its controversial

A situation in which the federal government simultaneously prosecuted the majors for alleged conspiracy and courted them to enter a government-designed consortium was obviously awkward.

The formula ultimately adopted in late 1954 attempted to relieve some of the tensions between considerations of domestic and foreign economic policy. American firms were assigned a 40 percent interest in the new consortium: 35 percent of the total was equally distributed between the five majors and 5 percent was allocated to a group of smaller "independents" that had not formerly conducted operations on a significant scale overseas.[20] Members of the consortium were authorized to produce and explore for oil in southern Iran and to operate the Abadan refinery. The National Iranian Oil Company (a newly organized government monopoly) was recognized, however, as the legal owner of Iran's oil reserves and refinery assets.

The opening provided in this formula for the smaller American independents testified to the U.S. government's concern for an industrial structure that approximated competitive conditions more closely.[21] Meanwhile the attorney general in an opinion on January 21, 1954, held that the proposed consortium plan would not in itself constitute an un-

---

nature." (Minutes of the Cabinet Meeting of January 23, 1953, Whitman Files, Cabinet Series, Box 1, DDEL.) Subsequently the Department of Justice terminated the grand jury proceedings but filed a civil complaint on April 21, 1953, alleging that the five majors were in violation of the Sherman Anti-Trust Act and were "engaged in an unlawful combination and conspiracy to restrain interstate and foreign commerce of the United States in petroleum and products imported into the United States, and to monopolize trade and commerce in petroleum and products between the United States and foreign nations. . . ." As cited in *The International Petroleum Cartel, the Iranian Consortium, and U.S. National Security*, p. 36.

20. The so-called independents participating in the Iranian Oil Consortium were Richfield, American Independent Oil Company (which was owned by nine U.S. domestic companies), Sohio, Getty, Signal, Hancock, Atlantic, Tidewater, and San Jacinto; collectively these new independent entrants to the Iranian scene were referred to as IRICON. Other allocations were distributed as follows: 40 percent to the Anglo-Iranian Oil Company; 14 percent to Shell (which was controlled by British and Dutch interests); and 6 percent to Compagnie Francaise des Pétroles (the French national oil corporation).

21. Events in the 1970s, however, revealed an unintended consequence of this decision. The leverage of the Organization of Petroleum Exporting Countries over oil pricing was greater with the independents established in the Middle East than it would have been had the international majors continued to preempt the field. On this point see Raymond Vernon, ed., *The Oil Crisis* (Norton, 1976), especially pp. 3–7.

reasonable restraint of trade. One of the provisions of the agreement worked out among the participants did, however, offer scope for its members to act collectively in restricting crude oil production.[22]

The Eisenhower administration itself added a further dimension to the international discussion of energy questions with a dramatic announcement in December 1953. In his "Atoms for Peace" speech before the General Assembly of the United Nations, the President set out an imaginative plan for international cooperation in developing the peaceful uses of nuclear technology. "Peaceful power for atomic energy is no dream of the future," he declared. "That capability, already proved, is here—now—today."[23] The challenge of the future was to use this potential to lighten the burdens of mankind. For its part the United States was prepared to take the lead in sharing nuclear materials and scientific knowledge in ways that promised to solve the world's long-term energy problems. In the climate of 1953, however, this message was designed primarily as a statement on foreign policy, not on energy policy.[24] Its

22. This provision was to be a matter of some controversy in the Department of Justice and to have implications of considerable import for the later prosecution of the cartel case. The issue was presented in a memorandum from Kenneth R. Harkins to Assistant Attorney General Stanley N. Barnes on September 15, 1954. "I have searched the documents diligently for indication wherein these arguments differ from the arrangements attacked in the cartel suit. I have found no significant deviation but on the contrary have found many indications which lead me to believe that these arrangements manifest a continuation of the cartel pattern. In the light of the information we have in the cartel case, I do not believe that we can properly assume that the participants will market this oil in a lawful matter. In view of this, I do not see how the Attorney General can approve these arrangements consistently with the position he has taken in the cartel suit. Therefore, I cannot recommend that the Attorney General sign a letter which states that these arrangements 'do not constitute a violation of the antitrust laws nor create a violation of antitrust law not already existing.' I discussed this memo with the Attorney General today—he stated that he felt he had already crossed this bridge on January 20, but that he agreed that approval of the consortium was inconsistent with the cartel case as the complaint is drawn and that necessarily the case must proceed with emphasis on the marketing aspects and not on the production control aspects." As reprinted in *The International Petroleum Cartel, the Iranian Consortium and U.S. National Security*, p. 91.

23. "Address before the General Assembly of the United Nations on Peaceful Uses of Atomic Energy, December 8, 1953," *Public Papers: Dwight D. Eisenhower, 1953* (GPO, 1960), p. 820.

24. The basic strategy underlying the development of the U.S. position appears to have emerged from a proposal of the President's, which he did not believe "anyone had yet thought of." On September 10, 1953, White House Special Assistant Robert Cutler, writing on behalf of the President, requested the comment of Lewis Strauss and C. D. Jackson on the following propositions: "Suppose the United States and the Soviets were each to turn over to the United Nations, for peaceful use,

text was shaped more by the experts on psychological warfare (who sensed an opportunity for diplomatic gains in the post-Stalin phase of the cold war) than by the experts on nuclear technology. Nevertheless, the Eisenhower speech and the response of other nations to it aroused new expectations that the United States was not only committed to leadership in the development of peaceful uses of atomic power, but that it would also share the fruits of its endeavors with others.

The Changing Climate of Policy in 1954

The broad principles by which the administration sought to guide the conduct of domestic and foreign economic policy initially had been reasonably clearly articulated, though at a high level of generality. But the operational strategies they called for were to be tested and in some measure recast by events in 1954. Circumstances of recession demanded attention, and the attention they received was to have a number of further consequences for the structure and functioning of the energy industries and for the subsequent development of policies toward them.

Despite its professed distaste for the "new economics" of a Keynesian variety and for enlarged participation of government in economic life, the senior leadership of the Eisenhower administration was persuaded that economic stabilization was a responsibility the federal government was obliged to discharge. Moreover, it was abundantly clear to the President, as it was to some of his closest advisers, that the Republican party could not prudently preside over the onset of another major depression. The question was not whether the federal government should provide recession buffers, but rather the forms they should take.

At the macroeconomic level the task of economic stabilization in 1954 called for stimulants to aggregate demand. The President, though opposed to "slam-bang" measures, insisted on the importance of "keeping in a high state of readiness all applicable plans for combatting, or rather preventing, depression or serious deflation."[25] His list of eligible

---

X kilograms of fissionable material. The amount X could be fixed at a figure which we could handle from our stockpile, but which it would be difficult for the Soviets to match." Cutler to Strauss and Jackson, September 10, 1953, Whitman Files, Administration Series, Box 5, DDEL.

25. Eisenhower to Arthur F. Burns, February 2, 1954, Whitman Files, Cabinet Series, Box 3, DDEL.

items in such contingency planning included public power projects. The longer-term need for such projects should of course be established, and care should be taken to ensure that spending by government did not displace spending that would otherwise be undertaken by private investors. Within that framework the Council of Economic Advisers was charged to coordinate the work of various agencies and departments in developing worthwhile programs of public spending to stimulate the economy.

These circumstances in turn stimulated a further look at the investment-absorbing capacity of the energy economy, particularly in those of its components most directly subject to government influence. The CEA accepted the Paley Commission's estimate that the nation's requirements for electric power were likely to be three and a half times greater by 1975 than they had been in 1950 and held that a strong case could thus be made for speeding development of hydroelectric capacity in areas where a power deficit was anticipated (notably in the Pacific Northwest and on the Niagara River).[26] It did not necessarily follow that the federal government should finance these projects, but it was essential that the government should not obstruct them. CEA Chairman Arthur Burns pointed out that this was not an imaginary concern. Delays in the Federal Power Commission had already frustrated promising proposals for hydroelectric projects on interstate waterways. He recommended to Sherman Adams that the FPC be authorized to enlarge its staff in order to "expedite and stimulate private investment in power. This is a very desirable goal. Can we do anything to push it along?"[27]

There was also a hint that the time might be auspicious for investment in developing less conventional sources of energy. Over the longer term the CEA expected real costs of oil and natural gas to rise. Similar cost trends were projected for hydroelectric power since the most attractive sites had already been tapped. If the nation's requirements for the next quarter-century were to be met, radically new processes for the generation of electrical power deserved to be entertained—for example, nuclear, solar, and wind energy sources.[28] As events unfolded, however, the form of countercyclical public spending that had the most to recommend it to the Eisenhower administration had greater impact on the

26. CEA Staff Working Papers, n.d., Neil Jacoby Papers, Box 1, DDEL.

27. Burns to Adams, August 17, 1954, Central Files, Box 193, DDEL. Adams in turn requested that Rowland R. Hughes, director of the Bureau of the Budget, review this situation carefully. Adams to Hughes, September 6, 1954, ibid.

28. CEA Staff Working Papers.

long-run demand for energy than on its long-run supply. To conservative tastes, support for the construction of an interstate highway system was especially attractive. This form of spending could readily be turned on and off with business conditions. It was a sphere of activity in which no preemptive competition with private investment could arise. Moreover, the increased efficiency in transport it could promote could contribute both to the growth of productivity in the private sector and to strengthening the nation's defense capabilities. Yet another consideration in its favor was that the financing of this program could be handled on a trust fund account and would not unbalance the visible administrative budget. This particular option also stood high in presidential favor.[29]

But recession also prompted a rethinking of economic strategy in general—and toward primary-fuel industries more particularly—in yet other ways. Shrinking markets predictably evoke appeals from distressed industries for special treatment. Moreover, such anxieties are likely to be especially acute when the distress of recession is compounded by fears of major structural changes in the market environment. In 1954 two industries in the primary fuel sector, coal and oil, felt themselves to be doubly vulnerable.

The coal industry regarded itself as uniquely disadvantaged. In the postwar years it had witnessed a shrinkage, both relatively and absolutely, in its position as a supplier of the nation's energy needs. Whereas it had contributed 51 percent of domestic requirements (as measured in Btu equivalents) in 1945, its share had fallen to less than one-third by 1954. Total production had declined by roughly one-third, or about 200 million tons, from the peak year in 1947. Meanwhile unemployment in the coal mining areas had risen dramatically. Much of the market space formerly occupied by coal had been claimed by the remarkable increase in the utilization of natural gas. To a lesser extent its declining fortunes were attributed to displacement by residual fuel oils. In the opinion of the coal industry's spokesmen, corrective action by the government was called for because the government itself had aggravated the industry's difficulties. According to the industry, government had placed coal at a competitive disadvantage by tolerating arrangements that allegedly had permitted natural gas to be sold in interstate commerce at

29. Eisenhower's personal interest in this matter is reflected in a longhand memorandum written to Sherman Adams on May 11, 1954. "Where do we stand on our 'dramatic' plan to get 50 billion dollars worth of self-liquidating highways under construction?" Whitman Files, Administration Series, Box 1, DDEL.

prices below its cost of production.[30] Moreover, the regulatory apparatus of government, through the actions of the Interstate Commerce Commission, had discriminated against coal in the setting of freight rates. But that was not all. Federal action was held to be responsible for subsidizing rival energy sources, for example, hydroelectrical power and, at least prospectively, nuclear energy. Meanwhile the coal interests asserted that national security was closely linked to their fate. Unlike the other primary fuels, the known reserves of coal were more than ample to satisfy demands over any reasonable time horizon. If the nation were to rely on coal as its principal energy source, there could never be a threat of supply interruption in the event of a national emergency.

The grievances of the oil industry took a different form. Production in this industry had declined with recession and was well below capacity levels of operation.[31] But this was not the only source of its concern. Even more troublesome was the rising volume of imports: by 1953 net imports of crude oil had risen to 10 percent of domestic production, compared with 5 percent in 1946. Moreover, there was every reason to expect this trend to continue. Not only could crude oil be procured abroad at substantially lower cost than at home, but the growing penetration of American firms into the rich fields of the Middle East was thought likely to increase shipments to the American market. The increased flow of oil imports was already putting pressure on the mechanisms worked out in the domestic industry to adapt production to demand. In particular the prorationing system administered by various state regulatory bodies had been brought under considerable strain. This system, though justified as a conservation measure, had effectively operated as a price-stabilizing mechanism when state regulatory agencies had been empowered to adjust "allowable" production rates with an eye to forestalling surpluses that might put downward pressure on prices. The most strategic component of this production and price control system

30. This indictment referred to the sale of "interruptible" gas distributed through interstate pipelines. In view of the seasonal fluctuations in the demand for natural gas and the technical necessity to maintain a regular flow of gas through the pipelines, a practice had developed whereby industrial users were quoted subaverage rates in the off-peak seasons on condition that their supplies could be terminated when requirements of households increased.

31. In Texas, for example, the annual average of monthly production "allowables," which had been 100 percent of the maximum efficient rate of extraction in 1948, was reduced to 65 percent in 1953 and to 53 percent in 1954. See Douglas R. Bohi and Milton Russell, *Limiting Oil Imports: An Economic History and Analysis* (Johns Hopkins University Press for Resources for the Future, 1978), p. 31.

was the Texas Railroad Commission, which had jurisdiction over wells producing nearly half of the nation's domestic crude oil supply. The commission, in company with similar regulatory authorities in most other oil-producing states, was accustomed to soliciting monthly "nominations" by which refiners indicated their anticipated requirements for crude oil. Allowable production rates could thus be targeted to preclude a reduction in crude oil prices.

Unrestrained oil imports posed a threat to these arrangements. They not only displaced domestic output that otherwise would have been forthcoming (though at higher supply prices) but also tended to erode the state regulatory system itself. The Texas Railroad Commission attempted in 1953 to prop up the price support features of the prorationing system by requesting oil importers to provide it with information on their import plans. But such information, even if accurately reported, would offer slight comfort to domestic producers. Although it could enable the regulatory bodies to adjust the allowable production rates to preclude any substantial erosion in price, this action also implied that the volume of domestic production would be contracted as imports increased.

In June 1954 a Supreme Court decision added another element of complexity to an already confused picture. When handing down its decision in *Phillips Petroleum Company* v. *Wisconsin,* the Court ruled that the FPC should henceforth regulate the field prices of natural gas. To both the administration and the FPC this additional regulatory assignment was unwelcome. Within the framework of the official doctrine, the gathering of natural gas in the field was entirely an intrastate transaction and not properly a matter of federal concern. The judiciary in combination with the general state of the economy had thus created a situation in which a rethinking of at least some aspects of the initial approach to the problems of energy was called for.

Revamped Strategy toward Energy Industries, 1954–55

Whether or not the executive branch chose to redress the grievances of distressed components of the energy economy, it could not ignore them, not least because influential voices in Congress were raised in their behalf. But direct intervention by government to support these industries posed a difficulty. The official doctrine maintained that government had already intervened excessively in private markets. The suggestion that it should add to the market shelters available to particular producer groups was not compellingly attractive. Such proposals were more entertainable, however, if they touched concerns for national security. The United States, of course, had been reminded in World War II and again during the Korean action of the importance of satisfactory energy availability to the successful conduct of military operations. Even in the absence of hostilities the acknowledged centrality of the United States to the security of the free world implied that national defense considerations could not be excluded from discussion of domestic policies toward the energy industries.

The first of the energy industries to receive formal official recognition along these lines was coal. Following White House sessions with industry representatives and with members of the congressional delegations from coal-producing states, the President announced the formation of an interdepartmental committee to study coal's problems in late June 1954. The language setting out the terms of reference for this study struck a characteristic note.

The soft coal industry is, of course, a very important part of our defense mobilization base. Despite the ever increasing demand for mechanical energy, the utilization of coal has actually dropped over the last several years and there is danger of a serious loss in our capacity to produce coal in the event of a major emergency in the future. . . . [T]he function of [the committee] shall be to determine the nature and extent of the danger to the strength and well-being of the nation created by present conditions in the coal industry and to recommend such remedial action as can and should be taken.[32]

Nor was the decision to designate the director of the Office of Defense Mobilization to head the coal study an uncalculated one. Tactically there was much to commend approaching these matters as problems of defense policy rather than of economic policy.

But the creation of a special committee to address the difficulties of a single industry could not long remain an isolated event. Other producer groups were quick to petition for comparable treatment. ODM Director Arthur S. Flemming informed the cabinet on July 29, 1954, that the announcement of the coal committee had generated "pressures . . . for having other similar committees created."[33] Accordingly he recommended that a new committee be formed with a broadened mandate: that is, to study "all factors, including regulation, pertaining to the continued de-

32. Eisenhower to Arthur S. Flemming, July 6, 1954, OF, Box 679, DDEL.
33. Minutes of the Cabinet Meeting of July 29, 1954, Whitman Files, Cabinet Series, Box 3, DDEL.

velopment of energy supplies and resources and fuels in the United States, with the aim of strengthening the national defense, providing orderly industrial growth, and securing supplies for our expanding national economy and for any future emergency."[34]

This proposal evoked a lively cabinet discussion. It was strongly endorsed by Secretary of the Treasury George M. Humphrey who noted "the major problems besetting all 'energy' industries, unemployment problems, and the forthcoming Iranian oil settlement." Attorney General Herbert Brownell, Jr., and Secretary of State John Foster Dulles were markedly more cautious. Brownell was concerned lest the proposed committee add to the confusion surrounding "judiciary decisions concerning petroleum" (that is, the pending oil cartel case). Dulles on the other hand expressed "serious concern over the coincidence of the appointment of this Committee with the Iranian oil settlement" and feared that its formation would be interpreted as a move to "stave off an influx of Iranian oil." He urged "that special effort . . . be made to keep this Committee from foreshadowing import quotas, higher tariffs, etc.," noting that "such implications would create panic in South America." He believed that it would be "more desirable to forego the Iranian settlement than to run the risk of losing South American good will." For his part the President emphasized to the cabinet that he was "determined not to be a party to the creation of a steel wall of tariffs around the United States." ODM Director Flemming reportedly "reassured the Cabinet with the announcement that the Committee need not foreshadow higher tariffs or import quotas."[35]

With some modifications, Flemming's proposal was adopted. A Cabinet Committee on Energy Supplies and Resources Policy was authorized; it was to be chaired by the ODM director, and the secretaries of the Departments of Defense, the Interior, Commerce, Labor, State, the Treasury, and Justice were to be its members. There was one noteworthy omission from this list: the CEA was not invited to participate in the deliberations.

Adoption of the proposal suggested that the formulation of a more comprehensive approach to energy problems was in the offing. In fact, however, the agenda for the Cabinet Committee was considerably less than all-embracing. It was charged to investigate matters pertaining to

34. This memorandum, prepared for cabinet discussion, was transmitted by Flemming to Maxwell Rabb on July 28, 1954 (ibid.).
35. Minutes of the Cabinet Meeting of July 29, 1954.

the major sources of energy, including "coal (anthracite, bituminous, and lignite, as well as coke, coal tars, and synthetic liquid fuels) and petroleum and natural gas."[36] Electric power was not included in its terms of reference, nor was any mention made of nuclear energy.

This group, which was aided by special industry consultants, drafted a report and made it available for the consideration of the full cabinet in mid-January 1955. In its basic structure this document reflected a shift from the orientation toward energy issues offered earlier by the Paley Commission. The Paley Report had invited attention to the long-run adequacy of crucial energy inputs at acceptable costs. The Draft Report of January 1955 foreshortened the time perspective and also placed the emphasis, not on the terms of resource availability, but on the climate of incentives for resource development. One of the central conclusions of the external advisers was accepted by the committee: that "overall energy supplies, assuming adequate incentives to development and a healthy economic climate generally, will be adequate, not only for economic growth, but also for at least the first year or two of full mobilization, should that become necessary any time during the next ten years."[37]

The Draft Report addressed more specifically the problems facing producers of each of the primary fuels. With respect to natural gas it recommended that the Supreme Court's decision in the Phillips case should be legislatively annulled by eliminating the field pricing of natural gas from the FPC's regulatory jurisdiction. The committee further proposed that the power of eminent domain be conferred for the development of underground storage reservoirs for natural gas. This was intended as a device for relieving some of the problems associated with seasonal fluctuations in demand for natural gas, and it spoke indirectly to one of the grievances of the coal industry. If natural gas could be held in inventory near the sites of its ultimate consumption, much of the rationale for pricing interruptible gas at a discount would be removed. But there was also a further bow toward coal in the recommendation that sales of natural gas by interstate pipelines at prices below actual cost "plus a fair proportion of fixed charges" should be forbidden. This practice was held to be contradictory to a "basic principle": that "the regulation of natural gas and the use of alternative energy sources should be as

36. As reported in "Energy Supplies and Resources Policy: Report of the Cabinet Committee," January 19, 1955, p. 2, Whitman Files, Cabinet Series, Box 4, DDEL. This document is discussed in the text as the Draft Report.

37. Ibid., p. 2.

far as possible that of free choice by the consumer and free and fair competition among suppliers." Sales below cost "which drive out competing fuels constitute unfair competition and are inimical to a sound fuels economy."[38]

Further measures for the relief of the coal industry were also proposed. Steps to remove any handicap to coal's competitiveness arising from excessive rail freight charges were suggested. The railroads were to be advised to adjust their rate schedules voluntarily. Should their response to such an appeal be unsatisfactory, the committee recommended that the Interstate Commerce Commission be directed to issue compulsory orders "to remove the excessive and disproportionate contribution that coal rates are making to meet the cost of other unprofitable services of the railroad industry."[39] In addition the government was urged to promote coal markets abroad by urging foreign governments to reduce restrictions on the access of U.S. suppliers to their markets and by counseling the Export-Import Bank to regard the financing of coal exports sympathetically. Cooperative efforts involving the coal industry and state and local governments were also called for to spur research into potential new uses for coal.

By far the most arresting finding of the Draft Report pertained to the treatment of oil. The Cabinet Committee stated its belief that "if the imports of crude and residual oils should exceed the respective proportions that these imports of oils bore to the production of domestic crude oil in 1954, the domestic fuel situation will be seriously impaired from the standpoint of the strengthening of national defense, making provision for orderly industrial growth, and assuring supplies for our expanding national economy and for any future emergency."[40] Accordingly it recommended that the President should "propose appropriate measures" to ensure that the required relationships between domestic production and imports on the 1954 base be maintained.

While the recommendations of the Cabinet Committee were artfully balanced to speak to the grievances of the producers of the three primary fuels, its approach lacked something in intellectual consistency. The recommendations for natural gas and coal had stressed the virtues of the competitive process and the importance of reduced federal regulation, except when regulation could perfect the market; the recommendations

38. Ibid., p. 3.
39. Ibid., p. 5.
40. Ibid., p. 4.

for oil, to the contrary, had called for controls to override a market solution. Similarly the recommendations for coal had called for reductions in barriers to the free movement of goods in international commerce, while the recommendations for oil had called for the erection of new ones.

Some of this inherent tension was reflected at the meeting of the cabinet on January 21, 1955, at which the report of the committee was presented for review. It was well understood that the imposition of formal import controls could not be readily reconciled with the administration's general posture and would create problems in the conduct of foreign relations. A general appeal for voluntary restraint by oil importers was the obvious alternative, though there was reasonable ground for doubt about its success. Secretary of the Treasury Humphrey predicted that "voluntary action would eventually be ineffective because of the increasingly bad situations in domestic energy industries," though he accepted that this course was the best available at the moment. Even so, admonitions to oil importers to exercise restraint were not thought to be trouble-free. The attorney general observed that schemes to encourage the oil industry to restrict imports might easily run afoul of the antitrust laws and cautioned that "any discussions by Government officials with officials of private oil companies must be limited to merely pointing out the consequences of failure to limit imports voluntarily."[41]

CEA chairman Arthur Burns read the matter differently. In a memorandum of January 21, 1955, Burns reminded the President that "the Council did not participate in any way in the report of the Cabinet Committee on Energy Supplies and Resources Policy, nor did we have an opportunity to see the report before its submission to you and the Cabinet. On the basis of a casual reading and the discussion that I heard at today's Cabinet meeting, I have formed the impression that this report deserves further study before you decide to accept it as an expression of your policy."[42]

Subsequent drafts of the Cabinet Committee's report attempted to smooth some of the rougher edges. Deregulation of the field prices of natural gas was presented as essential to the longer-term welfare of consumers.[43] The overtly restrictionist tone of the original was muted some-

41. Quotations in this paragraph are from Minutes of the Cabinet Meeting of January 21, 1955, Whitman Files, Cabinet Series, Box 4, DDEL.

42. Burns to Eisenhower, January 21, 1955, OF, Box 684, DDEL.

43. This amendment responded to the President's suggestion at the cabinet meeting of January 21, 1955, when he had insisted that "any public statement should stress the need for continued exploration in the long-range interest of the consumer." Minutes of the Cabinet Meeting of January 21, 1955.

what with the observation that "both domestic production and imports have important parts to play; neither should be sacrificed to the other."[44] The importance to national defense of checking oil imports in excess of the 1954 ratio to production was also qualified. The original draft had asserted that the importation of crude and residual fuel oils beyond this limit would imply that the domestic fuel situation "will be seriously impaired"; the final version indicated that such a result would suggest that "the domestic fuels situation could be so impaired as to endanger the orderly industrial growth which assures the military and civilian supplies and reserves that are necessary to national defense. There would be an inadequate incentive for exploration and the discovery of new sources of supply."[45] Editorial concessions were also made in the discussion of proposed control mechanisms. The original draft contained the recommendation that oil imports beyond the 1954 limit would call for the President to "propose appropriate measures that will bring about the required relationships." In the final version the committee concluded that "imports should be kept in the balance recommended above [the 1954 ratios]. It is highly desirable that this be done by voluntary, individual action of those who are importing or those who become importers of crude or residual oil. The committee believes that every effort should be made and will be made to avoid the necessity of governmental intervention."[46]

But an even more fundamental difficulty was inherent in the structure of the Cabinet Committee's recommendations if they were to constitute an official posture toward oil imports. The committee's case rested on a national defense rationale that had been asserted but not documented. It was by no means self-evident that the nation's security interests would be served best by a strategy that encouraged a more rapid rate of depletion of domestic reserves. On the contrary, it was certainly arguable that the conservation of exhaustible resources would improve the nation's capacity to meet the requirements of an emergency, particularly when the current needs of consumers could be met at lower costs by imports than by domestic production. This was a point of view that had the President's sympathy. At the cabinet meeting of January 28, 1955, he reminded his colleagues of "an old suggestion of his" for which he had been unable to obtain any support: that low-cost foreign oil should be

44. "The White House Report on Energy Supplies and Resources Policy," reprinted in U.S. Cabinet Task Force on Oil Import Control, *The Oil Import Question: A Report on the Relationship of Oil Imports to National Security* (GPO, 1970), p. 165.

45. Ibid., p. 166.

46. Ibid.

purchased for storage in exhausted wells.[47] This proposal, to be sure, would not quiet the clamors of the domestic industry, though it clearly offered a route through which the alleged national security objectives could be reconciled with the objectives of international economic policy.

Despite reservations, Eisenhower did not stand in the way of the distribution of the amended report, which was released to the press on February 26, 1955. But he did insist that its status be downgraded. It was now to be treated as the report of a presidential advisory committee rather than of a cabinet committee.[48] In this form its release did not imply presidential endorsement of its conclusions. Meanwhile he continued to press his colleagues to consider alternative approaches.[49] The President

47. Minutes of the Cabinet Meeting of January 28, 1955, Whitman Files, Cabinet Series, Box 4, DDEL.

48. This decision was transmitted to relevant cabinet members by Maxwell Rabb, secretary to the cabinet, in a memorandum of February 5, 1955, in which he observed: "In the future, the President does not wish to have the title, 'Cabinet Committee,' used in connection with the study groups he has set up on Water, Transportation, Telecommunications and Energy. He would like to have them designated as 'Presidential Advisory Committees.'" Rabb to Douglas McKay, Sinclair Weeks, and Arthur Flemming, February 5, 1955, OF, Box 684, DDEL.

49. In a memorandum to Lewis Strauss, AEC chairman, on February 15, 1955, he offered the following analysis: "a) The Mid East, particularly Iran, is producing oil at a tremendous rate. b) In the interests of Iranian development and free world security, there should be a growing market for Iranian oil. c) The world's current markets for oil are glutted, particularly in the United States. Any increased imports in this country would cause us a very considerable economic difficulty; specifically we would be damaging the numerous independents and wildcatters through whom is conducted the great mass of our oil exploration activities. European countries are only slowly converting industry to the use of fuel oil. d) In Iran crude or fuel oil can be purchased at something like 80¢ a barrel, including royalties. In the United States it costs $2.75 a barrel to produce. e) The world's needs in energy constantly mount. In certain areas, possibly including some within the United States itself, the production of power through traditional methods is impractical. In other nations in which we are vitally interested, this truth has much wider application than in our own country. The necessity for solving power problems in these countries is urgent. f) Nuclear science provides a way in which energy can be stored or stockpiled for periods of indefinite length. To produce and store nuclear energy we should have an abundance of cheap power. g) The proved reserves of uranium and other materials needed for the production of nuclear energy continue to grow. My question is couched in several parts. a) Could we not use the growing quantity of uranium, and cheap oil of Iran, to produce 'stored energy'? b) Could we not use the plentiful labor in Iran to erect and operate at the least possible cost, the plants necessary to produce this stored energy? It would appear that transportation costs would be insignificant. c) By so doing would we not be assisting in achieving the desired objectives cited above?" Eisenhower to Strauss, February 15, 1955, Whitman Files, Eisenhower Diary Series, Box 6, DDEL.

was apparently struggling for a formula to promote the growth of the world's energy supplies, but in ways that would shelter the American market from imports without controls. Though nothing was to come of this search, there could be no doubt about Eisenhower's eagerness to explore options beyond those his advisory committee had presented to him.

Technically the administration was not committed to any specific course of action on the bothersome question of import restrictions by the publication of the committee's final report. The premises of this document, however, were a considerable distance removed from the principles of the initial official doctrine. The basic perspective on energy matters was thus in the process of being reshaped. The concern of the Paley Commission for long-run resource availabilities at the lowest possible costs had faded further into the background. The framework that was now to dominate the approach to energy problems gave greater weight to protecting the market positions of established producers. The potential implications for resource exhaustion and for increased supply prices of key energy inputs were largely dismissed. Within the world of official thought, the best assurance of invulnerable long-run supplies was to be found in guaranteeing the profitability of continued exploration. Under the cover of defense essentiality, it was held that this result could be accomplished by widening the market space available to private energy suppliers at home.

The subsequent unfolding of the Eisenhower administration's approach to the primary fuels was shaped by the premises set out in early 1955. The treatment accorded to particular industries was neither neutral nor uniform, and in particular cases the evolution of policy took unexpected turns. The approaches of policymakers to the various pieces of the energy puzzle call for individual consideration.

Voluntary Oil Import Controls: Phase I

Though the report of the Presidential Advisory Committee on Energy Supplies and Resources Policy had dealt with the three primary fuels, the centerpiece of the exercise was oil. An optimum ratio of imports to production had been prescribed, but whether it would be achieved depended on the response of the industry. There was, however, more than a hint that exhortation, should it prove to be ineffective, would be supplemented by other measures. A provision of the Trade Agreements Extension Act, passed by Congress in June 1955, gave the government additional leverage for inducing compliance. Section 7 of this legislation contained the following stipulation:

. . . whenever the Director of the Office of Defense Mobilization has reason to believe that any article is being imported into the United States in such quantities as to threaten to impair the national security, he shall so advise the President, and if the President agrees that there is reason for such belief, the President shall cause an immediate investigation to be made to determine the facts. If, on the basis of such investigation, and the report to him of the findings and recommendations made in connection therewith, the President finds that the article is being imported into the United States in such quantities as to threaten to impair the national security, he shall take such action as he deems necessary to adjust the imports of such article to a level that will not threaten to impair the national security.[50]

Though the language of this section was perfectly general, the legislative history of this provision leaves no doubt that it was drafted with the circumstances of the oil industry in mind.

Behind the scenes it had been made clear to the White House from the earliest days of the administration that the failure of the executive branch to take steps to assure the health of the domestic oil industry would lead to congressional action to accomplish this purpose. This message had been conveyed through the intermediation of Robert Anderson, then deputy secretary of defense, who served as White House liaison with the Democratic congressional leadership. The interest of Congress in these matters was by no means confined to delegations from oil-producing states. Support could also be enlisted from members elected from some states without known oil deposits; there was always a hope that a big discovery might be made that would enrich the revenue base. Whether this happy result would occur seemed to depend on the vitality of the domestic independent producers. The international majors—with ample low-cost reserves available to them abroad—had little interest in financing prospecting at home. Hence the appeal for protecting the interests of the small men (that is, the independent domestic producers and wild-catters) touched a substantial constituency.[51]

ODM Director Flemming acted with dispatch in using the authority assigned to him by section 7 of the Trade Agreements Extension Act of

50. 69 Stat. 166.
51. The insights developed from personal conversation with Robert Anderson are gratefully acknowledged.

1955. In a letter to oil-importing companies on August 5, 1955, he called attention to his new responsibilities and reminded them of the conclusions of the Presidential Advisory Committee. Oil importers were requested to supply information on the volume of their imports during 1954–55 and on import quantities projected for the first half of 1956. The responses to this solicitation were disquieting. The ODM analysis of the returns yielded the following conclusions: "(a) that imports of crude and residual oil had increased more rapidly than the domestic production of crude oil, (b) that half the companies reporting imports of crude oil had exceeded the ratio recommended by the Advisory Committee and three-fourths of the companies reporting imports of residual oils had exceeded that ratio, and (c) that unless company policy changes were made, imports would continue to be substantially above the standard recommended by the Advisory Committee."[52]

When reconvened to consider this situation, the Presidential Advisory Committee modified its earlier position on two points of administrative detail. In the first place, it elected to treat imports of crude and of residual fuel oils separately. In light of this distinction, Flemming informed oil-importing companies on October 29, 1955, that it was now the considered judgment of the committee that "with respect to residual fuel oils, actual and planned imports for the period April 1–December 31, 1955 appear to be in accord with the Committee recommendation, on the basis of information now available."[53] There is reason to believe that the additional information provided to the committee when it was reaching this conclusion had been brought to its attention by New England consumers of residual fuel oil who sought unconstrained access to imports; the evidence on residual import volumes during this period does not indicate that the targeted ratios were being regarded with respect.[54]

The second procedural modification at this point involved a differentiation of oil imports by source. Importers were advised by Flemming that the Presidential Advisory Committee had now determined that "with the exception of oil of Canadian and Venezuelan origin, and assuming

52. "Summary Review of Developments with Respect to Oil Imports," Cabinet Paper Prepared for the Meeting of November 22, 1955, p. 1, Whitman Files, Cabinet Series, Box 6, DDEL.

53. Ibid., p. 2.

54. In this connection it may be noted that residual fuel oil imports amounted to approximately 129 million barrels in 1954; the import figure rose to about 152 million barrels in 1955 and to nearly 163 million barrels in 1956. See Bohi and Russell, *Limiting Oil Imports*, p. 146.

that imports from these areas do not rise appreciably above present levels, importers of oil from other areas should further reduce their planned imports of crude oil for the period April 1–December 31, 1955 by approximately 7 per cent, if substantial conformity with the Advisory Committee recommendation with respect to crude oil is to be achieved."[55] This pronouncement indicated that the origin of imported oil should no longer be regarded with indifference. The text of the original report had not spoken explicitly to this issue, though it had figured prominently in the cabinet deliberations preceding its release. The State Department had expressed particular concern about any program of import restriction that might jeopardize the position of Western Hemisphere producers. It was feared, however, that constraints on oil imports, whether voluntary or otherwise, that were blind to the country of origin would mean that Venezuelan and Canadian suppliers would lose out in competition with the Middle East. If this undesirable result was to be avoided, some preferential arrangements for Canada and Venezuela would be required. Such treatment was held to be justified by, and indeed to follow directly from, the rationale for import restrictions in the first instance: Western Hemisphere sources could be regarded as part of the national mobilization base. But this procedure clearly implied that the major international adjustments necessitated by U.S. oil import policy would be made in the Middle East.

Not surprisingly, the reactions to these programmatic modifications were decidedly mixed. With the exception of the Texas Company, the international majors indicated that they were prepared to comply with the new recommendations. Some half-dozen importing companies, however, reported imports or import plans that were substantially outside the recommended limits, and a number of companies with significant operations in the Middle East protested the "discrimination" against their products. These departures were welcomed, however, by the New England Council, which expressed its gratification that "the requested reduction in crude oil imports will not apply to oils of Venezuelan origin which are so essential to the industrial life of the New England community."[56]

The adequacy of exhortation in restricting oil imports was increasingly called into question by events in early 1956. Imports continued to rise and at rates well outside the targeted volumes. On June 26, 1956, the

55. "Summary Review of Developments with Respect to Oil Imports," p. 2.
56. Quoted in ibid., p. 3.

director of the ODM issued a further plea for compliance and reported that the optimum ratio of imports to domestic production indicated that imports in the third quarter of the year should be shrunk by 4 percent from the levels of the first half of 1956. (This admonition, however, referred only to oils other than those of Canadian or Venezuelan origin.) But the operational structure of the voluntary scheme underwent a further administrative modification at this time. The oil import program was now adapted to take account of differing circumstances in various regions of the country. Following a procedure used by the Petroleum Administration for War in World War II, the country was divided into five districts. Districts I–IV embraced the territory east of the Rocky Mountains, which was regarded as an oil surplus region; that is, oil-producing capacity available in these districts was underutilized. District V (the area west of the Rocky Mountains), on the other hand, was treated as an oil deficit region because its consumption requirements could not be satisfied even when its productive capacity was extended to the limit. Imports to District V were essential to assure adequacy of supply; by contrast, imports into Districts I–IV were regarded as bumping domestic producers from markets they had the capacity to supply. Accordingly the further "voluntary" reduction recommended in June 1956 was intended to apply only to imports into Districts I–IV. In this scheme of thinking the aggregate market was compartmentalized into two distinct geographical subdivisions regarded as having no transfers between them.

By September 1956 it had become apparent that the request issued in June had been ill-heeded. Though some reduction in imports had occurred, its magnitude had fallen short of the official recommendation. The director of the ODM took note of this outcome in a further communication to oil importers on September 7, 1956: "I would be less than frank if I did not say that this is a disappointing result. In view of the importance of this matter, we felt that we would obtain a better over-all response than we have received by appealing for action on an individual voluntary basis."[57]

But the ODM was not alone in observing trends in oil imports. In August 1956 the Independent Petroleum Association of America filed a formal petition with Director Flemming calling on him to initiate the

57. ODM press release, September 7, 1956, containing the text of the letter of Director Arthur Flemming to oil importers, Whitman Files, Administration Series, Box 16, DDEL.

investigations called for by section 7 of the Trade Agreements Extension Act of 1955 when imports appeared to threaten the national security. In addition the association's president, Robert L. Wood, took its case directly to the White House. In an audience with Eisenhower on September 11, 1956, Wood maintained that excessive oil imports meant that exploratory activities were being severely curtailed, particularly among the "thousands of individual operators and small companies that drill more than 75 per cent of all the wells completed." Moreover, "higher costs and inadequate prices" had been responsible for an increase of 40 percent or more in the number of oil well abandonments in Kansas, Oklahoma, and Texas. Increased oil imports, in turn, had "forced state conservation agencies to restrict domestic production below economic levels." In consequence, an increasing volume of domestic producing capacity had been "shut in" for lack of a market. The conclusion appeared to be obvious: that the government should take whatever steps were necessary to make the 1954 import-production ratio the effective reality.[58] When responding to this suggestion the President indicated that the problem was "not an easy one." The imposition of import quotas, he noted, might involve antitrust considerations and might also lead to price fixing in the sense that the industry "might be practically free to set prices without regard to consumer interests."[59]

Though public hearings on the complaint lodged by the Independent Petroleum Association were held on October 22, 1956, an ODM judgment of its merits was delayed by events in the Middle East. The derangement of the international oil market brought by the French-British-Israeli military intervention at Suez and the closure of the canal in late

58. Memorandum supplied to the President by Robert L. Wood, September 11, 1956, Whitman Files, Eisenhower Diary Series, Box 10, DDEL.
59. Memorandum, A. J. Goodpaster, "Conference of the President on September 11, 1956, with Robert L. Wood and Arthur Flemming," Whitman Files, ibid. Evidently the President's reference to price fixing in this context was informed by a memorandum submitted by Flemming in preparation for this conference. Flemming reported that he had been informed by the attorney general that "if we endeavored to establish such a relationship by formal action [that is, the 1954 oil import-to-domestic-production ratio] on the part of Government, it would give rise to serious anti-trust problems. The Attorney General calls attention to the fact that domestic production is limited by actions taken by such agencies as the Texas Railroad Commission. If in addition the Government should attempt to put into effect a formal quota system on imports, he believes that the industry might be in a position where it could fix prices without regard to the interests of the consumer." Flemming to the President, September 11, 1956, Whitman Files, Administration Series, Box 16, DDEL.

October preempted the attention of those with official oversight of oil matters. A supply crisis loomed in Western Europe. Once the withdrawal of military forces from the Suez area had been assured, the President directed the secretary of the interior to authorize fifteen U.S. oil companies to collaborate in organizing shipments of petroleum to members of the NATO alliance.[60] Communications were also sent to the various state regulatory bodies requesting them to increase allowable production rates to serve extraordinary needs in Western Europe. By the fourth week in November 1956 the flow to Europe from U.S. ports in the Gulf of Mexico had risen to 300,000 barrels of crude oil a day from zero at the beginning of the month.[61] Preparation of longer-term contingency plans was also stimulated by the Suez emergency. On October 12, 1956, the President authorized ODM Director Flemming to investigate the feasibility of constructing a supertanker fleet in American shipyards with government support. It was carefully noted, however, that this "study should proceed, of course, on the assumption that plans which are developed are to be consistent with the requests you have made to oil importers to voluntarily keep imports of crude oil into this country at a level where they do not exceed significantly the proportion that imports bore to the production of domestic crude oil in 1954."[62]

When deliberation on the petition filed by the Independent Petroleum Association was resumed in the spring of 1957, the climate in which it was conducted had been reconditioned by the fallout from the Suez crisis. Regulatory commissions in the oil-producing states, having increased production allowables at federal request, were understandably reluctant to cut them back. Meanwhile the smaller independent producers were fearful that concern for their interests in official circles had

60. Though a plan for an oil lift had been worked out in midsummer 1956 (following Egyptian nationalization of the Suez Canal in July), it was not put into operation until late November of that year. Eisenhower's first reaction to the military intervention of the British and the French was "that those who began this operation should be left to work out their own oil problems—to boil in their own oil, so to speak." Within his official family he did not disguise his extreme anger with actions taken without the foreknowledge of the U.S. government, actions he regarded as violations of "agreed undertakings such as the Tri-Partite Declaration of 1950." Memorandum, A. J. Goodpaster, "Conference with the President," October 30, 1956, Whitman Files, Eisenhower Diary Series, Box 11, DDEL.

61. Cable, Under Secretary of State Herbert Hoover, Jr., to all embassies and legations, November 29, 1956, Confidential Files, Box 79, DDEL.

62. Eisenhower to Flemming, October 12, 1956, Whitman Files, Administration Series, Box 16, DDEL.

waned. This suspicion was fed by the fact that the Department of the Interior had worked closely with the large international firms in organizing the supply lift from the Middle East to Western Europe. Texas Governor Price Daniel reflected this view in a telegram to Sherman Adams in February 1957.

For best interests of the President and all concerned I strongly urge he invite General Thompson [Chairman of the Texas Railroad Commission] and possibly two or three other oil state administrators for conference and suggestions. Whether right or wrong the impression is being left that the President is seeking aid and advice only from private oil interests and mostly the major companies. My suggestion would offset this and would show his recognition of and desire for suggestions and cooperation from the official regulatory bodies.[63]

Adams subsequently met with Lieutenant General Ernest O. Thompson, whose view of the appropriate next steps in oil import policy was well settled. The Texas legislature, he noted, was "already counting on spending the increased revenues due to added oil production. Therefore, the repercussions here will be great if our production has to be reduced again due to excessive refinery runs and excessive imports of oil into the United States."[64]

Formally, the next round of public debate on oil imports opened in March 1957 when Flemming reminded oil importers of his legal obligation to act on the complaint filed by the Independent Petroleum Association "as soon as the situation in the Middle East permits a return to normal oil movements in international trade." Information was again requested from companies on their plans for crude oil imports to enable the government to determine the steps necessary to "maintain the desirable relationship between oil imports and domestic production."[65] The responses to this request led Gordon Gray (Flemming's successor as ODM director) to report to the President on April 23, 1957, that he had "reason to believe that crude oil is being imported into the United States in such quantities as to threaten to impair the national security."[66]

Under the terms of section 7 of the Trade Agreements Extension Act of 1955 this finding required the President to call for an immediate investigation. The President indicated his intention to do so when ac-

63. Telegram, Daniel to Adams, February 13, 1957, OF, Box 650, DDEL.
64. Thompson to Adams, February 20, 1957, Central Files, Box 680, DDEL.
65. Letter, Flemming to oil-importing companies, ODM press release, March 6, 1957, Whitman Files, Administration Series, Box 16, DDEL.
66. Gray to the President, April 23, 1957, Philip Areeda Papers, Box 14, DDEL.

knowledging Gray's report of April 23.[67] The investigative committee, however, was not appointed until June 26, 1957. The group formed for this task was designated the Special Committee to Investigate Crude Oil Imports; its membership consisted of the secretaries of state, defense, treasury, commerce, interior, and labor; and it was charged as follows:

In carrying out this vitally important investigation, the special committee should view the national security in its broadest terms, and seek to balance such general factors as our long-term requirements for crude oil, the military, economic and diplomatic considerations involved in obtaining crude oil from various foreign areas, the maintenance of a dynamic domestic industry that will meet national needs in peace or war, and any special significance of imports in different regions of the country.[68]

Pressures for more forceful restrictive measures were steadily mounting. The President personally remained cautious. The tenor of his thinking at the time is conveyed in his remarks to a senatorial delegation (composed of Frank Carlson of Kansas, Everett M. Dirksen of Illinois, and Joseph C. O'Mahoney of Wyoming) that had called for prompt action to restrict oil imports. In response Eisenhower observed that he "was not only interested in the health of the domestic industry but was also concerned with the effect, on national defense and on the states' income, of depletion of our reserves, and that he wished to encourage exploration without causing the marketing of too much domestic oil and thereby unduly reducing our domestic reserves—in other words, he felt that a nice balance should be obtained." He further expressed his doubts about the effectiveness of the voluntary program "because of the inability of persuading two of the companies, Sun Oil and Tidewater, to participate." On the other hand the suitability of other arrangements was not clear. It was the President's opinion that the tariff alone "would not do the job." A quota system might be preferable, though he emphasized "the necessity for finding a flexible formula." In his judgment it was important to find space in any quota arrangement to "take care of new discoveries," such as the development of fields in North Africa or Brazil.[69] The trade-offs affecting judgments on next steps were becoming

67. Eisenhower to Gray, April 25, 1957, ibid.
68. Eisenhower to the Secretaries of Defense, Treasury, Commerce, Interior, Labor and State, June 26, 1957, OF, Box 683, DDEL.
69. Wilton B. Persons, Memorandum for the Record of the President's Appointment with Senators Carlson, Dirksen, and O'Mahoney, June 3, 1957, Whitman Files, Eisenhower Diary Series, Box 14, DDEL.

more intricate. But there was at least a nagging doubt about the wisdom of measures that might accelerate the depletion of domestic oil reserves.

Voluntary Oil Import Controls: Phase II

The Report of the Special Cabinet Committee to Investigate Crude Oil Imports submitted to the President on July 29, 1957, marked a further tilt toward protectionism.[70] In large measure its recommendations had been shaped by a four-member team of consultants composed of Herbert Hoover, Jr., Arthur Flemming, Robert Anderson, and Dillon Anderson. The consensus of this task group was that the scheduled import rate for the last half of 1957 would oblige Texas to restrict pumping to thirteen days a month and "that such a depressed producing rate, if continued for such an extended period, would threaten to impair national security"; however, the group agreed that "an import rate that will permit a 15-day allowable in Texas would eliminate the threat of impairment to the national security." It was hoped that import limitations sufficient to achieve this purpose could be accomplished by individual voluntary action, but the consultants recommended that mandatory controls be imposed if requests for compliance failed.[71]

The Special Committee prefaced the findings of its formal report with a restatement of the national security rationale for import limitations, but in a form that spoke to some of the President's reservations. The proposition that increased importation of petroleum might be prudent in the interest of conserving domestic reserves was dismissed as unsound on the ground that it would discourage private exploratory activity and hence would deny the nation the opportunity to "make a sound appraisal of its petroleum resources because it would not know the extent to which our reserve capacity could be developed."[72] Failure to keep the capacity

70. "Petroleum Imports" (issued as a press release), reprinted in Cabinet Task Force on Oil Import Control, *The Oil Import Question*, app. C-2, pp. 181–90.

71. As reported by F. X. Jordon, Office of Oil and Gas, to the Secretary of the Interior, July 16, 1957, Fred Seaton Papers, Oil, Gas, and Mineral Series, Box 4, DDEL. It is worth noting that confidence in the success of a voluntary solution was far from complete. Gordon Gray, ODM director, reported to the President, for example, that he was "by no means sure a workable basis for a voluntary program can be developed." Gray to the President, July 10, 1957, ibid., Box 5.

72. Special Committee to Investigate Crude Oil Imports, "Petroleum Imports," p. 184.

for exploratory activities in the United States in full health and vigor would expose the nation to crippling costs in the event of an emergency. Eisenhower's earlier suggestion that crude oil imported at low cost might usefully be stockpiled in depleted fields was rejected with the assertion that "the practical problems of cost and the physical problems connected with the storage of crude oil would make this solution impracticable from the standpoint of industry and government alike."[73] Similarly the committee saw no merit in proposals that the government itself might assume the responsibility for keeping exploratory capacity in a state of readiness. According to the committee, "such a course would be costly to an already overburdened government and would be contrary to the principles of free enterprise which characterize American industry."[74]

But there was still an awkward corner to be negotiated. The committee was mindful that its view would not be applauded by consumer interests. It recognized that "the low cost of imported oil is attractive," but it cautioned that "excessive reliance upon it in the short run may put the nation in a long-term vulnerable position. Imported supplies could be cut off in an emergency and might well be diminished by events beyond our control. This vulnerability could easily result in a much higher cost, or even in the unavailability, of oil to consumers. It is therefore believed that the best interests of domestic consumers, as well as of national security, will be served if a reasonable balance is maintained between domestic and foreign supplies."[75]

To strike that balance, the committee proposed that specific guidelines be established for each oil importer stipulating a maximum import volume. While compliance was not compulsory, this was still a distinct step beyond generalized admonition. The import target now set for Districts I–IV worked out to be 12 percent of domestic production. District V was again treated separately; the recommended import volume there was to be calculated as "the difference between demand and the domestic crude oil that can be made available to the area on a reasonably competitive basis."[76] The Special Committee added that the ratio of imports to domestic demand (rather than to domestic production) should henceforth be regarded as the operationally useful statistic; on

73. Ibid.
74. Ibid.
75. Ibid., p. 186.
76. Ibid., pp. 187–88. In District V this implied an import-production ratio of 29.8 percent and an import-demand ratio of 23.5 percent.

this basis of calculation the new guidelines yielded a figure of about 9.6 percent as the import maximum in Districts I–IV.[77]

These aggregate figures in turn were broken down into specific guidelines for each importing company. For this purpose oil importers were divided into two categories: the first, designated as "established importers," were those who had imported in substantial volume and had done so since 1954;[78] the second, designated as "new importers," included those firms that had begun importation after 1954 or whose import volume in 1954 was less than 20,000 barrels a day.[79] The formula for recommended import maxima was calculated differently for each of these categories. The established importers were requested to "cut back 10% below their average crude oil imports for the years 1954, 1955 and 1956." The new importers, on the other hand, were to be allowed to import the quantities projected in their submissions to the ODM as of July 1957, subject to the restriction that future imports should not exceed actual imports in 1956 by more than 12,000 barrels a day. This differential treatment was defended on grounds that the smaller late entrants "should have the opportunity to participate in the United States market on a basis more equitable than if the above cutback [to be applied to the established importers] were applied to them." These formulas yielded the result that the established importers in Districts I–IV would be obliged to cut back their programmed imports for the last half of 1957 by about 20 percent (from the scheduled rate of 630,100 barrels a day to 493,100 barrels a day). For the new importers the formula called for a reduction in imports of more than 25 percent from the programmed levels reported in the schedules earlier submitted to the ODM. Nevertheless, there was a sharp shift in the relative weights of these two categories. The new importers, according to the formula, would be authorized to import more than a third of the aggregate volume landed in Districts I–IV. By contrast, their share of the import market in 1954 had been approximately 12 percent and had been only slightly in excess of 20 percent in 1956. It was also noteworthy that the burden of adjustment was not uniformly distributed between firms. Only three of the

77. In the interests of continuity with the formula used during Phase I of the voluntary program, the target percentage for imports in relation to domestic crude oil production was still reported.

78. This group included seven firms: the five international majors plus Atlantic and Sinclair.

79. Fifteen firms were included in this category for Districts I–IV.

fifteen new importers would be obliged to reduce their planned imports in the last half of 1957 in order to comply, though all the established importers were subject to cutbacks.[80]

The new oil import program still lacked teeth, but there was an implicit threat that its failure would lead to an escalation in the control mechanisms. For the time being at least, the application of more direct techniques had been forestalled. And one control device, the tariff, had been explicitly considered and rejected. Secretary of State Dulles was particularly outspoken in his opposition to this tactic. At the cabinet meeting of July 24, 1957, he had argued that a tariff would be "the worst possible measure from a security standpoint since it would keep out Canadian and Venezuelan oil but let in Arabian oil—a development that would make the United States dependent on Mid-East oil."[81] The position set out in the report of the Special Committee—and announced as state policy on July 29, 1957—made no specific reference, however, to oil imports by country of origin. The historical basis for the assignment of quotas to importing companies was thought to convey an automatic preference to western hemisphere suppliers. One other omission was noteworthy: the new program did not apply to residual fuel oil, of which Venezuela was the principal supplier.[82]

This turn of events brought the federal government one step closer to a formal alliance with regulatory commissions in the oil-producing states

80. Information and quotations in this paragraph are from Special Committee to Investigate Crude Oil Imports, "Petroleum Imports," pp. 186, 187, 190.

81. Minutes of the Cabinet Meeting of July 24, 1957, Whitman Files, Cabinet Series, Box 9, DDEL.

82. Eisenhower personally was more comfortable with the position outlined in the report than he had been in February 1955 when the original recommendations of the Presidential Advisory Committee had been presented. To Dillon Anderson (who had served as a consultant to the Special Committee to Investigate Crude Oil Imports) the President wrote that he hoped "that our long term national objectives in this field can be spelled out and formalized so that they will mean something —in other words, that they will encourage maximum exploration in our country and use of imports as a supplemental, not a ruinous substitute, for our own production." He also offered a comment on an opinion Anderson had supplied concerning the risks of excessive dependence on Middle Eastern oil. Eisenhower concurred in the observation that "an adequate supply of oil to Western Europe ranks almost equal in priority with an adequate supply for ourselves." While the Western Hemisphere, he noted, could "on an emergency basis meet the short term requirements of the entire free world," this was impossible over the longer term. Hence "should a crisis arise threatening to cut the Western world off from Mid East oil, we would *have* to use force." Eisenhower to Anderson, July 30, 1957, Whitman Files, Eisenhower Diary Series, Box 14, DDEL.

in buttressing the prices of domestically produced crude. Free entry of imports had for some time posed a threat to the survival of this price support mechanism. The federal government now seemed prepared to come to its rescue. Some suspicions lingered that these steps were not totally in harmony with the procompetitive spirit of the official doctrine or with the antitrust laws.[83] But certain features of the revised voluntary program helped to quiet them. Its structure, it could be noted, encouraged increased competition in the oil-importing business. Preferential treatment had been accorded to smaller firms, and there was an indication that hospitality would be accorded to new entrants, though potential newcomers would be expected henceforth to file notice of their plans with the Department of the Interior at least six months in advance. The Department of the Interior would then make a determination "as to the extent these importers should share in the market initially, and as to whether room can be made for them as a result of the increase in permissible imports arising out of the increase in domestic demand or whether it will be necessary for older importers to decrease their imports in order to make room for the new companies."[84] This bow in the direction of newcomers was not enthusiastically welcomed by the established importers, particularly the international majors. The administration, however, could offer them some compensatory satisfactions. On September 19, 1957, the attorney general reported that "the government's anti-trust suit against Standard Oil of New Jersey has been settled by a consent decree, conditional however, upon SONJ obtaining the approval of its joint operator, Socony Mobil Oil, before December 1." The effect of this decree would be to forbid henceforth joint marketing operations between Standard of New Jersey and other companies and would pro-

83. The attorney general counseled the secretary of the interior (who was responsible for the administration of the voluntary import restriction program) on August 5, 1957, that when "requesting voluntary compliance by any one importer, care should be taken that each importer makes his decision regarding compliance independently and without agreement with other importers. In other words, no importer should condition his compliance on any assurance of identical assent by all other importers. Thus minimized is any possibility that voluntary compliance with the formula stems from agreement among the importers. Finally, the Government should insure that responsibility for insuring compliance with the formula should be—not with the importing companies—but with the Government itself." Quoted in a draft letter from William P. Rogers to Frederick H. Mueller, n.d., Rogers Papers, Box 29, DDEL.

84. Special Committee to Investigate Crude Oil Imports, "Petroleum Imports," p. 187.

hibit price fixing, allocation of territories, and restrictions on imports and exports. The attorney general further reported that "an effort will be made to reach consent decrees with the other oil company defendants in the cartel case."[85]

The second phase of the voluntary oil import control program was ill-starred from its beginning. Its announcement roughly coincided with another downturn in economic activity. As the demand for crude oil in the aggregate diminished, further cutbacks in import allowables were called for if the ratio of imports to domestic demand set out in the policy statement of July 29, 1957, was to be maintained. But importers to whom allocations had been originally assigned in July 1957 were subject to further curtailment in their allowables for another reason. Not surprisingly, the new scheme had attracted a considerable number of new entrants. In a climate in which overall demand was shrinking, market space for the new entrants could be created only at the expense of allocations that had formerly been assigned. By early March 1958 there were some indications that the resulting strains on the system threatened its very survival.[86] It was also alleged that the unwillingness of one firm, the Tidewater Oil Company, to cooperate in the import restriction program was a major contributor to this erosion. The President thought it probable that "some system of mandatory import controls would have to be worked out and put into effect."[87] To his associates the President made no secret of his "dislike of a situation where a recalcitrant company could deviate without punishment from a generally agreed program."[88]

For the import allocation period beginning on April 1, 1958, further downward adjustments in allowables were called for. The demand estimates for the next six-month period prepared by the Bureau of Mines indicated that the desired ratio of imports to demand required a reduction of 10 percent from the import volume of the preceding period in Districts I–IV. The cutback would be even more severe for the importers of record in July 1957. The number of newcomers had swollen from

85. Special Staff Note, September 19, 1957, Whitman Files, Eisenhower Diary Series, Box 16, DDEL.

86. This was reported as the generally agreed upon assessment of participants in a White House meeting of March 3, 1958, which included the President, Governor Allan Shivers of Texas, and Secretaries Weeks and Anderson. Memorandum for the Files, Gerald D. Morgan, March 3, 1958, ibid., Box 19.

87. Ibid.

88. Minutes of the Cabinet Meeting of March 21, 1958, Whitman Files, Cabinet Series, Box 10, DDEL.

fifteen at that time to thirty-three by March 1958. This implied still further reductions in the initial quota assignments, a step the Special Committee considered essential. "Our private enterprise system," it reported
on March 24, 1958, "must allow freedom to individuals to engage in
productive pursuits and not be frozen out of any legitimate area. Within
the framework of any voluntary plan there must be room to some extent
for such newcomers with immediate requirements and also to take care
of hardship cases that may develop."[89]

In the face of mounting symptoms of disarray the government made a
modest attempt at this time to strengthen its capacity to induce compliance with the import guidelines. On the recommendation of the Special
Committee, the provisions of the Buy American Act of 1933 were applied to the oil procurement policies of federal agencies and departments.
Sellers of petroleum products to the government were henceforth to be
required to "furnish a certificate from the Administrator of the Voluntary
Import Program that the materials that they proposed to furnish, if
partly of foreign crude origin, have been or will be imported in full compliance with the voluntary program."[90] It was noted at the cabinet level
that this move would add to the government's costs. Secretary of Defense
Neil H. McElroy, for example, observed that it was likely to increase
defense costs by $10 million to $20 million a year.[91] Although incremental burdens for the budget were assured, the utility of this measure
in accomplishing its primary purpose was not. Eisenhower revealed his
thoughts in a longhand note: "Bob Anderson and I are not confident that
the scheme will work."[92]

By the late spring of 1958 it had become apparent that a stable equilibrium was not in sight for yet another reason. The program had been
constructed to restrict the importation of crude oil but had been silent
on the imports of petroleum products at various stages of refinement.
This gap in coverage had not passed unnoticed in the industry. On
May 28, 1958, Gordon Gray, the new ODM Director, reported to the
President that reports had recently come to his attention indicating that
"projected plans of some importers which if carried through, could

89. "Supplementary Report of the Special Committee to Investigate Crude Oil
Imports," March 21, 1958, transmitted to the President by Weeks in a memorandum,
March 24, 1958, Whitman Files, Administration Series, Box 42, DDEL.

90. Ibid., p. 5.

91. Minutes of the Cabinet Meeting of March 21, 1958.

92. This inscription appears on a memorandum from Weeks to the President,
March 24, 1958, Whitman Files, Administration Series, Box 42, DDEL.

bring about a substantial increase in the level of products importation, which would seriously affect the voluntary program as now established." It was his recommendation that "cognizance of the whole field of petroleum and its products" was now in order and that the Special Committee should be instructed to expand its jurisdiction for this purpose.[93] The Special Committee further reported on June 4, 1958, its belief that "if commercial imports of unfinished gasoline and other unfinished oils increase beyond the currently prevailing level, such imports may constitute a threat to the voluntary program. The Committee therefore recommends that importing companies voluntarily limit their imports of such unfinished gasoline and other unfinished oils to this level during the remainder of the calendar year 1958."[94] Accordingly the scope of the voluntary program was expanded to include this category of imports. Residual fuel oils, however, remained untouched.

From the point of view of tidy administration of the voluntary restriction scheme another matter was even more bothersome. Authorization to import petroleum and its products with official blessing was obviously profitable. Applications from potential new entrants continued to mount. So also did the grievances of importers with established market positions whose quota allocations were subject to still deeper cuts. A system that effectively penalized those who complied but failed to punish those who did not was inherently unstable. Amendments in the allocation procedure that promised to make the system more manageable thus had an obvious attraction.

On September 12, 1958, Captain Matthew V. Carson, Jr., administrator of the Oil Import Program, offered a radically different approach for consideration. Quotas would henceforth be assigned to refiners on

93. "Memorandum for the President," reprinted in Cabinet Task Force on Oil Import Control, *The Oil Import Question*, p. 194. The surge in imports of petroleum products at this time was also influenced by an unexpected ruling by the Bureau of Customs. Early in 1958 the bureau amended its treatment of unfinished oils; for purposes of the calculation of import duties, they were henceforth to be charged at the low rate assigned to crude oil. Trends in the importation of unfinished oil were reported as follows by Captain Matthew V. Carson, Jr., administrator of the Oil Import Program, on February 19, 1959: imports ran at the rate of 57,000 barrels daily in 1956 and at 73,000 barrels a day in 1957 but had reached almost 350,000 barrels a day in 1958. For a discussion of this point, see William A. Peterson, *The Question of Governmental Oil Import Restriction* (Washington, D.C.: American Enterprise Association, 1959), especially pp. 24 and 25.

94. "Report on Imports of Petroleum Products by the Special Committee to Investigate Crude Oil Imports," reprinted in Cabinet Task Force on Oil Import Control, *The Oil Import Question*, app. C-2, p. 192.

the basis of the size of their runs (whether or not their inputs were of foreign or domestic origin) and the importing history of firms would be scrapped as an allocative criterion. This proposal had at least one highly attractive feature: it would permit the administrator to deal with a less volatile population. Public reaction to this proposal, invited by publication of the proposal in the *Federal Register,* was generally hostile, but the idea itself survived. It subsequently was incorporated into a proposal prepared by Under Secretary of Commerce Frederick H. Mueller and Herbert Hoover, Jr., now a special consultant to the State Department, in which the two allocative criteria were blended. But this compromise proposal was not without flaws. In the view of the Justice Department the proposed amendments appeared to be "a series of concessions designed to secure compliance from individual companies, rather than a Government program grounded on national security considerations presented to the industry for its compliance." Moreover, the alleged substantive merits of this proposal were questionable. There was a "probability" that the consequences would be "harmful to competition." The major integrated companies were dominant at the refining level. Linking import quotas to refinery operations would work to their benefit and to the disadvantage of the smaller independents.[95]

While debates in the executive branch continued over the next steps in oil import policy, pressures for a further tightening of restrictions gathered force elsewhere. There could be little doubt that Phase II of the voluntary program had failed to accomplish one of its primary purposes; crude oil production in the United States in 1958 was less by some 460,000 barrels a day than it had been a year earlier and exploratory drilling had also declined. Though imports of crude oil had simultaneously fallen (by about 69,000 barrels a day), this reduction had been more than offset by increased imports of finished and unfinished petroleum products (from about 77,000 barrels a day in 1957 to 248,000 barrels a day in 1958).[96] Even in District V, which had been regarded as the region of the country in which full operations were assured, "shut in" capacity had emerged.[97] Meanwhile the leverage available to pro-

95. Draft letter, Attorney General Rogers to Under Secretary of Commerce Mueller, n.d., Rogers Papers, Box 29, DDEL.

96. *Report of the National Fuels and Energy Study Group on an Assessment of Available Information on Energy in the United States,* S. Doc. 159, 87 Cong. 2 sess. (GPO, 1962), p. 422.

97. "Report of the Special Committee to Investigate Crude Oil Imports," June 30, 1958, Whitman Files, Administration Series, Box 42, DDEL.

ponents of tighter import restrictions was greater in late 1958 than it had been earlier. Section 8 of the Trade Agreements Extension Act of 1958 imposed a more stringent requirement on the executive branch than had section 7 of similar legislation in 1955. The President was now obliged, not just to initiate fact-finding proceedings, but to act to ensure compliance with programs certified by the ODM director as essential to the national security. Failing a reversal of the ODM's position on oil imports, the voluntary restriction program was doomed.

By mid-December 1958 a program of mandatory oil import controls was under active and sympathetic consideration by the Special Cabinet Committee. In principle another choice was available: a reassessment of the national security rationale and of the import restrictions defended in its name. The most eloquent spokesman for this position was Clarence Randall, chairman of the Council on Foreign Economic Policy, and his views were strongly seconded by Don Paarlberg of the White House staff. Randall put the case as follows:

In order to keep the record straight . . . let me say that I think that the placing of any restrictions on oil imports is wrong. I am not qualified to judge as to whether this program is required as a matter of domestic politics, but I am of the opinion that it cannot be justified on grounds of security or those of economic policy. Ostensibly, the program is based upon national security, but if domestic petroleum reserves are required for our defense in war, or our recovery after war, I do not see how we advance toward that objective by using up our existing reserves. It seems to me that our policy should be to conserve that which we have, rather than to take measures which would cause our supplies to be exhausted more rapidly.[98]

Randall further noted that "in terms of economics, import quotas increase the cost of petroleum products in many areas of the United States. This places a burden upon the consumer, who has no one to lobby for his protection. Large companies benefit, and the individual of modest means is penalized." Furthermore, the nation's position as a leader in the reconstruction of the international economic order would be compromised as "we . . . are seeking the reduction of trade barriers, and the elimination of discriminations by other nations. This step will inevitably further weaken GATT [General Agreement on Tariffs and Trade], which is already under threat from other sources."

The year 1958 closed with the issue still in suspense. In late December quota allocations for the period beginning January 1—which by prece-

98. Randall to Dulles and Strauss, December 26, 1958, Don Paarlberg Papers, Box 7, DDEL.

dent were assigned for the subsequent six months—were announced as unchanged until February 28, 1959.[99] This breathing space brought no relief from clamor elsewhere for more forceful restrictive measures. Further discussion was fueled by the report of a Texas oil imports study commission, appointed by Governor Price Daniel, which called for mandatory controls. Spokesmen for the coal industry also joined this chorus. In February 1959 a National Coal Policy Conference was convened in Washington representing the coal operators, the United Mine Workers Union, and the railroads, and it endorsed direct controls over all categories of petroleum imports, including residual fuel oil.[100] Nor was congressional opinion indifferent on this matter. Senator O'Mahoney of Wyoming signaled his intention to introduce a bill to impose mandatory import quotas on crude oil and its derivatives and three Pennsylvania congressmen (John P. Saylor, James E. Van Zandt, and Thomas E. Morgan) representing coal-mining constituencies introduced bills that would compel limitations on imports of residual fuel oil.

The administration chose to follow the procedural route prescribed in section 8 of the Trade Agreements Extension Act of 1958. The old ODM, renamed the Office of Civil and Defense Mobilization (OCDM) was requested to undertake a further study of the national security implications of the importation of oil and its products. Its director, Leo A. Hoegh (formerly governor of Iowa), submitted his findings to the President on February 27, 1959, concluding that "crude oil and the principal crude oil derivatives and products are being imported in such quantities and under such circumstances as to threaten to impair the national security."[101] Hoegh observed that it was "apparent" to him that "in the current world oversupply situation, excessive quantities of low-priced oils from off-shore sources are seeking the United States market. In such a situation, without control of production in relation to demand by the countries of origin, it is to be expected that there would be substantial economic incentives to increase imports into the United States."[102] The director's conclusions applied to all categories of oil imports. The position of the OCDM staff that imports of residual fuel oil constituted no

99. "Interim Report of the Special Committee to Investigate Crude Oil Imports," December 22, 1958, Areeda Papers, Box 14, DDEL.

100. On these points, see Peterson, *The Question of Governmental Oil Import Restrictions,* pp. 29–30.

101. Memorandum, Hoegh to the President, February 27, 1959, OF, Box 683, DDEL.

102. Ibid.

threat to national security was overridden in the report of findings submitted to the President.

Supporters of the vision of a more liberal international economic order and of noninterventionist solutions to domestic economic problems had been outflanked. But some rearguard actions could still be fought. Attorney General William Rogers was far from satisfied with the case Hoegh had presented. In a lengthy analysis Rogers advised the President that Hoegh had not established "a solid foundation upon which to base his conclusion." Deficiencies in Hoegh's position were dissected in some detail. "To provide a solid foundation for correct decisions which can be ultimately defended," wrote the attorney general, "all the facts directly relevant to these considerations must be faced and analyzed whether they support the same conclusions or not. Thus, the statute requires consideration of, among other matters, (1) domestic production needed for projected national defense requirements, and (2) the capacity of domestic industries to meet such requirements. Yet the Director's memorandum contains no conclusions as to either of these matters." Moreover, it failed to state "on what basis it is determined that a quantity is 'excessive' or a balance is 'reasonable.' " But these were not the only weaknesses. Rogers further observed that the statistics cited on a decline in the number of wells drilled in 1958 had no significance in isolation from "other relevant factors." He argued: "Such factors would include an estimate of the amount of reserves necessary to meet the extraordinary demand which might be created in time of war. This, in turn, would require some estimate of the shut-in producing capacity currently available in the United States as a reserve for emergency needs. It would also involve consideration of the extent to which the existing and projected rate of exploratory drilling would maintain such necessary reserve." Rogers also reported that he had been informed that the new reserves discovered in 1958 had exceeded the growth in domestic demand.[103] Moreover, the argument that residual fuel imports involved a national security risk was particularly suspect.[104]

103. Rogers to the President, n.d., Whitman Files, Administration Series, Box 35, DDEL.

104. Rogers quoted and apparently endorsed a communication from the National Oil Jobbers Council that had observed: "No one has successfully maintained that the United States petroleum industry can supply the demands of residual oil at reasonable prices after giving due regard to good conservation practices and economic management of domestic refineries. Such being the case, it is impossible for us to understand why even the slightest consideration is being given to restricting residual oil. . . ." Ibid.

The attorney general made clear that it was not within his competence to judge the larger questions of policy at stake in the matter; it was instead his concern to ensure that the requirements of law had been fully satisfied. This he regarded as a matter of extreme importance, as he anticipated that mandatory controls would be challenged in the courts. Nevertheless, there could be no doubt that in his judgment a persuasive case had not been made.

A note of caution was also sounded by the Council of Economic Advisers. Its chairman, Raymond J. Saulnier, advised the President that mandatory restrictions on oil imports would be in conflict with the administration's counterinflationary objectives. On February 26, 1959, he observed: "Should it become necessary to embark on a program of mandatory oil import controls, I suggest that explicit account be taken in any proclamation or statement that is issued at that time of the possible price effect of such controls." He regarded it as "inevitable that the control program will have a price effect (at least to hold prices at a level higher than would otherwise obtain). . . ." The administrators of any program that might be initiated should be charged "to limit its price effect to what is clearly essential for the accomplishment of national security objectives."[105]

The die, however, had already been cast. Even before the OCDM director had reported his findings, the Special Cabinet Committee had anticipated the likely contents of his message and had agreed unanimously to recommend a mandatory control program if the OCDM statement took the expected form. Secretary of Commerce-designate Lewis Strauss spoke for the committee before the full cabinet on March 6, 1959. The voluntary restriction program, it was suggested, was effectively bankrupt. "Noncompliance by a few companies," he maintained, "had tended to demoralize those that did comply to the extent that some of the latter now intended to withdraw from the voluntary program." Moreover, any attempt to bolster the voluntary system might run afoul of the antitrust laws.[106]

105. Saulnier to the President, February 26, 1959, Whitman Files, Eisenhower Diary Series, Box 24, DDEL.

106. Minutes of the Cabinet Meeting of March 6, 1959, Whitman Files, ibid., Box 25. The Special Committee's report itemized the following factors as compelling mandatory action: "excessive imports by companies who have not complied with the Voluntary Program; a threat to the success of the Voluntary Program because of increased importation of unfinished oils and products; the likelihood of increased noncompliance by companies now having allocations when they are asked to cut back imports voluntarily in order to provide allocations to newcomers to the pro-

Though the recommendation to go forward with mandatory controls covering all categories of oil imports was adopted, this step was not taken without reservations. The attorney general again expressed his fear that there would be "serious problems" in the legal defense of the government's position. Under Secretary of State Christian A. Herter questioned the basis on which "the defense essentiality concept could be applied to residual" and noted the serious impact on relations with Venezuela that might follow from this decision. But the most doleful note was sounded by the President himself. He expressed his concern over the "tendencies of special interests in the United States to press almost irresistibly for special programs like this" that were "in conflict with the basic requirement on the United States to promote increased trade in the world." He indicated that he "did not wish to be pessimistic about the nature of free government," but that he wanted to "caution about the trouble that might develop from too many cases of this sort."[107] Despite discomfort with the position then adopted, it was feared that inaction by the executive branch would produce an even less acceptable result. In view of congressional restiveness on oil imports, it was thought likely that mandatory restrictions would be legislated on terms that would provide little or no latitude for administrative interpretation.

Oil Policy under the Regime of Mandatory Controls

With the issuance of Presidential Proclamation 3279 on March 10, 1959, the federal government closed the remaining gap in a regulatory apparatus supporting the price of domestic crude oil. Henceforth imports of petroleum and its products could not legally be brought into the United States without a license issued by the secretary of the interior. In determining the total volume of import allowables, the administrator of the control program was charged to ensure that imports did not exceed a predetermined proportion of expected domestic demand for petroleum and petroleum products. In the first instance, the proclamation set the

gram; and the impossibility of working out a desirable and legally permissible revision of the Voluntary Program acceptable to this committee which will take care of these requirements." "Report of Special Committee to Investigate Crude Oil Imports," reprinted in Cabinet Task Force on Oil Import Control, *The Oil Import Question*, app. C-3, p. 203.

107. Minutes of the Cabinet Meeting of March 6, 1959.

maximum import allowable for crude oil, unfinished oils, and finished products in Districts I–IV at approximately 9 percent of projected total demand. In District V on the other hand the volumes eligible for license were to be governed by the differences between expected demand and local production. Differential treatment was accorded, however, to various categories of petroleum products. Most notably, imports of residual fuels in Districts I–IV were subject to a different rule: they were excluded from the general quota, but were to be limited to the import quantities reported in 1957.

In administrative design, much of this apparatus bore the marks of experience accumulated during the second phase of the voluntary restriction scheme. On one significant point, however, procedure was radically revised. The essential concept of the Mueller-Hoover plan, which had been canvassed during the autumn of 1958, was now resurrected. Not only were "historical" importers eligible for quota allocations, so also were refiners, whether or not they had had any experience as importers. In Districts I–IV the blanket inclusion of refiners in the allocation scheme meant that seventy-six new firms were added to the list of eligible license holders. Though the number of recognized claimants thus grew, the aggregate number of barrels to satisfy them did not. For the first allocation period under mandatory controls, imports were authorized nationally at 936,770 barrels a day (738,570 for Districts I–IV and 198,200 for District V).[108] By contrast, actual levels of importation of crude oil and finished and unfinished petroleum products (excluding residual) had amounted to 1,099,000 barrels a day in 1957 and 1,201,000 barrels a day in 1958.[109]

These steps clearly marked a victory for the protectionist interests in the domestic oil industry and to a lesser extent in the coal industry. But there could be no disguising the fact that they also marked a retreat from the administration's professed commitment to strengthened competition and to the reduction of barriers to international commerce. Nor could it be concealed that the interests of the consumers had been compromised.[110]

108. Department of the Interior press release, March 17, 1959, reported in Peterson, *The Question of Governmental Oil Import Restrictions*, pp. 31–34.

109. *Report of the National Fuels and Energy Study Group*, p. 422.

110. Reactions of consumer interests were not long delayed. Members of the New England congressional delegation deplored the inclusion of residual fuel oils in the control program, and Senator William Proxmire introduced a bill on March 25, 1959, that would rescind the President's proclamation and give Congress a veto power over any similar restrictions in the future.

At the same time, the new system was not massively protective. Oil imports had not been totally excluded. Instead, the mandatory program presupposed a coexistence of domestic and foreign oil in the American market, even though its terms were less than perfectly competitive. Indeed, a formula linking allowable imports to total demand would assure a growing volume of imports in an expanding economy. Nor had the administration's interest in more vigorous competition been completely abandoned. The design of the control program had made a bow in its direction by a progressive scaling of import quotas to refiners: smaller refiners were entitled to import a larger proportion of their requirements than were larger ones.[111] Moreover, part of the potential hardship to consumers could be relieved by administrative discretion. The import allowables, after all, were determined by estimating future demand—a procedure permitting some flexibility—rather than being tied to levels revealed in a prior base period. A concession was also made to consumers of residual fuel oil with the understanding that the imports in this category, though subject to control, were not to be charged against quota allocations assigned to importers of crude and other partially finished petroleum products. Moreover, the allowables for residual fuel were to be reviewed with some frequency.

A reconciliation of mandatory import controls with the administration's broader defense and foreign policy strategies posed even more intractable problems. Whereas the later stages of the voluntary restriction scheme had sheltered Canadian and Venezuelan suppliers, Proclamation 3279 had not mentioned imports by source. Nor was it clear how discrimination in favor of western hemisphere suppliers (and against those in the Middle East) could be incorporated into the mandatory program without flagrant violation of the GATT rules. Nevertheless, steps that would rebuild western hemisphere relations were held by the State Department to be urgent.

This matter headed the agenda of a White House Conference on April 27, 1959, at which Under Secretary of State Douglas Dillon noted that the present restrictions provided "an added inducement for the Canadians to build an uneconomic pipeline from their western oil fields

---

111. This was a matter of importance to the competitive position of the independent refiners. They had been obliged to purchase crude oil at prices established above competitive levels. Refineries operated by integrated firms with access to their own supplies of imported crude had been able to acquire feedstocks on more favorable terms. On this point, see Edward H. Shaffer, *The Oil Import Program of the United States* (Praeger, 1968), p. 16.

to the Montreal market. This would cut into Venezuelan oil shipments to Montreal and upset the market generally."[112] The President accepted the recommendation that this case should be given exceptional treatment, subject to "an understanding with Canada to the effect that if imports should loom excessively large, or if the Venezuelans should be blocked from Montreal, this would be dealt with as a new situation."[113] An amendment to Proclamation 3279 was issued on April 30, exempting as of June 1, 1959, further restrictions on the importation of crude oil and petroleum products "entering the United States by pipeline, motor carrier or rail from the country of production." The White House press release on this occasion emphasized that "this exemption applies to petroleum from sources which would be accessible from overland transportation in the event of an emergency."[114] This modification in the program thus could be seen to follow directly from the larger national security rationale for controls. Technically, oil from Mexico would qualify for exempt status under the provisions of this amendment, though it was not then anticipated that imports from that source would be more than trivial.

The "overland exemption" formula restored special status directly to one of the western hemisphere suppliers, but it spoke at best only indirectly to the interests of the other. The President tried to accentuate the positive when addressing President Romulo Betancourt of Venezuela on April 28, 1959. The proclamation, as amended, would

improve the operation of the program and serve the interests of the Western Hemisphere. While the relatively small amount of Canadian oil sold in the North Central and Northwestern part of the United States does not compete with Venezuelan oil, the amendment will, we hope, reduce the serious risk of a permanent loss to Venezuela of its Montreal market. At the same time, I hope you will agree that our governments should continue their discussions looking toward broader hemisphere arrangements. The United States has been Venezuela's largest market and I am confident that it will continue to be so on an expanding scale.[115]

Venezuela's special concern for residual fuel oil, which accounted for about 45 percent of its export sales to the American market, was par-

112. Paarlberg to Ann Whitman, Memorandum on the Conference of Secretary of the Treasury Anderson, Secretary of the Interior Seaton, Under Secretary of State Dillon, and others with the President, April 27, 1959, Whitman Files, Eisenhower Diary Series, Box 25, DDEL.

113. Ibid.

114. White House press release, April 30, 1959, Areeda Papers, Box 14, DDEL.

115. Eisenhower to Betancourt, April 28, 1959, ibid.

ticularly noted. The President observed that he had "asked the Administrator of the program to keep this aspect particularly in mind, and I assure you that it will receive careful attention."

By July 1959 the Department of State was persuaded that further steps to improve Venezuela's position were essential and proposed that the control system "be revised through some procedure which will have the effect of decontrolling imports of residual fuel oil."[116] Action along such lines was held to be needed, not only because of Venezuela's historic position as a principal supplier to the American market, but—and no less importantly—because of the possible unfortunate consequences over the longer term of Venezuelan animosity. The Venezuelan government, it was noted, was proclaiming that the restrictive oil policies of the United States justified other oil-producing nations in adopting interventionist solutions of their own.

There was a tone of foreboding in the State Department Staff Paper of July 22, 1959, commenting on the possible implications of the Venezuelan initiative in convening a meeting in Cairo to consider the formation of an Organization of Petroleum Exporting Countries. The following assessment was then offered:

Given the nationalistic climate which today prevails in Venezuela, it is doubtful, once the present world oil arrangements are effectively broken, that the line in Venezuela can be held at any point short of total government control, if not expropriation, or that the pace of increasing intervention can be held within limits consistent with orderly economic development. And if Venezuela demonstrates that it is capable of taking these measures without suffering any loss of revenue, it would be wishful thinking to assume that the line could be held in the Near and Far East where nationalistic aspirations are equally strong, if not yet so publicly defined. It seems clear therefore that we must in our own national self-interest make an effort to prevent this from happening and to provide appropriate encouragement to an evolution of Venezuelan thinking along lines which would be more promising of benefit for Venezuela and more compatible with petroleum interests of friendly countries as a whole.[117]

By September 1959 a more specific proposal for the de facto decontrol of residual fuel imports had been developed. The State Department then recommended that an "additional allocation" be issued monthly that would entitle importers to bring in residual fuel oil in the amounts

116. State Department Staff Paper, "Revision of the Oil Import Control Program and U.S. Position in Further Discussions with Venezuela Concerning Petroleum," July 22, 1959, p. 1, ibid.
117. Ibid., pp. 8, 9.

necessary to fill any unused storage capacity. This modification, it was maintained, could be accomplished by administrative regulations and would not require an amendment to Proclamation 3279. It would, however, have the practical effect of removing restrictions, even though residual fuel oils would technically remain under the import control program.[118] And it was hoped that it would have a further consequence: that of dampening anti-American fervor in Venezuela that might contaminate the environment for the international oil industry, not only there, but elsewhere.

This bit of formula engineering came to naught. The proposal received a hostile reception from other departments. The Interior Department opposed this recommendation on the ground that "the petroleum industry would consider effective decontrol of residual as the first sign of weakness in the administration of the program." Moreover, the coal industry was severely depressed and "the high degree of substitutability between residual fuel oil and coal in the areas of primary competition between the two fuels (the Eastern Seaboard) could lead to a further undermining of coal's marketing position in the United States."[119] The Commerce Department was also negative, noting that the action of the secretary of the interior increasing allowables of residual oils for the third and fourth quarters of 1959 "should be sufficient to indicate to them [the Venezuelans] that the United States is desirous of assuring them increasing access to this market." The recommendation of the State Department could "only be justified by an agreement with Venezuela not to take any further punitive actions against private oil interests by further tax increases or encroachment on presently operative management prerogatives."[120]

Though the State Department's recommendations on policy toward residual fuels were not followed, quota allowances were later liberalized for other reasons. Flexibility in the administration of these allowances was recognized as necessary to meet the needs of the Northeast in periods of unseasonably cold weather. A more relaxed attitude toward imports

118. Memorandum, Assistant Secretary of State Thomas C. Mann to Under Secretary of the Interior Elmer F. Bennett, September 1, 1959, Areeda Papers, Box 14, DDEL.

119. Seaton to the President, September 12, 1959, Paarlberg Papers, Box 7, DDEL.

120. Mueller to the President, September 11, 1959, ibid.

was also prompted by improvements in the technology of petroleum refining. Refiners naturally sought to maximize their outputs of the higher-valued petroleum products. In the domestic industry yields of residual per barrel of crude oil processed thus continued to fall and the gap between domestic demand and supply continued to widen. In these circumstances rigid limitations on residual fuel imports implied burdens on consumers without compensating benefits to domestic oil producers. The interests of coal producers alone were advanced.

But the mandatory control program was under further attack from some segments of the oil industry itself. The larger firms, especially those with investments in crude production overseas, protested that the system discriminated against them unfairly. Those who had assumed the risks of developing fields abroad were now being penalized. In their view the inclusion of independent refiners in the import authorization (whether or not they had ever before used imported crude) was a technique of income redistribution that rewarded those who were risk-averse. When responding to such charges the Department of the Interior attempted to broaden the national security rationale for controls. The health of both domestic producers and of refiners, it argued, should be kept in view.[121] At the same time, it was noted that the retention of a "historical" principle in the allocation formulas had placed a protective floor beneath the position of long-established importers.[122]

The rules governing the use of quotas assigned to refiners were also subjected to challenge. By its very nature the control system conferred an economic asset of considerable value on entitlement holders. (In view of the price differential between domestic and foreign crude oil, the value of quota allocation was approaching $1 a barrel.) Moreover, this windfall was made available to all refiners, whether or not they had used imported crudes in the past or had any intention of doing so.

121. Secretary of the Interior Seaton to Ralph G. Follis, Chairman of the Board of the Standard Oil Company of California, July 10, 1959, Whitman Files, Administration Series, Box 36, DDEL. Follis entered a letter of protest on these points directly to the President, and it was referred to the Department of the Interior for reply.

122. In March 1959 the allocations for Districts I–IV set quotas for importers of record under the voluntary program that were to be no less than 80 percent of their former entitlement. In the second allocation period (the last half of 1959) a reduction in the historical entitlement to 75.7 percent was required. Otherwise, space for allocations to refiners could not be found.

The regulations provided that a quota holder could exchange imported for domestic crude oil as long as such transactions took the form of barter (rather than sales) and were reported in advance to the secretary of the interior. Arrangements of this sort were particularly attractive to inland refiners, whose operations had been set up to handle domestic crudes. Though the reliability of information reported to the Interior Department on the terms of barter transactions is in some doubt, there could be no question that income distribution within the oil industry had again been tampered with. In defense of the decision to assign quotas to all refiners, including those with no use for imported crude, the Department of the Interior argued that "we could not support a program confining the privilege of importing crude oil to a special class of refiners." It was further asserted that the exchange procedure ensured that "the competitive advantages are allowed to fall where they may, in accordance with the free play of economic forces. . . . If the exchange is on a favorable basis, the result is that the cost of the crude supply of the newcomer-refiner is less. Similarly, importers which can use imported crude obtained through such exchanges are free to do so and can reap whatever economic benefits are involved."[123]

Though prepared to defend the mandatory control system from its external critics, the administrators of the program in the Department of the Interior were themselves pressing for a number of reforms. On October 15, 1960, Under Secretary Bennett reported to the President that "experience under the mandatory oil import program indicates that the present formulae have resulted in a ratio of petroleum imports to domestic crude production above that contemplated when the program was initiated."[124] Indeed, there was considerable evidence that the original purposes of the control scheme were not being served successfully.

123. Seaton to R. G. Follis, July 10, 1959. Senior members of the Department of the Interior were acutely aware of the sensitivity of the industry on this point. Under Secretary of the Interior Elmer F. Bennett, for example, took up the matter in an address to the National Petroleum Association in Cleveland, Ohio, on April 21, 1960: "I am sure that many of you have heard—even possibly support—the sentiment that an allocation granted to an inland refiner is a 'windfall' or unearned gift from the Federal Government. . . . The real windfall would, in fact, accrue if the Federal Government by administrative decree protected the import position of a refiner solely because of geography or overseas productive capacity and denied access to all others." Prepared text, pp. 10, 12–13, Elmer Bennett Papers, Box 13, DDEL.

124. Bennett to the President, October 15, 1960, Bennett Papers, Box 7, DDEL.

Drilling activity in the United States had continued to decline; meanwhile crude production had fallen and crude oil imports had increased.[125] In the view of the Interior Department corrective action was called for, and it might usefully begin with revisions in the formula for calculating allowable imports. The department proposed that the appropriate ratio should be imports to domestic production, rather than imports to total demand. The former relationship, it was argued, was "one of the most valid and reliable measures of the effectiveness of the program . . . since domestic production is an indicator of the climate in which domestic exploration and development must be conducted."[126]

But should the demand approach be retained, other steps to reduce the slippage in the control system were held to be essential. The first concerned the position of residual fuel oil in the determination of other allowables in Districts I–IV. In the mandatory scheme as first laid down, quota authorizations for crude oil and petroleum products (*excluding* residual fuel oil) were calculated at approximately 9 percent of total demand for all petroleum products (*including* residual fuel oil). With the relaxation of controls over imports of residual, this approach had meant that the base for calculating allowables for crude oil and other petroleum products had been swollen. The Interior Department pressed for an amendment in the proclamation that would permit a downward adjustment in crude oil allowables to offset imports of residual fuel in excess of the amounts imported in the base year 1957.[127]

The demand formula as applied in District V had also permitted another evasion of the control apparatus. Import quotas had been established there to cover the deficit between demand and domestic supply. When this scheme had been put in place, it was presupposed that the region west of the Rocky Mountains was isolated from the rest of the U.S. petroleum market. It now appeared that this assumption could no

125. Data prepared by the Department of the Interior indicated the following: the number of active drilling rigs in the United States on November 21, 1960, was 1,858 (down from 2,206 on November 23, 1959). Crude production in 1959 had been recorded at 6,211,000 barrels a day. In 1960, on the other hand, the production had averaged 6,185,000 barrels a day. Crude oil imports had risen from 730,000 barrels a day in 1959 to 745,000 barrels a day in 1960. Memorandum, Royce A. Hardy, Assistant Secretary of the Interior for Mineral Resources, to Under Secretary Bennett, December 7, 1960, Bennett Papers, ibid.

126. Ibid.

127. Bennett to the President, October 15, 1960.

longer be made with confidence. As Under Secretary Bennett described the problem to the President:

Transfers of crude oil and finished products from District V, under the existing formula, are part of the demand for petroleum in District V. The import level for that District is set to meet the difference between demand and domestic supply. Therefore, transfers from District V to Districts I–IV generate a corresponding increase in the level of imports of crude oil into District V. To a large extent, such transfers from District V to Districts I–IV have the effect of additional imports of oil into the latter Districts.[128]

A third complication had been generated as a by-product of the ex ante approach to demand in Districts I–IV. The Bureau of Mines had been charged to produce forward estimates of demand for each allocation period. In practice the bureau had often overestimated future demand and thus had permitted higher import volumes than could have been justified ex post. The Department of the Interior accordingly sought authority to adjust the allowables of subsequent periods to take account of errors of estimation.[129]

A further feature of the control system called for attention. The market environment shaped by import restrictions had increased the attractiveness of natural gas liquids. By December 1959 the rate of production of natural gas liquids had increased some 120,000 barrels a day over the preceding year.[130] This was additionally troublesome because natural gas liquids were counted as part of the total demand formula; import allowables had thus been further inflated.

The Interior Department insisted that the changes it sought should be regarded as "technical adjustments." There could be no doubt, however, about their basic intent: to restrict imports still further. The reaction of the State Department was sharply negative. Under Secretary Dillon described the new proposals as constituting a major shift in the structure of the program that could only properly be "founded on a clearly demonstrated merit directly related to the national security. No such foundation is laid in the case at hand."[131] He further cautioned that action along the proposed lines "would be widely regarded abroad by our friends and allies as a denial of, or default on," the assurance contained in the original proclamation that controls would be administered to avoid disrup-

128. Ibid.
129. Hardy to Bennett, December 7, 1960.
130. Ibid.
131. Dillon to Maurice H. Stans, December 1, 1960, Bennett Papers, Box 7, DDEL.

tion of the normal patterns of international trade. He concluded that "to make further modifications of a restrictive nature without deliberate study, without full discussion and agreement among the interested agencies, and, above all, without a clearly demonstrated national security foundation, could only magnify the present difficulties."[132] Clarence Randall also recommended disapproval of this action.[133]

The arguments on oil import policy in the last days of the Eisenhower administration were echoes of the debates that had raged two years earlier. In the earlier round the proponents of increased protection had won. The final round was a standoff. The mandatory control program remained in place, but—apart from winning approval for quota adjustments to compensate for errors of demand estimation—the restrictionists made no further gains.

Formulating Policy toward the Natural Gas Industry

The development of policy toward oil had been the source of much intellectual anguish to the Eisenhower administration. In principle the case of natural gas presented no similar complications. A policy strategy for this component of the energy sector appeared to be readily compatible with the administration's basic predisposition toward greater reliance on market solutions.

The Supreme Court decision in *Phillips Petroleum Company* v. *Wisconsin* confounded the issue. This judgment handed down in May 1954 held that the basic intent of the Natural Gas Act of 1938 could be carried out only if the Federal Power Commission regulated the pricing of natural gas inputs distributed through interstate pipelines. Formerly the FPC had regarded its regulatory jurisdiction as limited to the service functions of pipelines when transmitting and distributing natural gas. In the Phillips case the Supreme Court had directed the FPC to regulate the gathering and collecting of natural gas in the field as well. This judgment was clearly at odds with the administration's preference for less federal regulation rather than more. The decision also ran counter to the administration view of the optimal division of powers between various echelons of government: prices established for natural gas in the field

132. Ibid.

133. See memorandum, David W. Kendall, Special Counsel to the President, to Arthur B. Focke, General Counsel to the Bureau of the Budget, December 20, 1960, Areeda Papers, Box 14, DDEL.

should be regarded as intrastate transactions and thus appropriate for regulation by the states but not by federal authorities. At the practical level a further complication arose. In the judgment of the FPC the standard approach to regulatory rate-making—that is, through the calculation of a fair rate of return on capital—could not usefully be applied in this instance. Though it worked reasonably well in the regulation of services, such as those provided by electric utilities and pipeline companies, this technique was held to be unsatisfactory in setting fair prices for a product supplied by a large number of firms facing widely divergent cost conditions.

The original Cabinet Committee on Energy Supplies and Resources Policy had recommended in January 1955 that the additional regulatory requirements imposed by the Supreme Court be overturned by new legislation. The preparation of a bill with the desired specifications, however, presented an interesting problem in political tactics. There could be little question that a proposal to deregulate field prices would be interpreted by some partisan groups as a probusiness and anticonsumer move. When this matter was first brought forward for full cabinet consideration, Vice-President Richard M. Nixon counseled that the administration would be well advised to leave the initiative for the introduction of a bill amending the Natural Gas Act to members of Congress from gas-producing states (such as Senator Lyndon Johnson) who were under considerable pressure to get such a bill enacted.[134] The administration was able to reserve its position when two bills to deregulate natural gas in the field were introduced in the 1955 session by Congressman Oren Harris and Senator J. William Fulbright, both Democrats of Arkansas.

The deregulation proposals sparked the expected controversy. The White House heard the consumer view from a delegation led by Senator Alexander Wiley of Wisconsin, who argued that the "scuttling" of the Phillips decision would expose 60 million users of natural gas to unreasonable rates and that it would add from $200 million to $400 million a year to the burdens of consumers.[135] Senator Paul Douglas of Illinois was even more forceful in opposing the amendment to the Natural Gas Act. In a lengthy presentation before the Senate Interstate and Foreign Commerce Committee of June 9, 1955, he maintained that the very structure of the natural gas industry precluded competition from being

134. Minutes of the Cabinet Meeting of January 21, 1955.
135. "Statement by Representatives of Consumers to President Eisenhower Opposing Destruction of Consumer Protections under the Natural Gas Act," March 18, 1955, OF, Box 726, DDEL.

an effective force for consumer protection. Though the industry included a large number of producers (some 5,000 sellers were recorded as producers of natural gas in the FPC records), its dominant characteristic was its concentration. The bulk of interstate pipeline transmissions was controlled by a small number of companies, many of them also major oil producers. Deregulation, he insisted, would soon be followed by higher prices from which the consumer—who was effectively a captive—had no escape. Regulation was thus a prerequisite for consumer protection. The regulatory process, however, could be improved. Douglas proposed that the effort to regulate field prices be focused on the 175 or so producers who supplied approximately 90 percent of the gas moved through interstate pipelines. The smaller producers, representing about 96 percent of the firms in the industry, could safely be exempt from the FPC's jurisdiction. Consumer interests would not be harmed by this modification, he maintained, but the work of the FPC could thereby be made more manageable.[136]

The senior ranks of the administration were not unanimous on the appropriate position toward the Harris-Fulbright Bill when it was presented for the President's signature in February 1956. The ODM strongly supported the bill. The views of the consumer lobby were dismissed on the ground that its members "ignore or belittle the basic advantage of unregulated commodity prices in a free market and the national policy against Government interference with private enterprise."[137] The FPC also endorsed the bill. Fears of hardships for consumers were held to be groundless; consumers were adequately protected by the provision directing the commission to take into account "the reasonable market price" for natural gas when determining the rate structures it allowed to pipeline distributors. This approach, it was argued, was far superior to current regulatory requirements. Moreover, the FPC asserted that it could not possibly make the cost studies required by the Phillips decision.[138] As of April 1955 it reported that some 10,000 rate schedule filings from

136. Statement of Paul H. Douglas, *Amendments to the Natural Gas Act,* Hearings before the Senate Committee on Interior and Insular Affairs, 84 Cong. 1 sess. (GPO, 1955), pp. 1517–27, 1534.

137. "Comments on the Statement Left with the President Expressing Consumer Opposition to Amendment of the Natural Gas Act," transmitted by Arthur S. Flemming to Gerald D. Morgan, March 31, 1955, OF, Box 726, DDEL.

138. FPC Chairman Jerome K. Kuykendall to Director of the Budget Bureau Rowland R. Hughes, February 10, 1956, Morgan Papers, Box 20, DDEL. It was estimated that natural gas producers numbered about 8,000 in 1954 but that only 5,557 were large enough to report to the FPC and that 197 firms produced nearly 97 percent of the gas sold. Staff Memorandum, n.d., ibid.

some 2,000 producers were before it and the backlog was continuing to mount.[139] General support for the bill was also forthcoming from the departments of Commerce and the Interior.

But there were also voices of dissent within the administration's senior ranks. The most outspoken among them was that of Secretary of Labor James P. Mitchell, who urged a veto of the Harris-Fulbright Bill, arguing that state regulatory authorities were not satisfactory substitutes for federal controls. "There is little reason to expect producing States to regulate in the interest of consumers in other States," he argued. Nor was "the reasonable market price" test to be applied in evaluating pipeline rates an adequate protection for consumers. Mitchell cautioned that "where proposed rates are in line with prevailing prices the Federal Power Commission will find it difficult to go behind those prices."[140] Skepticism about the soundness of the bill's "regulatory philosophy" and its protections for consumers was also registered by the Bureau of the Budget.[141]

The Harris-Fulbright Bill was vetoed by the President but for reasons that had more to do with the circumstances surrounding its passage than with its substantive merits. Evidence had come to light of an attempt by a lobbyist to "bribe" a senator and both the Senate and the Department of Justice were investigating the matter. The President reported to the cabinet on February 13, 1956, that he "thought that any good bill ought to be passed without having a terrible stench connected with it."[142] He reiterated this concern in a session with the Republican legislative leaders the following day, noting that he was "sensitive to the tendency of labeling Republicans as the party of big business," and that he "hated to have any part of the Administration program open to the charge that business could get this bill by throwing sufficient money around."[143]

139. Kuykendall to Raymond Saulnier, April 26, 1955, CEA Files, Box 17, DDEL.

140. Mitchell to the President, n.d., Morgan Papers, Box 20, DDEL.

141. Hughes to the President, n.d., ibid.

142. Minutes of the Cabinet Meeting of February 13, 1956, Whitman Files, Cabinet Series, Box 6, DDEL.

143. Legislative Leadership Meeting Supplementary Notes, February 14, 1956, Whitman Files, Eisenhower Diary Series, Box 7, DDEL. The President's comments in a conversation with his special assistant Gabriel Hauge on February 13, 1956, are also noteworthy. The President then noted that he "was greatly irritated with business" because of the gas bill and that he wanted to "give businessmen an honorable place, but they make crooks out of themselves." Record of conversation with Hauge, February 13, 1956, ibid., Box 8.

In his veto message the President expressed his hope that legislation containing many of the features of the rejected bill would be passed at a later session. Congressman Oren Harris took up this invitation in 1957, and the President was requested to offer his views on the shape an appropriate bill might take. In testimony on this matter before the House Committee on Interstate and Foreign Commerce, Charles H. Kendall, general counsel of the ODM, carried the administration's brief. The administration, he reported, wished to reaffirm its support for the general principle of "free competition in the sale of a commodity," but it also believed that "new legislation should include specific protection for consumers in their right to fair prices." Though the "reasonable market price" formula was broadly endorsed, it was also recommended that the FPC be authorized to limit "step-up clauses" in existing contracts and that it be empowered to consider cost data at its discretion when arriving at judgments on reasonable prices. The administration also indicated its support for two proposals submitted by the Presidential Advisory Committee in 1955 that had not found a place in the Harris-Fulbright Bill: that the FPC be authorized to prohibit sales of natural gas via interstate pipelines "at prices below actual cost plus a fair proportion of fixed charges" and that interstate pipelines be awarded power of eminent domain to facilitate the development of underground storage reservoirs. These proposals had been designed to address grievances of the coal industry, whose spokesmen had insisted that coal's position in the national energy market had been unfairly jeopardized by the "dumping" practices of a competing fuel.[144]

Attempts to deregulate the field prices of natural gas continued throughout Eisenhower's second term, but they remained stalled in Congress. Meanwhile the FPC's case backlog of rate-schedule filings continued to grow. Of the hundreds of cases before the commission, only ten had been completed by 1960.[145] The FPC announced the formulation of a new procedure in 1960, one that attempted to assess a fair rate of return on the basis of cost patterns generally applicable throughout a natural gas field rather than on a firm-by-firm basis. Experimentation with this procedure was begun in the natural gas fields of the Permian Basin in West Texas and New Mexico.

144. Statement of Charles Kendall in *Natural Gas Act (Regulation of Producers' Prices)*, Hearings before the House Committee on Interstate and Foreign Commerce, 85 Cong. 1 sess. (GPO, 1957), pt. 1, pp. 30–32.

145. On this point see Stephen G. Breyer and Paul W. MacAvoy, *Energy Regulation by the Federal Power Commission* (Brookings Institution, 1974), p. 68.

The Approach to the Problems of Coal

Of the three primary fuels, coal stood lowest in the Eisenhower administration's priorities. No case could be made that the profitability of the industry should be guaranteed to provide the incentive for the discovery of new reserves: the known reserves were already more than adequate for any foreseeable contingency. Nor could a case be made that the federal government should improve the regulatory environment affecting coal production; the conditions of coal supply were already closer to the specifications of the competitive model than were those of oil or natural gas. The circumstances of coal were still not free of troubles. This component of the energy sector was obviously in decline. At the margin, the domestic market had already revealed its preference for competing fuels. There was no compelling reason why government should override that preference.

The administration, however, had recognized that the competitive position of coal in the national energy market was less than perfect. It was conceded that coal had been handicapped by excessive rail charges and by the discount-pricing of interruptible supplies of natural gas. On these points the administration—as evidenced by the report of the Presidential Advisory Committee on Energy Supplies and Resources Policy and by its position on reform of the Natural Gas Act—had expressed a sympathetic concern. Though this concern had not been reinforced by effective action, the coal industry could at least derive some satisfaction from the inclusion of residual fuel oils in the program of mandatory import restrictions.

For most practical purposes the Eisenhower administration treated the coal industry as an unemployment problem, not as an energy supply matter. As a contributor to unemployment, it was by no means a trivial source of worry. Nevertheless, it was not self-evident that the distress of jobless miners could best be relieved by giving artificial respiration to a declining industry. Other social programs were available for this purpose. When the administration had attempted to prop up the demand for coal by special intervention, as it did in 1954, the results had not been altogether happy.[146]

146. A special program for this purpose, for example, was initiated in 1954 with the objective of increasing coal exports by 10 million tons. This program lapsed, however, in mid-1955. The administrator of the International Cooperation Administration

But there were still options to be explored. Staff studies undertaken by the CEA, in collaboration with the Interior Department's Bureau of Mines, suggested that an increase in employment in the coal industry from approximately 205,000 in 1954 to more than half a million by 1965 (and with a growth in output from 390 million to 740 million tons) was possible if the development of new uses for coal was pressed with vigor. These projections presupposed that the government would support accelerated research programs in directions such as the following: the conversion of coal into synthetic liquid fuels; the conversion of coal into chemicals; the enrichment of coal gas to the same Btu content as natural gas; the underground gasification of coal; and the development of a coal-fired gas turbine locomotive.[147]

This agenda received a cool reception at the higher levels of the administration. Much of this activity was construed under official doctrine as primarily a matter for private rather than public action. A bill calling for the creation of a research and development commission for coal did manage to pass Congress in 1959 but was disapproved by the President. The veto message argued that government involvement in such research activities should be controlled by the Department of the Interior, not by a separate research agency. The President did indicate, however, that he would be prepared to support a scheme that would authorize the secretary of the interior to negotiate contracts for coal research.[148]

In the 1960 session of Congress, a bill to establish an Office of Coal Research in the Department of the Interior was passed with the President's signature. This organization was authorized to "contract for, sponsor, co-sponsor and promote the coordination of research with

---

then reported: "A certain amount of coal must be bought in the ordinary course of events to supply some of the countries in which we have aid programs. This, under present regulations, will be bought in the world market, and I am hopeful that we shall not have to consider a special coal program again for the industry in this country. I should like to point out that under the coal program certain areas were picked out as the source of supply. This antagonized the Members of Congress from every state where coal is produced which was not on the list for procurement. This attitude was uniform even though coal could not possibly be competitive in price. From the political point of view I think we get more ill will by trying to satisfy a few clamorous areas because at the same time we antagonize many more people whose constituents complain that they are being discriminated against." John B. Hollister to Sherman Adams, September 26, 1955, Central Files, Box 679, DDEL.

147. Memorandum, Irving H. Siegel to the Council of Economic Advisers, July 15, 1955, CEA Files, Box 6, DDEL.

148. Presidential Memorandum of Disapproval, September 16, 1959, Central Files, Box 679, DDEL.

recognized interested groups, including but not limited to, coal trade associations, coal research associations, educational institutions, and agencies of States and political subdivisions of States."[149] In the waning months of the Eisenhower administration, an Interior Department official marked the creation of the Office of Coal Research with the words: "no steps beyond this program have been taken to assist the coal industry except as such assistance may derive from the oil import program."[150] Indeed, the neglect of coal had been so complete that the recommendations for this industry submitted by the Presidential Advisory Committee on Energy Supplies and Resources Policy in early 1955 had been ignored. When an Interdepartmental Committee on the Soft Coal Industry was reconvened in 1960, its members noted that no directives to implement these recommendations had been issued and that the status of the recommendations themselves was "unclear." Accordingly the Interdepartmental Committee concluded that "the decision with respect to its continuation, its scope, or its dissolution should be deferred for consideration by the new Administration."[151]

During the Eisenhower years coal continued to lose ground to rival fuels in the national marketplace. By comparison with its rivals, it also competed unsuccessfully for governmental favor. Spokesmen for coal, however, had not failed to notice the style of argument that had been so effectively deployed by the oil interests. Special treatment appeared to be more easily won when the importance of the industry as a contributor to the nation's emergency needs could be demonstrated. In the late 1950s spokesmen for coal took the lead in calling for a new and comprehensive "national fuels policy." Priority, it was maintained, should be assigned to two objectives: (1) the conservation of those fuel resources most vulnerable to exhaustion (oil and natural gas) and the utilization of the fuel least vulnerable to supply interruption (coal); and (2) the maintenance of an activity level in the nation's least vulnerable fuel industry that would assure that capacity was at hand to respond to any emergency. It was thus suggested that the national interest would be best served if a domestic market for a minimum of 450 million tons of coal a year were guaranteed.

149. 30 U.S.C. 662.

150. Memorandum of Jack L. Spore to Royce A. Hardy, Assistant Secretary of the Interior for Mineral Resources, October 24, 1960, Bennett Papers, Box 1, DDEL.

151. "Report of the Interdepartmental Committee on the Soft Coal Industry," submitted by Leo A. Hoegh, Chairman, January 5, 1961, Seaton Papers, Oil, Gas, and Mineral Series, Box 2, DDEL.

This appeal for a new approach to an energy policy was something less than disinterested. But so also was the interpretation of "competition" used by its rivals when disputing this doctrine. A minimum target for coal consumption was regarded by the spokesmen for oil as a call for "end-use control" that was incompatible with consumer sovereignty. The oil industry might be less than comfortable with the same principle if consumers were to be allowed complete freedom to choose between oil of domestic and foreign origin; interfuel competition in the American market, however, was apparently a different matter. There was more than a touch of irony, for example, in comments of the Texas Railroad Commission in 1960 on the proposals of the coal industry for a congressional inquiry into a new national fuels policy:

Our Nation already has a national policy toward the development of its fuels, and a policy of the type sought by the coal industry interests ultimately would lead to governmental control of both production and pricing of all fuels. Neither Federal nor State regulation has ever denied the citizens a freedom of choice from among the various fuels. The continuation of this consumer sovereignty is essential in our American economy. It is clear that the coal industry's real objective is not an impartial study but the establishment of a Federal agency designed to limit competition from oil and gas with coal in industrial uses. The fact that there is intense competition for fuel customers is entirely consistent with our American private enterprise philosophy, and equally as consistent with our principles of conservation.[152]

Policies for Developing Electrical Energy from Conventional Sources

Officials of the Eisenhower administration were persuaded that the long-term demand for electrical energy would continue to expand and quite possibly at accelerating rates. The issue dominating their concern in this area was the role the federal government should properly play in providing the capacity to serve the nation's needs. The administration's basic position on this point had been set out in the power policy statement issued by the Department of the Interior in August 1953. It had then been made clear that the federal government henceforth expected the major responsibility for power development to rest with private industry

152. *Energy Resources and Government,* Materials Submitted to the Subcommittee on Automation and Energy Resources by Federal and State Regulatory and Developmental Agencies of the Joint Economic Committee, 86 Cong. 2 sess. (GPO, 1960), p. 582.

and with state and local public authorities. Should their effects fall short, the federal government was prepared to assist as a "partner," but the first moves should be made by others. Eisenhower reiterated his understanding of this position when dedicating the McNary Dam in the state of Washington in September 1954: "It is not properly a Federal responsibility to try to supply all the power needs of our people. The Federal Government should no more attempt to do so than it should assume responsibility for supplying all their drinking water, their food, their housing, and their transportation. To attempt such a centralization of authority and responsibility always starts a deadly cycle." He warned "that monopoly is always potentially dangerous to freedom—even when monopoly is exercised by the Government. . . . The American people do not want and do not need to have any such monopoly, nor do they want a system leading toward it. They know they can have all the power capacity of our streams developed, as needed, without forfeiting the advantages of local responsibility and participation."[153]

But there was at least the possibility of a disjunction between the articulation of fundamental principles and the actual creation of needed generating capacity. In several regions of the country, but most particularly in the Pacific Northwest, a power deficit seemed to be in prospect. This possibility, in the view of Secretary of the Interior Douglas McKay, was directly related to misguided judgments of earlier administrations. "In areas in which the Federal Government has been a major producer of power," he reported to the House Committee on Interior and Insular Affairs in 1955, "the threat of shortages has become almost chronic." The moral of the tale was clear: in view of the "large expenditures required to assure that our power needs will be fully met," the major financial burden should be borne by private investors and by non-Federal units of government.[154] Nevertheless, a practical question remained: was "partnership" likely to mean the effective withdrawal of the federal government from new power undertakings?

Budget Director Rowland Hughes highlighted the problem. Writing to Sherman Adams on May 26, 1955, he reported his sense that the "power program of the Administration has not been accepted by the general

153. "Address at the Dedication of the McNary Dam, Walla Walla, Washington, September 23, 1954," *Public Papers: Eisenhower, 1954* (GPO, 1960), pp. 859–60.
154. Statement of Secretary of the Interior Douglas McKay in *Discussion of Budget Circular A-47 and the Related Power Partnership Principle,* Hearings before the House Committee on Interior and Insular Affairs, 84 Cong. 1 sess. (GPO, 1955), p. 43.

public." A massive selling campaign needed to be undertaken that would point out that the Eisenhower program is consistent with "an expanding economy . . . one on which no artificial limits are imposed. Dependency on government and government financing, to the exclusion of all else, *in any field,* put[s] a ceiling on how far we can go." But he added: *"The most effective method of salesmanship is a demonstration of the product. If the program is to succeed there must be some actual construction undertaken before the 1956 elections."*[155] The President shared this concern. To the cabinet he stressed his "desire to get started on some one necessary and large multiple-purpose project"; at the same meeting it was the view of Ambassador Lodge, among others, that it would be particularly useful if a "dirt-turning" ceremony could be held before the close of 1955.[156] Of all the candidates for early action, the Upper Colorado River Storage Basin Project seemed to have the most to recommend it.[157] This project, authorized by Congress in 1956, was one of the few significant new power ventures involving substantial commitments of federal money during the Eisenhower administration. Even so, it was regarded primarily as an irrigation scheme; power generation was but an incidental by-product.

The official doctrine had spoken with even greater clarity on the approach to be followed in the major instance in which the federal government was a monopoly supplier of an area's needs for electricity: no further federal monies should be committed to subsidizing consumers in the Tennessee Valley. This judgment had informed the decision to contract with a private utility to supply the additional power needed by the Atomic Energy Commission's facilities in this area. The intent of this arrangement (the Dixon-Yates contract) was to permit the TVA to satisfy its preference customers (municipalities, cooperatives, and rural

155. Hughes to Adams, May 26, 1955, Morgan Papers, Box 21, DDEL.
156. Minutes of the Cabinet Meeting of May 20, 1955, Whitman Files, Cabinet Series, Box 5, DDEL.
157. The President's interest in this project was long-standing. In a memorandum on February 16, 1954, to Budget Director Joseph M. Dodge, he observed: "The project of course is appealing to me because of its comprehensiveness; as you know, I am completely convinced that our river projects should treat the entire river valley as a single project and that each unit developed therein should have a proper relationship to the whole. This seems to be the case in this particular project, and mere approval of the whole thing, regardless of the speed with which we undertake its construction, would be reassuring to the West. In addition, to get a start on a project of this size would help provide us an 'ace in the hole,' if we wanted to accelerate public construction at any time in the future." Eisenhower to Dodge, February 16, 1954, Whitman Files, Administration Series, Box 13, DDEL.

electrification authorities) without calling on the U.S. Treasury to finance additional capacity. In the controversies that raged around the Dixon-Yates episode, the administration's nose was bloodied a bit.[158] When the city of Memphis decided in mid-1955 to proceed with the construction of a facility to supply its requirements, the administration was able to make a strategic withdrawal. With claims on the TVA's facilities thus relieved, the albatross of the Dixon-Yates contract could be cast away. In his personal diary notes for July 14, 1955, the President appraised the outcome: "Philosophically this is a great victory for the Administration because it signifies acceptance on the part of the inhabitants of that region that the Federal Government will not be responsible for the construction of power plants that will be needed in that area in the future."[159]

Over the longer term it remained the administration's view that further growth in demand for power in the TVA's service area should be met without additional federal financing. Henceforth new capacity should be funded from the retained earnings of the system or through the issue of revenue bonds placed in the private capital market. The administration made clear its desire for legislation authorizing this procedure in proposals submitted to Congress in 1955, but action was delayed. Two points had proved to be particularly troublesome. The administration had insisted that legislation authorizing revenue bond financing should specifically restrict the TVA's service area to the territory in which it already had established operations: no encroachments on the private domain should be tolerated. Second, it was regarded as a matter of constitutional principle that TVA revenue bond issues be subject to prior presidential approval. The rationale for this position was that a coordinated fiscal policy demanded that the executive branch have control over

158. On November 11, 1954, the Atomic Energy Commission contracted with the Mississippi Valley Generating Company, an organization sponsored by the Middle South Utilities Company (of which Edgar H. Dixon was president), and the Southern Company (of which E. A. Yates was board chairman) to construct a 650,000-kilowatt steam power plant at West Memphis, Arkansas, across the Mississippi River from Memphis, Tennessee. The propriety of this contract was challenged by Democratic members of Congress and the matter became a lively partisan issue. It emerged that Adolphe H. Wenzell of the First Boston Corporation, who had served as an adviser to the Bureau of the Budget on cost factors involved in the AEC's use of private power, was also advising the Dixon-Yates group on their financing problems as a representative of the First Boston Corporation. Some of the administration's internal anguish over this situation is reflected in a memorandum from Rowland Hughes, Director of the Bureau of the Budget, to the President, n.d., Whitman Files, ibid., Box 12.

159. President's Diary Entry, July 14, 1955, Whitman Files, Eisenhower Diary Series, Box 6, DDEL.

the approaches of public corporations to the private capital market. This view implied, however, that the TVA—though expected to behave more like a private utility—would lack some of the freedoms that private businesses would take for granted. Legislation in 1959 ultimately satisfied the President on both these points.

Though the Eisenhower years were not distinguished for new federal initiatives in the development of electric power, the administration did continue to fund projects that had been planned and authorized by its predecessors, and it could claim general satisfaction with the results of its stewardship. The Pacific Northwest, for example, had been regarded in the early 1950s as a region of impending power deficit. By late 1960, however, the Department of the Interior could appraise its situation as follows:

In seven years, the Federal Government's Columbia River power system grew from two multi purpose dams, with an installed capacity of 2,630,000 kilowatts, to 17 multi purpose projects completed or under construction, with an ultimate installed capacity of 8,077,000 kilowatts. Non-Federal hydro-electric power projects in the Pacific Northwest, representing an installed capacity of 2,012,130 kilowatts in 1953, today have projects completed or under construction representing an installed capacity of 7,506,310 kilowatts. Today, the Pacific Northwest region has 161 hydroelectric plants with nearly 10,600,000 kilowatts of installed capacity—two-thirds of them completed or placed under construction under this Administration.[160]

For the nation as a whole the achievement of these years was also impressive. Between January 1, 1953, and December 31, 1960, the installed capacity of the electrical utility system in the contiguous forty-eight states more than doubled (from 82,226 megawatts to just over 168,000 megawatts). The federal government's component of this capacity—despite the administration's position on initiating major projects—expanded at an even faster rate (from 9,678 megawatts to 22,350 megawatts).[161]

The Case of Nuclear Power

During the Eisenhower years debates over the place of nuclear energy in the nation's energy complex were dominated by doctrinal controversies over the proper mix of public and private activities. The administration attached no particular urgency to the development of nuclear

160. "Accomplishments of the Department of the Interior, 1953–1960," ibid., Administration Series, Box 36.
161. U.S. Bureau of the Census, *Statistical Abstract of the United States, 1954* (GPO, 1954), p. 543; and ibid., *1964* (GPO, 1964), p. 531.

sources to meet prospective growth in domestic demand. Rival primary sources of energy, even if the terms of their availability were to deteriorate, were still held likely to be more attractive for a considerable time ahead. In much of the rest of the world the situation was expected to be different. Countries less well-endowed with conventional energy sources were thought to be more promising for the civilian application of this novel technology. With the Atoms for Peace address in December 1953 the U.S. government had indicated its intention to support such innovation in friendly countries and to maintain a position of leadership in peaceful uses of nuclear power for that purpose.

The Atomic Energy Act of 1954 embodied the administration's basic doctrine on the proper place of government in the nuclear power business. The Atomic Energy Commission was thereby authorized to distribute fissionable materials on license to private utilities and to make prototype designs of reactors available to private manufacturers. The impact of this move for the nation's energy supplies was uncertain, however. It was recognized that much would depend on the technical results of the AEC's five-year reactor development program (launched early in 1954) and on the response of private investors to this new opportunity. On these points official opinion was divided. An estimate circulating in the CEA suggested that nuclear generating costs could be competitive with conventional fuels within the next two decades in the higher-cost fuel areas of the nation and that from 2 to 10 percent of the nation's electricity might be supplied by nuclear sources by 1975.[162] The director of the Budget Bureau was more skeptical. When amendments to the atomic energy legislation had been discussed in 1953, Dodge had offered the opinion that "there is reason to doubt that industry can afford at this time, without some form of Government subsidy, to invest the funds required to develop atomic power and to build the first few full scale reactors (at $50 million–$150 million each)."[163] Similarly there were

---

162. Irving H. Siegel to the Council, October 7, 1954, CEA Files, Box 17, DDEL.

163. Dodge to Shanley, "The Atomic Energy Act of 1946," April 21, 1953, OF, Box 523, DDEL. Dodge further noted that "in opening up the Act to amendment at this time there is a risk of unacceptable amendments—e.g., a long-term Government commitment to purchase plutonium at a fixed price." This concern reflected the type of reactor development then under consideration that called for "dual purpose" units producing both power and plutonium. For security reasons the government wished to maintain close control over plutonium. Its right to be the preemptive buyer of this by-product was unchallenged: the issue outstanding was the price at which these transactions would be accomplished and whether or not a substantial subsidy would be concealed within it.

doubts about the willingness of electrical equipment manufacturers to venture into the production of reactors, particularly to serve the international market. Before the new approach to atomic development was a year old, special presidential assistant Nelson Rockefeller insisted that such bearishness was ill-informed. He reported to the President that his contacts with industrialists were encouraging. Contrary to reports that had been circulated that "power reactors for overseas use were five to eight years off, and that we were building up false hopes around the world by our statements," it appeared that one firm at least was prepared to begin deliveries of smaller reactors within two years and estimated that it would be able to build seven 10,000-kilowatt power reactors for a price "possibly as low as $4 million apiece" for delivery within three years.[164] The government's willingness to stimulate development both at home and abroad was further signaled by the President's announcement on February 22, 1956, that the United States stood ready to make available for sale or for lease some 20,000 kilograms of uranium 235 for use in power and research reactors abroad as well as 20,000 kilograms, principally for power reactors, for licensed civilian programs in the United States.[165] Though the federal government was not prepared to enter the civilian nuclear power business itself, it was in earnest about providing technical reinforcement to those who did.

The basic administration position concerning the appropriate mix between public and private activities in the development of civilian nuclear power, however, was not shared by the Joint Committee on Atomic Energy. Much of its membership was persuaded that a more aggressive development program should be undertaken and that the government's direct financial commitment to it should be enlarged. This view was embodied in identical bills in the House and Senate sponsored by Senator Albert Gore and Congressman Chet Holifield that were debated in Congress in 1956. According to the bills' provisions the AEC would not only be directed to accelerate the development of promising new reactor designs (a step held to be essential if a position of international leadership was to be maintained), but also to construct large-scale prototype reactors for power production on its own account. This position was clearly

164. Rockefeller to the President, May 16, 1955, OF, Box 524, DDEL.

165. "Statement by the President Announcing Determination to Make Uranium 235 Available for Peaceful Uses, February, 1956," *Public Papers: Eisenhower, 1956* (GPO, 1958), pp. 258–59. According to the AEC's calculations the value of the 40,000 kilograms of uranium 235 was approximately $1 billion. See Lewis L. Strauss, *Men and Decisions* (Doubleday, 1962), p. 362.

at odds with the official executive branch view that "AEC's power program should emphasize research and development, while the construction of prototype power plants to demonstrate economic feasibility should
be undertaken by private industry, perhaps with some Federal aid."
Moreover, the goal of policy should be "economic nuclear power and not
an immediate 'kilowatt race' with other nations."[166]

From the administration's perspective there appeared to be adequate
ground in 1956 for general satisfaction with the initial results of the
AEC's strategy. In the public presentation of the commission's case, Admiral Lewis L. Strauss, chairman of the AEC, served as its point man.
The response to government's invitation to private industry, he insisted,
had been gratifying. Within the span of two years, the AEC's Reactor
Demonstration Program (which provided some federal assistance to the
start-up costs of private firms) had produced ten proposals for nuclear
power plants with an aggregate capacity of 400,000 kilowatts. At least
seven more plants, to be financed entirely by the private sector, were
being planned. "Such is the faith of these companies in the inevitability
of atomic power," he asserted, "that they are prepared to invest in the
neighborhood of $250 million or $300 million in those seven plants with
a total capacity of 900 thousand to a million kilowatts of atomic power."
The "goal for progress," however, was not one of "building an arbitrary
number of plants, or a fixed figure of installed kilowatts of generating
capacity." The objective instead was to "develop the *technology* of nuclear power reactors of various types and sizes, to the point where they
will be economic in competition with kilowatts produced from conventional fuels." A comprehensive construction program involving a variety
of new designs was important if the technical and economic knowledge
required for an economically viable nuclear power sector was to be
gained. Strauss was determined that private industry should be given "the
first opportunity" to undertake the construction of the new generation of
reactors. But he added a qualification: "If acceptable proposals were not
forthcoming on all the specified types within a reasonable period of time,
the Commission would take prompt and positive steps to build those reactors on its own initiative."[167]

The mood of satisfaction with nuclear power progress, however, was

166. Budget Director Percival V. Brundage to Gerald Morgan, July 6, 1956,
Harlow Papers, Box 7, DDEL.

167. Quotations in this paragraph are from Lewis Strauss, speech delivered to the
American Nuclear Society, December 11, 1956, pp. 6, 8, 10–11, Morgan Papers, Box
2, DDEL.

not universal in the AEC itself. The most outspoken in-house dissenter was Thomas E. Murray, who had been appointed to the AEC by President Truman. In an appearance before the Joint Committee on Atomic Energy on February 19, 1957, Murray expressed his conviction that "our present policies and programs for the development of industrial atomic power" are "not adequate."[168] Murray insisted that

private industry is not prepared to provide more than a portion of the financial support to the power reactor development program which the national interest requires. We are constantly being told that private industry is ready and willing to assume responsibility for building large power reactors without direct government support. However, these assurances carry no guarantee as to when such projects will be completed. The experience of the past year gives evidence of this. The schedules given you last year have proved to be over optimistic.[169]

It was clear to Murray that "industry can hardly be expected to support an effort beyond that required to meet its own needs on its own time schedule. Industry's time schedule is set primarily by this country's needs for electric energy. But the time schedule required by the national interest is much shorter. It is set by the crisis in nuclear weapons and the world need for nuclear power." Moreover, he noted that estimates of construction costs of the reactor portion of the premier plant (at Shippingport, Pennsylvania) had overrun the estimates by about 50 percent. Similar cost overruns were also observable in other projects currently under way. It was thus to be expected that industry would become increasingly cautious about future commitments. Despite their fears of excessive public intervention, private utilities could soon be expected to welcome increased federal participation. Failure to act without delay would mean, he maintained, that "industrial atomic power will not be developed soon enough to enable us to meet our responsibilities as a nation." Europe would soon face a serious power shortage that could be averted if the United States could provide the reactor equipment needed there. It now appeared unlikely that this would be possible.[170]

Against this background Murray recommended that the federal government finance construction of reactor types that "we presently feel confident can be made to operate successfully as large-scale projects." Once

168. *Development, Growth, and State of the Atomic Energy Industry,* Hearings before the Joint Committee on Atomic Energy, 85 Cong. 1 sess. (GPO, 1957), pt. 1, p. 56.
169. Ibid., p. 57.
170. Ibid., pp. 57, 59.

the feasibility of these reactors had been established, it was his hope that "the burden for meeting our Nation's responsibilities will be assumed by private industry."[171] In Murray's judgment, however, "our vision must surely penetrate beyond the restricted view that measures the national interest in terms of our own domestic energy needs."[172]

Despite divided counsel the AEC did not alter course. In the view of Chairman Strauss the general response of the private sector continued to be heartening. By the close of 1957 six atomic reactors designed for civilian power had been brought into operation across the United States, and five of them were delivering electricity.[173] Four additional commercial plants of large scale were under way and negotiations were proceeding for another twelve or thirteen units. In the aggregate these twenty-three reactors would offer a total capacity of about 1.3 million kilowatts. Special attention could be drawn to the fact that of the "23 plants in operation, under construction or for which plans are announced, eight are being financed entirely by private capital without any direct financial contribution from the American taxpayer, even though nuclear power is not yet competitive in the United States."[174] In February 1958 Strauss added that the Pacific Gas and Electric Company had decided to build a 60,000-kilowatt reactor in Eureka, California, without any government funding and that this facility would "approach competitive costs for power in the area in which the plant is to be located—8.1 mills per kilowatt hour for power produced by the nuclear reactor as against 8.0 mills for conventionally produced power."[175]

Even so, there were some clouds on the horizon. Strauss reported to the President on February 25, 1958: "Unfortunately, the decline in general business levels seems to have been a factor in persuading some of the manufacturers, even some of the large companies, to testify in favor of Government construction or subsidy to nuclear power plant construction. They do not seem to realize what the consequences of the adoption of such a policy would mean. It is making it a little harder to hold the line."[176] In these circumstances it appeared to be prudent for the administration

171. Ibid., p. 60.
172. Ibid., p. 62. It should be noted that Murray did not share this statement with his AEC colleagues before its presentation.
173. Statement of Lewis L. Strauss for release on January 8, 1958, Central Files, Box 253, DDEL.
174. Ibid., p. 4.
175. Strauss to Adams, February 25, 1958, OF, Box 525, DDEL.
176. Strauss to the President, February 25, 1958, Whitman Files, Administration Series, Box 5, DDEL.

to prepare some contingency plans. If a shortfall in private activity occurred, the government should be in a position to act as the spender of last resort. This matter was debated in the context of the AEC's request for a supplemental appropriation in the 1959 budget. Within the executive branch it was determined that a sum of $60 million should be reserved for the construction of a gas-cooled reactor by the commission. This procedure won the President's approval, subject to an understanding "that the funds would *not* be used unless intensive efforts to get the job done by private industry met with failure. The $60 million in question would be held in reserve by the Bureau of the Budget during the period of negotiation with private industry."[177]

But there was a hint that all was not well in Strauss's final report to the President at the completion of his term as AEC chairman. In June 1958 he wrote: "Serious problems remain to be solved before we have a self-sustaining nuclear power industry. It is not yet clear that a nuclear power plant can be built to generate electricity as economically as a conventional plant in the United States. In Europe, nuclear power can be competitive almost immediately. We hope, by building reactors for our friends in Europe who need them, to learn how to build and operate reactors that will be economical in the United States."[178] Acting AEC Chairman Willard Libby saw the linkage between nuclear power development at home and abroad somewhat differently. He urged the President to take steps to promote further international cooperation, particularly with Britain, in the civilian power field. Though an agreement with the United Kingdom had already been concluded, it was Libby's judgment that its coverage should be extended because "the British most likely have knowledge and techniques in the generation of atomic power that they do not transmit to us and which we may not now have and probably need."[179] Libby reminded the President of the AEC's plan to construct a gas-cooled reactor of advanced design

in the event that private industry does not accept the challenge to build one in a reasonable time. Our planned expenditures might be quite different if we could obtain the British information, for it is just this family of atomic power reactors in which they specialize and in which they are most expert. We think our types of atomic power reactors are better than theirs, but we are not certain, and we feel we must fill this gap in our knowledge. In view of the fact

177. Wilton B. Persons, Memorandum for the Record, May 5, 1958, ibid.
178. Strauss to the President, June 30, 1958, Central Files, Box 253, DDEL.
179. Libby to the President, July 9, 1958, Whitman Files, Administration Series, Box 5, DDEL.

that we are exchanging information on nearly every other aspect of atomic energy, it seems a shame that we have to spend the money which might be saved or more wisely spent by full exchange.[180]

Congressional deliberation of the AEC's budget for fiscal year 1959 again put the White House and the Joint Committee on Atomic Energy at loggerheads. In this round the AEC itself was more sympathetic to an expanded role for government than had earlier been the case.[181] The AEC authorization bill specifically provided for the construction of a plutonium reactor at the expected cost of $145 million. It also provided $51 million for the controversial gas-cooled power reactor. The terms of both these arrangements were at odds with the President's program. The plutonium production reactor was held to be undesirable on the grounds that its "dual purpose" character—producing both plutonium and power—was unwise. Department of Defense requirements for plutonium were thought to be already well cared for, and a design that would make this reactor convertible to the generation of electric power exclusively was held to be needlessly expensive. Similarly the terms of the authorization for the gas-cooled reactor, which the administration wished to regard as a last-resort precaution, contained conditions thought likely to discourage proposals from private industry. Though the President approved the AEC authorization bill on August 4, 1958, he still questioned its merit. He suggested to Congress that appropriations for these projects be withheld and urged greater vigilance "against the ever present tendency to burden the government with programs, . . . the relative urgency and essentiality of which have not been solidly determined." He reaffirmed his willingness, however, to request appropriations for construction of the gas-cooled reactor "should it develop that a satisfactory industrial proposal will not be forthcoming in a reasonable time."[182]

180. Ibid.

181. Commenting on the AEC requests for supplementary obligational authority, Budget Director Maurice Stans observed: "The proposed acceleration of atomic power and development is defended by AEC as necessary both to achieve competitive nuclear power in the United States long before economic need for it exists and to fortify the U.S. position of world leadership. AEC appears to be acceding to new pressures for atomic power acceleration from the Joint Committee on Atomic Energy, which is intruding itself deeper and deeper into the detailed administration of the Atomic Energy Program." Stans to the President, n.d., Whitman Files, ibid., Box 37.

182. "Statement by the President upon Signing Bill Authorizing Appropriations for the Atomic Energy Commission, August 4, 1958," *Public Papers: Eisenhower, 1958* (GPO, 1959), p. 583.

The AEC took a deeper look at the longer-term objectives of its civilian power program in 1959. The AEC's Ad Hoc Advisory Committee on Reactor Policies and Programs directed attention to the basic policy issue: "Since the development of nuclear power is in fact proving to be difficult and expensive, the Government has been faced with a hard choice. Either this country continues its leadership at the cost of heavy expenditure or it accepts the probability that there will be no significant nuclear power industry in this country until the technology has been developed elsewhere and can be reintroduced here."[183] In the climate of the post-sputnik era, this challenge could not be lightly dismissed. The Ad Hoc Advisory Committee recommended that the primary objective of policy should be to fortify the American position of leadership in civilian nuclear power technology. The emphasis assigned to the importance of widespread private participation in earlier statements of goals was absent from this document.

The AEC absorbed much of this message, though in its formulation of objectives, announced in February 1959, the maintenance of American leadership in reactor technology dropped from first to fourth in the ordering of priorities. Precedence was instead assigned to reducing the cost of nuclear power to "levels competitive with power from fossil fuels in the high energy cost areas of this country within 10 years" and to assisting "friendly nations now having high energy costs to achieve competitive levels in about 5 years."[184] For the first time, performance targets with specific time schedules were thus set out. It should be noted, however, that the commission's definition of competitive nuclear fuel would be satisfied "when utility executives can decide to build nuclear power stations based on economic considerations."[185] The actual generation of nuclear power might thus lag the achievement of costs competitive with conventional fuels by four to five years.

At the close of the Eisenhower administration, AEC Chairman John A. McCone summarized the achievements of the past eight years: "Ten nuclear power plants have come into full operation and 22 have been au-

183. "Civilian Nuclear Power," Report by Ad Hoc Advisory Committee on Reactor Policies and Programs, Washington, January 2, 1959, in *Development, Growth, and State of the Atomic Energy Industry,* Hearings, app. 2, p. 513.
184. Statement of John A. McCone, Chairman, Atomic Energy Commission, in *Development, Growth and State of the Atomic Energy Industry,* Hearings, p. 39.
185. On this point see Philip Mullenbach, *Civilian Nuclear Power: Economic Issues and Policy Formation* (Twentieth Century Fund, 1963), p. 309, note.

thorized for construction either by Government or by industry." It was expected that 1.1 million kilowatts of electricity would be on the line by the end of 1963. The goal of achieving economic nuclear power by 1968 in regions of the country with high fuel costs was reaffirmed. It was further noted that "in certain specific parts of the country, such as in Southern California, it is now possible to design plants which when constructed and placed on line will produce electric power at costs competitive over their lifetime with conventional fuels in that area."[186]

Despite these achievements, tensions remained. The conflict between private and public power interests—highlighted by the diverging views of the administration and the majority of the Joint Committee on Atomic Energy—had not been resolved. At the same time, a disjunction between the domestic and the international objectives of the administration's program had become increasingly apparent. It was far from clear, for example, that reliance on private industry would be sufficient to achieve a desirable rate of development. Nevertheless, the view persisted that nuclear energy was far more important to less well-endowed parts of the world than to the United States. Nuclear energy was essentially a standby resource for the American economy, but one that could be perfected through experience gained abroad.

Policies toward Synthetic Fuels

During the Truman years a variety of experiments with the development of synthetic fuels had been assigned a high priority. In February 1953 Louis C. McCabe, chief of the Fuels and Explosives Division of the Bureau of Mines, could report that this work had produced "general technical agreement that liquid fuels may be produced from oil shale in large-volume operations at costs approximating those from crude petroleum," but that opinion differed on the costs associated with the production of liquid fuels through the hydrogenation of coal and that the economic status of the gas synthesis process was as yet "undetermined." He concluded that "our long-range economic needs and national security may make it desirable to accelerate our progress toward commercial production of synthetic liquid fuels." McCabe recommended that appropriations for these investigations be sustained, adding that further funding might

186. McCone to the President, January 3, 1961, Whitman Files, Administration Series, Box 5, DDEL.

"be necessary in order to facilitate the construction by private industry of prototype plants."[187]

The Eisenhower administration made a different reading of these matters. Following midsummer conferences with representatives of the oil industry, the Department of the Interior took the position in October 1953 that the operation of large-scale pilot plants for synthetic liquid fuels should be discontinued "as soon as possible" and that the government's activities should be limited "to research and developmental projects which private industry cannot be expected to undertake within the foreseeable future."[188] This approach was of a piece with the administration's general thinking on the appropriate role of government in the economy. Accordingly laboratory research was to be continued on the conversion of coal to oil, oil shale, and coal gasification, but the demonstration plants for shale oil refining (at Rifle, Colorado) and for liquid fuel production from coal (at Louisiana, Missouri) were to be closed. The plant at Rifle, Colorado, however, was to be maintained in a standby condition.[189] Meanwhile the word was passed to senior executives in the oil industry that "the Department of the Interior would like very much to see industry undertake the needed development work that would lead to the utilization of our oil shale resources." Large-scale development work was held to be "primarily the responsibility of industry, both in a financial and working sense, as it would definitely fall within the competitive realm of commerce."[190]

During the mid-1950s further experimental work on oil shale was conducted by the Union Oil Company of California at an operation near the

187. Statement of Louis C. McCabe, prepared for presentation before the House Committee on Interstate and Foreign Commerce, February 17, 1953, File 11-34, Bureau of Mines, Minerals–Synthetic Fuels, pt. 9, NA. Presentation of this statement was approved by Secretary of the Interior McKay, though it contained the qualification that the secretary had "expressed the need to familiarize himself more intensively with its details before he can express his views on these measures."

188. F. E. Wormser, Assistant Secretary of the Interior, to the Director of the Bureau of Mines, "Departmental Policy with Respect to Synthetic Liquid Fuels Programs," October 2, 1953, File 11-34, ibid., pt. 11.

189. This disposition was endorsed by an Interior Department study group in 1954 and supported by the National Petroleum Council's Committee on Shale Oil Policy in its report to Secretary McKay on January 25, 1955. See "Resource Progress: 1953–56, Responsibilities of the Interior Department," n.d., Seaton Papers, Ewald Research Files, Box 1, DDEL.

190. F. E. Wormser to A. C. Rubel, Vice-President, Union Oil Company of California, November 10, 1953, File 11-34, Bureau of Mines, Minerals–Synthetic Fuels, pt. 11, NA.

Interior Department's facility at Rifle, Colorado. Though the technical feasibility of converting oil shale into petroleum derivatives was established, the commercial competitiveness of the product remained moot. Secretary of the Interior Fred A. Seaton reported to the President on February 26, 1960, that "the Union Oil people have informed the Bureau of Mines that Union ran the plant for sufficient time to find out what they wanted to know about their process. They are now analyzing and making economic studies based on their data developed during the running period."[191] It was understood in the Department of the Interior that preliminary results of these investigations indicated that "the new process is unable to compete with imported oil." Reports reaching the department were silent, however, on the competitive position of shale-derived synthetics in relation to domestic oils. Secretary Seaton's analysis of this matter suggested that the decision of the Union Oil Company to terminate further research had been influenced by quite different market factors. He advised the President that it "might be significant in this connection . . . that the Gulf Oil Company has recently acquired a substantial interest in Union Oil. Gulf has an extremely strong petroleum reserve position in the Middle East, particularly in Kuwait. This fact may have led to reduced interest on the part of Union in the Colorado shales."[192]

A further consideration was also held to be pertinent to the assessment of the prospects for oil shales. The Department of the Interior estimated in 1960 that an investment on the order of $8 billion would be required to establish this industry on a viable footing. Such a commitment of capital was not likely to be forthcoming without modification in the tax code. Oil shale was eligible for a depletion allowance at the same rate as coal, 15 percent. By contrast, percentage depletion was allowed at the rate of 27.5 percent for oil and natural gas. The secretary of the interior had recommended in 1958 that the depletion rate for oil shale be increased to 27.5 percent and that it be calculated on the basis of the value of the processed product rather than on the value of crushed shale ready for shipment.[193] This recommendation had been vigorously opposed by the Department of the Treasury and no action was taken on it.

191. Seaton to the President, February 26, 1960, Whitman Files, Administration Series, Box 36, DDEL.

192. Ibid.

193. Office of the Secretary of the Interior, press release, April 16, 1958, Whitman Files, Administration Series, Box 36, DDEL. A similar recommendation was made on the tax treatment of coal used to produce synthetic fuels.

Interest in oil shale did not lapse completely. In August 1960 the AEC conducted experiments to determine the feasibility of breaking oil shale with nuclear explosives at the mine at Rifle, Colorado. The primary objective of this test undertaken with conventional explosives was to establish the extent to which radioactive gases might migrate through the shale. The AEC initiated this exercise, not the Bureau of Mines. No further experiments with oil shale were scheduled.[194]

A Closing Word

The invitation to a great debate on the shaping of a "comprehensive" energy policy issued by the Paley Commission in 1952 largely went unheeded during the Eisenhower years. From the internal perspective of the administration there appeared to be no compelling urgency to mount a debate. The immediate reality seemed to be dominated more by concern for sustaining the market position of domestic producers of the key primary fuels than with preparing for a world in which the terms of their availability might become less attractive.

Though energy matters in the large did not figure prominently in the thinking of policymakers, the administration did not lack for policies toward individual energy industries. At the doctrinal level its basic commitment held that the invisible hand should be the primary adjudicator of the terms of competition in the energy sector and the major determinant of the rates at which capacity should be extended and new technologies introduced. The application of this doctrine, however, lacked something in consistency. The most conspicuous break with principle occurred in the treatment of oil. In this instance the signals of the price system were redirected by administrative intervention. The approach adopted toward other components of the other energy sector was generally more compatible with the premises of the official doctrine. With respect to the pricing of natural gas, however, a gap between the administration's desires and the regulatory reality remained unclosed. There were growing signs also of a possible incompatibility between the domestic and the international presuppositions of the administration's approach to nuclear energy.

194. Memorandum, October 20, 1960, Briefing Book, Current Issues, Bennett Papers, Box 1, DDEL.

These piecemeal policies, in turn, left their legacy. The American position on oil imports gave momentum to forces elsewhere to reshape the international petroleum market. At home, mandatory controls added to the tensions between rival producer groups and between producers and consumers. Moreover, this intervention, though reluctant, committed the nation to a "drain America first" strategy. These were to be among the problems inherited by the Eisenhower administration's successors.

CHAPTER FOUR

Studied Inaction in the Kennedy Years

WILLIAM J. BARBER

In 1960 the concerns of a decade earlier about the long-run adequacy of energy supplies for a growing American economy had largely vanished. The economy was operating well below its potential, and excess capacity in two of the nation's primary fuel sectors, coal and oil, presented awkward problems. In this environment it was understandable that little urgency was attached to the formulation of a comprehensive energy policy for the longer term. The immediate fact of life was deficiency in demand rather than in supply.

Even so, the political process could not afford to be indifferent to the state of the energy economy. Candidate John F. Kennedy had recognized this in positions taken before regional constituencies. In Maine, for example, he had urged the development of the Passamaquoddy power project (involving the harnessing of the tides) as the antidote to the state's economic decline. This bold undertaking, he had insisted, was essential to the industrial renewal of northern New England.[1] Before audiences in the Southwest he had called for the reversal of the Republican administration's "no new starts" policy toward multipurpose river developments, asserting that "with the exception of one project—the Colorado River Storage Project—the product of the imagination and planning of Oscar Chapman [secretary of the interior under Truman]—there has not been one single multi-purpose, basin-wide project by the United States government in the past eight years."[2] To audiences in

The bulk of the primary material used in this chapter was drawn from collections in the John F. Kennedy Library, Waltham, Massachusetts. The author very much appreciated the assistance of the library's staff, particularly that of E. William Johnson. In the footnotes to this chapter the library is referred to as JFKL.

1. Address of Senator John F. Kennedy at the Maine Democratic Party's Issues Conference Banquet, Augusta, Maine, November 15, 1959, Pre-Presidential Papers, Box 1031, JFKL.

2. Remarks of Senator John F. Kennedy to the Western Conference at Albuquerque, New Mexico, February 7, 1960, ibid.

North Dakota he had castigated the Eisenhower administration for lagging in pursuit of the great national objective of bringing low-cost electricity to farmers through the Rural Electrification Administration. He maintained that "REA rates must remain low—more generating capacity must be developed—the vast resources of nuclear energy must be tapped —your high-grade lignite mines must be utilized—and the guiding spirit of [Senator] George Norris must prevail."[3] In Montana he called for the creation of a Council of Resources and Conservation Advisers within the Executive Office of the President to conduct "long-range, continuing, and comprehensive surveys" and among other things, to plan "how we might link the power systems of the Columbia and Missouri Rivers"; he further pledged to "restore America's leadership in atomic development and [to] protect the public's tremendous investment in this source of energy which must be tapped for the public good."[4] In West Virginia he pointed toward a new future for the coal-mining regions with the development of "coal by wire." In this vision:

Great steam plants, located near the coal reserves which will drive them, can profitably use ton after ton of coal every day of the week in manufacturing electricity to serve the ever-increasing needs of the four great metropolitan areas which lie within a 500 mile radius of central West Virginia—Chicago, Detroit, Philadelphia and New York—four of the five largest metropolitan areas in the United States. If, with Federal help, West Virginia can make the most of her strategic location and your abundant coal reserves, the future of coal and the future of West Virginia can both be bright.[5]

These remarks were in a venerable tradition of campaign oratory. They signaled that a Kennedy administration would be more favorably disposed than its predecessor had been toward an interventionist role for the federal government. But the remarks still reflected piecemeal approaches to local grievances. One set of campaign comments, however, suggested that a more general strategy toward energy was now in order. Speaking in West Virginia in April 1960, Kennedy asserted that "we must immediately establish a National Fuels Policy—a policy which will take the vast, intricate, and often contradictory network of laws and regulations which govern the nation's fuel industry and weld them into

3. Remarks of Senator John F. Kennedy to the Young Democrats Luncheon, Bismarck, North Dakota, February 6, 1960, ibid.
4. Remarks of Senator John F. Kennedy, Billings, Montana, September 22, 1960, Senate Files, Box 911, JFKL.
5. Remarks of Senator John F. Kennedy, Morgantown, West Virginia, April 18, 1960, Pre-Presidential Papers, Box 1031, JFKL.

a sound and logical whole."[6] Some of this language was reminiscent of the Paley Commission's appeal for a comprehensive energy policy, but in West Virginia in 1960 audiences understood these words as having a more specific meaning. The call for a national fuels policy was heard as an assurance of expanded market space for coal and of the relief of poverty in Appalachia.

Energy and the 1961 Policy Agenda

Candidate Kennedy's characterization of government intervention in the fuels economy as "intricate and often contradictory" was on target. Like Topsy, it had "just growed" over the preceding decades. But what priority should be assigned to developing a coordinated approach toward energy? Within the ranks of the new administration few were prepared to take up the challenge to weld policy into "a sound and logical whole."

One of the exceptions was James M. Landis, adviser to the President-elect on the regulatory agencies, who subsequently joined the White House staff as a special assistant. In his view government was at fault for its failure to attend seriously to this matter. He noted that the prospective exhaustion of natural gas resources "within a foreseeable period," though worrisome, had been neglected. Nor had systematic study been given to the development of alternative sources of energy. Landis held that research into hydrogenation of coal and oil-bearing rock should be stimulated. In this connection he observed that in "the opinion of many" an "all-out national effort similar to that which harnessed atomic energy" should be mounted. But, he reported, "inter-agency mechanisms for planning or even suggesting such projects are absent."[7]

In this reading of matters reorganization of the governmental structure was also called for to ensure wise utilization of existing energy sources. "Government," Landis observed, "actually controls to a considerable extent the degree to which these fuels are competitive and the exercise of these controls can affect to a great degree the rate of consumption of our resources."[8] Yet no proper coordination of govern-

6. Remarks of Senator John F. Kennedy, Logan, West Virginia, April 25, 1960, ibid.

7. James M. Landis, "Report on Regulatory Agencies to the President-elect," December 1960, p. 29, ibid., Box 1072.

8. Ibid.

mental activities occurred. Authority was unhappily fragmented. Landis surveyed the scene as follows:

Surface transportation of oil, coal, and liquified gas lies within the purview of the Interstate Commerce Commission and the Federal Maritime Board, and surface transportation of fuels is of enormous consequence in view of the importance of transportation costs in the pricing of the product. Natural gas is a concern of the Federal Power Commission. Electric power in its various forms falls within the purview of the Federal Power Commission, the Department of the Interior, the Corps of Army Engineers, the Tennessee Valley Authority and similar entities. The derivation of energy from fissionable materials is the business of the Atomic Energy Commission. General concern over the conservation of resources from which energy is developed rests primarily with the Department of the Interior, whereas the State Department and the Tariff Commission are factors in dealing with the extent to which our foreign investment is concerned with the production of fuel abroad as well as the extent to which these fuels should enter the domestic market.[9]

The system cried out for rational ordering.

This was decidedly a minority view. The bulk of those appointed to senior posts in the new administration believed that energy issues per se did not merit a high position on the policy agenda. From their perspective the central task was to improve the aggregative performance of the U.S. economy. The overriding priorities were the restoration of full employment and the strengthening of the balance of payments. Opinions within the administration differed about which steps would be most appropriate for reaching these goals—and indeed on whether these objectives could be readily reconciled. Nevertheless, a macroeconomic orientation dominated the approach of those charged with shaping the administration's basic economic strategy. Within that framework the distresses of excess capacity and unemployment in the energy sector were held to be best relieved by deploying monetary and fiscal policies to stimulate aggregate demand. As for longer-term worries about supply constraints, technological progress could be expected to take care of them. On this matter official thinking was dominated by a sense of high confidence that the nation stood on the brink of scientific achievements that would banish for all time any worries about resource limitations affecting the availability of energy. Indeed, scientific advisers counseled the incoming secretary of the interior that his major problem in the energy field was to prepare for an era in which nuclear power would be so ridiculously cheap that it would be inefficient to meter its consumption.

9. Ibid., p. 28.

Despite its predisposition in favor of macroeconomic strategies the Kennedy administration could not isolate itself from some of the parochial concerns of particular energy producers. The New Frontier had projected a vision of new dynamism in the domestic economy and of a reassertion of American leadership in international affairs. But the translation of the grand vision into reality confronted political constraints. Kennedy had come into office by the narrowest of electoral margins. Even though Congress was nominally controlled by the President's party, its receptivity to innovative policies was less than complete. Both public and congressional attitudes were crucially shaped by the importance of "fiscal integrity." Kennedy had recognized this fact in his pre-inaugural commitment to the congressional leadership to submit a balanced budget for the fiscal year beginning in July 1961 (a commitment his appointees to the Council of Economic Advisers learned about after the fact). Similarly those proposing initiatives in international economic policy were obliged to reckon with the strength of protectionist sentiments. In light of these realities the attitude of government toward the domestic energy industries had an added significance. To those at the center of economic policymaking, energy issues on their merits did not matter that much. But they could not be totally ignored. Legislative approval of the programs the administration cared most about was likely to require the support of senators and congressmen who had a stake in the prosperity of energy producers in their constituencies.

The National Fuels and Energy Study

On assuming office new administrations face two types of problems: those inherited from their predecessors and those they themselves have created in the contest for power. Kennedy's pledge to support a national fuels policy was of the latter type. This line had played well in the West Virginia primary and had subsequently been incorporated into the Democratic Party's national platform. From the later vantage point of the White House this issue looked different. It was not clear that there was a compelling need for such a policy. But it was apparent that the attempt to devise one would touch some politically sensitive nerves.

If Kennedy ever entertained the notion that the expression "national fuels policy" had a neutral connotation, he was disabused of it in early 1961. The American Petroleum Institute, for example, took exception to this project, noting that it was "subject to grave question" and was the "source of deep concern to many segments of the industrial community and the public." The coal industry was described as the "leading supporter" of this proposal and its motives were alleged to be less than disinterested. The coal industry's objective, it was maintained, was to steal a march on its competitors via the "imposition of Government-enforced end-use controls . . . despite overwhelming consumer preference for cheaper and more convenient oil and gas."[10]

Though there could be no going back on a campaign pledge, the White House was not eager to press this matter. But any lack of enthusiasm in the executive branch was more than compensated for by Congress. Both houses sought to sponsor inquiries into national fuels policy. (A joint congressional study, however, had been disapproved by Speaker Sam Rayburn.) The Senate got to the starting line first with the passage of a resolution brought forward by Jennings Randolph of West Virginia—which was cosponsored by sixty-two other senators—supporting the creation of a special Senate Committee on a National Fuels Study.

Despite this manfestation of interest, skepticism persisted about both the necessity and the likely objectivity of such an inquiry. Those doubtful on the latter point were not reassured by the arguments advanced by principal advocates of the fuels study in the hearings to consider it in June 1961. Senator Robert C. Byrd of West Virginia, for example, insisted that a "fuels policy" was essential to contain the "jungle warfare for markets" that resulted in the "reckless depletion" of the nation's most limited energy resources, oil and natural gas. A new approach was obviously called for to ensure their conservation and to promote the health of producers of "our most basic and most enduring natural fuel—coal." The coal industry's difficulties, he argued, were mainly attributable to "cutthroat competition in such wasteful market practices as the dumping of valuable natural gas for steam boiler use and in the excessive imports of residual oil from abroad, priced to sell along Atlantic coast ports at any figure necessary to undersell domestic coal."[11] The interpretation to be assigned to the objectives of a national fuels policy was further enriched by the testimony of George H. Love, chairman of the Board of Directors of the National Coal Policy Conference (as well as chairman of the board of the Consolidation Coal Company). He insisted that charges to the effect that the coal industry

10. Letter, Frank M. Porter, President of the American Petroleum Institute to President-elect Kennedy, January 17, 1961, reprinted in *National Fuels Study,* Hearings before the Senate Committee on Interior and Insular Affairs, 87 Cong. 1 sess. (Government Printing Office, 1961), p. 172.

11. Statement of Senator Robert C. Byrd, *National Fuels Study,* Hearings, p. 35.

was interested in developing governmental end-use controls over particular fuels were groundless. At the same time, he was persuaded that imports of residual fuel oil into New England were damaging to the domestic coal industry and that import restrictions on residual fuel oil should be tightened.[12]

But skepticism about the wisdom of pursuing a study at all was not lacking. Morgan J. Davis, president of the Humble Oil and Refining Company who testified on behalf of the American Petroleum Institute, the Mid-Continent Oil and Gas Association, and the Western Oil and Gas Association, put the case as follows: "Fundamentally, no basis exists at this time for concern about the soundness of relying on competition among fuels to serve the public interest, since it appears obvious that this policy has resulted in development of an abundance of energy at reasonable prices." He added: "No shortage of domestic fuels exists or is remotely in prospect, provided adequate incentives are maintained. . . . [T]here is no basis in the past record or present situation to require any new policy with respect to fuels and energy."[13]

The scope of any study that might be undertaken was a further point of contention and one to which the New England senatorial delegation was particularly alert. Senator John Pastore of Rhode Island spoke for his colleagues from that region when urging that the terms of reference of any study be drafted to emphasize the importance of consumers' interests. "No study of our national fuel policy and no recommendations which might flow therefrom could be complete or meaningful without adequate consideration of the effect of those recommendations upon the public at large. After all, the purpose of fuel production is not simply to create profits for

12. In this connection the following exchange was noteworthy:

"THE CHAIRMAN [Senator Clinton P. Anderson of New Mexico]. You say: 'We are strong in our belief that every consumer should have free choice in the fuel he desires to use.' If you believe in it, why don't you want the New England States to have free choice?

"MR. LOVE: They are having it. I repeat again that we believe there should be some limitation.

"THE CHAIRMAN: You either believe in free choice or you don't. You say you do. Do you?

"MR. LOVE: I believe this, sir, I believe there should be a sound coal industry in this country. Now, if that means that there should be some restriction of residual oil, if that means that, then let the consumer, New England or wherever he may be, have a choice of that much residual oil as opposed to coal, but not unlimited.

"THE CHAIRMAN: I think this helps to explain the resolution." (Testimony of George H. Love, ibid. p. 51.)

13. Statement of Morgan J. Davis, ibid., pp. 159–60.

fuel producers, or in fact to create jobs for a very limited number of workers in the fuel industries. The basic purpose is to supply fuel to meet the
needs of America's dynamic economy." Failure to keep the public interest
in the foreground could only result in "unwise and discriminatory policies."[14]

For its part the administration sought to adopt a controversy-minimiz-
ing posture. Secretary of the Interior Stewart L. Udall served as its
spokesman before the Senate committee and expressed his strong support
for a study that would be "thorough, intensive, and balanced." He further
held that the charge to a study group should be broadened: all energy
sources, not just the primary fuels, should be examined. Udall added that
"we should weigh carefully all the implications of the fact that we have
become on balance an energy-importing Nation. . . . [W]e should take action now to insure against an energy gap in the period ahead. A study of
fuels and energy by a Senate committee, and appropriate action based
upon its recommendations, would go far toward assuring all Americans
that they will never be faced with such a gap."[15]

The Senate inquiry was authorized to proceed as a study of fuels *and*
energy resources. But the atmosphere in which it was conceived suggested
that it might do more to heighten tensions between rival producer groups
and between producer and consumer interests than to yield a coordinated
strategy to guide the nation's long-range plans. Meanwhile, the administration was obliged to develop its position toward individual components
of the energy complex on a more immediate timetable.

Oil Policy Dilemmas in 1961

The oil policy the Kennedy administration inherited fell short of satisfying any of the contending interests. Despite the imposition of mandatory
controls, excess capacity in the domestic industry had continued to grow.
Meanwhile consumer interests, particularly in New England, were becoming increasingly vocal in their opposition to a scheme that redistributed
income to their disadvantage. Nor was it clear that the national security
justification for import restrictions was well grounded. Nearly two years
of mandatory restrictions had resulted in a further decline in new well
drillings in the United States.

14. Statement of Senator John Pastore of Rhode Island, ibid., p. 140.
15. Statement of Stewart L. Udall, ibid., p. 38.

The Kennedy administration brought a new cast of characters to the consideration of these issues. Even so, some continuities in departmental viewpoints remained—most particularly, the commitments of the Department of the Interior to the overriding importance to the national security of a prosperous domestic oil industry. But a striking modification occurred with a change of command at the Office of Civil and Defense Mobilization, redesignated the Office of Emergency Planning (OEP) in mid-1961. During the Eisenhower years the OCDM had been quick-triggered when invited to validate import restrictions on national security grounds. By contrast, Kennedy's OEP was uncomfortable with the findings of its predecessor and receptive to invitations to review them. In the intra-administration infighting on next steps in oil policy the central protagonists were to be the Interior Department and the OEP.

The bureaucratic skirmish lines formed initially over the place of residual fuel oils in the scheme of controls. The administration's first intervention in this matter occurred before it was a month old, when Secretary Udall announced that he had authorized an increase of more than 200,000 barrels a day in the quotas for residual fuel oil for the remainder of the first quarter of the year. This was presented as a response to emergency conditions created by unusually cold weather and thus was designed to maintain—but not to upset—the status quo in residual fuel inventories. Udall insisted that no decision had yet been reached on the larger issues of policy, but that it was his "present position" that direct controls were "necessary" unless he was "convinced otherwise."[16] This announcement touched off immediate reactions. Senator Byrd registered his "vigorous objection" with the White House, asserting that this relaxation in controls would "adversely affect the whole coal industry and related industries" and was incompatible with the President's "distressed area program and with national security requirements."[17] But voices favoring still greater freedom to import were also heard. The New England senatorial delegation petitioned Frank B. Ellis, director of the OCDM (and later of the OEP) to reappraise the national security rationale for the continuation of restrictions on residual fuel imports.

Soon afterward the OCDM became the OEP, which moved with dispatch in response to this request. As required by statute, the OEP invited submissions from interested parties and was prepared to report the results

16. Transcript of the Press Conference of Stewart L. Udall, February 17, 1961, Myer Feldman Papers, Box 23, JFKL.
17. Telegram, Byrd to the White House, February 17, 1961, ibid.

of its investigations to the President in mid-November 1961. Its conclusions, transmitted to the White House in draft form, were unambiguous: "the continued inclusion in the oil import control program of residual fuel oil, for use as a fuel, is not warranted on grounds of national security."[18] Accordingly decontrol was recommended. This judgment, the draft report noted, was reinforced by the opinion of the Department of Defense that "as residual fuel oil production continues to decline in continental U.S. refineries we feel that imports should make up the deficit, which will have to be done in national emergencies. . . . We cannot see wherein residual fuel oil imports can seriously endanger the national security."[19] Improvement in U.S. refinery techniques had indeed meant that consumption requirements could not be satisfied by domestic suppliers. By the first half of 1961 the residual yield of crude oil refined in Districts I–IV had fallen to 8.7 percent (from 16.5 percent a decade earlier), and there was no reason to expect this trend to be reversed.[20] The case for welcoming residual fuel imports, especially from Venezuela, was thus strengthened. State Department support for this position, which had been voiced during the Eisenhower administration, was now expressed even more vigorously. But there was a further justification for decontrol (in which the Department of Commerce concurred): the existing program had increased residual fuel oil prices to the hardship of consumers.

In presenting the case for decontrol the OEP report anticipated objections from the coal interests. But, it insisted, the distress of the coal industry was not "chargeable primarily to residual." The decline in the demand for coal could be accounted for largely by the dieselization of the railroads and by reduced coal consumption on the part of households, commercial establishments, and smaller industrial concerns. In none of these markets was residual fuel oil the prime competing fuel. Where coal and residual fuel oil were in the most direct competition—that is, in the electric utility market—coal had recorded its only major gain of the preceding decade.[21]

Meanwhile the Interior Department had prepared a quite different set of proposals for modification of existing import controls. In its view the decline in exploratory activity signaled the need for more stringent restric-

18. Frank B. Ellis to the President, November 14, 1961, p. 37, ibid.
19. Letter, Department of Defense to Office of Emergency Planning, as quoted in Ellis to the President, Draft Report as revised November 21, 1961, p. 17, ibid.
20. Ibid., p. 12.
21. Ibid., pp. 23–24.

tive measures. Its recommendations for amendments to Presidential Proclamation 3279, circulated within the executive branch on October 12, 1961, called for the reduction in "allowables" of crude oil and petroleum products (other than residual) in Districts I–IV by a further 50,000 barrels a day. This objective, it was maintained, could be achieved through several procedural changes. In the first place, the basis of calculation of quotas should be changed from a percentage of total demand in these distiricts to a percentage of domestic crude oil in refinery runs. The proposed formula also called for a change in import quota percentages, from 9 percent of demand to 10.25 percent of the refinery runs of domestic crude. This liberalization in import percentages, however, would be more than offset by the redefinition in the base. Under the proposed formula natural gas liquids (which had been counted as a component of total demand) would be excluded. This was by no means a trivial matter. The consumption of natural gas liquids had continued to rise and was currently running at the rate of 800,000 barrels a day. Consideration was also given to a further reduction in import allowables by changing the interpretation of the overland exemption. It was suggested that imports in this category might henceforth be deducted from the total allowable volume. The impact of such a change could also be expected to be substantial. Canadian shipments had increased from about 60,000 barrels a day to about 110,000 barrels a day since the overland exemption had been introduced. Meanwhile, imports via Mexico—which initially had been negligible—had run at the rate of 30,000 barrels a day since April 1961.[22]

In defense of its position, the Interior Department argued that the original national security rationale for mandatory controls should be extended. The case was now put, not solely in relation to the defensive capability of the western hemisphere in the event of war, but in terms of potential claims on the American industry to satisfy the free world's requirements for petroleum. It was regarded as "evident that one of the first strategic targets of conventional warfare will be the Middle East, which now supplies the bulk of Europe's liquid energy requirements, as well as large volumes of petroleum to Canada, Australia, the Far East, and the United States. Realistically, our planning must contemplate the probability that the free world will be denied a large portion of petroleum from this source." But the case was further enlarged with the argument that a relax-

22. The Interior Department's views, it may be noted, had much in common with the recommendations pressed by the department in the last year of the Eisenhower administration.

ation in restrictions would increase the strategic vulnerability of domestic refinery capacity. This conclusion was inferred from the fact that "those areas of the world newly participating in oil exploration can deliver oil at prices well below the mature industry in the United States." It was thus reasonable to assume that import volumes would be swollen considerably "were we to permit economics to take their course." The benefits of cheaper imports would not, however, be uniformly distributed geographically. Refiners with ready access to overseas supply would gain, but those situated in the hinterland would be unable to survive. The first casualties in the competitive struggle would be refineries in "the most dispersed locations." From the perspective of national security, it was argued, these refineries had a "strategic significance out of proportion to their capacity."[23]

While the Interior Department's main preoccupation was with the importation of crude oil, it also registered its opposition to the OEP's position on residual fuel oils. Part of its concern was that decontrol in any phase of the mandatory program, even in one acknowledged to be of marginal significance to the domestic oil industry, might not easily be contained and that pressures to scrap the entire control apparatus would be intensified. But it was also argued as a rejoinder to the State Department's position that decontrol of residual would eliminate a "significant safeguard" to Venezuela's interests. The historical basis for the assignment of allocations, it was maintained, was biased in Venezuela's favor. In a regime of open competition, it was likely to lose out to lower-cost producing areas (such as the Middle East).[24]

In the executive branch the cleavages on oil import policy ran deep. The circulation of the Interior Department's draft amendments to Proclamation 3279 did nothing to close them. The Budget Bureau, for example, was outspokenly hostile to the department's position: "The present proposals appear to have grown out of domestic industry pressures rather than defense considerations." The national security rationale presupposed that import controls would accelerate the discovery of new reserves. But

23. Quotations in this paragraph are from "Statement by John M. Kelly, Assistant Secretary of the Interior, in Support of Proposals to Amend the Oil Import Program," n.d., pp. 1–2, 3, 4, Feldman Papers, Box 23, JFKL.

24. Kelly to Feldman, October 22, 1961, ibid., Box 24. It should be noted that the validity of this argument was not unquestioned. In the view of many commentators at the time, both inside and outside government, the qualitative differences between Venezuelan and Middle East crudes meant that the latter were not likely candidates to be suppliers of residual to the U.S. market.

current conditions provided little basis for confidence in the capacity of the private oil industry to increase exploratory activities substantially. Despite shelter from imports, "shut-in" capacity in the domestic industry had continued to grow. There was thus little incentive to undertake major expenditures to expand productive capabilities. It could, of course, be argued that import controls should be tightened to the point that shut-in capacity was eliminated and incentives to exploration stimulated; this indeed was the premise of some of the industry's spokesmen. But this would involve both a trade-off of future for present consumption and an unacceptable tax on domestic consumers. The control program had already added an estimated $2 billion a year to the oil bills of consumers. In view of these factors the Budget Bureau suggested consideration of a radically different approach. If the stockpiling of proved reserves was the objective, it might be achieved more efficiently by other means, that is, through governmental subsidies to oil prospecting. It was further suggested that the bulk of the costs of such a program might be financed through the elimination (or at least the substantial reduction) of the oil depletion allowance.[25]

The alleged merits of mandatory controls were challenged for other reasons as well. The Justice Department expressed concern about the anticompetitive effects of the current program—particularly the handicaps suffered by independent suppliers and refiners when attempting to survive in competition with integrated companies enjoying easier access to low-cost imports.[26] The State Department continued to be uneasy about the incompatibility of restrictions with the broader goal of reducing barriers to international commerce. And it occurred to some that relief from the $2 billion burden imposed on the economy by domestic oil prices above world market levels would provide a healthy stimulant to economic expansion.

In late November the White House attempted to mediate these divergent intra-administration views. Representatives of interested agencies and departments were gathered by Theodore Sorenson, but no consensus on policy changes emerged from their discussions. In such circumstances postponement of decision can readily be regarded as the better part of wisdom. Delay in this instance also had other considerations to commend it. As Director Ellis of the OEP insisted, the national security justification for

---

25. The quotation and information in this paragraph are from Staff Memorandum, Bureau of the Budget, "Oil Import Quotas," November 16, 1961, ibid., Box 23.

26. Memorandum, J. H. Mayer to the Director of the Bureau of the Budget, "Proposed Proclamation on Oil Import Quotas," November 29, 1961, ibid.

mandatory controls over imports of crude and its derivatives (other than residual) had not been properly investigated. A proclamation change at this point would place a premature stamp of approval by the Kennedy administration on a program it had inherited.[27] But there were substantive as well as tactical reasons for deferring a decision. Even those most critical of the Interior Department's approach to the problem were not prepared to dismiss a national security rationale for restrictions over crude oil imports out of hand. Ellis, for example, believed that the growth of shut-in capacity threatened to curtail exploratory drilling to a point that "could be seriously damaging to the national security in an emergency."[28] In a similar vein the Budget Bureau, in spite of its discomfort with the prevailing system, recognized "more subtle defense aspects in the existence of the control program than the assurance of profits to certain domestic producers." If the control program were to be scrapped entirely, the geographical pattern of oil imports could be expected to shift toward heavy reliance on the Middle East.[29]

The 1961 round of debates over oil import policy was brought to a close with the White House announcement on December 2 that the President had charged the director of the OEP to lead a "comprehensive study of petroleum requirements and supplies in relation to national security objectives." Pending the completion of that study, allocations of oil import quotas would "continue to be made under the existing proclamation."[30]

27. Ellis to David E. Bell, Director of the Bureau of the Budget, November 14, 1961, ibid.

28. Ibid. As Ellis diagnosed matters: "State regulatory commissions and bodies, of necessity, have imposed such rigorous production quotas and allowables that the pay-out period, particularly in the drilling of deep wells, makes it virtually impossible for oil operators to develop reserves through the normal channels of commerce. For example, the operator without large cash reserves who normally would finance drilling operations through banking institutions, is unable to do so today because of the high cost of drilling, coupled with the low daily return of a producing well; thereby making the pay back period to the bank so onerous and stringent that normal commercial loans are difficult, if not impossible, to obtain." It should be noted that these judgments were those of Ellis, not of his staff. The staff insisted that "the economic condition of an industry can provide a basis for controlling imports only as that condition bears on the national security" and that the Interior Department's case was "not . . . supported by any showing that the change is needed in the interest of national security." (Letter, Ellis to Bell, OEP staff draft, n.d., Joseph Lerner personal files.)

29. Staff Memorandum, Bureau of the Budget, November 16, 1961, Feldman Papers, Box 23, JFKL.

30. White House press release, December 2, 1961, ibid.

The wording of this announcement had been carefully chosen. In the original discussion of the formation of a new study group, it had been suggested that the group's work should be completed early in 1962. The White House press release, however, called for completion by mid-1962. Timing posed a problem of some delicacy. The Budget Bureau had drawn attention to the "importance of a longer due date for the study" to ensure that this matter did not "come to a head during the slam-bang period of the trade legislation fight" anticipated to occur in the next congressional session. Deferral to mid-1962, in the view of the Budget Bureau, had an "openendedness" that was "intended to finesse the problem as much as possible."[31]

The Petroleum Study Committee of 1962

With the formation of the Petroleum Study Committee (PSC), the administration had bought time.[32] But how that time was to be deployed was another matter. The White House had attached a high priority to a trade agreement bill in 1962 that would give it a freer hand in negotiating tariff reductions and that would also support the strengthening of the European Economic Community (including British membership in it). Congressional approval of this legislation was far from assured. Protectionist sentiments were a fact of life, and congressional delegations from energy-producing constituencies were particularly alert to them.

The decision to stand pat on oil import controls, pending the scheduled completion of the PSC's work in mid-1962, was not fully satisfying to either of the main contending parties in the debates of 1961. Ellis, as director of the OEP and chairman of the PSC, maintained that the residual fuel oil component of the program had already been sufficiently studied, that this aspect of the problem need have no place on the agenda of the committee, and that the President had adequate warrant to suspend controls over residual on March 30, 1962 (at the end of the current allocation pe-

---

31. Kenneth R. Hansen to Feldman, November 30, 1961, ibid.

32. The director of the OEP served as PSC chairman; the committee's members included representatives of the Departments of State, Treasury, Defense, Justice, Interior, Commerce, and Labor. Representatives of the Bureau of the Budget and the Council of Economic Advisers, and the deputy special assistant to the President for national security affairs were designated as advisers; representatives of the Central Intelligence Agency and the Federal Power Commission participated as observers.

riod). Though this interpretation was accepted as technically correct, it was also the case that the committee had been directed to undertake a comprehensive review of oil policy. On this ground further delay of action on the OEP's recommendations to decontrol residual could be justified. But there were other reasons for tabling this recommendation. Myer Feldman, the member of the White House staff who followed energy matters most closely, presented them to the President in February 1962, noting that a decision to free imports of residual would provoke "a great political debate in Congress at the wrong time" and "could considerably affect our trade program." This issue, he observed, was a "highly sensitive matter to coal producing states—particularly West Virginia." Feldman proposed that "the Office of Emergency Planning file a report with us setting forth the facts without making any recommendation. These facts would indicate that present quotas have maintained a stable price and provided residual oil for any user that wants it. The clamor for elimination of quotas has not been severe during the past year because there has been more oil available this winter—under quota restrictions—than was used."[33]

Keeping residual within the framework of controls was deemed important, but it did not follow that import quotas could not be adjusted upward. Feldman urged—with the concurrence of the Interior Department —that residual quotas be increased by about 10 percent for the allocation period beginning April 1, 1962. This increment could be justified on the basis of estimates prepared by the Bureau of Mines, which indicated that both a further reduction in domestic supply and an increase in domestic demand were in prospect in the next allocation period.[34] In the supporting brief prepared by J. Cordell Moore, administrator of the Oil Import Administration, the consequences of this liberalization in allocations were appraised as follows: "There can be little doubt that the increase in the level for the coming year will be criticized by the coal industry. It would appear, however, that the criticism will be tempered by the fact that controls still remain in effect notwithstanding the serious efforts that have been made to remove them." Moore expected that fuel oil marketers and consumers, particularly in New England, would not be satisfied with any-

33. Feldman to the President, February 26, 1962, Feldman Papers, Box 23, JFKL.
34. This worked out to be an increment in allowables of 46,000 barrels a day over the 461,000-barrel allowable in the 1961–62 allocation period. For the allocation period beginning on April 1, 1962, the daily reduction in domestic supply was expected to be of the order of 7,000 barrels, while the increase in demand was projected at 39,000 barrels a day.

thing less than a complete scrapping of the control system. He observed, however, that "some of the Fuel Oil Marketers appear to be less vocal in their objections to controls than heretofore, apparently because of the uncertainty of competitive conditions which would exist were controls to be removed." In addition he noted that the reaction in Venezuela would be favorable inasmuch as the historical basis for quota assignments would ensure that it would be the main beneficiary of the increased authorization.[35]

The Interior Department was restive, however, about the treatment accorded to other aspects of the oil program. Its recommendations on tightening restrictions on imports of crude and its primary derivatives had also been tabled. By early February 1962 it appeared unlikely that the PSC would complete its work before the next quota allocations for this category of imports—scheduled to take effect on July 1, 1962—would need to be determined. Udall urged Kennedy to redefine the mandate of the PSC by instructing it "to move immediately to an examination of the existing program and an analysis of ways and means to improve the program within the general framework of the existing structure." A foreshortening of the timetable for completion, Udall maintained, was imperative because of "the certainty that the next three or four months will be critical to your trade program, and some spokesmen for the industry have already demanded that fixed quotas be written into the trade bill."[36] The Interior Department had no doubt about the appropriate course of action. When Udall's plea for a delimitation in the scope of the PSC study was not acted on, the department proceeded to prepare its own recommendations for amendments to Proclamation 3279. The department's proposals in May 1962 did not differ fundamentally from those circulated in October 1961: restrictions were to be tightened by shifting the base of calculation from total demand to the refinery throughput of domestic crude, and imports via the overland exemption were to be charged against quotas. Though the quota percentages were to be enlarged—to 12 percent of refinery use of domestic crude (as opposed to the 10.25 percent figure proposed in the preceding autumn)—the net effect would be a reduction of total imports into Districts I–IV by about 100,000 barrels a day from the level of the first half of 1962.[37]

35. Moore to Kelly, February 26, 1962, Feldman Papers, Box 23, JFKL.
36. Udall to the President, February 2, 1962, ibid.
37. Memorandum for the Files, May 7, 1962, ibid.

The White House failed to share a sense of urgency about an early completion of the PSC's deliberations. Indeed it was quite comfortable with an extension of the reporting deadline to September 1, 1962.[38] Further delay had its advantages. Not only did it permit the administration to stall on proclamation changes affecting both residual and crude oil, but with luck it also might mean that congressional action on the trade bill would be completed before next steps on import controls would need to be openly debated.

While the White House was not eager to speed completion of the PSC report, it was far from neutral about the shape of its ultimate contents. Passage of the trade bill was the administration's top priority for the 1962 congressional session. This required courting key congressional figures. Kennedy made an early start in this lobbying effort. In mid-December 1961 he met with Senator Robert S. Kerr of Oklahoma, indicating to him the importance of export markets to the economic health of his state. The background paper prepared for presidential use on that occasion indicated, however, that "of course, under the proposed trade legislation, the existing restrictions upon imports of crude oil would remain."[39] In subsequent months the administration broadened its campaign. Myer Feldman indicated its direction when reporting to the President on conversations with Congressman Homer Thornberry (Democrat of Texas) on June 25, 1962. Feldman and Assistant Secretary of the Interior John Kelly had

38. From all appearances PSC's work had not been organized to submit a report on a more timely basis. No staff director was appointed in the early months, and various agency participants in its proceedings were serving only part-time while continuing their regular duties. In late April 1962 one observer commented on the status of the committee's work as follows: "We do not yet have a clear basis for relating the price structure to costs. Neither is there a realistic basis for relating current production to capacity (or reserves). The basis for industry compilation of statistics is not clear, even to Interior staff. The defense aspects appear to be quite general, particularly since planning must increasingly take a global viewpoint. The balance of payments approach so far appears unrealistic, and the importance in the economy of petroleum products is so diffuse that it cannot be related to any other particular products, except possibly petro-chemicals and alternative fuels." (J. H. Mayer to Kenneth Hansen, "Progress Report: Petroleum Task Force Study," April 23, 1962, ibid.) There were also some indications that the progress of the study was slowed by reluctance on the part of Interior Department officials to supply statistical data and to explain their estimating and projecting procedures to members of the group. See Joseph Lerner, Memorandum for the Record, "Petroleum Study Committee Task Force Questions for Department of the Interior," June 19, 1962, Lerner personal files.

39. Feldman to the President, "Items Which May Be Discussed at Your Meeting with Senator Kerr," December 14, 1961, President's Office Files, Box 63, JFKL.

visited the congressman to "receive his assurances" on a vote on the trade bill in the Rules Committee. As Feldman reviewed their discussions:

We related to him the substance of the conversations in your office with Congressman Mills and with Senator Kerr when they asked questions concerning our oil policy. At the conclusion of our discussion we summarized our intentions as follows:

1. The Administration had appointed a committee to study the national security aspects of oil production and consumption in the United States. This committee, headed by Ed McDermott [the successor to Ellis as OEP director], would report before September 1st.
2. We were certain that a system of import quotas for oil would be retained.
3. Under the system of import quotas we would establish allocations on the basis of domestic crude production rather than on the basis of estimated demand. This sounds technical, but it is very important to the oil producing states. It will enable the producers and the state regulatory bodies to plan future production.
4. On or about July 15, the Department of the Interior will initiate discussions with their counterparts in the Canadian Government, looking toward a voluntary limitation of exports of Canadian oil to the United States. The State Department was advised of the exchange of letters which took place last year calling for these discussions.[40]

Though Feldman insisted that "no commitment was made regarding the actual number of barrels which should be specified as an import quota" and that he believed a "flexible position" to have been maintained, it was nonetheless clear that the deliberations of the PSC were now largely redundant.[41] The chairman of the Petroleum Study Committee, Director Edward A. McDermott of the OEP, was apprized of the White House position after the fact. On June 29, 1962, McDermott observed to Feldman that he understood "that you have announced an extension on the broad petroleum study to September 1, 1962." McDermott added: "I believe it important that I know of any representations, commitments, or understandings that may have been made with reference to crude oil imports incident to current Congressional activity. If you have that information, I would like to discuss it with you at your convenience."[42]

The PSC report, which was sent to the President on September 4, 1962, was a contorted document. The mandatory control program, it noted, had imposed considerable burdens on consumers; estimates made available to

40. Feldman to the President, "Program for the Oil Industry," June 25, 1962, Feldman Papers, Box 23, JFKL.
41. Ibid.
42. McDermott to Feldman, "Residual Fuel Oil Study and Petroleum Study," June 29, 1962, Feldman Papers, Box 23, JFKL.

the committee suggested that crude oil prices would be about $1 a barrel lower without controls.[43] It added that "since the total demand for petroleum products in the United States is about 3.5 billion barrels annually, it is apparent that the present system of controls involves a large cost to consumers."[44] Nor was the committee comfortable with the implications of the existing system for the allocation of resources within the industry. Oil import licenses were estimated to be worth about $1 million a day to their recipients. The distribution of such largesse by the federal government was bound to affect "the financial return of individual companies, the structure of the industry, the functioning of the economy, and other national objectives." Moreover, these benefits were conveyed to an industry already uniquely favored by tax breaks: Treasury Department estimates were cited that indicated that the revenues forgone by percentage depletion (as opposed to cost depletion) amounted to about $1 billion a year. In addition the competitive position of American industries in export markets was handicapped by fuel costs inflated by government intervention. These considerations, however, were set off against the less happy consequences that might follow any radical departure from the status quo. "Petroleum is basic to the economies of the principal producing States," the PSC observed, "affecting levels of employment, business activity, and the revenues of State governments. . . . A sharp decline in the level of prices or of production would create pockets of economic distress and unemployment."[45]

Despite evidence of some strain, the PSC made major accommodations to the requirements of higher authority. It advised that the mandatory control system should be retained and that the formula for calculating allowable oil imports should be shifted from a total demand to a domestic production base. For Districts I–IV, however, the committee recommended that the production formula should include all liquid hydrocarbons (condensate and natural gas liquids as well as crude oil), as opposed to the Interior Department's proposal that the allowable should be linked to the

43. "A Report to the President by the Petroleum Study Committee," September 4, 1962, p. 2, ibid. The draft of this report, which had been sent to the White House on August 24, 1962, had indicated that "domestic crude oil prices are substantially higher (on the order of 25 percent of current delivered prices) than they would be in the absence of import controls. . . ." This language was deleted from the final text. "Petroleum Study Committee Task Force Report," draft, August 22, 1962, ibid.

44. "A Report to the President by the Petroleum Study Committee," p. 2.

45. Quotations in this paragraph are from ibid., pp. 2 and 3.

refinery use of domestic crude exclusively. Note was taken of the overland exemption with the recommendation that the secretary of state, assisted by the secretary of the interior, should "discuss this problem with the Goverment of Canada with a view to obtaining coordination of United States and Canadian policies relating to North American petroleum security." While the PSC called for the retention of the mandatory control apparatus, it recorded its judgment—from which the Interior Department dissented —that "a modest increase in the level of licensed crude oil imports above that which would be provided by the present program for Districts I–IV can now be undertaken."[46]

The PSC had accepted the import control system as a response to "extraordinary" conditions. But it also insisted that longer-term measures should be shaped that would eliminate the need for such controls. The committee held it to be "imperative that domestic petroleum costs be reduced to permit a narrowing of the difference between the United States and foreign prices."[47] This was important, not only to the interests of consumers, but also for balance-of-payments reasons. This objective could not be achieved, however, through federal action alone. Prices and production in the domestic oil industry were fundamentally determined by the actions of state regulatory bodies. The current situation had intensified "state curtailment of crude oil production to a point where it adds substantially to real costs and raises serious question as to the equity of its impact on producers."[48] The prorationing system, after all, had been designed to protect the marginal producers by requiring cutbacks in the same proportion in the outputs of high- and low-cost wells. This in turn meant that average production costs in the American crude oil industry were needlessly inflated. The PSC held that rationalization of this system was overdue and recommended that the secretary of the interior initiate discussions with the Interstate Oil Compact Commission (the body coordinating the activities of various state regulatory agencies) on steps that might reduce production costs in the domestic crude oil industry and enable it to hold its own in the domestic market without protection. If sufficient productivity improvement could be achieved over the longer term, import restrictions would ultimately be pointless.

In the interim the PSC suggested that the administrative procedures

46. Information and quotations in this paragraph are from ibid., pp. 8, 9.
47. Ibid., p. 3.
48. Ibid., p. 5.

used in the present control system should be reviewed. The committee observed that tariffs were "generally considered preferable to quantitative restrictions by reason of their simplicity and the larger scope they allow to market forces." This technique for restriction was not regarded as "feasible at this time"—primarily because of "possible adverse effects in this hemisphere."[49] Fees and auctions were held to be worthy of consideration as devices for allocating import licenses. Indeed it had been the view of the PSC's task force that the exchange of oil under the control program "should emphasize the sale of such oil." It was argued that "valuable information bearing on the operation of the program" could be obtained if the sale of the import license itself were permitted.[50]

Though the PSC's basic conclusion that oil imports could be increased without imperiling national security had been presented in muted form, the committee's findings fell short of satisfying the White House. The press was informed that the report had been delivered, but its contents were not publicly released.[51] As far as the Department of the Interior was concerned, the PSC might just as well have not existed. Shortly after the release of the report, the department renewed its campaign for amendments to Proclamation 3279 that would tighten the apparatus of restriction. The particulars of its recommendations in the autumn of 1962 were essentially the same as those canvassed a year earlier. Allowables were to be cut by shifting the basis of calculation from domestic demand to domestic production, and imports via the overland exemption were to be charged against the quota assignments. The likely impact of these proposed changes for import volumes in the first half of 1963 was variously estimated. The OEP calculated that the added "degree of restrictiveness . . . could well be on the order of 40–60 thousand barrels a day."[52] The Budget Bureau estimated that the Interior Department proposal, "while slightly increasing quotas over 1962 levels, represents a reduction of 71,000 barrels per day

49. Ibid., p. 3.

50. Lerner to McDermott, "Petroleum Study Committee Task Force Suggestions," August 24, 1962, Lerner personal files.

51. In response to a question at the White House Conference of Business Editors and Publishers on September 26, 1962, Kennedy observed: "The report was not wholly accepted by me, so that I don't expect any announcement will be made about the matter at the present time." *Public Papers: John F. Kennedy, 1962* (GPO, 1963), p. 715.

52. McDermott to Hansen (signed for McDermott by Joseph Lerner), "Proposed Letter from the President to the Secretary of the Interior Concerning Oil Import Programs," November 9, 1962, Feldman Papers, Box 24, JFKL.

from the level which would be established if the present demand formula were to continue unchanged."[53]

The reaction of other agencies and departments to the Interior Department's draft amendments to Proclamation 3279 was largely a replay of debates of late 1961. But there was one difference: the work of the PSC had been completed in the interim. In fundamental respects, as the OEP pointed out, the department's position was "incompatible with the September 4 report of the Petroleum Study Committee."[54] The OEP protested that "the benefit of the vast amount of work which has been devoted to petroleum should not be thrown aside in haste" and that further instructions to the secretary of the interior should "reflect the findings of the Petroleum Study Committee, except as [they] may be expressly modified by the President." Specific exception was taken to the increased restrictiveness of the Interior Department's proposals, which flew in the face of the majority recommendation that a modest increase in crude oil imports could safely be allowed. Objection was also raised about the proposal to charge overland exempt imports against the total allocation; the PSC had chosen to handle this problem by continuing to exclude Canadian oil from quota allowables, though it had recommended that the secretary of state discuss voluntary curtailments with the Canadian government. The State Department again registered its objections, noting that "from the point of view of our foreign relations and our trade policy, it would be most desirable to put into effect the recommendation of the majority of the members of the Petroleum Study Committee that there be some moderate increase in the rate of petroleum imports in the next period."[55] The department noted that it had already indicated to the Canadian government its desire to initiate discussions on the coordination of the oil policies of the two countries, but that it was unreasonable to expect those discussions to be completed within the next few days. The Department of Commerce reported its preliminary judgment that the proposed amendments to the proclamation were likely to mean that prices of crude oil would

53. Hansen to Feldman, "Oil Import Quota for Districts I–IV," November 29, 1962, ibid.

54. McDermott to Hansen, "Proposed Letter from the President to the Secretary of the Interior Concerning Oil Import Programs."

55. William H. Brubeck, Executive Secretary of the Department of State, to Myer Feldman, "Petroleum Import Policy," November 16, 1962, Feldman Papers, Box 24, JFKL.

rise by about 5 cents a barrel and that the cost to U.S. consumers "would be in the neighborhood of $180 million."[56]

Despite these protests the Interior Department's position carried the day. On November 30, 1962, the President issued a proclamation amending 3279 along the lines the department had proposed. Effective January 1, 1963, the basis for quota allocation in Districts I–IV for crude oil and petroleum products (other than residual fuel) was to be calculated as 12.2 percent of the quantity of crude oil and natural gas liquids "produced in these districts during the period of six months which ends six months prior to the beginning of the allocation period."[57] Imports subject to the overland exemption were henceforth to be charged against the total allowable. In addition the basis for assigning quotas to particular importers was to be revised to accelerate the phasing out of the historical importers. This change in procedure was held to be a necessary reinforcement to competition in the industry and to the position of smaller importers and refiners.

The losers in this policy battle went down fighting. Kenneth R. Hansen, assistant director of the Bureau of the Budget, mounted a rearguard action by drawing attention to an anomaly in the Interior Department formula for calculating import allowables. The selection of 12.2 percent as the operational figure had been justified on the ground that it reproduced the actual ratio of imports to domestic production in 1961. But that year had been one of abnormal stock accumulations of refinery products. If imports in 1961 were expressed as a percentage of domestic production consumed in 1961, the resulting figure worked out to be 12.4 percent. The logic of the department's position, Hansen maintained, called for a larger quota percentage than had been stipulated in the amended proclamation. This would imply an increase of about 15,000 barrels a day in the allowables for the first half of 1963. Hansen urged that the Department of the Interior be directed to amend its procedures along these lines, noting that "this much of an increase would seem to represent a more favorable posture for the administration to take at a time when changes are being made in the proclamation which will have restrictive effects on licensed petroleum imports."[58] This attempt to win a bit more freedom of maneuver was frustrated. When this proposition was submitted to the Department of the

56. Daniel L. Goldy, Acting Assistant Secretary for Domestic and International Business, Department of Commerce, to Feldman, November 29, 1962, ibid.

57. "Proclamation 3509, Modifying Proclamation 3279, Adjusting Imports of Petroleum and Petroleum Products," *Federal Register,* vol. 27 (December 5, 1962), p. 11985.

58. Hansen to Feldman, November 29, 1962, Feldman Papers, Box 24, JFKL.

Interior its assistant solicitor offered the opinion that "the Secretary is not empowered to vary the percentage expressly fixed in the proclamation and I am quite clear that any level set by the use of a different percentage would be indefensible from the legal standpoint. . . .[T]he Secretary . . . is not at liberty to take stock changes into account in determining the 'quantity of crude oil and natural gas liquids produced' in Districts I–IV during any particular period of six months."[59]

The attacks both on the basic structure of the control system and on restrictiveness in its administration were thus resisted. The mandatory program continued without significant modification for the remainder of the Kennedy administration. A modest cosmetic change in the formula for arriving at the total quota volume was introduced for the allocation period in the second half of 1963. Its effect was the dropping of the ex post basis for determining quotas and the calculation of the allowable as 12.2 percent of the Bureau of Mines estimates of domestic production in the next semiannual allocation period. This was still quite different from the procedure followed before the proclamation amendment of November 30, 1962, when estimates of total demand had been the controlling factor.

Though the position of the majority of the PSC had largely been ignored, not all the committee's recommendations were stillborn. In early 1963 representatives of the Department of the Interior initiated conversations with the Interstate Oil Compact Commission, pointing out the interest of the administration in "making domestic oil as competitive as it possibly could be with foreign oil."[60] By June the governors of the states included in the Interstate Oil Compact Commission had agreed to the formation of a study committee (to be headed by Governor Matthew E. Welsh of Indiana) to examine "all aspects of conservation, economics, regulatory practices, and legal and technical factors affecting the petroleum industry on a world-wide basis."[61] Preparation of this report was expected to take some time, though it was hoped that a preliminary document could be submitted to the governors for study in late November or

59. Bruce Wright, Assistant Solicitor of the Department of the Interior, to John F. O'Leary, Special Assistant to the Assistant Secretary for Mineral Resources, Department of the Interior, December 5, 1962, ibid.

60. Notes on conference with Assistant Secretary John Kelly and his Assistant, Jerome J. O'Brien, on February 12, 1963, as reported by F. Allen Calvert, Jr., February 13, 1963 (Calvert was the Oklahoma representative to the Interstate Oil Compact Commission), White House Central Files, Box 645, JFKL.

61. Udall to the President, August 27, 1963, President's Office Files, Box 80, JFKL.

early December 1963. No federal agencies or departments were to be involved in the work of this group.

The Vexed Question of Residual Fuel Oil

The debates over the future of the oil import control program in 1961 and 1962 had left the fate of residual fuel oil dangling. The proclamation of November 30, 1962, which tightened the control network over imports of other petroleum products, had not spoken to this issue. Meanwhile the OEP inquiry launched in May 1961 in response to a challenge to the national security rationale for continued controls was still pending. Though the OEP had been prepared in November 1961 to release a report calling for the decontrol of residual fuel imports, its findings had been suppressed on the ground that a final determination on this matter should await the finding of the Petroleum Study Committee. In the discussions of February and March 1962 the White House had again insisted that this boat should not be rocked. The structural status quo was maintained, though more generous quota allocations were then permitted. In late June 1962 the OEP had again indicated that it would shortly be ready to move. McDermott reported to Feldman that "the residual fuel oil study will be ready for submission to you in draft form soon for release in accordance with our earlier understanding."[62] But the White House continued to prefer postponement.

These delays had not passed unnoticed. Joseph E. Moody, president of the National Coal Policy Conference, brought them to McDermott's attention in late August 1962 by recording his dismay on reading a report in the *Oil and Gas Journal* of August 27, 1962. Its substance was that a decision on the future of residual import controls was being deliberately deferred as a political strategy. Moody reported that the *Journal* had predicted that the matter would be disposed of shortly after congressional action had been completed on the Trade Extension Act and had asserted that "the Administration has sought to get the trade bill through Congress without stirring up the opposition it fears would come from announcing a decision on the resid program." Moody also noted that the *Oil Daily* of August 30, 1962, had reported that "a study and recommendation on the future of residual oil imports was 'wrapped up' months ago and pigeon-

---

62. McDermott to Feldman, "Residual Fuel Oil Study and Petroleum Study," June 29, 1962, Feldman Papers, Box 23, JFKL.

holed until the Trade Bill crossed the finish line."[63] In response Mc-Dermott pleaded that staff resources had been preempted by the PSC. As soon as this work was completed, staff attention would be "addressed to the residual study, with the objective of completing and submitting that report as promptly as possible thereafter."[64]

The OEP honored that commitment. On September 7, 1962, three days after the PSC report was transmitted to the President, the OEP submitted a redraft of its findings on residual fuel oil to the White House. The conclusion of the preceding year was reasserted: that import controls over residual should be terminated. In the interagency correspondence that followed the circulation of this version of the OEP's findings within the executive branch, a familiar argument reemerged. Advocates for the preservation of controls maintained that their removal would be harmful to Venezuela by eliminating its automatic "historical" preference. The OEP found no merit in that claim. The viscosity of oils from the Middle East and North Africa was ill-suited to yield residual fuel oils for the American market. It remained the OEP's settled conviction that a case for continued controls over residual could not be sustained.

But a further argument for keeping residual within the framework of mandatory controls could be introduced in the autumn of 1962. The PSC had recommended that the control apparatus should be kept in place for other categories of oil imports (though it also called for liberalization in quota authorizations). For reasons of symmetry, it was not unreasonable to suggest that an analogous approach to residual be adopted. This indeed was the view pressed by the White House. From its vantage point, there was much to be said for retaining the control system (as a reassurance to the coal interests) while expanding import quotas (as a bow to the interests of consumers). The OEP was urged to recast its findings to recommend a "meaningful relaxation," but not the elimination of controls. But what was a "meaningful relaxation" to mean? The OEP answered that question in its further drafts in December 1962 by proposing the exemption of electric utilities from import controls.

On February 13, 1963—almost exactly two years after the original petition for an investigation into the justification of controls over residual fuel imports had been filed—OEP Director McDermott reported to the President that "a careful and meaningful relaxation of controls would be consistent with national security. . . . Such a relaxation should be designed

63. Moody to McDermott, August 30, 1962, ibid.
64. McDermott to Moody, August 31, 1962, ibid.

to achieve the maximum reduction of the burden on the economy, given the import levels resulting from the easing of controls."[65] Reference to the exemption of electric utilities was deleted from the final version. Contrary to its better judgment, the OEP had again yielded to higher authority. Its conclusions, though calling for increased import volumes, did not directly challenge the de jure apparatus of controls. This accommodation had been painful. No less distressing to the OEP were indications that the report of its findings was being proclaimed as a validation of controls. On this point McDermott protested to Feldman:

To interpret my Memorandum as basically justifying controls rather than as providing for the substantial reduction of controls would be a misreading of the document. To do so would also probably lead to many petitions for investigations under the national security clause. . . . [T]he only national security reason given in the Memorandum for not ending controls on residual fuel imports is that such action might alter the primacy of Western Hemispheric sources. That reservation itself is somewhat tenuous. The investigation and all of the contributions to it developed no information indicating that removal of controls would bring in residual fuel oil from other areas.[66]

McDermott also put on record his view of the way his memorandum to the President should be read. He observed that "higher imports . . . because of an increase in the gap between projected demand and domestic availability of residual fuel oil from all sources would constitute not a relaxation of controls, but a continuation of present controls. A change in the means of allocating imports alone would also not constitute a relaxation of controls."[67]

On this issue the White House drew fire from other quarters as well. Senator Jennings Randolph of West Virginia spoke for the coal interests when denouncing the administration from the Senate floor for its softness toward residual fuel oil imports. Whereas it had been his impression that the import control program would be "stabilized," the administration was diluting its effectiveness.[68] In these circumstances Feldman recommended that a new program be shaped that would

authorize the Secretary of the Interior to issue import licenses for residual fuel oil to any applicant who can demonstrate to the satisfaction of the Secretary

65. McDermott to the President, February 13, 1963, as quoted in the attachment to memorandum, O'Leary to Feldman, n.d., ibid., Box 24.

66. McDermott to Feldman, February 26, 1963, ibid.

67. Ibid.

68. *Congressional Record* (February 19, 1963), pp. 2550–54. Feldman briefed Kennedy on the background as follows: "When the Trade Bill was before Congress . . . I met with Senator Randolph and assured him (1) that he would have a chance to

(a) that he has a bona fide requirement for the oil, (b) that there is no evidence of dumping or any other malpractice, and (c) that he can use at least a tanker load. This means that we can continue controls over the program, but the relaxation would be so substantial that it would cause a gradual price decrease. Under this procedure, we could also be assured the source of the oil would remain Venezuela and not the Middle East.[69]

Feldman indicated that the complete elimination of controls was a possible option, though one he regarded as "too drastic a step at the present time." This course, he acknowledged, had been the "real recommendation" of the OEP, but it had been modified at his insistence "so that we could continue controls."[70]

The Kennedy administration kept residual fuel oils within the jurisdiction of the oil import administrator, but it did open more space for imports. Quota authorizations were further liberalized in the allocation period beginning April 1, 1963. Even the Department of the Interior, which had pushed most vigorously for tighter restrictions over other categories of petroleum imports, had no difficulty with this approach. In its view, improvements in refining technology had made this a matter of trivial concern to the domestic industry. As the department noted on March 3, 1963, "residual fuel oil yields have declined to the point where this fuel is not a major factor in refinery economics in the area served by imports."[71] The coal constituencies, to be sure, were far from indifferent. To mend fences with them, Feldman suggested the following points could be emphasized:

We will not follow the OEP recommendation of banning residual oil import controls. . . .We will give some stability to the industry by making the necessary allocation a one-year allocation instead of a 6-month allocation. . . .We will not have any increase in the allocation beyond what is essential to prevent prices from rising. . . .We are about to sign a contract for the construction of a $10 million plant at Cresaps, West Virginia, for the liquefication of coal (making gasoline out of coal). This is part of an accelerated coal research program.[72]

---

see the OEP report on residual fuel oil before it was published, (2) that he would be consulted in connection with the new residual fuel oil program, and (3) that any program adopted would provide for a continuation of controls. Senator Randolph voted with us at critical times. We have kept our word. . . ." (Feldman to the President, "Residual Fuel Oil Imports," February 27, 1963, Feldman Papers, Box 24, JFKL.)

69. Feldman to the President, "Residual Fuel Oil Imports."

70. Ibid.

71. Kelly to Feldman, March 3, 1963, Feldman Papers, Box 24, JFKL.

72. Feldman to Kennedy, "Meeting with Tony Boyle, President of the United Mine Workers," March 7, 1963, President's Office Files, Box 63, JFKL.

McDermott, director of the OEP, suggested an alternative expression of the administration's sympathy for coal:

> . . . it may be helpful to recall that Federal support of interstate coal pipelines has had a very favorable impact on the competitive position of the coal industry. A number of responsible industry people feel that the President's support of legislation concerning eminent domain for the acquisition of rights-of-way for coal pipelines has been of more direct assistance to the coal industry than any other program now under way. The coal pipeline program assumed an air of reality with the Administration's support of needed rights-of-way legislation. This stimulated the railroads to adopt innovations in coal transportation which have reduced coal costs to consumers in the range of 75¢ to $1.00 per ton.[73]

But it was still open to dispute whether or not the course of action chosen in March 1963 constituted the meaningful "relaxation of controls" the OEP had found to be consistent with national security. The Steuart Petroleum Company thought not. It brought suit against the secretary of the interior, charging that the increases in quota allocations then announced did not satisfy this requirement.[74]

Coal: Concessions and Disappointments

Of the various components of the nation's energy complex, the coal industry occupied a position of special sensitivity to the Kennedy administration. The campaign of 1960 had raised high expectations among the coal mining communities. Candidate Kennedy had been quite unambiguous in his expressions of sympathy for the plight of these distressed areas and of his determination to improve their lot. A brighter future for coal had been outlined with indications of the use of new technologies—for example, the "coal by wire" technique for electrical transmission and generation and the further widening of market space for coal through the construction of pipelines to convey it more efficiently to consumer markets. In addition candidate Kennedy had pledged to support the congressional National Fuels and Energy Study to which the coal interests had assigned such importance.

73. McDermott to Feldman, "Residual Oil—Coal Discussions," March 7, 1963, Feldman Papers, Box 5, JFKL.
74. See memorandum, Bruce Wright to John Kelly, June 10, 1963, ibid., Box 24. In April 1965 counsel for the Steuart Petroleum Company and for the Interior Department agreed to terminate this proceeding, and the case was dismissed without a judicial opinion on its merit.

In the early going the administration had shown earnest on these commitments. The Office of Coal Research (authorized by Congress and approved by the President in 1960, though it had not been staffed by the Eisenhower administration) was launched with the charge that it should "expand, through research, the uses of coal in order that this abundant, but under-developed, natural resource will make its maximum contribution to the welfare and progress of the nation."[75] Similarly, the administration had endorsed the National Fuels and Energy Study to be undertaken by the Senate Committee on Interior and Insular Affairs (though it had been less than eager to mount this inquiry within the executive branch). In the spirit of its campaign pledges, the administration had also worked to promote export markets for coal, in the first instance those that could be influenced by government contracts. When Congressman Daniel Flood of Pennsylvania pointed out to the President that the armed forces in Germany were supplied with German coke (when American anthracite could be used as a substitute), Kennedy regarded this as "a legitimate gripe" and requested the Defense Department to review its procurement policies.[76] On August 23, 1961, the White House announced that the Defense Department would invite bids from suppliers of coal and coke exclusively in the United States to cover the needs of the armed forces in West Germany for the last three-quarters of the fiscal year.[77] Meanwhile American missions abroad were instructed to be on the lookout for coal markets and, in France particularly, these efforts met with some success. The Office of Coal Research underwrote the export-expansion effort by commissioning the consulting firm of Robert R. Nathan Associates to survey the market potential for U.S. coal abroad. The optimism of the findings led the President to direct the secretary of the interior to "take the lead within the Federal Government in developing, in conjunction with the affected industries, a program to stimulate our coal exports. The significant social and economic benefits to the coal producing regions of the

75. White House press announcement, April 9, 1961, President's Office Files, Box 79, JFKL.

76. Theodore Sorenson to Roswell L. Gilpatric, July 11, 1961, Feldman Papers, Box 5, JFKL.

77. "White House Announcement of Plans for Supplying U.S. Coal and Coke to the Armed Forces in West Germany," White House press release, August 23, 1961, ibid. This decision, however, was not enthusiastically endorsed throughout the government. The State Department feared that trade negotiations with Germany—which promised to increase opportunities for American coal exporters through regular commercial channels—would be compromised.

United States, as well as the advantages to this Nation from the standpoint of its balance of payments, need hardly be underscored."[78]

In domestic markets the administration also encouraged innovations that would strengthen coal's position in interfuel competition. In this connection one of the central points of discussion in early 1962 was a proposal designed to remove legal obstacles to the construction of a coal pipeline from West Virginia to New York. A coal pipeline plan had been developed by the Pittsburgh-based Consolidation Coal Company and the Texas Gas Transmission Corporation and its technical feasibility was well established; an intrastate coal pipeline had already been brought into successful operation in Ohio. The West Virginia-to-New York project had been held up, however, by the refusal of railroads to grant rights-of-way to a competitor. It appeared that this obstacle could be overcome only through federal legislation awarding rights of eminent domain to carriers of coal by pipeline. On March 20, 1962, the President submitted a draft bill to Congress proposing that such legislation be enacted. His message noted that this legislation would grant to coal pipelines the privileges already enjoyed by distributors of natural gas.[79] Despite administration sponsorship, this proposal was not acted upon favorably by Congress.

The administration had also far outdone any of its predecessors in support for research into new uses of coal. The Office of Coal Research had financed pilot projects for the conversion of coal into gaseous and liquid fuels and the initial results appeared to be encouraging. By March 1963 the Office of Coal Research estimated that success with the first commercial plants designed for these conversions could add some 11 million tons a year to the demand for coal.[80] Inquiries were also projected into the

78. Kennedy to Udall, October 11, 1963, ibid.

79. "Letter to the President of the Senate and to the Speaker of the House Transmitting a Bill to Stimulate Construction of Coal Pipelines," *Public Papers: Kennedy, 1962*, pp. 249–50. In making his recommendation the President had rejected views expressed by the Bureau of the Budget that such authority should be conveyed by the states, not the federal government. West Virginia, it was noted, had already changed its law to award rights of eminent domain to the builders of coal pipelines, though parallel action by other states on the route to New York was more problematic. The wisdom of the proposed federal intervention was also challenged for another reason. No provision had been made for federal regulation of entry into the coal-pipeline industry. Interstate carriers of natural gas, by contrast, were regulated by the Federal Power Commission. See Philip S. Hughes, Assistant Director for Legislative Reference, Bureau of the Budget, to Feldman, January 29, 1962, Feldman Papers, Box 6, JFKL.

80. George A. Lamb to the Special Assistant to the Assistant Secretary for Mineral Resources, Draft Memorandum, March 11, 1963, Feldman Papers, Box 5, JFKL.

feasibility of "mine-mouth" generation of electricity, that is, the "coal by wire" proposal.

The grievances of the coal constituencies were still far from placated, and the Senate National Fuels and Energy Study did nothing to relieve them. The coal interests had been the prime movers in the initiation of this study and it had been their thinly disguised hope that its findings would validate claims for preferential treatment for coal. From their perspective, the results were profoundly disappointing. The report, issued on September 21, 1962, concluded that there was no cause for concern about energy availabilities through 1980: "The Nation's resource base, in terms of each fuel, is adequate to meet projected requirements for the period covered by this study—i.e., to 1980." Coal was abundantly available and the nation had the "ability to be self-sufficient in oil if it so wills," though the achievement of self-sufficiency would depend on accelerated exploratory drilling and on increased attention to secondary recovery techniques. The domestic supply of gas appeared to be "well above the projected requirement" and it was held that "oil shale may in fact be yielding oil well before 1980, and coal may be yielding gasoline." No problems were anticipated in the availability of electrical energy. Nuclear power was accepted as "an accomplished technological fact," though some technical problems would need to be solved before its full potential could be realized.[81]

Moreover, the study group made light of a concern expressed by the Paley Commission a decade earlier: that the United States faced the prospect of substantially higher costs in its energy supplies. The study group proclaimed its faith, "albeit faith based on the record," in "the ability of continued technologic progress to hold costs within limits." It noted

that information on costs is elusive and inconclusive, but at least for oil and gas jointly there seems to be little discernible trend either upward or downward in real terms (dollars of constant value). None of the three principal fossil fuels seems likely to price itself out of any major markets within the time span of this report. In any case the cost of oil from shale should place an upper limit on the price of crude oil, and the cost of gasifying coal a limit on the price of natural gas; all these will impose restraints on the price of coal.[82]

Nor was there comfort for coal in the study group's treatment of the industry's complaints about the pricing of natural gas and the importation

81. *Report of the National Fuels and Energy Study Group on an Assessment of Available Information on Energy in the United States,* Senate Committee on Interior and Insular Affairs, S. Doc. 159, 87 Cong. 1 sess. (GPO, 1962), p. 12.
82. Ibid., p. 13.

of residual fuel oil. The study group acknowledged that the prices of inter-ruptible gas were below those charged to customers with "firm service." But this pricing arrangement, it maintained, "at least covers the cost of the gas itself plus the out-of-pocket costs of transportation and distribution. Thus this type of service makes a contribution toward fixed charges that would otherwise be borne by firm customers." This contribution to fixed charges was estimated at $400 million nationally in 1960. It was further acknowledged that the rising domestic consumption of imported residual fuel oil amounted to the equivalent of about 40 million tons of coal on the East Coast alone. But in the judgment of the study group, it did not follow that tighter import restrictions offered a solution to the unemployment problems of coal communities. On this matter, the study group concluded: "Elimination of interruptible gas sales and of the importation of heavy fuel oil would increase employment in the coal industry, but for a number of reasons (among them that part of the vacated markets would be taken by domestic oil and by firm gas and that the current coal work force is used less than full time) the gain would be small—perhaps a few thousand men—in terms of the gross problem."[83]

The conclusions of the Senate National Fuels and Energy Study Group were compatible with OEP thinking on the subject of controls over residual fuel imports. For its part the White House had done its best to mediate between the sensibilities of the coal constituencies and the in-terests of consumers of residual. Despite the weight of argument in favor of decontrol, residual imports were kept within the surveillance of the administrator of the mandatory import control program, though this concession had greater symbolic than practical significance.

Natural Gas and Its Regulatory Apparatus

The natural gas industry presented problems quite different from those of either oil or coal. It was clearly a growth sector. From the perspective of the Kennedy administration, the problems of this component of the energy complex were primarily ones of regulatory reform. Its diagnosis, however, contrasted markedly with the one offered by the Eisenhower administration. The objective of the latter had been to get the federal government out of the business of regulating the field prices of natural gas —a responsibility thrust on the reluctant Federal Power Commission by

83. Ibid., pp. 15, 16.

the Supreme Court's disposition of the Phillips Petroleum case in 1954. The Kennedy team had no desire to undo the Phillips decision; in its view priority should instead be assigned to simplifying and expediting the regulatory process—while strengthening protections to consumers—and on improving the quality of the personnel serving the FPC.

In the opinion of those closest to the President on these matters, most particularly James M. Landis, the FPC in the 1950s had failed to do its job. Petitions on rate schedules and on authorizations for new pipeline construction had been allowed to accumulate. Neither the legitimate interests of consumers in reasonable prices nor of producers in the expansion of the industry had been properly attended to. Landis maintained that the "problem of rate backlogs could largely have been avoided." In his judgment the FPC in the mid-1950s had "trod water," hoping that deregulation bills pending in Congress "would eliminate all these cases by removing federal control over rates of natural gas producers." When the law had not been changed, he maintained that the FPC had "deliberately sought to prove that rate regulation of natural gas production was an administrative impossibility."[84]

One of the consequences of the FPC's backlog was that rate increases had "pancaked" outrageously. The law permitted natural gas distributors and producers petitioning for approval of increased rates to charge their customers at the higher rate if a regulatory decision was not reached within six months of the date of filing. Firms doing so, however, would be required to pay refunds in the event the FPC ruled the new schedules to be unwarranted. There was nothing to prevent successive rounds of rate increases from pancaking. In February 1961 Landis estimated that the "*annual* amount being collected by the pipeline companies by rate increases whose reasonableness had not been determined is over $418 million. In the gas production field the annual amount of similar rate increases is over $170 million."[85] He further noted that the aggregate sums collected from rate increases that were subject to a possible refund to the

84. Landis to the President, February 20, 1961, President's Office Files, Box 78, JFKL. Landis had made the same point in his earlier report to the President-elect. In December 1960 he had written: ". . . the Commission appears to have refrained from any real effort to deal with its docket on the theory that the passage of these bills [the deregulation bills presented to Congress during the Eisenhower years], in the manner of a *deus ex machina*, would relieve them totally and finally of this sudden accretion in their business." (James M. Landis, "Report on Regulatory Agencies to the President-elect," December 1960, p. 7, Transition Files, Box 1072, JFKL.)

85. Landis to the President, February 20, 1961.

public was "beginning to approach the figure of one billion dollars"; this estimate was later revised upward to about $1.2 billion.[86]

But this was not the only evidence of unsatisfactory regulatory performance. Delays in the FPC were held to be responsible for holding up pipeline construction permits valued at $800 million.[87] In addition uncertainties about rate schedules were estimated to have reduced investment in pipelines by the order of $100 million. In Landis's judgment, this was "a sad matter in these days of unemployment."[88]

In general form the President's Special Message to the Congress, April 13, 1961, addressed these matters with a suggestion that legislation might be appropriate that would authorize the FPC to exempt small independent producers of natural gas from its jurisdiction. The attention of the commission could thus be concentrated where it mattered most. Only about 17 percent of the nation's natural gas production was supplied by small firms, but their rate applications accounted for over 80 percent of the total case load.[89] This approach followed lines proposed by Senator Paul Douglas as early as 1955 in the first round of post-Phillips debates on natural gas regulation. Though an administration bill with this intent was introduced in 1961, it died in Congress. From the outset Landis had been bearish about its prospects. In his opinion this proposal would "evoke certain opposition on the part of the large producers who want to maintain the screen of the small producers against any effective regulation of their prices."[90]

Another approach to regulatory reform in natural gas was canvassed in 1962. An "anti-pancaking" rule, which would prohibit a pipeline company from filing for a rate increase while a previous rate proceeding was pending, was included in Senate bill 666. Members of the FPC—all five of whom had been appointed by President Kennedy—opposed this provision, though they expressed sympathy for its objective. The FPC preferred instead to approach this problem by revising the statute to permit the period of suspension of a proposed rate increase to be extended from six months to a year. It hoped that such an amendment would largely preclude pancaking by giving the FPC a somewhat longer period to process the cases before it. Opposition to an outright prohibition of pancaking was

86. Landis to Senator Hubert Humphrey, June 19, 1961, White House Central Files, Box 171, JFKL.

87. Ibid.

88. Landis to Kennedy, February 20, 1961.

89. Ibid.

90. Landis to Feldman, May 24, 1961, Feldman Papers, Box 9, JFKL.

registered, however, on grounds that the FPC, despite its best efforts, was unlikely to be able to dispose of the massive backlog it had inherited for some time to come. The commission saw some merit in the argument offered by natural gas companies that "they must secure relief from increasing costs after a reasonable time if they are to remain solvent and if they are to attract the capital required for expansion of facilities for growing gas demands. . . . The natural gas companies can justifiably ask that S. 666, as well as the FPC alternative proposal, must be appraised on the assumption that backlogs will be with us for some years to come."[91] FPC Chairman Joseph C. Swidler also reported: "It is hard for the Commission to forget its responsibility not merely for rates but for supply and for the economic soundness of the industry. We are dealing with the fifth largest industry in the country, representing an investment of over 20 billion dollars and serving 34 million consumers." He did not feel assured that an outright prohibition against pancaking "would not gravely jeopardize the industry." In this connection he noted that

rate cases which have been disposed of in recent months have resulted in refunds of about forty per cent of the suspended amounts. Put another way, on the average, the natural gas companies were entitled to about sixty per cent of the amount of the increases for which they filed and some of them to much larger proportions of their filings. I see little basis on which we could provide positive assurances that the natural gas companies' justified need for rate increases is likely to be different in the future.[92]

Proposals submitted in 1962 to amend the Natural Gas Act were again stalled in the legislative pipeline. Within its authority, the FPC did attempt to accelerate the disposition of natural gas cases. In November 1962 it introduced major changes in its regulations that were designed to speed up the processing of petitions for rate increases by requiring companies to submit more detailed information at the time of filing. These measures were intended to eliminate many of the lengthy field investigations that would otherwise be required of the commission's staff. By early 1963 the commission could report that cases disposed of since July 1, 1961 (when the influence of Kennedy appointees to the FPC began to be felt) had "brought to $350 million the amount of refunds by pipeline companies . . . and reductions of approximately $62 million per year in their rates for the future. At the same time, independent producers have been ordered to refund more than $29 million, and to reduce their rates by approximately

91. Joseph C. Swidler, Chairman of the Federal Power Commission, to Feldman, February 15, 1962, White House Central Files, Box 489, JFKL.
92. Ibid.

$21 million per year."[93] It could also be reported that the commission had approved "the largest pipeline rate refund order in its history" in December 1962 when ordering the Tennessee Gas Transmission Company to refund more than $134 million.[94]

Nuclear Energy in the Policy Mix

The inauguration of the Kennedy administration brought high hopes that the civilian nuclear power program would be advanced in the scale of national priorities. Throughout the Eisenhower years, the Democratic members of the Joint Committee on Atomic Energy had held that a Republican administration had been much too cautious in its budgetary commitments to civilian nuclear power development and much too confident that the private sector would take the lead in applying this promising new technology. A change in political leadership seemed to suggest that more dynamic government initiatives would now be undertaken.

Like its predecessor, the Kennedy administration was mindful of budgetary constraints. Formally, it lent its support to the prime candidate in 1961 for nuclear power appropriations—the new production reactor at Hanford, Washington.[95] But it was not overly dismayed when the project died in the House of Representatives. Meanwhile, the Atomic Energy Commission—with explicit presidential approval—made some modest administrative changes designed at least in part to make nuclear power generation more attractive to private investors. Its base charges for enriched and depleted uranium were reduced from $13.50 a pound of natural uranium oxide to $8 a pound. At the same time, however, the use charge rate on nuclear material leased by the AEC to private firms was

93. Swidler to the President, January 14, 1963, White House Central Files, Box 171, JFKL.

94. Ibid. The pancaking of charges by this company had caught the President's eye in the early days of his administration. Kennedy sent a note to James Landis on February 15, 1961: "Kefauver and Gore informed me that there have been five increases in rates in the Tennessee gas transmission without any action by the Federal Power Commission. Are they getting away with murder? If so, what can we do about it?" Kennedy to Landis, February 15, 1961, President's Office Files, Box 78, JFKL.

95. This project had been authorized during the Eisenhower years for the production of weapon-grade plutonium, but the additional expense required to adapt the facility to civilian power production had then been regarded as lacking in merit. The Kennedy White House staff reported this phase of the proposal as only "marginal-to-feasible" when judged "from a strictly economic standpoint." Memorandum, "New Production Reactor," March 4, 1961, White House Central Files, Box 10, JFKL.

increased from 4 percent to 4.75 percent a year to reflect an increase in long-term government borrowing rates since these charges were first set in 1954. It was the judgment of AEC Chairman Glenn T. Seaborg that the "net effect" of these revisions would be "a significant reduction in the cost of nuclear power (by several tenths of a mill per kilowatt hour)," though he added that this was "not likely to have a decisive impact on the nuclear-power industry at the present time."[96]

The Kennedy appointees to the AEC were eager to press boldly toward a nuclear future. In public addresses in the autumn of 1961 Chairman Seaborg offered a vision far more ambitious than that presented by his predecessors. His view was that nuclear power should be made competitive in all areas of the country (as opposed to the previously announced goal of economic nuclear power in the higher-cost fuel areas by 1968). Accelerated development was held to be important because of the nation's growth in demand for power and the exhaustibility of its oil and gas reserves. Seaborg added his voice to those who were calling for a national policy on fuel utilization and conservation. His perspective, however, was essentially a technocratic one. Such a policy, in his judgment, should

take into account the available resources, both fossil and nuclear, and the demands upon these resources for electric power, propulsion, industrial process and home heating, chemical and other applications which appear to be essential and inevitable. A policy of this type might, for example, reserve oil for supplying personal type mobile energy requirements, where no suitable substitute exists. Natural gas might be preferred over oil, coal and nuclear fuel for residential heating. Under such priority conditions, nuclear fuel and coal might possibly be better suited for the production of electricity than gas and oil.[97]

He concluded that "it behooves us, therefore, to speed developments which will make nuclear power cheap enough so that it can be selected over other valuable and versatile materials and thus hasten the day when we can realize the many benefits which will undoubtedly be derived from a future national fuels policy."[98]

National defense considerations, Seaborg maintained, strengthened his case. Electrical energy was obviously essential to the nation's survival, yet conventional electric power facilities were highly vulnerable to attack. Nuclear plants, on the other hand, were constructed with containment

96. Seaborg to the President, May 18, 1961, ibid.
97. Glenn L. Seaborg, "The Country's Civilian Reactor Program," speech prepared for delivery to the Association of Land Grant Colleges and Universities, Draft of November 3, 1961, p. 19, ibid., Box 907.
98. Ibid., p. 20.

shieldings which could withstand "war type dangers" without exposing the population to radioactive hazards. Moreover, they could be made still more impregnable if constructed underground, which could be done with "relatively little cost penalty." But the attractiveness of nuclear power was enhanced by another of its characteristics. Conventional electric genera-tion placed heavy demands on a transport system that was also exposed to disruption by enemy action. By contrast, nuclear plants had a "tre-mendous advantage. They can operate for many years with the fuel on hand and when refueling is required, only a token transportation system would be adequate to handle shipments."[99]

Despite the case being made within the AEC, with sympathetic support from the Joint Atomic Energy Committee, proposals to accelerate the nuclear power development program were received less than enthusias-tically elsewhere in the administration. The budget prepared for fiscal year 1963 made no provision for reactor construction. Two projects proposed by the AEC for 1962 had been axed by the Budget Bureau. This deletion was explained by Kenneth R. Hansen, assistant director of the bureau: "We had hoped to receive from AEC last fall a clearer statement of the objectives of the atomic power program and the needs to be met in the context of overall energy needs. We wanted this because the program had never been related to the larger problem of overall needs and resources and because we believed, therefore, that no really rational basis existed for the 1968 timetable which had been established by AEC some years ago." Hansen enumerated the considerations that

appear to underscore the need for a clarification of needs and objectives before launching into further expansion and new construction: (1) Much will be learned from the operation of reactors not yet completed. (2) The short-term 1968 goal, whether rational or not, appears to have been reached already. A private utility in California (Pacific Gas and Electric) proposes, without Gov-ernment financial assistance, to build a 325 megawatt atomic powerplant on the grounds of economic attractiveness. (3) No rational basis has yet been established for intermediate range (say 1980–1990) or long range (twenty-first century) objectives, relative to overall energy needs and resources, in-cluding the coal and oil problems. (4) The true potential of atomic power for extending energy resources lies, not in the perfection of existing types, but rather in much longer-term concepts, such as breeders. . . .[100]

But the AEC had an ally in the Joint Committee on Atomic Energy. Its chairman for 1962, Congressman Chet Holifield of California, com-

99. Quotations in this paragraph are from ibid., p. 17.
100. Hansen to Lee C. White, February 13, 1962, Lee White Papers, Box 2, JFKL. In this context it was further noted that applications of atomic energy to outer space exploration had "taken priority" over civilian atomic power.

plained to the President on February 13, 1962, that "this Administration will be vulnerable when it can be shown that it is de-emphasizing atomic power development more than the previous Eisenhower Administration." He insisted that

the downgrading by the Administration of the atomic power program has gone much too far. As a matter of fact, the technology for atomic power plants is actually looking more promising. During the next couple of years we will be at the stage where we really need to begin some practical demonstrations, both of large scale plants which will be almost economic, and of follow-on prototypes of more advanced systems such as the sodium graphite reactor. . . . In view of the fact that we have invested almost a billion dollars in atomic power development and have only a relatively short way to go to achieve economic nuclear power, I believe it is incumbent upon this Administration to continue efforts to foster atomic power development through the prototype stage. One of the great achievements during your term of office could be the achievement of economic competitive kilowatts from fission. The cost of obtaining such an entirely new and almost inexhaustible source of energy will seem very small a few years from now.[101]

At this point Kennedy elected to follow the recommendation of the Budget Bureau by instructing the AEC to "take a new and hard look at the role of nuclear power in our economy" and to submit a report to him on this matter by September 1, 1962. Its terms of reference were set out as follows in a letter from the President to Chairman Seaborg of March 17, 1962:

Your study should identify the objectives, scope, and content of a nuclear power development program in the light of the Nation's prospective energy needs and resources and advances in alternate means for power generation. It should recommend appropriate steps to assure the proper timing of development and construction of nuclear power projects, including the construction of necessary prototypes. There should, of course, be a continuation of the present fruitful cooperation between Government and industry—public utilities, private utilities, and equipment manufacturers.[102]

It was noted that two related studies were also in existence or in prospect: one by the National Academy of Sciences (conducted at the President's request) on the nation's longer-term energy needs and a study soon to be undertaken by the Federal Power Commission on long-range power requirements.

But concessions were also made to those who pushed for a more

101. Holifield to Kennedy, February 13, 1962, White House Central Files, Box 164, JFKL.
102. Kennedy to Seaborg, March 17, 1962, reprinted in *Nuclear Power Economics—1962 through 1967*, Report of Joint Committee on Atomic Energy, 90 Cong. 2 sess. (GPO, 1968), p. 97.

vigorous approach to nuclear power development. On May 21, 1962, the President transmitted to Congress an amendment to the 1963 budget involving an increase of more than $200 million in the AEC appropriation. Included in this request was provision for detailed studies of the technical and economic attractiveness of a new type of reactor design, as well as funding for the construction of a prototype organic power and heat industrial reactor to be developed in cooperation with private industry.[103] Meanwhile the Hanford, Washington, project (which had been defeated in 1961) was reactivated, though on terms that would not involve federal appropriations to build the power plant nor federal participation in its operation. On this basis the new production reactor won the approval of both houses of Congress and of the President in September 1962.

Though the AEC did not meet the presidential deadline of September 1, 1962, for the completion of its report, it did offer a document in November.[104] Nuclear energy, it was again asserted, was crucial to an invulnerable national defense. Moreover, its economic importance was vital in the face of supply limitations of exhaustible fuel resources. A no less important consideration was that nuclear energy held the key to economic growth in lagging regions of the country. "High cost power areas would no longer exist," it was argued, "since, in the absence of significant fuel transportation expenses, the cost of nuclear power is essentially the same everywhere. This would be an economic boon to areas of high cost fossil fuels and, by enabling them to compete better, should increase the industrial potential of the entire country." This report maintained that "continuation of the Commission's present effort, with some augmentation in support for the power demonstration program, would . . . provide industry with the needed stimulus to build a significant number of large reactors in the near future, would bring nuclear power to a competitive status with conventional power throughout most of the country in the 1970s, and would make breeder reactors economically attractive in the 1980s." By the year 2000 nuclear power could be expected to contribute half of the generating capacity of the country and to satisfy subsequent increments in power demand. This rate of progress in the twenty-first century was held to be "an important step in conservation of the fossil fuels and, unless breeders lagged the converters much more than we pre-

103. "White House Announcement of a Budget Request for the Atomic Energy Commission," White House press release, May 21, 1962, President's Office Files, Box 70, JFKL.

104. U.S. Atomic Energy Commission, "Civilian Nuclear Power: A Report to the President, 1962," reprinted in *Nuclear Power Economics*, pp. 95–252.

dict, would raise no problems in nuclear fuel supplies." Lest producers of conventional fuels be alarmed, it was pointed out (though in a footnote) that FPC estimates suggested that the aggregate demand for power would have grown tenfold by the year 2000; thus "fossil fuel consumption for this purpose would still increase by a factor of from four to five."[105]

For the intermediate term the report called for a construction program in the next twelve years involving seven or eight power-producing prototype reactors (most of which would be financed by the AEC) and assistance to the capital costs of industry for ten to twelve full-scale power plants of improved design. Meanwhile it was expected that industry would carry all the costs of many more units of established design.[106] In the climate of the time this faith seemed to be soundly placed. Late 1962 and 1963 witnessed an apparent breakthrough in the technology of commercially feasible nuclear power. Two of the major electrical manufacturers, General Electric and Westinghouse, competed vigorously in offering to supply entire nuclear generating facilities to utilities at a preestablished price. When the first of these "turnkey" offers was accepted in December 1963 (by the Jersey Central Power and Light Company for its Oyster Creek plant), the new era seemed genuinely to have arrived. It was then asserted that the latest phase in nuclear technology could generate electricity at this site at costs below those of any alternative technique.[107]

Despite the contagion of its optimism, the AEC report of 1962 was hardly an analytic study. It was written in the style of a promoter's prospectus. Nuclear power was depicted as the solution to a host of problems. Not only could its use reduce the drain on exhaustible conventional fuels, it would also spur revitalization of remoter industrial communities and contribute to improvement in the international balance of payments. In his letter transmitting the final version of the AEC report to the President, Chairman Seaborg summed up its reading of the situation with the observation that "nuclear power promises to supply the vast amounts of energy that this Nation will require for many generations to come, and it probably will provide a significant reduction in the national costs for electrical power." In addition, he pointed to yet another consideration favoring supplementary governmental support for the nuclear power

105. The quotations in this paragraph are from ibid., p. 111.
106. Ibid., p. 112.
107. For a useful discussion of the expectations associated with turnkey nuclear power projects, see Irvin C. Bupp and Jean-Claude Derian, *Light Water: How the Nuclear Dream Dissolved* (Basic Books, 1978), especially chap. 2.

program. Unless further new starts on atomic power plants were stimulated, he feared that the "atomic equipment industry will probably dwindle
down to fewer manufacturers than would be desirable for a healthy and
competitive nuclear industry."[108]

If the White House had hoped for a detached appraisal of the nation's
long-run energy position from the AEC, it could only have been disappointed with this document.

The Interdepartmental Energy Study Group and the National Power Survey

The AEC report on civilian nuclear power, transmitted to the President
in its final form on November 20, 1962, failed to meet White House
needs. The Budget Bureau's concerns about the adequacy of the rationale
for an accelerated nuclear program had not been systematically addressed.
The AEC had chosen instead to lobby for greater appropriations without
demonstrating their necessity. But this appeal was not likely to find ready
favor with an administration attempting to restrain expenditures and finding other programs, such as the exploration of outer space, more compelling.

Kennedy's response to the AEC report was to put the issue on "hold"
by commissioning another study. A presidential directive of February 15,
1963, created an Interdepartmental Energy Study Group to be chaired by
the director of the Office of Science and Technology, with the chairman of
the Council of Economic Advisers serving as vice-chairman; other members were to be drawn from the AEC, OEP, FPC, Bureau of the Budget,
National Science Foundation, and Departments of Interior and Commerce. The charge to this group was to undertake a "comprehensive study
. . . of the development and utilization of our total energy resources to aid
in determining the most effective allocation of our research and development resources." More particularly this group was directed to consider
questions the AEC had "considered inappropriate to cover in its report"
or had dealt with only implicitly; that is, "the possible effects of major
research efforts on the economics of nonnuclear energy sources, or on improved transmission methods for either nuclear or nonnuclear produced
energy" and "the size and characteristics of future demands for energy,
possible price trends for fuels, and available alternative technical ap-

108. Seaborg to Kennedy, November 20, 1963, reprinted in ibid., p. 96.

proaches to the problem of supplying the long-term energy requirements of the Nation."[109] An interim report from the interdepartmental group was requested by September 1, 1963.

This disposition of matters called for some interpretation to the nuclear power enthusiasts in Congress. Jerome Wiesner, director of the Office of Science and Technology, supplied it in testimony before the Joint Committee on Atomic Energy on February 20, 1963. Though "highly interesting and significant," the AEC report, he maintained, needed "to be viewed in the broader context of our total energy picture." The question remaining to be answered was "what degree of urgency the Nation should attach to nuclear power development in the light of the projected availability of conventional energy sources, which should last well into the next century."[110] The Interdepartmental Energy Study Group was designed to address it. In the executive branch Wiesner subsequently counseled that it would "seem inadvisable to make any major public statements on Administration policy on energy developments in general, and on nuclear power developments in particular" before the results of the new study were available to the President.[111]

At its first meeting on March 11, 1963, the Steering Committee of the Interdepartmental Energy Study Group agreed that its central objective should be "to provide a broad, long-term strategy for research and development related to energy, based on most fruitful apparent opportunities for pay-offs." But opinions diverged on the particulars. Some members held that projections twenty-five years forward were too long, while others maintained that a time perspective of less than half a century was too short.[112] By mid-July the plan of the study was still a point of contention. In the judgment of William M. Capron, the Council of Economic Advisers staff member working most closely with the Steering Committee, "the outline is a shopping list—it includes every conceivable topic under the heading 'energy.' " He further noted that the economic discussion was

109. Memorandum, Kennedy to the Secretary of the Interior and others, February 15, 1963, reprinted in *Development, Growth, and State of the Atomic Energy Industry*, Hearings before the Joint Committee on Atomic Energy, 88 Cong. 1 sess. (GPO, 1963), pt. 1, pp. 69–70.

110. Testimony of Jerome B. Wiesner in *Development, Growth, and State of the Atomic Energy Industry*, Hearings, pp. 56–57.

111. Wiesner to McGeorge Bundy, May 3, 1963, White House Central Files, Box 10, JFKL.

112. "Office of Science and Technology Summary, March 11, 1963 Meeting of Steering Committee of the Interdepartmental Energy Study," Walter Heller Papers, Box 38, JFKL.

"relegated to a separate chapter which looks as if it would be a primer on principles, not an application of economic analysis to the subject matter of the report."[113]

When the first draft of the report (prepared under the general direction of Ali Bulent Cambel, head of the Department of Mechanical Engineering at Northwestern University) was circulated for comment in late September 1963, neither its form nor its content was entirely satisfying to the agencies represented on the Steering Committee. Though it was a massive compendium of technical details, it lacked something in integration. Nor was it clear that the findings were internally consistent. On the one hand it suggested that a major push should be mounted in energy research and development (particularly in the nuclear sector); on the other, the findings indicated that energy supplies were likely to be ample for the foreseeable future. No resolution of these perspectives was readily in sight. Disputations over various drafts of the Interdepartmental Energy Study Group were to outlive President Kennedy.[114]

The Approach to Electric Power from Conventional Sources

Though debate about the appropriate place of nuclear energy commanded most of the limelight in deliberations about the nation's long-range power supplies, consideration of the future of electricity generated by conventional techniques still retained a place on the agenda. In the early going the Kennedy administration made it clear that it was more sympathetic than its predecessor had been to an enlarged federal role in this sphere. The President's special message on natural resources in February 1961 reaffirmed a federal responsibility for the development of hydroelectric power "in all multiple-purpose river projects where optimum economic use of the water justifies such action" and asserted that the price of federal power would be set "to encourage widespread use and to prevent monopolization."[115] The strategy being put in place at this time, however, assigned significant weight to a further governmental function:

113. William M. Capron to CEA Chairman Walter W. Heller, July 17, 1963, ibid.

114. On the fate of this inquiry, see chapter 5.

115. "Special Message to the Congress on Natural Resources, February 23, 1961," *Public Papers: Kennedy, 1961* (GPO, 1962), p. 118.

the use of federal authority as a catalyst to efficiency in the nation's electric power system. This objective, it was maintained, could best be served by stimulating the development of regional interties in the distribution of electric power.

In line with this thinking the secretary of the interior was charged to prepare plans for "national cooperative pooling of electric power, both public and private."[116] Priority in this exercise was assigned to the study of interconnections linking the Pacific Northwest and the Pacific Southwest, though investigations were also projected into the feasibility of other regional interties (for example, between the Bonneville Power Administration Area and the Missouri Basin, between the Southwest Power Administration Area and the Missouri Basin, and between the Southwest Power Administration Area and the Tennessee Valley Authority). In the course of this activity the Department of the Interior opened discussions in 1961 with nonfederal utilities on the collaborative use of transmission facilities by private and public systems.[117]

The vision of a fully coordinated national power network was given further impetus with the launching of the National Power Survey by the FPC in January 1962. One of the central goals of this undertaking was to demonstrate the economies that could be realized through integrated planning and "to encourage all power systems to accelerate their coordination efforts."[118] Though the results of this inquiry were not published until after Kennedy's death, its findings seemed abundantly to support the expectation that a federal commitment to promote interties between regions and between privately and publicly owned facilities was wise. On the assumption that the nation's electric power requirements would more than triple between 1962 and 1980, it was calculated that full coordination would permit power needs in 1980 to be satisfied at costs more than 25 percent below those that would be incurred if the same output were to be delivered under the conditions of 1962. Coordination would yield a significant narrowing of differential costs of electricity between regions. (These calculations presupposed that a downward trend in the delivered costs of fuels used in electricity generation could be expected in most

116. Ibid.

117. Orren Beaty, Jr., to Lee C. White, "Department of the Interior: Preliminary Statement on Plans and Programs Responsive to the President's Special Message on Natural Resources, February 23, 1961," November 29, 1961, White Papers, Box 12, JFKL.

118. Federal Power Commission, *National Power Survey, 1964* (GPO, 1964), vol. 1, p. 29.

locations and that some 13.3 percent of the nation's generating capacity would be nuclear by 1980.)[119] Even so, this prospect was not universally applauded. Spokesmen for the American Public Power Association, for example, questioned whether or not the savings projected from interconnections would be passed on to consumers and registered their fear that this trend would accelerate mergers and promote dangerous concentrations of economic power in the hands of private utilities.[120] Concern from the same quarters was also expressed about a potential threat to the public interest in the arrangements being worked out by the Department of the Interior for the "wheeling" of power generated at federal facilities in the Upper Colorado River Storage Project over transmission lines owned by private companies.

While the power policies of the Kennedy administration were distinguished more by enthusiasm for efficiency gains through coordination than by an interest in funding major additions to capacity, two new hydroelectric power schemes still captured its attention: a Columbia River Basin project (requiring collaboration with Canada) and the Passamaquoddy tidal power project (proposed for siting in the bay on the U.S.-Canadian border between Maine and New Brunswick). Action on the first of these was stalled by the failure of the Canadian Parliament to ratify the Columbia River Treaty, which had received the endorsement of the U.S. Senate in 1961. Though the Passamaquoddy project (in combination with the construction of a hydroelectric station on the Upper Saint John River in Maine) was supported by the Department of the Interior as "both desirable and economically feasible" in mid-1963,[121] it was greeted with skepticism elsewhere in the executive branch. The Army Corps of Engineers took the position that alternative projects "would produce power more economically."[122] This conclusion was shared by the Department of Commerce, which maintained that other means for meeting the power requirements of upper New England, particularly atomic energy, had not been satisfactorily evaluated.[123]

119. Ibid., pp. 62, 215, 285–88.

120. In this connection see the speech of Alex Radin, General Manager of the American Public Power Association, to the Conference of the California Municipal Utilities Association, March 8, 1962, White Papers, Box 15, JFKL.

121. Udall to the President, July 1, 1963, President's Office Files, Box 80, JFKL.

122. Major General R. G. MacDonnell, Acting Chief of Engineers, to Cyrus R. Vance, Secretary of the Army, July 3, 1963, White Papers, Box 14, JFKL.

123. Franklin D. Roosevelt, Jr., Acting Secretary of Commerce, to Elmer B. Staats, Deputy Director, Bureau of the Budget, September 13, 1963, ibid., Box 15.

A Closing Word

The senior leadership of the Kennedy administration liked to think in terms of grand strategies, and it managed to formulate them for the conduct of macroeconomic policies. The Kennedy years also generated considerable discussion about "comprehensive" and "coordinated" approaches to the energy sector. But there was a disjunction between rhetoric and reality. At the highest levels of government energy was not perceived as a significant economic concern. The problems of various components of the energy sector were instead regarded primarily as challenges to political management. This attitude, in turn, was sustained by the widely held presupposition that the adequacy of energy supply over the longer term was not a problem. If any mistakes were made in the short term, they would be erased by the era of technological salvation that was about to dawn.

The Kennedy years certainly did not lack for governmentally sponsored inquiries into longer-range energy strategies. But most of them were set in motion primarily as devices for pressure-group containment. The search for a national fuels policy in 1961 (which the White House was content to pass to the Senate) was designed to deflect some of the pressures from coal. The work of various petroleum study committees and the manner in which their findings were recast, deferred, or ignored reflected an attempt to minimize disturbance to the complex of interests with a stake in oil import policies. Similarly the charge to the Interdepartmental Energy Study Group in 1963 was inspired as a technique for containing the AEC's expansionist aspirations. Of the several inquiries into energy matters in these years, only the National Power Survey represented a systematic exercise in forward planning. Its scope, however, was necessarily restricted and its calculations accepted the prevailing premise that the prices of primary fuels would continue to decline.

Up to November 22, 1963, the impact of the intellectual energies applied to energy problems was slight. Only cosmetic changes were made in the programs the Kennedy administration inherited. Whether or not the outcome would have been different if the Kennedy presidency had not been prematurely terminated is a question history will never answer. During the thousand days, however, energy policy for most purposes was a strategy of studied inaction.

CHAPTER FIVE

Energy Policy in the Johnson Administration: Logical Order versus Economic Pluralism

JAMES L. COCHRANE

ENERGY is the capacity to do work or, more narrowly, to power mechanical equipment and provide heat in other economically useful ways. The conventional list of nonhuman energy sources embraces a wide variety of materials, from hydrocarbons, such as petroleum, natural gas, and coal to nuclear fuels, falling water, and sunlight. (Although often referred to as a secondary energy source, electricity is a method of converting and transmitting energy.) During the 1960s the utilization patterns of these sources were expected to continue into the indefinite future, without price increases. Therefore little effort was made to focus on *interaction* among sources. It is unfortunate that this was so but not surprising. The central theme of this essay is that the Johnson years represent shaky and hesitant steps in the transition from individual fuel policies to energy policies. During the 1960s the need for logical order—an internally consistent

I AM GRATEFUL to Harry J. Middleton, Director of the Lyndon B. Johnson Library in Austin, Texas, for his encouragement and material assistance, and to the Library's staff. Phyllis Ball of Special Collections of the University of Arizona Library assisted with the Udall papers. Richard L. Hewlett, historian of the U.S. Department of Energy, made it possible to gain access to former Interior Department materials now in the custody of the Department of Energy. Robert W. Anderson, records officer in the Office of the Secretary of the Interior Department, not only made the Office of the Secretary files from the 1960s available but also suggested ways of locating records from the 1960s no longer in Interior Department custody. Preliminary drafts of this essay were read by William J. Barber, George Fumich, Craufurd D. Goodwin, Gary L. Griepentrog, Stewart L. Udall, Lee C. White, and Joseph A. Yager. Their advice and assistance, along with that of Janet Hardy, is greatly appreciated.

In the footnotes to this chapter the Lyndon B. Johnson Library is referred to as LBJL.

energy policy—was increasingly evident. The distortions caused by cling-
ing to policies focused solely on one particular energy sector became obvious. More people recognized that economic pluralism, a narrow sectoral
orientation, would have to give way to a broader view. Such a broader
view called for recognition that a healthy and orderly domestic petroleum
market required knowledge of interrelations among energy sources. And
each energy source had its protective belt of policies and bureaucratic apparatus.

Missed Chances

During the 1960s various federal agencies served the energy needs of
their constituents. The Atomic Energy Commission promoted nuclear
power for generating electricity. Subcomponents of the Interior Department burrowed into specific areas of responsibility; the Office of Coal Research served coal users and producers, while the Office of Oil and Gas
served the petroleum and natural gas companies. The State Department
consistently took a deep interest in the international activities of the large,
integrated petroleum firms, particularly in the Middle East and most particularly after the Middle East war in June 1967. The Federal Power Commission devoted considerable effort to large-scale production of cheap
power as well as to the technology and politics of transmitting power from
one area of the country to another, especially from the Pacific Northwest
to urban California. But no central administrative unit in the executive
branch devoted itself to unifying these disparate activities. In the absence
of such a mechanism the Johnson administration failed to develop a coherent energy program. There is, in retrospect, a program, but it is an ex
post amalgam of individual operating practices of various independent
government agencies, each more or less independent of the other. Nevertheless, there were at least two exceptions to this general state of affairs.

First, the Council of Economic Advisers was not bound by a constituency. The CEA, if and when it chose to do so, could serve as the focal
point for the development of a Johnson administration energy policy.
Some CEA activities during this period moved the executive branch in the
right direction, but the CEA was small and overextended and lacked sufficient clout to overcome the entrenched powers. The Interior Department's assistant secretary for mineral resources, for example, enjoyed the
firm and steady support of a well-organized external constituency.

The second exception to this administrative vacuum was the Office of Science and Technology. During the Johnson years the OST was as close to being a focal point for energy policy as any organization in the executive branch. But OST officials did not have the internal weight or external leverage to accomplish much. They tried nonetheless and provided some embryos for the next administration to fertilize.

The OST and Energy Policy

Throughout the Johnson years the OST was led by Donald F. Hornig. A short time before President Kennedy was assassinated, he announced Hornig's appointment as his special assistant for science and technology, succeeding Jerome B. Wiesner. After a period of being lost in the transition chaos, Hornig was appointed and confirmed and took office on January 24, 1964.[1] While Hornig was preparing to join the administration in late 1963 the "science structure" of the Executive Office of the President was firmly established into a quadripartite apparatus. Hornig actually inherited four hats from Wiesner. He was the president's special assistant for science and technology, a post created by the Eisenhower administration in autumn 1957 after the sputnik shock. Second, Hornig chaired the President's Science Advisory Committee (PSAC), created in November 1957 by transferring the Science Advisory Committee of the Office of Defense Mobilization to the White House. (During this transfer James R. Killian, Jr. was given the "science job.")[2] Third, Hornig was responsible for lead-

1. Hornig received an undergraduate degree (1940) and a Ph.D. (1943) from Harvard. During 1943–44 he worked on explosives at Woods Hole, Massachusetts. In 1944 he moved to Los Alamos, New Mexico, to work on a triggering device for the atomic bomb under the direction of Robert Oppenheimer. Between 1946 and 1957 he was a chemistry professor at Brown University, maintaining his government ties, working on such things as the application of infrared to warfare and lobbying for the Sidewinder missile. In 1957 he moved to Princeton University, in 1960 President Eisenhower asked him to join the Science Advisory Board, and in 1961 he served on a Kennedy space policy task force. After serving through the entire Johnson administration Hornig became vice-president of Eastman Kodak and professor of chemistry at the University of Rochester. In the early 1970s he became president of Brown University. Following a tour at Brown, he joined the faculty of Harvard's School of Public Health.

2. The PSAC consisted of about twenty people who had performed well on its ad hoc external panels. Committee work absorbed about forty days a year; appointments were for four years. Committee members represented one of four categories: general science, industry, life sciences and medicine, and behavioral sciences (added autumn 1966). After repeated discussions two-thirds of the PSAC agreed to support "the nomination of a well-known economist with experience in government." (They

ing the Federal Council for Science and Technology, a product of the 1958 PSAC report *Strengthening American Science*.[3] The council was an internal operation, drawn from agencies such as the OST, the National Aeronautics and Space Administration, the National Science Foundation, and the Atomic Energy Commission, with observers from the less technical portions of the executive branch such as the CEA. Hornig's fourth responsibility was the OST itself, established on June 8, 1962, by Kennedy Reorganization Plan 2. Hornig provided more leadership than anyone during the Johnson years in the search for a policy and a policy apparatus to supersede the bits and pieces of administrative practice current at the time. But even before Hornig came to the OST several lines of work were being pursued that would fall under the general heading of "energy policy," as William Barber noted in the preceding chapter.

In August 1961 the Senate Committee on Interior and Insular Affairs began an assessment of available information on energy. The committee established an analytical unit, the National Fuels and Energy Study Group, that was fully operational by November 1961 and worked for approximately ten months, submitting its report to the committee on September 7, 1962.[4] The Interior Department assembled an internal group to assist and react to the Senate inquiry, and the department's Ad Hoc National Energy Policy Staff held its first meeting in January 1962. The meeting was initially run by the assistant secretary for mineral resources, John M. Kelly.[5] Kelly briefly outlined the concept of the energy policy study as he and Secretary of the Interior Stewart Udall saw it. The primary mission of the ad hoc staff was to have "the departmental position prepared, or in preparation, by the time the Senate's National Fuels and Energy

---

had Carl Kaysen in mind.) The idea went nowhere, however, for the one-third against the idea was a *strongly* negative minority. In autumn 1967 "the committee agreed, as a matter of principle, to recommend the addition of one social scientist with roots in both the physical and social sciences": they had Herbert Simon in mind and Simon was appointed. (Office of Science and Technology, "Administrative History," vol. 1 (1968), LBJL. Toward the end of the Johnson administration each unit in the executive branch was ordered to prepare an administrative history as well as a collection of critical documents.)

3. U.S. President's Science Advisory Committee, *Strengthening American Science* (Government Printing Office, 1958).

4. *Report of the National Fuels and Energy Study Group on an Assessment of Available Information on Energy in the United States,* Senate Committee on Interior and Insular Affairs, 87 Cong. 2 sess. (GPO, 1962).

5. Kelly was a highly respected petroleum engineer with substantial government and industry experience in New Mexico.

Study" was complete.[6] Kelly turned the meeting over to Thomas B. Nolan, director of the Geological Survey, who was to serve as staff chairman. The ad hoc group consisted of the Interior Department's operational chiefs, including the directors of the Bureau of Mines, the Office of Coal Research, and the Office of Oil and Gas and their deputies. The ad hoc staff achieved its primary mission, working in harness with the staff of the Senate committee, although at times the two groups were at odds.

The Interdepartmental Energy Study

During 1962 the leadership of the Interior Department found it convenient to expand the mission of the Ad Hoc National Energy Policy Staff. For example, Secretary Udall agreed on April 25, 1962, to cooperate with the Atomic Energy Commission in preparing a report on the role of nuclear power in the U.S. economy. The AEC was particularly interested in obtaining data on fossil fuel resources, their transport costs, the cost of using them to generate electric power, consumption rates by consumer class, and anticipated interconnection patterns for the large electrical grids. The Office of Oil and Gas, operating through the ad hoc staff, prepared a report for the AEC, "Supplies, Costs and Uses of the Fossil Fuels," transmitted on June 29, 1962. The Interior Department was quite proud of this report and decided to make mimeographed copies public in February 1963. The AEC submitted the report to President Kennedy on November 20, 1962, and simultaneously released it with a separate volume of appendixes to the public.[7]

Interaction between the Interior Department staff and the AEC staff during the production of these documents reflected the basic conflict of interest between the two groups. They disagreed substantially on some very basic numbers. The AEC considered the department's estimates of potential fossil fuel reserves too optimistic. Certainly these estimates were larger than similar ones received from the Federal Council for Science and Technology. Internally the Interior Department staff explained the discrepancies by pointing out that both the department and the OST used the same basic data provided by the Geological Survey but that significant definitional problems were involved in sorting out what the data really

6. Minutes of the Ad Hoc National Energy Policy Staff Meeting, January 25, 1962, Files from the Department of the Interior's Energy Policy Staff, 1962, currently in the custody of the Department of Energy.

7. U.S. Atomic Energy Commission, *Civilian Nuclear Power: A Report to the President, 1962* (GPO, November 20, 1962).

meant. In August 1962 the energy policy staff advised Assistant Secretary Kelly that some of the misunderstanding was because the Interior Department was still modifying its "philosophy as to what constitutes a resource." The staff was concerned that the AEC would fail to recognize that U.S. potential resources of the fossil fuels were enormous and that there was every reason to believe that technology could be developed to make these resources economically exploitable.[8]

This flurry of activity that involved the Interior Department, the OST, and the Senate committee and that resulted in other contemporary studies led Kennedy on February 15, 1963, to order a large-scale interdepartmental energy study.[9] After receiving the AEC civilian nuclear power report on November 20, 1962, President Kennedy asked the director of the Budget Bureau to recommend the most effective ways of dealing with the issues addressed in the AEC report. The staff of the Executive Office of the President, including key personnel at the Bureau of the Budget, the OST, the National Security Council, and the CEA, considered the report a most useful document but "greeted with some consternation . . . a flavor in the AEC report" that suggested the AEC was seriously contemplating a major, long-term commitment of federal funds to nuclear research and development. It was not clear that massive *public* expenditures "would be necessary or desirable to secure the future advantages of nuclear power."[10] This was a continuation of the public versus private nuclear power industry debate that had soured relations between Eisenhower's AEC and pronuclear Democrats in Congress. AEC Chairman Glenn T. Seaborg had transmitted a report to President Kennedy recommending movement toward a nuclear future based on a possible program through the mid-1970s that would include the construction of seven or eight power-producing prototype reactors, half-advanced converters and half breeders, plus as-

8. Memorandum, Energy Policy Staff to Assistant Secretary for Mineral Resources, "Estimates of Potential Fossil Fuel Resources," August 23, 1962, Files of the Office of Oil and Gas, 1962, in custody of the Department of Energy.

9. Seven special reports on natural resources had been produced for the Committee on Natural Resources of the National Academy of Sciences–National Research Council, including one by an energy resources study group chaired by M. King Hubbert (*Energy Resources,* NAS-NRC, 1962).

10. OST, "Administrative History," vol. 2, Documentary Supplement, "Energy Policy." CEA staff economist Michael Brewer examined the November 1962 AEC study for Chairman Walter W. Heller. The CEA concluded that the AEC study "could not be evaluated without a much broader assessment of energy demand and supply," helping to make the case for the White House to direct the president's science adviser and the CEA to prepare a broad-based energy study. Council of Economic Advisers, "Administrative History," vol. 1, chap. 5, LBJL.

sisting the private sector in building about a dozen full-scale power plants of gradually improving design. Specific development programs, especially at the breeder sites, would be coupled with a general research and development effort to develop the underlying technology. In short, the AEC was prepared to lead the charge into a nuclear future.

Responding to Kennedy's request, Budget Director Kermit Gordon had Assistant Director Charles L. Schultze prepare a draft presidential memorandum, working with the OST and the CEA. Gordon, Walter Heller of the CEA, and Wiesner decided that the memorandum should designate the OST director as chairman of an Interdepartmental Steering Committee to explore the foundations and implications of the AEC report.

President Kennedy directed the following to form a committee, with the OST director as chairman and Walter Heller as vice-chairman: the secretaries of the interior and of commerce; the chairmen of the AEC, the CEA, and the Federal Power Commission; the directors of the Bureau of the Budget, the National Science Foundation, the OST, and the Office of Emergency Planning. As time passed Defense Secretary Robert S. McNamara was added to the group responsible for implementing President Kennedy's memorandum. This group of ten formed the Interdepartmental Energy Steering Committee that operated in an on-again-off-again fashion for the next three years.

In response to the directive of February 15, 1963, the Interdepartmental Energy Study Group formed a large consortium of consultants under the leadership of Ali Bulent Cambel, an expert in gas dynamics and head of the Department of Mechanical Engineering at Northwestern University. The economics side of the external research was directed by Robert Strotz of Northwestern University. The basic organization plan of the internal and external personnel of the Interdepartmental Energy Study Group called for the OST and Cambel to be responsible for the overall study and for the technical side of energy matters, and for the CEA and Strotz to be responsible for the economics of energy. William Capron, CEA staff economist, played a major role in launching this study as well as serving as initial liaison between Strotz and the government. When Capron left the CEA in the fall of 1963 Edwin S. Mills became CEA liaison with Cambel and the staffs of the other steering committee members. In 1966 Paul MacAvoy replaced Mills.

Throughout 1963 and 1964 the executive branch participants in the study attempted to reach agreement on a single statement pertaining to federal policies in energy research and development. Meanwhile the

Cambel work proceeded. (During the 1964 presidential election campaign Cambel took time out to serve in a group called Scientists and Technicians for LBJ.)

The external Cambel-Strotz work as well as the internal Interdepartmental Energy Steering Committee work was essentially complete by the summer of 1964, although it would be argued over until the autumn of 1966. The Cambel-Strotz work was intensely debated at a staff level during 1963 and 1964, with everyone taking offense at something. Although Cambel's report was formally transmitted to Hornig on June 5, 1964, it would not be published until the following year.

Cambel was a prodigious worker and drew heavily from the staffs of government agencies as well as from colleagues at Northwestern. By the end of summer in 1963 a 1,200-page, double-spaced, typewritten manuscript had been prepared—an encyclopedic review of both the state of the art and the apparent opportunities in every conceivable aspect of energy production and use. Cambel and his colleagues buttressed the view of the future underlying the 1962 AEC report. They advocated a major public effort in energy research and development, particularly in nuclear breeder reactors.

The Cambel document went through an extensive process of internal analysis. At the CEA, for example, James T. Bonnen provided Walter Heller with a six-page, single-spaced evaluation, with special reference to the economic content of the report. Bonnen observed something that would plague the drafters of the report throughout its gestation: "The present draft is far too long, and not well organized or focused. One is left with no clear rationale for one matter being taken up and another omitted. I suspect that the many consulting panels' reports were simply pieced together with little or no editing." Bonnen informed Heller that the report's basic conclusion was that the United States had "adequate energy supplies in view for the foreseeable future with no increase in . . . prices." This result led the authors of the report to wonder about the need for government research and development in energy, including the impregnable nuclear program. In fiscal year 1964 government energy R&D was about $310 million, of which $244 million was accounted for by the AEC, a probable imbalance. Bonnen had a wide range of reservations about the draft report including the use of a 12 percent interest rate in benefit-cost computation of government R&D investment, based on the argument that "the funds come from industry sources in absence of Federal expenditure and that the opportunity costs must be translated through a 52 percent marginal corporate tax rate." Bonnen also questioned whether the CEA would want its share of a proposed tripartite body consisting of the CEA, OST, and Budget Bureau and known as the Advisory Commission for Energy Research and Development.[11]

The difficulties continued through 1964. The reaction of AEC Commissioner James T. Ramey is indicative of the difficulties associated with getting material everyone could accept and keeping the multidepartmental work moving, avoiding the obvious trap that some agencies would feel less consulted and less pleased with the chapters than other agencies. Ramey informed Hornig that "although each successive draft of these chapters represents an improvement, the chapters still do not present a comprehensive and objective discussion of the problems involved in estimating resources and applying economic analyses to energy research and development problems." Commissioner Ramey argued that in the AEC's opinion "the penalties to our society of over-estimating our energy resources and under-estimating their costs may be considerably greater than the costs we may incur by working somewhat harder to assure abundant energy resources at low cost." The AEC staff's reaction to Strotz's work was that it was founded on an exaggeration of available fossil fuel resources and overoptimism about the emergence of new discovery and production techniques. The AEC argued that the Department of the Interior's estimates of fossil fuel resources, particularly oil and coal, were perennially shown to be gross exaggerations. The AEC staff was concerned about this because they believed there was more risk in failing to develop "optimal energy policies" if resources were overstated than if they were understated.[12]

By early November 1964 Hornig was able to send a "very preliminary draft" of a steering committee statement and galley proofs of the Cambel Report to his nine committee colleagues. He asked for written comment by November 30.[13] As the winter of 1964–65 wore on, the Cambel Report generated little enthusiasm. In mid-January 1965 Edwin Mills of Gardner Ackley's CEA staff met with Budget Director Schultze and Robert Bar-

---

11. Bonnen to Heller, October 8, 1963, CEA Microfilm, Roll 6, LBJL.

12. Ramey to Hornig, September 30, 1964, with attachments, CEA Microfilm, Roll 22, LBJL.

13. Hornig to Interdepartmental Steering Committee, November 4, 1964, ibid. The draft steering committee statement was written by Stephen L. McDonald of the University of Texas for then CEA Chairman Heller to be transmitted via Sam H. Schurr of Resources for the Future, Inc. The McDonald draft was politicized by the committee. (McDonald interview with the author, August 4, 1978.)

low of Hornig's OST staff. Mills advised Ackley that the report was "in pretty bad shape."[14] On January 5, 1966, Hornig sent an "extensively revised" draft steering committee statement to his colleagues and called a meeting for January 24. He hoped it would "be possible to bring the study to a satisfactory conclusion either at this meeting or as soon thereafter as humanly possible." But the "as soon thereafter" turned out to be the better part of a year.[15]

Election Interlude: The Resources Task Force

During the 1964 campaign the Johnson administration created many task forces designed to achieve several simultaneous objectives. First, the process engaged a variety of active Americans in analyzing problems in which they had demonstrated special interest and expertise. This represented an extraordinary mobilization of talent and gave the Johnson candidacy an enviable combination; incumbency coupled with a massive harnessing of new ideas and fresh legislative thrusts, with the activists kept active in wholesome, output-oriented pursuits. The second, and explicitly stated, mission of the task forces was to provide a series of recommendations in virtually every area in which federal policy could touch. The task forces were to produce statements of problems with concrete suggestions about how these problems might be solved either directly by administrative action or indirectly by executive branch submission of appropriate legislation to Congress.

One of these election year task forces was given the job of preparing a report entitled "Resource Policies for a Great Society." This task force, chaired by Joseph L. Fisher, President of Resources for the Future, Inc., included several other people from RFF, including Sam H. Schurr. Lee White of President Johnson's staff and William Capron, then of the Budget Bureau, served as liaison between the task force and the Executive Office of the President. The Interior Department and the Agriculture Department were represented on the task force. On November 11, 1964, immediately after the Johnson landslide over Senator Barry Goldwater, the task force submitted a ninety-page report on natural resources to the President.

14. Mills to Ackley, January 18, 1965, CEA Microfilm, Roll 22, LBJL.
15. Hornig to Interdepartmental Energy Study Steering Committee, January 5, 1966, ibid.

The report covered numerous resource policies ranging from needs for improved forestland management to pollution and flood control. The task force offered eleven basic categories of recommendations based on areas identified as policy issues; the eleventh one was energy policy. The task force began with the premise that it was "important to realize that there is widespread substitutability among the Nation's basic energy resources —coal, oil, natural gas, water power and nuclear power. As a result, policies affecting any one of these resources will inevitably also produce important consequences for the others."[16]

Task force members realized that the post–World War II growth areas for primary energy sources in the United States were oil and natural gas, which were far less abundant than coal. They perceived that a major problem facing the United States was how the continued growth in demand for liquid and gaseous fuels could be met. Once this particular problem was introduced, they addressed a bold list of policy fields, including national security, foreign trade, R&D, and regulatory practices. They noted that restrictions on crude oil imports ran counter to general U.S. foreign trade policy. In addition the restrictions on crude oil importation did not serve the interests of "friendly nations which are economically dependent upon their export trade in oil." Also, it was recognized that the import restrictions led to Americans paying higher prices for crude oil products. The task force was greatly concerned that natural gas, the fuel in most limited supply, was also the fastest growing component of U.S. primary fuel.[17]

The task force recommendations were shaped by the members' belief in the need for a special presidential commission on energy policy to achieve a set of goals, including the preparation of a statement of the national objectives of U.S. energy policies. The task force argued that it would be undesirable to have members of the industries involved in the commission and provided the President and his advisers with six short papers dealing with a representative sample of problems a presidential energy policy commission might consider.

The first of these short issue papers was directed to the Cambel line of inquiry, federal energy R&D expenditures. The main federal effort had been in the area of nuclear power, and assuming that nuclear power was now competitive with other fuels, it was unfair to continue the imbalance.

16. "Resource Policies for a Great Society: Report to the President by the Task Force on Natural Resources," November 11, 1964, FG 600/T*, LBJL.
17. Ibid.

An equitable approach to financing federal R&D energy efforts could be developed if there were an overall, coordinating agency immune from constituency pressure.

The second issue was the quarrelsome one of federal taxation and the mineral fuels industries. The task force simply recognized that differences of opinion existed about whether special tax treatment, such as depletion allowances, of extractive industries served as an incentive for exploration and development.

Third, the task force addressed the problem of oil import regulation, noting that the basic fact of life in this area was that the landed price of foreign crude oil in the United States was significantly less than the price and cost of domestic crude. The task force felt that only a presidential commission could successfully take on an established program involving such deeply ingrained special interests.

Fourth, artificial restrictions administered by the Interior Department were holding imports of crude oil and oil products to about 20 percent of total U.S. oil consumption. Oil prices in the United States were substantially higher than they would have been if free trade were permitted.

Five, the task force argued that a presidential commission could address several very basic questions: (1) What percentage of total oil consumption could be imported by the United States without endangering its national security? (2) What advance provisions should be made to cope with interruptions in oil supply? (3) Was there a national security justification for restricting importation of residual fuel oil?

The sixth and last energy policy recommendation of the task force was the prescient observation that the United States should thoroughly investigate the extent to which the country would be placed at risk "by the emergence of an organization of oil exporting countries for concerting policy and action."[18]

In December 1964 the Interior Department prepared a response to the task force report on the basis of the department's views and comment by the Department of Agriculture. The combined Interior-Agriculture response was a recommendation-by-recommendation reaction to particular task force proposals and was about as long as the task force report itself. Ten general areas were analyzed, including minerals policy, general energy policy, and electrical energy policy. A basic premise of the response was that the ongoing internal work of the executive branch was by definition of greater depth than anything that could be produced externally

18. Ibid.

during an election year summer. The response stated that analysis by the federal government of R&D in the field of energy resources—the internal and external work associated with the Cambel-Strotz effort—had been under review for the past two years by the presidentially appointed steering committee. It pointed out that "persons who have reviewed the Interdepartmental Energy Study Report in its present semi-final draft judge it to be a work of substantial merit—both as to scope and depth." The Interior Department reacted strongly to comments about the U.S. Oil Import Program: To "throw open the U.S. domestic oil market for free entry of oil from any and all foreign sources is not an economically viable policy." The department saw no urgency for interagency examination of the Oil Import Program but stated that it would continue to consult with the State Department in the development of oil import policies.[19]

Expressing a widespread but generally unstated complaint, the Interior Department observed that the "proposed establishment of a Committee on Energy Policy will probably come chiefly from certain professional persons who have felt for a long time that a truly comprehensive approach to energy policy is urgently needed." The department noted that although it was difficult to judge just what organized groups could be expected to lend support to such "professional persons," they would not have a strong constituency behind them. The coal industry and railroads, it was argued, might conceivably be natural constituencies for such "professional persons," since these two industries had already sustained "heavy losses by competition from other energy materials." The "strongest opposition would probably come from the oil and gas industry, from the private electrical utilities, from interests committed to the rapid development of civilian nuclear power, from the guardians of 'states rights,' and probably from a number of agencies who felt their regulatory functions were likely to be threatened."[20]

The Interior Department's response (the Agriculture Department had not taken a position on this matter) concluded with a summary of the "fundamental issues involved."

Whether a society like our own needs to develop a "National Energy Policy" that would be thoroughly consistent throughout its entire structure is apparently the main question at issue.

Persons schooled in the academic disciplines tend to want more logical

19. Quotations in this paragraph are from "Resource Policies for a Great Society," Brief on the Report to the President by the Task Force on Natural Resources, December 1964, FG 600/T*, LBJL.
20. Ibid.

order and pattern than our pluralistic economy is likely to favor. It may be that the United States has no "National Energy Policy" that would pass inspection on the basis of academic criteria. But the United States does operate under the terms of a rough consensus regarding energy matters. That consensus continues to change from year to year in response to economic, social and political forces. It is therefore not a choice of "policy or no policy," but rather of policy articulated in a written statement that would meet standards of logical consistency—or policy informally recognized by consensus and accommodation.

If the Nation's energy economy was in a state of disarray and not functioning in a reasonably satisfactory manner, rigorous across-the-board investigation by a Commission on Energy Policy would be indicated. But no such conditions prevail nor are they immediately in prospect.[21]

This was the mentality of the technicians and bureaucrats running the various fuel programs at the Interior Department. Their approach was ad hoc and they were proud of it. They distrusted those searching for aggregate and intertemporal coherence. Through "consensus and accommodation," real people—people who knew their segment of their industry down to the last Hughes drilling bit and Louisiana salt dome—should make decisions. There was no need for "policy articulated in a written statement" that could stand muster with theorizing generalists.[22]

The Interdepartmental Committee Grinds to a Conclusion

During the period before the fall of 1966, as the executive branch deliberated about an internal set of consensus recommendations to be submitted to President Johnson, the Interior Department had an advantage because of its Energy Policy Staff, created in 1962 to work with the Senate's National Fuels and Energy Study Group. For example, by January 1966 the Energy Policy Staff was chaired by William T. Pecora, the new director of the Geological Survey who reported to the assistant secretary for mineral resources that the staff had "comprehensively reviewed the proposed draft of the Interdepartmental Energy Study" and that it was "the consensus of the group that the report is scientifically and technically inadequate." The Energy Policy Staff felt that the report was "superficial" and presented "a distorted picture of our overall energy position."[23]

21. Ibid.
22. Ibid.
23. Pecora to the Assistant Secretary for Mineral Resources, "Interdepartmental Energy Study," January 20, 1966, Files of the Interior Department Energy Policy Staff in the custody of the Department of Energy.

An additional example of how the Interior Department's Energy Policy Staff was able to respond effectively to other agencies' initiatives is reflected in its response to and participation in a meeting of the Energy Committee of the Organisation for Economic Co-operation and Development on January 10–12, 1966. As reported by one of the U.S. delegates to the meeting, "the specific suggestions submitted by the U.S. delegation were nearly all accepted," and the U.S. delegation reflected the views of the Interior Department.[24]

The Interdepartmental Steering Committee had great difficulty in resolving the difference of opinion about the optimal role for the public sector in energy R&D. The drafters of the Cambel Report, the Interior Department, and the AEC were bold; the CEA, Budget Bureau, and OST staffs proposed caution. The executive agency staffs, particularly at the OST, were especially unenthusiastic about spending federal money on petroleum research and development. An early OST redraft of the Cambel Report took such a hard line on petroleum that John O'Leary of the Interior Department asserted flatly that Udall "will not sign the report in its present form."[25]

During the Interdepartmental Energy Steering Committee deliberations Interior Department officials worried about alternative ways of approaching energy policy formulation and execution. A series of news stories reported Secretary Udall's proposal that a single federal agency be established for coordinating energy policy and empowered to develop a specialized energy staff capable of reviewing policy questions objectively and making policy recommendations.

The Interior Department prepared an internal memorandum on the general subject of interagency coordination, picking up their story with Udall's general proposal. In an eleven-page, single-spaced memorandum, department officials presented a case for the need to centralize energy policies.[26] They made the rather remarkable observation that there was a need to formulate energy policy in a comprehensive framework because "resources used to produce energy are competitive in the unique sense that one resource may be substituted for another in a substantial portion of the

24. V. E. McKelvey, Memorandum for the Report, "Results of Paris Meeting of OECD Energy Committee," attached to Interior Department Energy Policy Staff agenda for a meeting on January 20, 1966, ibid.

25. OST, "Administrative History," vol. 2, "Energy Policy."

26. The memorandum is attached to a letter from Deputy Director Elmer B. Staats of the Budget Bureau to CEA Chairman Gardner Ackley, February 6, 1966, CEA Microfilm, Roll 22, LBJL.

industrial market. Therefore, positive federal action to advance one source of energy may have a negative effect on others." They pointed out five ways to develop a centralized approach to formulating energy policy. The first was to "assign central responsibility to Interior." In the discussion of the pros and cons of the alternative ways of centralizing energy policies, it was observed that the Interior Department was the primary federal agency "with respect to the traditional energy resource industries: coal, oil and natural gas."

All the department's various interests in energy matters from the leasing of public lands and the regulation of oil imports to such esoteric things as administering the Helium Gas Act were listed to make the case that the department dominated the energy resource field. It was noted that the necessary information concerning resource industries was available in the department and that the department was capable of dealing in-house with many interindustry resource matters. A remarkable piece of understatement pointed out that the department's "relationships with the traditional energy resource industries would facilitate consultations with industry leaders on issues affecting their interests." On the negative side, the department confessed to some empirical shortcomings, particularly relating to such matters as demand projections and transportation trends outside the resource industries, and admitted that its "ability to take an objective view on issues, such as atomic energy and oil imports, which affect the industries within its cognizance would be suspect." It concluded that current issues in the field of energy warranted the establishment of a Presidential Commission on Energy Policy. An interagency committee would be capable of operating within the framework of the commission and would temporarily finesse the problem of where a central staff on energy policy would be permanently located. The Interior Department recommended that the commission be composed of private citizens and have a broad charter to develop and analyze information concerning energy and to make policy recommendations. Furthermore, the CEA chairman should be designated chairman of the interagency committee.

Paul MacAvoy provided CEA reaction to the proposal. MacAvoy was critical of the fact that a commission or interagency committee would not have the means for seeing that policy proposals were carried out. MacAvoy pointed out that this would paralyze the formulation of policy; there were no gains to be made or lost from compromise. He observed that the Interior Department would not be appropriate for coordinating research, pricing, and subsidy policies in the energy field because of strong organizational ties to oil, gas, and coal interests. The Office of Emergency Preparedness and the Department of Commerce, he said, had failed to perform well in the past and could not be relied on in the future. MacAvoy's suggestion was "to put coordination where the money is—in the Bureau of the Budget." A committee could then be formed from the CEA, OST, and Office of Emergency Planning, all of which were capable of unbiased analysis, to produce periodic advice for the Budget Bureau in this area.[27]

On August 18, 1966, Hornig wrote a memorandum to the nine other steering committee members concerning the status of the Interdepartmental Energy Study. He observed that the study had been "reviewed and re-reviewed by all the agencies involved" and that a final draft of a steering committee statement to the President could not be expected to meet "all of the points of interest to all of the participating agencies." He stated that a "long process of compromise" had taken place in attaining the present version of the draft and that in his opinion "it would not be useful to carry this forward any further." Therefore Hornig called a meeting of the steering committee for August 24, 1966, to consider any further issues that might arise concerning the final draft statement. He hoped the meeting would be "the terminal session."[28]

On October 7, 1966, Hornig transmitted to the President the consensus of the ten federal agencies participating in the interdepartmental study. Later the document was published as an eighteen-page pamphlet and released with the more detailed and comprehensive volume resulting from the Cambel group effort.[29]

The committee's findings and recommendations were fairly optimistic. The premise of the report was that "the Nation's total energy resources seem adequate to satisfy expected energy requirements through the re-

27. The MacAvoy memorandum appears as an attachment to the letter, Staats to Ackley, February 6, 1966.

28. Hornig to Steering Committee, Interdepartmental Energy Study, August 18, 1966, Chron File, Box 4, Donald F. Hornig Papers, LBJL.

29. *Energy R&D and National Progress: Findings and Conclusions* (GPO, 1966); and *Energy R&D and National Progress,* Prepared for the Interdepartmental Energy Study by the Energy Study Group under the direction of Ali Bulent Cambel (GPO, 1965). The latter, although printed in 1965, was not circulated until the publication of the former in 1966, when both were released simultaneously accompanied by a mimeographed note that shed little light on the discrepancy in dates. One measure of the Cambel volume's long-run impact is that ten years later the Ford Foundation Energy Policy Project's authors working in the field failed to mention it in the text of the report or in their extensive bibliography. See J. Herbert Holloman and Michel Grenon, *Energy Research and Development* (Ballinger, 1975).

mainder of this century at costs near present levels."[30] It was noted that the exhaustion of liquid petroleum and natural gas could be anticipated but that fossil fuel alternatives, based on shale oil, tar sands, and liquefaction of coal, would "certainly be available." The Interdepartmental Energy Study Steering Committee advised President Johnson that because of the high risks, large capital expenditures and long times involved, the federal government would be justified in continuing a reasonable level of effort to develop advanced nuclear power plants with improved fuel utilization. The committee informed the President that its conclusions were partly based on the in-depth analysis carried out by Cambel and the Interdepartmental Energy Study Group; this analysis had involved more than 500 people inside and outside the federal government.

The OST, Resources for the Future, and S. David Freeman

When Hornig completed his work on the interdepartmental study, presidential assistant Joseph A. Califano, Jr., directed him to chair a task force to evaluate alternative methods for conducting studies of nonfuel minerals resource policy, energy resources, and subsurface excavation technology. Califano asked that the task force include representatives from the Interior Department, the Budget Bureau, the CEA, and anyone else Hornig considered appropriate. He gave Hornig and his task force a little over a month to produce some detailed conclusions and recommendations, asking that consideration be given to the notion of a presidential commission.[31]

Hornig chose to work with CEA Chairman Gardner Ackley; Carl Schwartz, chief of resources and civil works in the Budget Bureau; John O'Leary, deputy assistant secretary of the Interior Department; Walter Hibbard, director of the Bureau of Mines; and Federal Power Commission Chairman Lee C. White. The five men met in Hornig's office on October 19, 1966, to begin their task. David Beckler of the OST served as liaison between Hornig and the other members of this group.[32]

The group met again on October 31, 1966, and by this time had draft papers to consider that had been submitted by O'Leary and Hibbard as well as a member of Ackley's staff. O'Leary suggested that the economics

30. *Energy R&D and National Progress: Findings and Conclusions*, p. 4.
31. Califano to Hornig, October 7, 1966, Gaither Files, Box 1089, LBJL.
32. Hornig to Ackley and others, October 17, 1966, Chron File, Box 4, Hornig Papers, LBJL.

side of the mineral resource problem be integrated into a single study and turned over to the Brookings Institution. In a draft memorandum on the general problem of energy resources, Beckler noted that the "notion of a Presidential Commission on Energy Policy is rejected at this time on the grounds not only that considerably more groundwork needs to be laid, but that it is doubtful that a Presidential Commission in the energy area would enhance the chances of public acceptance of controversial recommendations." Nevertheless, Beckler noted that there was a "need for a presidential-level mechanism for analyzing energy issues and policies so that the best information and analyses can be brought to bear in weighing policy alternatives without being unduly colored by the parochial interests of the federal agencies involved. . . ." Beckler suggested that there were two ways of proceeding. The first was to recognize that it was unwise to initiate a government-sponsored study of energy policies until a central mechanism was established for dealing with these policy problems. Until such a mechanism was established, "it would be desirable to stimulate under private auspices a series of generalized studies of the energy questions facing the Nation." Such studies "could provide a better perspective and framework for public discussion and debate." The second approach was for the government to go ahead and contract "with a non-profit organization (preferably the Brookings Institution) for a study of issues of national energy policies that confront the government."[33]

By late November the Hornig task force was able to respond to Califano's memorandum of October 7, 1966. It concluded that broadly based studies of both the nonfuel minerals and energy resources were needed to guide government policy formation. In the case of the nonfuel minerals, Hornig and his colleagues argued that the study should attempt to develop a better understanding of the impact of technological change on the economics and incentives within the industry. Given this approach, the policy question was then to determine how government action could strengthen the industry's contribution to the U.S. economy. The task force accorded "highest importance to the creation of a small, senior energy policy staff in the Executive Office of the President to undertake and coordinate analytical studies of energy policy issues and to take the initiative and bring appropriate recommendations for their resolution to the Presi-

33. Draft memorandum, David Beckler, "Energy Resources," November 10, 1966, CEA Microfilm, Roll 22, LBJL. The Brookings Institution was not active in energy matters at this time, leaving the field to another research organization receiving substantial Ford Foundation support, Resources for the Future, Inc.

dent for decision." Before proceeding with the pair of energy studies, the task force recommended that a necessary first step was to solicit a study design or prospectus for each, recommending that the pair of study designs be "developed through contracts of private institutions with special competence and experience in the minerals and energy fields, such as Resources for the Future and the Brookings Institution." This would "assure that the necessary expertise and objectivity" would be brought to bear.[34]

Hornig submitted two brief statements with his memorandum: "Nonfuel Minerals Study" and "Energy Resources." The second document stated the basic problem: the U.S. government was organized in such a way that various governmental energy policies were interrelated only in their effects. There was no provision within the government for considering these policies within a comprehensive framework. Yet the effects bear on the responsibilities of a wide range of federal agencies and cut across diverse interests of domestic companies. It was observed that "positive Federal action to advance one source of energy may have a negative effect on others." The memorandum concluded with a statement that there was a need to approach an outside organization to offer a design for a study that would provide a comprehensive framework for analyzing and developing a national energy policy over both the long and short terms.[35]

The question of exactly where an energy staff would be located "was left for a BOB [Budget Bureau] study."[36] This task force had no better luck than earlier ones when addressing the dilemma of where to locate an energy staff. It "would be too small and too specialized to justify independent agency status" but at the same time, none of the existing offices, for example, the OST or CEA, wanted it. In addition "the Budget Bureau felt strongly (with positive assent from the other Offices) that there were already too many Executive Offices."[37] RFF went to work on its design reports "using outside consultants and knowledgeable persons from within government such as James Rettie of the Interior Department, Joseph Lerner of the Office of Emergency Planning, and Franklin Huddle of the Library of Congress."[38]

In response to a memorandum from Califano for draft material for

34. Hornig to Califano, "Natural Resources Study," November 23, 1966, Chron File, Box 4, Hornig Papers, LBJL.

35. "Energy Resources Study," Gaither Files, Box 1049, LBJL.

36. OST, "Administrative History," vol. 2, "Energy Policy," p. 16.

37. Ibid.

38. Ibid., p. 18.

the State of the Union Message in 1967, Hornig suggested that some language be included to indicate the President's concern about energy policies. He suggested the President point out that "although several Federal agencies are responsible for different aspects of energy resources development and utilization, there is no provision for considering energy questions within a comprehensive framework of national objectives—rapid economic growth, efficient development and use of resources, satisfactory international monetary and resource relationships, and adequate resources for national security." He suggested that the President "propose to establish within the Office of Science and Technology in the Executive Office of the President a small staff to analyze and coordinate the study of energy issues and to develop policy alternatives for decision-making, taking fully into account the interaction of the interests and objectives of the federal agencies involved." In his cover memorandum to Califano, Hornig pointed out that this statement "would also pave the way for congressional support for an increased staff for this purpose in the Office of Science and Technology."[39]

On January 30, 1967, President Johnson submitted a message to Congress entitled "Protecting Our Natural Heritage." In this message he stated that he had directed Hornig "to sponsor a thorough study of energy resources and to engage the necessary staff to coordinate energy policy on a government-wide basis."[40]

In early January 1967 Hornig contacted Joseph Fisher, RFF president, to discuss the government's need for broadly based studies dealing with nonfuel minerals and energy resources. It had been decided, he explained, that before proceeding with in-depth analysis, study designs should be produced to establish the nature and scope of the problems requiring examination. This preliminary work would include assessments of the organizational and fiscal requirements for following through on the studies themselves as well as an assessment of the time required for their completion.[41] In early March 1967 Hornig and Fisher signed a contract for RFF to prepare a report consisting of two design studies dealing with nonfuel minerals and energy resources, respectively. RFF agreed to provide the OST a report on the work program contem-

39. Hornig to Califano, December 20, 1966, with attachments, Chron File, Box 4, Hornig Papers, LBJL.

40. "Special Message to the Congress: Protecting Our Natural Heritage," January 30, 1967, *Public Papers: Lyndon B. Johnson, 1967* (GPO, 1968), bk. 1, p. 100.

41. Hornig to Fisher, January 5, 1967, Chron File, Box 4, Hornig Papers, LBJL.

plated for the design studies by May 1, 1967. Final reports would be delivered to the OST by October 1, 1967.

This agreement with RFF to do the design work represented the first element of the OST's execution of the President's directive of January 30 regarding energy policy analysis and coordination. Another element was permission to (try to) "engage the necessary staff to coordinate energy policy on a government-wide basis." In April 1967 Hornig advised Califano that the OST's fiscal 1968 budget included $200,000 for this purpose. He informed Califano that he had testified in early February before the congressional committee overseeing appropriations for independent offices and was scheduled to appear before Senator Magnuson's appropriations subcommittee on June 14, 1967. Hornig anticipated difficulties in getting congressional approval for the $200,000 and advised Califano that "support from the White House may be needed."[42]

During the spring and summer of 1967 Hornig worked hard in both the House and the Senate to obtain fiscal 1968 appropriations for the various components of the program set forth in President Johnson's message of January 30, 1967. For example, the nonfuel minerals study was put into the Bureau of Mines budget. The Bureau of Mines requested $500,000 for the study, the Senate approved appropriations of $250,000, and the House disallowed funds entirely. Hornig lobbied to get at least the Senate amount restored to the Bureau of Mines budget. By early October 1967 Hornig was able to circulate copies of two preliminary draft study designs prepared by RFF. He sent them to David S. Black at the Interior Department, Lee White at the FPC, Carl Schwartz at the Budget Bureau, and Gardner Ackley at the CEA for comments and observations. He wanted to get reactions RFF could use when preparing its final version. Independently RFF sought comments on the draft from a number of persons both within and outside the government.

By November RFF provided final design proposals and budgets. Hornig's concern was finding a way to finance this work. The budget for the OST was relatively small. In fiscal 1967 the OST had $1.2 million in appropriated funds. Hornig was unhappy about how Congress had treated his request for $200,000 for 1968 to add energy policy coordination capabilities to his staff. Having had this problem with Congress during the summer of 1967, he was very reluctant to have the two studies designed by RFF appear in his 1969 budget. It would represent a rather extraordinary percentage increase. Thus Hornig recommended that $1

42. Hornig to Califano, April 19, 1967, ibid., Box 5.

million be included in the 1969 Interior Department budget to finance the energy study the President had requested be undertaken under Hornig's direction. He asked Budget Director Schultze to act favorably on this recommendation as the best way of assuring that these two studies could move forward in 1969 or even earlier.[43]

Hornig was pleased that the RFF energy study proposal was an excellent beginning in defining the range of problems faced by the federal government. He had asked RFF to put together a recommended study program, based on $1 million and a two-year time horizon. The nonfuel minerals effort, on the other hand, had not yet moved to this stage. Hornig observed that responsibility for this study was explicitly the Interior Department's and that the action he wanted at the moment was "to provide the funding for the energy study, which will be carried out under OST's direction." The Interior Department was the logical place because the "visibility and hence vulnerability" of the amount would be lower in the budget of a larger agency.[44]

On November 22, 1967, Hornig informed President Johnson that he had "looked hard for the right man" to be responsible for the presidential directive of January 30, 1967, to the OST to assemble a staff to coordinate energy policy. He informed Johnson he believed he had found the right man in S. David Freeman, who was "highly recommended by Lee White, Dave Black and others" and whose appointment to Hornig's staff had "been approved by John Macy." Macy was chairman of the Civil Service Commission and personally cleared high-level appointments for Johnson. Hornig asked for and received Johnson's approval to announce this appointment and further asked the President to provide Freeman "with the kind of prestige and visibility which you alone can give him" because the role Freeman was being asked to play was worthy of Johnson's personal attention. Associating Freeman with the aura of the presidency would help him be effective in dealing with the array of agencies and industries concerned with energy.[45]

Over the Thanksgiving weekend, a press announcement was released from the Texas ranch announcing Freeman's appointment to head an Energy Policy Staff in the OST. Freeman's appointment, announced on November 25, 1967, became effective December 1.

43. Hornig to Schultze, November 6, 1967, ibid.
44. Ibid.
45. Hornig to the President, November 22, 1967, Chron File, Box 5, Hornig Papers, LBJL.

At the time of his appointment, Freeman was forty years old and practicing law in Washington, D.C., in partnership with former FPC Chairman Joseph W. Swindler. He had been assistant to the FPC chairman from 1961–65, playing a leading role in the commission's National Power Survey as well as handling congressional liaison. Before the Kennedy team took over, he had served as an attorney with the TVA in Knoxville during 1956–61.[46] Freeman's appointment raised some eyebrows around Washington, particularly in Congress. Inquiries also came from various trade associations. In late November 1967 Hornig responded to an inquiry from Joseph Moody, president of the National Coal Policy Conference (composed of coal companies, the United Mine Workers of America [UMW], the coal-carrying railroads, some electric utility companies, and coal equipment manufacturers) informing Moody that "Dave Freeman has amply demonstrated in the past an ability to work in close harmony with industrial organizations and groups such as yours."[47] In June 1968 Freeman acquired two staff assistants; Milton F. Searl, a former AEC economist, and J. Frederick Weinhold, Jr., an engineer recently trained at Princeton's Wilson School.[48]

During the Johnson administration Freeman and the OST were never able to carry out their intended mission because of a combined failure to receive adequate appropriations and the general winding down and "short-time" mentality of the other Johnson administration officials. It was difficult to get cooperation from the various internal operating organizations at the Interior Department, particularly after Johnson's political resignation on March 31, 1968. Hornig spent much effort from late 1967 until January 1969 trying to generate enthusiasm for the appropriation needed to develop centralized energy policy capabilities. On

46. Freeman, born in Chattanooga, Tennessee, received an undergraduate degree in civil engineering from the Georgia Institute of Technology and a law degree from the University of Tennessee in 1956. Before receiving his law degree, he had worked for the TVA as an engineer from 1948 to 1954. He remained at the OST after Nixon became president. After 1970 his title changed from director of the Energy Policy Staff to assistant director for energy, natural resources and environment. In August 1971 he left government service and became affiliated with the University of Pittsburgh where he worked on an energy book sponsored by the Twentieth Century Fund (S. David Freeman, *Energy: The New Era* [Walker, 1974].) He then assumed responsibility for the well-known and controversial Ford Foundation Energy Policy Study. After the 1976 presidential election he returned to the Executive Office of the President and then to leadership of the TVA.

47. Hornig to Moody, November 28, 1967, Chron File, Box 5, Hornig Papers, LBJL.

48. Interview with S. David Freeman, August 9, 1978.

February 9, 1968, for example, he wrote to Califano concerning the need to press Congress to include $500,000 in the 1969 budget to carry through the Energy Policy Study that had been under consideration for some time. He referred to this study as "a scaled-down Paley Commission report" and said that the eventual cost would be around $1 million. He unsuccessfully lobbied Congressman Joe L. Evins, chairman of the Subcommittee on Independent Offices of the House Appropriations Committee, and in a curious display of candor concerning public versus private needs, Evins's committee recognized "that *the government must be assured* that its energy policies are rational and reasonably consistent." But it decreed that the work should be done by existing staff with "the cooperation of industry."[49]

On February 20, 1968, RFF submitted a revised and expanded version of a design for an energy study that reflected consideration of comments made by persons inside and outside government.[50] In early March Hornig informed Joseph Fisher that the OST had had "a chance to study the final reports on energy resources and non-fuel minerals, as well as the annexes to each report" and thanked Fisher for "a job well-done."[51] RFF had now completed the work outlined in the contract of March 6, 1967, and the only remaining question was the publication of the two reports. It was the opinion of the OST that the annexes to each report were "not for publication" but that the reports themselves should be made available to the public. Since these reports were entirely the work of RFF, it seemed appropriate that they be RFF publications. Hence they appeared as a book in the spring of 1968 with a preface by Fisher summarizing the origins of the work.[52]

Lacking funds for a staff as strong as that needed to coordinate a national energy policy within the OST as well as to carry through the research project detailed in the RFF report, Freeman and Hornig had to rely on the voluntary cooperation of other agencies in order to do their work. Twice during 1968 Hornig signed memorandums, drafted by Freeman, to all heads of all agencies with any interest in energy matters. In mid-August 1968 Hornig asked his colleagues in the executive branch

49. *Independent Offices and HUD Appropriations Bill, 1969,* House Rept. 1348, 90 Cong. 2 sess. (GPO, 1968), p. 2.

50. Hornig to David S. Black, Lee C. White, and others, February 20, 1968, Chron File, Box 6, Hornig Papers, LBJL.

51. Hornig to Fisher, March 7, 1968, ibid.

52. Resources for the Future Staff Report, *U.S. Energy Policies: An Agenda for Research* (Johns Hopkins Press for Resources for the Future, 1968).

to help him prepare a report listing pending energy policy issues as well as those on the more distant horizon. He also asked his colleagues to identify significant issues that warranted discussion in the Executive Office of the President, stating that he believed "this initial report could serve as a useful basis for facilitating continuity in the coming Administration." He asked for responses by September 23, 1968.[53] Only a few agencies, such as the Interior Department's Office of Oil and Gas, bothered to respond. A short memorandum from Onnie P. Lattu, director of the Office of Oil and Gas, went up through the department's hierarchy. It listed several general pending issues, such as "the optimum level of oil imports consistent with the objectives of low energy cost and national security." Lattu concluded his memorandum with the statement that his "office has no energy studies underway at the present."[54]

In late November 1968 Hornig informed virtually everyone who had received the August 1968 memorandum that their response had not been overwhelming. He made the same general plea for assistance, observing that the material would "provide an important source of transition material for the next Administration." By that time it was known that the next administration would be that of Richard M. Nixon rather than that of Hubert H. Humphrey or George C. Wallace.[55] The response to the second request appears to have generated some activity in some agencies but no major responses. Again, however, the Office of Oil and Gas attempted to provide an appropriate response.

Hornig spent considerable effort trying to get the administration to include $500,000 in the 1970 budget for the energy study, but in mid-December 1968 he told Califano of his disappointment when the Bureau of the Budget informed him that President Johnson had eliminated the $500,000 from the OST's budget. Because Califano had an extraordinary influence over President Johnson in such matters, Hornig asked him to get the President to change his mind. He based his appeal to Califano on the fact that the study was Califano's idea as was the estab-

53. Hornig to the Secretary of State, Secretary of the Treasury, and others, "Request for Report on Energy Policy Matters," August 12, 1968, Chron File, Box 6, Hornig Papers, LBJL.

54. Lattu forwarded his draft reply to Hornig's memorandum of August 12, 1968, to Harry Perry, who was then working in the Office of the Assistant Secretary for Mineral Resources, U.S. Department of the Interior, Office of Oil and Gas, Energy Policy Staff. These records are currently in the custody of the Department of Energy.

55. Hornig to the Secretary of the Interior, Secretary of Agriculture, and others, November 26, 1968, Chron File, Box 6, Hornig Papers, LBJL.

lishment of an Energy Policy Staff in the OST.[56] In early January 1969 Hornig personally appealed to President Johnson to restore the $500,000, arguing that there was a need for "an effort that would result in a current, comprehensive report of energy policy issues resembling the Paley Commission report." He said it was imperative to "go ahead with this study to provide a sound basis for energy policy because so much time had elapsed since the Paley Commission report; the technology of energy production and consumption had changed so much; nuclear energy development had been plagued by so many problems; and the oil import policy, shale oil development, fossil fuel combustion pollution of the atmosphere, and so on, were such pervasive problems.[57] Unfortunately, the answer was no.

Nevertheless, the three-man Freeman group was able to accomplish something. During the Johnson years Freeman discussed energy policies with a large number of public officials, industry representatives, trade press reporters, the National Petroleum Council, the European Economic Community, and the Organisation for Economic Co-operation and Development, as well as British and French government officials.

When the Nixon administration took office, Freeman and his two assistants were retained in their positions by incoming OST Director Lee DuBridge. Using certain OST funds, with Hornig's cooperation, several external research projects were launched, including a contract with Charles River Associates to analyze the national security foundations of the oil import program (a major concern of the Nixon-era task force headed by George Shultz).[58]

Fuel Policies

Johnson administration energy policies can be discussed on a fuel-by-fuel basis, but such a discussion can never have the cohesive symmetry possible when discussing energy policies of the 1970s. By the mid-1970s interrelationships among energy sources and uses were much more explicit; particular policies toward all aspects of energy were treated at a common bureaucratic level. In the 1960s analysis of some energy sources,

56. Hornig to Califano, December 12, 1968, ibid.
57. Hornig to the President, January 3, 1969, ibid.
58. OST, "Administrative History," vol. 2, Documentary Supplement, "Energy Policy: Supplemental Report," inserted in file per memorandum from David Beckler to James B. Rhoads, January 22, 1969, LBJL.

such as solar power or natural gas, failed to surface at the White House or cabinet level. They were the special province of small bands of enthusiasts or small bands of regulators. The work of the enthusiasts or regulators was of insufficient interest in the higher reaches of the federal government to be viewed as part of a national energy policy. But the work was done, and in many cases the future was shaped.[59]

The Federal Power Commission, for example, continued to have regulatory authority over the production and gathering of natural gas, authority based on both the 1938 Natural Gas Act and the 1954 U.S. Supreme Court Phillips decision. (The Phillips case had extended FPC regulatory functions to natural gas sold for resale in interstate markets by companies engaged solely in production and gathering operations.) During the Kennedy-Johnson years the FPC attempted to solve the massive administrative burden associated with regulating over 4,000 independent producers on a company-by-company basis. In 1961 the Permian Basin Area Rate Proceeding was begun. The methodology in the Permian case was to allow producers to receive prices based on a variant of the utility rate-base, cost-of-service approach, using the *average* costs of all *area* producers and a 12 percent rate of return. This approach was being used in 1965 and was blessed by the Supreme Court in 1968; it was extraordinarily difficult to implement, in part because natural gas was a joint product. Second, the Permian case methodology also attempted to provide an exploration incentive by "vintaging"—permitting a higher price for "new" gas than for "old" or "flowing" gas. The result of the FPC's activity appears to have been an even greater decline in the U.S. natural gas reserves-production ratio than would have happened without the FPC's successful efforts to keep natural gas priced at artificially low prices.[60]

Nuclear Energy and the Generation of Electricity

The production and distribution of electricity naturally was a concern of the Johnson administration, given the President's past attachment to

59. The written records of the enthusiasts and regulators themselves sometimes survive, although more often they do not or they are not yet accessible to researchers. The Department of Energy has much of this material, but it is in a rather extraordinary state of disarray. The department's Historian's Office is simply the old AEC Office. It is difficult for the staff to cope with all the records the department inherited from predecessor agencies, especially the various fuel bureaus in the Interior Department.

60. See Paul A. MacAvoy, "The Regulation Induced Shortage of Natural Gas," *Journal of Law and Economics*, vol. 14 (April 1971), pp. 167–99.

rural electrification. The transmission of electric power was one of the major interregional conflicts during the 1960s. Cheap electric power was produced in the Pacific Northwest by the Bonneville Power Administration, part of the Interior Department. Production levels were well above the region's demand for electricity, and future demand for this power would be in the Pacific Southwest, particularly in Los Angeles. With Johnson administration guidance, the issue was resolved in Congress. Stimulated in part by the power failure in the Northeast in November 1965 and in part by general preparation for the first session of the Ninetieth Congress, the Executive Office of the President established a Task Force on Electric Power. This task force, chaired by Hornig, recommended moving in the direction of regional planning and systems integration. This could be achieved either by a voluntary program or by giving appropriate mandatory powers to the FPC. The majority of the task force members recommended the second approach but appreciated the political problems. Hornig complained that "within the time available" it was impossible "to come to clearcut conclusions."[61]

But in retrospect the most important electricity issue during the Johnson years was the emergence of a commercially successful nuclear industry. As discussed earlier in this chapter, the AEC had enthusiastically outlined a nuclear future for President Kennedy in November 1962. During the Kennedy-Johnson transition several independent lines of activity were bearing fruit, all stimulating the use of nuclear power to generate electricity. (During the last two years of the Johnson administration nuclear power plants accounted for nearly half of the new steam-generating capacity announced by utilities.) The Private Ownership of Special Nuclear Materials Act became law in August 1964, enabling the industry to move toward a system of private ownership of fuel for nuclear reactors. In 1963–64 the AEC, under a new director of reactor development, reviewed more promising plans for future power reactor development and decided to stress the liquid-metal-cooled fast breeder reactor. The OST and the Budget Bureau remained unconvinced about the economics of this approach, and the debate continued throughout the Johnson years. This was a debate about the long term, about power reactors requiring years of federal support before even a successful demonstration stage was reached.

61. OST, "Administrative History," vol. 2, Documentary Supplement, Reference Documents, File J, "Energy." This file includes a memorandum, Califano to Hornig, October 14, 1966, detailing an agenda for inquiry, and Hornig's task force response to Califano, December 2, 1966.

In the meantime a nuclear present suddenly emerged. The Atomic Energy Act of 1954 gave the AEC a mandate to develop (and supervise) a commercial nuclear power industry. Between 1954 and 1961 the AEC and some electric utilities financed a number of small reactors, with the light-water reactor being established as showing the most immediate promise. Almost all observers assumed that LWR commercialization required a much greater scale, at least in the 200–400 megawatt (electric) range. The utilities were unwilling to move alone, and the AEC was reluctant to provide subsidies. The congressional Joint Committee on Atomic Energy broke this deadlock in 1962 by explicitly directing the AEC to use $20 million of previously authorized funds to assist utilities to design and develop large-scale LWRs. This intervention resulted in two Westinghouse contracts: Connecticut Yankee (December 1962) and San Onogre I (January 1963). Both were turnkey contracts, with Westinghouse assuming all design, construction, and licensing responsibilities at a specified price.

The status quo was dramatically altered in December 1963 with the announcement that General Electric would produce a large nuclear electric-generating plant for Jersey Central Power and Light Company with no AEC subsidy. This Oyster Creek, New Jersey, plant was priced at $132 per kilowatt of capacity. It not only would have a fuel cost advantage over the conventional alternative (coal), but its capital costs—$110–$160 per kilowatt capacity—would compare favorably as well. This was the first instance of private economic considerations alone leading to a choice of the nuclear option.

On June 10, 1964, President Johnson gave a commencement address at Holy Cross College and spoke glowingly about "an economic breakthrough in the use of large-scale [nuclear] reactors for commercial power."[62] Although the Oyster Creek decision was followed by a lull during 1964–65, by 1966 orders were booming. Twenty-one contracts for nuclear power plants were awarded in 1966 and thirty the following year. By the beginning of the Nixon administration, utilities had ordered over sixty-five large nuclear plants (with capacity in excess of 500 megawatts), thirty of which were already being built. The rush to a nuclear future was on, not as a result of present or future policy but as a result of an economic click, the culmination of past policies and programs. Of course, it all turned out to be based on extraordinarily optimistic estimates of construc-

62. "Commencement Address at Holy Cross College, June 10, 1964," *Public Papers: Johnson, 1963–64* (GPO, 1965), bk. 1, p. 764.

tion costs. In addition nuclear power would be identified by many with everything perceived to be wrong with society. As a surrogate for what many distrust and dislike about their economic and political life, nuclear power would have to bear a tremendous and perhaps insupportable burden.[63]

Coal Transformation

All fossil fuel industries were concerned about federal R&D spending on energy. The coal industry in particular felt threatened by government support received by a major competitor, the nuclear power industry (primarily Westinghouse and General Electric). The National Coal Association could not be expected to be sanguine about the AEC "spending tax dollars" to find ways of making nuclear power an economically feasible fuel source for the generation of electricity. As the AEC succeeded, the coal industry was directly hurt. Nevertheless, the coal industry did have an R&D arm within the federal government. The Office of Coal Research, embedded in the Interior Department, had been authorized by Congress in 1960 but had never been staffed by the Eisenhower administration. The Kennedy administration put the OCR into operation. Although it had a modest staff, its personnel were able to draw on other parts of the Interior Department, especially the Bureau of Mines, and of course they relied on consulting firms for analysis. The OCR came under the general responsibility of the assistant secretary for mineral resources; its chief during the Johnson years was George Fumich, Jr. It had to work very closely with the appropriate congressional committees and also with its own General Technical Advisory Committee composed of coal producers and users as well as other interested parties. It was not surprising to see the National Coal Association as well as the UMW enthusiastically participating side by side in OCR activities, including GTAC meetings. (Interestingly enough, R&D for labor-replacing technical change, such as innovation in strip-mining techniques, were not on the OCR agenda.)

Coal is dirty to produce and to use and it is awkward to transport. The major thrust of the OCR was to find solutions to these unattractive attributes. For example, the "coal-by-wire" idea of generating electricity right

63. For a critical review of this "turnkey" or "bandwagon" era see Irvin C. Bupp and Jean-Claude Derian, *Light Water: How the Nuclear Dream Dissolved* (Basic Books, 1978). For a thorough layman's guide see "Nuclear Fission as an Energy Source," in Lon C. Ruedisili and Morris W. Firebaugh, eds., *Perspectives on Energy,* 2d ed. (New York: Oxford University Press, 1978), pt. 3.

at the mine site was an attractive one and stimulated the OCR to contract for solutions to problems associated with high-voltage transmission. Much of the OCR's effort was to transform coal into a more easily transportable product, either liquid or gas. Furthermore, the OCR was interested in ways to extract the potential waste product in raw coal before the coal was shipped. If, for example, 12 percent of a given type of raw coal would turn into unusable ash when burned, it made sense to search for economically feasible ways of removing the ash content at the mine site. This would solve several problems simultaneously, including reduction of transportation costs and elimination of the problem of disposing of the ash at the use site, probably an urban area at which the disposal costs would be relatively high. Also, of course, ash-free coal would burn more cleanly.

The history of the OCR during the Johnson administration is best characterized by rather extraordinary bursts of optimism concerning the economic feasibility of the various ways of solving the unattractive aspects associated with raw coal. In the area of coal gasification two early OCR demonstration projects were thought to yield encouraging results. An M. W. Kellogg Company pilot project and a Chicago Institute of Gas Technology pilot project were thought to demonstrate that pipeline gas could be produced from coal at a price ranging from 50 cents to 60 cents per thousand cubic feet.

Perhaps one of the most extraordinary experiences the OCR had during the 1960s was with one of their large contractors, the Consolidation Coal Company of Pittsburgh. (Consolidation would eventually be acquired by Continental Oil Company.) The Consolidation Coal Company received $9,963,000 to develop a synthetic liquid fuel process, Project Gasoline, in a pilot plant at Cresap, West Virginia, in a highly industrialized area of the Ohio River about twenty miles downstream from Wheeling. Throughout the early and middle 1960s Consolidation Coal and the OCR were optimistic that gasoline could be manufactured from coal at competitive prices. This optimism reached a peak in the middle 1960s. At a GTAC meeting on January 27, 1965, Eric Reichl of Consolidation Coal reported that the Cresap pilot plant would produce 100 octane (premium) gasoline that could be sold at a price ranging from an optimistic 11 cents a gallon to a pessimistic 13.6 cents a gallon. These potential prices were computed to be comparable with the prices at which petroleum refineries would sell gasoline, at the refinery, to large-quantity buyers. Consolidation Coal compared its range of prices with the prevailing price of 100-octane gasoline in various parts of the United States. It found that Consolidation's process was expected to yield coal-derived gasoline that would be competitive with petroleum-derived gasoline, then priced at about 13 cents a gallon. Taking Grand Rapids, Michigan, as an illustrative case, the delivered wholesale price in 1965 of gasoline was 18 cents, the refinery price of 13 cents plus 5 cents for transportation. Consolidation Coal had built in a 6 percent rate of return on the capital required for the coal conversion process, which was comparable with the rate of return then prevailing in petroleum refining. Reichl noted that Project Gasoline was a potential economic success, based on a price of coal of $3.80 a ton, even though coal and petroleum had differential depletion allowances.[64]

By early 1967 Consolidation Coal was still optimistic but reported some problems. First, the Cresap pilot plant was turning out to cost more than estimated, a provisional guess in 1967 was that it would be over 30 percent above the original estimate. Second, engineering problems plagued several steps of the process. Third, there were some basic difficulties associated with the chemistry of the process, pertaining to the catalyst, zinc chloride. Potential labor problems at the Cresap plant were taken care of by a UMW representative serving on the GTAC, Michael Widman, Jr. In his report to the GTAC on January 10, 1967, Eric Reichl thanked Widman profusely for helping negotiate a contract with UMW District 6.[65] The difficulty was that they were breaking new ground in coming up with a labor contract for a continuous chemical plant. It was quite fortunate for Consolidation Coal to have a UMW representative serving on the committee. And of course, G. A. Shoemaker, the president of Consolidation Coal was also a member of the GTAC, so when Reichl made reports and then left the room, his boss remained in the room as a GTAC member.

In early 1967 there was much optimism for the Consolidation Coal project, including plans for a spring dedication of the pilot plant at Cresap. As time went by, however, it became increasingly clear that the plant was not a success. Some learning took place, and thus the experiment did yield benefits. There is some doubt about whether all stages of the process had ever operated simultaneously, as well as substantial feeling that the entire project was in a way a tribute to the position of Senator Robert Byrd of

64. GTAC meeting, OCR, "Official Report of Proceedings," January 27, 1965, Washington, D.C., p. 29, in the custody of the Department of Energy.
65. Ibid., p. 32.

West Virginia, who was chairman of the Senate Appropriations Committee, which passed on the OCR's budget. The plant was shut down in the early 1970s, then reactivated in the mid-1970s as an experimental facility. The instructive thing about this episode is the extent to which all the per-gallon-cost estimates were roughly the same. The contractor, independent consultants, and OCR staff all disagreed about what the per gallon costs would be, but all the estimates were within a few pennies per gallon of each other. All were operating with the same data base and the same perceptions of the possibility of engineering success.

Another OCR program that apparently had strong congressional overtones was a contract with Spencer Chemical Company, a subsidiary of Pittsburg & Midway Coal Mining Company, later acquired by the Gulf Oil Corporation. In August 1962 Spencer Chemical obtained a $1.4 million OCR contract to develop a process producing a liquid fuel from coal that resembled coal tar pitch. Essentially what Spencer Chemical was doing was extracting all the carbon from coal. As late as January 1965 the GTAC was unexcited about Spencer's results. The process seemed technically sound but economically unfeasible. An analysis of the Spencer project by the Battelle Memorial Institute was very negative concerning the potential market for its fuel.[66] Nevertheless, as time went by, the OCR continued to support this project, resulting in what was known during the 1970s as the Great Transcontinental Coal Shuttle: the conversion plant is located in Fort Louis, Washington, using coal from Kentucky, producing a liquid fuel to be burned in New York City. This bizarre state of affairs is apparently attributable to the political clout of Congressman Floyd Hicks, first elected to Congress in 1964 from the district that then included the plant site. Congressman Hicks was able to convince two fellow Washingtonians, Senator Henry Jackson and Congresswoman Julia Butler Hansen, to support the Fort Louis site. Hansen was chairman of the Subcommittee on the Interior of the House Appropriations Committee, Senator Warren Magnuson of Washington was chairman of the Senate Committee on Commerce, and Senator Jackson chaired the Senate Committee

---

66. In the summer of 1978 the Department of Energy proclaimed great enthusiasm for a technique known as solvent coal refining, which promised to yield a nearly ideal substitute fuel for oil-burning utility and industrial boilers. The department asked Congress for authority to take $33 million from elsewhere in the fiscal 1978 budget to put into this program. In addition the department announced an intention to spend another $23 million in 1979. This technique emerged from the OCR contract granted to the Pittsburg & Midway Coal Mining Company in 1962.

on Interior and Insular Affairs. In short, the state of Washington had an extraordinary amount of leverage to bring to bear on the OCR.[67]

It was unfortunate that the OCR was apparently forced into economically unsound but politically necessary decisions in order to maintain its thin reed of congressional appropriations. Congress never was particularly enthusiastic about the OCR's efforts, and certainly the owners of oil leases and petroleum refineries could not be expected to have *their* well-placed congressmen and senators push for a massive coal transformation program.

During fiscal 1963 Congress appropriated $3.45 million for OCR activities. By fiscal 1969 this amount was increased to $13.7 million. Nevertheless, given the nature of OCR operations, this increase was grossly insufficient. It did not permit the OCR to maintain promising projects, much less to initiate new ones. The difficulty was that once the OCR made a commitment to a particular project, many years of support were required. Thus for the OCR to have a dynamic program, its budget would have to grow exponentially. And the leaders, represented by the GTAC, were unable or unwilling to develop the congressional support for such exponential budget growth. Two major contracts, the one to make gasoline from coal and another to transform coal into pipeline gasoline were axed in 1968 for budgetary reasons. As the Johnson administration wound down, the OCR was frustrated because it was engaging in pilot projects that could not be demonstrated as commercially feasible on a large scale until one or two decades had passed. Nevertheless, OCR technicians felt their work was paying off, since the major petroleum companies were reserving coal properties and some companies had begun coal conversion research on their own.

Shale Oil

Releasing oil from shale was of substantial interest to both government and industry during the 1960s, an energy problem cutting across a wide range of issues, including state-federal conflict, horizontal concentration of "energy" companies, and the proper role of the federal government in energy research. There are vast reserves of shale in North America, and the technology involved in their exploitation as an energy source is simple. Some of the petroleum formed in the bottom of seabeds never escaped as a liquid or gas but instead oozed into surrounding clay sediment and

67. "Coals to Newcastle," *Barron's,* May 15, 1978.

became a flaky, soft rock—shale. There are vast reserves of shale, particularly in North America. The technology involved is extraordinarily simple. To release the oil, the shale needs to be crushed and heated to 480° centigrade. There are environmental problems, however. For example, conventional shale oil technology requires extensive earth removal and large quantities of water and produces massive amounts of waste rock. To finesse these basic problems the industry and the government explored the possibilities of in situ technology that would permit cracking and heating shale in place, underground.

During the Johnson administration the potentialities of shale oil were explored with enthusiasm, but with little payoff. Several major studies of oil shale development were done during the period. Interior Secretary Udall appointed an Oil Shale Advisory Board during the summer of 1964 to identify and evaluate the major public policy questions relating to the development of oil shale. It was obvious to Udall that federal government involvement was inevitable in any oil shale program for a multitude of reasons. For example, a great deal of available shale was on federally owned land. Second, the shale oil technologies satisfying private sector economic criteria involved extensive land and water damage, a major concern to environmentalists. The government's chief activity in the oil shale field was the long-term experimental plant at Rifle, Colorado. This operation dated back to World War II, using raw material from a nearby naval oil shale reserve. A major private program was also being carried out by The Oil Shale Corporation (TOSCO), a company financed 30 percent by Lehman Brothers. TOSCO was mining shale on a very substantial basis using privately owned land. By 1965 it had bought enough rights to private tracts of land to have the potential to recover 5 billion barrels of oil.

On February 15, 1965, Udall's Oil Shale Advisory Board produced an interim report. The board was chaired by RFF President Joseph Fisher and included former New Dealer Benjamin V. Cohen and John Kenneth Galbraith. The major political issue addressed by the six-member board was whether or not President Johnson should rescind a thirty-five-year-old presidential directive forbidding the leasing of federally owned shale oil lands, a directive resulting from the Teapot Dome scandal. Unfortunately the board was split 3-3; Fisher, Cohen, and Galbraith were against releasing the federal shale oil lands, and the other three members favored releasing some lands on an experimental basis. In May 1965 Johnson was advised to accept the general recommendation of the board to defer the issue since "the art of extracting oil from shale is not yet developed to a point where it is commercially competitive," and "until it is, there is no need for the Government to enter into a large scale leasing program."[68]

In April and May 1967 the Subcommittee on Antitrust and Monopoly of the Senate Judiciary Committee held hearings on shale oil, including the issue of shale retorting on the surface as well as a proposed underground nuclear detonation. The latter plan, known as Project Bronco, had surfaced as a scheme endorsed jointly by the AEC and the Interior Department in December 1966. The work was to be done by the CER Geonuclear Corporation. The Senate subcommittee hearings indicated the wide diversity of interests in this matter, however. The general conflict seemed to be the need to develop the oil shale resources versus the fact that such development would add to the oligopolistic nature of the industry. One suggested way around this problem was to offer the oil shale lands at high annual rentals but to demand very low production royalties. A variety of ownership schemes were proposed, ranging from TVA-style public agency development to a quasi-public corporation similar to the Communications Satellite Corporation (Comsat) to private development along TOSCO lines. In addition substantial conflict of interest arose between the states and the central government over the division of royalties. Finally, testimony indicated that the oil companies were not anxious to exploit the oil shale lands, because if they were successful they would lower the value of their own petroleum leases.

Petroleum

Prorationing, that is, state control over crude oil output to match estimated demand, was a federal as well as a state issue during the Johnson years. The major producing states, Texas, Louisiana, Oklahoma, New Mexico, and Kansas each have regulatory commissions to establish the "allowable" amount of oil that can be produced and sold at current prices. These regulatory commissions base their decisions on a number of factors, including the Bureau of Mines forecasts of crude petroleum demand. At least in the case of the Johnson administration, the Executive Office of the President directly intervened in the decisionmaking process of the regulatory commissions.

An example is provided by Johnson's actions during the inflation-fighting days of early 1966. The future course of the Vietnam War was uncer-

68. Harry McPherson to the President, May 28, 1965, Office Files of DeVier Pierson, "Oil Shale," LBJL.

tain. The price indexes were rising. Johnson and his domestic advisers used the federal apparatus to postpone and suppress price increases. In March Joseph Califano provided the President with a three-part memorandum on actions taken, actions recommended, and other possible actions. The first item in the second category was "gasoline, petroleum, and coal." The recommended action was to "have Udall continue to prod Texas and Louisiana Commissions to continue to increase allowables." Beneath this recommended action was a place for the President to check yes or no. He checked yes, underlined the word Texas, and wrote in the margin "I passed this to Udall."[69] In late May Udall reported to the President that he had "touched base again today with Ben Ramsey of the Texas Railroad Commission to check on the recent slight decrease in allowables." Ramsey had explained this temporary adjustment to Udall's satisfaction and had assured Udall that "he and the Commission are most anxious to keep supplies fully adequate." Califano attached a brief cover note to Udall's memorandum and sent it to the President, who returned the material to Califano after having noted that "we need to get Bur[eau] of Mines to give [a] most generous estimate of needs."[70]

As is the case with much of the regulation of the petroleum industry, prorationing was developed to handle a problem of *surplus*. Indeed, one of the major aspects of the present energy crisis is the fact that the United States' present body of legislation, executive orders, and judicial decisions evolved over a century of surplus. The so-called Connally Hot Oil Act of 1935 (15 U.S.C. 715), which prohibited interstate shipment of oil in excess of state production quotas illustrates this surplus orientation. Prorationing is one of three general areas of special government treatment of the petroleum industry. The taxation of oil and gas operators has differed from that of other businesses in that certain capital costs were deductible immediately rather than over the life of the assets. In addition the annual deduction for depletion was related to income rather than to asset cost.[71]

Of course, the major petroleum story during the Johnson administration was management of the Mandatory Oil Import Program, which was created by the Eisenhower administration. The 1957 voluntary program

69. Califano to the President, March 16, 1966, BE 5, LBJL.

70. Udall to the President, May 24, 1966, with covering note by Califano, BE 5-2, LBJL.

71. See Thomas G. Moore, "Petroleum," in Walter Adams, ed., *The Structure of American Industry*, 4th ed. (MacMillan, 1971); Raymond Vernon, ed., *The Oil Crisis* (Norton, 1976); and Consad Research Corporation, *Effects of Special Tax Provisions on Selected Aspects of Oil and Gas Industry*, Special Report to the U.S. Treasury (Consad, 1967).

to restrict crude oil imports was made mandatory in 1959 by Proclamation 3279. The legal foundation for the mandatory program was a mixture of defense statutory authorities as well as sanctions given in the Buy American Act of 1933. When President Eisenhower decided to intervene on March 20, 1959, crude oil prices in the United States were depressed and drifting downward. The Interior Department strategy on crude oil import quantity was to limit imports to 12.2 percent of domestic consumption and on crude oil pricing was to maintain 1959 prices. The pricing side of this strategy was certainly successfully carried out during the Johnson years. The average price of crude oil in the United States in 1959 was $3.09 a barrel. During the summer of 1966 the average price was $3.06. That is, the nominal price of crude oil was constant, enabling producers and users to expect this steady price as a fact of life and work around it.

Even though the nominal price of crude oil was relatively stable during the 1960s, prices of products made using crude oil were not. Price increases of gasoline were of particular concern to the Johnson administration since consumers seemed to be keenly sensitive to the cost of "filling it up." During 1966 John E. Robson, on loan to the White House from the Justice Department, devoted a substantial amount of his inflation-fighting efforts to halting gasoline price hikes. During 1966 the U.S. oil industry charged the highest pre-tax service station prices since 1957, the year the voluntary stage of the oil import program was introduced. In 1966 average pre-tax service station prices of gasoline rose to 21.5 cents a gallon, up from 20.7 cents in 1965 and 19.98 cents in 1964. Frank N. Ikard, president of the American Petroleum Institute, explained the price increases in demand terms: strong aggregate economic activity, increased vehicle registrations, and increasing leisure automobile use because of travel promotion.[72] But the price of the industry's basic raw material was virtually unchanged.

Realizing that consumers were sensitive to gasoline prices even in excess of the product's 3 percent weight in the consumer price index, Robson attempted to improve the situation by increasing competition in gasoline production and distribution, contemplating changes in the oil import regulations as sticks and carrots. He and his associates at the Justice Department, Office of Emergency Planning (OEP), and CEA did not try to develop a program to increase the volume of oil imports above the 12.2 percent ceiling but rather to make effective adjustments in the *disposition* of existing import flows. Robson tried to break the system of allocations based on historical patterns. Donald F. Turner, head of the Justice De-

72. *Wall Street Journal*, December 28, 1966.

partment's Antitrust Division, provided Robson and his boss, Califano, a detailed set of suggestions. For example, Turner recognized that 700,000 barrels a day, or roughly 12.5 percent, of petroleum used east of the Rockies was imported and that 250,000 barrels a day of this imported oil were allocated on a strictly historical basis, with the lion's share going to the large, integrated firms. Even modest adjustments of the historical quota scheme would free about 75,000 barrels a day for redistribution to small refiners. Members of Turner's staff and of the OEP and the CEA worked through the mechanics of several schemes of altering the allocation patterns in ways that would make petroleum refining more competitive. But the Interior Department was able to thwart their efforts. The oil import program was their turf, and the unholy alliance of inflation fighters at the CEA and the White House, misplaced zealots at the OEP and trustbusters at the Justice Department were not about to be permitted to fiddle with the smoothly oiled apparatus of the Interior Department's assistant secretary for mineral resources, the Office of Oil and Gas, the Oil Import Administration, the Oil Import Appeals Board, and the department's petroleum advisory arm, the National Petroleum Council. Robson was grateful simply to be "able to prevent the oil import program from being made *more* restrictive."[73]

Unfortunately for the Interior Department and its agencies responsible for implementing the import quotas, the program was increasingly battered by pressure from people wanting exemptions. Any exemption from existing quotas permitted producers to take a product that cost very little and sell it at a handsome profit in the American market. Profits from imports were extraordinary because the marginal cost of producing crude oil, particularly in the Middle East, was almost zero while prices in the United States were artificially high. Producers could extract crude oil, particularly in Saudi Arabia, at virtually zero marginal cost. Many categories of exemptions developed over the years. Each has been discussed thoroughly in the literature.[74]

73. Robson to Califano, "Oil Import Program," with attachments, December 28, 1966, Robson-Ross Pricing Files: Oil, LBJL.

74. See, for example, Kenneth W. Dam, "Implementation of Import Quotas: The Case of Oil," *Journal of Law and Economics,* vol. 14 (April 1971), pp. 1–60; and Douglas R. Bohi and Milton Russell, *Limiting Oil Imports: An Economic History and Analysis* (Johns Hopkins University Press for Resources for the Future, 1978). The costs and benefits of various components of the U.S. oil import program as well as the distortions caused by economic analysis focused on the quantitative rather than the qualitative side of the program are analyzed in Yoram Barzel and Christopher D. Hall, *The Political Economy of the Oil Import Quota* (Hoover Institution Press, 1977).

During the late 1960s the temptation to bring pressure to bear on the Department of the Interior became very great. And as one segment of the industry obtained relief from the 12.2 percent rule, the damaged portion of the industry would howl with anger. At the same time, more and more individuals would see an exemption granted and dream up their own exemption to be taken to the department. The official monitoring agencies of the program, the Oil Import Administration and the Oil Import Appeals Board within the department, were kept very busy with increasingly complex and adventurous schemes to get around the spirit of Proclamation 3279. When it served their interest, petitioners brought other economic arguments to bear, particularly the balance of payments. The U.S. petrochemical industry, for example, attempted to obtain an exemption for import petroleum feedstocks on the basis of a balance-of-payments argument. Petrochemical industry spokesmen claimed that the mandatory quotas forced them to buy relatively high-priced feedstocks. Therefore they could not compete with competitors around the world, because of the mandatory quotas. The petitions of the petrochemical industry were fought by the petroleum industry, the suppliers of the feedstocks.

One of the most extensive areas of exemptions was the so-called Islands Program. In these cases, companies petitioned the Interior Department for an exemption based on the need to develop offshore U.S. holdings, particularly Puerto Rico and the Virgin Islands. The petitioners, such as Phillips Petroleum and the Sun Oil Corporation argued that there was a need to develop refining capacity in the islands as a stimulus to local economic development. As a result, they obtained the assistance of political and business leaders in the islands. Major concessions were made to exempt crude oil flowing into Puerto Rico and the Virgin Islands during the 1960s. The refined products could then be moved from the islands into lucrative mainland markets. In some cases, such as the Sunoco project in Puerto Rico, a per barrel contribution to a conservation and development fund was mandated so that the company was required to provide financial support for island development directly as well as indirectly.

One of the most interesting exceptions from a political point of view was the attempt to use foreign trade zones within the continental United States as centers for refining companies, exempt from the 12.2 percent rule. There was a substantial history of companies successfully and unsuccessfully seeking exemption based on proposed operations in a free trade zone. The most controversial and unresolved case, involving Occidental Petroleum, arose toward the end of the Johnson administration. Occidental's chairman, Armand Hammer, wanted an exemption for a refining program at Machiasport, Maine. He had the support of the governor of Maine and the other New England governors, the twelve senators of the New England states, and many congressmen. Hammer also had a wide range of opponents, including the large, integrated oil companies. Unfortunately for Hammer, right before the 1968 election Congressman Hale Boggs, the House Democratic Whip, accused three Occidental Petroleum Corporation executives of attempting to bribe him in order to assist with their proposed Machiasport project. Of course, Boggs was from Louisiana, and many of the opponents of the Machiasport project were from Boggs's home state. Hammer referred to Boggs's charges as "false and outrageous."[75] After the 1968 election the Johnson administration found it impossible to resolve the Occidental petition, which became part of the incoming Nixon administration's agenda.

The Occidental petition was important because it represented the potential difficulties of the multinational firms operating in the Middle East. Armand Hammer had bought Occidental in 1956 when it was a sleepy Los Angeles company. Ten years after the purchase Hammer had aggressively penetrated Libya and had achieved an excellent round of concessions from the government of King Idris. There was immense feeling about this sort of penetration among the major traditional producers in the area. Companies such as Occidental were considered to be threats to the existing order. They represented potential overproduction of petroleum. If permitted to market petroleum in the United States, they would upset the price-quantity balance so carefully developed over the years. The major producers were angry because small independent companies enjoyed a tax advantage in their Middle East operations. The small independent companies paid taxes on the basis of the actual market price of crude oil while the majors paid royalties to the producing countries (that is, "taxes") on the higher, officially posted prices. In 1963 the major producers had tried to use the Organization of Petroleum Exporting Countries against the independent companies. Armand Hammer's major breakthrough in Libya helped to develop Libya's petroleum economy, a development that led to the September 1969 overthrow of King Idris by Colonel Mu'ammar el-Qadaffi.

Of course, the chronic issue in the Johnson years was the national defense justification for limiting crude oil imports. After all, forgetting the protectionist argument, the basic energy justification for restricting the flow of crude oil into the United States was the need to protect the existing

75. William M. Blair, *New York Times,* October 12, 1968.

U.S. production and refining capability in case of conventional war. The experience during World War II was still fresh in everyone's mind. The possibility of interdiction of tankers to the United States by a foreign power buttressed the argument that the United States could not become dependent on foreign oil supplies. The June 1967 Arab-Israeli war strengthened the position of those using national defense as a justification for what was really a protectionist policy. The ability of U.S. producers and refiners to adjust to the temporary Arab oil embargo in 1967 and the closure of the Suez Canal led policymakers to agree that it was in the interest of the United States to maintain the spirit of Proclamation 3279 and to tighten up the exemptions. Nevertheless, as years went by the exemptions became increasingly imaginative, reaching a low-comedy climax in what was known as the Brownsville Loop. Put briefly, the Brownsville Loop took advantage of a loophole in the oil import program that was the first amendment made to Proclamation 3279, an attempt to accommodate Canada and Mexico. Since the oil program was based on the potential danger of tankers being sunk by an enemy of the United States, it made no sense to employ the same restrictions on oil moved by pipeline from Mexico and Canada. So Mexico and Canada were treated as special cases. There was a general overland exemption for oil that was not moved by ship. Companies took advantage of this rule in many ways, the most infamous being the Brownsville, Texas, U-turn operation. The Brownsville Loop was the movement of Mexican oil by tanker to Brownsville, Texas, which is on the Mexican border. The oil was then trucked back into Mexico. Then, it was trucked from Mexico back to Texas. In this way it satisfied the overland exemption rule. In 1967 the Sea Line Corporation petitioned the Department of State to replace the U-turn truck movement with a pipeline. The petition was opposed by virtually everyone, including the governor of Texas. As J. Cordell Moore, assistant secretary of the Interior Department observed, approval of this application could "embarrass the President" by giving positive approval to what was a bizarre use of a gap in the law.[76] The application was rejected, but that it appeared at all indicates the deterioration of the mandatory program.

The deteriorating oil import program would become a major Johnson legacy to the Nixon administration. The monitoring agencies of the Interior Department were thought to have become more sympathetic to petitioners toward the end of the Johnson era; the Oil Import Appeals Board

76. Moore to Stanford Ross, September 13, 1967, Robson-Ross Pricing Files: Oil, LBJL.

changed from having a "heart of stone" to a much lower "threshold of sympathy."[77] Nevertheless, the Nixon administration inherited a *quantitative* program, with quotas expressed in terms of so many barrels of (any) crude oil. Not only was the program increasingly a nightmare to administer and a drain on American petroleum consumers, it resulted in some subtle distortions of import patterns, particularly importation of higher quality oil than would have been imported in the absence of a *quantitative* import program.[78]

The Political Economy of Energy: Coal and Residual Oil

Of all the individual fuel stories that could be developed based on the record of the Johnson administration, perhaps the most fascinating one is that of the efforts of the administration and interested parties to find a compromise between imported residual oil and coal. This particular case is of further interest because it does not directly involve the large integrated oil companies, the companies often perceived as the villains in any energy story. The large integrated firms were disinterested in this particular issue because of the nature of the products involved. Residual oil is a family of distilled fuels—including no. 4, bunker C, and navy special fuel oil—characterized by very high boiling points. It can be used as a fuel, but it commands lower prices than other distilled products such as gasoline.

The fraction of any particular barrel of oil turned into residual oil depends on a number of factors, including the nature of the crude oil itself. Some very thick high-sulfur crudes, such as those from Venezuela, have a high percentage of residual content. Other crudes, such as those from Libya, are much more attractive as far as the economics of distillation are concerned; a much smaller percentage would be left at the bottom of the barrel. Moreover, the percentage of a given barrel of oil becoming residual oil depends on the demands for the end products of the refining process. For example, in 1944 approximately 28 percent of U.S. refinery yield was residual oil. As the demand for lighter products, such as gasoline, increased following World War II, the residual refinery yield declined until by 1964 it was significantly below 10 percent.

77. "Watching Washington," *Oil and Gas Journal*, October 7, 1968, p. 85.

78. This is one of the basic arguments made in Barzel and Hall, *The Political Economy of the Oil Import Quota*. They note that the prices of two "barrels" of oil can differ by over 100 percent owing to factors such as differential API gravities, sulfur content, bottom sediment, and water content.

The demand for residual oil is centered on the East Coast of the United States. East Coast consumption of residual oil being used to fire industrial boilers as well as boilers of electric utilities has remained relatively constant at approximately 1.2 million barrels a day. During the late 1950s and early 1960s residual oil imports doubled, to take up the slack caused by the decline in domestic refinery yields of this distillate. There was nothing mischievous in this particular activity. The changing composition of the demand for refined products simply caused more and more of a given barrel of oil to be turned into products such as gasoline. Little effort was made to expand the demand for residual oil, and the slack between domestic consumption and production was taken up by increased imports. Nevertheless, the coal industry was able to make a case against the residual oil suppliers because the standard practice in the oil industry was to sell the "bottom of the barrel" at a price virtually below cost. The standard pricing practice was to push as much total production and distillation costs as possible on to other products such as gasoline. Thus residual oil could be sold at a relatively low price, a price that angered U.S. coal producers.

Residual oil was subject to the regulations of the Eisenhower mandatory import program, Proclamation 3279. As the years went by, it became standard practice to gradually raise the import quota for residual oil, and as domestic production declined, to maintain a steady supply. Soon after President Johnson assumed office the conflict between residual oil and coal became more intense. In the spring and summer of 1964 the coal industry launched a major campaign against the continuously increasing ceilings on residual oil imports. On March 6, 1964, Interior Secretary Udall announced that his department was again raising the maximum import levels for residual oil. Representatives from the bituminous coal industry immediately weighed in with angry protests. Even the residual suppliers were not happy with Udall's action, because they felt it did not go far enough in resolving the discrepancy between supply and demand. Edward M. Carey, president of the Independent Fuel Oil Marketers of America, Inc., wrote to Udall suggesting the entire program be abolished and that American businessmen be permitted to supply unlimited amounts of residual oil to industrial and utility users. Carey argued that the time has come "to return this market to our traditional enterprise system." His letter was followed by a barrage of communications from the Independent Fuel Oil Marketers' executive director, John K. Evans, and these arguments were buttressed by a joint response from the two senators from New York, Jacob K. Javits and Kenneth B. Keating. Javits and Keating had sent a series of formal letters to Udall arguing that restrictions on residual oil imports were forcing utilities in New York and other Atlantic Coast states to convert from residual oil to coal. This conversion was not only costly, it was inconvenient and lowered air quality.[79]

One of the first coal officials to react to Udall's increase in the ceiling level for residual oil imports was Tony Boyle, president of the UMW. Boyle wrote a formal letter to President Johnson on March 12, 1964, expressing great concern about the impact of residual oil on the U.S. coal industry, recommending that the increase in import levels for the fuel year beginning April 1, 1964, be rescinded in the interest of American coal workers. The Johnson administration took Boyle's letter quite seriously. Presidential assistant Myer Feldman sent the letter to Orren Beaty, Jr., Udall's primary personal assistant. Beaty oversaw the production of a draft response for Johnson's signature; it was based on the argument that in fact the increasing imports of residual oil were taking up the slack in domestic production and were in no way taking jobs away from American coal miners. The Interior Department's position was that it "cannot be assumed that coal would be used in place of No. 6 fuel oil, in all instances, if the latter were unavailable."[80] The response to Boyle noted that many consumers of no. 6 fuel oil had no economically feasible way of converting to coal, because of the capital outlays required, the time required for conversion, and the structural lack of coal storage space. Furthermore, some of the conversion might well be to natural gas rather than to coal if residual oil were unavailable. The draft questioned the employment stimulus that would be provided by even a total abolition of residual imports, noting that since the Kennedy-Johnson administration had come into office in January 1961 bituminous coal production had increased by more than 12 percent, while average daily employment in the industry had declined by more than 4 percent. Output per man in the coal industry had risen rather dramatically in the early 1960s. It was definitely unclear that further demand for coal would stimulate employment.

On the day Udall announced the increased ceilings a UMW delegation met with him; J. Cordell Moore, then head of the Oil Import Administration; and John O'Leary, then deputy assistant secretary of the interior for mineral resources. Boyle urged Udall to rescind his action since it was in-

---

79. Correspondence on this matter between Udall and all interested parties are in the files of the Office of the Secretary, Department of the Interior, Minerals and Fuels, Exports and Imports, Inquiries, pt. 1, January 6, 1964 to April 17, 1964.

80. Beaty to Feldman, March 19, 1964, ibid.

consistent with President Johnson's War on Poverty. He argued that a similar increase in March 1963 had led to a substantial elimination of jobs in U.S. coal mines. Boyle hinted that "pressure for a massive march on Washington of unemployed mine workers was hard to resist." Secretary Udall responded that the "residual fuel oil control program was inherited from the previous administration" and that he "had done his best to maintain it in a bold manner in the face of extremely heavy opposition from New England." He also pointed out that the higher maximum levels announced on March 6, 1964, were "entirely predictable to anyone who had examined the history over the past three years." That is, the Kennedy administration had been systematically increasing the ceilings on residual fuel oil imports.[81]

On March 24, 1964, Secretary Udall reported to the President that the announcement of the new residual oil quotas a few weeks before had aroused the usual cross fire of charges and countercharges. He informed Johnson it was "plain that the extra blast that we received from the UMW was largely related to the internal politics of that union."[82] But contrary to this assumption, the problem did not go away and complaints about the relaxation continued to come from other quarters. The conflict between the residual oil importers and the coal industry began penetrating the trade newspapers, and Interior Department officials became increasingly nervous that President Johnson would fail to support them. There was some concern that the President would cave in to pressure from the coal industry and from Boyle. Secretary Udall took very seriously the oral delegation of power the President had given him immediately following the Kennedy assassination. In Udall's mind, Johnson had decided to divorce himself totally from oil matters, to avoid any charge of presidential conflict of interest. Johnson's close association with the industry was widely known. Since he had been a U.S. Senator from Texas, it was natural to associate him with the industry. Johnson never put this delegation of power in writing, but it had been made orally, and it had received widespread publicity.[83]

On April 25, 1964, Secretary Udall felt it necessary to write Myer Feldman expressing strong opposition to "*any* and all concessions or

81. "Memorandum of Conversation," copy sent to Walter Jenkins by Walter Pozan, March 16, 1964, TA 6/Oil, 3/1/64–4/8/64, LBJL.

82. Stewart L. Udall Papers, Box 115, University of Arizona.

83. See, for example, "President Turns Oil Policy-Making over to Udall," *Washington Post,* December 10, 1963; and "President Gives Udall Oil Power," *New York Times,* December 10, 1963.

promises" made by the President to "Boyle and the coal people." Udall
believed that any promises or concessions made by the President would
be regarded by everyone "as an indication that the President has personally assumed control of the oil programs and oil decisions" in direct con-
tradiction to his delegation of petroleum matters to Udall on December 9,
1963.[84]

A few days later Udall sent a substantive memorandum to Feldman
outlining the nature of the residual oil program, reminding Feldman that
the Interior Department had consistently adhered to the policy established
in the spring of 1963 during a series of White House discussions. The
policy was to maintain the status quo, neither tightening the program to
meet the demands of the coal people nor relaxing it to meet the demands
of the residual oil consumers. He did not see the 1964 adjustment as a
relaxation but rather as a continuing adjustment to maintain equilibrium
of supply and demand. He pointed out to Feldman that politically this
course of action was a balanced one because relief was given neither to
congressional representatives of the coal-producing states nor to the congressional representatives of the residual-consuming states, particularly
New England, the Middle Atlantic region, and Florida.[85]

In early May 1964 Joseph E. Moody wrote to Secretary Udall about
how his policies were creating an oversupply of residual oil on the East
Coast and that this in turn was creating chaotic conditions in all fuel markets.[86] Udall's increase in the residual quota for the fuel year beginning
April 1, 1964, by 20 million barrels, according to Moody, was producing
a significant oversupply and some price discounting. Moody asked Udall
to take another long, hard look at the 1964–65 quota.

In June 1964 members of the National Coal Policy Conference met
with President Johnson. The operators, railroads, and utilities doing business in Appalachia offered to invest $1.5 billion during the next few years
if they could be assured that residual oil imports would be maintained at

84. Udall to Feldman, April 25, 1964, Udall Papers, Box 115, University of
Arizona.

85. Udall to Feldman, "Residual Fuel Oil Import Control Program," April 28,
1964, ibid. One technological fact of life not mentioned in the various government
memorandums at this stage of the conflict was that many users of residual oil, particularly in New England and Florida, would be incapable of switching to coal because of the absence of appropriate railroad facilities. Maine and Florida in particular did not have the railroad capability to become major coal users. Residual
oil could be brought in by truck; it would be economically inefficient to truck in
coal.

86. BE 5-5/CO1, 11/22/63–7/31/64, LBJL.

current levels. On June 15, 1964, the conference formally proposed that the President change residual oil import quota policy to stabilize imports by limiting the maximum amount that might be imported into the United States east of the Rockies to 50 percent of domestic consumption during the corresponding quarter of the previous year. The conference argued that 18,000 additional mine jobs and 15,000 additional railroad jobs in Appalachia would be stimulated by 1973.

Feldman advised Johnson that Udall had "turned down this offer" and had talked "privately in terms of releasing all controls on residual oil imports next year." Feldman informed Johnson that he had been discussing this matter with Moody and with Moody's counsel and had concluded that the best solution was to seek an alternative program "designed to deal with all the problems of the fuel and energy industries of the United States." One provision of such a program would be the establishment of a "permanent National Energy Commission." As a preliminary step, Feldman suggested that Johnson appoint an appropriate cabinet-level committee chaired by Udall. Feldman pointed out that the coal industry would be unhappy if Udall were designated as chairman, probably preferring the secretary of commerce.[87]

On June 24, 1964, President Johnson formally appointed a special cabinet committee composed of the secretaries of state, defense, interior, commerce, and labor. The state stimulus for the creation of the committee was the recently released report of the Appalachian Regional Commission. Johnson directed the committee to "determine what steps can and should be taken now by the executive departments, to carry forward the policy of developing, within the framework of private enterprise, new and additional markets for the Appalachian coal industry and assuring its participation in the national energy market on a fair competitive basis."[88]

Thus President Johnson had found it necessary to turn over this problem to his number one troubleshooter, Defense Secretary McNamara, who became chairman of the committee and would presumably be immune from the various special interests involved. Not only would McNamara be capable of independent judgment, but he would be able to secure a staff of people who would not be oriented or bound to a particular constituency.

The formation of the Cabinet Committee on Appalachian Coal was a

87. Ibid.
88. Johnson to McNamara, June 24, 1964, BE 5-5/CO1, 11/22/63–7/31/64, LBJL.

rather closely held secret in the Johnson administration. There were a few references to it in the press, particularly in an article in *Forbes,* which had the story a little bit twisted but which generally recognized that McNamara was in charge and that the objective was to do something about the bituminous coal industry in Appalachia. *Forbes* reported that McNamara had been told by President Johnson "to push coal for all it's worth." That may have been the impression that coal officials had; and certainly the article was based on interviews with coal officials. But McNamara was given the job because he represented a potentially objective point of view. *Forbes* reported that at the same time McNamara received his instructions, Johnson told the U.S. representative to the General Agreement on Tariffs and Trade negotiations in Geneva to give coal top priority and to persuade nations that had trade barriers against U.S. coal to lower them.[89] *Petty's Oil Letter* of September 26, 1964, said President Johnson had assigned consideration of coal's place in the U.S. economy to a cabinet-level committee headed by Defense Secretary McNamara. The publication argued that it was "a takedown for Udall to have LBJ hand the coal study to McNamara" and that it would be even worse "if LBJ accepts McNamara's recommendations."

During November and December 1964, after the election, the McNamara group moved in several directions. On November 14, 1964, McNamara, Udall, and McNamara's special assistant, Joseph Califano, met with officials of the Humble Oil and Refining Company. Assistant Secretary of the Interior for Mineral Resources John M. Kelly was also present. McNamara and Udall wanted Humble's views on the current residual oil quota system, the competitive relationships between residual oil and coal on the East Coast, and the potential competition among atomic energy, coal, and residual oil. They had asked the chairman of the board of Humble to be prepared to explain how the price of residual oil exported from Venezuela into the United States was determined. Similar meetings were held with coal producers as well as with coal users, such as the Consolidated Edison Power Company. There was a substantial exchange of correspondence from the oil industry to the government and from the coal producers and users to the government. The correspondents were given an opportunity to address issues raised in their rivals' submissions.

By February 20, 1965, the Cabinet Committee had prepared a draft report for the President's consideration. After some internal deliberations

89. "Coal: To the Rescue?" *Forbes,* September 15, 1964, p. 17.

the committee transmitted this report to the President with a four-page cover memorandum by McNamara. Basically the committee rejected the National Coal Policy Conference proposal that the residual oil import quotas east of the Rocky Mountains be reduced. It had found that the conference's assertion that this proposed change in the residual oil policy would create 33,000 additional jobs was incorrect, and it unanimously recommended rejection of the proposal. With the exception of Secretary of Labor W. Willard Wirtz, the committee members in fact believed that continuation of residual oil import quotas was "not in the national interest and that they should be removed." Wirtz disagreed with the view of the majority because in his opinion elimination of quotas would adversely affect the Appalachian economy and the "impact on labor interests might be particularly adverse."[90]

One of the basic conclusions of the McNamara report was that nuclear power, not residual oil, was the true, long-run competitive threat to the coal industry and that the National Coal Policy Conference had chosen the wrong villain. Given the federal government's extraordinary support for nuclear research and development, there was no need to tell the coal people what they should have known anyway. The McNamara report was closely held. In fact, Secretary Udall told the press that the report was not yet complete during a news conference on the 1965–66 residual oil quotas.[91]

As the time for decisions for the new fuel year was drawing close, the residual oil import program again became of major interest in the press and a problem for the Executive Office of the President. Udall had the McNamara report behind him as government policy but was unable to make the existence of the report known. He had to appear to make decisions about the future of the residual oil program as if he were acting entirely on his own and as if the McNamara group were still working on the problem. In late March and early April 1965, when the new residual oil program was announced, Udall went through one of the toughest peri-

90. McNamara to the President, March 17, 1965, with attached report of the Cabinet Committee on Appalachian Coal, March 8, 1965, BE 5-5/CO1, 10/1/64–, LBJL. The McNamara report was classified "confidential" and was not made available to the public until February 1978, when the Department of Defense acted favorably on a Freedom of Information Act request to declassify the document.

91. Presidential Assistant Harry McPherson sent a copy of the McNamara report to CEA Chairman Gardner Ackley on April 12, 1965, with a covering note that said: "Jack Valenti asked me to pass this on to you. So far as the world is concerned, it doesn't exist." BE 5-5/CO1, 10/1/64–, LBJL.

ods of his public life. A wide range of interests actively sought to influence his decision as well as to take advantage of the decision once it was made. For example, if he decided to permit more imports of residual oil, the State Department wanted to maximize its advantage. It wanted to be able to help cement relations with the Venezuelan government in any way it could. The department proposed to permit the Venezuelans to take a great deal of credit for any relaxation in the residual oil program, in order to help them improve their own relations with their constituents. The Johnson administration was rather nervous about this particular course of action, considering it to be potentially dangerous. The parties damaged by any relaxation would then argue that the United States had caved in to a foreign government. During this period a substantial volume of cable traffic passed between the U.S. embassy in Caracas and Washington in an attempt to find some way of permitting the Venezuelans to take advantage of any relaxation policy. The same line of activity took place between Washington and the American embassy in Ottawa.

President Johnson had given Secretary Udall "full control over oil matters" fifteen months earlier. Much effort was spent "for the sake of the President staying neutral on oil matters."[92] It was inevitable that Johnson would find it impossible to keep from knowing about and intervening in oil issues.

On March 30, 1965, in his weekly report to the President, Udall reported that the oil import program would expire in two days and that he was going to announce a new program at a press conference on the afternoon of April 1. He informed the President that the "quota controls presently penalize the East Coast residual oil consumers" and that the "most inequitable feature in the existing program is the penalty effect of the program in those areas—Florida and New England—where coal and oil are not in competition." To "eliminate this gross inequity" Udall informed the President that he was "placing Florida and the five New England states under 'open end' controls." Strict quota controls would be continued in the Middle Atlantic states. Udall concluded by observing that he had "serious doubts whether we can justify this program in the future 'on national security' grounds." On a cover memorandum to W. Marvin Watson, special assistant to the President, Udall noted that the Florida and New England "Congressional people will applaud long and loud." The Interior Department had held hearings on the program in early March, and a num-

92. Memorandum, Jake Jacobsen to Marvin Watson, March 18, 1965, TA 6/Oil, 3/1/64–4/8/64, LBJL.

ber of New England senators, including Edward M. Kennedy of Massachusetts and Edmund S. Muskie of Maine, felt sufficiently strong about the program to appear in person at the hearings. Udall observed that the coal people, the two West Virginia senators, and Tony Boyle would "attempt to see the President in an effort to persuade him to reverse the decision." Udall advised Watson to get "ready for some emotional phone calls" and also observed that members of Congress from the Middle Atlantic area would "be mildly disappointed." Senators Jacob Javits and Robert F. Kennedy of New York had appeared at the early March hearings and would undoubtedly be disappointed at the maintenance of strict control quotas in their region. At 7:00 P.M. on March 30 presidential assistants Harry C. McPherson, Jr., and Lee C. White met with Secretary Udall and, according to White's report to the President, "advised him that a number of us had discussed the residual oil situation and concluded that it could be politically disastrous for the President to go forward with the lifting of quotas for New England and Florida."[93]

Udall informed the two men that "he would do whatever [they] told him to do." White informed the President that Udall had nevertheless "made a persuasive case" not to reverse his position. He had already "contacted New England and Florida senators indicating what he was likely to recommend." A sixty-page booklet describing the new program was already "printed and held under tight control" and could "be destroyed"; such a decision was "difficult to keep secret in a large department where oil and gas reporters have contacts at every level." Should Udall reverse his decision, according to White, it would "be widely and easily interpreted as a decision by the President or the White House reversing the Secretary of the Interior who had publicly been proclaimed as the one to make these decisions."

After White had summarized the pros and cons of the reversal of Udall's program, he advised the President: "Although your decision [to reverse Udall] was firm and unequivocably obvious and rests upon your sound political instinct, I have the impression that we were not fully aware of how far this had proceeded and, therefore, were unable to judge the political disadvantages of forcing a reversal on Udall." Udall *was* prepared to reverse himself but White considered that the new information warranted bringing the matter back to Johnson again. White concluded his memorandum to Johnson with some observations about Udall's team

93. Material in this and the succeeding five paragraphs is from TA 6/Oil, 3/1/64–4/8/64, LBJL.

behavior: "When we confronted him with our view that he should reverse his decision, he said, 'I will do whatever you tell me to do—I am the President's boy.' " The next day, March 31, White informed Johnson that he had talked again with Secretary Udall. Udall proposed that the existing program be continued for a year but that there be "some increase to adjust for the decline in domestic production and for the growth of the residual share of the total growth and demand for all fuels throughout the past year." In response to anticipated questions, Udall would indicate that "the President was not personally involved in the matter."

Udall defended his maintenance of the old program and failure to promulgate the new program on the legal grounds that his own departmental lawyers, as well as counsel at the Department of Justice, the Bureau of the Budget, and the White House had advised that the secretary of the interior was not authorized to institute such a change since it "ran counter to the whole business of the proclamation which rested on a finding by President Eisenhower that the national security would be impaired unless there were import controls." (It might be noted that the *Wall Street Journal* reported at the time that the attorney for the New England Council had submitted a legal brief early in 1965 pointing out that the proposed Udall revision was not only legal but consistent with the whole program. The lawyer was Charles W. Colson.)

In early April Udall's announcement received the expected response. On April 4 Lee White informed the President that the senators from New England believed "they have been given the run around and have been tricked." Senators Javits and Kennedy of New York wired Johnson urging him to cancel the Eisenhower proclamation, an action that would undercut Udall's defense of his reversal. (White refers to a confidential McNamara Committee Report, but there is not enough information in his memorandum to indicate that this is the ad hoc committee referred to above.)

In late April the President continued to be bombarded with requests from New England senators to see him to discuss the question of residual oil. On April 29 presidential assistant Jack Valenti informed Johnson of constant pressure on the White House to give Democratic senators some time with the President to discuss the matter. On Valenti's memorandum Johnson wrote the following: "I must not bring oil into W.H. and tell them not to insist—Ask them to see [Bufford] Ellington [director of the Office of Emergency Planning] if they won't see Udall." (As noted above, the OEP was as responsible as any agency for energy policy before the

Nixon years, although particularly after Kennedy and McNamara had transferred its civil defense functions to the Defense Department, OEP's mission was rather limited. In the Nixon administration it would blossom dramatically under the name of the Office of Emergency Preparedness during the 1971 wage-price freeze. It was killed in 1973.)

This story has a denouement: oil import restrictions were caught up in the administration's effort to restrain price increases during late 1965 and early 1966. Until 1964 the price of refined petroleum products had been generally declining from the peaks reached during the Suez crisis in 1957. During 1964 and 1965 crude oil prices had not risen, but the prices of refined petroleum products had. And during 1965 stocks of refined petroleum products declined. The administration reacted to this tightening of the domestic oil situation in many ways, including action between December 1965 and March 1966 to add to the quotas even before the beginning of the new fuel year on April 1, 1966.

On November 25, 1965, CEA Chairman Gardner Ackley reported to presidential assistant Califano on the petroleum industry and price stability. He noted that petroleum had been one of the sources of price pressure during 1965, that earnings in the industry were also up, that the supply of foreign petroleum was determined by the U.S. oil import quotas, and that except for the East Coast, residual fuel oil imports were held at 1957 levels. The OEP was undertaking a thorough examination of the national security basis of the program, he said, and was trying to determine if the practice of setting levels of residual fuel oil imports to the East Coast to fill the estimated gap between ex ante supply and demand should be continued. Ackley argued that termination of the program "would cut coal production by about 1 percent or less than half a year's normal growth."[94]

On December 17, 1965, Cailfano informed the President that he had "worked out the residual oil situation" in such a way that Secretary Udall would announce that there would "be substantial relaxation (but *not* decontrol of imports)" and that there would "be no indication of terminating the program." Califano argued that this "should keep the coal people and the New England people both from getting too unhappy" and would be "a step that will enable us to lift controls about a year from now if that is the right thing to do."[95]

The Department of the Interior raised permissible imports of residual

94. BE 4/0, LBJL.
95. BE 5-2, 11/17/65–12/28/65, LBJL.

fuel oil by 50 percent, effective from December until April 1, 1966. This increase was justified on the basis of the need to restrain oil and coal prices.

On March 22, 1966, Udall informed Johnson that he had met that day with Attorney General Nicholas Katzenbach; Postmaster General Lawrence F. O'Brien; Ferris Bryant, OEP director; Califano; and Jake Jacobsen about the new program for residual oil. He told Johnson that under the old program the Department of the Interior "would announce before April 1 a maximum import level for the entire heating year. Quotas would then be allocated to a relatively small number of firms." The new program, which Udall and his conferees had proposed to implement, would expand eligibility of quota licenses and would in general add a great deal of flexibility to the quota program. The new program followed the recommendations of Speaker of the House John McCormick and other members of the New England congressional group. Califano had forwarded Udall's memorandum to the President with a covering note in which he observed that the New England and Florida congressional delegations would "be delighted" and that members of Congress from coal-producing states "should not be too unhappy because the quota system remains (in a nominal sense at least)—and this is more than the coal people realistically expect." Califano noted that under the new program Udall would set an overall annual import level that residual oil users would not be expected to consume and that this was essentially what had been done since December. It was part of the administration's strategy to show that in fact unlimited residual imports would not seriously affect the coal industry. At the same time, as long as the quota system remained in effect in a nominal sense, the secretary of the interior could "always tighten the screw should there be some serious adverse affect on the coal industry."[96]

Among other things, the narrative above indicates that even when the President explicitly asked his advisers and lieutenants to keep him out of the oil picture, it was impossible for them to do so. Johnson could ask his people not to "bring oil into the White House," but it was simply too important to be kept out.

Concluding Reflections

The Johnson administration was a transitional one for U.S. energy policies. The theme of energy and fuels policy in the Johnson era is charac-

96. Information reported in this paragraph is found in CF TA 6/Oil, LBJL.

terized by a lack of any notion of impending scarcity or price increases. This tended to subordinate energy issues to other political or economic issues. The Johnson era was a high-water mark for technological optimism, permitting decisions to be made on grounds of politics or regional equity.

Donald Hornig, S. David Freeman, and their OST colleagues sought to unify national energy policies and policymaking. They did not succeed, but seeds were planted. The Interior Department tried to protect the fossil fuel industry from itself, particularly from the lure of cheap foreign crude. The AEC turned a corner in the road to a nuclear future for electricity and pressed to go faster and widen the road. All these lines would intersect in the 1970s, taking energy policies from the background to center stage.

CHAPTER SIX

Energy Policy under Nixon: Mainly Putting Out Fires

NEIL DE MARCHI

IT IS COMMONLY believed that serious thinking about energy in the Nixon administration began only with the crisis of 1973. On the contrary, the ingredients of a good program were at hand in 1971 and 1972. The precise date, however, is of secondary importance, since neither earlier nor later schemes came to anything like a comprehensive *implemented* policy. Several things stood in the way.

First, the government eventually came to acknowledge the adverse effect of its own regulatory policies; those, for example, over natural gas in interstate commerce. But it could not reverse consumer sentiment quickly or accustom people (or Congress) to the notion that energy prices must be much higher in the future. The rationale behind utility rates policy and control of natural gas pricing was that energy should be available at "fair" (competitive) prices; but over the years this had come to mean relatively low prices.

THANKS ARE DUE to Doris Dewton, Charles J. DiBona, John A. Hill, William A. Johnson, Rodney Weiher, Roy Niemuller, Robert Plett, John F. Schaefer, and Robert Shepherd, with whom I was able to discuss various aspects of energy policy-making in the Nixon years. William Johnson was especially helpful in the early stages of my work, and he generously opened his extensive personal files to me. I further gratefully acknowledge the cooperation of Robert Anderson, records officer in the Department of the Interior; Richard G. Hewlett and his staff, especially archivist Roger M. Anders, in the Historian's Office of the Department of Energy; Jack Best, who guided me through the Gerald L. Parsky papers in the Treasury Department; and Jerry Hess and Michael Leahy and their associates, who supplied similar services with respect to the records of the Economic Stabilization Program and the Office of Science and Technology at the National Archives and Records Service in Washington, D.C.

In the footnotes to this chapter, the National Archives, Washington, D.C., is referred to as NA, and the Gerald R. Ford Library in Ann Arbor, Michigan, is referred to as GRFL.

Second, turning this assumption around was made more difficult by the government's equivocation about the oil industry. There was a long history of involvement, mostly toward the end of sustaining a strong domestic production capability. But in the 1970s the public felt entitled to know why, if prorationing, special tax provisions, and a Mandatory Oil Import Program (MOIP) had been so essential to maintaining domestic capacity in the industry, there was now a decline in drilling, refinery capacity had been increasingly exported, and still higher prices were said to be needed to stimulate domestic exploration and production. By allowing imports to increase whenever shortages occurred, and through the granting of exceptions to imported products, the government had gone a long way toward undermining its own case for supporting the domestic industry.

Third, the government found that it had been moving in the wrong direction concerning coal, acceding to environmentalists' requests for cleaner air, encouraging a switch from coal to oil and gas-fired boilers, and thereby exacerbating the pressure on oil and gas supplies. But retracing its steps and pressing for an accelerated program of nuclear power production and of strip-mined coal proved difficult. Along that path lay confrontation with the same environmentalist coalition the administration had succored in its first years in office.

Fourth, the effect of government regulatory programs typically is not only to distort the allocation of resources but to vest certain interests in the continuation of particular programs. And the vested interests are not only those of immediate beneficiaries but also of the bureaucracies established to run the programs. In addition to vested interests and program bureaucrats, and completing what one writer has called "the iron triangle" are those members of Congress who control the shaping of legislation and appropriations.[1] Although in its first years the Nixon administration sought a more coordinated structure for dealing with energy issues, its efforts were unsuccessful, since the iron triangle made major reorganization difficult. At a somewhat later stage, when President Nixon's integrity was impugned and his ability to lead was seriously questioned, when a midterm election swept into Congress a large number of freshmen Democrats and the Democratic caucus succeeded in diminishing the power of committee chairmen, and when not only the freshmen but many other congressmen felt no special obligation to the White House, the problem mani-

1. John C. Whitaker, *Striking a Balance: Environment and Natural Resources Policy in the Nixon-Ford Years* (American Enterprise Institute for Public Policy Research, 1976), chap. 3.

fested itself differently. Anti-White House and anti-Big Oil sentiments then appeared, further complicating the workings of the already cumbersome congressional committee system, making it virtually impossible for a coherent energy policy to be accepted as an administration initiative in the national interest and to be allowed to pass unscathed into legislation.

Finally, while the administration and Congress did move with alacrity at the time of the embargo in 1973, the programs adopted and the authority granted to deal with the crisis were not those best suited to resolving the long-run energy problems of the nation. With the setting up of mandatory allocation programs, the simultaneous creation of groups who would wish to see the programs extended in scope and time was inevitable. This turned out to be an important constraint on the kinds of proposals the administration could realistically present to Congress. For its part, Congress, which before 1973 had displayed a serious concern with designing a long-term policy, now busied itself with finding and enacting suitable punishments for the party it identified as most culpable in the matter of shortages and the crisis, namely the major oil companies.

These will be recurring themes in the story that follows. The story will be told, however, from the perspective of an administration trying to devise and implement energy policy. Despite the steady decline in presidential power over the period 1969–76 (and beyond), it seems best to try to account for the series of executive branch initiatives in the energy area as a way of imparting a measure of coherence to an otherwise impossibly complex history. A further simplification has been adopted: where it is possible or desirable to choose between alternative versions of what the "energy problem" is, the standpoint taken is that of the economist. Shortages are defined in terms of prices that are in some way constrained, and solutions are spoken of as either efficient or not. Since this is not an essay in policy assessment, the main reason for adopting one standpoint is to provide a line of reference, not to award praise and blame. Nonetheless, telling the story from an economist's point of view will alter it in various ways from the story that an environmentalist or a specialist in international relations might tell, and the reader is alerted to this fact at the outset.

One further word of explanation and a disclaimer. The account of energy policy under Nixon runs into that of energy policy under Ford. This is desirable in the sense that there were strong elements of continuity in the two administrations. The style of the two presidents was very different, however, even when the substance of their initiatives was the same.

These differences were important, and they are deliberately preserved by making the account of the Nixon years more episodic and that of the Ford years more systematic. One resulting peculiarity is that no attempt is made to define the energy problem until the discussion of Ford in chapter 7. A second is that many Nixon initiatives are not mentioned until they can be set in the context of the corresponding Ford initiative, though by then it becomes more natural to regard them merely as preludes. By way of final warning, while the aim in undertaking this study was to provide a more or less comprehensive statement on the development of energy policy under Nixon and Ford, the study's limitations reflect those of the records available. In some cases access has been restricted; but even where very full written records exist and have been opened to the public, it is not certain that they accurately convey the flavor of debate and the true process of decisionmaking.

Benign Neglect: "Industry Is Responsible"

When Nixon took office signs of an energy emergency were already present. Electric power difficulties had been experienced in the form of brownouts. Natural gas was recognized widely as being in short supply. The potential environmental costs of increasing energy supplies were flashed before a startled nation in news reports of loss of birdlife and damage to beaches from a blowout in a Union Oil Company well in the Santa Barbara Channel when Nixon was barely eight days into his presidency. Nonetheless, by the standard of the hectic pace normal to recent administrations, the period January 1969–January 1973 was a relatively quiet one on the energy front, providing opportunity at least for a serious look at the nation's energy needs and prospects, free from overriding exigencies.

An early concern that persisted throughout Nixon's five years and Gerald Ford's two years in office was the organization and coordination of energy policy. What Nixon inherited was a system in which energy oversight was dispersed along lines justified in part simply by usage, and where coordinated high-level discussion, insofar as it took place at all, was usually no more than a response to some immediate problem.

The nature of policy responsibilities as they were understood toward the end of the Johnson administration had been explained in 1967 by J. Cordell Moore, assistant secretary of the interior, in some remarks to the Energy Committee of the Organisation for Economic Co-operation and Development. Moore stated that by energy policy the U.S. government meant

that industry is responsible for production, distribution, marketing and pricing, except in markets where fair prices cannot be guaranteed by competition, such as, for example, gas and electricity in interstate commerce. The Federal Government attempts to establish a climate favorable for the growth of the energy industries. It tries to stimulate initiative, to help advance technology, and to encourage and maintain competition. It monitors the overall energy situation to be sure that the national security and the broad interests of the public are protected, it applies constraints to the operations of the private sector where the public interest so requires, and it makes liberal use of the instrument of persuasion at times to influence the course followed by the private sector. But the Federal Government does not control production, it does not direct the efforts of industry, and it does not involve itself in company affairs. Even in the regulatory field its posture is mainly reactive rather than positive. Information on costs, reserves, processes, and plans is generally closely guarded by the companies and they are not required to divulge it. . . . I stress our lack of authoritative knowledge concerning these matters because it is a basic part of our policy. . . .[2]

This now reads curiously like a statement from another age, but it was basically the position taken in the early years of the Nixon administration. Government's proper role was to monitor the energy situation with an eye to the national security, to coping with emergencies, and to ensuring that the consumer's interest would be served by maintaining an environment favorable to the growth of the energy industries, subject only to price controls being used where competition seemed naturally not strong enough to guarantee "fair" prices.

Not surprisingly, agency and departmental responsibilities reflected the several goals of this policy. Reliable sources of imports and a strong domestic energy industry (chiefly oil) were complementary objectives. The Departments of State and Defense were primarily concerned with security and, in particular, oil import and naval oil reserves policy. The Office of Emergency Preparedness (OEP) watched over the import program and stockpiles, though the MOIP itself was operated from within the Department of the Interior, where expertise in the oil industry was concentrated. As James Cochrane has noted earlier, during the Johnson years it was customary to think of individual fuels, not of "energy," and

---

2. *Energy Policy Papers*, Committee Print, Senate Committee on Interior and Insular Affairs, Serial no. 93-43 (92-72), 93 Cong. 2 sess. (Government Printing Office, 1974), pp. 350–51.

on into the Nixon period the department had responsibility for coal and for mineral leasing policy. Separate energy interests were also represented in part by special offices in the department. Much coal technology and related research was funded by the Office of Coal Research and the Bureau of Mines, while the problems of the oil and gas industry formed a large part of the responsibilities of the Office of Oil and Gas. Research on the civilian uses of nuclear energy, meanwhile, was the special province of the Atomic Energy Commission. The task of maintaining "fair" prices for interstate gas and for electricity fell to the Federal Power Commission, while surveillance of the competitive climate in the energy industries was exercised by the Federal Trade Commission and the Antitrust Division of the Justice Department. Numerous other agencies, offices in the executive branch, and departments claimed some authority or undertook oversight of certain energy-related matters.[3]

There was nothing irrational about this dispersion of tasks, but it was an arrangement best suited to a situation in which there were no energy-environmental conflicts and in which the separate segments of the energy industry were in a healthy supply condition. Any change in these circumstances, apart from a strictly temporary shortage in one fuel alone, was likely to prove the system inadequate.

Energy Policy by Default: The Task Force on Oil Imports

Ironically, the first step toward direct cabinet-level involvement in energy policy was taken without any centralizing or coordinating purpose in view. On February 20, 1969, Nixon announced that he was assuming direct responsibility for oil import policy and that the MOIP was to be reviewed by a cabinet task force. This action was in one sense merely restoring to the White House the directional control over federal oil policy that Texan Lyndon Johnson had felt it prudent to relinquish in favor of the Interior Department. But the review of the quota system itself was a move to stem a rising tide of criticism in Congress and elsewhere.

Several anomalies in the import program had been receiving embar-

3. For a more or less complete tabulation of responsibilities, though of slightly later date, see *Federal Energy Reorganization: Historical Perspective,* prepared by the Congressional Research Service for the Senate Committee on Interior and Insular Affairs, Serial no. 94-46 (92-136), 94 Cong. 2 sess. (GPO, 1976), pp. 54–55 and discussion in the several analyses forming pt. 1.

rassing publicity. Among the more puzzling developments were the existence of "el loophole," and the rights granted several companies to refine cheaper foreign oil in Puerto Rico and even in the Virgin Islands and to export the refined products to the United States in competition with fuels derived from higher-priced domestic crude oil and at the expense of the import quotas of other companies. Free imports of residual fuel oil into Petroleum Administration for Defense District I (New England) were also troublesome, as was the fact that industry outlays for oil exploration, the drilling rate, and investment in refineries had all begun to decline (elsewhere they were increasing), while the justification for the import program was supposed to lie in the encouragement it gave to the home industry.[4] Moreover, the pressure to grant still more exceptions continued unabated. The New England Congressional Caucus in particular had been asking why there should not be an extension of the privileges accorded refiners in Puerto Rico and the Virgin Islands in the form of a free trade zone in Maine to allow construction of a refinery there using imported oil exclusively. In addition the costs of the program to the consumer had come under scrutiny. Senator William Proxmire, for example, had begun serious probes into the cost of maintaining the system, expressing concern that "unlike almost every other government program" the transfer costs in this case were not screened by any budgetary process.[5] Finally, some of the major oil-producing companies themselves, whose share of imports under the program suffered with every exception granted the petrochemical producers, had been reduced to urging a review of the whole set of arrangements.[6]

Energy was not one of Richard Nixon's concerns. In this instance, as in many others, it seems likely that he acted to forestall something worse on the part of Congress, as well as to cultivate the image of an active, bold President. Whatever his true reasons, he was unprepared for what transpired. Secretary of Labor George P. Shultz was appointed to head the Cabinet Task Force on Oil Import Control, and he promptly set in train a typical economist's investigation. To remove the inquiry above special interests Schultz hired a team of outside economists and a professional

4. See chapter 5 in this volume; also Allan T. Demaree, "Our Crazy, Costly Life with Oil Quotas," *Fortune,* June 1969, pp. 105–07, 175–76, 180, 182.

5. William Proxmire to George P. Shultz, November 5, 1969 (copy), Secretary of the Interior's Files, Subject File: Minerals and Fuels–Exports and Imports, Permits, Department of the Interior.

6. "White House Assumes Import Reins, Orders Program Review," *Oil and Gas Journal,* vol. 67 (February 24, 1969), p. 42.

staff. The task force accepted its primary concern as being national security but proceeded to ask how this goal might be accomplished "with minimum cost and maximum advantage to the economy, to various regions of the country, to consumers and producers, and to other segments of the industry." Furthermore, it declared, "We also seek minimum disruption to and maximum opportunity for the free play of competitive market forces."[7]

The framework of the investigation having been thus defined, it was predictable that a tariff would be deemed preferable to quotas as a means of controlling imports. Not that this was the unanimous view of the task force. The secretaries of the interior and of commerce submitted a dissenting report in which they argued that removing volume controls and the consequent lowering of the price of domestic crude that would occur would have serious disincentive effects on domestic exploration and production. John N. Nassikas, chairman of the Federal Power Commission, added that since the production of natural gas depends for the most part on the oil companies and independent producers of oil and gas, reserves of natural gas also would be reduced.

Industry reaction to the task force recommendations was overwhelmingly negative, and a hundred congressmen signed a letter to the President warning against action that would reduce domestic crude prices.[8] Just one year after ordering the most comprehensive review of the MOIP to date, Nixon announced that he was deferring any major change in it. At the same time, he followed one of the task force's suggestions by creating an Oil Policy Committee. This was to be under the direction of Brigadier General George A. Lincoln, who also headed the Office of Emergency Preparedness, and was to include all members of the task force, plus the attorney general and the chairman of the Council of Economic Advisers, but with the significant exception of Shultz. The new committee was to consider "interim and long-term adjustments that will increase the effectiveness and enhance the equity of the oil import program."[9]

Setting up the Oil Policy Committee may have been intended simply as

7. U.S. Cabinet Task Force on Oil Import Control, *The Oil Import Question: A Report on the Relationship of Oil Imports to the National Security* (GPO, 1970), p. 8.

8. "What a 30-Cent Crude Price Cut Would Do to U.S. Oil," *Oil and Gas Journal*, vol. 68 (January 26, 1970), pp. 81–86.

9. "Statement about the Report of the Cabinet Task Force on Oil Import Control, February 20, 1970," *Public Papers: Richard Nixon, 1970* (GPO, 1975), p. 195. For a discussion of these maneuverings see Douglas R. Bohi and Milton Russell, *Limiting Oil Imports: An Economic History and Analysis* (Johns Hopkins University Press for Resources for the Future, 1978), pp. 189–200.

a way of shelving politically difficult decisions.[10] But General Lincoln, as director of the OEP, was already seriously occupied with energy monitoring on a broad front, and it now seemed that he was to assume *policy* responsibility for oil imports. This gave an inducement to the OEP to develop a more coordinated approach to energy supply problems than had hitherto been pursued anywhere outside the Department of the Interior. This was reinforced in September 1970 with the creation of an interagency Joint Board on Fuel Supply and Transportation, also under Lincoln. The board was to identify emergency problems and coordinate appropriate remedial action. Its meetings were attended by agency representatives of at least assistant secretarial standing, so that it complemented the Oil Policy Committee as a high-level forum on energy questions.

Lincoln's formal responsibility was quite circumscribed, however, and did not include initiating changes in the MOIP beyond those that had been agreed on by the whole Cabinet Task Force. All decisions were taken after full consultation with Peter M. Flanigan in the White House, Hollis Dole in the Interior Department, and other members of the Oil Policy Committee. When the need for energy policy, as distinct from fuels programs, began to surface, Lincoln's OEP staff emerged as the only group that was both nonaligned and capable of producing general analyses of energy issues. Its analytical and coordinating services were first-rate, but lacking departmental status, it still fell short of being a full policymaking force.[11]

10. During the spring and summer the House Interior Subcommittee on Mines and Mining, the Senate Subcommittee on Antitrust and Monopoly, and the House Ways and Means Committee all heard testimony basically critical of the task force proposals. On August 13, 1970, General Lincoln, with the concurrence of the Oil Policy Committee, recommended to the President that all thought of moving to tariff control of oil imports be discontinued since radical changes in the system might prove to be ill-timed because of certain improvements already effected in the quota system and uncertainties to do with the timing of Alaskan oil, the effect of the environmental program, the prospect of increased imports from insecure sources, and possible changes in the world energy market. Nixon accepted this advice. See Bohi and Russell, *Limiting Oil Imports,* pp. 200–03.

11. This is the combined assessment of several OEP staff members (Wanda Porterfield, Robert Shepherd, Robert Plett, and Doris Dewton) as expressed during conversations with the author. A chronological record of OEP memorandums and actions kept by Dorothy K. Clark and now in her possession confirms their impressions. Lincoln may have been inhibited from moving more aggressively to influence policy because there never was a formal executive order delegating to him even policy responsibility for the MOIP. Lincoln was bothered about this, and Clark's historical file is replete with summaries of memorandums on the subject that passed between Lincoln and Flanigan for several months. Lincoln was a master at involving others but seemed unable to decide whether he personally was in a decision-making role, whether it was the Oil Policy Committee as a whole, or whether a simple majority of the principals on the committee was sufficient.

It quickly became clear to Lincoln that if the nation's security and future energy supplies were to be assured, a range of action was required, beginning immediately and extending far beyond an improved oil import program or the occasional price increases for domestic crude that had been allowed in the interest of security. Nothing short of a coordinated look at energy R&D, energy and environmental conflicts, and the investment needs of the energy industries would do. Lincoln tried without apparent success to draw the attention of the President in this direction.[12]

Science Advising and Energy Policy

Lincoln's was not quite a lone voice in the executive branch. From very early on in the new administration the Energy Policy Staff of the Office of Science and Technology, under S. David Freeman, had engaged in a whole range of energy studies. These included a planning program for oil shale development (in cooperation with the Department of the Interior and the Bureau of the Budget), several environmental impact studies (relating to unleaded gasoline, control of sulfur dioxides from stationary sources, and the impact on the environment of expanded electricity production), and critical surveys of available energy forecasting methods and data. Freeman brought to his task several explicit concerns. He was critical of energy supply estimates since they were mostly volumetric and unrelated to prices. He was bothered about the lack of any high-level agency being charged with developing new energy supply systems and not already having some commitment to present sources (an implied criticism of the Interior Department and the Atomic Energy Commission). He wanted a high-level agency also to ensure that a proper balance would be realized between securing future energy supplies and enforcing environmental standards. And he was perhaps the earliest, certainly the most forthright, spokesman in the administration for energy conservation.[13]

Freeman's concern for a high-level, truly disinterested energy policy

12. Letter, Lincoln to the President, April 15, 1971, accompanying OEP, "Report on Crude Oil and Gasoline Price Increases of November 1970" (copy), Secretary of the Interior's Files, Subject File: Minerals and Fuels—Commodities and Products, Petroleum, Department of the Interior.

13. See, for example, S. David Freeman to Hubert Heffner, March 12, 1970, OST Box 960, Subject File 1970: Energy; OST press release, March 12, 1970, OST Box 1105, Subject File 1972: Energy, OST records; all in NA. See also Freeman, "Towards a Policy of Energy Conservation," *Bulletin of Atomic Scientists,* vol. 27 (October 1971), pp. 8–12.

body was expressed in OST submissions to the Advisory Council on Executive Organization (the so-called Ash Council).[14] Freeman made a case for a Department of Natural Resources, which would include the AEC's civilian nuclear R&D functions. His case for the new overarching department rested on five arguments. First, no single agency, he noted, currently was responsible for looking at new ideas or new energy sources, and since there was a need also for evenhanded treatment of competing energy sources in the allocation of R&D monies, a new structure, without the ties to industry that existed in the AEC and the Department of the Interior, seemed desirable. Second, the government could not avoid becoming much more directly involved in energy and resource policy, since more than 50 percent of estimated future domestic oil and gas resources lay on federal lands or the outer continental shelf. Third, it had to be recognized that coal, oil, gas, and uranium are to some extent substitute sources of energy. Private industry had already reorganized to conform to the realities of the marketplace by moving to form horizontally integrated companies, and it was imperative that the government also adopt a comprehensive approach to planning. Fourth, Freeman charged, government energy programs were a mess. Many had been designed to foster specific forms of energy or to meet specific energy needs (for instance, the Rural Electrification Administration). Not only was it not at all clear that the problems to which these programs were addressed still existed, but abundant evidence indicated that no thought was given to the effect of one program on another or to the effect on the energy industry itself of the fragmented, unbalanced, and often conflicting arrangements. Finally, the line between federal responsibility and private initiative was not clearly drawn, yet industry needed clear indications as to the federal role, plus a harmonious, rational policy in areas such as taxation, imports, and antitrust.[15] This point, the damaging effects of uncertainty about government policies on investment in exploration and research, became an oft-repeated theme in explanations of the nation's energy difficulties.

14. Roy L. Ash, president of Litton Industries, was brought in to develop a plan to increase efficiency in the Executive Office. See Rowland Evans, Jr., and Robert D. Novak, *Nixon in the White House: The Frustration of Power* (Random House, 1971), pp. 237–41. At the start of Nixon's second term Ash was made director of the Office of Management and Budget.

15. Memorandum, Freeman and Bruce Netschert to Amory Bradford, Executive Director of the Ash Council, "Energy and Mineral Resources Agencies," March 11, 1970, OST Box 949, Subject File: Cabinet, Reorganization, Ash Council, vol. 2, 1970, OST Records, NA.

The Ash Council reported late in 1970. It endorsed arguments of the sort that Freeman presented, and the President decided to press for the suggested new Department of Natural Resources.[16]

Meanwhile Freeman's chief, OST Director Lee DuBridge, had been urging that a cabinet-level energy committee be formed. Although Du-Bridge did not have direct access to the Oval Office, he did eventually persuade Domestic Council Director John D. Ehrlichman to form such a committee.[17] On July 30, 1970, while Nixon was still deliberating on the Ash Council proposals, Ehrlichman alerted various department heads that he was establishing a subcommittee of the Domestic Council to deal with energy problems.

Ehrlichman's motivation can only be guessed at, but certain developments had been pointing up an urgent need for some such forum for co-ordinated discussion and planning. The winter of 1969–70 turned out to be the coldest for thirty years and no. 2 heating oil, natural gas, and liqui-fied petroleum gas were all in short supply, though the industry insisted that these problems were only local and temporary. More ominous was a warning in February 1970 by the Texas Independent Producers and Royalty Owners Association that the nation was fast losing its surplus producing capacity. Moreover, in February the demand for low-sulfur crude oil showed a 38 percent increase over 1969. This was largely due to a switch from coal to oil by power plants. Then in July Libya, in a dispute with the oil companies, cut its supply of sweet (low-sulfur) crude by 400,000 barrels a day. In addition the Trans-Arabian pipeline had been cut, with a loss of 500,000 barrels a day to the West, via the Mediterranean. Tanker rates soared as demand shifted to the Persian Gulf to supply the shortfall of nearly 1 million barrels a day and as the need arose to route it around the African cape. This made the price of imported crude more or less equal to the price of U.S.-produced crude, and the import tickets held by inland refiners became unsalable, creating specific supply difficulties for them. At home the summer was marked by brownouts up and down the Atlantic seaboard; and the prospect once again was for tight supplies of fuel oil and natural gas for the coming winter.[18]

16. For more details see Whitaker, *Striking a Balance*, pp. 61–68.
17. Robert Gillette, "Energy: The Muddle at the Top," *Science*, December 28, 1973, pp. 1319–21.
18. "Severe Cold Puts Real Zip in Demand," *Oil and Gas Journal*, vol. 68 (February 2, 1970), pp. 70–72; and "U.S. Fuel Shortage," *Facts on File*, vol. 30 (October 8–14, 1970), p. 735.

The Domestic Council's Energy Subcommittee

Ehrlichman's move to create an energy subcommittee in the Domestic Council was made public in a White House press release on August 6. The subcommittee was charged (1) with making recommendations to alleviate the threatened acute shortage of clean fuels for the winter of 1970–71 and (2) with assessing the longer-term (five-year) energy outlook. It was to comprise the secretaries of state, interior, and health, education, and welfare; the directors of the OST, OEP, and Office of Management and Budget (OMB); the chairmen of the Council of Economic Advisers, Council on Environmental Quality, FPC, and AEC; and the special assistant to the President for consumer affairs. Paul W. McCracken, CEA chairman, was to chair the subcommittee, chosen, as he would have it, because "I brought to the subject that objectivity which came from total ignorance about it," and because he represented no threat to members of the cabinet.[19] McCracken's reticence notwithstanding, the subcommittee was to become the first effective energy policy body of the Nixon administration.

The subcommittee's first task was to decide on a plan of action to alleviate the fuel shortages expected during the coming winter. To that end suggestions were solicited from the various departments and agencies represented on the subcommittee, a meeting was held with Washington representatives of the major power, fuel supply, and fuel transportation organizations, and a report was requested from the National Petroleum Council on the short-term fuel outlook. On September 29 McCracken and Lincoln issued a joint statement which explained to the public how the shortages had arisen, outlined steps being taken by the federal government, and warned that sterner measures might be needed if combined industry-government actions failed to avert a crisis.[20]

Since this was the first message to the public dealing with the broader questions of energy supply and demand, it is of interest to notice how McCracken and Lincoln defined the problem. Their statement identified four elements underlying current difficulties: a recent surge in demand for energy, increased demand for clean fuels in particular to meet national

19. Paul W. McCracken, *Reflections on Economic Advising: A Paper and an Interview*, Original Paper 1 (Los Angeles: International Institute for Economic Research, 1976), p. 7.
20. Paul W. McCracken and George A. Lincoln, "The Fuel Situation for the Winter of 1970–71," September 29, 1970, OEP.

air pollution standards, increased demand combined with inadequate exploration and development of natural gas, and pressure on fossil fuels because nuclear power plant construction had fallen behind schedule. Neither the first nor the third item was explained in more detail. That is to say, no acknowledgment was made openly that federal regulatory programs may have contributed to the difficulties mentioned. Only a vague reference was made to "changes in the price structure" of fuels that could be expected and that would provide the necessary incentives to adjust relative supplies.[21] Subsequently, in a statement before a more restricted audience McCracken argued that the virtually free importation of residual fuel oil since 1966 and the fact that its sulfur content can be reduced readily to meet environmental standards, plus a combination of improved refinery technology and effective import restrictions on imported light products, had together created an undue dependence on imported residual, especially on the East Coast.[22]

Turning to the second task of the subcommittee, at its first meeting on August 11, 1970, six working groups were established to study aspects of the longer-run situation and to form the basis of long-run proposals. It became clear to some in the White House that these proposals might usefully be incorporated into a presidential statement on energy problems and policies. That message was eventually delivered on June 4, 1971. But the more immediate effect of the subcommittee's work was that it prodded the Department of the Interior into pressing ahead with its own coordinated studies. This was a belated effort to regain the initiative in an area in which the department possessed great expertise and experience but in which it had exercised this expertise in a selective rather than an encompassing way. The department had already requested the National Petroleum Council to undertake a major study of U.S. oil and gas requirements for 1970–85 and to report on general trends to the year 2000, and the council was now asked to extend this study to other energy forms.[23]

21. Ibid.

22. Paul W. McCracken, "The U.S. Fuel and Energy Situation," *The Conference Board Record,* vol. 8 (March 1971), pp. 37–40.

23. Letters, Hollis Dole to Jack H. Abernathy, Chairman of the National Petroleum Council, January 20, 1970, and Secretary of the Interior Walter J. Hickel to E. D. Brockett, Chairman of the National Petroleum Council, August 31, 1970. Both letters appear in the NPC's final report, *U.S. Energy Outlook: A Report of the National Petroleum Council's Committee on U.S. Energy Outlook* (NPC, December 1972), app. 1. An interim report, *U.S. Energy Outlook: An Initial Appraisal, 1971–1985,* had been published in July 1971. After July 1971 the NPC's investigation focused on policy alternatives and trends to the end of the century, and the

It also began a crash internal study related to short-term needs and meant to contribute to the subcommittee's five-year projections, and initiated a more broad-based national energy study of its own. This last, directed by John J. McKetta, Jr., of the University of Texas at Austin was intended by Secretary Walter Hickel "to make available information from which a national energy policy may be derived." Hickel asked the McKetta group "to develop a supply curve for all of the principal forms of energy which are expected to be available between now and 1980 . . . [and to] review . . . the influence of the various government policies, such as taxation, leasing, incentives, and so forth on the availability of the various forms of energy . . . [both questions] to be considered in the light of environmental consequences."[24]

The First Message on Energy

The President said that his energy message of June 1971 was "the first time that a message on energy of a comprehensive nature has been sent to the Congress by a President of the United States";[25] it was delivered before either the McKetta report or the National Petroleum Council study was available. With two exceptions, the McCracken subcommittee had contributed most directly to its substance.[26] The message addressed the long-run problems and possibilities tackled by the subcommittee's working groups. The long run, McCracken and Lincoln had said in September 1970, was where "the government can play the greatest role," and the subcommittee had been asked to judge "how programs to assure an adequate supply of energy ought to be divided between the public and private

findings are discussed in the final report. A preliminary summary, "U.S. Energy Outlook: A Summary Report of the National Petroleum Council," was released earlier and appears as chapter 1 in the final report.

24. Hickel to McKetta, September 30, 1970, Secretary of the Interior's Files, Subject File: Minerals and Fuels–Commodities and Products, Department of the Interior. The McKetta group report appeared as Advisory Committee on Energy, *U.S. Energy: A General Review,* Report to the Secretary of the Interior (U.S. Department of the Interior, June 1971).

25. "Remarks about a Special Message to the Congress on Energy Resources, June 4, 1971," *Public Papers: Nixon, 1971* (GPO, 1972), p. 703.

26. An additional reason why the subcommittee had more influence than the Interior Department was that Nixon had dismissed Hickel as secretary of the interior toward the end of November 1970. Six of Hickel's appointees followed after a two-day lag.

sector," and "the extent to which tax incentives relative to other approaches ought to be used in the public sector."[27] In addition it had handled a series of technical papers submitted by various agencies and dealing with specific R&D or conservation programs.

In the message itself a prominent place was given to an expanded civilian nuclear program (successful demonstration of the liquid metal fast breeder reactor and expanded uranium enrichment capacity) and an expanded program to convert coal into a clean gaseous fuel. Other proposals involved an accelerated outer continental shelf program, an oil shale reserves leasing program, support for sulfur oxide control demonstration projects, reaffirmation of an earlier proposal that Congress tax leaded gasoline, and a strong plea for the centralization of energy functions within a Department of Natural Resources. This last, and the general emphasis on *clean* energy in the long term, reflected the work of David Freeman, who as OST representative on the subcommittee contributed more than any other person to the substance of the message.

The CEA and the OMB opposed the nuclear and coal gasification proposals on the ground that neither had been justified economically, but both were retained at Nixon's behest. This followed strong lobbying by the American Gas Association and an "understanding" reached between the White House and Democratic Congressman Chet Holifield of California whereby the latter, as chairman of the House Government Operations Committee, would not stand in the way of Nixon's energy reorganization plans (though his own preference was for an independent AEC developing nuclear energy in the manner of a Manhattan-style project), provided Nixon pushed the breeder reactor.[28]

The message was intentionally silent about the short term, and its longer-term emphases did not stem from a comprehensive and consistent review of all the R&D possibilities. Freeman was well aware that energy R&D studies had skirted the difficult questions of what total amount should be invested and of what balance should be struck between competing technologies. The energy message directed the President's science

27. McCracken to members of the Domestic Affairs Council Subcommittee on the National Energy Situation, December 7, 1970, Secretary of the Interior's Files, Subject File: Minerals and Fuels–Commodities and Products, Department of the Interior.

28. Gillette, "Energy: The Muddle at the Top." For a summary of Holifield's views see "Energy III: Government Reorganization," *National Journal Reports,* October 13, 1973, p. 1519. The complexities of devising an economic evaluation of nuclear breeder reactor research strategies are discussed at length in Paul W. Mac-Avoy, *Economic Strategy for Developing Nuclear Breeder Reactors* (M.I.T. Press, 1969).

adviser to provide an assessment of R&D that could serve to guide future policy. On the adverse impact of government regulations on energy availability, the message was also almost silent. The FPC was praised for its recent rate changes to encourage exploration for natural gas and commitments of gas to interstate markets. But energy pricing was not directly addressed except for a pronouncement—again probably reflecting Freeman's views—to the effect that the nation must be educated to stop wasting energy by being faced with prices that reflect the full social costs of energy production.

Congress ignored the energy message and within the administration, too, it was quietly laid aside. This was partly because no immediate crisis was in sight, partly because the President had become rather sensitive to advice from scientists containing implied criticism of administration policies, and partly because there were other developments just then that captured more attention. Among these were the exciting prospect of renewing contact with Peking and, in the economic sphere, balance of payments difficulties, concomitant pressure on the dollar, and a surge of interest by Congress and businessmen in wage and price controls.

A mandatory wage and price freeze was implemented in August 1971 as part of the Economic Stabilization Program. Controls in general continued until April 1974 and on petroleum products for much longer. These controls were to play an important role in constraining energy policies.

There is an inherent conflict between the need to keep prices down as part of an anti-inflation campaign and the need for prices to rise to cover incremental cost increases and stimulate expanded output. It was a peculiarity of the oil industry however, that price increases there were often interpreted as rapacious. Administration officials generally believed that while oil prices might temporarily rise, they should tend downward in the not-too-distant future. This belief did not rest on a presumed suspension of the principle of diminishing returns but on the simple fact that world oil prices stood well above costs, and on the expectation that with the entry of increased numbers of producing countries into world trade, competition would tend to depress prices.[29] U.S. domestic producers were

29. The Cabinet Task Force on Oil Import Control adopted price assumptions directly in line with this reasoning: see, for example, the assumptions specified in *The Oil Import Question,* pp. 39 and 124. It was also a view fully endorsed by the Department of the Interior. An Office of Oil and Gas report, "Cost of the Oil Import Program to the American Economy," January 14, 1969, exemplifies the point. Secretary of Interior's Files, Subject File: Minerals and Fuels–Exports and Imports, Permits, Department of the Interior.

insulated from this pressure by the oil import program, which placed the government in a strong position to jawbone the industry over price increases occurring before the imposition of mandatory controls. But the belief in a downward tendency was sufficiently widespread that when the embargo and the oil shortages of 1973 occurred, many felt that price controls on crude were no more than just, since it was entirely possible that the shortages were a weapon the oil companies had wielded to maintain higher than competitive prices.[30] This belief was an additional constraint on policymaking.

Peter Flanigan and the Domestic Council Subcommittee

After the energy message of June 1971 the McCracken subcommittee fell into disuse. The proposals in the message were meant for the most part to be for the long run, but unexpected difficulties were experienced with virtually every one, further delaying the date of their expected realization. It took three years before the Department of the Interior had completed an environmental impact statement on the oil shale program. Acceleration of outer continental shelf leasing ran into environmental litigation and not until 1973 did the annual acreage leased exceed 1 million acres, a figure Nixon said would have to be tripled by 1979. The proposal to create a Department of Natural Resources foundered in Congress. In June 1973 the President substituted for it a Department of Energy and Natural Resources and subsequently accepted the compromise of an Energy Research and Development Administration, with a restructured nuclear energy agency, the Nuclear Energy Commission (later renamed the Nuclear Regulatory Commission), performing regulatory functions only, both of which came into being in October 1974. At that time the idea of a super energy department was still alive, but Ford abandoned the struggle in the face of conflicting interests in Congress early in 1975.[31] Coal gasification and the fast breeder reactor remain at the pilot or demonstration stage today, despite substantial budget allocations, especially to the latter.[32]

30. Two examples may be cited out of many: Les Aspin, "The Oil Company Blues," *New York Review of Books,* March 7, 1974, pp. 27–28; and "How to Create an Oil Shortage," *Consumer Reports,* March 1974, pp. 206–08.

31. Whitaker, *Striking a Balance,* pp. 66–70, 228, 273, 275.

32. John Hagel III, *Alternative Energy Strategies: Constraints and Opportunities* (Praeger, 1976), chaps. 3, 4; and U.S. Energy Research and Development Ad-

In January 1972 Paul McCracken resigned from government service, and presidential assistant Peter Flanigan undertook to revive the subcommittee and to formulate options for a comprehensive energy policy statement. This was largely his own initiative. Initially Flanigan took over from McCracken as chairman of the subcommittee. That job subsequently went to Secretary of the Interior Rogers C. B. Morton in May, but Flanigan remained de facto head of energy policy planning for the remainder of 1972, a fact that illustrates a curious disjunction between official titles and roles in the energy area that marked both the Nixon and Ford administrations. Flanigan had been active in the Oil Policy Committee and the Joint Board on Fuel Supply and Transportation and over time had made himself the White House expert on energy issues. This imparted a precious element of continuity and coherence to policy discussion in an area where fragmentation and "ad hoccery" would otherwise have reigned supreme.

Planning went on apace under Flanigan, though little was decided and nothing made public until after Nixon's resounding election victory in November. Flanigan initiated a new series of task force studies early in 1972, covering natural gas pricing (led by Edward Mitchell of the CEA); gas stimulation from "tight" sands (Richard Balzhiser of the OST); outer continental shelf leasing (William Pecora of the Interior Department); coal (Hollis Dole of the Interior Department); oil shale, tar sands, and heavy Venezuelan oil (Dole); and conservation (Lincoln of the OEP). There was also a special study on deep water ports and supertankers (William A. Johnson, CEA). At a later stage several additional special studies were added.[33] The intention was to combine the work of the task forces with environmental impact studies and to draw up a program of specific legislation. The effort was well-conceived, honest, and open. Issues were identified at the secretarial or assistant secretarial level; the task force and environmental impact studies were coordinated by White House aides James Loken and John Schaefer; and congressional leaders were told what was going on.

Flanigan brought distinctive new emphases to tackling the energy prob-

---

ministration, *A National Plan for Energy Research, Development and Demonstration: Creating Energy Choices for the Future,* vol. 1: *The Plan* (GPO, 1975). In 1979 the first commercial coal gasification plant was on the drawing boards for Mercer County, N. Dak.

33. Background materials for the meeting of the Domestic Affairs Council Subcommittee on the National Energy Situation, Thursday, November 9, 1972, circulated to members by Peter Flanigan. Copy in William Johnson's personal files.

lem. The various R&D proposals in the 1971 message had no possible payoff before about 1985. In the face of well-publicized consumption trends suggesting that by the early 1980s more than 50 percent of U.S. petroleum needs would have to be met by imports, Flanigan decided that it was imperative to find practical ways to increase domestic production, especially of oil and gas, in the near term. In choosing this emphasis he was fully prepared to bear its implied consequences: higher prices (hence costs to consumers) to guarantee a reasonable rate of return on investment and increased risks to the environment.[34]

The political sensitivity of these issues dictated that no announcement of policy be made before the election. But by October clear statements came from two FPC commissioners (although not Chairman Nassikas) and from General Lincoln and Flanigan himself in favor of natural gas price decontrol.[35] Flanigan stressed the importance of being sure that supply would respond to a price increase, and without too long a delay. The preliminary "Task Force Report on Natural Gas Pricing" (July 31, 1972) was returned with a request that there be further checks to see that estimates of the elasticity of supply made by several academic economists were not overly optimistic, given the lower numbers implied by at least one industry study. In fact, the report made use of six supply-response studies, three from industry. The separate estimates were fairly consistent, and special reasons could be adduced for more pessimistic results projected by the National Petroleum Council and by a model developed for the Cities Service Oil Company (the CITGO model).[36] Flanigan also sought help from Paul W. MacAvoy of the Massachusetts Institute of

34. Richard Corrigan, "Energy Report: Administration Readies 1973 Program to Encourage More Oil, Gas Production," *National Journal Reports,* October 21, 1972, pp. 1621–32.

35. Nassikas favored a combination of the FPC approach and support for administration-backed sanctity of contract bills (S. 2405 and H.R. 2513). At the time, the FPC was involved in promulgating an "optional-pricing" system (approved by the commission on August 3) under which producers were invited to argue the case for higher prices. Under the two bills new price contracts would be protected against future price cuts initiated by the FPC. (Corrigan, "Energy Report," p. 1623.) Nassikas clearly presented his position in FPC, "Energy Resources Policy," remarks before the Forty-third Annual Meeting of the Independent Petroleum Association of America, Dallas, Texas, October 18, 1972.

36. This information is from a CEA report, "The Phasing of the Output and Price Impacts of Decontrol of Natural Gas," author and date unknown, but most likely a response to questions raised at the November 9 meeting of the Energy Subcommittee of the Domestic Council. (Copy in Johnson personal files.)

Technology, who was in the process of developing the first general equilibrium (supply and demand) model for natural gas. MacAvoy was able to provide the subcommittee with estimates of the likely market-clearing price of gas under various schemes for decontrol, making due allowance for reductions in demand as well as supply increases following upon higher prices.[37]

The Department of the Interior was less concerned to press the matter of natural gas price decontrol, but on oil prices Hollis Dole, assistant secretary for mineral resources, argued publicly that "the case for increasing the domestic oil supply is every bit as cogent as that for gas . . . [and] the proper objective of policy ought to be to permit the free movement of domestic oil and gas prices within a market afforded some protection from foreign competition."[38] More so than in the case of natural gas, the agency controlling oil prices, in this instance the Price Commission, whose mandate did not include resolving the nation's energy problems, was unenthusiastic.[39] It stood alone against a virtually unanimous administration.

The President had made it known in August 1970 that the MOIP would remain in place, although with an understanding that flexibility would be exercised in determining the precise ceilings. He had also reiterated on April 30, 1972, in a statement at the ranch of Texan John B. Connally, his continued support for the oil depletion allowance.[40] Accelerated leasing of the outer continental shelf, it will be recalled, was a component of the June 1971 message.

A combination of these prior commitments with the new stress on incentives to increase domestic oil and gas production would have constituted a controversial but integrated package as one way to meet the nation's medium-term energy needs. However, although more specific options were still being drafted and sorted through, the cast of energy principals changed dramatically, and after numerous modifications the second presidential energy message delivered to Congress on April 18, 1973, bore only a distant resemblance to the proposals Flanigan had envisaged in the fall of 1972.

37. MacAvoy to Flanigan, February 20, 1973 (copy in Johnson personal files).
38. *Oil Daily,* July 24, 1972; compare the statement by Gene P. Morrell, Director of the Office of Oil and Gas, in *Trends in Oil and Gas Exploration,* Hearings before the Senate Committee on Interior and Insular Affairs, 92 Cong. 2 sess. (GPO, 1972), pt. 1, pp. 74–81, especially pp. 76–77.
39. Corrigan, "Energy Report," p. 1624.
40. Ibid.

Energy Officially Returns to the White House

Up until December 1972 Flanigan remained firmly in charge. Loken and Schaefer had prepared a fat book of options, and in conjunction with briefings by Flanigan these had been passed before the members of the cabinet, albeit without capturing much interest. At this point Loken left and Flanigan seconded James E. Akins, director of the Fuels and Energy Office in the Department of State, to help develop the proposals further and to frame legislation. Akins brought ideas of his own: a proposal to modify the MOIP by auctioning licenses, a much expanded energy R&D effort, a gasoline tax. For a while this slowed things down. He managed to convince Flanigan on the first two issues, although not the third. At any rate the White House group soon reached a new consensus, and by January or February the first fat option book had been trimmed and work was proceeding on legislative initiatives to accompany the new energy message.

Before this John Ehrlichman had intervened, having decided that it was a propitious moment to reassert his own control over the energy concerns of the Domestic Council. The election, after all, was over and energy was promising to develop into the number one issue in 1973. Moreover, as the President's businessman up front, Flanigan had had to fend off repeated charges of conflict of interest, so that it may have seemed to be inviting trouble to allow him to head up an energy program embodying both higher prices for oil and gas and an enlarged federal involvement in energy R&D. Flanigan's office was moved from the White House to the Old Executive Office Building. Akins worked through three drafts of an energy message but could get no positive response from Ehrlichman, and he finally gave up the unequal struggle and simply sat out a period of waiting until given a diplomatic appointment.[41]

Organizational changes followed each other with disturbing rapidity in early 1973. On January 5 the President gave George Shultz, then secretary of the treasury, the additional title of assistant to the President for economic affairs. It was understood that Shultz's jurisdiction would include such energy-related matters as oil prices and imports. On February 7 control over the oil import program was formally transferred to the Treasury Department and Deputy Secretary of the Treasury William E.

41. Interview with John Schaefer, Houston, Texas, December 12, 1978; and letter, James Akins to the author, August 23, 1978.

Simon was named chairman of the Oil Policy Committee. This move was part of Executive Reorganization Plan No. 1 of 1973, whereby among other things the President assumed all functions vested by law in the OEP. The same plan abolished the OST and transferred its functions to the National Science Foundation. Darrell M. Trent, who succeeded General Lincoln and presided over the OEP in the months before its final demise at the end of June 1973, later pointed out to those concerned about the difficulties of quickly erecting an emergency fuel allocation authority to cope with the effects of the embargo that the OEP had existed precisely to deal with such situations.[42] In January Nixon also indicated that Secretary of Agriculture Earl L. Butz would become presidential counselor for natural resources.

Finally, on February 23 the President made public the remaining details of his new White House energy advisory organization. A triumvirate of advisers, comprising Shultz, Ehrlichman, and Henry Kissinger, in his role as national security adviser, was to be known as the White House Special Energy Committee. Charles J. DiBona, president of the Center for Naval Analyses, was appointed as the President's special consultant on energy. He was expected to take a year to become familiar with the issues and increasingly to act as coordinator of energy analyses being conducted in the various agencies and departments. Only a small staff was envisaged for DiBona—it never did exceed five or six—and his group was to be known collectively as the National Energy Office.

Butz's appointment was part of a presidential plan to install four super cabinet officers as a shortcut to the reorganization that was still awaiting congressional action. It was conceivable that he might act as referee in the event of intractable divisions in the energy triumvirate, though he did not in fact exercise any influence over energy policy in the brief period before the organizational arrangements changed yet again. It is also possible that Butz was used simply to draw attention away from the Interior Department and the close associations between many of its offices and the oil and gas industry at a time when these were beginning to come under public scrutiny. Certainly considerations of neutrality played a role in DiBona's selection: on his own admission he was largely innocent on energy issues.

Contrary to his expectations, DiBona found himself thrust into the

42. Trent to Simon, n.d., Gerald L. Parsky Files, Box 2, folder: FEO–Admin. 1973–74, U.S. Treasury. Trent had coordinated an interagency group working in the spring of 1973 on contingency plans for petroleum conservation and allocation.

business of preparing an energy message. Even before his appointment was official he was asked by Ehrlichman to comment on the trimmed-down set of energy option papers put together by Schaefer. These consisted of the six task force reports and the special study on deep water ports initiated by Flanigan, plus new option papers on the MOIP, power plant siting, the international aspects of energy problems, and the recent National Petroleum Council report offering projections of oil imports under various technical and policy assumptions.[43]

DiBona's discussion of the option papers showed clearly two dominant elements in his own thinking: first, a concern with the issue of national security, and second, an analyst's enthusiasm for the logic of market processes. He noted that fossil fuel deposits are a finite resource and that expanded domestic oil and gas production (favored by Flanigan and Akins) must therefore be at the expense of future "oil in place." "The point of reserves is to have them," he said, "not to use them. By this analysis, the use of imported oil under normal conditions contributes to national security."[44] This general perspective led him to question several of the assumptions held by Flanigan and Akins and underlying those of the option papers that he had inherited from them. The most obvious of these assumptions, according to DiBona, included:

—World oil prices will continue to rise rapidly.

—Even if the OPEC cartel collapsed, we would achieve only a short period of relative ease as it would lead to an exhaustion of Middle East oil and a world-wide shortage of energy.

—There is little flexibility of foreign output other than in Saudi Arabia and Iraq.

—There is significant [midterm] flexibility in U.S. output.

—The security of the U.S. would be jeopardized by reliance on imports from the Eastern Hemisphere.

—Oil from the Canadian Athabasca Tar Sands and the Venezuelan Orinoco Heavy Oil Belt can be developed at prices not significantly above domestic oil prices.[45]

If these assumptions were correct, DiBona granted, they would imply more intensive development of U.S. energy resources, increased reliance on Western Hemisphere secondary sources, and R&D for the more dis-

43. Interview with John Schaefer, December 12, 1978. Schaefer remained at the White House after Flanigan's removal to the Executive Office Building and served on DiBona's staff.

44. Interview with Charles DiBona, Washington, D.C., April 13, 1978.

45. DiBona to Ehrlichman, "Comments on Energy Option Papers," February 5, 1973 (copy in Johnson personal files).

tant future. DiBona's own preference was for (1) strong action (unspecified) to weaken OPEC; (2) liberal imports even if world prices should increase and remain high; and (3) policies designed to provide direct incentives, not to U.S. development and production, but to the creation of a substantial U.S. reserve or shut-in proven capacity to meet future security needs.[46]

As to the form policies should take, DiBona favored market solutions. The authors of the task force report on natural gas pricing (reflecting mainly the views of Ezra Solomon and Edward Mitchell at the CEA) had opted for decontrol of "new" gas only, to avoid political opposition from those who might view total decontrol as a giveaway to producers.[47] DiBona initially argued that total decontrol would be "the simplest solution and most likely to work in bringing about continuous re-adjustment" and should therefore be chosen over the partial decontrol alternative. Subsequently he conceded that this might be politically infeasible. He was adamant, however, on the choice of conservation measures: "tax and price options," such as automobile excise taxes and increased electricity prices, would be more effective than simply giving hints and information to consumers, and should be used. So too with import policy. Freeing imports of crude oil probably was the most desirable policy, but if some means for controlling imports had to be used, then at least it should be one that could work through the price mechanism to serve the main end: secure and adequate supplies in the near term. DiBona therefore argued for a policy whereby possession of unused new (proven) reserves would be made a condition for receiving import tickets. Probably a conviction about the power of the market also lay behind DiBona's feeling that OPEC should be challenged. He requested information about the theory and practice of cartels from old colleagues at the Center for Naval Analyses and was able to derive some support from their response, especially the advice that consuming nations should not be panicked into making unnecessary concessions but should shop for better terms from individual members of the producers' group and should seek through R&D and the adoption of substitutes to lessen their real dependence on the cartel.[48]

When it came to presenting summary advice for the energy message to Shultz and Ehrlichman, DiBona moved more cautiously. He argued that

46. Ibid.

47. "Natural Gas Pricing," Task Force Report, July 31, 1972 (copy in Johnson personal files).

48. DiBona to Ehrlichman, "Comments on Energy Option Papers"; and Arnold Moore to Charles DiBona, March 12, 1973 (copy in Johnson personal files).

if world prices remained high but there was strong reason to believe American R&D efforts would pay off in a timely way, then domestic energy production should be pressed forward on all fronts. On the other hand, if world prices fell and there was reason to fear that R&D efforts would not pay off in a timely manner, clearly imports should be increased and domestic resources preserved. Rather than rest his case on one or the other of these clear-cut positions, DiBona offered what he called a "hedged program"—a list of suggestions that touched all bases and in the process lost focus. Thus he recommended that domestic production of oil and gas should increase, under the stimulus of higher prices, but the rate of development and depletion of reserves and the effectiveness of monies directed into R&D for alternative energy sources should be monitored lest balance of payments and national security problems be merely deferred rather than solved. Imports should be allowed to make up shortages, to a greater extent if world prices should fall (OPEC weakens) than otherwise. Constraints on the use of coal should be minimized, consistent with "reasonable" environmental constraints.[49] And so on.

The DiBona hedged program lacked all elements of the bold "big play" that so appealed to Richard Nixon, and the pallor of the energy message of April 18, 1973, suggests that it was more or less foisted on a President dazed or at least distracted in the midst of the first round of problems to do with the Watergate cover-up. The President reiterated the steps taken since his 1971 message. He called for decontrol of natural gas from new wells, gas newly dedicated to the interstate market, and "old" gas after existing contracts had expired. Outer continental shelf leasing was to be stepped up by a factor of three before 1979. A plea was registered with Congress to put no further obstacles in the way of the Alaska pipeline. The President spoke of the shale oil program, geothermal leasing, nuclear energy, and coal, in the latter case urging that the states apply the provisions of the Clean Air Act of 1970 judiciously and "for the 'general welfare' "; that is, so that virtually all coal produced would be used. Important changes in the MOIP were announced. Tariffs and direct controls were suspended, to be replaced by a quota-fee system whereby a fee would be levied for imports in excess of 1973 levels. Import fees would be higher on refined products, and three-quarters of crude requirements for new domestic refinery capacity were to be free, as an incentive to the much-needed expansion of U.S. refining strength. Legislation to license deep water ports was proposed, conservation urged, international cooperation

49. DiBona to Ehrlichman, ibid.

vaguely appealed to, and a number of specific R&D options mentioned. Finally, the organizational changes of January and February were confirmed, and the President promised legislative proposals to establish a Department of Energy and Natural Resources (in place of the earlier Department of Natural Resources), as well as ordering several new energy-related offices to be established in the Interior Department.[50]

The message was full of useful items and suggestions, but like the June 1971 message, its list of R&D proposals was makeshift. DiBona had complained to Ehrlichman that there was no way to choose among the R&D options he had seen, since they were not presented in a way to make economic comparison possible. He had nonetheless supported Akins's idea of a substantial injection of funds into existing research. This was scotched, probably at the insistence of Ash, on the grounds that the President could not properly initiate large outlays on anything at the very time that he was refusing to spend funds up to the limit authorized by Congress.[51] At any rate, at the last minute DiBona received an instruction to alter the R&D portions of the message; Shultz was unavailable to provide guidance, and Ehrlichman was totally involved with the President over Watergate. The result was a 20 percent increase in R&D in the form of a series of nods in the direction of several worthy areas, but no clear-cut policy.

The New Oil Import Program of 1973

The only proposal spelled out in some detail in the April 18 message or its accompanying proclamations was the new oil import policy. This was a late addition, debated right up·to the last minute and designed to address industry problems and their political repercussions at a level no less important than, but very much below, that of DiBona's contending energy philosophies.

It was widely accepted by the industry and the administration that some change in the MOIP was inevitable. The program had been designed to control the spillover of an abundant world supply into the United States. Since 1970, however, U.S. excess capacity for crude production had been pared to close to zero, while domestic refinery capability had not expanded. Liberalizing imports of both crude and petroleum products

50. "Special Message to the Congress on Energy Policy, April 18, 1973," *Public Papers: Nixon, 1973* (GPO, 1974), pp. 302–19.
51. This is DiBona's understanding of the events.

seemed to many—especially those in the industry—to be the only way to protect against domestic shortages. There was even a sort of consensus in the industry that given the shortage of domestic refining capacity in the short term, "the U.S. government will respond to every impending crude and product crisis by raising the import quotas."[52] And the most optimistic projections had net U.S. oil imports rising from roughly 23 percent of U.S. oil supplies in 1970 to over 40 percent by 1975.[53] Both the industry concensus and the projections were supported by a steady weakening of the quota system in the early years of the decade. Following recommendations by the Cabinet Task Force on Oil Import Control, import levels were raised above the official limit—12.2 percent of U.S. production—by an arbitrary amount in 1970. A further 100,000 barrels a day were added to the crude oil quota in 1971. Failure to predict a drop in domestic production in 1972 plus unexpected increases in demand stemming from natural gas shortages and environmental regulations led to shortages in feedstocks suffered by independent refiners, and the 1972 quota was twice raised (to 4.4 million barrels a day, up from an initial estimate of needs in September 1971 of 1.6 million); while in late 1972 the Oil Policy Committee conceded that a quota roughly 40 percent above the highest point reached during 1972 probably would be necessary in 1973.[54]

The main problem during 1972 was that of the independent refiners, who found that they could no longer obtain feedstocks. Traditionally supplies to this group had been secured by the Texas Railroad Commission simply increasing allowable production levels when shortages threatened. This action would increase oil stock levels above normal, inducing majors to reduce their inventory through sales to the independents. But by March 1972 it was clear that production in Texas and Louisiana was not responding sufficiently to allowable increases, and stocks of crude were falling rapidly. Federal action seemed to be indicated, but it was not obvious how best the government should respond to this unusual situation. If more import tickets were allocated, this would mean that the majors would have

52. Memorandum, John Schaefer to M. R. "Duke" Ligon, "Refinery Capacity," December 8, 1972 (copy in Johnson personal files).

53. National Petroleum Council, *U.S. Energy Outlook* (December 1972), p. 272. Estimates reflect case I assumptions (of four cases analyzed). The assumptions are stated in broad terms in ibid., pp. 17, 20.

54. Phillip L. Essley, Jr., to William Simon, "Report Requested by Senator Jackson Concerning Crude Oil Import Levels in 1972 and 1973," October 5, 1973 (copy in Johnson personal files); and Dorothy Clark's personal file of Oil Policy Committee actions.

less need to purchase the tickets owned by independents, and the independents' lifeline—a positive market value of tickets—would be squeezed. If the federal government chose to allocate by manipulating quotas, the ensuing delays in securing adjustment to needs could be as long as three to four months, compared with a ten-day production lag in the days when the mechanism of allowed increases worked.

The plight of the independent refiners was compounded by other factors in the overall import situation. U.S. refiners as a whole, but especially the independents, were short of low-sulfur crude; thus increased imports of nonsweet crude would not resolve this specific problem. Moreover, in early 1973, for a variety of reasons, including a continued need to ship crude around the cape and the diversion of some combination tankers to serve the export of wheat to Russia, landed prices of Saudi Arabian and Iranian crude were close to U.S. levels for comparable grades, while Libyan sweet crude stood above the domestic price. This reduced to zero or near-zero the value of tickets.

It was clear to the members of the Oil Policy Committee in late 1972 and early 1973 that the MOIP had broken down and that a simple increase in quotas would not meet the situation. Drastic changes of a quite different sort seemed to be needed, and alternatives were under study, principally at the OEP (which sponsored a scheme to auction import licenses) when the President announced the abolition of the OEP and transferred the chairmanship of the committee to the Interior Department.[55] The OEP auction scheme was not enthusiastically received by the Oil Policy Committee. When the chairmanship again moved, to Simon at the Treasury, more radical schemes were considered before a modified fee approach finally was agreed to.[56]

On February 21 John Ehrlichman publicly denied that the administration was considering total suspension of the MOIP. During the same week William Johnson, who had moved from the CEA to become energy adviser to Simon, was dissuading his boss from pursuing that very course.[57] Johnson had no love of quotas but was concerned about the political and security implications of abandoning the program. What had become quite clear by this time was that with OPEC's price having risen to the U.S. level, no more than a token fee, if any, on crude imports was needed. The main

55. Clark personal file of Oil Policy Committee actions.
56. William Johnson to Ezra Solomon, "Mandatory Oil Import Control Program," January 3, 1973; and "Forthcoming OPC Meeting on an Auction System for Oil Import Quotas," January 5, 1973, CEA (copies in Johnson personal files).
57. *Oil Daily*, February 21, 1973.

problem was overcoming artificial subsidies to product imports, in the form of Export-Import Bank loans, and domestic environmental restrictions on refinery construction. These subsidies encouraged the export of U.S. refining capacity, and they were the only good reason for creating any sort of price differential between imported and domestic crude and products.

It was eventually settled that the program would be retained but with quotas replaced by a "license fee." (Charles Owens, director of the Energy Policy Division of the Cost of Living Council [COLC], coined this term to avoid possible challenges to the constitutionality of a "tariff" and to avoid stirring memories of the abortive efforts of Shultz and the task force during 1969–70.) According to the license fee plan, devised by Phillip L. Essley, Jr., of the Treasury; Schaefer; Akins, Owens; and Johnson, the fee would be split (1 cent a gallon on crude oil, residual fuel oils, and gasoline; 2 cents on unfinished oils and all other finished products—later reduced to 0.5 cent and 1.5 cents respectively) so as to create a differential of 42 cents a barrel in favor of *domestic* refined products. In the first year refineries would qualify for free allocations up to their 1973 allocations, so long as they maintained 1973 refinery input levels, with this exemption to be phased out over seven years. New refineries and additional capacity would be granted free allocations, to be phased out over eight years.

The sliding scale that had given disproportionate advantage to small refiners was abolished, but the Oil Import Appeals Board was authorized to respond to special hardships that might be experienced by all independent refiners and marketers by, for example, issuing crude tickets to independent marketers to be used in exchange for products in cases where majors would not accept product tickets.[58] The Interior Department was not convinced about some aspects of this set of changes, but the Oil Policy Committee accepted the plan, and the President approved it.

The new import policy went some way toward establishing incentives for the repatriation of refining capacity: industry representatives claimed

58. Draft memorandums, Phillip Essley, "Oil Import Policy Action Plan," March 27 and April 3, 1973; and memorandums for the record of Oil Policy Committee meetings of March 30 (by Essley) and April 6, 1973 (by Patricia L. Spencer); copies in Johnson personal files. A complete analysis of the decision to change MOIP has been conducted by Linda S. Graebner, consultant with Griffenhagen-Kroeger, Inc., Public Management Consultants, *The Decision to Suspend All Quotas on U.S. Imports of Foreign Oil (1973)* (Commission on the Organization of the Government for the Conduct of Foreign Policy, 1975). This study gives details of the various options considered, personalities involved, and so forth.

it was now economic to expand existing capacity, though not to build new refining capacity in the United States. But the program did not help the independents at all. The reason was Special Rule No. 1 of the COLC. In the same Oil Policy Committee meeting at which the import plan was accepted, Simon noted that "balancing the needs of the economic stabilization program against our energy needs [is] difficult."[59] The point was underscored in a mailgram sent by the Atlantic Richfield Company the same day and addressed to Simon, Johnson, and M. R. "Duke" Ligon, director of the Office of Oil and Gas in the Interior Department. Investment in new refineries would not be encouraged, the mailgram noted, unless investors could be assured that the additional cost increments involved in purchasing foreign crude as feedstock could be passed through onto product prices, and under the existing price control regulations that was by no means assured.[60] The new import policy removed an important element of uncertainty surrounding the government's intentions in this area, but in the months that followed, conflict between the needs of the stabilization plan and the dictates of energy shortages did much to negate this gain.

Fighting Inflation versus Curing Energy Ills

Phases I and II of the Economic Stabilization Program worsened specific fuel shortages and caused difficulties for some segments of the oil industry.[61] But Phase III, which began on January 11, 1973, was more significant, partly because it built on the effects of Phases I and II and partly because by early 1973 public, congressional, and administration priorities had switched from fighting inflation to dealing with energy shortages. Phase III rules stood in the way of realizing explicit goals laid down in the President's April 18 message.

The Price Commission was eliminated at the end of Phase II and its functions were taken over by the COLC. The basic principles of price regulation remained those enunciated in Phase II: prices were to be con-

59. Memorandum for the record, Patricia L. Spencer, April 6, 1973.

60. Mailgram, W. F. Kieschnick, Jr., Vice-President for Planning, Atlantic Richfield Co., to William E. Simon, William A. Johnson, M. R. Ligon, and David Oliver, April 3, 1973 (copy in Johnson personal files).

61. William A. Johnson, "The Impact of Price Controls on the Oil Industry: How to Worsen an Energy Crisis," in Gary D. Eppen, ed., *Energy: The Policy Issues* (University of Chicago Press, 1975), pp. 99–121; and Bohi and Russell, *Limiting Oil Imports*, pp. 208–17.

trolled by monitoring profits on a firm-by-firm basis. Permission to average price increases over products covered by term-limit pricing agreements was allowed in general, though not for gasoline, no. 2 fuel oil, or residual fuel oil; and the prices of such excluded products were frozen.[62]

Phase III introduced some flexibility into a firm's choice of period for estimating its base profit margin, and the controls were to be self-administered. Unfortunately this took no account of the distortions created in Phases I and II. In the summer of 1971, just before the initial freeze of prices (Phase I), stocks of fuel and heating oils had been unusually high, even allowing for the seasonally lower summer demand. This meant that the price of such oils was frozen at an abnormally low level. Furthermore, a Phase I ruling (the "reseller rule") that increases in costs on imported items could be passed through only if the imports and comparable domestic products were kept physically separate right up to the point of final consumption complicated the business of importing enough to discourage imports of crude and product, including fuel and heating oils. In addition, since ceiling prices at retail were higher than at wholesale, majors began eliminating the customary discounts on large purchases of gasoline by independent marketers and marketed the product through their own outlets. This action had the effect of increasing the profit differential between gasoline and middle distillates and moved refiners to concentrate more heavily on gasoline. These several factors, together with an unusually severe winter, resulted in a critical shortage of fuel and heating oil during the early months of 1973. As McCracken had pointed out in mid-1971, though in reference to residual fuel oil, "It would be hard to think of a more effective way of creating a fuel crisis than to decree U.S. price ceilings . . . below those prevailing in the world market."[63]

Not surprisingly, when Phase III was introduced retail fuel oil prices quickly registered a sizable (7.4 percent) increase. Following mandatory hearings, the COLC ruled on March 6 that while these particular price increases could be cost-justified, the major oil companies henceforth must justify any price increase greater than 1 percent above base prices. Increases between 1 and 1.5 percent above base would be subject to a requirement for new cost justification. Increases above 1.5 percent would involve prenotification, and profit margin limitation rules would apply.

62. A convenient summary of the main price regulations affecting the oil industry before December 1975 is contained in Federal Energy Administration, *Plain Language Overview: FEA Price Regulation* (FEA, January 1976).

63. McCracken, "The U.S. Fuel and Energy Situation," p. 39.

The effect of this ruling—Special Rule No. 1—combined with the exogenous rise in world oil prices was sufficient to check imports. This contributed to the decline to zero in the value of import licenses, as noted earlier. Whole segments of the April 18 message were thus negated by the price control program. According to Bohi and Russell: "Conditions had been created wherein there was no market incentive to raise domestic production, no incentive to reduce consumption, and no incentive to increase imports."[64] The problems of independent refiners were exacerbated since crude oil import costs had to be charged against overall allowable price increases, and this reduced the incentive of majors, for whom crude bought for resale was a low margin item, to swap domestic crude against import tickets or licenses. At the same time, independent marketers and jobbers were being hurt because the majors were finding it to their disadvantage to supply other low-margin items like gasoline and liquified petroleum gas.

The COLC guarded itself against possible criticism by announcing (also on March 6) that a new version of the reseller rule would be forthcoming. This amendment to Special Rule No. 1 would allow cost pass-through so long as the customary initial percentage markup was preserved.[65] This modification to the rule was advertised in the *Federal Register* on May 14, 1973. However, it did not meet the difficulty that imported crude or products had to maintain their separate identity to qualify for cost pass-through, nor did it eliminate the uncertainties associated with prenotification or provide any positive incentives to increase crude or product imports to allow expanded refinery runs. DiBona and his staff therefore asked for a still more liberal approach, even urging that the situation was so bad as to warrant complete exemption from controls of petroleum and its products on the allowable ground that this was "necessary for efficient allocation or to maintain adequate levels of supply."[66]

64. Bohi and Russell, *Limiting Oil Imports*, p. 218.

65. Charles Owens to Charles DiBona, "Reseller Rule under Special Rule No. 1," April 26, 1973 (copy in Johnson personal files). Before moving to the Federal Energy Office Owens had been director of the COLC Energy Policy Division. Subsequently he wrote a history of petroleum price controls covering the first year of special regulations applying to petroleum products. This was published as part of U.S. Department of the Treasury, Office of Economic Stabilization, *Historical Working Papers on the Economic Stabilization Program, August 15, 1971–April 30, 1974* (GPO, 1974), pt. 2, pp. 1223–1340. Owens makes use of many internal memorandums, which give the history a special value since the records of Owens's division are not among the substantial COLC records transferred to the National Archives when the council ceased to exist.

66. DiBona to John T. Dunlop, May 5, 1973 (copy), Parsky Files, Box 1, folder: Oil (May 1973) (2), U.S. Treasury.

John T. Dunlop, director of the COLC, dismissed this call for liberalizing the controls over the oil industry. In testimony before the Senate Banking Committee on May 11, 1973, he implicitly argued that since covered companies could raise prices by up to a 1 percent annual weighted average increase to cope with any given cost increases without profit margin limitations being invoked, and since there was no maximum for price increases on individual lines, within the weighted average increase provision, Special Rule No. 1 would in effect "assure oil companies flexibility under phase III to respond to market conditions in the United States and abroad in order to maintain adequate supplies of crude oil and petroleum products in this country. . . ."[67]

Despite this public disavowal that anything was amiss, the COLC did develop a proposed Special Rule No. 1A. This would have imposed a ceiling on domestic crude prices, with provision for the ceiling to rise gradually toward the higher price for imported oil. The ceiling, however, would apply to old oil only, or production on a property up to the level attained in the base year, 1972. For output from a property above this base level, or new oil, there would be no ceiling; and for each barrel of new oil a barrel of old would be freed from the ceiling provision. Part of the logic behind this two-tier price system was that price increases had already taken place in domestic crude, apparently cost-justified, but also in an amount sufficient (in the COLC's judgment, based on industry comment) to stimulate additional exploration. More basically, it was meant to provide incentives to production only at the margin. Unrestricted price increases would be merely inflationary and would provide rents to existing producers. Moreover, if domestic prices were to be left free to rise to foreign price levels this would probably trigger further increases in imported crude prices. To avoid inequities the scheme provided that sellers of crude should prorate price increases on old oil among all purchasers when old oil was freed from ceiling limitations by the production of a like amount of new oil.[68]

The reaction to this proposal by Simon's advisers at the Treasury and the Office of Oil and Gas was largely negative. Doubt was expressed about the accuracy of the assumptions underlying the case for a two-tier system.

67. Statement of John T. Dunlop in *Petroleum Product Shortages*, Hearings before the Senate Committee on Banking, Housing and Urban Affairs, 93 Cong. 1 sess. (GPO, 1973), pp. 413–18, especially 416–17.

68. Charles Owens to Dunlop, May 24, 1973, "Ceiling on Domestic Crude Petroleum Prices: Extension of Special Rule No. 1" (copy in Johnson personal files).

And criticism of its substance ranged from charges that the proposal betrayed ignorance of the workings of the crude market (where purchasers, not producers, post the price) to the view that with multiple ownership of leases each might qualify for a different price, creating nearly impossible accounting and legal problems for purchasers. It was also pointed out with some prescience that compliance would be difficult to enforce since new and old oil need not be sold in separate transactions; thus a false combined price could be created through fictitious purchases of new oil at very high book prices.[69]

Special Rule No. 1A was not put into effect during Phase III but was introduced as part of Phase IV price controls in August 1973. I will return to the stabilization program somewhat later. Before Phase IV was begun the nation had experienced a voluntary allocation program for crude and refined products and was moving rapidly toward a mandatory allocation program.

Allocation and the Independent Marketers and Refiners

The impetus behind allocation schemes was the complaints, channeled very effectively through congressmen, of independent marketers and terminal operators. Protecting these independents (and the independent refiners) was *the* energy issue of 1973, not the Arab embargo. This was partly because the legislation enacted to cope with the embargo had in fact been devised to help the independents, and provisions designed for the latter purpose tended to restrict the administration severely in responding to the enforced shortage of crude. More generally it can be said that the significance of the allocation experience for energy policy is not that it was part of a strategy to resolve underlying problems. It is, rather, that it highlights the catch-as-catch-can way that energy issues arose and were dealt with. Long-term neglect was at the heart of the administration's difficulties. This was overlaid with a lack of a strong, centralized, and stable organization to design energy policy; unforeseen political shocks (Watergate and later Arab intransigence); incompatible programs (as

69. Phillip Essley, Jr., to William Johnson, May 30, 1973, "Comments on a Memorandum to Dr. Dunlop from Charles Owens Dated May 24, 1973, Relative to the Domestic Crude Oil Petroleum Prices—Extension of Special Rule No. 1"; and Duke Ligon to William Simon, June 1, 1973, "Ceiling on Domestic Crude Petroleum Prices" (copies of both in Johnson personal files).

illustrated by the conflicts between stabilization policies and energy policies); and the political consequences of past policies and present shortages, all of which guaranteed that the administration would find itself throughout 1973 doing little more than trying to manage crises.

The problem of the independent marketers made itself felt in the spring of 1973. Independent gasoline marketers—primarily those who historically had operated in the spot market—found their supplies cut off. This was a direct consequence of eliminating excess refinery capacity through increased demand. In general those independent marketers with good long-term relations with majors continued to be supplied. Nonetheless, those who did not have long-term contracts were most vocal and effective in drawing attention to their difficulties.

A second set of difficulties was experienced by independent refiners. The reasons have been discussed above. The predicament of the refiners was the subject of a special meeting of the Oil Policy Committee Working Group in February, and the committee itself considered it at a meeting on April 6. The matter was sensitive politically and multifaceted.

One relevant consideration was that the independent refiners, with a few exceptions, qualified as small businesses and were in principle on every administration's favored list. Related to this, the Justice Department sensed a threat to competition should the independents be eliminated. On the other hand most lacked economies of scale, possessed only outdated downstream processing equipment, and in a free struggle certainly would not survive. The government faced a series of no-win options. Many small refineries sometimes accounted for a significant proportion of all employment in small communities, and they tended to supply out-of-the-way places; if the government did nothing to help them it would certainly be held culpable. But since these refiners mostly lacked the equipment for refining unleaded gasoline, even with short-term help in securing feedstocks, the Environmental Protection Agency's regulations could bring about their death just as effectively as lack of crude. As one of Simon's advisers put it: "If we do nothing, and a number of independents do fail . . . then the Government will be charged with their death. Conversely, if we keep them alive and they later die from lead poisoning, their blood will also be on the Government's hands."[70] Over and above all these factors the health of the *inland* refiners was linked to the health of Midwest agriculture; while the East Coast independent terminal operators were critical

70. Essley to Johnson, "Providing Feedstocks for Inland Refiners," March 19, 1973 (copy in Johnson personal files).

in the supplying of pipeline-poor New England. In both cases powerful congressional voices could be and were raised as soon as the independents cried danger. Many independents had become wealthy on special arrangements for import quotas or on the spot market, and they were not slow in seeing to the protection of their interests.

No one, therefore, seriously suggested that the independents be allowed to die. Several plans were offered for saving them. The Department of Justice suggested that the majors' rights to import be made conditional on their supplying the independents with crude. Phillip Essley of the Treasury also favored this idea on the ground that it would forestall a mandated allocation scheme during the year. Another approach, suggested by the OEP, involved an import license fee rebate to majors who would sell crude to inland, nonintegrated refiners. Simon's advisers favored a stopgap proration scheme to apportion sufficient crude to the coastal independents to allow them simply to remain in business. A fourth possible approach was to give the Oil Import Appeals Board authority to deal with special cases of hardship. At the Oil Policy Committee meeting of April 6, 1973, Simon expressed a desire to err on the side of generosity concerning the East Coast terminal operators but indicated that new categories of exemptions, hence any special allocation to the inland refiners, was something he wanted to avoid. The fourth approach was the one incorporated into the modified MOIP announced by the President two weeks later. One reason for selecting this solution may have been a fear that since all the other options pointed to intervention in the market on a programmed basis and to the abrogation of certain freedoms and rights, legal battles could be avoided only if a state of emergency were declared. But that in turn might create an atmosphere of panic that the administration wanted to avoid. It was simplest and quietest to make use of the authority already vested in the Oil Import Appeals Board.[71]

It is doubtful whether Simon believed that the new oil import program would resolve the problems of the independents. In one respect—raising a tariff on imported products—it clearly ran counter to the interests of those

71. Moreover, DiBona, unmindful of the mood of Congress, vetoed all the other options. W. C. Truppner, Chairman of the Oil Policy Committee Working Group to members of the committee, "Options Paper for Possible Actions to Deal with Shortage of Crude Oil for Mid-Continent Refiners," February 28, 1973; memorandum for the record (minutes of the committee meeting on April 6, 1973), Patricia L. Spencer; and Essley to Johnson, "Suspension of Import Controls and Problems of Inland Independent Refiners and Independent Marketers," April 2, 1973 (copies in Johnson personal files).

independent jobbers having to rely on imported products.[72] At any rate no sooner was the new program announced than plans were set in motion for a voluntary crude allocation scheme. The Oil Policy Committee felt itself under a good deal of political pressure, and there are repeated references in the files to a feeling that if the administration failed to act on the problems of the independents, it would find itself outflanked by Congress and involved in a mandatory allocation program by the fall. There was good ground for such fear. Senator Thomas F. Eagleton had introduced an amendment to the bill to extend the life of the Economic Stabilization Program, under which the government would have power to allocate crude oil supplies among refiners and refinery output among marketers. Nixon signed this into law on April 30 (Public Law 93-28). It was still more disturbing that Senator Henry Jackson in the meantime had introduced another bill (Senate bill 1570) containing additional authority to allocate *all* fuels, even at the retail level. And on another level, Simon adviser Phillip Essley in more than one memorandum warned that complaints by motorists forced to buy gasoline at higher prices from majors' outlets, pressure by the 13,000 independent oil jobbers, and a widespread public desire to "get in a few licks" at the expense of the majors, might produce legislation to divorce pipelines from the majors and even antitrust action against them.[73]

In forming the voluntary allocation plan, the first thought was to use incentives and avoid all appearance of compulsion. Hence the rebate idea, giving to integrated refiners fee-exempt licenses to import for crude supplied to the independents on the basis of past allocations, surfaced once again.[74] In testimony before the Subcommittee on Consumer Economics of the Joint Economic Committee on May 2, Simon reiterated his preference for incentives only and hinted that if it were to come to mandatory allocation, the administration already had all the authority it needed in the Eagleton amendment.[75] A few days later an allocation plan was ready.

72. Johnson to Simon, "The Probable Impact of the Proposed Changes in MOIP on Various Interest Groups," March 28, 1973 (copy in Johnson personal files). Johnson guessed there was likely to be "a mixed reaction with continuing demands for additional help" from both independent refiners and terminal operators, while from jobbers he expected "to hear a number of complaints."

73. Essley to Johnson, "Suspension of Import Controls."

74. Johnson to Simon and others, "Proposal to Encourage Sharing of Oil with the Independents through the License Fee System," April 20, 1973 (copy in Johnson personal files).

75. *The Gasoline and Fuel Oil Shortage,* Hearings before the Subcommittee on Consumer Economics of the Joint Economic Committee, 93 Cong. 1 sess. (GPO, 1973), pp. 79–97.

Each refiner, marketer, jobber, and distributor was to agree in writing to supply to each state, to each main class of customers, and to each unaffiliated purchaser the same percentage of its total supply of crude and products as in the corresponding quarter of the base year (October 1971– September 1972), less a 10 percent set-aside for possible allocation by the Office of Oil and Gas to priority users.[76] This plan was made public on May 10 and was further explained by William Johnson at special hearings on oil product shortages on May 11.[77]

No sooner was the scheme announced than some of the majors complained that they could not comply without reneging on contracts.[78] The first step toward mandatory allocation was taken in response to these complaints. Johnson suggested to Simon that general guidelines be published, that compliance be voluntary, but that majors be required to submit a detailed plan showing how they intended to meet the guidelines. Force majeure clauses could be invoked, he argued, in the light of current shortages, relieving companies of any liability for violation of contracts.[79] This plan was not implemented. Instead, an enormous number of manhours was devoted to finding supplies for individuals or companies who complained to their congressman or directly to Simon. Public hearings were held, June 11–14, on the effectiveness of the voluntary program. Testimony, plus a continuing deluge of complaints received by the Office of Oil and Gas, then moved Simon in the direction of mandatory allocation.

This was against Simon's personal philosophy (and that of DiBona in the White House) and seemed to him an inevitably futile effort when viewed in relation to the need to increase energy supplies. Writing to Senator Thomas J. McIntyre at the end of June he warned that mandatory allocation not only would not increase supply but "may actually reduce output. . . . In allocating crude oil and product we have a situation not unlike the passengers on a sinking ship fighting for top position at the mast head. Unless we increase production we shall all sink sooner or later." Simon pointed a finger at past enactments and at proposals to regulate the energy industries as causing more problems than an allocation scheme could resolve. He referred in particular to air quality standards that

76. Johnson to Simon, "Allocation of Crude Oil and Refinery Products," May 8, 1973 (copy in Johnson personal files).

77. Department of the Interior, Office of Oil and Gas, news release, May 11, 1973 (copy in Johnson personal files).

78. Harry Bridges, President, Shell Oil Company, Houston, Texas, to Duke Ligon, May 29, 1973 (copy in Johnson personal files).

79. Johnson to Simon, "Possible Modifications in the Voluntary Allocation Program," May 18, 1973 (copy in Johnson personal files).

virtually necessitated the use of low-sulfur crude and to proposed legislation in the form of a requirement that the majors divest themselves of their
marketing operations.[80]

Love's Labor: Resisting Allocation to the End

The decision whether to move to a mandatory allocation program was
not Simon's alone to make. Shortly after the April 18 energy message John
Ehrlichman left the administration and Roy L. Ash, Director of the Office
of Management and Budget, moved to have the President restructure the
Executive Office energy organization. Ash felt it important to plug an
obvious gap and to forestall Senator Jackson, whose proposal (Senate bill
70) to create an Energy Council on the lines of the Council on Environmental Quality had already passed the Senate. A desire to have the OMB
more directly involved and DiBona less prominent was also present and
but poorly disguised. Pending the creation of a Department of Energy and
Natural Resources, and to guarantee that the executive branch would
retain the initiative in energy policy, Ash proposed that the President
create an Energy Policy Council. The council might comprise four executive branch members, four congressional representatives, and four non-
government members. A restructured National Energy Office would be the
coordinating arm of the council, would supply staff analysis, and would
comprise DiBona (reporting to Shultz) and one representative each from
the National Security Council, the Domestic Council, and the OMB. Ash
specified a number of matters that he considered urgently needed attention, among them (surprisingly) a negotiating posture with the Arabs and
related oil policy questions such as import levels and rationing, further
decisions on the expansion and direction of energy R&D, environmental-
energy conflicts, regulatory and licensing constraints and delays, and
energy conservation.[81]

Ash's proposal supplied the thrust of Executive Order 11726, issued on
June 29, whereby an Energy Policy Office, not a council, was established.

80. Simon to Senator Thomas J. McIntyre, Chairman of the Subcommittee on
Financial Institutions of the Senate Committee on Banking, Housing and Urban
Affairs, June 28, 1973 (copy in Johnson personal files).

81. Ash to Shultz and others, "Organization of Energy Policy Development
and Implementation," May 17, 1973 (copy in Johnson personal files); and Ash to
Haig and others, "Executive Branch Energy Organization," May 22, 1973, Parsky
Files: Box 4, folder: Energy Organization 1973, U.S. Treasury.

After a search, and partly reflecting a heightened White House awareness of regional conflicts of interest in a time of energy shortages, Governor John A. Love of Colorado was asked to head the new office, with DiBona acting as his assistant. The President also indicated in his statement that there would be a much expanded R&D program ($10 billion over a five-year period) for energy; he stressed conservation in a way not done before (a specific target of a 7 percent saving of energy within the federal government was set for the following twelve months); and he announced that he would seek congressional approval of an Energy Research and Development Administration (ERDA), incorporating the research functions of the AEC, and a Nuclear Energy Commission to direct the licensing and regulatory activities of the AEC.[82]

The Department of Energy and Natural Resources proposal from the April 18 message was not abandoned, but it had run into intractable opposition in Congress. Members of the Interior and Insular Affairs committees of the House and Senate favored a super Department of the Interior, at the expense of the AEC. On the other hand the Joint Committee on Atomic Energy held that many of the Interior Department's energy-related responsibilities should move to an expanded AEC. The members of the Joint Committee feared that nuclear energy concerns would be swamped by the commitments to fossil fuels in the department, but they were prepared to accept the demise of the AEC as long as their committee retained jurisdiction over the ERDA. Conversely, members of the Interior and Insular Affairs committees were ready to relinquish oversight of R&D to ERDA provided near-term fossil fuel development, leasing policy, and other scattered natural resource and conservation functions remained within their purview. Nixon's decision to press for ERDA plus the Nuclear Energy Commission was in part an acknowledgment of these political realities. A further factor influencing his decision was the clear need for a specialized agency, such as ERDA, to coordinate and direct the greatly expanded R&D effort that he envisaged.[83]

To Simon's dismay, Governor Love shared DiBona's naive optimism that Congress would not impose allocation, if need be, to rescue the independents. Ironically he found himself fighting for the acceptance of some-

82. "Statement Announcing Additional Policy Measures, June 29, 1973," *Public Papers: Nixon, 1973*, pp. 623–30.

83. This paragraph draws heavily on Whitaker, *Striking a Balance*, pp. 67–68. See also the excellent discussion in "Energy III: Government Reorganization," *National Journal Reports*, October 13, 1973, pp. 1517–26.

thing he also abhorred but which he (though not Love or DiBona) believed inevitable under the circumstances. Love and DiBona were not absolutely opposed to the implementation of a mandatory allocation program, but their prognoses were less pessimistic than Simon's, and they registered their views by holding off for as long as possible and by raising objections that in some cases at least were not fully in touch with reality. For example, objecting that the schemes under consideration involved a "dangerous precedent," since greater intervention was envisaged than during previous crises when the oil companies themselves had largely managed the problem, took no account of the fact that unprecedented elements were currently involved. The United States was now more dependent on imports than in 1967, for example, while there was no excess domestic refining or production capacity worth speaking of. In addition the government was already much more heavily involved in programs that directly affected oil supplies and demands (clean air regulations, COLC rules, and so on).[84] These and other objections notwithstanding, the Energy Policy Office was less negative about proposed schemes that would be administered by the states. But this, as Stephen A. Wakefield, assistant secretary for energy and minerals at the Interior Department, pointed out, raised the specter of not one but fifty distinct programs operating with different degrees of efficiency and success.[85]

From where Simon sat, as chairman of the Oil Policy Committee, and from the perspective of the Office of Oil and Gas in the Interior Department (both in the direct line of fire from anguished independents and congressmen), the Energy Policy Office must have seemed at times to be involved in a different energy crisis. Had he been under less pressure, however, Simon would no doubt have acknowledged that Love's analysis had considerable merit. As Love put it: "I have tried at all times to keep the petroleum situation in its proper perspective. . . . To do otherwise is to fall victim to the 'jigger with this then tinker with that' syndrome rather than to delineate and solve the overall problem." While the voluntary allocation program might be less than ideal, Love allowed, "I am not convinced that [its] shortcomings . . . can best be corrected by adopting a

84. A list of these and other possible objections that could be raised was compiled by John Schaefer, "Rationale for Not Adopting a Mandatory Allocation System," July 9, 1973 (copy in Johnson personal files).

85. Wakefield to Schaefer, "Comments on the July 20 Draft Allocation Program," July 20, 1973, Secretary of the Interior, Secretary's Files, Subject Files: Minerals and Fuels–Commodities and Products, Petroleum, Department of the Interior.

mandatory fuel allocation system." That judgment was offered at a news conference on August 9, where Love also listed the steps he thought should be tried before moving to mandatory allocation:

1. Review federal and state environmental regulations to consider adjustments that would permit the increased use of coal and high-sulfur crude oil.

2. Seek changes in price control rules to encourage imports.

3. Adopt conservation measures to decrease demand.

These suggestions commanded wide support in the administration. Rather less compelling was Love's additional suggestion that the independent segment of the industry could best be protected by the Antitrust Division of the Justice Department.[86]

Bowing somewhat to the inevitability of circumstances, Love also unveiled "a possible mandatory allocation program" on August 9. Love added emphatically that the government was not now or at any specific time in the foreseeable future planning to implement the program but was looking for comment. The aim of the program was "to facilitate operations by small refiners at levels of at least 90% of capacity." The Office of Oil and Gas would see to this by ordering exchanges where necessary between major refiners, who would report crude availability, and small refiners, who would report their net needs. Exchanges would take place on a posted price basis (plus transport and handling costs and a markup). Imported crude and new discoveries would be exempt. As to products, bulk purchasers would be allocated 100 percent of the same quantities they had received in 1972, or a pro rata share in the event of absolute shortage, with allowance for those not in business during the entire base year and for growth since 1972. A priorities list would be superimposed, similar to the one adopted under the voluntary program. Love was adamant in his comments to the press that end-use (for example gasoline) rationing would "not be contemplated unless the situation is indeed desperate."[87] In this respect, at least, he echoed Simon's sentiments.[88]

This proposed program differed from an earlier one devised by Simon's staff, both in applying to small refiners only and in disallowing major refiners the right to charge the higher replacement cost of imported crude

86. Office of the White House Press Secretary, "Statement of Governor John A. Love on the Current Fuel Situation and Mandatory Fuel Allocation Program," August 9, 1973.

87. Ibid.

88. U.S. Treasury Department news release, "No Gasoline Rationing, Oil Policy Chairman Says," July 3, 1973.

for lower-priced domestic crude they would be obliged to give up.[89] The latter provision was also subjected to strong criticism by majors.[90]

Love continued for a time on the course he had outlined early in August. He followed up with a statement on August 27 that the Eagleton amendment was to be used to block further coal-to-oil conversions and to delay shifts to lower-sulfur-content fuel oils except where to do otherwise would violate primary air quality standards.[91] In a press conference following his announcement Love also suggested that he had met with some success in trying to get the COLC to change its Phase IV rules. These rules established ceilings on gasoline, no. 2 fuel oil, and diesel oil prices and allowed cost pass-through on imports—subject, however, to the weighted average of price increases remaining within ceiling limits. Since complete cost pass-through on higher-priced imports was thus disallowed, suppliers of heating oil made up largely of imported product, such as many in the Northeast, continued to be at a competitive disadvantage relative to those with access to more domestic product. With the help of Shultz, Love was able to get the COLC to modify its restrictive interpretation of the pass-through regulations.[92]

Meanwhile, too, the President's interest in energy was quickening, and a veritable spate of statements was issued from the White House during September and October. Twice Nixon urged Congress to act on bills affecting the Alaska pipeline, deep water ports, deregulation of natural gas and strip mining. In addition he spoke of executive actions to relax emission standards, dismissed "the old wives' tales and horror stories that are told about nuclear plants and all the rest" and recommitted the administration publicly to expanded nuclear research. He also requested action on his

89. Johnson to Simon, "Mandatory Allocation Program," June 25, 1973; and Johnson to Charles J. Cullen, Office of Oil and Gas (comments on proposed Mandatory Petroleum Allocation Program), September 7, 1973 (copies in Johnson personal files).

90. "Report of the Task Force to Evaluate Comments on the Proposal for a Mandatory Petroleum Allocation Program" (working group draft), September 18, 1973 (copy in Johnson personal files).

91. Office of the White House Press Secretary, "Statement of Governor John A. Love on Establishment of Priorities of Use and Allocations of Supply for Certain Low Sulphur Petroleum Products," August 27, 1973.

92. Office of the White House Press Secretary, "Press Conference of John A. Love and Charles J. DiBona," September 8, 1973; Johnson to Simon, "Phase IV Regulations—Meeting with Sec. Shultz at 5 p.m. Today," August 6, 1973 (copy in Johnson personal files); and Love to Dunlop (on proposed Phase IV regulations), August 6, 1973, COLC Deputy Director's Files, Box 41, folder: Oil 1973, COLC Records, NA.

energy reorganization plans, on proposals to streamline the process of determining the siting of power plants, and on his request to allow leases in the Santa Barbara Channel to be canceled and production to be expanded instead within Naval Petroleum Reserve No. 1 (Elk Hills). On October 9 and 11 came special announcements about conservation and the establishment of an Energy Research and Development Advisory Council to assist Love.[93]

During September internal efforts to arrive at a policy toward allocation were intense. In mid-September a draft memorandum for the President in the names of Ash and Love argued that a mandatory allocation program was almost certain to emerge from Congress; hence the main issue was "which program gives us the best political posture." The position taken in the draft memorandum was to announce that a mandatory program would be implemented by early October and to state at the same time that there would be major conservation efforts, steps to obtain "variances" in environmental standards, and significant relaxation or complete removal of petroleum price controls.[94]

It was reported that this general line was acceptable to Russell E. Train, administrator of the Environmental Protection Agency, Simon, and the staff of the Domestic Council. Counselor to the President for Domestic Affairs Melvin R. Laird, White House speech writer Bryce N. Harlow, presidential assistant William E. Timmons, Peter Flanigan, and Rogers Morton were said to prefer to wait for and reluctantly accept a program if enacted by Congress, since they doubted an allocation plan could be made to work well, and this tactic would at least transfer part of the blame to Congress. Shultz was said to be opposed to a mandatory program and to have the support of Commerce Secretary Frederick B. Dent and Secretary of the Department of Transportation Claude S. Brinegar. In a separate memorandum Kenneth R. Cole, Jr., executive director of the Domestic Council, expressed strong opposition to mandatory allocation on the ground that no such program would prevent a heating oil shortage during the coming winter, and the administration would therefore be blamed whether it initiated allocation or merely responded to con-

93. "Statement Following a Meeting with Energy and Environmental Advisers on Energy Conservation, October 9, 1973," and "Statement about Additional Funding for Energy Research and Development Programs in Fiscal Year 1974, October 11, 1973," in *Public Papers: Nixon, 1973*, pp. 851–52, 862.

94. Love and Ash to the President, "Decision Regarding Mandatory Fuel Allocation Program," September 15, 1973, COLC Deputy Director's Files, Box 41, folder: Oil 1973, COLC Records, NA.

gressional initiatives. The proper stance would be to oppose mandatory allocation, stressing other elements in the energy program such as those argued for in the draft memorandum from Ash and Love, plus a continuation of the existing voluntary arrangements together with provision for distress relief.[95]

Both the options and the preferences were somewhat more differentiated by September 21, when a second draft memorandum from Love and Ash to the President indicated that in addition to the three short-term measures earlier proposed in lieu of mandatory allocation the President might (1) propose a gasoline tax of 10 cents a gallon or (2) consider a mandatory program for crude only. The latter might force available crude to independent refiners, in turn causing majors to raise their imports and ultimately, if indirectly, addressing the problems of the most vocal segment of the industry, the independent marketers. This memorandum identified the most pressing problems as a supply shortage of natural gas, propane, and distillates plus disruption of traditional distribution patterns, with especially adverse consequences in some areas, notably the Northeast. Hence a third possible option was to move to mandatory allocation for propane and home heating oil only. General agreement was reported among advisers that a program for propane was inevitable. As a way of showing that the administration was concerned and at the same time expressing its real fear that a full-blown program would involve the government for the three-to-five years needed to expand refinery capacity, Love was said to favor a program for distillates, plus the other short-term solutions, excepting a gasoline tax. Ash in the meantime had apparently been persuaded to Cole's view. Simon was reported as holding to his view that a mandatory program was necessary to preempt Congress; and this time he had Morton's support.[96]

A week later the situation had again changed in that the substance of the

95. Ibid., and Kenneth Cole to the President, "Mandatory Fuel Allocation Program," in COLC Deputy Director's Files, Box 41, folder: Oil 1973, COLC Records, NA.

96. Love and Ash to the President, "Fuel Shortages/Allocation Systems," September 21, 1973 (copy in Johnson personal files). Morton's shift may have been due to very explicit advice from his own key assistants in the energy area. See Ken Lay, Deputy Under Secretary of the Interior for Energy, to Morton, "Follow-up to Lunch with Bryce Harlow on Energy Situation," September 17, 1973, Secretary of the Interior's Files, Subject Files: Minerals and Fuels—Commodities and Products, Petroleum, Department of the Interior.

House report on Jackson's bill was known and the lineup of advisers was also altered in consequence. Love, Ash, and Laird now favored announcing a mandatory program, but for heating oil and propane only. A more general program was preferred by Shultz, Morton, and Simon. There was virtual unanimity on the additional short-term measures, with the exception of a gasoline tax and a proposal to make the type of conservation regulations applied in the Northwest nationwide.[97]

The President chose to move to a partial program. On October 2 Love, at Nixon's direction, announced the establishment of a mandatory allocation program for home heating oil and propane gas whereby supplies would be made available to purchasers in accordance with individual sales between October 2, 1972, and April 30, 1973, after deduction of sales to a list of priority customers.[98] The propane problem was enormously complex. Propane is a clean fuel, and growing shortages of natural gas had sharply increased the demand for propane as a substitute. There were a number of brokers who bought propane at very high prices, primarily for industrial users whose gas supplies had been curtailed on orders from the FPC. Most propane sold to farmers and trailer dwellers, however, was bought from distributors whose suppliers were the major oil companies. The majors, historically, purchased the 70 percent of propane stripped from natural gas and added it to their own 30 percent from refining. But Special Rule No. 1 made this highly unprofitable. Thus while demand had risen, propane remained price controlled as if still in excess supply, and the efforts of the COLC made the shortage worse. Farmers, rural households, and their suppliers together had created strong pressures for an allocation program. But allocation was physically difficult to effect from Washington. Propane was distributed beyond the gas pipeline system, and this meant that supplies were difficult to trace on short notice. Moreover, propane requires transport and storage under special conditions, so that price was sensitive to the place of sale. DiBona and Love had argued that if their office was to handle energy policy, diffuse authority over pricing decisions must cease. They now felt that for their pains they had been thrown a problem that was quite intractable.[99]

97. Love to the President, "Fuel Shortages/Allocation Systems," September 27, 1973, COLC Deputy Director's Files, Box 41, folder: Oil 1973, COLC records, NA.

98. Office of the White House Press Secretary, Statement by Governor John A. Love, "Mandatory Propane Allocation Program," October 2, 1973.

99. Interview with Charles J. DiBona, April 13, 1978.

Phase IV and Antitrust and Energy Policy

For all the intensive effort that went into deciding the allocation issue, this remained primarily a short-term political expedient. No one in the administration was lulled into thinking that mandatory allocation could cure the underlying ills: increasing energy demand, declining domestic production of oil and natural gas, declining exploration and limited refinery capacity, a failure to develop alternative sources of energy. At the same time, it should not be thought that allocation was a problem apart. The year 1973 spawned a host of special, interrelated difficulties demanding some response from the administration. Two of these became mixed up with the question of the survival of the independents, hence directly or indirectly with allocation, and may usefully be singled out for notice at this point. They are the Phase IV rules of the COLC and charges that the difficulties of the independents stemmed from the machinations of the major oil companies.

In a petition to the Oil Policy Committee in March 1973 the New England Fuel Institute—an association of 1,143 independent retail heating oil distributors, wholesale distributors, and independent terminal operators—spoke of their position relative to that of the majors in the event of a move to a system of auctioning import licenses, likening it to "David against Goliath with David being bereft of his sling."[100] Whatever the aptness of the analogy in this instance, it sums up a persistent and much more commonly held feeling about the major oil companies that frequently seems to have amounted to little more than an equating of bigness with venality.[101]

In the circumstances of the spring of 1973 much more specific charges could be laid at the majors' door. Not only did they cut product supplies

100. Charles H. Burkhardt, Executive Vice-President of the New England Fuel Institute to Duke Ligon, Executive Secretary of the Oil Policy Committee, March 13, 1973 (copy in Johnson personal files).

101. This was the case, for example, when Senator Edward Kennedy, in a letter also signed by others, complained to Interior Secretary Hickel of increasing costs of no. 2 fuel oil and home heating oil to New Englanders, blaming the "growing market power of the major oil companies" and saying that "New England is a captive market." The explanation in this particular instance turned out to be wider margins being taken by distributors in the New England area. Kennedy to Hickel, February 17, 1969, and Hickel to Kennedy, May 7, 1969, Secretary of the Interior's Files, Subject Files: Minerals and Fuels–Commodities and Products, Petroleum, Department of the Interior.

to some independent distributors, but the changes made by the Oil Policy Committee in the MOIP, whereby imports could be had by all who could afford the license fee, laid the administration open to the charge that it was aiding and abetting the majors in decimating the independents.

This was implausible in that context, since the Oil Import Appeals Board was given carte blanche to help importers, especially independents, in financial distress. Nonetheless, just such a charge was made for or by independent retail (principally gasoline) marketers in another context. The occasion was the COLC's announcement in July of its Phase IV regulations. These involved price ceilings at the retail end, with the intention that pressure would be exerted backward onto costs. The ceilings promised to affect major oil company outlets less, however, because of the majors' greater overall financial base and access to credit; while the possibility was quite remote that independent marketers could exert pressure on their major suppliers. This aside, the new rules allowed major company retailers to compute ceiling prices based on May 15, 1973, markups, whereas January 10 was the date applied to independent retailers. In January many petroleum dealers and jobbers had been involved in price wars, so this choice of date was unfortunate.[102] In a letter to John Dunlop in July 1973 Senator Edward W. Brooke of Massachusetts interpreted the choice thusly: "Given the impact on independents, one can only surmise that the Phase IV plan is being proposed by those who do not care whether the independent petroleum marketer survives. It is an unsupportable, anticompetitive proposal."[103]

Anticompetitive behavior was also a charge made directly against the majors, and not only by those outside the administration. In mid-1973 the Federal Trade Commission completed an investigation into concentration in specific fuels and the overall energy industry. In the resulting staff report and in a separately filed complaint the majors were accused of "manipulating the existence of a shortage to the competitive disadvantage of independent refiners and marketers."[104] James T. Halverson, director of the

102. Johnson to Simon, "Probable Reaction by Marketers to Phase IV Regulations," September 11, 1973 (copy in Johnson personal files). Johnson records that one independent attributed this disparity to a sell-out by COLC to the majors.

103. Brooke to Dunlop, July 31, 1973, COLC Deputy Director's Files, Box 41, folder: Oil 1973, COLC Records, NA.

104. See Federal Trade Commission, "Preliminary Staff Report on Its Investigation of the Petroleum Industry," July 2, 1973. The report was prepared in response to a request by Senator Jackson, as Chairman of the Senate Permanent Subcommittee on Investigations, May 31, 1973, for a study of the role of the petroleum in-

FTC's Bureau of Competition, repeated the accusation in testimony before the Senate Judiciary Committee and the Senate Committee on Commerce.[105] This provoked William Simon to point out to the chairman of the FTC that the independents had come into existence largely because of surplus crude and refining capacity in years past, and that the disappearance of this surplus could hardly be attributed to a predatory policy on the part of the majors.[106] The FTC in turn suggested that Simon and his staff were trying to obstruct the commission in its adjudicative function and were being the not wholly unwitting tools of the majors.[107] These incidents serve to illustrate once again the sensitive nature of energy issues and the sometimes unexpected repercussions that attended apparently simple regulatory decisions.

---

dustry in the development of the fuel shortage. The FTC report was based on a wider investigation of the industry begun late in 1971. It was made available to members of Congress and released by Jackson on July 12. On July 18 the FTC issued a complaint against the eight largest oil companies (Exxon, Texaco, Gulf, Mobil, Standard Oil of California, Standard Oil of Indiana, Shell, and Atlantic Richfield) charging the majors with a variety of anticompetitive practices used to control the supply of crude to independent refiners and potential entrants into the refining business.

105. *The Natural Gas Industry,* Hearings before the Subcommittee on Antitrust and Monopoly of the Senate Judiciary Committee, 93 Cong. 1 sess. (GPO, 1973), pt. 1, pp. 223–74; and *Fair Marketing of Petroleum Products Act,* Hearings before the Subcommittee on Consumer of the Senate Commerce Committee, 93 Cong. 1 sess. (GPO, 1973), pp. 224–38.

106. Simon to Lewis A. Engman, July 30, 1973, Parsky Files, Box 2, folder: Oil-FTC 1973–4, U.S. Treasury.

107. This was implied in a letter from Halverson to Simon, September 7, 1973, and stated more openly in "Proposed Statement on FTC Oil Company Antitrust Case," May 1, 1974, by the FTC attorney in the first prehearing conference on the oil company antitrust case that the FTC subsequently brought. (Both in Parsky Files, ibid.) The episode raises the important issue of the availability and reliability of data in the energy field; most of what was supplied to the government had for years been what the oil industry voluntarily collected. The FTC hoped that one result of its bringing an antitrust suit against the majors would be to "subject the operations of the industry to the rigorous examination of an adversary proceeding. We will be able to substitute fact and careful analysis for myths and superficial rhetoric." (Halverson to Simon, September 7, 1973.) It is doubtful, however, whether the drawn-out proceedings of the suit and moves to secure divestiture, which might be regarded as the congressional counterpart to those proceedings, were necessary on that account. The embargo later in 1973 and the increasing experience in the field of petroleum pricing and regulation accumulated since early 1973 were quite sufficient to convince federal agencies of the need for better and "untainted" data, and by early in 1974 concerted moves were being made by the administration to correct past deficiencies.

Drifting into the Embargo

Just as President Nixon was putting before the nation his April 18 package of energy palliatives and noting in particular that the new import policy "should help to meet our immediate energy needs by encouraging importation of foreign oil at the lowest cost to consumers,"[108] Sheik Ahmed Zaki al-Yamani of Saudi Arabia was warning the United States that his country would find it difficult to increase oil production for export to the United States if Washington did not help in settling the Mideast problems to the satisfaction of the Arab states.[109] This was by no means the first threat of the Organization of Petroleum Exporting Countries to cut off supplies.[110] Yet well into 1973 the State Department had no clearly formulated negotiating stance with the Arabs, far less plans to deal with a possible embargo.

The State Department, of course, was well aware of the growing importance of the Middle East as a supplier of crude to the United States. So far as one can judge, given the paucity of documentary evidence in this area, its response was threefold: (1) avoid overt actions that might offend the Arab producing nations;[111] but at the same time (2) encourage increased domestic production and (3) attempt to negotiate some sort of pact with the industrialized consuming nations that might be used as a countervailing force to contain or even weaken OPEC. Unfortunately these three broad principles seem not to have been worked out in any detail, and they were not pursued with equal enthusiasm, so that policy fell short of being quite coherent. The first implied quiesence rather than policy initiatives, though the State Department's lead in having the Western Hemisphere preference (affecting Canada and Venezuela) eliminated from the MOIP might be interpreted as reflecting the belief that it would be regarded as a signal that the United States was interested in multilateral agreements rather than preferential bilateral arrangements with Western neighboring

108. "Special Message to Congress on Energy Policy, April 18, 1973," *Public Papers: Nixon, 1973*, p. 312.

109. "Saudi's Link Oil Flow to U.S. Policy," *Facts on File*, vol. 33 (April 22–28, 1973), p. 329.

110. See M. A. Adelman, "Is the Oil Shortage Real? Oil Companies as OPEC Tax-Collectors," *Foreign Policy*, no. 9 (Winter 1972–73), pp. 69–107.

111. Ibid., especially pp. 79–82. Adelman turns this into the charge that the State Department more or less openly acquiesced in OPEC moves early in the decade to raise taxes on foreign companies producing in the Middle East.

producer countries.[112] If encouraging increased domestic production was taken seriously, it certainly was not a concern of high-level officials in the department. Individuals such as James Akins, it is true, strongly advocated increased domestic supply and R&D expenditure to lessen U.S. dependence on oil, but Secretary of State Kissinger took no active interest in the President's energy message of April 18, 1973, although he was a member of the energy triumvirate ostensibly responsible for its substance. Perhaps the most actively pursued strategy was the third one listed. It seems to have been the view of those in charge at the State Department that in the long run OPEC could be broken, and Under Secretary of State John N. Irwin II was involved in discussions with other national representatives on the Oil Committee of the Organisation for Economic Co-operation and Development from early 1971 onward to try to create a united front among the consuming nations.

No threat from the consumers could be credible unless massive efforts were made at the same time to increase domestic production (in the case of the United States) and to conserve. Akins understood this and saw both the strength of OPEC in the short term and the need to reduce U.S. dependence on imports in the longer term. Hence the first and second policies were for him inseparable. As early as the spring of 1970 Akins's Fuels and Energy Office put together the implications of reduced reserves of domestic natural gas and the success of Libya in negotiating better terms from the oil companies and began predicting a price for crude at the Persian Gulf of $4.50 by 1980. Three years later Akins warned publicly that OPEC was in an uncommon position for a cartel, since it controlled a product that was virtually irreplaceable in the short run.[113] Kissinger had neither a taste nor a head for economics. Eventually, however, he saw the need to link his grand international schemes to practical domestic policies and by late 1974 was a leading supporter, if not instigator, of Project Independence to achieve self-sufficiency in energy and of the tariff and conservation proposals espoused by Ford. But through most of 1973 (and beyond) his thinking seems to have been dominated by the general truth that cartels are unstable, and Akins found himself a prophet without honor at the State Department.

The department was unprepared for the action in the fall of 1973 of

112. The State Department's role in this is spelled out in Linda Graebner's analysis (see note 58).

113. James E. Akins, "The Oil Crisis: This Time the Wolf Is Here," *Foreign Affairs,* vol. 51 (April 1973), pp. 462–90.

the Organization of Arab Petroleum Exporting Countries (OAPEC), as for that matter, were most others in the administration.[114]

Responding with a Reorganization

Throughout 1973, as the energy problem escalated, so too did the number of organizations hurriedly put in place to contain it. The tiny National Energy Office gave way to the Energy Policy Office, five times its size. But before the year was out the Energy Policy Office was exceeded in size by a single task force set up to study and devise an allocation program, and the task force in turn was absorbed by and became but one office out of seven in a new structure, the Federal Energy Office.

The mandatory allocation program for propane and distillates was in place by November 1. But before then—on October 16—the war in the Middle East had supplied occasion to OAPEC to activate Yamani's earlier threat and to cut off supplies of oil to the United States. On November 7 the President conceded to the nation that a crisis—in earlier statements there were problems and "a challenge" only—was upon them all. In an urgent message Nixon warned that at least 10 percent of anticipated demand for petroleum would not be met. He urged a series of voluntary practical steps, ranging from turning down thermostats to car-pooling. Congressional authorization was required for stronger measures, and the President asked specifically for the freedom to open the Naval Petroleum Reserves, to relax environmental standards, and to halt the tendency of power plants to switch away from coal. He also asked for quick enactment of a bill already under consideration and designed to equip the administra-

114. There were some notable exceptions. Mention has already been made of the interagency task force under Darrell Trent that prepared contingency plans in the spring of 1973. These plans were not wholly lost with the demise of the OEP. In July William Johnson already had initiated inquiries concerning the administration's authority to build up a stored reserve to minimize the impact of a possible disruption of foreign crude supplies, by mid-August the Treasury had assembled data to provide a rough estimate of U.S. vulnerability in the event of an Arab cutoff, and by the time the embargo was imposed a full set of draft contingency plans had been drawn up, including a plan for fuel oil and gasoline rationing that resurrected earlier work by Trent's task force. Robert Nipp to William Simon, "Significance of Arab Country Oil to the U.S. Economy," August 13, 1973; and Office of Energy and Natural Resources, Department of the Treasury, "Contingency Plans in Response to Curtailment of U.S. Oil Imports," October 9, 1973 (copies of both in Johnson personal files).

tion with authority to ration energy supplies. In the meantime, he promised, the administration would prepare a contingency rationing plan. The President also ordered the Emergency Petroleum Supply Committee into action, and he dropped his request for a Department of Energy and Natural Resources but implored Congress to enact enabling legislation for the ERDA and the Nuclear Energy Commission.[115] Finally, the President turned from "crisis" measures to a more optimistic discussion of the energy "challenge" ("We can take heart . . . that we . . . have half the world's known coal reserves") and he ended with a call for dedication to a new national endeavor, Project Independence. "Let us set as our national goal, in the spirit of Apollo, with the determination of the Manhattan Project, that by the end of this decade we will have developed the potential to meet our own energy needs without depending on any foreign energy sources."[116]

With this rhetoric the President at a stroke, though inadvertently, set a time limit on and implicitly defined quantitative goals for energy R&D policy. By implication, too, Nixon committed the nation to supporting a new coordinating agency and bureaucracy to formulate the plan for Project Independence and to see it through.

The message embodied just that confident and decisive tone Nixon counted so important to an administration. It hid a not inconsiderable amount of disarray in energy policy, however; and with respect to Project Independence it promised more than had been studied and agreed upon. Only when war broke out in October did Love and Kissinger get together with other senior administration officials to prepare a contingency plan. By October 30 Love was ready to outline options to the President in preparation for a public statement. Love pointed out that it would take at least forty-five days to prepare a rationing scheme, though it would be important to announce an intention to draw up plans, as an incentive to voluntary conservation. Love also stressed that of the expected 600,000-barrel-a-day shortfall, actions such as reducing the highway speed limit and more minor energy-saving schemes would still leave a deficit of 450,000 barrels a day. This might be dealt with by a gasoline tax of 20 cents a gallon, allocation at the retail level, and a reduction in demand

115. See Richard Corrigan, Claude E. Barfield, and James A. Noone, "Energy Report: Administration, Congress Move Swiftly to Counter Shortages of Fuel Supplies," *National Journal Reports*, November 17, 1973, pp. 1722–30.

116. "Address to the Nation about Policies to Deal with the Energy Shortages, November 7, 1973," *Public Papers: Nixon, 1973*, p. 920. Both the Manhattan Project and the Apollo program analogies were by this time in fairly common use to suggest the kind of action needed on the energy front.

"forced" by permitting customers to wait in line at service stations or by use of a coupon system. These and other possible lines of action were put to the President in an unhurried manner,[117] and there is some reason to believe that both Love and the President reacted to the embargo as to a storm one hopes will pass quickly. For Nixon, long besieged and struggling to stay in office, it was a case of yet another unfortunate turn of events, and really something of a nuisance. By mid-November nothing had been done, save that the President had addressed the people. Love continued to seek advice among members of the cabinet, but positions were being taken and it began to look as if Love's gentlemanly pace and manner would not produce a consensus and the action needed.

Treasury economists studying the impact of the embargo on the economy concluded that if industry were to bear the brunt of the shortages, as had been proposed in an FPC list of priority users, that sector would experience a 25 percent shortfall, "resulting in massive unemployment, loss of production, and general social and economic chaos."[118] The CEA later translated this into an increase in the unemployment rate from 4.7 to 5.6 percent.[119] Herbert Stein, CEA chairman, and Shultz adamantly opposed gasoline rationing except as a desperation measure. They strongly favored a gasoline tax and wanted to see the FPC's priorities list inverted so as to make "nonproduction" sectors bear the brunt of the shortages. OMB Director Ash, on the other hand, preferred a modified rationing scheme whereby motorists would be guaranteed a certain basic supply of gasoline and could purchase more but at a higher price.[120]

In mid-November, frustrated at the lack of action and angered over the public airing of differences within the administration, presidential aide Alexander M. Haig, Jr., and Counselor for Domestic Affairs Melvin Laird took charge. An Energy Emergency Action Group was formed. Love was nominally in command, but he lacked staff, and an interagency working group was commissioned to serve the cabinet-level action group. The working group was based on a task force created in October under Eric R. Zausner, deputy assistant secretary of the interior for energy, and John A.

117. Love to the President, "U.S. Domestic Response to Arab Oil Boycott," October 30, 1973, CEA Records, Gary Seevers Files, GRFL.

118. Ron Bass to Simon, "Energy Shortages and the Economy," November 8, 1973 (copy in Johnson personal files). The FPC's priorities list is contained in FPC Order 493, September 21, 1973.

119. *Wall Street Journal,* November 30, 1973.

120. Corrigan, Barfield, and Noone, "Energy Report"; and Harry B. Ellis, *Christian Science Monitor,* November 16, 1973.

Hill, deputy director of the Management Division for Natural Resources, Energy and Science at the OMB, to design the mandatory allocation program for distillates. Convinced at that stage that the shortage problem was quite pervasive, Zausner and Hill, with the blessing of Love, John C. Sawhill (Hill's chief at OMB), Interior Secretary Morton, and Under Secretary John C. Whitaker, coordinated a sixty-five-person interagency task force under Hill to pursue broader allocation plans. This became the working group, or Energy Emergency Planning Group (as it was officially known).[121]

Shultz, for his part, continued to foster a Treasury-CEA version of an appropriate response to the crisis. The options explored included a gasoline tax, with a general tax refund channeled through the Internal Revenue Service withholding system, a crude oil tax, and moving toward market prices for crude and natural gas.[122] At the same time tax analysts in the Treasury were investigating these possibilities, members of Simon's energy advisory staff were quietly working with John Schaefer (without the knowledge of Love or DiBona) to write the propane and crude allocation programs.

Meanwhile Ash, Haig, and Laird had determined that the energy program implied by the President's November 7 message and the proposed Emergency Energy Act (Senate bill 2589), which alone would establish more than thirty operating programs, went far beyond the resources of Love and the Energy Policy Office. They worked out a plan for a new consolidating agency, its offices largely replicating those of the recently abandoned plan for the Department of Energy and Natural Resources.[123] Enabling legislation was required for the new agency, though an executive office could be created to perform the same functions in the interim. The President decided to move in that direction, and Shultz was able to see to it that not only would Love have no part in the new scheme but that he himself would be given responsibility for the office. Shultz promptly delegated his authority to Simon, in an attempt to secure a large measure of influence for the Treasury over whatever new policies might be adopted. As a quid

121. Frank V. Fowlkes and Joel Havemann, "Energy Report: President Forms Federal Energy Body with Broad Regulation, Price Control Powers," *National Journal Reports,* December 8, 1973, pp. 1830–38; and interview with John A. Hill, New York, October 25, 1978.

122. William Fellner to Shultz, "Suggestions Made in View of the Information Contained in the Treasury Papers Received from Assistant Secretary Hickman on November 21," CEA Records, Seever Files, GRFL.

123. Fowlkes and Havemann, "Energy Report."

pro quo, Simon was not given the freedom to choose his own deputy, but it was decided that this should be Sawhill from OMB. This particular share-the-influence compromise was doubly unfortunate. Simon and Sawhill were unable to work well together. Moreover, Simon's longer-range plans included a hope that he would succeed Shultz as secretary of the treasury, and he insisted on retaining his job as deputy secretary while also heading up the new energy office. This imparted a peculiar bias to the style of the new office, since Simon determined that he would do nothing to compromise his chances of being confirmed by the Senate in the Treasury job. As it turned out this placed the office at the mercy of a host of special interests and pleas from individual Congressmen, especially Senators. Sawhill, for his part, sensed a power vacuum, shed the mantle of fiscal restraint typically worn by deputy directors of the OMB, and devoted himself to securing the growth and sustained influence of an agency that had never been meant as more than a temporary and emergency structure.

The Federal Energy Office (FEO) was created by executive order on December 4, 1973. Simon was named executive director of the Energy Emergency Action Group, which (under Nixon's nominal chairmanship) would "continue to oversee all major policy issues relating to energy."[124] He was also designated FEO administrator and charged with advising the President "with respect to the establishment and integration of domestic and foreign policies relating to the production, conservation, use, control, distribution, and allocation of energy and with respect to all other energy matters."[125] There had been energy czars before, but Simon was the first expected to be omniscient and omnipresent, and he was given almost unlimited staff and budgetary resources.

The new FEO, conceived in crisis, began its life with an awesome inheritance of problems. In the first place, the emergency authority sought by the President had been granted in a form that exceeded his intentions. The Emergency Petroleum Allocation Act of 1973 (Public Law 93-159), signed by the President one week before the establishment of the FEO, obliged the administration to prepare and implement allocation plans for crude oil and for all petroleum products, not just propane and heating oil —all within thirty days. It even contained authority to move to gasoline rationing. Next, the legacy of COLC Phase IV regulations and the still

124. "Federal Energy Office, Executive Order 11748, December 4, 1973," *Weekly Compilation of Presidential Documents*, vol. 9 (December 10, 1973), p. 1391.

125. "Remarks Announcing Establishment of the Federal Energy Office, December 4, 1973," *Public Papers: Nixon, 1973*, pp. 990–91.

unresolved problems of the independents became the FEO's direct responsibility. Third, it had to bring forth a plausible plan for energy self-sufficiency by 1980.

Allocation Woes

Proposed allocation regulations were published for comment in the *Federal Register* on December 13, 1973, and the final rules, though still incomplete, were promulgated early in January with the notice that they would be effective January 15, 1974. With some technical changes these regulations formed the basis of petroleum regulatory policy throughout 1974 and also during Gerald Ford's two years in the White House.

The December 13 proposals followed closely the plan already in place for middle distillates. In effect supplier-purchaser relationships as of a specified base month or period were to be maintained between crude producers, refiners, wholesale resellers of petroleum, wholesale consumers, and certain specified end-users. The year 1972 was suggested as the most appropriate base year. Superimposed on this fixed pattern of relationships was a list of priority users. In the event of absolute shortfall pro rata allocation among priority users would apply. Only defense requirements and certain agricultural and medical space-heating needs were to be fully met under all circumstances. Provision was made for the FEO to try to find suppliers for new purchasers unable to secure a commitment from suppliers.

The plan differed in no important respect from that first issued for comment by Love on August 9, 1973. At that time the administration had felt itself torn between two possibly opposed goals: securing equitable distribution on the one hand and stimulating supplies on the other. Largely because of political pressures reflecting the lobbying of independents, it opted for equitable distribution as the primary purpose of the program.[126] The August 9 proposed program for crude oil allocation addressed this point directly. It would have required major refiners (175,000 barrels a day or more) to share their domestic crude with small refiners to the extent necessary to keep the latter operating at 90 percent of that portion of their feedstock needs met by domestic crude in 1972. A sharing arrangement was later mandated under the Emergency Petroleum Allocation Act, embodying the definition above of "small" refiner and extending the plan also

126. Love to the President, "Fuel Shortages/Allocation Schemes," September 27, 1973, COLC Deputy Director's Files, Box 41, folder: Oil 1973, COLC Records, NA.

to independent refiners (those obtaining less than 30 percent of their crude from "captive" sources). Allocations were to be reduced on a pro rata basis if the aggregate amount of domestic and imported crude fell below the total for the corresponding period in 1972. The intention was to enable each refiner to run his refineries at the same percentage of capacity.

It is not my purpose to discuss all aspects of the allocation program or to detail its many implications.[127] From a policy as well as an operational perspective, however, this element in the act warrants further comment.

First, certain inequities resulted from this supposed "equity provision." Some refiners, such as the Standard Oil Company of Ohio (Sohio) and Ashland Oil, Inc., ranking thirteenth and fourteenth in refining capacity when the plan was put into effect, qualified as independents because they happened to be crude-poor. They thus obtained purchasing rights over domestic crude, while many of their smaller competitors did not. This not only ran counter to the spirit of the provision—to aid small businesses— but actually rewarded companies that had earlier followed a policy of investing in downstream activities and depending on (cheaper) foreign oil at the expense of companies that had invested in domestic exploration and production. This bias seemed particularly ironic at the time of the embargo.

Second, the act's liberal definitions of "small" and "independent" refiner encompassed too many large refiners. In addition to Ashland and Sohio, Amerada Hess Corporation and Phillips Petroleum Company also lobbied hard to qualify; all four had capacity in excess of 175,000 barrels a day. In fact, only fourteen refiners in all failed to qualify. As a result, large amounts of crude had to be purchased and sold quite outside normal distribution channels, just to meet the allocation requirements.

Third, shortages of specific products resulted from the buy-sell requirements. For instance, refiners who traditionally produced jet fuel were required to sell 42 million barrels of crude, while only 9 million were purchased by refiners who traditionally produced jet fuel. Specialized refining capability was thus idled and the airlines experienced a serious shortage of jet fuel. A similar problem, traceable to the same basic cause,

127. This is done more fully in a number of places. See, for example, Stephen A. Wakefield, "Allocation, Price Control and the FEA: Regulatory Policy and Practice in the Political Arena," *Rocky Mountain Mineral Law Institute*, vol. 21 (1975), pp. 257–84; Paul W. MacAvoy, ed., *Federal Energy Administration Regulation: Report of the Presidential Task Force*, Ford Administration Papers on Regulatory Reform (American Enterprise Institute for Public Policy Research, 1977); and Arnold Moore and Susan Hodges, "How Oil Price and Allocation Regulations Actually Work" (American Petroleum Institute, July 1978).

was experienced with petrochemical feedstocks and gasoline on the East Coast. In the latter case refiners who could readily and normally distribute products along the East Coast were allowed to purchase 32 million barrels of crude under the allocation regulations, whereas other refiners who could do the same were required to sell 50 million barrels, resulting in an 18-million-barrel shortfall.[128]

These and other difficulties quickly persuaded Simon that amendments to the allocation act would be desirable or, better still, that the crude program should be eliminated from the act altogether. On February 19 Simon asked for the latter.[129] New plans were devised by the FEO, but the Emergency Petroleum Allocation Act remained intact, and the FEO and its successor, the Federal Energy Administration (FEA), were forced to seek indirect ways around the difficulties. This search led to the entitlements program, of which more will be said in due course.

Gasoline Rationing?

End-use allocation was not required under the Emergency Petroleum Allocation Act, and the crude and products allocation plans stopped short of guaranteeing supplies to end-users. That was where conservation and disincentive policies were supposed to take effect. More precisely the President made job preservation the overriding goal, and given that constraint, the administration generally acknowledged that cutbacks in gasoline consumption were the single best way to achieve energy saving.[130]

But how best to curb gasoline consumption? Five options had been discussed at a meeting on November 30, 1973, of the Energy Emergency Action Group, with the President in attendance. A gasoline tax and price decontrol were aired but rejected, partly on the ground that short-term demand probably was of low elasticity and therefore either directly (as with the tax option) or indirectly the poor would suffer.[131] Further, should

128. Johnson to Simon, John Sawhill, and William Walker, "Impact of the Crude Oil Allocation Program," February 22, 1974 (copy in Johnson private files).

129. Federal Energy Office, "Simon Calls for Elimination of Crude Oil Allocation Program in the Emergency Petroleum Allocation Act," public affairs release, February 19, 1974 (copy in Johnson private files).

130. Fowlkes and Havemann, "Energy Report."

131. An optimistic view of "elasticity pessimism" in the energy field is to be found in George P. Shultz and Kenneth W. Dam, *Economic Policy beyond the Headlines* (Norton, 1978), pp. 186 ff.

demand turn out to be inelastic, there could be an undesirable drain of purchasing power. Moreover, in the case of price decontrol refinery output would have to be controlled and (for political reasons) so too would oil company profits. A proposal to cut gasoline allocations by some given percentage met no great show of enthusiasm because of the probable resulting inconvenience to consumers forced to seek out a gas station with supplies and because of the possibility of favored treatment for selected customers. Two rationing options were also considered, one employing a white market in coupons, the other involving a general gasoline tax but combining this with coupons that could be turned in to defray the tax on purchases up to some maximum weekly allowance. Purchases above the allowance would be at the full (tax-inclusive) price. The meeting generally favored a white market coupon scheme.[132]

Simon, to whom the decision fell after December 4, had an abhorrence of rationing. He also had a strong preference for tax or price incentives. But tax alternatives would have required additional legislation, and price decontrol would have cast him as a friend of "Big Oil." Simon had no option but to implement the mandated allocation programs, but he stopped short of allocation to final consumers.

The decision for any sort of allocation scheme virtually guaranteed that Simon and his staff would spend much time dealing with hardship cases channeled through congressmen (they as well as DiBona and Love had had to do this to make the voluntary allocation program work some months previously). The effect of the decision and the significance of the allocation program for gasoline, therefore, was that they diverted the FEO from addressing medium- and long-term problems. Once again, crisis management was the order of the day.[133]

It has been suggested by one critic that the gasoline allocation program would have been less disruptive had the FEO taken a more optimistic view of the duration of the embargo and not tended to focus on anticipated reductions in oil imports rather than on current stocks, being loath to

132. Fowlkes and Havemann, "Energy Report."

133. Simon himself painted in graphic detail the hectic character of his reign as energy czar in William E. Simon, *A Time for Truth* (McGraw-Hill, 1978), chap. 3. Simon offered a rationalization of his role somewhat different from that given in my text, arguing that he chose a businessman's strategy rather than a bureaucrat's, or that he chose to be directly responsive to reality and to solve problems rather than merely to follow rules (ibid., p. 55). In the assessment of outsiders and of some within the FEO, this approach led Simon into promising the impossible to a whole series of individual congressmen.

allow the latter to run down to compensate for reduced imports.[134] This assessment neglects the facts that the United States was more than two months into the embargo before the FEO received authority to allocate and that decisions on stocks were taken in the first instance by the industry, not by the FEO. Nor was it at all clear at the time that the embargo would be short-lived, and prudence required that a bulwark be maintained against potential economic collapse. More to the point is that the FEO labored under severe limitations. Initially it accepted an estimate of imports by a panel of oil industry experts that was much publicized by the National Petroleum Council. This involved a shortfall of roughly 3–3.5 million barrels a day. For various reasons, including warm weather, the success of conservation measures, a slowing of the economy, and effective redirection of world oil flows by the majors, this figure proved to be about 1 million barrels a day too high. Partly for this reason the FEO's allocation programs were more severe than the situation warranted.

It was also to be expected that in the FEO's brief and hectic life lessons would be learned when it was almost too late to do much in the way of correction. One such instance may be given. Under COLC Phase IV rules raw material cost increases could be passed through as price increases once each month. During the embargo cost increases were substantial. The FEO allowed these to be passed through on the first of each month, with the result that toward the end of each month retailers hoarded gasoline and gas lines lengthened in a regular monthly cycle, a pattern that became obvious only by the end of February.[135]

Price Controls and the Embargo

Phase IV rules, it will be recalled, set ceilings at retail on the prices of three so-called special products, which together amounted to about 70 percent of refined products. The three were gasoline and the no. 2 oils (diesel and home heating oil). Crude oil was also treated in a special way. A novel two-tier pricing system was introduced (basically the scheme developed by Charles Owens some months previously). Old crude was

134. Richard B. Mancke, *Performance of the Federal Energy Office* (American Enterprise Institute for Public Policy Research, 1975).

135. Johnson to Simon, Sawhill, and Parsky, "Impact of Price Controls on Gasoline Stock Levels," March 21, 1974 (copy in Johnson personal files).

subject to a ceiling (initially set at $4.25 a barrel). New crude, that is production on a property over and above 1972 levels and oil from new wells, was exempt. By a provision added in the allocation act, from December 1973 "stripper" production was also exempt. Refiners were permitted automatic pass-through on a dollar-for-dollar basis of increased product costs; and increases could be allocated over products at the discretion of the refiner. In the case of the three special products, however, costs could be allocated only in proportion to the volume of sales of the products themselves. Thus if 30 percent of a refiner's production was no. 2 oils, only 30 cents of a $1 increase in crude costs could be allocated to no. 2 oils. The automatic pass-through of cost increases was an acknowledgment that the United States had become more dependent on imports of both crude and products, whose price were beyond the control of the COLC. The exception of special products from the pass-through, however, operated during the embargo in such a way as to worsen the shortages.

During the fall of 1973 and especially after the embargo was in force, foreign crude prices rose steeply, as did the prices of many refined products. Importers felt caught in every way—unable fully to pass through these cost increases on special products or faced with allocating the increases to some extent over other products, but then with the possibility of raising prices on those products above the prevailing domestic level and thus facing loss of sales. The result was that imports were reduced.[136]

A second effect of the COLC rules that had policy implications stemmed from a provision that in transactions between affiliated entities the cost of product and transportation be computed according to accounting procedures generally accepted and historically applied by the firm concerned. In January 1974 the FEO's Office of Policy Analysis was ap-

---

136. This was not the only result. Since cost pass-through on special products, once allowed to fall below the allowable level, was not permitted to regain the allowable level, the tendency over time was for joint costs of production to be allocated disproportionately to other products. For this reason, propane prices rose very sharply. See Johnson to Simon and Sawhill, "Propane Price Regulations," January 29, 1974 (copy in Johnson personal files). Johnson waged a protracted but losing battle over the special products problem, arguing from the outset that they should simply be classed with "other products." Also see Johnson to Simon and Sawhill, "Distillate and Propane: Pricing Problems and Solutions," January 29, 1974; and Johnson to Simon, Sawhill, and Parsky, " 'Special' Product Pricing Rule Is Backing Out Imports," March 26, 1974 (copies in Johnson personal files). The FEA finally proposed in September 1974 that the three products most directly affected by the rule (though not propane) would revert to being "other products."

proached by two oil company officials who said this ruling would mean they could book imports at the posted price of $11.65 a barrel f.o.b. Persian Gulf, although their actual processing costs were only about $8. In the days of lower-priced foreign crude, competition in the international market had prevented them from charging the higher prices posted domestically. Now, with foreign crude at a higher price, applying their historical accounting procedures would give them a per barrel profit of $3.25. Assuming this would be done industry-wide, there could be added to net revenue in 1974 some $3 billion over and above any ordinary profits (that is, a 31 percent increase over 1973 profits). Noting that this would be politically explosive, the officials suggested total elimination of the various foreign tax credits enjoyed by oil companies (since a windfall profits tax would not touch the problem). The rule was changed, effective June 1, 1974, but it is ironic that in this instance the very price controls that were viewed as an essential guard against the oil companies making extraordinary gains due to foreign crude price increases worked in just the opposite manner, at least for some.[137] This was but one of many instances when companies informed the FEO of inordinate profits being made by some as a result of COLC regulations.

Project Independence

It was suggested above that the FEO was very little involved in planning and very much engaged in seeing to it that allocation schemes worked on a day-to-day basis. Some consideration was given to postembargo strategies for pricing and allocation, but the really significant planning effort, stemming from the President's "Project Independence" pledge, took place outside the FEO.

One serious step toward self-sufficiency had been taken on June 29, 1973, when the President announced an injection of $10 billion over five years for energy R&D.[138] Good data are not readily available, but one investigator has determined that this would have amounted to government funding of about 54 percent of all energy R&D during fiscal year 1975, or "more than double the comparable percentage figure for all nondefense

137. Johnson to Simon and Sawhill, "Possible Oil Industry Profits in 1974" (copy in Johnson personal files).

138. "Statement Announcing Additional Energy Policy Measures, June 29, 1973," *Public Papers: Nixon, 1973,* pp. 623–30.

and nonspace R&D."[139] Up to mid-1973 there had been only sporadic efforts to integrate R&D policy in the sense that technical specifications were matched against an economic assessment in such a way as to make projects comparable. DiBona had complained of this deficiency in the options presented to him in connection with the April 18 energy message. This is not to say that individual agencies failed to make cost-benefit calculations but that it was beyond the capacity of DiBona's tiny staff to undertake all the reworking of data required to express these calculations in strictly comparable form. Nor was this the greatest deficiency in R&D studies. The absence of a clearly specified set of energy goals and a time frame within which they were to be achieved had precluded development of a meaningful strategy for energy R&D, in the sense of a single consistent ranking of competing technologies and an estimate of the total investment likely to be necessary.

Given this lack, no high expectations were generated when Nixon also announced on June 29 that AEC Chairman Dixy Lee Ray would "undertake an immediate review of Federal and private energy research and development activities, under the general direction of the Energy Policy Office, and . . . recommend an integrated energy research and development program for the nation."[140] Much the same request had been made of the President's science adviser in the course of the first energy message, back in mid-1971. The Ray report, in fact, made great strides in the right direction, partly because by the time it was to be put together the energy R&D problem had been well defined. First, the President set a figure of $10 billion to be spent over five years beginning in fiscal 1975. Subsequently, with the proclamation of Project Independence, an implicit quantitative goal for oil production was added to these two givens: total additional federal spending and a time frame. This at last made it possible to list the major categories of alternatives (increased domestic production of oil and gas, nuclear energy, and so on) in the order in which their contributions to self-sufficiency would begin to materialize and to make some judgment as to a "reasonable" balance among Federal outlays in the

139. John E. Tilton, *U.S. Energy R&D Policy: The Role of Economics*, RFF Working Paper EN-4 (Resources for the Future, 1974), p. 75. An excellent historical review of earlier studies and an assessment of the difficulties in the way of arriving at a rational R&D program is *Energy Research and Development: Problems and Prospects*, Committee Print, Senate Committee on Interior and Insular Affairs, 93 Cong. 1 sess. (GPO, 1973).

140. "Statement Announcing Additional Energy Policy Measures, June 29, 1973," p. 627.

light of past and ongoing programs, technical constraints, and anticipated outlays by private industry.[141] This approach still did not deal with the *desirable* proportions of federal and private expenditure or with possible constraints that were not strictly technological such as water for shale oil development and an adequate energy transportation system.

There was no reason to expect that the President's proposed Energy Research and Development Administration would do better on those fronts. In the first place there was so general a consensus that energy R&D is a good thing that funding for energy research might easily be viewed as an end in itself, and the creation of a special energy R&D agency would throw the weight of bureaucratic self-interest behind this notion. Somewhat related to this, a separate ERDA might lend strength to the false idea that energy R&D policy could or should be determined independently of energy policy as a whole.[142]

Project Independence, by contrast, held out a prospect of eliciting the first truly integrated study of the nation's energy goals and options. The goal itself bore little relation to technical or economic realities. Even before the announcement Nixon's own energy and budget advisers had been extremely wary about target dates and accomplishments, and there is also little doubt that the announcement was in part simply a response to press criticism about the lack of an R&D policy in the April 18 message and to a proposal of Senator Jackson (Senate bill 1283) to devote $20 billion of federal funds toward achieving self-sufficiency by 1983.[143] But this does not detract from the fact that a unique opportunity was opened up on November 7 with the announcement of the target of self-sufficiency by 1980.

Toward the end of January 1974 Simon solicited comment from other agencies on a plan and schedule for Project Independence. The document bears the marks of Simon's market orientation. Self-sufficiency by 1980 was interpreted by Simon to mean, not zero imports, but that imports should come from a sufficient range of sources and be of sufficiently small magnitude in relation to needs to ensure that a future embargo by some

141. Excerpts from the Ray report, "The Nation's Energy Future: A Report to Richard M. Nixon, President of the United States," is readily available in Library of Congress, Congressional Research Service, Environmental Policy Division, *Materials Shortages: Selected Readings on Energy Self-Sufficiency and the Controlled Materials Plan,* prepared for the Permanent Subcommittee on Investigations of the Senate Committee on Government Operations, 93 Cong. 2 sess. (GPO, 1974), pp. 25–45. The report itself appears not to have been published.

142. Tilton, in *U.S. Energy R&D Policy,* chap. 5, offers an extended discussion of these and related points.

143. Corrigan, Barfield, and Noone, "Energy Report."

foreign suppliers would not seriously disrupt the economy. A figure of 15 percent for total oil and gas imports was suggested. Simon retained the overall goal of complete self-sufficiency for the 1980s, as suggested in the Ray report. As a means to this end, Simon suggested moving to a free market in energy—an end to both allocation and price control programs for oil and an end to natural gas price control—and he warned against any direct government involvement in the production of energy.[144]

A very simple and elegant economic specification of the problem to be solved in achieving energy independence was put forward by the OMB staff under John Hill in the Division of Natural Resources, Energy and Science. This formulation recognized an increasing cost (insecurity) involved in relying more heavily on imported oil, as well as a rising marginal cost curve for domestic energy. The task of those responsible for designing a Project Independence Blueprint was thus to identify the point at which the security risk of additional imports was just balanced by the cost of additional output from domestic sources, and to select instruments to bring the nation to that position.[145]

Neither the FEO nor the OMB had much influence on the form and evolution of the Project Independence Blueprint.[146] Its form was set before Hill's specification of the problem at hand was circulated late in April. The course of its development was influenced primarily by technical and bureaucratic considerations rather than by a need to find answers to policy questions.

The task of preparing the Project Independence Blueprint was given to Eric Zausner, at this time assistant administrator for data analysis in the FEO and subsequently assistant administrator for policy and analysis in the FEA. When he moved from the Interior Department to the FEO, Zausner gathered a team of highly qualified economic modelers, among

144. "Project Independence Plan and Schedule," FEO Staff Paper, February 28, 1974, distributed by Simon to members of the Economic Policy Group (copy in Johnson personal files).

145. This conception of the problem was first developed by George Patton of Frank Zarb's OMB staff and circulated to the Deputies Group of the Committee on Energy. Subsequently it became the basis of a more extensive analysis of the problem facing the Project Independence Task Force. See a paper by John A. Hill, Deputy Associate Director of the OMB for Natural Resources, Energy and Science, "Energy Independence—an Overview," May 2, 1974. This and related memorandums are contained in FEA records at the Department of Energy, Files of Deputy Administrator Eric Zausner, Project Independence—Policy Evaluation folder.

146. Up to the last minute the product of the task force was referred to as a blueprint, but the published version was called a report to avoid giving the impression that national energy policy was already set. It is discussed further in chapter 7.

them Bart Holaday, David Wood, and William Hogan. During the embargo the group busied itself with a short-term petroleum forecasting model and with exploring available energy models, with a view to adapting one or more to develop an analytical framework for Project Independence. By March 1974 the team was ready to meet with Zausner and decide on the precise approach to be used.[147] Zausner wanted a framework that would be ready in time to serve as an input into the 1975 State of the Union Message. This meant a November deadline. The chosen framework also had to be one that would permit fairly quick examination of alternative policy strategies by congressional committees if need be and by other interested parties. The latter constraint argued for a computer-based model or set of models. The group decided to use a set of models, combining an existing macromodel (such as the Data Resources, Inc., or Chase Econometrics Associates' model) with a separate framework for examining the energy sector. The macromodel would supply economy-wide parameters (GNP, unemployment, and so on) to the energy model, or models, and the economic implications of the energy sector analysis could be compared with the starting parameters as a consistency check.

For analyzing the energy sector itself, the group agreed to use distinct demand and supply models, the latter to be a linear programming model that would indicate the marginal supply prices implied by an attempt to meet the fuel outputs corresponding to postulated demand-prices, at minimum cost. An acknowledged disadvantage of using a single linear programming model on the supply side was that average, as distinct from marginal supply-prices, could not be calculated. For that reason the model's prices could not be regarded as a good proxy for energy prices set by regulatory agencies.[148] Hogan argued that the linear programming approach also possessed an offsetting advantage, namely, that it was a process analysis, which would allow resource constraints, such as manpower, water for shale oil, drilling and platform equipment, capital for utilities, and so on, to be incorporated.

The group recognized that their chosen sequential approach whereby

147. My description of the evolution of the Project Independence Blueprint is based in part on the detailed knowledge of Robert W. Blanning of the Owen Graduate School of Management, Vanderbilt University. Professor Blanning has examined the Project Independence Evaluation System effort closely and has interviewed many of the participants. He does not necessarily agree with the construction I have placed on events.

148. As a matter of fact, William Hogan found a way around this by interrupting the ordinary simplex system and introducing appropriate modifications.

demand-prices would be postulated and the implied quantities fed into the linear programming model—which in turn would yield a set of supply-prices—might result in two sets of prices and that these might or might not converge with further iterations. And even if there were convergence, it might involve an unmanageably large number of iterations. Nor could the team members promise Zausner that they would have the time and resources to incorporate substitution between energy products, or policy time lags. It was clear to all that it would be necessary to go beyond the immediate output of the energy demand-supply analysis. For that would yield at best a set of equilibrium prices, whereas what was required for the blueprint was an analysis of the impact (principally on imports) of changes in the energy sector resulting from various government actions to reduce import vulnerability. There was some disagreement about how far the team should try to go in breaking down the energy analysis by regions. Zausner, given the time constraints, opted for a fairly aggregated study using political units (states), while team members felt a more refined analysis would be desirable.

The modeling group designated their effort the Project Independence Evaluation System (PIES). As the brief outline above suggests, it was an ambitious undertaking, and as the work progressed, Zausner and FEA Administrator John Sawhill accepted, not with dissatisfaction, that it was absorbing many resources. By September 15 the Project Independence Blueprint staff, mostly borrowed from other agencies, had grown to 500, and the team was hopeful that PIES might not only be used in preparing the 1975 State of the Union Message but that it also might be accepted as the standard tool for subsequent analyses of presidential initiatives in the energy area.[149] Through the summer doubts were expressed about whether the modeling system could be made to work in time to fulfill even the first of these expectations. To meet the November deadline the scope of the enterprise was severely curtailed. The number of possible policy scenarios was reduced to four, only a few of the many hundreds of possible constraints that had been identified were incorporated after all, and a good deal of "manual adjustment" was needed to cope with the inevitable unfortunate results, such as elasticities that had the "wrong" size or sign.

---

149. PIES was one of several energy modeling systems being developed at about this time outside the administration, and the PIES modeling team could not expect their approach to be used exclusively in the future. In fact, they were more interested in technical modeling problems than in policy analysis. It was Zausner who pressed the team to do more in the policy direction.

Eventually the *Project Independence Report*—a massive document of nearly 800 pages backed by volumes of technical reports and data—was produced and unveiled by Sawhill with much pride on November 12. The modeling team had not been able to fulfill its intentions. For example, the demand model was not broken down by regions, no iterations were done to test for convergence between the economic parameters used as inputs to PIES and the economic implications of PIES, no constraints on free market behavior had been incorporated to approximate the effects of regulation in various energy markets, and substitution between energy products was not allowed for.[150] The PIES approach nonetheless marked a turning point in the assessment of policy options. The chief significance of the approach lay in its general equilibrium character. In principle this should have eliminated two sources of error in previous efforts to put numbers to policy options: an inherent tendency to double counting when the technique used was simply to add up the separate effects of individual policies, and the need to make some ad hoc adjustment for substitution effects in the absence of a single model framework integrating demand and supply and incorporating substitution.[151] In fact, as has just been noted, the modeling system was not so completely developed as to guarantee improved results.

Questions, too, remain about whether partial analysis with judgmental allowance for cross effects will always be less accurate a basis for making policy when practiced by those with a good knowledge of the energy sector. (As it happened, the integrating system converged to a set of market-

150. Limitations of PIES are mentioned in FEA, *Project Independence Report*, pp. 418–21. "Closing the loop," or performing economic impact studies and checking to see whether after appropriate modifications these results would converge to the values of the parameters used as economic input into the energy demand and the supply and integration models, was not taken very seriously by Hogan and the operations researchers on the team. He argued that since energy inputs amount only to a small percentage of GNP, any inconsistencies between input and output probably would amount to less than the errors in the macroeconometric model used to give the inputs in the first place. A different implication of failure to close the loop is suggested by Askin in A. Bradley Askin and John Kraft, *Econometric Dimensions of Energy and Supply* (Lexington Books, 1976), chap. 7. Askin argued that assuming convergence, failure to perform the iterations "probably overstates the differences among alternative energy scenarios" (p. 97).

151. On this point see Thomas H. Tietenberg, *Energy Planning and Policy* (Lexington Books, 1976), p. 73. Tietenberg also extensively described PIES and its strengths and weaknesses. Two years after PIES was developed, double counting because of the use of partial analysis was still a charge that could be leveled at ERDA. Philip K. Verleger to Paul W. MacAvoy, "ERDA Presentation," August 2, 1976, CEA Records, Alan Greenspan Files, GRFL.

clearing prices after a few iterations, but had this not occurred and had a more complex price adjustment rule also not helped, Hogan was prepared to replace all such adjustment rules with a person familiar with energy economics.) Inadequate or unavailable data were serious problems for the modelers, just as for anyone using a simpler method of analysis. Moreover, given the simplifications inherent in the modeling process, plus possible errors of specification and identification problems, the meaningfulness and trustworthiness of the crucial matrix of demand elasticities in the system were by no means self-evident.

Objections very similar to those just mentioned were raised at the time by, among others, Phillip Essley of Simon's staff, on the basis of his experience with similar modeling efforts.[152] The Treasury contingent in FEO was from the beginning quite skeptical of Zausner's enterprise, and Simon eventually moved to curb the FEA and to restore his own position in the energy hierarchy. A month after Nixon signed the Federal Energy Administration Act of 1974 on May 7, handing the FEO's responsibilities over to the new administration, he was also under pressure from the Treasury to establish by executive order a cabinet-level Committee on Energy. The Energy Emergency Action Group of late 1973 had not been disbanded, though it had ceased to function. The new committee was to succeed this body and perform the same coordinating and review tasks as Love's Energy Policy Office. That is to say, overall energy policy *and* formal responsibility for Project Independence were to rest not with the FEA but with this committee. Simon was to be its chairman and his executive assistant, Gerald Parsky, was to head a working group to provide staff support.[153]

There was at work here a strong element of personal animus, a determination by Simon to block Sawhill. But the move would also have been a normal response in any administration to a situation in which one agency moves too far ahead and looks as if it might start shaping policy on its own. That fear was not merely academic in the summer of 1974 when the White House turned in upon itself. Late in August, after Nixon had resigned the presidency, Simon moved again to ensure that the new incumbent be made aware of the basic principles that in his view must underlie sound energy policy. Parsky distributed a memorandum in which he stressed that

152. Essley to Sawhill and Zausner, "Project Independence Blueprint," April 10, 1974 (copy in Johnson personal files). See also Ben Massell to Gary Seevers, "Possible Talking Points for E-1," May 9, 1974, CEA Records, Seevers Files, GRFL.

153. Simon to Kenneth Rush, Counselor to the President for Economic Policy, "Energy Policy Committee," June 4, 1974, Parsky Files, Box 13, folder: Committee on Energy–Meetings, U.S. Treasury.

whereas at $2.50 a barrel an increasing national dependence on imported oil was to be expected, if oil were to sell at $10 a barrel, there would be automatic conservation as well as greater production both at home and abroad. A useful Project Independence Blueprint, Parsky urged, must reflect this basic fact, and that meant clearing out of the way of normal price incentives the major obstacle to short- and medium-term efficiency in production and allocation, namely the U.S. government and its regulation of various sectors of the energy industry. Specifically, therefore, Project Independence must embody (1) decontrol of domestic crude oil prices, coupled with a windfall profits tax; (2) deregulation of natural gas; and (3) imposition of a gasoline tax. Parsky added that the FEA should cease to exist as an independent agency and its functions should revert to various offices in the Interior Department; when Project Independence was worked out and regulations were ended, there would be no reason for being for the FEA.[154]

The Battle over Entitlements

Nothing short of an order from the President could have stemmed the momentum attained by Zausner's team in its modeling activities, and that order was unlikely in the dying days of the Nixon administration or in the hiatus that followed. In this respect the Treasury strategy was misconceived. On the desirability of a return to the market, Sawhill and Simon were at one. Sawhill even conceded in principle that the FEA should eventually cease to exist. But he had a genuine fear of inflation should energy prices rise; he was aware that congressional pressures would make it difficult to move to deallocation and decontrol of prices; and he had nurtured from infancy to adulthood both a tool and a bureaucracy for policy planning and was not inclined to let either languish or die, their promise unfulfilled. Sawhill's chosen strategy for handling decontrol gave due weight to these concerns. They led away from the Treasury's market orientation, and the administration found itself still deeper in the regulatory mire.

The issue of price decontrol as a step toward solving the nation's shortage of crude oil had been seriously debated within the administration in mid-December 1973. The Treasury and the CEA had argued for abandon-

154. Parsky to Simon, "Meeeting with the President on Energy Policy and Project Independence," August 28, 1974 (copy in Johnson personal files). As of August 27 no executive order had been issued and Parsky was urging the new President to issue one. The Committee on Energy functioned, it seems, without authorization.

ing the two-tier price system for domestic crude and for establishing a short-run ceiling price at about $12 a barrel, coupled with a windfall profits tax that would net producers a price of roughly $6.50 a barrel. This last amount was thought to be in the range of the likely long-run equilibrium price, while $12 a barrel was reckoned to be high enough "to avoid the need for rationing" in the short term.[155] It was acknowledged by these two agencies that under decontrol the price of crude would rise sharply at first, because of immediate limitations on drilling supplies and external pressures. The tax proposal was meant to capture paper profits attributable to the externally induced shortage. A graduated scale of tax rates would apply to different segments of the difference between actual selling price and the base price of $4.02 on May 16, 1973. To allow for inflation and long-run increases in demand, the whole scale would be allowed to float upward over time at some chosen rate. As supplies increased and crude prices fell back toward their long-run equilibrium level, the taxable amount would also fall back toward zero, and it was thought that the tax would be unnecessary after three years. The possibility of refunding the tax to producers was held open, on condition that it would be plowed back into energy-producing investment. And a coupon system was proposed, to return to consumers part of the extra amount they would pay under an uncontrolled price system. Coupons for gasoline and fuel oil would be issued to consumers, who could turn them in to any bank for a cash equivalent determined from month to month in accordance with the national goal of conservation and an intention of allowing long-run fuel prices to rise. Because higher prices should stimulate supplies, it was thought that decontrol would actually contribute to fighting inflation.[156]

John Dunlop strongly opposed immediate decontrol for reasons that included a fear that a large initial jump would further escalate bidding in the international markets, foster consumer and organized labor protest, and result in a serious disruption of the administration's anti-inflation program.[157] Dunlop's preferred strategy was a step-by-step approach to

155. William N. Walker to John T. Dunlop, "Notes on the 9:00 A.M. Meeting, Concerning the Price of Domestic Crude Oil," December 18, 1973, COLC Deputy Director's Files, Box 41, folder: Oil 1974, Records of the Economics Stabilization Program 1971–74, NA.

156. U.S. Treasury Department news release, "Proposal for a Windfall Profits Tax," December 19, 1973.

157. Dunlop to Shultz, "The Pricing of Domestic Crude Oil," December 19, 1973, COLC Deputy Director's Files, Box 41, folder: Oil 1974, Records of the Economic Stabilization Program 1971–74, NA.

long-run price levels. He also pointed out that the Emergency Petroleum Allocation Act prohibited price decontrol for petroleum products except upon a finding by the President that, among other things, there is no shortage of the products in question. Such a finding was unlikely to survive the congressional review also provided for in the act.

Caution prevailed and on December 19 the President announced a $1 increase (to $5.25) in the base price of old crude. At the same time, Nixon promised a legislative proposal for a windfall profits tax.[158]

Prospects for implementing the Treasury-CEA proposals diminished as the embargo continued. Disclosure was made of sharply rising oil industry profits and public and congressional suspicions were voiced more frequently that the majors in effect had induced the shortage.[159] It also came to light that almost 10 percent of Nixon's 1972 campaign receipts had come from 413 directors, senior officials, or stockholders of 178 oil and gas companies, and the interpretation placed on this information was such that the administration would have found it difficult to sustain an argument that higher prices were in the national interest and only incidentally to the advantage of the President's supporters.[160] The vexed questions of special foreign and domestic tax privileges for the oil industry also were reopened, and moves were begun in Congress to subpoena oil company records and to eliminate the remaining 22 percent oil depletion allowance. Repeated efforts were made to force a rollback of oil prices.

On April 30 the House Ways and Means Committee approved a bill that would increase federal taxes on the oil industry, phase out the depletion allowance by the end of 1976, and tighten control over the oil companies' foreign earnings. The bill also included the Treasury's windfall profits tax and a modified version of its plow-back proposal, but as committee staffer Robert A. Best pointed out in a meeting with OMB and FEO officials on April 11, while the committee was "primarily interested in self-sufficiency," and not in "reforming tax laws or punishing oil companies," still the "market place cannot be relied on . . . for incentives," because

158. "Statement Proposing Enactment of an Emergency Windfall Profits Tax, December 19, 1973," *Public Papers: Nixon, 1973,* pp. 1018–19.

159. "The Energy Crisis: Oil Profits Cited," *Facts on File,* vol. 34 (January 26, 1974), p. 44; "The Energy Crisis: More Quarterly Profit Reports," ibid. (February 23, 1974); and "Energy: Oil Companies Report Quarterly Profits," ibid. (May 25, 1974), p. 419.

160. The disclosure was made by Congressman Les Aspin. See "Nixon Said 'Tied' by Oil Firms," *Facts on File,* vol. 34 (January 1, 1974), p. 6.

"Congress keeps voting for rollbacks and controls in two years may be worse than they are now."[161]

Best's assessment was prophetic. Both the Emergency Petroleum Allocation Act of 1973 and the Federal Energy Administration Act of 1974 stipulated that amendments regarding deallocation or price decontrol would require a finding by the President that no domestic shortage existed in the product in question, that continued regulation would be unnecessary to fulfill the purposes of the acts, and that no adverse effect was likely to be felt on the supply of any other product; moreover, Congress must concur in the President's judgment on all these matters. Since part of the force behind at least the former of these two acts was the problems of the independents, and since these had not been resolved outside the framework of allocation schemes, a finding that the purposes of the acts would be fulfilled *without* allocation would find no support in Congress. Moreover, deallocation and price decontrol were inseparable in practice. The two-tier price system necessitated allocation to protect crude-poor refiners, while domestic price ceilings helped create the shortages that allocation schemes were supposed somehow to alleviate. Thus quite apart from the problems of the independents, deallocation would not be practicable if price controls remained, and nothing was more certain than that they would remain as long as no greater villain than the oil companies appeared on the scene.

The FEA in the spring of 1974 developed a strategy thought to be least likely to provoke Congress into extending the allocation act, which was due to expire on February 28, 1975, or into tightening controls. To obviate the congressional review provisions, a product-by-product approach was to be followed, with relaxation measures stopping short of outright exemption. The success of each partial step toward deallocation would, it was hoped, gradually defuse the whole issue. The first products to be tackled were those thought least liable to shortage before February 28, 1975, those not viewed by priority users as threatening their preferred position, and those that would not lead to serious dislocations elsewhere or threaten the market shares of independents. According to these criteria, residual fuel oil, jet fuel used by the military, and some other products (but not gasoline, heating oil, or crude itself) seemed to qualify. Movement toward

161. Memorandum for the record, Phillip L. Mann, "Energy Taxes—Conference with Senate, OMB and FEO Representatives, Held April 11, 1974," April 12, 1974, Office of Tax Policy, U.S. Treasury, folder 552 (b (5)) no. 3, U.S. Treasury.

deallocation was to proceed in tandem with certain other measures, such as the elimination of the special products rule. Sawhill reiterated his support in principle of the Treasury view on raising the ceiling price of old oil to free market levels, coupled with a windfall profits tax; but he also ruled it out as impractical: it "does not provide a solution to the immediate problem," he said, and in a memorandum to other senior officials concerned with energy he listed several alternatives that he would prefer to see tried first.[162]

Of the alternatives to complete decontrol of old oil, the one that received most attention in the FEA itself was a plan first proposed by John Kaneb of Northeast Petroleum Industries, called a "domestic tickets system." The plan amounted to a method of distributing low-cost domestic old oil among all refiners so as to equalize their feedstock costs. Tickets would be issued to refiners in an amount representing the percentage of capacity that could be sustained by available low-cost crude, with a slight bias in favor of small refiners. A ticket would be necessary to refine a barrel of low-cost crude. Refiners with more old oil than their allocation of tickets could sell it at a controlled price plus a 10 cent resale markup or buy tickets from other refiners at the difference between old and new crude prices.[163]

The domestic tickets scheme was espoused by Charles Owens, who was then FEA deputy assistant administrator for policy, planning, and regulation. He renamed Kaneb's scheme the "entitlements scheme." Owens was convinced that something like this was necessary to solve the problems created by the two-tier price controls system. The controls meant that certain refiners and marketers were forced to undercut competitors who did not have access to low-cost oil. If deregulation with a tax was ruled out as unlikely or unworkable, then entitlements (tickets) seemed like an attractive alternative way to resolve the distribution problems caused by controls.

The scheme was criticized elsewhere in the administration because it failed to attack the problem of equalizing U.S. and world prices; without such equalization, allocation would continue to be necessary to protect the independents. Treasury economists continued to press for complete price decontrol (with a windfall profits tax) as an essential first step toward

162. Sawhill to Ken Rush and others, "Petroleum Deallocation Strategy," June 10, 1974 (copy in Johnson personal files).

163. Joel Havemann, "Energy Report: FEA Considers Assistance to Independent Oil Companies," *National Journal Reports,* May 25, 1974, pp. 777–82.

phasing out allocation.[164] They were supported by OMB Director Ash and by CEA staff who expressed a fear that the entitlements plan would merely create a new set of vested interests, which in turn would attempt to block decontrol for as long as market-clearing prices remained above $5.25 a barrel.[165]

The Treasury view seemed to prevail after meetings in August 1974 of the Deputies Group of Simon's Committee on Energy, at least in the sense of a consensus in favor of direct decontrol, provided that seemed feasible. It was also acknowledged that an interim equalization scheme would be necessary if decontrol were to be judged by the committee to be politically infeasible. On August 12 Sawhill distributed a memorandum outlining four variants of such an interim arrangement, but before the committee could meet, the FEA submitted for publication in the *Federal Register* a proposed set of regulations that amounted to the domestic tickets system without the tickets. Alternative schemes were mentioned in an appendix. The FEA's rationale for taking this step was that it would provide an opportunity for comment and allow for implementation as early as October.[166] As it turned out, when the committee next met, Morton, Ash, Brinegar, and even Virginia H. Knauer, the President's adviser on consumer affairs, strongly opposed the FEA's preferred plan. It was agreed that the deputies should try to come up with plans for ways to increase domestic production, including ways to change the ratio of new to old oil and to stimulate increased production of old oil. The Treasury, FEA, Department of the Interior, and OMB would set out a written plan for decontrolling old oil, with accompanying legislation to prevent excess profits: "a program to decontrol," as one CEA attendee put it, "not a program to control like FEA entitlements."[167] Gerald Parsky noted after the meeting

164. Sam van Vactor to Douglas McCullough, "Decontrolling Crude Oil and Petroleum Product Prices," August 5, 1974; and a Treasury submission to a meeting of the deputies of the Committee on Energy, "A Program to Equalize the Prices, and to Increase the Supply, of Domestic Crude Oil," August 7, 1974 (copies of both in Johnson personal files).

165. Covering letter from Gary Seevers to Gerald Parsky, August 12, 1974 (referring to a CEA memo, Bob Dohner to Seevers, "Cost of Crude Price Decontrol," August 12, 1974); also Ash to Sawhill, June 18, 1974 (copies in Johnson personal files).

166. Simon to members of the Committee on Energy, "Meeting on Decontrol or Price Equalization of Crude Oil," September 4, 1974, Parsky Files, Box 13, folder: Committee on Energy, Meetings, U.S. Treasury.

167. Notes on the September 4 meeting of the Committee on Energy by unnamed CEA staff member, CEA files; and memorandum for the record, Parsky, "Summary of the Meeting of the Committee on Energy," September 6, 1974 (copy in Johnson files).

the committee's conviction that the entitlements plan would involve a degree of regulation greater than that currently in force, would present numerous administrative difficulties, and would create vested interests, but would not increase domestic production.

So far as the FEA was concerned, however, the die was cast. On July 21 twenty-eight senators, led by Senator Philip A. Hart of Michigan wrote to Sawhill urging him to adopt the entitlements plan as something essential to fulfilling a statutory obligation (under the allocation act) to "preserve the competitive viability of independent refiners, small refiners, and non-branded and branded independent marketers." Sawhill was also concerned about estimates by his own staff economists showing that decontrol could contribute from 0.2 to 0.3 percent annually to inflation of the consumer price index. In this concern he was joined by Department of Commerce officials. This plus the sharp reminder by the Senate Democrats was enough to make him doubt the wisdom of pressing for immediate decontrol. On August 8 he wrote to Senator Henry Jackson indicating that the FEA would support an extension of the Emergency Petroleum Allocation Act for four months, till July 31, 1975, "for the sole purpose of facilitating a smooth transition back to an uncontrolled market." After FEA hearings in September it was announced that the administration would move ahead with an entitlements scheme.[168]

On November 29 the FEA promulgated the Old Oil Entitlements Program, which was to go into operation in January 1975. Under the program the FEA would establish each month a national average ratio of old crude supplies to crude runs to stills and imported products. All refiners would be issued entitlements—access to price-controlled old crude oil—equal to the national average, though with extra entitlements going to small-scale refiners (those with a capacity under 175,000 barrels a day). Refiners with less than the national average ratio (based on actual crude runs, not refinery capacity) would then sell entitlements that refiners with more old crude than the national average would have to buy in order to secure the

168. The information in this paragraph was drawn from a press release, office of Senator Hart, July 21, 1974; Sawhill to Jackson, August 8, 1974; FEA, Office of Economic Impact and Office of Regulatory Policy, "Alternative Crude Oil Price Responses to Decontrol," August 23, 1974; Department of Commerce, Paper for Deputies Group of Committee on Energy, "Comments on Deallocation and Decontrol of Petroleum and Petroleum Products," August 7, 1974 (copies in Johnson files). See also "New FEA Rules May Lower Gas Prices; Morton Gives Price Equalization Plan," *National Journal Reports*, November 2, 1974, p. 1661. The Emergency Petroleum Allocation Act asked for everything, urging protection for the independents, efficiency, and minimization of interference in markets.

right to process all the old crude in their possession. In this way it was hoped to reduce feedstock cost differentials between refiners. The program would cover imported products as well as crude, so as to address the problems of refiners and marketers who depended on imported products and who had experienced difficulty under the price controls in selling their higher-priced imported products.

There was a strong feeling among members of the Committee on Energy that Sawhill and the FEA had stolen a march on them in advertising that regulations of this sort would be forthcoming. Sawhill was replaced as head of the FEA in October, and as Rogers Morton explained matters, Sawhill had been found wanting in "executive compatibility."[169] At the same time, a reason must be found to explain the fact that Sawhill was not overridden and his decision to go ahead with the entitlements plan reversed. For that inaction a good deal of credit must go to the New England Congressional Caucus, which labored for six months to get the entitlements program, putting pressure not just on Sawhill but on Morton.[170]

Project Independence involved three things: increasing domestic energy supplies, conserving energy, and developing alternative sources of energy and new technologies for fossil fuels. Higher energy prices were prerequisite for all three, as the President had made clear, though in muted tones, in his statement of December 19, 1973. The entitlements program, if anything, *encouraged* consumption and helped perpetuate U.S. dependence on imported oil by subsidizing companies that imported oil; it secured rough cost equivalence for refiners at the expense of efficiency by protecting uneconomic small refiners; and it established a constituency for the extension of price controls and allocation programs. This last was to dog the Ford administration in its efforts to secure decontrol.

169. Joel Havemann, "Energy Report: Ford Rearranges Organization to Give Morton Policy Control," *National Journal Reports,* November 2, 1974, pp. 1655–56.

170. Congressmen Thomas P. O'Neill, Jr., and Silvio O. Conte, Cochairmen of the New England Congressional Caucus, to Morton, November 14, 1974; also R. T. Sutton, Commissioner, Department of Conservation, State of Louisiana, to Congressional Delegation, "Energy Related Legislation and Other Matters," January 17, 1975 (copies in Johnson personal files). Part of the latter memorandum quotes from a statement issued by O'Neill and Conte: "In 1974, the Caucus achieved the biggest price breakthrough for our hard-pressed region in years. Interior Secretary Rogers Morton's decision in late November to allocate a larger than expected share of price controlled 'old oil' entitlements to New England and the East Coast followed an unremitting six-month effort by the Caucus."

CHAPTER SEVEN

The Ford Administration:
Energy as a Political Good

NEIL DE MARCHI

RICHARD NIXON left the White House on August 9, 1974. Watergate had claimed its most prominent victim, but its repercussions for policy had been felt for months before, measured in indecision, lack of clear lines of authority, and sheer neglect. Energy policy suffered along with others. During most of Nixon's second term, but especially in his last months in office, little had been done at the highest level in the way of energy planning. Pronouncements had been made and several important initiatives had come from the White House: a move to reconsider the adverse effect of the Clean Air Act of 1970 on domestic energy supply, proposals to stimulate coal production and exploration of the outer continental shelf (OCS), an effort to arrive at a rational energy R&D policy, and Project

I WISH to thank Milton Russell, John A. Hill, James Reddington, Frank G. Zarb, and Charles A. Cooper for helpful discussions about energy policymaking under President Ford. This chapter draws most heavily on Federal Energy Agency records assembled for my use by Roger M. Anders of the Historian's Office in the Department of Energy; Council of Economic Advisers records made available by William J. Stewart and his staff at the Gerald R. Ford Library in Ann Arbor, Michigan; and the personal files of Milton Russell. Although the FEA and CEA records are extensive, a peculiarity of the Ford administration was that the two men who most directly influenced the President's thinking on energy, FEA Administrator Frank Zarb and CEA Chairman Alan Greenspan, were in such close and frequent communication with President Ford that they felt no need to record much that is important to the history of energy policymaking in 1974–76. My account may therefore be biased in ways not easily identified because it makes such extensive use of the FEA and the CEA records. A serious effort has been made to preserve balance by consulting persons in other departments or offices of the executive. I am particularly grateful to Thomas O. Enders for commenting on a draft of the role of the Department of State in specific energy policy initiatives, and to Rodney Weiher of the Office of Management and Budget for reading a penultimate draft of the chapter.

In the footnotes to this chapter the Gerald R. Ford Library is referred to as GRFL.

Independence. But these represented at best spasmodic interest by the President in energy, and the initiatives, each significant in itself, were neither coordinated nor monitored from the top with any sense of urgency. At the agency and department levels energy problems were dealt with in the manner of brush fires to be contained and put out. Moreover, not only was direction from the President lacking, but sometimes its absence caused fierce power struggles to develop (such as the running battle between William Simon and John Sawhill), to the detriment of morale and efficiency. Partly for these reasons the period 1973–74 is recalled by those who were heavily involved in it as one in which energy operations bordered on the chaotic.

Gerald Ford inherited a patchwork of unfulfilled energy plans, a handful of hastily contrived authorizations to manage energy emergencies, and a set of energy advisers busily working out some combination of personal ambitions and solutions to "the energy problem," defined according to their own best lights, in a context of ideational and territorial disputes.

The Energy Problem, Vintage 1974

While the long-run energy problem had been little affected by executive action in the period to August 1974, events had made its outline progressively sharper. Domestic oil production had peaked in 1970 and had declined from 11.3 million barrels a day in that year to 10.5 million in 1974. Oil imports grew from 22.7 percent of total oil supply in 1970 to 35.9 percent in 1973.[1] It had come to be widely accepted that half of U.S. oil needs would have to be met by imports by 1980. As to natural gas, consumption had been running at twice the rate of discoveries since 1968, and curtailments (expected to amount to 10 percent of demand in 1974) had become a part of the annual burdens of winter.[2]

Part of the problem with oil lay in the price controls that had been applied since 1971 (though these postdated the peak in production). Similarly, the problem with gas stemmed partly from its long-standing artificial cheapness (in 1972–73 the wellhead price of gas was about one-third that of oil, on a Btu basis). But opinions differed widely on the likely effects of

1. Federal Energy Administration, Project Independence Blueprint, Interagency Task Force on Oil, *Oil: Possible Levels of Future Production*, Final Task Force Report, pt. 5 (Government Printing Office, 1974), p. II-9.

2. Federal Power Commission, Bureau of Natural Gas, *National Gas Supply and Demand, 1971–1990* (GPO, 1972), p. 3.

decontrol for both oil and gas, reflecting different perceptions of the causes of the shortages. On the one hand some viewed the oil and gas industry as basically competitive and believed that one could expect substantial increases in supply from higher prices. On the other hand it was suggested that the industry was anything but competitive, that prices for years had been higher than they need have been, that recent shortages were artificial, and that one could expect little except sharply increased profits in the event of decontrol.

The two most promising alternative sources of energy for the near term and midterm (1978–85)—coal and nuclear power—suffered under severe disadvantages. Coal was plentiful but dirty. The industry, sometimes called "the stepchild of the fossil fuel family," had been neglected (in 1960 coal supplied 23 percent of gross domestic energy consumption, but by 1974 this had fallen to 18 percent).[3] Active research and technical and tertiary instruction in mining technology had been reduced to minimal proportions, "surge" capacity in existing mines was limited and a lead time of about three years was reckoned to be necessary to introduce new capacity. A combination of court challenges and general opposition by environmentalists to strip mining had brought Interior Department leasing to a halt in 1971 (in 1974 federally leased coal production amounted to only 4 percent of national output) and rendered prospects for developing the 88 percent of the nation's low-sulfur coal concentrated in the western states quite uncertain.[4]

By 1973 nuclear power accounted for only about 5 percent of the nation's electricity, though the Atomic Energy Commission was optimistically predicting a rise to 22 percent by 1980. By the end of 1974, however, the industry's research program, largely concentrated on the liquid metal fast breeder reactor, had run into difficulties, and the 22 percent target was expected to be reached only in 1985, and then on some rather optimistic assumptions.[5] Cost overruns on the first breeder demonstration plant at Clinch River, Tennessee, were of the order of 250 percent above estimates,

---

3. Hermann Enzer, Walter Dupree, and Stanley Miller, *Energy Perspectives: A Presentation of Major Energy and Energy-Related Data,* U.S. Department of the Interior (GPO, 1975), p. 36. Federal government ownership of the total coal reserve base amounted to 40 percent, rising to 70–80 percent for western coal alone. Ibid., p. 142.

4. Ibid., pp. 144, 150.

5. The 22 percent figure assumed $11 a barrel for oil (ibid., p. 170) and the "business as usual" case in Federal Energy Administration, *Project Independence Report* (GPO, 1974), pp. 64–65.

and the timetable for that project had slipped by two years to 1982.[6] Moreover, problems of waste disposal and safety (especially in regard to safeguarding the fuel product, plutonium) remained unresolved.

Synthetic fuels from coal, oil shale, and tar sands were the next most promising alternative for the midterm, but they were far from clean and environmentally neutral and seemed to remain tantalizingly *un*economic, even as the price of crude oil rose.[7]

In short, it looked as if oil and natural gas would remain the chief sources of fuel for the rest of the century. That was one side of the picture. The other was that key parameters in the oil (and gas) energy balance situation had changed during Nixon's presidency.

In its 1970 report the President's Task Force on Oil Import Control had assumed the following:

—Foreign crude oil would remain less expensive than domestic.

—The risk of oil imports being interrupted for political reasons was low.

—Imports from Canada and the western hemisphere would increase.

—Oil from the North Slope of Alaska would reach the U.S. West Coast in 1973.[8]

All four assumptions had proved incorrect. In 1972 spot prices for some foreign crudes had topped U.S. prices for the first time. In the period January 1973 through February 1974 imported crude quadrupled in price, while domestic "old" oil remained under strict price controls. Further, the Organization of Arab Petroleum Exporting Countries had successfully implemented a politically motivated embargo against the United States and the Netherlands, and OPEC as a whole showed every sign of being a

6. *Project Independence Report*, p. 118; and James G. Phillips, "Energy Report: Breeder Reactor Continues to Receive Administration Priority," *National Journal Reports*, March 1, 1975, pp. 305–13.

7. A Treasury staff comparison of studies in early 1973 suggested possible prices of $4–$6.50 a barrel (delivered) for oil from shale and a slightly lower figure for oil from tar sands (both projected for 1980). Liquefied coal was estimated as likely to cost $8–$9 a barrel (projected for 1985). (Robert Dohner to William Johnson, "Projected Prices for Various Energy Sources," February 2, 1973, CEA Records, Gary Seevers Files, GRFL.) By 1976 the break-even price for oil from shale and coal had been revised to $16–$18. In 1979 oil from tar sands was being produced for about $16, but cost estimates ranged from $22 (shale) to $45 (for synthetic gas and liquids from coal). "Synthetic Fuels," *The Economist*, June 30, 1979, pp. 91–92; and "Why Carter's Energy Prayers Will Not Be Answered," ibid., July 21, 1979, pp. 95–96.

8. Cabinet Task Force on Oil Import Control, *The Oil Import Question: A Report on the Relationship of Oil Imports to the National Security* (GPO, 1970), pp. 20–21, 33, 34–35, 39 (and note 38), 48.

healthy and stable cartel.[9] As to Canadian imports, the United States in the early 1970s had maintained a policy of limiting imports from western Canada until such time as the Canadians took steps to avert the danger of interruptions in supply from foreign sources to its own eastern provinces. But not long after Ford took office, the Canadian government announced that starting on January 1, 1975, Canada would implement an eight-year phaseout of *all* exports to the United States. During 1974 Venezuela, the main western hemisphere supplier to both Canada and the United States, took steps to nationalize oil production and to impose curbs on its output of crude.[10] Meanwhile, U.S. dependence on oil from the Middle East had reached 24.7 percent of imports and this percentage was expected to grow.[11] Finally, far from having North Slope oil flowing by 1973, construction of the pipeline from Prudhoe Bay to Valdez did not receive congressional approval until that year.

The problem to which these facts and events bore witness had been correctly identified in early discussions of the direction to be taken by the Project Independence Blueprint. If, as seemed to be the case, the marginal social cost of expanding domestic output of fossil fuels was an increasing function of quantity, and if the same was true of increased reliance on insecure imports, then the aim of policy should be to balance domestic production and imports at the point where the sum of these two costs would be minimized.[12] If policy could be directed also to positioning the curves more favorably, then the kinds of policies needed were those to increase domestic output and reduce imports, while at the same time improving conservation and increasing the security of imports. Security could be further enhanced and long-term dependence on fossil fuels (domestic and imported) lessened by promoting appropriate kinds of energy R&D.

It proved to be easier to identify these rough building blocks of a ra-

9. To this must be added two qualifications. The international oil companies effected a redistribution so that even the embargoed nations suffered no very marked deprivation. Moreover, the restriction of production associated with the embargo was not a collective act, and it was still not clear, therefore, whether OPEC was somehow exceptional and would escape the instability inherent in cartels.

10. "Venezuela: Oil Production Cut," *Facts on File,* vol. 34, April 20, 1974, p. 313; "Venezuela: Nationalization Announced," ibid., July 6, 1974, p. 543; "Venezuela: Oil Cutbacks, Nationalization Plan," ibid., September 28, 1974, pp. 798–99; "Canada: Phase-out of Oil Exports to U.S.," ibid., November 30, 1974, p. 984.

11. Enzer, Dupree, and Miller, *Energy Perspectives,* p. 95.

12. John A. Hill, "Energy Independence: An Overview," May 2, 1974, FEA Records, Eric Zausner Files, folder: Project Independence–Policy Evaluation, U.S. Department of Energy.

tional energy policy than to shape specific policy measures and to get them into place. These two stages, the second especially, were complicated by conflicting goals and interests. First, a trade-off had to be considered between environmental quality and increased domestic exploration and development, particularly of oil, gas, and coal. A second complication, already apparent when Ford took office, arose out of state claims to revenues and to compensation in the event of adverse consequences from increased exploration and development, especially of coal lands and areas of the outer continental shelf. Moreover, as noted above, there were conflicting expectations and beliefs about the efficacy and equity of relying more heavily on the market mechanism, hence conflicts (most obviously within Congress) between advocates of price incentives to production and conservation and proponents of physical controls (for example, quotas) and uniform mandatory standards (for example, for emissions).

Devising a salable package of energy initiatives in late 1974 was still further complicated by short-run concerns on the one hand—record postwar unemployment, persistent inflation, sharply (hence in many eyes suspiciously) increased profits in the oil and gas industry, and a desire to preserve the small and independent segment of that industry—and by a more perennial problem on the other: the multiplicity of sectional interests affected by virtually any piece of energy legislation. This latter fact could and did give rise to a host of rather fluid coalitions, in which the administration might find itself on one issue opposed by the very same groups that, on another, were its allies. A case in point is the concurrence of interests of the utilities and of environmentalists in 1975, when both lined up against the Ford coal conversion plan.

Grasping the Organizational Nettle

Ford quickly took steps to centralize control over energy policy. In an address on October 8 before a joint session of Congress he announced the creation of an Energy Resources Board, with his old friend and House colleague Rogers Morton in charge. The executive director and coordinator of the new board was to be Frank G. Zarb, associate director at the Office of Management and Budget for energy, natural resources, and science. Immediately thereafter Congress passed the Energy Reorganization Act of 1974, establishing the Energy Research and Development Agency and a Nuclear Regulatory Commission and providing for an Energy Resources Council. Ford signed the bill into law on October 11, accepting the slight change of name for his erstwhile board; the council was charged with developing "a single national energy policy and program."[13] Sawhill was made to understand that his resignation as administrator of the Federal Energy Administration would be welcomed; he stepped down, and on November 25, after the President's nominee to succeed Sawhill had failed to be confirmed because of conflict of interest, Zarb was designated the new administrator.

Zarb and the FEA were to become much more important to energy policy formulation and implementation than the Energy Resources Council and other agencies, a development that resolved some territorial disputes but brought with it new problems of two sorts.

First, it so happened that a core of senior FEA officials was supplied by the OMB. The exodus started with Sawhill, but Zarb and John Hill, later to be FEA deputy administrator, followed the same course. Moreover, the OMB supplied staff work for the council under Zarb's general direction. Thus by early 1975 a situation had arisen whereby, according to Milton Russell, energy economist in the Council of Economic Advisers: "OMB staff are faced with proposals made in the name of persons they know, respect, and to whom they have only recently reported."[14] The result, he noted, was a blurring of lines of authority in the OMB and a weakening of one of the main checks in the executive branch to an agency staff exercising its natural penchant to expand.

The second kind of problem arose out of a conflict between responsibilities within the FEA itself. On the one hand the FEA was—or was soon to become—the lead agency for initiating and influencing energy policy, and in the Ford administration this involved striving after free markets for fuels. On the other hand the FEA inherited, to some extent developed, and to some extent had imposed upon it by Congress various responsibilities of a regulatory sort. Hubris is an occupational hazard of regulators, and the energy technocrats in the FEA had no special immunity. It may be that interventionists are more inclined to join an agency with regulatory functions. Whatever the case in that regard, the FEA was prodded in the interventionist direction by several forces. The very way the energy problem was perceived—as a need to cut imports and reduce energy consumption

---

13. "Address to a Joint Session of the Congress on the Economy, October 8, 1974," *Public Papers: Gerald R. Ford, 1974* (GPO, 1975), p. 231.

14. Milton Russell to Gary Seevers, "Energy Legislation," January 20, 1975, CEA Records, Staff Files, GRFL.

—gave occasion to those so inclined to devise instruments to see that both would happen. Congress, if anything, encouraged that kind of thinking. Another more subtle influence operated in the postembargo period, when public and congressional sentiment ran strongly against the major oil companies and "Control the giants in the public interest" became a sort of rallying cry. Given the climate, it would have been an exceptional regulator who did not succumb to the argument that interventions, however cumbersome and distorting they may be, are least harmful when administered by disinterested public servants. Finally, the need to strike bargains with certain interest groups in order to get energy legislation through Congress, gave a fillip to interventionism. For example, when President Ford proposed to levy a tariff on crude oil imports, energy-intensive industries and various parties in the Northeast protested. The FEA responded with a suggestion to tilt the passing on of the increased fees to products in such a way that gasoline prices would rise disproportionately. As noted within the Council of Economic Advisers, an implication of this proposal was that it "would solidify the FEA bureaucracy by giving it something to do even if prices were decontrolled. It would require continued monitoring of refinery operations and limit flexibility."[15]

The combined effect of these influences was such as to make it unlikely that the FEA would strive wholeheartedly to put itself out of the regulatory business. And in the absence of an effective OMB check, the balance of forces clearly favored the continued growth of the agency; so much so that in retrospect the eventual evolution of the FEA into an independent Department of Energy under Carter seems to have an air of the inevitable about it.

The Ford Plan

Those responsible for producing the Project Independence Blueprint clearly hoped that their report would become the basis for any energy initiatives that President Ford might undertake. In addition to devising a general and internally consistent modeling framework for forecasting U.S. energy demand and supply and the resulting "necessary" imports, they had wanted to be able to specify and assess alternative policy options. As it turned out, time did not allow much to be done toward meeting this sec-

15. Milton Russell to Alan Greenspan, "Energy Program Modifications," February 18, 1975, CEA Records, Greenspan Files, GRFL.

ond goal. The resulting report therefore focused on predicting the likely import gap in 1985, postulating possible prices for foreign oil delivered to the United States of $7 and $11 a barrel.[16] It made use of four specifications of the policy context but did not attempt to evaluate the assumptions behind these specifications in relation to widely different alternatives.

The four policy contexts considered were (1) a base case, assuming decontrol of energy prices and a relaxation of pollution standards so as to allow an increased use of coal; (2) an "accelerated development" case, involving increased OCS leasing and exploitation of the Naval Petroleum Reserves; (3) an "energy conversation" case, exploring the impact of a package of conservation and demand management measures; and (4) a combination of 2 and 3. While most attention was devoted to accelerated development and conservation, the assumptions lying behind the base case (misleadingly called the "business as usual" case) involved significant departures from current government policy, and as a subsequent analysis by the Massachusetts Institute of Technology (MIT) Energy Laboratory showed, the effects of their failing to be realized seemed likely to far outweigh the positive results that could be achieved by accelerated development or conservation.[17] The key assumptions were phased deregulation of natural gas; the removal of price controls on oil; revisions in the Clean Air Act of 1970 that would allow tall stacks, intermittent control systems, and certain compliance delays so that high-sulfur coal might continue to be used until stack gas scrubbers could be introduced; and retention of the depletion allowance. In addition the authors of the report assumed that the supply curve of foreign oil was fully elastic, that foreign supplies would be unaffected by any change in the U.S. demand-supply situation, and that world prices would approach a given level smoothly and would remain there. In other words, the report skirted the problem of assessing the likely behavior of OPEC and its response to the U.S. drive toward independence.

These deficiencies in the FEA study were keenly felt elsewhere in the

16. As noted in chapter 6, the product of the task force was known as a blueprint until publication, when it became a report, to avoid giving the impression that national energy policy was already set. The *Project Independence Report* also included projections at an assumed price of $4 a barrel, but in the discussion this price was given relatively little attention.

17. This paragraph draws on "Projections of U.S. Energy Supply and Demand" (MIT Energy Laboratory analysis of *Project Independence Report* data), December 12, 1974, CEA Records, Greenspan Files, GRFL. A more detailed critique from the same perspective is Jerry A. Hausman, *"Project Independence Report:* An Appraisal of U.S. Energy Needs up to 1985," *Bell Journal of Economics,* vol. 6 (Autumn 1975), pp. 517–51.

administration, and nowhere more so than at the Treasury and in the Council of Economic Advisers, where fears were expressed that the import-centric focus and the stress on accelerated development and on conservation would bias policy away from a free markets approach and toward intervention.[18] Some critics said the report's emphases were due to the use of supply projection techniques that underestimated interfuel substitution. The result was an overestimate of the share of oil and an underestimate of the shares of gas and coal in demand. The prices of gas and of coal were said to be underestimated for the same reason, and the overall energy price index used to calculate total energy demands by sector was thereby biased downward; as a consequence likely energy consumption at market-clearing prices was overstated. On this view, the Project Independence modelers had been led to make an unnecessarily pessimistic prognosis for oil imports.[19] This bias was further reinforced by the organization and management orientation of Eric Zausner, who in directing the Project Independence study was inclined to stray from the early tight specification of the problem as one of optimization and to issue long lists of unresolved "issues," to be "staffed out" and analyzed.[20] By

18. Some of these shortcomings were foreseen in the early days of Project Independence. (Ben Massell to Gary Seevers, April 19, May 3, and May 9, 1974, CEA Records, Gary Seevers Files, GRFL.) The MIT Energy Laboratory analysis of the *Project Independence Report* merely confirmed fears already held within the CEA. Milton Russell, reporting on an oral presentation of results by representatives of the MIT group, concluded darkly: "*PIR* leaves an impression that far more needs to be 'done' than the situation actually justifies: A reading of *PIR* implies the problem is far more serious than it actually is; that government policy need be more interventionist than is necessary; and that price can play a smaller role than MIT believes it can." Russell to Greenspan and Seevers, November 20, 1974, CEA Records, Greenspan Files, GRFL.

19. Hausman, *"Project Independence Report:* An Appraisal of U.S. Energy Needs," pp. 522, 524–32.

20. Numerous such lists survive in Zausner's files in FEA records. The disparity between the issues approach and the conceptual view enunciated by George Patton and John Hill (which was warmly received by economists in the agencies invited to comment) was clear almost from the start. In Zausner's lists an issue typically was linked with a specification of the necessary supporting run of the Project Independence Evaluation System model. Ben Massell commented: "The domestic market work is overly model oriented. The model is not an outgrowth of a need to find answers to policy questions, but a project with a life of its own. . . . The model was formulated long before the completion of Hill's paper, which defines the issues." (Massell to Seevers, May 9, 1974, CEA Records, Seevers Files, GRFL.) Seevers himself, commenting on a list of "general energy policy issues" prepared by Zausner, wrote: "My main reaction is that they do not seem to be structured in a way that is consistent with the [Hill] overview paper." Seevers to Sawhill, May 23, 1974, FEA Records, Zausner Files, folder: Project Independence–Policy Evaluation, Department of Energy.

late October 1974, when drafts of the report were circulated within the administration for comment, the import-centric approach and implications for interventionist solutions were so apparent that Gary Seevers, a member of the Council of Economic Advisers, was moved to express to Zausner his very great concern "that energy policy options not prematurely be precluded by the publication of this document."[21]

For a while, however, it looked as if the CEA had missed the boat. Just as Sawhill had outwitted the Treasury in the matter of entitlements, so he had already (on October 2) advised the new President that an energy policy should revolve around a reduction in petroleum imports of 1–2 million barrels a day, voluntary conservation plus certain tax and regulatory measures to the same end, and accelerated energy supply.[22] Ford's October 8 speech contained both a plea for voluntary conservation and a target for oil imports involving a reduction of 1 million barrels a day by the end of 1975.

Ironically, Ford's apparent acceptance of Sawhill's advice also marked the high point of influence for the Project Independence study. Rogers Morton, as head of the new Energy Resources Council, had no intention of sharing his advisory role with Sawhill. Morton and Zarb quickly formed a small team made up of John Hill and Edward Miller of the OMB, Milton Russell of the CEA, and Alvin A. Cook, Jr., of the FEA to take a fresh look at the options for energy policy and to present their suggested initiatives to the Energy Resources Council.[23] This sudden switch resulted in a package unified by a clear economic logic and with a market orientation.

The new team agreed on a program with six objectives. These included reduced reliance on insecure sources of energy, enhanced security against supply interruptions and rapid changes in price, and provision of funds for

21. Seevers to Zausner, "Preliminary Comments on Project Independence Blueprint," October 21, 1974, Milton Russell personal files.

22. Morton and Sawhill to the President, "Energy Measures for Inclusion in Economic Speech," October 2, 1974, CEA Records, Greenspan Files, GRFL.

23. Joel Havemann, "Energy Report: Ford Rearranges Organization to Give Morton Policy Control," *National Journal Reports,* November 2, 1974, pp. 1655–56. Although Morton and Sawhill in principle were jointly advising the President up till October 8, Morton disliked both Sawhill's attempts to build a constituency outside the administration and the impetus toward large government involvement that he saw implied in the *Project Independence Report.* Morton criticized the report as "a lot of fancy footwork with computers." (See Joel Havemann and James G. Phillips, "Energy Report: Independence Blueprint Weighs Various Options," *National Journal Reports,* November 2, 1974, pp. 1635–40.) Morton also had the Hill-Miller-Russell-Cook team working on options independently of Sawhill and the FEA *before* his own authority as chief energy adviser had been publicly clarified. In a strict sense the Ford program originated quite outside the normal framework of government.

necessary domestic energy supply initiatives. But there was also to be (subject to the constraint of using maximum amounts of source fuels) a free market in energy and (with an eye to the condition of the economy) maintenance of consumer purchasing power at prepolicy levels. And all was to be done "in an economically efficient manner."[24]

By mid-November the measures necessary to achieve these goals had been roughed out, and the FEA was ready to proceed with staff analyses. Apart from proposals to cut income taxes and to increase transfer payments so as to maintain taxpayer and nontaxpayer purchasing power, the measures comprised crude oil decontrol plus a windfall profits tax, a tariff on imported crude and products, deregulation of natural gas plus an excise tax (so as to equalize fuel prices on a Btu basis), a fund for energy development and conservation (financed partly by these several levies), an emergency storage program and changes in petroleum and natural gas tax provisions, including a tilt in aftertax fuel receipts in favor of secondary recovery, reduced incentives for U.S.-based companies to produce abroad, and repeal of the depletion allowance.[25]

Legislative measures embodying these proposals were discussed at Camp David in mid-December, in meetings between representatives of the Energy Resources Council, OMB, CEA, and others concerned with the economy and with energy matters. The President was briefed on the outcome of these discussions on December 19, and following further meetings with his chief advisers in Vail, Colorado, on December 27, Ford settled on a legislative package for energy policy.[26] He conveyed the sub-

24. Briefing paper, "First Morton Briefing" (circa early November 1974), Russell personal files.

25. Russell to Greenspan and Seevers, "Energy Policy Initiatives" (with attached outline of initiatives dated November 18, 1974), November 20, 1974, CEA Records, Greenspan Files, GRFL. Initially the team's proposals included a stiff gasoline tax. The idea was favored by Morton and Greenspan and approved by the Energy Resources Council. Ford, however, quashed the idea. A tax much above 10 cents a gallon was politically inconceivable, but at that level it was unlikely to be effective. Ford's position was in line with opinion polls taken in October in which a strong preference for rationing over higher gasoline prices was revealed. See Robert W. Rycroft, "The Federal Energy Administration: A Case Study of Energy Policy Making" (Ph.D. dissertation, University of Oklahoma, 1976), pp. 279–80. The gasoline tax idea remained alive in the face of presidential disapproval. At Camp David discussions in December a group of representatives from the OMB and the State Department unsuccessfully urged that such a tax be reinserted in the program, on the ground that a workable windfall profits tax was not likely to be passed and that World War II experience with such taxes had been fraught with difficulties.

26. The discussion of the making of the Ford program draws heavily on Joel Havemann, "Energy Report: Federal Planners Study Ways to Cut Reliance on Imports," National Journal Reports, December 14, 1974, pp. 1863–66; Richard Corri-

stance of his initiatives to the nation in his State of the Union Message in January 1975 and transmitted the core of his program to Congress in an omnibus bill entitled the Energy Independence Act of 1975.[27] The administration's energy bill comprised thirteen titles.

Title I requested authorization to develop the Naval Petroleum Reserves. The oil expected to flow from the development of three of these areas would be used to fill Defense Department storage tanks and to start a national strategic petroleum reserve, while revenues accruing from the development of the three designated areas would go to finance further exploration and development of the remaining reserve areas.

Title II asked for authority to set up a civilian national strategic petroleum reserve of up to 1 billion barrels to be funded largely from production from the Elk Hills Naval Reserve.

Title III requested authority to deregulate the wellhead prices of "new" natural gas and to place an excise tax on natural gas of 37 cents per 1,000 cubic feet (equivalent to a separately proposed tax of $2 a barrel on domestic crude oil).

Title IV amended the Energy Supply and Environmental Coordination Act of 1974 so as to enlarge and extend in time FEA authority to require power plants to convert to coal and to bar conversion away from coal to other fuels.

Titles V and VI involved amendments to the Clean Air Act of 1970 so as to delay until 1982 the original auto emission standards (which would otherwise take effect in 1977 and 1978) and to delay the requirement for certain plants to install and operate scrubber systems or convert to low-sulfur coal. Other proposed amendments would permit some plants to use intermittent control systems up to 1985 and would give the Environmental Protection Agency authority to grant extra time for certain regions to meet air quality standards.

Title VII requested that suspensions of proposed utility rate increases be limited to five months, that bans on utilities passing through increased fuel costs be disallowed, that utilities be enabled to include construction

---

gan, "Agreement on Policy Remains Elusive," ibid., January 4, 1975, p. 19; John Herbers, *New York Times*, December 28, 1974; "How Ford Drew up His Energy Program," *Business Week*, February 3, 1975, pp. 52–53; Thomas H. Tietenberg, *Energy Planning and Policy: The Political Economy of Project Independence* (Lexington Books, 1976), pp. 88–92; and conversations with Frank Zarb, Milton Russell, and John Hill.

27. This act was introduced in the House as H.R. 2633 and H.R. 2650 and was referred to four committees. In the Senate, Senator Hugh Scott introduced the act (S. 594).

costs and outlays for pollution control in their rate base, and that peak-load pricing be allowed. The President also proposed raising the invest-ment tax credit for utilities from 4 to 12 percent for one year (and for two additional years for utilities not burning oil or gas).

Title VIII asked that the FEA be authorized to oversee the develop-ment of a national plan to facilitate the siting, and to expedite the approval and construction, of energy facilities.

Title IX requested that the President be allowed to impose tariffs, quo-tas, or variable import fees on imported oil should foreign producers lower their prices enough to threaten investment in conventional domestic pro-duction.

The remaining titles involved mandatory thermal efficiency standards for buildings, the use of federal funds to assist in improving the energy efficiency of the homes of low-income persons, product labeling, and standby authority for the President to control private resources and stocks in the event of an embargo or other energy emergency. In addition to these requests, Ford promised to levy a duty on imported crude oil and products at an initial rate of $1 a barrel but rising in successive months to $3 a barrel and promised that he would move to decontrol domestic petroleum.

Very little of this was new. Although Congress had declined to make significant changes in the Clean Air Act of 1970 when requested to do so by Nixon at the height of the shortages in the winter of 1974, Ford sub-mitted a virtually identical request. The same may be said of his proposals to decontrol natural gas and oil. And there were strong similarities with earlier approaches even where the content of the Ford package was new. Thus Ford's stern pronouncement in his message of October 8, 1974, re-peated in less threatening language on January 15, 1975, in his State of the Union Address, that the automobile industry would achieve a 40 percent improvement in gas mileage ratings over four years whether by agreement or by law, smacked of the "legislated technology" strategy that had been used earlier in relation to auto emissions.[28]

What the package did possess that was striking was consistency, born of a conviction shared by Ford and his advisers that moving to a free mar-ket in energy was the single best contribution they could make toward resolving the nation's energy problems. Higher prices for fuels should at

28. "Address before a Joint Session of Congress Reporting on the State of the Union, January 15, 1975," *Public Papers: Ford, 1975* (GPO, 1977), bk. 1, p. 42. On legislated technology see John C. Whitaker, *Striking a Balance: Environment and Natural Resources Policy in the Nixon-Ford Years* (American Enterprise Institute for Public Policy Research, 1976), pp. 93–105.

once encourage conservation and stimulate supply. The free market part of the program was balanced by a proposed windfall profits tax on oil industry profits and tax rebates to ease the burden of higher energy prices on the consumer. A third supporting pillar of the program was security, and this, together with the stress on efficiency and equity, meant that the whole was both comprehensive and balanced.

That at any rate was the view of the White House, where it was correctly perceived that this program was significantly more coherent than earlier efforts, and where—incorrectly—it was felt that Congress and the nation would be grateful for this contribution by the executive branch. Neither Congress nor the public at large believed in an energy crisis, except in the sense of contrived shortages, and the administration was to discover during 1975 and 1976 that designing a sensible energy policy, even with all the constraints that had to be taken into account, was considerably more straightforward than getting it enacted.

Several reasons for this—sectional interests, regional and energy-environmental conflicts, doubts about the market mechanism, distrust of "Big Oil"—have already been mentioned. Some of these reasons will be illustrated at greater length in later sections. But the interaction of Congress and the executive over some of Ford's key proposals also warrants separate and detailed examination. For not only did dealing with Congress over energy absorb the best efforts of Ford and his advisers for a whole year, but that extended episode raises an issue of more general nature. This is the problem that occurs whenever legislation must be enacted by representatives subject to reelection and when conflicts exist between the immediate and longer-term interests of the electorate, or between its real and perceived interests.

Congressional Alternatives to the Ford Package

A national energy policy had been a major concern of Congress for rather longer than it had occupied an equally high place on the agenda of the administration. The initiative had come at first from the Senate. Early in 1971 Senators Henry M. Jackson and Jennings Randolph, with forty-eight other members of the Senate, cosponsored a resolution to authorize the Senate Interior and Insular Affairs Committee to conduct a study of national policies affecting energy.[29] Under the authority for the National

29. S. Res. 45. Ex officio representation was later extended to the Senate Committees on Aeronautical and Space Sciences, Commerce, Finance, Foreign Relations, Government Operations, Labor, and Public Welfare.

Fuels and Energy Policy Study, as it came to be known, Jackson commissioned and published an extensive series of reports; compilations of relevant materials; and option studies encompassing national goals, the legal basis of existing energy policies, policy alternatives, responsibility for energy policy in the government structure, energy R&D, energy and the environment, and so forth. Documents continued to appear under the auspices of the study throughout the Nixon and Ford years, although the initial limited aim had been to produce only a report of findings, together with recommendations for legislation, for the Senate by September 1, 1972. Over the period 1971–76 Senator Jackson was involved in numerous legislative moves connected with energy problems, and his efforts to evolve a national energy policy were unquestionably sincere. Yet the only visible result of the study was an enormous outpouring of words. When Ford presented his plan to Congress in January 1975 not only was there no prepared alternative, but subsequent attempts to shape one disclosed serious disagreements among Democrats about the best ways to address the energy issues.

The first Democratic version of an energy plan was unveiled just hours before the President made public his own proposals in a nationally televised address from the White House on January 13. The Democratic plan was drawn up by a Speaker's Task Force on Energy and Economic Policy, headed by Congressman James Wright of Texas. Whereas Ford had decided to use the price mechanism, the House Democrats, expressing concern about recession, inflation, and conservation of energy more or less in that order, instead opted for mandatory allocation of petroleum (including gasoline rationing), or conservation without price controls. The task force also recommended higher taxes on gasoline and on "gas guzzler" autos, gasless days, subsidies for home insulation, and a restructuring of utility rates to discourage the use of electricity. Whether mandatory allocation and tax-price incentives were to be regarded as alternatives or complements was left open in the report. But the dual set of control and market devices did not sit well together, and Speaker Carl Albert asked for a further effort to work out a plan.[30]

This time Wright's group was matched by another in the Senate under Senator John Pastore of Rhode Island. The two groups worked out separate proposals, then met to formulate a joint program that was released on

---

30. The task force proposals are in *Energy Conservation and Oil Policy*, Hearings before the Subcommittee on Energy and Power of the House Committee on Interstate and Foreign Commerce, 94 Cong. 1 sess. (GPO, 1975), pt. 1, pp. 117–21.

February 27 as *The Congressional Program of Economic Recovery and Energy Sufficiency*.[31] The hallmarks of the joint program were skepticism concerning the market and the price-responsiveness of oil and gas supplies and an insistence that energy problems not be divorced from the condition of the economy. Together these emphases dictated that the preferred strategy would involve only moderate price increases, if any, but substantial new authority to mandate changes in production and consumption. As its prime target the program specified economic recovery, coupled with a lower rate of inflation.

To the Democrats, fighting inflation meant rejecting the President's tariff on imported oil, his excise tax on domestic production of oil and gas, and decontrol of petroleum. The (secondary) energy targets—conservation, increased supply, management procedures for coping with shortages—were so specified as to imply more federal involvement in the energy industries. The administrative centerpiece of the program was to be a newly created National Energy Production Board (long favored by Jackson), fashioned after the War Production Board of World War II. The board would be funded by a gasoline tax of 5 cents a gallon and would have authority "to break energy bottlenecks" on the side of production, plus extended allocatory powers meant partly to protect the independent segment of the oil industry. In addition the board would be responsible for a national system of strategic oil reserves and storage and would have standby authority to restrict imports and to ration in the event of another embargo. The program called for taxes only in that area of petroleum use (58 percent of the total) that was nonwork related. A stiff mandatory improvement in auto fuel efficiency was to be coupled with a system of tax penalties and incentives to buyers.[32]

This compromise plan was not acceptable to all Democrats. Many of the freshmen Democrats in the Ninety-fourth Congress favored energy price *decreases,* and during March forty members of this group issued an alternative plan that would have extended allocation and price controls and imposed a price rollback of domestic crude oil prices.[33]

31. *The Congressional Program of Economic Recovery and Energy Sufficiency* (GPO, 1975).

32. Ibid., pp. 3–4, 17, 22, 27.

33. See Russell Warren Howe and Sarah Hays Trott, "The 'Watergate Babies'," *Saturday Review,* May 31, 1975, pp. 11, 48. Examples of the views of some of the more outspoken freshmen Democrats are to be found in the statement of Congressman Andrew Maguire of New Jersey in *Energy Conservation and Oil Policy,* Hearings, pt. 1, pp. 159–61, and in the questions of Maguire and Congressman Toby Moffett of Connecticut in ibid., passim.

Congressman Al Ullman of Oregon, newly installed as chairman of the House Ways and Means Committee, also took an independent line. On March 2 Ullman outlined some proposals that had been formulated by eight task forces of the committee's Democrats and shaped into a program by freshman Congressman Joseph L. Fisher, who could call upon his former experience with the CEA during the Truman administration and as president of Resources for the Future. The ten-point plan differed in important respects from both the President's program and that of the Democratic leadership (the Wright-Pastore plan). A gasoline tax was recommended, but for conservation, not just for revenue, as the leadership program proposed. Starting at 5 cents a gallon the tax would rise over four or five years to a steep 40–50 cents on gasoline consumption in excess of 10–15 gallons a week. Uncertainty about the effectiveness of raising the price of imports and concern about inflation led the Ullman group to prefer quotas above a tariff, but with import licenses to be auctioned. The administration's windfall profits tax was endorsed but combined with a rebate linked to a plowback of profits into investment aimed at increasing oil supplies. In general the plan moved further in the direction of the market than the other Democratic alternatives to the President's program, but it stressed the importance of changing price signals slowly rather than in the abrupt manner implied by the administration's proposals.[34]

Despite the divisions among the Democrats, there was also considerable agreement on the desirability of protecting the consumer and the economy as a whole from higher energy prices. This concern made it inevitable that attempts would be made to quantify the inflationary impact of Ford's program and that the FEA would be drawn into comparing the President's plan with alternatives involving a gasoline tax or rationing schemes to reduce gasoline consumption, or with a combined quota-allocation program consistent with the President's goal of reducing oil imports by 1 million barrels a day.

The net result of FEA efforts was to discredit the administration. The FEA's early estimates of the impact of Ford's program on consumers were unrealistically low.[35] Moreover, comparing alternative programs for their

34. *Alternatives for Consideration in an Energy Program,* Committee Print, House Committee on Ways and Means, 94 Cong. 1 sess. (GPO, 1975).

35. Jackson's staff suggested that the increase in energy prices implied by the Ford program would cost the average family $800. The FEA responded with an estimate of $235, later raised to $275. (FEA, Office of Economic Impact, Office of Analysis, "The Impact of the President's Proposed Energy and Economics Program on Net Energy Costs to Consumers," n.d.) Treasury Department staff pointed out that

impact on oil imports and on GNP, prices, and unemployment gave the impression that the President had selected his own measures on this basis, which was untrue.[36] The objectives of the Ford plan, to repeat, were to reduce imports, establish a free market in petroleum, maintain purchasing power, provide revenue for energy R&D, and to achieve these goals in an economically efficient manner. Decontrol of oil and gas satisfied the goals, as to some extent did devices such as a tariff on imported oil, an excise tax on natural gas to eliminate curtailments, and a motor vehicle fuel tax. But the architects of the Ford program preferred decontrol, since that would mean a free market in petroleum and natural gas, and they thought of a tariff and the other measures as second best, useful in the event that decontrol proved to be infeasible.[37] That the final Ford program included both decontrol and some of the other devices merely gave room for negotiation and retreat. Quotas and rationing or allocation schemes were ruled out, not because they involved a greater impact on consumers or on prices, but because they were not efficient solutions to the problem. In making its numerical comparisons, the FEA was doing the administration a disservice

---

FEA estimates depended heavily on there being no increase in intrastate natural gas prices and coal prices. (Sam van Vactor to Douglas McCullough, "Logical Inconsistencies in the FEA Estimates of Increased Cost to Consumers of the President's Energy Program," January 30, 1975, William Johnson's personal files.) John Hill counters this criticism by pointing out (1) that the FEA could show that coal and oil prices had not tracked each other closely over long periods of time; (2) that a lot of gas was still under controls, but that even if gas prices were allowed to rise, this would occur slowly; and (3) that since the utilities used residual fuel oil, the bulk of which was imported and at a price close to the international price, utility rates would not increase much as a result of the program. (Interview with John A. Hill, New York, October 25, 1978.) The Treasury critique added, however, that even assuming constant coal and gas prices, the FEA was stretching credibility, since its estimates still required that business absorb all remaining price increases in lower profit margins. Van Vactor to McCullough, "Logical Inconsistencies."

36. "A Contrast of Energy Policy Alternatives" (draft), FEA Technical Report 75-8, March 3, 1975; and Allan Pulsipher and Milton Russell to Greenspan, "FEA's Paper on Energy Policy Alternatives," February 28, 1975; both in Russell personal files.

37. In an undated "Summary of Analysis and Policy Conclusions" (of issue papers prepared by various agencies for the Camp David meetings in mid-December 1974) Milton Russell structured the set of import control options into three categories: (1) desirable policies (for example, decontrol) that restrict imports to an appropriate level in the absence of a positive import restraint policy; (2) policies that do this, assuming decontrol to be infeasible (for example, a tariff); and (3) instruments to implement a policy of restriction beyond the level implied by market-clearing prices (for example, a motor vehicle fuels tax with rebates, quotas). CEA Records, Greenspan Files, GRFL.

on several counts. First, the estimated differences between the alternatives were no greater than the ranges of probable error in the estimates themselves. Second, once the defense of Ford's plan was altered from efficiency with supplementary devices to safeguard equity to that of least short-run, direct impact on prices, output, and unemployment, the way was opened to make ad hoc adjustments to lessen—supposedly—the impact on particular groups, industries, or regions.[38] The so-called gasoline tilt, already mentioned, was one such compromise. The political advantages of some ad hoc adjustments were not lost on the President, nor was the FEA interventionist faction averse to changes that would enhance its regulatory role. But once things began to move in this direction the basis of the original program was weakened, and the issues on which decisions affecting energy policy were to be made were much obscured.

Problems that arose from the divisions among the Democrats resulted in the first place in a postponement of serious consideration of any and all energy programs. The first two months of the Ninety-fourth Congress saw only delaying actions in both House and Senate in the form of challenges to the President's claim that he possessed authority unilaterally to impose tariffs under section 232 of the Trade Expansion Act of 1962, which was addressed to national security. On January 22 Ford made good on his claim, announcing a tariff of $1 a barrel on imported crude oil, effective February 1. He had earlier promised to start the process of oil price decontrol on April 1. But on January 23 Senators Kennedy and Jackson introduced a resolution (Senate Joint Resolution 12) to suspend for ninety days the President's powers regarding tariffs. The same resolution included a ninety-day postponement of oil price decontrol. On the following day the House Ways and Means Committee approved a ninety-day delay in the tariff increase and on February 5 the full House approved House bill 1767, which called for suspending the President's authority to change tariffs for that length of time and to negate all such actions that might be taken concerning petroleum tariffs after January 15.

The President responded by vetoing the bill on March 4, though in making that decision public he said also that in the interest of accommodation he would postpone till May 1 the second of two more tariff increases of $1 a barrel originally scheduled for March 1 and April 1. Ford further promised that he would not submit a plan for decontrolling old oil before

38. Pulsipher and Russell to Greenspan, "FEA's Paper on Energy Policy Alternatives"; and Russell to Greenspan, "Energy Program Modifications," February 18, 1975, CEA Records, Greenspan Files, GRFL.

May 1. He gave as one reason for his compromise actions that the congressional leadership had asked for more time to "work out the specifics" of their own plan.[39] He also noted, though without comment, that this plan, the Wright-Pastore compromise, was very different from the Ullman plan. It was undoubtedly preferable for Ford to postpone price decontrol and further tariff increases than to turn the debate over energy policy into a test of strength between Congress and the administration. But it was also unavoidable in the sense that without an agreed upon congressional alternative program the administration simply did not know with whom and over what it should be negotiating.

This particular uncertainty was to persist for many months. It was compounded of several elements, some specific to the Ninety-fourth Congress and others, such as jurisdictional conflicts between committees, recurrent. As noted above, the influx of "Watergate freshmen" injected a more independent strain into congressional deliberations on energy. This particular group of representatives owed their election in part to public feeling against the oil companies and disenchantment with the Nixon style of government. They had nothing to gain from supporting higher oil or gasoline prices, even if this option had the approval of senior Democrats, and especially not if it was part of a White House plan. The Democratic caucus, strengthened by the influx, pushed through important reforms. These included deposing (mostly conservative) committee chairmen, enlarging certain committees, making committee appointments, and rendering committee hearings more open. The latter three of these changes affected the House Ways and Means Committee, which occupied a critical position with respect to energy policy by virtue of its control of energy tax legislation and the tax status of the oil industry. At this time the chairman of the committee, Congressman Wilbur D. Mills, resigned, and his replacement, Ullman, found himself with an expanded committee (thirty-seven, up from twenty-five) and one less inclined to accept directives from the chairman, more open in its deliberations to public scrutiny, and less directly influenced by outside lobbying interests, but one that also was less influential in the House, having lost its power over committee appointments.

One early result of the changed nature and status of the Ways and Means Committee was the repeal of the long-standing oil depletion allowance in March 1975. Traditionally a Ways and Means bill could not be amended once it reached the floor of the House. In 1974 this tradition

39. "Veto of a Bill to Suspend the President's Authority to Set Oil Import Fees, March 4, 1975," *Public Papers: Ford, 1975*, p. 315.

had been challenged in connection with an attempt to put a repeal amendment before the House. Mills had been able to circumvent the move simply
by keeping his bill from the floor. When a similar attempt was made in
1975 Ullman was unable to withstand the groundswell for reform.

Moreover, as the session progressed it became clear that Ullman would
not gain acceptance of more than a token gasoline tax by his own committee, let alone the House.[40] The early Ways and Means proposals had
been accepted by the administration as a basis for discussion, and after
extensive sessions with Frank Zarb, Ullman presented to his committee a
scaled-down version of the initial task force plan, minus a windfall profits
tax. House bill 5005 retained the President's initial $1 tariff on imported
oil but would have switched the means of control to quotas beginning in
1976. It would also have imposed a gasoline tax rising ultimately to 37
cents a gallon and would have taxed inefficient autos and the industrial
use of oil and natural gas. Zarb felt that this went about 60 percent of the
way toward the tax goals of the administration's energy plan. But Ullman's
proposals were successively weakened, first in the committee, then in floor
debate. When the bill was reported out of committee and became the Ways
and Means bill in the House (House bill 6860), the initial $1 import fee
had been eliminated, the maximum increase in gasoline taxes was much
reduced, and the modest taxes retained on inefficient automobiles were to
apply only to the *average* fuel economy of a maker's whole fleet. On the
floor of the House, amendments were accepted that wholly removed the
provisions for higher gasoline taxes, and all tax schemes to achieve fuel
economy were abandoned in favor of a system of fines on auto manufacturers, paving the way for an easier route to challenges, delays, and exemptions through the courts rather than through Congress. The truncated
measure was passed by the House in mid-June as the Energy Conservation
and Conversion Act and was sent to the Senate Finance Committee. There,
following a few hearings, it was allowed to languish.[41]

40. For a discussion of depletion repeal and a gasoline tax see Tietenberg, *Energy
Planning and Policy,* chap. 8.
    41. Committee action on H.R. 5005 and the provisions of H.R. 6860 are detailed
by Tom Arrandale in the following: "Energy Report: Energy Taxes," *Congressional
Quarterly Weekly Report,* April 26, 1975, pp. 858–59; "Energy Report: Ways and
Means Approves Energy Tax Package," ibid., May 10, 1975, pp. 959–61; "Energy
and Environment: Divided Panel Reports Energy Tax Bill," ibid., May 17, 1975, pp.
1016–20; "Energy and Environment: House Kills Key Energy Bill Provisions," ibid.,
June 14, 1975, pp. 1268–70; "Energy and Environment: House Passes Stripped Down
Energy Tax Bill," ibid., June 21, 1975, pp. 1275–76. See also "Energy Report: Energy
Tax Deliberations Continue," ibid., May 3, 1975, pp. 952–54; and *Congressional

One lesson of this abortive effort to obtain congressional approval of some energy tax measures the administration felt it could support was that the character and mood of the House made it uncertain whether the congressional leadership or committee chairmen could deliver on agreements they might reach with the President or his advisers.[42]

Decontrol Once Again

After the early skirmish over Ford's tariff actions and proposals a second major issue quickly surfaced to dominate committee activity in both House and Senate. This was the matter of oil price decontrol. The history of efforts to reach a compromise on decontrol during 1975 contains the more general lesson already alluded to that in an electoral system it is the rule rather than the exception that good economics will be dominated by exigencies of the moment and by transitory political concerns.

It is useful to recall in this regard the history of price controls on petroleum from the Nixon years. The first special treatment of petroleum came with Phase III controls introduced early in 1973. At that time, while most controls were relaxed, the prices of gasoline and of no. 2 and residual fuel oils, for example, were frozen. By controlling these and other product prices it was expected that the price of domestic crude would also be held down. Subsequently under Phase IV (August 1973) a distinction was introduced between old and new oil, the latter being free from the price controls. There was an explicit provision that the ceiling price of old crude would be adjusted upward until it equalled the price of uncontrolled oil, at which time it was to be expected that all crude oil prices could be decontrolled. In December 1973 authority to control oil prices was trans-

---

Quarterly Almanac, 1975 (Congressional Quarterly, 1976), pp. 214–19. Two useful contemporary analyses of the debacle in the House are Elder Witt and Tom Arrandale, "Overestimating the Capability of Congress?" *Congressional Quarterly Weekly Report,* June 28, 1975, pp. 1343–46; and Richard Corrigan, "Energy Report: Ford Position Strengthened by Lack of Consensus in Congress," *National Journal Reports,* June 7, 1975, pp. 837–41.

42. This was only one aspect of the problem. Intercommittee relations were also complicated by the stance of the Democratic freshmen. In Ullman's case, his position and his usefulness to the administration were limited because the Subcommittee on Energy and Power of the House Committee on Interstate and Foreign Commerce and its clientele outside Congress simply did not trust Ways and Means to write a windfall profits tax that would not be full of loopholes. Interview with John A. Hill, New York, October 25, 1978.

ferred from the Cost of Living Council to the Federal Energy Office, and while the Economic Stabilization Act expired, oil remained under this two-tier system. The rationale for this was that in a time of shortage the administration did not want to cause inflation or create a windfall on existing output but only to give an incentive to production at the margin. During 1974, instead of immediate decontrol, the administration introduced the entitlements program. Its main purpose, like that of the allocation programs devised in 1973, was to protect the independent refiners. The FEA argument used in support of entitlements was that although shortages no longer existed and it was desirable to do away with the allocation schemes, this could not be accomplished without risk to the independents so long as there was a price disparity between different crudes (old and new). But immediate price decontrol would be likely to raise gasoline prices and provoke action by Congress to extend the life of the Emergency Petroleum Allocation Act. The effect of entitlements was to subsidize oil imports and small refineries and to create new reasons for some independent, and even some major, oil refiners to want to retain the act. Entitlements also took some of the pain out of the price controls program and in this way lessened the political opposition to them.

This brief listing of the major developments up to 1975 suggests several observations. First, controls were intended to siphon off the rents that would otherwise have accrued to domestic producers in the wake of foreign crude price increases. Only production at the margin was to be encouraged, and consumers and independent refiners were intended to be the main beneficiaries of the controls. Further, although controls were meant to be only temporary, the possible adverse impact of decontrol on consumers, on the economy, or on the competitive structure of the oil industry, or the political backlash that might result, could always be cited as arguments to quash the option of immediate decontrol. Finally, to close the circle, with decontrol effectively eliminated as an option, there was both an opportunity and a need for additional layers of controls to paper over the most glaring ill effects of the existing controls as these came to light.

The 1975 battle over decontrol was a logical extension of the prior history of controls and the precedents and tendencies it had established.[43]

43. Within the administration this view was cogently expounded by SEA economists on whose analyses the foregoing paragraphs draw. John Davis and Milton Russell to Greenspan, "Review of Energy Decisions: A Prelude to the Conference Energy Bill" (draft), December 12, 1975, Russell personal files.

Controls originally were due to lapse in February 1975, but Congress secured an extension of the Emergency Petroleum Allocation Act, shifting the date of expiration to August 31, 1975. The Ford program, as I have stressed, was premised on full decontrol of oil, and the President intended to submit a decontrol plan to Congress by April 1. After discussion with the House leadership he agreed to a one-month delay; but then a cat and mouse game began in which Congress pounced each time decontrol showed its head.

Ford announced the one-month delay on March 4. But on March 7 the Senate Interior and Insular Affairs Committee reported out a bill (Senate bill 621) sponsored by its chairman, Jackson, under which either chamber would be given thirty days instead of five in which to review and reject proposed changes in oil price controls. A week later the House Interstate and Foreign Commerce Committee approved a bill sponsored by John D. Dingell of Michigan, chairman of the committee's Subcommittee on Energy and Power, to extend the review period to fifteen days. The Dingell Bill (House bill 4035) also would have extended the date of expiration of controls legislation by four months, to December 31, 1975. Senate bill 622, a companion to Senate bill 621, had been approved by the Senate Interior Committee on March 5. That measure, similar to Jackson's Emergency Energy Act of 1974, which Nixon had vetoed, embodied certain standby powers, as requested by Ford in his own legislative proposals. But Senate bill 622 also provided for congressional review and possible veto of the President's use of them. In addition the bill extended the allocation act of 1973 through March 1976 and prohibited any increase in the price of old oil and any exemption from price controls of crude, residual, and refined products without review and approval by Congress.[44]

Late in April Ford agreed to a further delay in his own plans for decontrol, and at that time House bill 4035 was withdrawn from the House calendar. A month later, however, Ford again foreshadowed proposals for ending controls, and spurred by this announcement, both chambers quickly approved House bill 4035 and Senate bill 621.

Meanwhile the Energy and Power Subcommittee of the House Com-

44. Details of S. 621 and S. 622 and of committee and floor debate are given in "Energy Report: Emergency Standby Powers," *Congressional Quarterly Weekly Report,* March 15, 1975, pp. 511–12; "Energy Report: Oil Price Review Policy," ibid., pp. 516–18; and "Energy Report: Senate Approves Standby Energy Powers Bill," ibid., April 19, 1975, pp. 783–84.

merce Committee had completed hearings and was engaged in marking up an (unnumbered) energy bill, hoping to meet the President's challenge to the Democrats to come up with a program by May 1. The marked up version was presented to the full Commerce Committee as House bill 7014. In the debate on this bill decontrol was once again the central point of contention. The subcommittee had voted eight to seven for a four-year phaseout of controls, subject to enactment of a windfall profits tax. Chairman Dingell's vote created the majority, but as the vote suggests, the subcommittee was deeply divided. Its Democratic majority included seven freshmen, among them such outspoken critics of the oil industry and of decontrol as Congressman Andrew Maguire of New Jersey and Congressman Toby Moffett of Connecticut. In the full committee the language of the subcommittee was rejected, and on May 15 the committee also moved to disapprove Ford's first decontrol plan, which had been disclosed on April 30 when he directed the FEA to prepare a schedule for phasing out controls over twenty-five months.[45]

Frank Zarb reminded Ford at this point that a vote for decontrol would require a large number of House Democrats to vote with the administration. Even before the Commerce Committee's disapproval of the decontrol proposal Zarb advised against sending the plan to Congress, pending efforts to put together a coalition of Republicans, oil state Democrats, and the New England delegation (whom it was hoped would be appeased by an indefinite delay in adding a second dollar to the $1 import fee imposed by Ford on January 22.)[46]

Subsequently Ford put forward two more decontrol proposals. One, on July 14, extended the phaseout from twenty-five to thirty months and set a ceiling of $13.50 on the 27 percent of domestic output in the categories of new and released oil. A second, on July 25, would have eliminated controls over thirty-nine months, with most of the price increases coming after the 1976 elections, and with a ceiling price on all domestic oil of $11.50 a barrel. The administration believed this plan was acceptably close to an amendment that had been offered by Dingell in debate on House bill 7014. (The amendment involved an $11.50 ceiling and decontrol of old oil over five years.) The House, however, was not satisfied. Ford had vetoed House bill 4035, which not only extended controls

45. "Energy and Environment: Oil Price Decontrol," *Congressional Quarterly Weekly Report,* May 17, 1975, p. 1020.

46. Zarb (through Morton) to the President, "Decontrol and Import Fee Options," May 15, 1975, CEA Records, Greenspan Files, GRFL.

through December 1975 but set a maximum price of $11.28 a barrel on domestic oil not classed as old, thereby rolling that price back to the January 1975 level. While the House chose not to try to override the veto, on July 30 it passed a resolution disapproving the thirty-nine-month plan.[47] On the next day it passed Senate bill 1849 (a simple extension of price control authority for six months), and on August 1 it refused to include in House bill 7014 the thirty-nine-month plan, which had been presented as an amendment.

From this point on the administration's resolve steadily weakened. In submitting his thirty-nine-month plan Ford had said that he would veto an extension bill. On August 15 he affirmed that he would indeed veto Senate bill 1849, and the administration moved with alacrity to ensure that it would have the votes to sustain the veto, at least in the Senate. Ford promised to waive the existing import fee of $2 a barrel (a second dollar had been added on June 1) and to lift a 60-cent fee that had been imposed on imported products if his veto were sustained.[48] In addition to thus sweetening the pill the administration tried to quell fears about the fate of independent refiners under decontrol. John Hill, FEA deputy administrator, suggested publicly that the windfall profits tax as envisaged by the administration would take care of this problem. Since the tax

47. For the President's twenty-five-month and thirty-month decontrol proposals see *Executive Energy Messages,* Committee Print, Senate Committee on Interior and Insular Affairs, 94 Cong. 1 sess. (GPO, 1975), pp. 265–67, 321–28. His rejection of H.R. 4035 is contained in "Veto of a Petroleum Price Review Bill, July 21, 1975," *Public Papers: Ford, 1975* (GPO, 1977), bk 2., pp. 1007–08. See also "Ford Proposes $13.50 Lid on New Oil," *Oil and Gas Journal,* July 21, 1975, pp. 46–47. On July 30 Frank Zarb wrote to Republican Congressman Clarence J. Brown of Ohio expressing disappointment that the thirty-month plan seemed unacceptable to Congress. He also reported much confusion in the administration at the rejection of a proposal worked out in response to objections to the thirty-month proposal and following extensive consultation with Democratic members. Letter, Zarb to Brown, July 30, 1975 (copy in Johnson personal files).

48. The possibility of removing the 60-cent fee on imported products had been foreshadowed earlier. (FEA Energy News Release, "FEA Proposing Removal of 60-Cent Fee on Product Imports," July 30, 1975.) There was some confusion over whether the President intended to remove both fees, not only in the event that controls expired, but also if a compromise could be reached. In testimony before the Dingell Subcommittee, September 8, Zarb affirmed that in the event of a compromise on the basis of the President's thirty-month plan, the $2 tariff would remain. *President's Decontrol Proposals,* Hearings before the Subcommittee on Energy and Power of the House Committee on Interstate and Foreign Commerce, 94 Cong. 1 sess. (GPO, 1975), pp. 736–37.

would be levied on the difference between market prices and notional long-run equilibrium prices, integrated companies that might otherwise have charged themselves a lower-than-market price for crude and in turn would have undercut independents on product prices would have no incentive to do so, because they would be paying the tax in any case. It is not clear how the administration thought it would get a windfall profits tax enacted at this stage. Ullman had not included such a tax in the Ways and Means package, having agreed to wait and see what sort of decontrol proposal came out of the Commerce Committee. But neither was there a profits tax in House bill 7014. The Senate Finance Committee, under Senator Russell B. Long of Louisiana, had readied a windfall profits tax, but this had not been passed by the Senate before the summer recess. In any case when Congress resumed its session, and with Ford's veto of Senate bill 1849 imminent, the administration hedged by promising new legislation that would soften the impact of decontrol on independent refiners and marketers as well as on service station owners. In the light of forecasts that natural gas would be in short supply during the coming winter and with the implication that propane prices would rise sharply if controls had lapsed by that time, the President also moved to still farm belt opposition to decontrol. It was announced that he would ask for standby powers to allocate propane and to control propane prices.[49]

The expected veto came on September 9, and it was sustained on September 10 in the Senate by a vote of 61 to 39. Of the Senators voting to sustain, seven were Democrats, all from oil-producing states. Seven Republicans, all from the Northeast, voted to override.[50]

49. Richard Corrigan, "Energy Report: Opposing Forces Battle for Votes on Oil Price Issue," *National Journal Reports,* August 23, 1975, pp. 1208–11; statement of John A. Hill in *Oil Price Decontrol,* Hearings before the Senate Committee on Interior and Insular Affairs, 94 Cong. 1 sess. (GPO, 1975), pp. 144–75; and testimony of Frank Zarb before the Dingell Subcommittee, *President's Decontrol Proposals,* Hearings, p. 738.

50. This vote illustrates the increased influence of local constituency interests relative to party that characterized the Ninety-fourth Congress. A study of this and other energy votes during 1975 confirms that the financial interests of members in the oil and gas industry seem not to have influenced voting. (See Elder Witt and David Speights, "Energy and Environment: Energy Holdings of Key Committee Members," *Congressional Quarterly Weekly Report,* September 20, 1975, pp. 2000–02.) But a study of voting on natural gas deregulation in 1976 suggests that neither party nor local interests explain the results as well as "ideology." Edward J. Mitchell, *Energy and Ideology* (American Enterprise Institute for Public Policy Research, 1977), Reprint 77.

EPCA: The Last Hurrah

On September 23 House bill 7014 passed the House, and after action on somewhat similar measures in the Senate a conference began early in October on House bill 7014 and Senate bill 622, known as the Energy Policy and Conservation Act (EPCA). Controls had formally lapsed on August 31, but the threat of retrospective price rollbacks kept prices from rising, and in September and again in November Ford agreed to temporary extensions of controls to facilitate accommodation to Congress and to allow the conferees to complete their work.

Within the administration the extensions of controls were supported on the understanding that there would be no retreat from the substance of the thirty-nine-month plan. The conferees quickly showed that they were set on rolling back prices, and they began working with the notion of a weighted composite price, to which the various categories of domestic oil collectively would be constrained as a composite entity in the first instance. Zarb made it clear to the conferees that even if there were such a composite price limit at the outset, it should not be lower than $13.50 a barrel at the termination of controls. Moreover, the starting price for new oil should not be less than $10.50. And the decontrol schedule should not be such as to increase, at any stage, dependence on imported oil more than was implied by the President's thirty-nine-month plan. Zarb further suggested that a starting composite price of $8 would be acceptable to the administration, This, together with the first two conditions specified above, implied a yearly price increase of 15 percent (over thirty-nine months).

Senator Jackson offered an alternative to these administration proposals involving a starting composite price of $7.55. It also provided for upward adjustment for inflation (no more than 6 percent annually), plus a 3 percent discretionary adjustment to bring on significant quantities of oil in high-cost, high-risk areas (for example, oil from Alaska and from stripper wells). John Hill, who by special agreement sat in on the conference sessions, said that he would recommend acceptance of this plan by Ford, provided stripper wells and Alaskan oil could be wholly exempted from the composite price. This offer and another involving a starting price of $7.35, excluding stripper wells, was rejected. Zarb then made further concessions, offering a starting price of $7.96 and an end price of $10.95. Ultimately the conferees settled on $7.66, with increased flexibility for the President to increase prices if justified for high-cost and enhanced recovery projects, and a total allowable adjustment of 10 percent a year. It was also agreed to postpone further discussion of Alaskan oil until April 15, 1977.[51] The administration thus made significant gains at the last minute. By comparison with its starting position, however, it conceded $2.55 on the end price and 5 percent on the allowable annual adjustment. Moreover, the FEA projected an increase in imports of 174,000 barrels a day, a $2-a-barrel lower end price and a 3-cent or 3.5-cent-a-gallon higher price for gasoline, all after three years and relative to what the President's thirty-nine-month program had been expected to achieve. The FEA judged that there would be no discernible difference in domestic production of oil after three years, comparing the two plans.[52]

The final pricing provisions of the EPCA as passed by both houses of Congress continued the two-tier structure for crude oil, maintained the price of old oil at $5.25 a barrel and placed a cap on the roughly one-third of "uncontrolled" domestic crude at $11.28 a barrel. It will be recalled that $11.28 was the ceiling earlier rejected by Ford in his veto of House bill 4035. Since the late November price of imported crude was $12.50 a barrel, in effect a third tier was created by virtue of the cap on previously strictly uncontrolled domestic oil. The weighted average price of $7.66 a barrel could be increased monthly at the President's discretion by an adjustment for inflation and one (not to exceed 3 percent a year) to provide a production incentive. The total adjustment was not to exceed 10 percent, though the administration could propose a higher figure on March 1, 1976, and every ninety days thereafter subject to disapproval by either house within fifteen days. The mandatory controls program would revert to standby after forty months, but the President would still have to take a positive act to achieve decontrol. The President was enjoined to dismantle as much as possible of the existing structure of price

51. This account of the conference negotiations is based on daily reports by Treasury observer W. E. Steger dated October 31, November 4 (two reports), 5, and 6, 1975 (copies in Johnson personal files), and on Caroline E. Mayer, "President, Congress End Energy Battle," *Oil and Gas Journal,* November 17, 1975, pp. 34–35. The written record of administration thinking is slight, though surviving documents in FEA Records, Inter-Office Memo Files, Department of Energy, attest to the accuracy of the Mayer account.

52. Zarb to the President, "HR 7014/S 622: The Energy Policy and Conservation Act," n.d. The FEA considered three cases: unfavorable, moderate, and favorable (that is, pessimistic, likely, and optimistic). The comparisons mentioned in the text are for the moderate case, which assumed that Congress would allow a 10 percent escalation throughout the forty months and that Alaskan oil would be exempt.

and allocation controls (excluding those on crude oil), each such action to be permanent (that is, not subject as before to congressional review every ninety days) unless disapproved by either house within fifteen days.[53]

After long hesitation Ford signed the act into law on December 22, 1975. The FEA was the leading advocate of signing. In his initial draft decision memorandum to the President late in November Zarb acknowledged that the EPCA was inferior to the administration's thirty-nine-month plan but pointed out that it probably was no worse than an extension of existing controls. Moreover, provided the other proposals in the President's total package were enacted, the EPCA was not inconsistent with a modest saving in imports over the decontrol period.[54] The CEA, on the other hand, the leading opponent of signing (except for the Treasury), strongly criticized Zarb's presentation on the ground that the true comparison—that between Ford's initial intention, or immediate and full decontrol at midyear, and the EPCA—was not made clear. By neglecting this comparison, the CEA contended, the full extent of the administration's concessions to Congress was minimized.[55] In fact, Zarb had made brief mention of immediate decontrol as "the best policy from an energy self-sufficiency point of view and the only *realistic* alternative to the Conference pricing provision."[56] But he did not initially introduce this alternative into his numerical estimates (as the CEA would have wished), and his comment on the decontrol option reveals that he implicitly dismissed it, not because it was bad economics or bad government, but because it conflicted with his assessment of the prevailing political climate and possibilities. "If decontrol is achieved through the sustaining of a veto of the Conference bill, the Democratic strategy would likely be to hold off on any further action until prices and profits went up, several independent refiners failed, propane prices and supplies became a serious

53. P.L. 94-163.
54. Zarb to the President, "HR 7014/S 622: The Omnibus Energy Bill" (draft), n.d. (almost certainly late November 1978), FEA Records, External Correspondence Files, Department of Energy. It was noted above that the FEA believed the EPCA would result in increased imports. The savings just mentioned are on the strict assumption that Ford's other short-term proposals (for example, coal conversion, increased output from Elk Hills, improved auto efficiency standards) would be accepted.
55. Greenspan to Zarb and Hill, "CEA Comments on FEA Analysis of Conference Energy Bill," November 25, 1975, FEA Records, Inter-Office Memo Files, Department of Energy.
56. Zarb to the President, "HR 7014/S 622."

problem for farmers and rural households, and the issue was debated in the primaries or general election campaigns."[57]

Zarb's assessment focused on the problems with which Ford had been dealing throughout his long struggle with Congress over decontrol and went far toward explaining why the administration had agreed, first, to delaying its submission of decontrol plans, then to a sequence of ever more extended decontrol periods and ever lower ceilings on domestic oil prices, then to a series of concessions and standby controls to safeguard special interests likely to be hurt by decontrol, then to successive temporary extensions of the Emergency Petroleum Allocation Act and finally had accepted, albeit reluctantly, what Senator John G. Tower acidly referred to as the "Cold Homes and Dark Factories Act," or the "Energy Dependence Act," or the "OPEC Relief Act of 1975."[58] For Ford was a vulnerable President from the beginning: not elected, facing an election within two years of taking office, threatened by Jackson, Ronald Reagan, and even by the suspected vice-presidential aspirations of one conservative Republican in his own administration, William Simon. He needed a bold issue, and "free markets for petroleum" was a watchword he might not in ordinary circumstances have accepted quite as readily as he did.

The reformist Congress Ford faced made negotiating compromises a tricky and unpredictable business and encouraged a wait-and-see attitude. The Democrat-dominated Congress, too, seemed bent on siding with the consumer, and Ford found himself cast unwittingly on the side of villainous Big Oil. Congress was undoubtedly backing the right horse: opinion polls in 1975 showed half the people believing that there never had been a real energy crisis and a growing percentage placing the blame for inflation, not on OPEC, but on the major oil companies.[59] Moreover, shortages had disappeared. As Ullman complained, when his Ways and Means bill was being cut to pieces in the House it was impossible to pass a gasoline tax after the gas lines had vanished and energy had become "an invisible crisis."[60] It is true that by August pollsters were reporting a majority prepared to accept the necessity of rising energy prices.[61] But by

57. Ibid.

58. "Energy and Environment: Congress Sends Ford Energy Policy Bill," *Congressional Quarterly Weekly Report,* December 20, 1975, pp. 2766–78.

59. Richard Corrigan, "A Decision at the Polls May Not Hinge on the Price at the Pump," *National Journal Reports,* April 3, 1976, pp. 440–45.

60. Richard Corrigan, "Energy Report: Ford Position Strengthened by Lack of Consensus in Congress," ibid., June 7, 1975, p. 837.

61. *Chicago Tribune,* August 4, 1975.

then, for other reasons Ford no longer possessed a lively option in decontrol. The inflation figures for July were bad—the consumer price
index rose 12 percent—and even Greenspan became concerned about
the possible inflationary impact of decontrol.[62] Simon, Zarb, and others
were worried about the prospect of higher propane prices should a serious
natural gas shortage develop during the coming winter. Oil company
profits meanwhile continued to rise even under controls, and the chances
for securing a windfall profits tax were remote. And all the while the
direct political pressures were growing stronger. Reagan was looking
dangerous, and the Democrats were presented with a plum in the form
of a win in New Hampshire's September Senate election—a victory that
Jackson readily attributed in part to the high price of gasoline.[63] Under
these circumstances it is not surprising that Ford in the end, as some
observers put it, traded Texas for New Hampshire and the momentum
he would get from winning the first primary.[64]

62. The CEA estimated that decontrol would have "a significant one-shot inflationary impact," though the effects on the economy as a whole would be slight if the
$2-a-barrel import fee on crude and the 60 cent fee on imported products were
dropped and modest fiscal and monetary support were provided. This might keep the
increase in gasoline prices down to 5 cents a gallon. The CEA admitted, however,
that the inflationary effects would be "complicated" by a possible $2 OPEC price in-
crease in the fall (this would increase the GNP deflator from 0.5–0.6 percent to 1.4–
1.6 percent through the third quarter of 1976). Greenspan to the President, "The
Economic Effects of Immediate Decontrol" (draft), August 1, 1975; and Tab A
(Macroeconomic effects of oil decontrol and OPEC price increases), CEA Records,
Greenspan Files, GRFL.

63. Richard Corrigan, "Energy Focus: A National Referendum on Energy," National Journal Reports, January 3, 1976, p. 27.

64. This "most shallow and cynical [of] arguments" for signing was denounced by
the Wall Street Journal on December 5, 1975. Ford's close political associates and
White House staff, counselor Robert T. Hartman, and advisers L. William Seidman
and James M. Cannon, argued against a veto on a variety of grounds, but the dominant
recurring theme was that the bill was marginally worth signing to end the national
uncertainty about energy and to show that "the oil companies do not control Washington." (Zarb to the President, "HR 7014/S 622: the Energy Policy and Conservation Act," n.d., with attached statements by Seidman, Cannon, and other advisers and
agencies, CEA Records, Greenspan Files, GRFL.) Ford had been set to sign the bill
immediately after its provisions were known; but the day after the conference ended
Senator John Tower and a group of Republicans (including Senators Dewey F. Bartlett of Oklahoma, Clifford P. Hansen of Wyoming, and some House Republicans) met
with Ford and several advisers, including Zarb and Greenspan, and denounced the
bill as a national betrayal. They also argued that acceptance by Ford would entail the
loss of Texas to Reagan. This drove a wedge where none had been before and precipitated the five weeks of doubt and uncertainty before Ford finally was won over by the
assurances of, among others, Kissinger and Arthur Burns. Within the administration
only the CEA and the Treasury opposed the signing. (Based on discussions with John
A. Hill, William A. Johnson, and Frank Zarb.)

Bypassing Congress on Natural Gas

The administration's efforts to win congressional approval of natural gas decontrol, of which brief mention must be made, foundered on the twin rocks of intransigence and a refusal to believe that natural gas shortages were other than contrived. In mid-1975 the administration backed a proposal submitted to the Senate by Republican Senator James B. Pearson of Kansas and Democratic Senator Lloyd M. Bentsen of Texas, under which measures already being considered to ease the curtailments anticipated for the winter of 1975–76 were linked with a plan to lift controls on new natural gas produced onshore and sold in interstate markets after January 1, 1975. Offshore gas would be decontrolled in stages by 1981. Senate Democratic leaders preferred to keep the short-term problem separate from long-term decontrol, but the Pearson-Bentsen measure (Senate bill 2310) passed the Senate on October 22. In the House, however, chairman Dingell of the House Interstate and Foreign Commerce Committee's Energy and Power Subcommittee, and Congressman John E. Moss of California, chairman of the same committee's Oversight and Investigative Subcommittee, absolutely refused to entertain long-run decontrol and deflected the attention of the House to investigating whether producers were not deliberately withholding supplies.[65]

The House Commerce Committee reported a bill (9464) to deal with the predicted winter emergency, but no further action was taken before

65. The Pearson-Bentsen proposals were a substitute for the original Senate bill 2310, sponsored by Democratic Senators Ernest F. Hollings of South Carolina, John Glenn of Ohio, and Herman E. Talmadge of Georgia and designed solely to deal with winter shortages. The administration supported the substitute because no acceptable action had been taken on its own decontrol proposal. (See Elder Witt, "Energy and Environment: Plans to Ease Natural Gas Shortage Debated," *Congressional Quarterly Weekly Report,* October 4, 1975, pp. 2144–46; Witt, "Energy and Environment: Senate Passes Two-Part Natural Gas Bill," ibid., October 25, 1975, pp. 2292–95; and Richard Corrigan, "Energy Focus: Natural Gas: Meanwhile, in the House . . . ," *National Journal Reports,* November 8, 1975, pp. 1553.) The 1975 debate was a replay of a Nixon battle for deregulation, with the added complication that the shortages in the winter of 1975–76 were expected to be much more severe than in 1974. The year 1976 saw yet another go-round. See James G. Phillips, "Energy Report: Congress Nears Showdown on Proposal to Decontrol Gas Prices," *National Journal Reports,* May 25, 1974, pp. 761–75; Richard Corrigan, "Energy Report: Natural Gas Pricing Bill to Undergo Senate Scrutiny," ibid., July 12, 1975, pp. 1021–26; and Corrigan, "Energy Report: Gas Deregulation Tripped Up by Compromise Measure," ibid., February 14, 1976, pp. 196–97.

the end of the first session of the Ninety-fourth Congress. Early in 1976 the House did consider a long-term deregulation measure, but when it came to a vote on House bill 9464 what was actually agreed to was a substitute proposal that ended price controls over small producers but extended regulation over major companies. The FPC was directed to set a national ceiling price for new natural gas sold both intrastate and in interstate commerce by large companies.

This bill did not appeal to senators who had fought for complete deregulation, and after first delaying on a conference, the Senate reported on May 18, 1976, a new bill (3422) that would have retained price controls but allowed prices on interstate gas to rise substantially above the 52 cents per 1,000 cubic feet allowed by the Federal Power Commission. This alternative in turn ran into opposition from consumers and from industry advocates of full deregulation.

The to-ing and fro-ing in Congress paralleled a certain ambivalence in the administration. Congress seemed bent on "allocating" shortages in an equitable way, without feeling that they should be eliminated. Up to the middle of 1975, at least, the FPC and the FEA seemed concerned to free the supply end of the market, urging that curtailed high-priority gas users be allowed to bid away gas from intrastate markets, yet they were unwilling to impose the costs of this on the consumer and busied themselves at the same time with plans for federal relief to pipeline companies that might be faced with a sudden rise in costs.[66]

Further legislative action was forestalled on July 27, 1976, when the FPC decided to raise the nationwide price ceiling for new interstate gas produced or contracted for after 1974 to $1.42 per 1,000 cubic feet. This step was taken by a commission that had undergone a virtually complete change of membership in a year, and after numerous less radical measures tried under former Chairman John Nassikas had failed to stop the steady decline in reserves. The decision was justified in part on the grounds that both drilling costs and taxes had gone up for gas producers.

---

66. An overview of issues and options prepared for the Camp David meetings on the administration's energy program, June 7 and 8, 1975, suggests that the FEA regarded the possible options as forced transfer of gas between pipelines, direction of purchase of gas in the field by industry and distributors, and direction of new gas supplies to those pipelines in the greatest difficulties. ("Energy Overview: Discussion Paper," n.d., CEA Records, MacAvoy Files, GRFL.) Milton Russell complained that options such as these "read as a preliminary to special Federal relief for pipelines or to Federal intervention in pipeline planning." Russell to Greenspan and MacAvoy, "Comments on Briefing Book for Camp David," June 6, 1975, ibid.

This was in line with the provisions of House bill 9464 under which the FPC in setting a national price was enjoined to take account of, among other things, the need for profits sufficient to provide adequate incentives to attract capital and encourage the exploration and development of new natural gas resources. A further justification was that the new interstate rate made new natural gas roughly equivalent in price (on a Btu basis) to the price of residual fuel oil and no. 2 home heating oil.[67] In this respect the decision must be viewed as a major victory for the advocates of deregulation in the administration. Not that price controls were eliminated, but there was at least an acknowledgment of the principle that, to facilitate efficient use of energy, substitute fuels should be priced at the margin so as to achieve Btu equivalence. The CEA had been urging acceptance of this notion.[68] In effect the FPC had done what Congress had repeatedly balked at doing.

The Nonpricing Provisions of the EPCA

I have concentrated on the frustrations of dealing with the Ninety-fourth Congress and have stressed the compromises made by the administration in order to secure a measure of agreement on oil decontrol.

67. The details of the debate on natural gas deregulation can be followed in "Energy and Environment: Natural Gas," *Congressional Quarterly Weekly Report,* September 13, 1975, p. 1944; Witt, "Energy and Environment: Plans to Ease Natural Gas Shortage Debated"; Prudence Crewdson, "Energy and Environment: Senate Rejects Natural Gas Re-Regulation," ibid., October 11, 1975, pp. 2205–06; Witt, "Energy and Environment: Senate Passes Two-Part Natural Gas Bill"; "Energy and Environment: Emergency Natural Gas Bill," ibid., November 29, 1975, p. 2601; "Energy and Environment: Natural Gas Bill," ibid., December 6, 1975, p. 2672; Corrigan, "Energy Focus: Natural Gas—Meanwhile, in the House"; Corrigan, "Energy Report: Gas Bill Stuck at Net in Congressional Ping-Pong Game," *National Journal Reports,* March 20, 1976, p. 369; Corrigan, "Energy Report: FPC's Gas Price Ruling Leaves Consumers Out in the Cold," ibid., November 13, 1976, pp. 1626–31.

68. "The important long-run question," Paul MacAvoy had written to Frank Zarb, commenting on S. 3422, "is whether the bill allows gas to work into an equilibrium relationship with other fuels, so that energy is used efficiently." MacAvoy went on to say that CEA calculations indicated that Btu equivalence between natural gas and oil for boiler fuels would not be achieved under the provisions of S. 3422. He suggested that the administration press for a modification of the Senate bill to achieve this equivalence. MacAvoy to Zarb, letter summarizing CEA's review of S. 3422, May 24, 1976, CEA Records, MacAvoy Files, GRFL.

But the EPCA was much broader than the oil pricing provisions alone. It dealt positively with five elements of Ford's initial program, and this was an additional reason for his signing in December.

The act authorized a strategic petroleum reserve (requested under title II of Ford's omnibus energy bill). This was not linked directly to expanded production from the Naval Petroleum Reserves, but the administration was hopeful that legislation being considered by a House-Senate conference in December would supply the link. The EPCA also provided standby authorities roughly similar to those asked for by the President (under title XIII). Further, it contained the necessary authorizations to enable the United States to participate in the International Energy Program (title IX). And it granted the authorities requested on coal conversion (title IV) and product labeling (title XII) virtually without verbal change.

Where the administration had qualms about accepting these and some other provisions—for example, import purchasing authority and materials allocation, and authority for the collection, verification, and transmission to Congress of energy data—the problem lay in the direction of Congress having undertaken more oversight and granted more powers than the President wanted. This was felt to establish a dangerous interventionist precedent.[69] For the same reason, the administration was disturbed that the act mandated an auto efficiency program, in place of a voluntary agreement Ford had reached with the auto makers earlier in the year; though, as noted above, in this instance Ford himself initially had used the threat of mandated standards to gain his "voluntary" agreement.

FEA principals were particularly pleased that the act actually enjoined the President to dismantle controls (other than on crude oil). And Zarb found it a positive feature of the legislation that it eliminated the requirement for congressional review and approval of each decontrol proposal every ninety days, as under the Emergency Petroleum Allocation Act (EPAA). This new freedom was quickly exploited, and during the spring of 1976 the administration succeeded—where it had failed in 1974—in decontrolling no. 2 and no. 6 fuel oils.

The administration's success in this direction was facilitated in no small measure by a change in the mood of some independents. In 1973 when shortages prevailed the independents were in difficulties, and the

69. Zarb to the President, "HR 7014/S 622."

EPAA had been enacted partly to mitigate their problems. In 1975 and early 1976 surpluses were once again the rule, and members of Congress found themselves being lobbied for repeal of the act by some of the very independents for whose protection it had been devised.[70]

The difficulties of matching legislation to the complexities and constantly changing state of the petroleum market are illustrated in another respect by the EPCA provisions designed to assist "small refiners." In the entitlements program, as promulgated in November 1974, refineries having a capacity of less than 175,000 barrels a day were granted additional entitlements. They also were granted exemption from the need to purchase entitlements on the first 30,000 barrels a day of crude runs to stills. This purchase exemption was intended to be phased out. Under the EPCA, however, the definition of "small refiners" was changed to those with a capacity of less than 100,000 barrels a day, and these refiners were given permanent exemption from purchase requirements on the first 50,000 barrels a day of crude oil run. The FEA had resisted requests by small refiners during 1975 for total exemption. The small refiners already enjoyed a disproportionate share of cheap crude, and complete exemption would have given them a still greater competitive advantage in the market for refined products. Once Congress had rewritten the provision governing small-refiner bias this expectation was realized, but the benefits were felt mainly by the group of small refiners who were exempted from buying entitlements and at the expense of other small refiners who had to sell. The exempt small refiners quickly expanded into the direct marketing of gasoline, and this threatened to undermine the goal of preserving competition at the retail level.[71] In other ways, too, this effort by Congress to dictate the behavior of the oil industry had predictable deleterious effects on efficiency. A direct incentive was given to potential entrants into the refining business to keep their investment "small," and the number of small refineries rose sharply

70. As early as May 1975 the National Oil Jobbers Council was asking Jackson, chief architect of the EPAA, to allow the allocation authority to revert to standby status. (Letter from Thomas Love, President, National Oil Jobbers Council, to Senator Jackson, May 20, 1975, copy in Johnson personal files.) The same letter was sent to Dingell. It should be noted that at the same time independent refiners, terminal operators, and marketers were among those asking for an *extension* of the EPAA.

71. "FEA Rejects Pleas to Exempt Small Refiners," *Oil and Gas Journal,* March 31, 1975, p. 54. In "How Federal Regulations Are Putting Independent Oilmen Out of Business," William A. Johnson discussed the expansion of "small" refiners into gasoline marketing. *Congressional Record,* daily edition, September 25, 1975, p. S16760.

over the next three years.[72] This meant that there was a relative expansion of that component of the industry *not* enjoying economies of scale. It also contributed to a·shortage of unleaded gasoline, which many of the small refiners lacked the ability to produce.

EPCA apart, there remain a number of initiatives under the original Ford program and problems in getting them accepted that need to be discussed. Other related matters occupied the administration more or less intensively, though they were not part of the initial package for energy independence. In particular, there was the whole issue of the role of government in energy, certain international aspects of energy policy, and a complex of conflicts between national and regional interests, equity and efficiency, and energy and the environment. Passing mention has been made of these conflicts. It is convenient to treat them, together with the remaining administration initiatives and problems, under general heads, though the discussion must be considered as indicative only and cannot pretend to be complete.

The Role of Government in Energy

The embargo of 1973–74 caused temporary inconvenience to many, but it fell short of being a disaster. That is to say, it was just irritating enough to give rise to a search for scapegoats without being so painful as to create a nationwide front in the face of adversity. The integrated oil companies came under suspicion early, since producers with downstream operations stood to gain from sales of crude at higher prices. Because most of the data on reserves, production, refinery capacity, and stocks were industry data, and because movement from the industry into government posts and vice versa was not uncommon, the administration shared in this presumed guilt by association.

Government Dependence on Industry Data, Personnel

The last time the government and industry worked together in an operational way was on the Libyan issue in 1970–71, when the U.S. com-

72. For a time in 1976 those refineries with a capacity of less than 10,000 barrels a day were given special entitlements equivalent to about $2 on each barrel of input. In 1976–77 thirty-six refineries were built in the United States, nineteen of them in this category and only one with a capacity in excess of 50,000 barrels a day. See Tom Alexander, "How Little Oil Hit a Gusher on Capitol Hill," *Fortune,* August 14, 1978, pp. 148–52.

panies sought to isolate Libya. With hindsight, this clearly was a mis-calculation. Thereafter both parties tended to be on the defensive against sniping and increasingly concerted attacks by Congress and consumer organizations. Thus even though various industry advisory bodies con-tinued to exist in name, they played no real role in policy throughout much of the period 1969–76.

The catalyst for public anger toward the companies was increased profits at a time of shortages (gasoline lines). (In the first quarter of 1974 twenty of the major oil companies showed an average 79 percent gain in profits; and the average return on equity of the twenty-two largest oil and gas companies was higher in 1973 by 4.2 percent than the average of the preceding ten years.)[73] But the attacks were mounted against two different targets: the administration's dependence on industry for data (and personnel), and the integrated structure of the majors. The desir-ability of having independent data was a point not lost on the adminis-tration, but when it came to whether it was necessary or useful to break up the majors, the administration and industry stood together against Congress.

Traditionally the government had relied on the American Petroleum Institute for up-to-date information on oil imports, refinery runs, and in-ventories; on the institute and the American Gas Association for oil and gas reserve data, and on the coal industry for statistics in that area. The data, given voluntarily, were rarely checked, if ever. Moreover, up to a point, checking was rendered impossible because of industry fears about the release of proprietary information. Such fears gave rise to protective habits, among them the publishing of aggregate data only, to preclude the identification of individual companies. The dependence of govern-ment extended to every agency. The FPC relied on industry when it needed cost data for decisions about gas prices, the Interior Department looked to leaseholders when it wanted to assess the potential value of fuel reserves on federal lands, and the Oil Policy Committee depended on informal links with industry sources for guidance—for example, in selecting the appropriate differential between imported crude and product prices when it wanted to introduce an incentive to domestic refining in 1973.

The shortcomings inherent in this system of data collection had been recognized for at least half a century. The 1962 Petroleum Study Com-

73. See "Huge Profits During Arab Embargo," and "Record Oil Quarterly and 6-Month Profits," in Lester A. Sobel, ed., *Energy Crisis*, vol. 2: *1974–75* (Facts on File, 1977), pp. 63–65, 93–94.

mittee under President Kennedy, plus several follow-up groups within government, had tried to initiate changes. But an Office of Energy Data and Analysis was not created (in the Interior Department) until May 1973, and Simon, as head of the Federal Energy Office, was the first to insist on disaggregated data on a weekly basis, obtained directly from the companies themselves. The Nixon administration sought new data-collecting authority in 1974. Additional powers eventually were granted —going rather beyond what the administration had sought—in the Energy Supply and Environmental Coordination Act of 1974, the EPCA, and the Energy Conservation and Production Act of 1976 (ECPA). Collectively these provided for the comptroller general to conduct verification examinations of private persons or companies required to submit energy information to the FEA, Department of the Interior, or FPC. The Securities and Exchange Commission was empowered to take steps to assure the development and observance in the oil and gas industry of accounting practices that would permit the compilation of an energy data base (with separate categories for domestic and foreign operations and separate calculations of capital, revenue, and operating cost information) pertaining to prospecting, acquisition, exploration, development, and production. Under the ECPA a statutory office was established in the FEA for energy information and analysis. As noted earlier, the Ford and Nixon administrations did not dispute the desirability of more data, independently verifiable. Differences with Congress centered on the extent to which such data should be made available to the public.

One of the ironies of the developments described here, and of the greatly expanded regulatory functions of government with respect to energy in general and the oil industry in particular after the embargo of 1973, is that these responsibilities could have been exercised and the new data interpreted and applied more astutely with additional help from industry experts. But as noted, these developments came at the same time that both government and the industry were becoming more sensitive to possible conflict of interest charges that might be leveled against such special employees as oil industry executives temporarily coopted by government as advisers. Thus—to give just one example—in December 1973 Frank Zarb, then in the Federal Energy Office, alerted Simon to the "critical need for on-site industry expertise both at the national level and in the field." Yet Zarb also had to report that the acting attorney general had advised that there could be no guarantee that industry advisers and their companies would be immune from conflict of interest and even antitrust charges, and that in the absence of such a guarantee, industry counsel were advising against releasing personnel for government service.[74]

Divestiture

A second lightning rod for congressional displeasure was the vertical integration of the majors. In 1973, it will be recalled, a Federal Trade Commission complaint was filed against eight majors, charging them with anticompetitive practices and seeking divestiture of some of their refineries and pipelines. The next year a ten-year Justice Department investigation resulted in the filing of a suit against a major pipeline owner (Colonial). Congress, following a tentative start in mid-1973, with a divestiture amendment attached to the Alaska Pipeline Bill, soon took over the running, and in the next three years a succession of attempts was made to legislate divestiture.

The charges were various.[75] Concentration ratios were but part of the evidence, and by no means an unambiguous part. Evidence on joint ventures and interlocking directorates was also marshaled against the oil

74. Zarb to Simon, "Industry 'Advisors': Conflict of Interest," December 24, 1973, Gerald L. Parsky Files, Box 2, folder: Industry Advisory Committees (1973–74), U.S. Treasury. An excellent discussion of the data problem and the differences between the Nixon administration and Congress on the extent to which private energy data should be released is to be found in Bruce F. Freed, "Energy Report: Government Seeks Ways to Verify Energy Data," *National Journal Reports*, February 23, 1974, pp. 278–85, on which the paragraphs above draw.

75. No attempt is made here to evaluate these charges. The divestiture movement in Congress can be followed in James G. Phillips, "Justice Report: Oil Companies Threatened by Moves to Force Their Breakup," *National Journal Reports*, March 9, 1974, pp. 343–52; Joel Havemann, "Regulatory Report 8: Crisis Tightens Control of U.S. Energy Production," ibid., April 26, 1975, pp. 619–34; Robert Walters, "Political Focus: Petroleum and the People," ibid., October 18, 1975, p. 1457; Richard Corrigan, "Energy Report: Oil Company Divestiture Gains Support in Congress," ibid., December 6, 1975, pp. 1657–63; Corrigan, "Energy Focus: Another Swipe at Big Oil," ibid., February 14, 1976, p. 208; Corrigan, "Energy Focus: Jumping on the Divestiture Bandwagon," ibid., February 28, 1976, p. 278; Corrigan, "Energy Focus: No April Fool's Joke," ibid., April 10, 1976, p. 490; "Washington Update: Oil Divestiture Squeaks by in Judiciary Committee," ibid., June 19, 1976, p. 869; and Louis M. Kohlmeier, "Regulatory Focus: The Future of Divestiture," ibid., September 11, 1976, p. 1292. For the issues see Shyam Sunder, *Oil Industry Profits* (American Enterprise Institute for Public Policy Research, 1977); W. S. Moore, ed., *Horizontal Divestiture: Highlights of a Conference on Whether Oil Companies Should Be Prohibited from Owning Nonpetroleum Energy Resources* (American Enterprise Institute for Public Policy Research, 1977); and William A. Johnson and others, *Competition in the Oil Industry*, Energy Policy Research Project, Occasional Papers on Energy Policy (George Washington University, 1976), vol. 1.

companies. And all of this, whatever it might amount to, was reinforced by indirect evidence from events of the recent past: independent gasoline retailers denied supplies, regional shortages of heating oil, and frustrated efforts by independent companies to build pipelines or connect with those owned by majors. The Federal Trade Commission's charges also included exploitation by the majors of the tax laws. It was argued that use had been made of the depletion allowance to maintain relatively low prices on products, thus making life difficult for the independent refiners.

The debate on divestiture dragged on throughout Ford's term, with three twists being added. First, the charge was made more frequently that the majors, by virtue of their possessing downstream operations as well as crude production capability, were not unwilling parties to OPEC price increases. Second, attempts were made to include horizontal divestiture and pipeline divestiture in the total package. Finally, restrictions were proposed on joint ventures.

After the Treasury response to the Federal Trade Commission's charges during 1973 (see chapter 6), the Nixon and Ford administrations each maintained silence on the divestiture issue. It was widely believed that Ford would veto a divestiture measure. But while the Treasury and later the FEA did prepare some papers on the structure and competitive behavior of the petroleum industry—largely skeptical of the criticisms commonly made—and the latter were discussed by the Energy Resources Council and the President's Economic Policy Board meeting jointly in March 1976, these groups did not proceed to offer policy advice.[76] No legislation actually came before Ford, and it was not an important preoccupation of his energy advisers, though the possibility of punitive legislation involving divestiture among other things was used by Zarb as a reason why Ford should accept the pricing provisions of Senate bill 622. It seems likely that the main effect of the divestiture debate was to heighten uncertainty in the industry and delay the needed increases in supply.

Government-Sponsored Production of Energy?

The issue of government involvement in energy went beyond pricing and allocation controls and beyond the need to respond to attempts to

76. Memorandum for Energy Resources Council/Economic Policy Board Executive Committee, Frank Zarb, "Congressional Divestiture Proposals," March 15, 1976, with attachments (FEA fact sheet, "The Structure and Competitive Behavior of the Petroleum Industry," and discussion paper, "Competition and Concentration"), CEA Records, Greenspan Files, GRFL. The meeting merely resolved that the matter be studied further by an interdepartmental group at the assistant secretary level. Russell to MacAvoy, "ERC Meeting, 3/16/76," CEA Records, MacAvoy Files, GRFL.

decide on the appropriate structure of the oil industry. The Ford administration inherited certain commitments in the form of energy R&D programs and had to decide whether it wanted to change the emphases or the degree of federal government involvement. For the most part Ford did not alter the broad research priorities as they had been established under Nixon, though the allocations to conservation and to coal research jumped sharply in fiscal year 1976, the funding for solar energy projects leapt in the same year by more than 500 percent, and Ford asked for a special loan guarantee authority of $2 billion for synthetic fuels research in a fiscal 1976 supplemental request.[77] But by far the most significant decision in this area was one to support a $100 billion Energy Resources Finance Corporation (ERFCO), as proposed by Vice-President Nelson Rockefeller. The central issue here was whether the federal government should take the initiative, and that on a massive scale, in supplying loan monies or guarantees to private industry for projects that the market had not underwritten. Much the same problem posed itself on a smaller scale in connection with the need to relieve the electric utilities from certain financial pressures. And the issue was again much the same, though tempered by other considerations, in the case of deciding whether part responsibility for the enrichment of uranium should be handed over to the private sector. These three matters—ERFCO, an electric utilities bailout, and uranium enrichment—will be discussed in turn as illustrations of aspects of a persistent concern of the Ford administration with the degree to which government should be involved in the energy sector.

Rockefeller requested the Domestic Council Review Group in May 1975 to identify five important energy projects that were delayed for financial reasons and to find appropriate financing mechanisms, using a proposed federal corporation, to speed their development (and at the same time attack unemployment). Commenting on this, CEA energy staff economist Milton Russell observed that to the extent that delays exist they are the result of bad regulation, uncertainty about prospective

77. The federal energy R&D budgets for fiscal years 1975, 1976, and 1977 are collected in *A National Plan for Energy Research, Development and Demonstration: Creating Energy Choices for the Future*, ERDA 76-1, Energy Research and Development Administration (GPO, 1976). Useful discussion is in Richard Corrigan and James G. Phillips, "Science and Energy: Research and Development Is Allotted $1.6 Billion of $2.24 Billion Power Total," *National Journal Reports*, February 8, 1975, pp. 205–08; and "Energy: New Programs Push Up Energy Budget, Including 30 Per Cent Hike for R&D," ibid., January 31, 1976, pp. 141–42.

government action, failures of state utility commissions, and poor economics (for example, projects are undertaken prematurely). Russell argued that an increase in federal funding would mask the real symptoms and induce inefficiency, as well as causing inflation and being a less effective means of helping against unemployment than a tax cut.[78]

In a joint memorandum one month later Russell and Paul MacAvoy drew attention to additional problems with an Energy Resources Finance Corporation. Commercial projects, they suggested, would go to ERFCO because the capital charges would be lower; but these projects would have eventuated anyway, so no net gain in energy production would result. Noncommercial projects would be dusted off and presented to ERFCO, resulting in wasted resources. R&D projects not yet at the commercial stage could be pushed too fast, with resulting accidents and cost overruns. In addition, should ERFCO succeed in lifting energy capacity, shortages would occur elsewhere. A cost would thus be imposed on society in terms of forgone outputs currently valued above energy. In other words, if energy capacity is to be increased via subsidies, the benefits must be over and above any direct gain in terms of extra capacity.[79]

CEA spokesmen were merely the most vocal of skeptics within the administration. They received muted support from the FEA and open support from Treasury Secretary Simon. A draft memorandum from OMB Director James T. Lynn suggests that support may also have come from the OMB. This memorandum pointed to some of the political dangers in a free-standing ERFCO: Congress would most likely give it an extended life and excessive resources and would channel its activities in particular directions (for example, by requiring certain allocations to help solar energy research).[80]

On the basic question of whether additional financing was needed, there

78. Russell to Greenspan, "Domestic Council Review Group: Energy and Resources Policy and Finance," May 7, 1975, Russell personal files.

79. MacAvoy and Russell to Greenspan, "Energy Resources Finance Corporation (ERFCO)" June 20, 1975, CEA Records, Greenspan Files, GRFL. A more detailed statement along the same lines was prepared later. Burton Malkiel and others to Greenspan, "Analysis of ERFCO," August 22, 1975, Russell personal files.

80. Zarb and John Hill of the FEA privately were as skeptical of ERFCO as were the CEA and the Treasury, but for obvious reasons they could not so openly dismiss Rockefeller's scheme. A hint of what the OMB's position might have become is in James T. Lynn to the President (draft), "Energy Resources Finance Corporation," August 8, 1975, Russell personal files. The Treasury's views are in Simon to Zarb, "Critical Analysis of the Proposal to Establish the Energy Resources Finance Corporation (ERFCO)," n.d. (copy in Johnson personal files).

was no disagreement in the administration on outside estimates that the energy sector seemed likely to require capital amounting to about 20 percent of total business fixed investment during the period 1975–84. This was in line with the post–World War II average. Why, then, was a special effort called for?

Despite these doubts from his own economic and budgetary advisers, Ford urged that the idea be pursued. By late summer an Energy Independence Authority had been conceived as the vehicle to carry out Rockefeller's plan. The President announced the new group at a meeting of workers of the construction trades on September 22, representing it as a stimulant to economic growth and a means to create new jobs, end runaway energy prices imposed by foreigners, and restore "control over our own destiny."[81] The Energy Independence Authority was to have $25 billion in equity (appropriated gradually by Congress) and $75 billion in government-backed borrowing authority. It would be self-liquidating over ten years.

Republicans in Congress reacted negatively to this plan. The idea of a fiscally conservative President proposing to allocate $100 billion of GNP over ten years with less than the usual congressional and budgetary review offended those who had been supportive of Ford's efforts to move to a free market in petroleum. Democrats also dismissed the plan, described by one as "grossly inflated, fiscally irresponsible and susceptible to political manipulation."[82] This combined opposition was sufficient to kill the administration's initiative.

Electric Utilities Bailout

The administration also found itself at odds with Congress over proposals to help the electric utilities out from under their financial difficulties, with Congress leaning toward the views of some consumer groups

81. Office of the White House Press Secretary, "Remarks at AFL-CIO Building and Construction Trades Meeting, San Francisco, California, September 22, 1975." See also Prudence Crewdson, "Energy and Environment: $100-Billion Energy Agency Formally Proposed," *Congressional Quarterly Weekly Report,* October 18, 1975, pp. 2237–38.

82. Congressman Henry S. Reuss, chairman of the House Banking, Currency and Housing Committee, quoted in Crewdson, "Energy and Environment: $100-Billion Energy Agency Formally Proposed," p. 2238. Senator Edward M. Kennedy was equally critical of the Energy Independence Authority proposal; *Congressional Record,* vol. 121 (October 8, 1975), pp. 32175–77.

that "subsistence" electricity should be supplied to families at low cost and that the utilities should not be granted the right to pass on increased fuel costs to consumers but should instead be urged to experiment with "inverted rate" structures.

The utilities question was brought to Ford's attention toward the end of 1974, by which time a serious cash flow problem in this sector had developed. The utilities had met the difficulty by deferring or canceling plans for new plants; but this stopgap solution at first sight seemed to threaten to upset the nation's future energy balance.

Ford himself, it will be recalled, had addressed the problems of the utility companies in his January energy proposals to Congress. He had asked that the investment tax credit be increased temporarily to 12 percent, a request that was subsequently met part way. Ford had also included a Utilities Act of 1975 as title VII of his omnibus energy bill. This act requested authority to reduce the regulatory lag at the state level and to allow the utilities to include construction work in progress in the rate base. During the first part of 1975 the President's Labor-Management Committee under John T. Dunlop pursued the matter further, as a challenge to the nation involving both energy supplies and jobs. On May 21 the committee submitted a package of recommendations, including a reiteration of the advice that the investment tax credit be increased to a full 12 percent for utilities, that the credit be extended to depreciation on construction outlays as they are made (provided such costs are included in the rate base), that pollution control facilities be granted accelerated write-off status and that tax liability be deferred on dividends reinvested in new issues of common utilities stock.[83]

During the spring of 1975 the Treasury and the FEA also investigated the problem. The Treasury reported that by the end of 1974, 235 plant deferrals or cancellations had occurred. Of this total, some 68 percent of all nuclear plant deferrals or cancellations and some 48 percent of fossil fuel plant deferrals or cancellations could be related in part at least to financial distress. The FEA judged that some 120,000 jobs might have been forfeited. One Treasury analyst suggested that the utilities needed

83. Decision memorandum, L. William Seidman to the President, "Labor-Management Committee's Tax Incentive Proposals for Electric Utility Construction," June 6, 1975, CEA Records, Greenspan Files, GRFL. This memorandum outlines the history of the administration's involvement with the problem and lists the Labor-Management Committee's proposals.

"substantial and timely financial relief,"[84] and the FEA decided that action additional to the provisions of the Utilities Act would be desirable. The most controversial of the FEA's recommended steps was a proposal to issue national guidelines for electricity rate-making. In a memorandum to the Energy Resources Council Zarb also listed several other far-reaching options, including a federal guarantee of utility debt, government purchase of utility stock, tax-free stock dividends, and government purchase or construction of power plants (to be leased back to utilities).[85] It was also proposed that legislation for a Utility Finance Corporation be prepared to be submitted to Congress should the other initiatives fail.[86] The feeling in the FEA was that if the administration did not propose some solution, Congress would fill the vacuum with a worse alternative, which made a Utility Finance Corporation the best means of dealing with the pressing needs of the utilities in a *politically* satisfactory way.

Amidst much administration opposition to the FEA's position, the CEA found itself once again in the role of chief nay-sayer. CEA staffers rejected the political cast given the problem by the FEA and questioned whether the whole issue had not been misperceived. They drew attention to the fact that industry projections of electricity demand were based largely on demographic trends, with inadequate allowance for the role of past reductions in the real price in stimulating demand. With a reasonable allowance for price, it looked as if "the currently well publicized cancellations and postponements of investment plans by utilities may be consistent rather than inconsistent with long term energy policy goals, i.e., the consequence may be to avoid a financially sicker industry rather than to retard the attainment of 'energy independence.' "[87] The CEA did not deny that revenues had failed to keep pace with costs and that a genuine cash flow

84. Alan M. Arsht to Simon, "Analysis of Utility Construction Delays," March 20, 1975, Russell personal files.

85. Zarb (through Morton) to the President, "Electric Utility Financing Problems: Additional Government Initiatives" (draft decision memorandum distributed to the Energy Resources Council, April 7, 1975), Russell personal files. A subsequent draft of the Zarb memorandum, dated May 21, 1975, is in CEA Records, Greenspan Files, GRFL.

86. Zarb favored a Utility Finance Corporation despite general reluctance in the Energy Resources Council to undertake radical interventionist or precipitate action. See Milton Russell to Greenspan, "ERC Meeting of 4/17," April 17, 1975, CEA Records, Greenspan Files, GRFL.

87. Allan Pulsipher to Seevers, "The Short Term Financial Difficulties of the Electric Utilities and Long-Run Energy Policy," September 12, 1974, Russell personal files.

problem existed. But it attributed the revenue shortfall to regulatory lags, a disinclination on the part of state utility commissioners to raise rates in the face of consumer opposition, and to a decline in expected sales due to higher rates and the current recession. Drawing its conclusions from this analysis, the CEA argued that no case had been made that the condition of the utilities was so desperate as to jeopardize needed supplies in the future. Moreover, even if that were a danger, the effects would fall primarily on the localities directly involved, and it was up to these localities to judge whether the effects of blackouts were more or less onerous than bearing the costs of adequate capacity. In short, no vital national interest was involved, and no convincing case had been made for any, let alone for federal, financial assistance or federal involvement in rate-making.[88]

The CEA's cautionary advice may have served to keep the Energy Resources Council from making precipitate decisions; at any rate the administration did not seek a new federal financing agency to help the utilities. In December 1975 Congress rejected an authorization for guarantees to implement a synthetic fuels commercialization program. In the light of this rebuff and the subsequent rejection of the proposed Energy Independence Authority, the administration's reticence seems wise. The matter of national guidelines for electricity rate-making, however, remained a live issue, even entering into the presidential campaign in the fall of 1976. By that time Congress had become actively involved with the problem, but less with the aim of bailing out the utilities than with effecting a shift toward peak-load pricing, eliminating rate advantages to bulk industrial users, and reducing the large average wastage (during 1975 the utilities averaged 49 percent use of capacity).[89] Here the lines of battle were drawn, but no legislative action was taken before the end of Ford's term.

Uranium Enrichment

The issue of uranium enrichment had been under study long before it was taken up in earnest by the Ford administration. The need for a decision arose out of earlier Atomic Energy Commission projections that one

88. Milton Russell to Greenspan, April 10, 1975, CEA Records, Greenspan Files, GRFL; also two memorandums dated April 18, 1975, both in CEA Records, Staff Files, GRFL, and one dated June 5, 1975, Russell personal files—all setting out Russell's views on the electric utilities bailout.

89. Robert J. Samuelson, "Economic Report: Battle Lines Are Being Generated for Reform of Electric Utility Rates," *National Journal Reports,* October 16, 1976, pp. 1474–78.

or more additional plants would be needed by 1980. Given lead times, this meant that a decision would have to be made in 1975.[90]

The CEA's position under both Nixon and Ford was that the nuclear fuel industry should be competitive. When the matter came to a head in mid-1975 the CEA's energy economists argued that the new enrichment facility should be in private hands and even that the existing three plants should be sold off.[91] In June Ford announced a proposal to allow the Energy Research and Development Agency to assist private firms to build and operate enrichment facilities. But a General Accounting Office study of this proposal, without taking sides on the issue of privatization, urged that the next increment of enrichment capacity be achieved by adding on to the existing government gaseous diffusion plant.[92] This was due in part to shortcomings the GAO felt characterized a specific proposal by Bechtel-Goodyear, operating as Uranium Enrichment Associates. The proposed legislation did not confine the Energy Research and Development Agency to dealing with the associates nor did it restrict discussions to the associates' first scheme, and the CEA felt that the argument should be about quite different things. It was not even appropriate to define the issue simply in terms of whether the next plant should be private. The CEA argued that the true question was: if the next plant is not privately built, will the diffusion technology to be employed not be foreclosed to private development in the future? For if the centrifuge technology ran into development problems and private companies were excluded from the diffusion technology, not only would privatization in the industry be pushed back in

90. A Presidential Task Force on Uranium Enrichment Facilities reported in August 1969, treating the question of private ownership of enrichment facilities in an open pro-con manner. By 1973 the Atomic Energy Commission, according to Peter Flanigan, was "proceeding with its efforts to increase the opportunities for industry to build the fourth enrichment facility," though the desired relationship between government and industry had still not been determined. Letter, Flanigan to Congressman Craig Hosmer, circa February 2, 1973 (copy), CEA Records, MacAvoy Files, GRFL. For a useful treatment of the background and issues see Thomas Gale Moore, *Uranium Enrichment and Public Policy,* AEI-Hoover Policy Study 25 (American Enterprise Institute for Public Policy Research and the Hoover Institution on War, Revolution and Peace, 1978).

91. Milton Russell to Greenspan, "ERDA Draft Bill," June 18, 1975, CEA Records, MacAvoy Files, GRFL.

92. Comptroller General of the United States, *Report to the Congress: Evaluation of the Administration's Proposal for Government Assistance to Private Uranium Enrichment Groups,* Report RED-76-36 (General Accounting Office, 1975).

time but the technical options open to it would turn on the centrifuge technology alone, with an added risk to the nation that the private companies might all turn out to be high-cost ones.[93]

In this instance industry itself was less than enthusiastic about taking on the $2 billion-plus plant without wide-ranging guarantees from the government. Moreover, the antinuclear lobbies across the nation mobilized during 1976. And when candidate Carter began to profess the greater concern on nuclear safety issues and the worldwide spread of nuclear energy (including enrichment and recycling technology), the Ford administration demurred on development at the back end of the fuel cycle.[94]

This is a further illustration of the way short-term political considerations deflected the course of energy policy. What stands out from the record, and the more so because of the way it contrasts with the FEA's pragmatic and often activist advice, is the purity and sophistication of the economic analysis of energy problems emanating from the CEA. Not that the issues were all economic in nature; but the CEA played a singular role in clarifying those that were and in separating economic from other considerations.[95] That some such source of purist advice was anything but superfluous emerges just as clearly as in the ways considered above when one turns from the FEA to the State Department's involvement with energy.

93. MacAvoy and Russell to Greenspan, "GAO Report on the Administration's Proposal for Assistance to Private Enrichment Groups," December 6, 1975, CEA Records, Greenspan Files, GRFL.

94. James G. Phillips, "Energy Report: 1976 Is the 'Go or No Go' Year for Nuclear Industry," *National Journal Reports,* January 24, 1976, pp. 91–97; and Richard Corrigan, "Energy Focus: A No-Go on Nuclear," ibid., November 6, 1976, p. 1608.

95. It is perhaps desirable to point out that "purity" in this context means neither knee-jerk "promarket" responses nor "blackboard" economics and theory without reference to institutional realities. Greenspan insisted on highly professional analysis by his staff, and he never discouraged the use of whatever the analysis might show from being used as a guide to policy. A belief in efficiency was a hallmark of the Greenspan CEA, but market solutions were the result of analysis rather than a starting point. What the CEA at times found itself opposing was policy initiatives in which the economic analysis was incomplete or so bound up with other considerations as to allow no separate weighting of the elements relevant to a decision to be made. In this regard a further qualification is in order. In such matters as energy the CEA was in the position of reacting to proposals made elsewhere. As a reactor, usually overwhelmed by other tasks, the CEA responded only when it had objections. A danger of relying on the CEA records is that one almost inevitably derives a picture of opposition that can seem both strident and unremitting. The other side of the story is that the records are blank when the CEA supported initiatives.

Energy and Foreign Policy

Henry Kissinger, it will be recalled, had an opportunity to influence energy policy in the spring of 1973 when, as assistant to the President for national security affairs, he was appointed along with Treasury Secretary George Shultz and John Ehrlichman to form an energy advisory triumvirate. The State Department's serious involvement with energy only began, however, many months later when Thomas O. Enders became an adviser to Kissinger after the latter became secretary of state.[96]

In May 1974 Enders became assistant secretary of state for economic and business affairs, but he had acted unofficially for some time before that. He personified the qualities that have always set the State Department somewhat apart: he had a first-rate mind and was able to regard domestic policy wrangling with a certain aloofness. When Kissinger recalled him from a post in Cambodia Enders set about identifying the chief areas of policy within which his division might expect to exert an influence. Energy was at the top of his list. In the midst of much ado and confusion about energy, the State Department was able to pitch in with an international program based on a few simple but sweeping ideas.

Kissinger was already enthused about the notion of energy independence, and Enders was able to persuade him that in order to inject some content into the idea of 1974 being the "Year of Europe," he needed an issue such as energy policy.[97] In the wake of the dismay produced by the embargo, the United States could take the lead in integrating energy policy in the Western industrialized nations.

96. In the absence of documents this and subsequent judgments about the origins of, and motives governing, State Department actions must be regarded as "conjectural history" at best. The discussion draws heavily on conversations with Charles Cooper and James W. Reddington. Thomas O. Enders offered helpful corrective comments on a draft of this section. For the State Department's initial response to the embargo see Tietenberg, *Energy Planning and Policy*, pp. 73, 84–88.

97. Kissinger unveiled the Year of Europe in a speech at the annual luncheon of the Associated Press in New York, April 23, 1973. One historian of American diplomacy described it as "an Atlanticist concept" or "an American project . . . for a sort of moral and intellectual redefinition of the Western alliance to see NATO into its second quarter-century (which began in 1974), and to take account of the enhanced strength and status of Japan, as well as Western Europe; perhaps even to parlay the Atlantic Alliance into a sort of Oceanic Alliance for the advanced industrialized non-communist world." Coral Bell, *The Diplomacy of Detente: The Kissinger Era* (St. Martin's Press, 1977), p. 105.

This idea fitted readily into what Kissinger was already advocating at the time of the embargo—some form of coordinated response to OPEC by the consuming nations. At a meeting of foreign and finance ministers of the United States, Japan, Norway, Canada, and the Common Market countries (except France) called by Kissinger early in 1974, an Energy Coordinating Group was established. Subsequent negotiations within the group led to an International Energy Program, whereby the members would maintain reserves of petroleum, develop mandatory demand restraints to be applied during future emergencies, and join an international allocation system for oil-sharing at such times. Such a program, if it ever was to work, would require careful organization and management. The Oil Committee of the Organisation for Economic Co-operation and Development was thought to be too rule-bound, and Enders suggested that an independent organization be formed within the OECD.

There is some suggestion that Kissinger and Enders saw the International Energy Agency, as the organization came to be called, as a sort of international Department of Energy. A national commitment to the International Energy Program was required by October 1974, and Kissinger and Enders, convinced that the United States would join, set about tailoring U.S. domestic energy policy, where necessary, to the needs of their international brainchild.[98]

This was most apparent in a dispute that erupted between Kissinger and Simon during the forming of Ford's initiatives in the fall of 1974. But it was reflected in less obvious ways as well. As successive drafts of the allocation formula under the International Energy Program were developed, the United States was under pressure to accept a change in the formula from import- to consumption-based weights. The former favored the United States, the latter, Europe. The CEA pointed out that for the case of a general embargo this could mean, under one proposed formula, that the United States would be under obligation to export 0.4 million barrels a day of domestic oil, as against an entitlement to imports of 1.9 million barrels a day under the import-based weights formula. This gave

98. The State Department's first move was to determine that accession to the International Energy Agency would be through an executive agreement and not by a treaty subject to Senate ratification. Assistant to the Secretary for International Activities to the Assistant Secretary, Energy and Minerals, "Briefing by the Department of State on Status of the International Energy Program," October 18, 1974, Secretary of the Interior's Files, Subject File: Minerals and Fuels–Commodities and Products, Petroleum, Department of the Interior.

rise to the question of whether the cost-benefit balance had not shifted so much as to call into question U.S. participation.[99]

Disagreement on the basis for sharing had bedevilled efforts to negotiate an emergency oil-sharing agreement between Europe and the United States during the 1950s and 1960s. Rather than allow the latest attempt to fail for the same reason, Enders sought to redirect the negotiations. Instead of pressing directly for a sharing arrangement he proposed that each government should undertake commitments as to how it would cut consumption in the event of a cutoff or enforced reduction in supplies and as to how much it would seek to build up emergency stocks. It turned out to be possible to reach agreement that stocks should be proportionate to imports, and once consumption cuts and emergency stock drawdowns were agreed upon, actual shares were determined without it being necessary to bargain over them.[100]

In the formulation actually adopted import weights turned out to be much more important than consumption weights. This made it no less desirable that the United States tighten its belt, and Kissinger became a strong supporter of import reductions as a key element in the Ford program. Conservation via import cuts also fitted State Department preconceptions in another way. The department acted as if it believed that world oil prices could be talked down. One premise underlying such a belief was that excess crude oil production capacity would put pressure on OPEC.[101] Conservation and increased supply in the United States itself could serve jointly to promote this end. But of these two complementary options, conservation was the more likely to make the threat to OPEC credible in the short term.

A second strand in State Department thinking was the desirability of maintaining international stability.[102] This made it important for the element of confrontation implicit in efforts to establish the International Energy Program to be balanced by certain assurances to OPEC members. Enders is said to have persuaded Kissinger that a guaranteed floor price

99. "CEA Comments on Latest (8/23/74) Draft of IEP," n.d., CEA Records, MacAvoy Files, GRFL.

100. Thomas O. Enders to the author, February 1, 1980. Compare memorandum, Enders to Rogers Morton, "IEA Long-Term Cooperative Program," December 11, 1975, CEA Records, MacAvoy Files, GRFL.

101. Compare with the views of M. A. Adelman, "Oil Prices in the Long Run (1963–75)," *Journal of Business,* vol. 37 (April 1964), pp. 143–61.

102. These two parts of the department's world view were spelled out in Milton Russell, "Comments on Briefing Book for Camp David," June 6, 1975, Ford-CEA Records, Staff Files, GRFL.

written into the program could serve both ends. If the consumer nations would agree to this idea, and it seemed likely that excess capacity would develop, then the argument could be used in negotiations with OPEC that the future world price in the absence of an International Energy Program (with floor price) might be substantially lower than the agreed upon minimum. The consumer nations might bargain for immediate price reductions in return for longer-term purchase agreements consistent with the built-in floor price. The floor price would thus strengthen the hand of the consumers while at the same time reassuring OPEC and guarding against possible punitive OPEC responses to the International Energy Program, with their destabilizing consequences. The floor price, in addition, could serve to guarantee domestic investment in expanded energy supplies, under conditions of rising costs.[103]

Treasury Secretary Simon, who favored aggressive attempts to break OPEC and bring prices down, objected to the floor price idea on the ground that it would introduce an unnecessary rigidity into oil markets. In particular it would prevent consumers from benefiting from possible future price reductions, and at the level of $7–$8 a barrel being suggested by the State Department, producers would be given an unnecessary subsidy. Moreover, a fixed tariff could be devised to achieve most of the supply incentive sought, without precluding consumers from enjoying future price reductions.[104]

At the Camp David discussions in mid-December 1974 on the options for energy policy one important agreement reached was that policy should be based on the assumption that OPEC would *not* be broken and that high prices would continue. This was a breakthrough for the CEA, which until then had been almost alone in arguing this position. CEA's Russell held that "no reliable inferences can be drawn with reference to OPEC disarray based on projections of surplus OPEC production capacity." The reason was that "the cartel may simply adjust its sharing or pricing rules whenever a member *approaches* the decision point, and hence avoid final rupture. . . . The cartel can continue indefinitely, adjusting to changing market con-

---

103. Tietenberg, *Energy Planning and Policy,* pp. 84–91. See also Richard S. Frank, "Energy Report: Ford Seeks Price Guarantees for Fuel to Aid U.S. Development," *National Journal Reports,* March 8, 1975, pp. 357–66.

104. Tietenberg, *Energy Planning and Policy.* See also Parsky to Simon, "Estimates of New Oil Production Costs and Major Arguments against Price Floor," December 20, 1974, Parsky Records, Box 12, Folder: Energy—New Oil Production Costs. This memorandum reflected the views of Treasury economist Thomas D. Willett.

ditions but retaining price above marginal cost by restricting output."[105] The CEA was aware that it could not support a strong conclusion to the effect that prices would *not* fall, but it was concerned to show that the State Department view of the world was also untested and that of the two positions, the department's was the more risky, since it implied that oil prices were a matter of politics only.[106]

Simon and Kissinger were parties to the Camp David decision, and in principle this should have ended their dispute over the floor price. The State Department, however, apparently had no intention of giving up the idea, and the debate continued throughout December and even in the President's presence during the December 27 discussions between Ford and his advisers at Vail. Ford settled on a compromise. Title IX of the Energy Independence Act of 1975 asked only for standby authority to use tariffs, quotas, or a price floor should prices decline sufficiently to threaten the commercial viability of substantial quantities of domestic petroleum from *conventional* sources.

It very soon became clear that the State Department was bent on pressing much stronger language on the International Energy Agency. In a February 3 speech to the National Press Club in Washington, D.C., Kissinger proposed that a common minimum price on imports be set in the immediate future for all parties to the International Energy Program. Kissinger gave as one reason for the proposal that it would help underwrite investment in conventional *and* alternative sources of energy. Two days after the speech Enders presented this proposal as U.S. administration policy to a meeting of the International Energy Program member nation representatives in Paris.[107]

105. Russell to Greenspan, "Inferences about OPEC Cartel Breakdown," December 5, 1974, and two complementary memorandums; Russell to Greenspan, "Conversation with James T. Jensen," December 11, 1974; and Russell to Greenspan, "Inferences about OPEC Cartel Breakdown," December 12, 1974; all in CEA Records, Greenspan Files, GRFL. Although it has been presented in the text as an argument about strategy toward OPEC, the debate between Kissinger and Simon at the same time reflected doctrinal (and personal) differences. Simon was persuaded that domestic decontrol would create a significant increase in oil supplies within a reasonably short period. He was also deeply concerned about introducing anything like commodity agreements into oil, since that might be taken as a signal for a continued general regulation of oil prices, which he believed to be undesirable. I am indebted to Thomas Enders for reminding me of this.

106. OPEC production cuts in late 1974 suggested, as Parsky put it, that OPEC was "not completely immune from market forces." Parsky to Simon, "Estimates of New Oil Production Costs." The CEA position was in line with this view.

107. Rowland Evans and Robert Novak, *Washington Post,* February 13, 1975; and Frank, "Energy Report: Ford Seeks Price Guarantees."

Kissinger had ample reason for pursuing the floor price plan. If the CEA were correct in assuming that prices would not fall, when it was still important to secure the International Energy Agency's acceptance of a minimum price in order to make sure that Great Britain, as producer-consumer, would support the International Energy Program. On the other hand should prices fall in the future, it would be useful to have secured Japan's adherence to the program, since it was known that the Japanese favored bilateral arrangements and could be expected to try to undercut the other consumer nations if the cartel broke. Either way, if the International Energy Agency was worth establishing—and Kissinger held to his initial view that it was useful to have a coordinated consumer group to undermine OPEC—then agreement on a price floor could only serve to cement relationships among the members.

The sequence of events just outlined really was extraordinary. The United States had been committed to the International Energy Program at the behest of the State Department. This virtually forced the United States to take steps toward conservation and reducing imports, even though it was not at all clear at the time that Congress would approve the use of *efficient* import control devices (such as price decontrol and tariffs). Moreover, the State Department, presumably with Ford's knowledge but not that of the Energy Resources Council, had moved to commit the administration to a floor price scheme, to take *immediate* effect. This meant that if prices later broke and the United States wished to import and consume more, holding domestic capacity in reserve, that option would be foreclosed. Finally, Kissinger's National Press Club speech seemed to commit the United States to a floor price sufficient to encourage not merely conventional energy sources, as administration supporters of title IX of the President's omnibus energy bill envisaged, but alternative sources as well. This could mean a price high enough to protect synthetic fuels. The President had set a goal in his State of the Union Message of achieving a capacity of 1 million barrels a day in synthetic fuels by 1985.[108] But in early 1975 it had not been decided how this might best be achieved. The matter was under study by an interdepartmental task force. Even so, the CEA's position, for one, was becoming clear: it would be preferable to use capital grants rather than price guarantees over the whole life of a synfuels plant in the case of such uncertain, but probably very high-cost, ventures. Finally, if price supports were to be granted, Congress could be expected to step in with requirements concerning oversight and probably pricing, which might delay or frustrate the return to a free market in

108. *Public Papers: Ford, 1975,* bk. 1, p. 42.

energy. In short, as a stunned Milton Russell reported in an open memorandum to the CEA shortly after Kissinger's February 3 speech, "under the guise of foreign policy endeavors . . . large segments of domestic energy policy are being set by the State Department."[109]

The administration was involved in international energy problems on several other fronts during 1975. The import policy on liquified natural gas was discussed in the Energy Resources Council on numerous occasions, concern being expressed about a possible gas cartel that, unlike OPEC, might *lower* the price so as to undercut synthetic gas from coal and Alaskan gas. One decision was that financial incentives to those engaged in liquified natural gas projects should be withdrawn.[110] In the fall an abortive round of negotiations ensued in an attempt to obtain Russian oil at a discount in exchange for wheat.[111] The administration also continued to be preoccupied with OPEC. A preparatory Producer-Consumer Petroleum Conference in April 1975 demonstrated consumer solidarity but reached an impasse when the delegations from OPEC and the less developed countries stood firm on a proposal to treat raw materials and development problems on an equal footing with energy.[112] The price floor eventually gained acceptance by the International Energy Agency but not without opposition. Members, after all, were left free to choose from a wide range of devices to make the floor price effective.[113] Skepticism within the administration about the State Department's approach to OPEC led to some moves, nominally coordinated by an ad hoc interdepartmental group, to explore ways of encouraging investment by OPEC members in the United States. One argument used in favor of this alternative approach to weakening OPEC was that for member countries with a low capacity to absorb

109. Russell to the CEA, February 13, 1975, CEA Records, Staff Files, GRFL.

110. Summaries by Zarb of Executive Committee meetings of the Energy Resources Council, March 7 and October 9, 1975, and January 5, 1976, CEA Records, Greenspan Files, GRFL.

111. Memorandums, Russell to Greenspan, October 31 and November 4, 1975, CEA Records, Staff Files, GRFL.

112. Russell to the CEA, "Producer-Consumer Conference," March 10, 1975, ibid.; unsigned memorandum by Russell, "International Energy Policy," April 23, 1975, Russell personal files; and Russell to Greenspan, "International Energy Issues in International Economic Reviews," May 1, 1975, ibid.

113. At a meeting on March 20, 1975, members of the International Energy Agency accepted the floor price concept but specified that the safeguard price should be aimed at stimulating and protecting investments in the bulk of *conventional* sources. It was also agreed that members would be free to use measures of their own choice to establish the safeguard price (for example, tariff, variable tariff, quotas).

oil revenues, the option of safe investments abroad might cause them to be less willing to accept production cutbacks.[114]

By year's end the State Department had lost interest and most of the action in the international sphere was over.

The concern expressed by CEA's Russell in his protests to Council members about the State Department's role had been twofold. On the one hand he felt it unwise for the nation to be led into energy decisions simply because they were implications of foreign policy initiatives. On the other hand he saw this as part of a larger problem, "namely, wide Administration consultation appears to be missing in formulating *domestic* energy policy."[115] The State Department, he seemed to be suggesting, might have been checked had the Energy Resources Council functioned effectively in coordinating agency opinion. This was an indirect complaint against the FEA. The CEA files contain much evidence of frustration at receiving position papers from the FEA (and from the Energy Research and Development Agency) too late for comments to make any difference or at having to defend dubious numbers once these had already been made public.

In the remaining domestic problems discussed below, the problem was not that consultation was inadequate but that there simply were too many parties to try to satisfy.

The Elusive Common Interest in Energy Matters

How did this come about? There is nothing surprising in the suggestion that conflicting claims are the stuff of political activity. And no special elaboration is needed to convince the reader that environmentalists saw the energy problem differently from the proponents of energy independence or that regions or states with energy resources often were at odds with consumer states. But it should also be apparent following the extended discussion of decontrol above and the account of the State Department's role in energy policy that energy had become highly politicized. From the congressional side, as has been noted, this meant that the real or

114. Russell to the CEA, "Producer-Consumer Conference." The interagency group was led by Gerald Parsky. It represented a continuation of overtures by Simon to Saudi Arabia immediately following the embargo. These earned him the opprobrium of Kissinger.

115. Russell to the CEA, February 13, 1975, CEA Records, Staff Files, GRFL.

perceived interests of consumers or business constituents were paramount in attempted resolutions of energy problems, with the general result that oversight, regulation, and transfer arrangements were extended in various directions to protect certain groups (such as small refineries) and to keep energy prices below their market level. From the side of the administration, while it was clearly seen that an efficient solution involved dismantling regulations and allowing market prices to clear energy markets, there was great reluctance to accept the full consequences of this view.

CEA's energy economist might point out, for example, that "the social cost of energy is the marginal cost of incremental supplies (foreign oil) *plus* an insecurity premium *plus* uncovered external costs of energy consumption (such as pollution)."[116] And the Ford administration could accept the fact that allowing domestic prices to rise to the international level and establishing a petroleum reserve against interruption to supplies were desirable in principle. But when it came to the problems associated with achieving clean air and with expanding offshore oil production, the administration seemed to balk at the implications of internalizing the uncovered external costs.

In principle, external costs can be internalized by making "polluters" pay. In the absence of a market, government can move to see that some sort of compensation is made to injured parties. Either way, prices, if allowed to reflect the action, should rise. Though it is nowhere recorded, the administration undoubtedly was sensitive to the likelihood that getting consumers to accept price rises to cover environmental externalities—that is, price increases over and above those implied by decontrol—would involve it in yet more battles with Congress and with consumers directly, either in the form of class action suits or at the polls in 1976. The administration's chosen strategy was to avoid broad confrontations of this sort in favor of smaller, concentrated battles. Thus it pushed ahead with expanding the use of coal by mandating a switch by utilities from oil to coal,[117] and it sought to accommodate the best organized or most vocal elements of opposition to OCS exploration and development. It was partly as a result of its own preferred strategy that the administration found itself having to deal with an impossible range of sectional interests.

116. Russell to Greenspan and MacAvoy, "Comments on Briefing Book for Camp David," June 6, 1975, CEA Records, MacAvoy Files, GRFL.

117. Philip Verleger to MacAvoy, "Material for the Report" (on regulatory reform), August 25, 1976, CEA Records, Greenspan Files, GRFL. Verleger judged the authority given the FEA to regulate fuel choice by utilities, in the Energy Supply and Environmental Coordination Act, "a net loss for regulatory reform."

That way of putting things is rather too sharp. Even if it had been de-cided that it was desirable to internalize all the costs of OCS exploration and development and of increased coal production and use, the grounds for controversy would still have been numerous enough. Should polluters pay for the amount of pollution they cause or meet certain absolute, uni-form standards? And what kind of penalty should be adopted?[118] More-over, different interests would still clash. A per ton fee on deep-mined coal would affect eastern deep pits differently from strip mines in the western states. And even if there were financial compensation for environmental damage, to the extent that the physical changes were irreversible residents in coastal or producer states would be bound to feel that in a sense a transfer in kind was being forced on them, benefiting those in consumer states.

That said, it remains true that the long-term consequences of the ad-ministration's acting as if these issues could be separated from price was to delay the realization by consumers generally that the full cost of the energy they used must rise and make it more or less inevitable that the shock of the 1973–74 embargo would have to be repeated. In the shorter term the approach also achieved little. The policy of dealing with opposi-tion on a piecemeal basis had some unexpected consequences, as when environmentalist groups united with the utilities to oppose the mandated switch to coal. It also proved to be difficult to limit the numbers of those claiming special consideration in discussions of compensation. And con-frontation with Congress was not avoided after all: Ford's term ended with federal plans for expanded OCS exploration having been killed in the House and proposed amendments to the Clean Air Act of 1970 stopped by the Senate.

Court challenges over the right to resources in OCS areas had been a thorn in the side of both the Nixon and Ford administrations. But in March 1975 the Supreme Court sided with the federal government in the case of the *United States* v. *Maine et al.,*[119] refuting the contention of the states that they possessed jurisdiction over and possession of the entire

118. The way in which these issues could divert attention from energy *policy* must not be underestimated. Frank Zarb, for example, accepted the desirability of "forcing" changes in the form of lighter autos with better mileage by making energy prices *across the board* reflect real costs. For that reason he opposed including a tax on gasoline alone in the Ford package at the end of 1974. But Zarb found himself fighting on the much more limited terrain of a voluntary 40 percent improvement in mileage by 1980 or a mandated 100 percent improvement by 1985.

119. 420 U.S. 515.

outer continental shelf. This opened the way for the Interior Department to push ahead with a plan to offer 19.1 million acres in 1975 (double the total leased in twenty years of OCS operations). The states with rights within the three-mile limit threatened in some instances to forbid the laying of pipelines ashore or to levy landing taxes; and they requested grants-in-aid to cope with the impact of offshore developments on the environment and economy of the affected areas. Under existing law, the 1920 Mineral Leasing Act, the federal government collected all revenues from offshore leasing, with states getting a fixed percentage of the bids, rents, and royalties collected by the federal government. During 1975 Congress discussed several bills that would provide additional federal monies in the form of grants or loans.[120]

Several government agencies favored loans or loan guarantees rather than grants—which the states preferred—and wanted to limit all transfers to direct impact aid to those persons or areas affected, when it was needed. In other words, revenue sharing, or a categorical federal grant role on a continuing basis, was rejected. The Interior and Commerce departments and the CEA agreed that nothing more than impact aid was "deserved." They argued on three grounds that it was a dangerous precedent to offer more. States might not stay "bought." Alternatively, buying off some political subdivisions might only encourage others to see themselves as possible claimants. And in general such a policy would run counter to long-run budgetary control by the OMB. This group also urged that if the states nonetheless intended to levy "landing taxes," federal aid should be unnecessary.[121] A majority in the Energy Resources Council overruled

120. A useful introduction to the main issues is "Energy Report: Offshore Oil—A National Treasure Hunt?" *Congressional Quarterly Weekly Report,* April 5, 1975, pp. 690–92. The evolution of thinking within the administration and congressional and state reaction can be gleaned from James A. Noone, "Energy Report: Industry Response Seen Pacing Offshore Leasing Expansion," *National Journal Reports,* April 20, 1974, pp. 592–98; Richard Corrigan, "Energy Focus: Interior Stressing Offshore Leasing," ibid., October 26, 1974, p. 1623; Corrigan, "Energy Focus: Ford Presses States to Drill Offshore," ibid., November 23, 1974, p. 1776; Arthur J. Magida, "Environment and Natural Resources: Outer Continental Shelf Development of Oil and Gas Leads Ford's Request," ibid., February 8, 1975, p. 209; Magida, "Environment Report: Major Changes Eyed in Offshore Development Plans," ibid., June 14, 1975, pp. 883–89; and "Washington Update: Congress Passes Coastal Development Aid Bill," ibid., July 10, 1976, p. 981. Whitaker, in *Striking a Balance,* also provides a full discussion of the OCS and other issues mentioned here.

121. Russell to Greenspan and MacAvoy, "Comments on Briefing Book for Camp David," CEA Records, MacAvoy Files, GRFL; Russell to MacAvoy, "OCS Leasing," October 9, 1975, Russell personal files; and James L. Mitchell, October 14, 1975, untitled memorandum giving OMB comments and suggestions to the President on OCS leasing bills (S. 586 and S. 521), CEA Records, MacAvoy Files, GRFL.

these arguments, believing that some form of revenue sharing was politically necessary. Late in 1975 an administration initiative was devised going beyond impact aid but still in the form of loans and loan guarantees.[122]

As noted above, no agreement with the interested parties and with Congress was reached before the end of Ford's term of office. The range of interests to be satisfied is illustrated by the following *partial* list taken from an OMB document prepared at Zarb's request for the Energy Resources Council in mid-October 1975 and referring to administration policy at that time.[123]

Concerns	*Proponents*
1. Need for impact aid not met	Sen. Hollings, Sen. Magnuson, Cong. Forsythe, National Governors' Conference
2. Need for revenue sharing not met	Sen. Johnston, Sen. Stevens, State of Louisiana, most major oil companies
3. Not only should OCS imports be met, but also those in the western coal and oil shale lands	Gov. Lamm, Western Governors' Conference
. . . .	
9. Leasing procedures enrich oil companies at expense of Federal Government	Environmental Policy Center, Natural Resources Defense Council
10. Liability for damage from spills not covered	Most of above
11. Government should do exploration	New Jersey

This list embraces not just the implications of the Interior Department's OCS leasing plans but the general issue discussed earlier, namely, the proper degree of federal involvement in energy. The question it raises also applies to both. How was it that national energy policy came to be bogged down in such details? The proximate answer is clear: political necessity. But the answer at one remove is more complex. In November 1974 Ford had said the OCS offers "the largest single source of increased domestic energy during the years when we need it most." He had added,

122. Russell to MacAvoy, "OCS Leasing," October 9, 1975, Russell personal files.
123. Mitchell, draft decision memorandum (see note 121). The insistence of the Western Governors' Conference on extending impact aid to synfuels development projects (item 3 in the list) illustrates the potential for escalation of claims inherent in the administration's decision to "buy off" offended parties.

"The OCS can supply this energy with less damage to the environment and at a lower cost to the U.S. economy than any other alternative."[124] What Ford failed to incorporate into his energy program was a clear explanation of what would be involved in internalizing the environmental costs. The FEA's calculations, and those by others, of the impact of the program concentrated on the effects of achieving market prices for petroleum and natural gas and on the cost of an emergency reserve. The environmental costs were implicitly treated as if they could be dealt with other than by raising prices. And the implication of this decision, to repeat, was that the administration found itself fighting a series of street battles without any clearly defined front.

This was very clearly the case in the fight to amend the Clean Air Act of 1970. Here the administration found itself continuing a struggle begun under Nixon early in 1974, and under terms laid down at that time. The difficulty was that in the first two years of the Nixon administration environmental quality had come to be accepted as an absolute good. Clean air and acceptable levels of emissions had come to be defined by uniform rules, rather than the option being given to would-be polluters to incur a cost according to the amount of pollution they created. The tendency to absolutize environmental quality and a failure to deploy market devices (taxes, emission charges, user fees) seemed to go together. Nixon's economic advisers urged him to seek market devices in the amendments to be submitted to Congress. But Nixon himself spoke of amendments that would "remove . . . roadblocks to energy production" and of "cancelling environmental inhibitions," as if these were so many physical obstacles to be chipped away or pushed aside.[125] And if this language seems to betray an incomplete grasp of the method of internalizing environmental costs in energy prices, that impression is strengthened by the list of non-market amendments eventually transmitted to Congress. The Energy Supply and Environmental Coordination Act dealt with Nixon's amendments only in a limited way, extending the timetable for achieving engine and

124. Statement following White House discussions with coastal states on accelerated OCS leasing, November 13, 1974, as reported in Corrigan, "Energy Focus: Ford Presses States to Drill Offshore," p. 1776.

125. Allan Pulsipher, "Questions and Answers on Energy Policy and the Environment, in Preparation for Joint Economic Committee Meetings [on CEA Report]," January 29, 1974, Russell personal files; and Kenneth Cole to the President, "Legislation on Environment and Energy," February 27, 1974, referring to directions given by the President during a meeting earlier that day, Parsky Files, Box 4, folder: FEO-Environment, 1973–74, U.S. Treasury.

vehicle emission standards and granting some authority to require power plants to convert to coal. Ford asked for changes in line with those requested by Nixon, also without much success. But the most striking similarity between the two administrations from the present point of view is that neither Nixon nor Ford placed the issue before the public in its true light, as a choice between more imported energy at international prices and with a security premium or more domestic energy with the environmental costs written into the price. The battles waged were over a postponement of improvements in auto emissions, over the lowering of the technically defined air quality standards, and over scrubbers versus intermittent controls in stacks, but not over the implications for energy prices of internalizing environmental costs.[126]

The case of strip mining is somewhat different. In this instance Ford found himself vetoing two bills, the second of which, in mid-1975, was acknowledged by White House staff to be close enough to the administration's own suggested compromise legislation to warrant acceptance.[127] The bill, which included a land reclamation fee on each ton of deep-mined coal, was vetoed, not because the administration refused to acknowledge in this instance the principle of internalizing environmental costs, but because at the time the nation was depending heavily on mines brought into operation only when demand was strong and prices high. The bill would have eliminated much of this so-called surge capacity and would have created a temporary coal shortage and serious upward pressure on prices. In addition utilities were using the unavailability of coal as a ground for resisting the FEA's coal conversion program, and given that the program was an important component of the Ford energy independence plan, the bill would have been self-defeating.

Ford's veto was widely held to be a further retreat from environmental protection, and it was ironic that the vetoed bill would have helped in one respect to internalize the environmental costs of coal production; but the timing was not right. Without the other elements of Ford's package in place, neither the congressional initiatives nor that of the administration itself would have done other than increase U.S. import dependence. Ford's veto was an expression of concern for the *short-run* price and oil import

126. John F. Burby, "Environment Report: New Committee Lineups Will Shape Clean Air Act Revisions," *National Journal Reports,* January 4, 1975, pp. 12–14.

127. James Cannon to the President (decision memorandum), "Strip Mining Bill," May 15, 1975, CEA Records, Greenspan Files, GRFL. For background to the bill and its provisions see Elder Witt, "Energy Report: House Passes Strip Mining Bill, 333–86," *Congressional Quarterly Weekly Report,* March 22, 1975, pp. 582–86.

effects, not for the long-run effects of stricter strip mine laws on costs.[128] This experience held a sharp reminder that piecemeal energy policy was no longer possible.

The Years 1969–76 in Review

The intense struggles during 1975 to secure a coherent, basically market-oriented energy policy had drained all who were closely involved. Despite the EPCA's shortcomings, the Ford administration was considerably relieved that a settlement of sorts had been reached. Energy could be pushed quietly into the wings and the 1976 campaign could be pursued in earnest.

By comparison with the previous year, then, 1976 was a quiet one on the energy front. One important piece of legislation was passed toward the end of the summer: the Energy Conservation and Production Act. The administration had submitted a request in January for a simple extension of the FEA's life for thirty-nine months. In the Senate, at Senator Edward Kennedy's behest, the necessary authorization was transformed into a vehicle for securing federal assistance to encourage energy conservation on a large scale. This included assistance in the weatherizing of homes— asked for by the administration—but also an authorization for the FEA to guarantee up to $2 billion for industry, state and local government, small business, and nonprofit institutions borrowing for the purpose of conservation. In addition, the ECPA deregulated stripper production of oil, en-

128. The administration was partly responsible for obscuring its own logic in this instance. Both the Interior Department and the FEA used arguments in defense of the veto that made it look as if the main issue was the unemployment that would follow closing some mines. The Interior Department provided estimates of the production and jobs likely to be lost during hearings on H.R. 25, the Surface Mining Control and Reclamation Act of 1975. Zarb also used the figures and the unemployment argument during a press conference on May 19 in explanation of Ford's veto. ("Energy and Environment: Strip Mining," *Congressional Quarterly Weekly Report,* May 24, 1975, p. 1065.) When congressional staff requested an explanation of the methods and assumptions behind the estimates, CEA economists were brought in. Milton Russell commented to Zarb that "they would require 20 pages to explain and even then could be attacked on the basis of someone else's 'judgement.'" (Russell to Zarb, "Draft Insertion: Testimony on Strip Mining Bill," May 30, 1975, CEA Records, Staff Files, GRFL.) Allan Pulsipher pointed out that the difference in unemployment effects between the "Administration's Bill" and H.R. 25 was "insignificant" and that the real basis for opposing control legislation at that time was quite different. (Pulsipher to Greenspan, "Strip Mining," May 23, 1975, Russell personal files.)

hanced recovery production of oil, and assured that crude prices could rise by 10 percent a year through March 1977 regardless of the rate of inflation. But this latter concession was given in exchange for an FEA commitment not to submit any new price increase proposals during 1976. The FEA was also no longer permitted to submit proposals removing products from price and allocation controls at the same time, which implied that it would be harder to remove price controls in the future. The ECPA required the Energy Resources Council to prepare a plan for the reorganization of executive branch activities involving energy and natural resources; and it established in the FEA an Office for Energy Information and Analysis, as mentioned above.

The FEA, whose statute had expired and whose existence—as the Federal Energy Office—was extended by the grace of an executive order, strongly recommended approval of the ECPA. The OMB and the Commerce and Interior departments also approved the act. The Treasury concurred but expressed concern about the growth in federal regulation and bureaucracy implied by the conservation provisions of the bill. A CEA staff economist concluded ruefully that "Hill and Zarb may have negotiated a 3–4% increase in crude prices (through March 77), stripper decontrol, enhanced recovery decontrol and a smaller conservation program in exchange for permanent price controls on products. It is not clear that the benefits are worth the cost. It is also not clear that CEA's opinion on this issue will be solicited."[129] It was not.

In the subsequent required study on energy reorganization, all the problems of the structure of energy planning in the Ford administration that have emerged in the course of my discussion, plus some that have not, were brought to light.

1. Inherent conflict within the FEA, which was required to formulate energy policy recommendations and simultaneously to regulate the petroleum sector.

2. Inherent conflict within the Energy Research and Development Agency, which was responsible for assessing the nation's energy needs but also for supporting and funding new types of energy technologies.

3. Lack of a central coordinating body: the Energy Resources Council

129. Philip Verleger to MacAvoy, "FEA Extension," August 9, 1976; and draft OMB decision memorandum for the President, "Enrolled Bill HR 12169—Energy Conservation and Production Act," August 13, 1976; both in CEA Records, Greenspan Files, GRFL. In the draft memorandum "approval," "no objection," or "no comment" was marked in for every department and agency with the exception of the CEA.

was controlled by the FEA because the latter supplied the analytical power.

These conflicts had produced three corresponding tendencies. First, the regulatory group in the FEA could function only with difficulty in a manner consistent with national energy policy. The Energy Research and Development Agency for its part was encouraged to act as a political organization with favors to distribute, since budgeting so as to minimize offences to its clientele meant funding all possible options.[130] Finally, to the extent that the FEA was dominated by an activist or regulatory mentality, and the Energy Resources Council by the FEA, effective control of energy policy was taken out of the White House and fell to an energy technocracy. This in turn meant that managing rather than resolving shortages became the order of the day.[131]

The ramifications of loss of control by the White House extended still further. Independent-minded departments, such as the State Department, were enabled to exert an influence over domestic energy policy as an indirect result of pursuing foreign policy objectives.

Moreover, the administration's own ambivalence about freeing energy markets and its hesitation about promoting the view that energy prices should reflect the full social costs of increased energy production contributed to making energy a political good—one systematically and persistently allocated at prices other than market prices and on grounds other than economic efficiency.[132] Congress's work is legislation, and Ford's omnibus energy bill comprised many and various proposals for interference as well for freeing energy markets. This supplied numerous

130. Verleger to MacAvoy, "ERDA Modelling Efforts," July 14, 1976, CEA Records, Greenspan Files, GRFL. Verleger commented that "the economist's role at ERDA appears to be to justify programs, not to determine levels or need." See also Verleger to Burton Malkiel, "Energy Reorganization Proposals," November 19, 1976; and Verleger to MacAvoy, "CEA Proposals to Energy Organization Study," June 18, 1976; both in ibid.

131. It should be mentioned, however, that the FEA participated in a presidential initiative to identify and assess the costs of regulatory interventions in the economy with a view to reform. A Domestic Council Review Group on Regulatory Reform was established, and Paul MacAvoy and Frank Zarb, with a task force under the direction of Donald Flexner of the Department of Justice, jointly headed an investigation of the FEA. MacAvoy subsequently edited a version of the report on the FEA, published as *Federal Energy Administration Regulation: Report of the Presidential Task Force*, Ford Administration Papers on Regulatory Reform (American Enterprise Institute for Public Policy Research, 1977).

132. See Arthur W. Wright, "The Case of the United States: Energy as a Political Good," *Journal of Comparative Economics*, vol. 2 (June 1978), pp. 144–76, 161.

pegs for legislation. Again the administration's less than wholehearted support for market-oriented policies, whether reflecting technocratic hubris or political expediency, *allowed* Congress to deflect discussion onto side issues such as oil company profits or the needs of "small" refiners. To the extent that regulation of production and prices or allocation of shortages was attempted, distortions resulted and these had to be corrected by still more regulations.[133] From the perspective of Ford's CEA under Alan Greenspan it seemed that the FEA and Congress were at times united in an effort to curb rather than enhance market incentives.[134]

These problems, many of them of the administration's own making, were exacerbated by others that were largely outside its control. Chief among these were OPEC, congressional intransigence, and public disbelief in the reality of an energy problem, as distinct from transient energy problems and the supposed machinations of the major oil companies.

Ford's task regarding public disbelief was not made easier by his having to follow Nixon. Watergate was very disturbing to the policy process. It took the White House out of the policymaking arena. It also reassured the public that it was right to be skeptical of administration pronouncements. And it drew congressmen in the direction of attending more closely to local and immediate grievances than to national and long-term needs. But Nixon's style left its mark more directly. Energy policy in the period 1969–74 comprised a series of messages and initiatives whose specific elements reflected current crises or presidential opportunism. Something would be advanced at one time, and something else the next. The action was not unlike that of a boxing match. This approach served to maintain the comfortable illusion that energy problems did not involve decisions about national goals and choices but could be dealt with by a quick sally and a rain of blows in the form of legislation, reorganization, or technical "fixes."

Ford, as noted, went a long way in the direction of an integrated policy based on principles. But the past exacted its price. Low-cost energy had

133. The difficulties of predicting the effects of regulatory interventions are nicely brought out in Rodney T. Smith and Charles E. Phelps, "The Subtle Impact of Price Controls on Domestic Oil Production," *American Economic Review*, vol. 68 (May 1978, *Papers and Proceedings, 1978*), pp. 428–35.

134. One positive element, running in the opposite direction, should be recorded. Natural gas deregulation was achieved under Carter with support from some of those very congressmen who had been most adamant in opposing Ford. This suggests that a process of education may have been begun under the one administration, coming to fruition only much later.

become an assumption of life, so much so that early in Nixon's presidency the nation had felt able to afford itself the luxury of environmental safeguards. While these were recent appurtenances, the subsequent suggestion that they be discarded was resisted quite fiercely. Part of the reason, perhaps, was that it struck at the more basic assumption of energy abundance. Nixon's style did nothing to disabuse those who held that belief, and it was an ungrateful task to have to reeducate the nation on so basic a subject. Ford saw the need more clearly than Nixon, who had little interest in energy anyway, but even Ford found the political costs intolerable and alowed himself to be maneuvered into acquiescing in an extension of controls on oil and into trying to avoid a confrontation with consumers over the passing on of external costs associated with expanding domestic production of oil and of coal.

Much of the foregoing has been concerned with successive reorganizations. It should not be necessary to add that correcting organizational deficiencies was not a guarantee that an appropriate energy policy would emerge. That much should be very clear from the account itself, in which the stress on organization and reorganization is only a reflection of just how much effort was spent on these things. Changes in the organizational structure of energy policymaking at times followed so hard one upon the other as to suggest that reorganization was a conditioned response to any new twist in the real world problem situation. To keep this in perspective, however, it must be added that reorganization as a response was only one aspect of what I have dubbed the Nixon style of addressing energy problems. Flamboyant gesture was another and perhaps more telling element, since it is something quite as characteristic of the Ford administration as of its predecessor. The Nixon gestures included numerous energy messages, plus items such as Project Independence and the proposed $10 billion injection into energy R&D. Ford's Energy Independence Authority, special pushes for the development of synfuels and solar energy, and even the International Energy Agency, with its plan for allocation among consumers and a floor price, for "dealing with" OPEC, have something of the same flavor. Gestures they were, in the sense that they were last-minute attempts to make complex problems seem simple and to give an impression that the long term could be reduced to the short term provided the right device could be found or enough funds and personnel could be marshaled to the task.

It is not difficult to account for the survival of this element of the Nixon style beyond his term in office. As the real energy problems became harder, more urgent, and more replete with institutional complexities and perceived resource trade-offs, pressures to "do something" increased. The long view is at all times a luxury for elected governments. And in the face of current shortages the leisurely exploration of the likely future incremental costs of alternative energy paths, with their implied decisions about goals and life-styles, simply became harder to defend. It is also more difficult for a government agency than for private advocates to defend a decision to devote resources to sorting out the implications of particular goals and values. For a variety of reasons it is deemed more acceptable to define long-term, strategic issues in technical terms. Certainly, under both Nixon and Ford there was an implicit preference for leaving to designated agencies (the Office of Science and Technology and the Atomic Energy Commission in the beginning, later the Energy Research and Development Administration) and their technical experts much of the planning of the nation's energy future. In the records I have been able to examine, which admittedly do not include those of the White House or the OMB where more of such evidence might be expected, there is almost nothing to suggest that broad-based "future think" exercises akin to those embodied in the report of the Paley Commission were pursued. The decision to avoid too explicit a consideration of values is in part an expression of a desire to quantify options; and this too limits the time horizon that can be entertained. For uncertainty increases very rapidly as one looks forward. In other words, even ignoring the obvious political pressures, it was difficult to resist looking to the quick fix, and there are reasons enough to understand why these tended to invoke technology or to take the form of a new program.

One additional element caused the Nixon and Ford administrations to lean toward such solutions. This was a widespread belief that the energy problem was in some sense much the same as those problems that had been successfully addressed by the Manhattan Project and the manned space flights program. The belief was of long standing. In earlier administrations faith in technology had been used to justify postponing serious thought about nonfossil, nonnuclear energy futures. Under Nixon and Ford events seemed to signal that the time had come to call up the spirit of Apollo.

CHAPTER EIGHT

Carter Energy Policy and the Ninety-fifth Congress

JAMES L. COCHRANE

JIMMY CARTER and Gerald R. Ford waged the first post–oil embargo presidential campaign. Carter carried a greater scientific background into the campaign than anyone had before him. His navy work in Schenectady and his extensive experience with Admiral Hyman G. Rickover's Nuclear Propulsion Division gave him a substantial advantage in that he could bring an engineer's understanding to the energy crisis. Admiral Rickover was an extraordinary influence on Jimmy Carter. In fact, Carter produced a consistent triad of names when asked who had influenced him the most. His response always included his mother, "Miss Lilian"; Julia Coleman, a Georgia high school teacher; and Admiral Rickover, the cantankerous architect of the U.S. nuclear fleet. In many respects Carter represented a combination never before seen in American politics, an engineer responsible for a Southern Baptist Sunday School class. Carter's campaign combined the love-trust ethic of his Southern Baptist Church with a methodical, analytical style and manner.

Energy Issues during the Campaign

After Carter captured the Democratic nomination for president and began the direct campaign against Ford, the energy issue fizzled; it failed

THE AUTHOR is indebted to several persons who took time to discuss the Carter energy program with him, especially officials at the Department of Energy and the Office of Management and Budget. A preliminary draft of this essay was read by William J. Barber, William Chappell, Neil B. de Marchi, John Fox, Craufurd D. Goodwin, Gary L. Griepentrog, Leslie Magerfield, Neva McElroy, William S. Rawson, Robert Rosen, Walt W. Rostow, Edwin H. Seim, Arnold Stebinger, and Ronald P. Wilder. Their advice and assistance, along with that of Janet Hardy and Elizabeth A. Clark, is greatly appreciated.

to capture the interest of the electorate. The general absence of energy issues was a major anomaly of the 1976 presidential campaign. There was little discussion about the price of fossil fuels, about strip mining, or about energy company divestiture. On September 21, 1976, Carter proposed the creation of a separate, cabinet-level Energy Department, but the announcement failed to cause much of a stir. He made one energy pledge during the campaign that would later haunt his administration. About three weeks before the election he wrote to the governors of Texas, Oklahoma, and Louisiana promising to "work with the Congress, as the Ford Administration has not been able to do, to deregulate new natural gas." In the same paragraph, after noting the exploration incentive and interstate sales benefits of deregulating producers' prices for *new* natural gas, he explained that his version of decontrol would "protect the consumer against sudden price increases in the average price of natural gas."[1] Of course these three states were important at all stages of the Carter candidacy. David L. Boren of Oklahoma was the first governor to endorse Carter. Democrats in Texas, the nation's third most populous state, delivered substantial campaign contributions to their fellow southerner whose anti-Washington and anticontrols themes played well in the suburbs of Houston and Dallas. And in November Carter carried Texas.

Nuclear power did become a campaign issue of sorts but a minor one. In May 1976 candidate Carter spoke at the United Nations, decrying the inexorable movement toward an international plutonium economy via reliance on breeder reactors.[2] On October 28, 1976, at the heated end of the campaign, President Ford altered his administration's policy by stating

1. Jimmy Carter to Governor Dolph Briscoe of Texas, October 19, 1976.
2. The U.S. breeder reactor program dates back to at least 1945 when the Argonne National Laboratory Division of the Manhattan District Metallurgical Laboratory initiated a mercury-cooled reactor program at Los Alamos. In 1949 the Atomic Energy Commission took hesitant first steps toward a commercial electric breeder reactor program; the program has been controversial ever since. Breeder reactors were the ultimate ambition in civilian nuclear power. In the process of using the initial fissionable charge, a new fissionable material, plutonium, was created. (Plutonium is also produced in light-water reactors but in small quantities and at very slow rates.) Breeders had the potential of yielding over one hundred times the amount of energy from a given amount of relatively scarce natural uranium than light-water reactors. France, the United Kingdom, and the Soviet Union have been successfully operating breeders for several years, with the French building a commercial prototype, the Super Phénix, rated at 1,200 megawatts (electric). For a critical review of the U.S. program, see Brian G. Chow, *The Liquid Metal Fast Breeder Reactor: An Economic Analysis* (American Enterprise Institute for Public Policy Research, 1975).

that the United States needed to be cautious about proceeding toward reliance on plutonium. This statement by President Ford, apparently delayed at the request of the French government, represented a potential reversal of the Nixon-Ford position. Presidents Nixon and Ford had supported the Clinch River Breeder Reactor, which was being built on Tennessee Valley Authority lines and which TVA had an option to take over. The Clinch River Breeder Reactor was designed to be the primary U.S. demonstration project in the field, an attempt to close the gap between European developments and lagging U.S. technology. Carter had expressed concern about terrorists obtaining plutonium and using it to blackmail the industrial democracies. He also worried about developing countries acquiring plutonium for weapons, thus increasing the number of countries capable of waging nuclear war.

During the latter half of 1976 energy was not a dominant campaign theme, but Carter's people realized it would be of major importance if they won in November. In late August it was reported that Joseph B. Browder, executive vice-president of the Environmental Policy Center in Washington, D.C., had "moved into the transition headquarters of the Carter organization to coordinate policy planning in the natural resources area."[3] Browder was described as an aide to Jack H. Watson, Jr., a Carter insider who would become cabinet secretary in the new administration. In addition Katherine P. Schirmer, formerly of the Envrionmental Protection Agency and aide to Senator Philip A. Hart, oversaw a task force drafting energy position papers, a job she would continue to do in the Carter administration, working for Stuart Eizenstat's Domestic Policy Staff. During the campaign and after the election several people emerged as Carter's chief energy adviser. Certainly throughout the autumn and early winter of 1976 various parts of the Carter entourage issued many statements concerning energy matters. The major pre-inaugural document seems to have been an energy policy paper prepared by S. David Freeman for Watson's transition team.

Before the inauguration many individuals and numerous organizations were at work on the energy problem. They were inspired to bring their work to a boil, to offer the incoming president advice. The legislative branch was no exception. Comptroller General Elmer B. Staats released a fifty-six-page report to the incoming Ninety-fifth Congress identifying eight critical national energy issues and summarizing, for each, the ques-

3. Richard Corrigan, "Energy Focus: Someone's Got to Lose," *National Journal*, August 28, 1976, p. 1224.

tions requiring analysis. The report also informed new executive branch officials that the General Accounting Office would be an active source of energy policy analysis. The GAO's report was cast in terms of the office's "ongoing and planned work" plus the need for everyone to get involved, "most particularly the Congress of the United States."[4]

Many outside organizations weighed in with advice. In January 1977 the Twentieth Century Fund released a report from a task force chaired by Herbert B. Cohn, vice-chairman of the American Electric Power Company.[5] The task force included Walter J. Levy, Morris A. Adelman, and John A. Love, three distinguished Americans deeply interested in energy matters. They advised the new administration to spur development of domestic energy sources by providing price incentives for oil and gas, to expand government-sponsored research and development, and to encourage the use of nuclear power and coal. They also urged speedy development of a crude oil stockpile, already mandated by Congress during the Ford administration. This Twentieth Century Fund task force was *production* oriented and placed substantial emphasis on development of the Alaskan North Slope and the outer continental shelf. Its report illustrated the "drain America first" policy. (This pejorative phrase had been coined by S. David Freeman in a chapter for *Beyond the New Deal: Democrats Look to the Future,* a volume produced by the Democratic Forum for distribution at the New York Democratic Convention in the summer of 1976.)

Another source of pre-inaugural advice came from the National Research Council's Committee on Nuclear and Alternative Energy Systems. This committee released an interim report on the day of Carter's inauguration describing some progress on an eighteen-month study begun about a year earlier using $3 million from the Energy Research and Development Administration.[6] The committee's interim report urged greater stress on conservationist government policies. Two opposite approaches to energy issues are embodied in these two reports: spurring production or reducing consumption.

4. Comptroller General of the United States, *National Energy Policy: An Agenda for Analysis,* Report to the Congress (Government Printing Office, 1977), p. 4.
5. *Providing for Energy: Report of the Twentieth Century Fund Task Force on United States Energy Policy* (McGraw-Hill, 1977).
6. The final report was not published until 1980. See National Research Council, *Energy in Transition, 1985–2010: Final Report on Nuclear and Alternative Energy Systems* (W. H. Freeman, 1980).

The First Ninety Days

On inauguration day Carter promised to send Congress a comprehensive energy plan in three months. The Carter administration's first winter was an extremely harsh one characterized by fuel shortages, particularly of natural gas. On January 26, 1977, President Carter sent Congress emergency legislation to provide temporary authority to shift natural gas from one interstate pipeline to another and to liberalize his authority to let interstate pipelines pay prices above federal ceilings for extra amounts of interstate gas. On January 30 Carter took his first trip as President, a helicopter ride to Pittsburgh, which had been hard hit by the weather and the fuel crisis. He used the trip to Pittsburgh as reason to say the United States was probably experiencing a "permanent, very serious energy shortage."[7] On February 2, 1977, President Carter had a "fireside chat" with the American people concerning the natural gas shortage, emphasizing national sacrifice. Congress gave the President the natural gas authorities he had requested, and the new administration could move on to more general energy problems.

Of course, existing policies and programs required immediate leadership. President Carter appointed John F. O'Leary to head the Federal Energy Administration; in early 1977 O'Leary was often in the spotlight for executive branch energy policy. He had been active in the government energy game since the mid-1950s, when he had served as an Interior Department commodity analyst. During 1962–67 he was deputy to J. Cordell Moore, assistant secretary of the interior for mineral resources. In 1967–68 he served as chief of the Federal Power Commission's Bureau of Natural Gas. In 1968 President Johnson made him director of the Bureau of Mines, a job he held until the Nixon administration fired him, apparently for overly careful readings of coal mine safety regulations. After serving as a private consultant, he was the Atomic Energy Commission's director of licensing during James R. Schlesinger's AEC chairmanship. He then had quick tours with the Mitre Corporation and the state of New Mexico before being asked by Carter to head the FEA. In sum, O'Leary was not an energy neophyte.[8] But while O'Leary was out front granting interviews, giving speeches, and running programs, *the* Carter energy pro-

7. *New York Times,* January 31, 1977.
8. See Richard Corrigan, "Energy Focus: The Man Who's Done It All," *National Journal,* January 29, 1977, p. 181.

gram was being hammered out by Carter's real energy adviser, O'Leary's former AEC boss.

In December 1976, well before the inauguration, Schlesinger and President-elect Carter established a strong bond of mutual admiration and trust. In meetings at Carter's home in Plains, Georgia, they began the process of identifying problems and potential solutions. Schlesinger and Carter were strikingly similar, both combining a keen analytical mind with a high sense of moral purpose. They shared a deep belief in the impending exhaustion of fossil fuels but saw this as an opportunity, a challenge, rather than just another element of doomsday. They saw the energy crisis as a means to revive traditional American values—"things like ingenuity and imagination," in the words of one Carter aide.[9] Thus with confidence derived from a common base of righteous pragmatism, Carter gave Schlesinger his head. Schlesinger's mission was to forge a plan to deal not only with immediate problems but to take the United States into the 1980s with sound energy programs, codified where necessary, and with sufficient administrative apparatus for their implementation.

Carter's "energy czar" was a Harvard-trained economist: A.B., summa cum laude, 1950; M.A., 1952; and Ph.D., 1956. When selected, he was more of a heavyweight than his predecessors (John Love, William Simon, John Sawhill, and Frank Zarb). He had taught economics at the University of Virginia, a generally right-leaning department, after leaving Harvard. From 1963 until 1969 he was associated with the RAND Corporation, serving as director of strategic studies, 1967–69. He rose quickly through the upper ranks of the Nixon budget office, becoming assistant director of the Office of Management and Budget in 1970. (During Schlesinger's early budget days, his intellectual zeal and moral fervor did not wear well: Richard Nixon once told an aide, "Never bring that guy in here again."[10] But he was quickly back in the oval office.) From 1971 until early 1973 Schlesinger served as AEC chairman. He reorganized the commission, ending some of the comfortable relationships the AEC and the Joint Atomic Energy Committee of Congress had developed with the industry. (During his AEC tour he supported the breeder reactor program.) Between February and July 1973 he served as director of central intelligence, presiding over a 10 percent reduction in Central Intelligence Agency (CIA) personnel. In the summer of 1973 Nixon made him secretary of defense. He managed to reverse a decade of declining real spend-

9. James M. Naughton, *New York Times,* April 22, 1977.
10. Ibid.

ing on peacetime forces.[11] He was relieved of this job by President Ford in November 1975, allegedly at the demand of Secretary of State Henry Kissinger who felt that Schlesinger's hard line toward the USSR was undermining Kissinger's détente.

According to some of his longest and closest associates, Schlesinger's views on national economic policy were closer to French indicative planning than to the invisible hand of Adam Smith, Alfred Marshall, or Milton Friedman. Cultivation of a spirit of cooperation between government planners and industry appealed to Schlesinger: government analysts would provide goals and then perhaps would tailor these goals as a result of feedback from industry. He saw the relationship between government and industry as cooperative rather than adversarial.

To develop a master plan for energy Schlesinger assembled a small band of workers. This team had to develop the plan's rationale and the plan itself and then cast the plan in appropriate legislative language for transmittal to Congress. Schlesinger assembled approximately fifteen economists, public administrators, and lawyers on the second floor of the Old Executive Office Building, next to the White House, with a support staff of twenty-five secretaries and clerks. The Schlesinger team was young, with a strong tilt toward university and public life. None of the group was from industry. Unlike President Ford's energy planners, they emphasized the role of government in solving energy problems. While Ford's people focused on stimulating supplies from energy producers, Carter's people focused on conservation, to alter energy users' demand patterns. The Carter team had all previously worked on *public* approaches to energy or else were known by Schlesinger to be sympathetic to such approaches. It was natural for Schlesinger to surround himself with former subordinates and people who had provided expertise to energy-conscious Democrats during the Nixon-Ford years.

Many of the team had significant ties to Schlesinger. George R. Hall had been associated with him off and on—at the AEC and the Defense Department, for example—ever since they were colleagues in the University of Virginia economics department. (He would become a member of the Federal Energy Regulatory Commission.) John F. Ahearne, a physicist, had been deputy assistant secretary of defense for manpower under Schlesinger. (He would eventually become a member of the Nuclear Regulatory Commission.) As noted above, John O'Leary had been with

11. See Edward Cowan, *New York Times,* April 27, 1977; and Juan Cameron, "James Schlesinger in Dubious Battle," *Fortune,* February 27, 1978, pp. 36–40.

Schlesinger at the AEC. William A. Morrill, a career public administrator, had worked with Schlesinger in the late 1960s at the Budget Bureau and was an assistant secretary for planning and evaluation at the Department of Health, Education, and Welfare. Morrill was influential in emphasizing the equity aspects of components of the energy package. Harry E. Bergold, a foreign service officer, had been Schlesinger's deputy assistant secretary of defense for NATO and European affairs. Frederick P. Hitz had been hired by Schlesinger at the Defense Department to help deal with the rambunctious "Congressional Class of 1974."

Schlesinger made Alvin L. Alm the team's leader. Alm had been assistant administrator of the Environmental Protection Agency during 1973–77. He served as ringmaster for the group and was Schlesinger's chief liaison with the environmentalists. Together they recruited people from congressional staffs. Roger D. Colloff had been a lawyer on Senator Walter F. Mondale's staff and had written a Carter transition team paper on creating a Department of Energy. Robert R. Nordhouse had spent much of his career drafting House bills. After his shift to the House Commerce Committee in 1975 he concentrated on drafting energy bills. Nordhouse was a strong influence in getting the group to think of solving the energy problem through taxation. S. David Freeman was recruited from the staff of the Senate Commerce Committee. He had just finished directing a controversial large-scale energy policy project for the Ford Foundation,[12] and he brought to his task a conservationist orientation plus what some critics would consider an anti-industry orientation. Certainly his work for the Ford Foundation, which was blasted so thoroughly by everyone from the editor of *Harper's* to market-oriented economists to the president of the Mobil Corporation,[13] demonstrated a very particular point of view toward the energy problem that was not shared by his production-minded colleagues in the Carter administration. Another member of the team was Leslie J. Goldman, a lawyer who had worked for Senator Adlai E. Stevenson III. Goldman was a regulator; part of his job was to carry the Carter message to special-interest groups.

12. *A Time to Choose: America's Energy Future,* Final Report by the Energy Policy Project of the Ford Foundation (Ballinger, 1974).

13. See Lewis H. Lapham, "The Energy Debacle," *Harper's,* August 1977, pp. 58–74. The Institute for Contemporary Studies, based in San Francisco, severely criticized Freeman's report in its lively *No Time to Confuse* (ICS, 1975). Officers of the Ford Foundation felt obliged to publish a rejoinder to *A Time to Choose* by a dissenting member of the Energy Policy Project's advisory board, Mobil president William P. Tavoulareas. For balance, a reaction to both Freeman and Tavoulareas by Carl Kaysen was also included in the publication (William Tavoulareas and Carl Kaysen, *A Debate on A Time to Choose* [Ballinger, 1977]).

Although Schlesinger's team met with people from industry and government agencies, they essentially operated in isolation. Carter and Schlesinger chose operating efficiency over the more time-consuming process of consensus building. The staff of Schlesinger's Office of Energy Policy and Planning worked long nights and long weekends to produce a plan President Carter could take to Congress by his self-imposed deadline of April 20, 1977.

The Carter administration attempted to obtain advice not only from persons in the upper echelons of industry and government but also from the American people in general. Soon after the inauguration the Carter administration placed a call for written comments and suggestions in the *Federal Register*. They also sent questionnaires with a cover letter from Schlesinger on White House stationery to 450,000 citizens—300,000 chosen at random from Census Bureau cross sectional data. The other 150,000 letters went to state and local officials, congressmen, businessmen, and environmentalists. The 450,000 citizens were told that "the President needs your response before March 21." Twenty-eight thousand responses were received, an impressive response rate. (The energy staff was pleased with this indicator of Americans' interest in energy policy.) The administration was advised to do everything from "Stop all plastic manufacturing for one year" to "Darken Las Vegas" to "Reduce the birthrate."[14] The FEA also conducted ten regional "town meetings" in mid-March that were attended by several thousand people. Schlesinger's Energy Policy and Planning Office conducted twenty-one small conferences.

Of course, the last thing a tiny, overworked staff needed while producing an energy plan in ninety days was 28,000 pieces of advice. The letter-questionnaire scheme was essentially a charade. There simply was not enough time to do much with even potentially valuable responses, assuming they could have been cut from the herd. In fact, there was not even much time to deal with major officials in the Carter administration itself. The energy planners ignored Brock Adams, Carter's secretary of transportation. The Office of Management and Budget followed Bert Lance's direction and stayed out of the Schlesinger team's way. Charles Schultze's Council of Economic Advisers had no idea what the Schlesinger team was producing. Laurence N. Woodworth, assistant secretary of the treasury for tax policy, was kept in the dark about tax and spend-

14. Executive Office of the President, Energy Policy and Planning, *The National Energy Plan: Summary of Public Participation* (GPO, n.d.); and Linda Charlton, *New York Times*, April 14, 1977.

ing aspects of the Schlesinger proposal; he was called over to the Old Executive Office Building to answer specific questions but was given no clues about the overall shape of the plan. And the Schlesinger team's energy plan would have substantial importance for U.S. fiscal policy, on both sides of the ledger. The fiscal leaders of Congress and everyone else on the Hill were left in a state of suspended animation, waiting for the Delphic utterance from the Old Executive Office Building.

Objectives of the National Energy Plan of April 1977

On April 20, 1977, President Carter delivered his first postinaugural address to a joint session of Congress, introducing his administration's National Energy Plan. Following Schlesinger's advice, he used William James's phrase, "the moral equivalent of war," to describe the energy crisis. The nature and scope of the National Energy Plan developed by the Schlesinger team was shaped by a specific perception of U.S. energy problems that had three dominant features: choice of a proper planning horizon, concern about oil imports, plus concentration on prices of domestically produced oil and natural gas.

The United States was thought of as poised at the critical state of a third historic energy transition. In the first transition during the 1860s wood, waterwheels, and windmills gave way to coal as the major source of energy. During the second transition following World War II the United States shifted from hard to soft hydrocarbons, from coal to oil and natural gas. The Carter administration's Energy Policy and Planning Office considered the present period to be a third transition, a period during which the United States was depleting previously abundant domestic and foreign sources of oil and natural gas. The mission of the Carter planners was to ease the transition to the 1980s, providing time for the United States to modify its stock of capital goods and thus preventing energy chaos during the 1980s. They wanted to assist American households and business to adjust the nation's housing, means of production, transportation equipment, and so forth to enable the United States to survive a potential catastrophe during the mid-1980s. The plan's components were thought through with 1985 as a planning horizon. This represented a concrete, middle-term definition of the relevant future. It was not a plan for the next two years or the next two decades but rather for the next half-dozen years.

To the Schlesinger team the most pressing problem within this 1985 planning horizon was U.S. dependence on imported oil.[15] While the plan was being formulated immediately after the Carter inauguration, U.S. oil imports were running at about 9 million barrels a day, representing roughly one-half of U.S. domestic consumption. Without action, the administration expected this number to increase to between 12 million and 16 million barrels a day by 1985. The Carter planners decried the fact that previous government policies had *stimulated* this demand via artificially low prices. The National Energy Plan was to have three stages: the period from 1977 through 1985, the mid-1980s transition, and the period beyond 1985. But the basic thrust of the plan was on the 1977–85 period. And the focal point of that thrust was on oil imports. The plan's components were analyzed using a common criterion—millions of barrels of oil a day not imported. Throughout the plan's complex legislative life, each component, regardless of its direct relevance to crude oil, was evaluated in terms of the millions of barrels of oil a day that would be "saved," that is, not acquired from abroad, particularly from OPEC, the marginal supplier to the United States. Thus the plan was focused on reducing U.S. dependence on imported crude and on reducing U.S. dollar flows for relatively expensive marginal supplies.

While petroleum import reduction was the primary criterion, the plan was grounded on other issues. One of the most important of these problems was that the United States needed to develop pricing systems for domestically produced oil and natural gas that satisfied at least three potentially conflicting goals. First, the systems should be "fair." In addition they had to provide producers with sufficient incentives to seek and extract new domestic sources of supply. And finally, at the same time, the pricing systems had to reflect marginal replacement costs more closely. There was simply too much spread between what Americans were paying for oil and natural gas and what it cost to replace the flows consumed, at the margin. OPEC had quadrupled the world price of crude oil; in addition the United States had become dependent on arti-

15. Ever since the days of President Nixon's Oil Import Control Task Force, U.S. officials had seriously discussed potential security problems arising from oil imports, and these discussions went beyond a mere "national security" cover for protectionism. The official discussion in the Atlantic Community began during the mid-1960s. For two prescient analyses see United Kingdom, Ministry of Power, *Fuel Policy*, presented to Parliament by the Minister of Power by Command of Her Majesty, November 1967 (London: Her Majesty's Stationery Office, 1967); and Royaume de Belgique, Ministere des Affaires Economiques, *La politique energitique en 1967–1975* (December 1967).

ficially low-priced natural gas. The equity orientation of the plan was explicitly developed. U.S. energy policy should capture the eventual increase in domestic petroleum and natural gas prices for the American people; the increase in values should not accrue only to the producers. The "distribution of the proceeds of higher prices among domestic producers and consumers must be equitably and economically efficient if the United States is to spread the cost fairly across the population and achieve its energy goals."[16] Prices in a market economy serve many simultaneous signaling functions, and the signals being emitted by the prices paid by Americans for oil and natural gas were false ones, leading to misallocations.

The Carter energy planners recognized other problems and therefore had other goals. One problem was how to solve the policy trade-off between the energy requirements of economic growth—problems of coal strip mining, coal burning, nuclear plant siting and nuclear waste disposal—and the environmentalists' challenge to develop a more livable atmosphere. The Carter planners had a full plate of problems; in April 1977 they had the President unveil their solutions.

President Carter attempted to establish the momentum required to push the program of his Office of Energy Policy and Planning through both houses of Congress without loss of component parts. The administration faced the immediate problem of convincing Congress (and the public at large) that there *was* an energy problem, that the administration's perception of the problem was accurate, and that its solution was sound. To buttress its case an unusual decision was made to publish a CIA report on the international energy situation a few days before unveiling the National Energy Plan.[17] One of the major themes of the CIA report was that USSR production of oil would peak in the 1980s. The USSR and the other Warsaw Pact nations would then begin requiring OPEC oil. The CIA report did not offer guidance about appropriate policies; it provided forecasts of supply and demand. Yet the implications were obvious. One could assume that the petroleum needs of the Warsaw Pact nations were helping shape their foreign policies in the Mediterranean and Africa. Just as the OPEC producers had become the mar-

16. Executive Office of the President, Office of Energy Policy and Planning, *The National Energy Plan* (Executive Office of the President, April 29, 1977), p. xi.

17. U.S. Central Intelligence Agency, *The International Energy Situation: Outlook to 1985* (GPO, 1977).

ginal suppliers of crude oil to the United States in the early 1970s, they would become the marginal suppliers to the Warsaw Pact nations during the 1980s. It was bad enough that the United States had developed adversary relationships with OPEC members as well as with its Western bloc competitors for OPEC oil. But adding the Warsaw Pact nations to the competition would be an additional complicating factor for U.S. foreign policy during the 1980s.

Although there were differences of opinion in the administration concerning USSR known reserves, the general point made in the CIA report was underscored by a City University of New York political scientist, Dankwart A. Rustow, in a *Foreign Affairs* piece during the spring of 1977. Rustow argued that the dangers of "physical shortages of oil throughout the non-communist world" had to be taken very seriously and speculated about a "second price jump comparable in amount to that of 1973–74."[18] Few shared the depths of Rustow's alarms; the possibility of another OPEC quadrupling of petroleum prices seemed remote. But the prospect of further substantial price shocks was part of conventional wisdom among President Carter's energy planners. The Defense Intelligence Agency of the Department of Defense criticized the CIA report for grossly underestimating USSR known petroleum reserves. (The CIA had put USSR known reserves at 35 billion barrels, roughly equivalent to that of the United States; the Defense Intelligence Agency estimated USSR known reserves at 85 billion barrels.) Nevertheless, the Carter administration effectively employed the drama of releasing a CIA report to underscore the international, long-term precariousness of the U.S. energy situation.[19] The administration's pessimism was supported by reports by

18. Dankwart A. Rustow, "U.S.-Saudi Relations and the Oil Crises of the 1980s," *Foreign Affairs,* vol. 55 (April 1977), p. 494.

19. The critical quantitative issue in the CIA report, as in any discussion of anticipated world oil production, was how many millions of barrels a day Saudi Arabia would be asked to supply and what the Saudi response would be. The CIA projections indicated that the demand for Saudi oil could be 7 million barrels a day in 1980, rising to 12 million in 1982, and to some 13 to 16 million in 1983. Unless demand were curtailed, Saudi Arabia would have to supply 19 to 23 million barrels a day by 1985, roughly double 1977 capacity. Although the CIA indicated that the Saudis have the reserves required to support these high rates of production, it doubted that expansions of this magnitude could be achieved by 1985 without a major shift in Saudi priorities. According to the CIA, if Saudi Arabia allowed production to reach 20 million barrels a day by the mid-1980s, output would begin to decline in the mid-1990s because of reserve depletion.

the secretary-general of the Organisation for Economic Co-operation and Development and by the Workshop on Alternative Energy Strategies of the Massachusetts Institute of Technology.[20]

The initial written version of the National Energy Plan took the form of a fact sheet issued April 20, 1977, and released by the White House as the President addressed the joint session of Congress. It was widely publicized in the press.[21] On April 29 Schlesinger's Energy Policy and Planning Office released a booklet that gave much more detail and background than the fact sheet and warned that if the United States failed to act, there would be "a severe economic recession in the mid-1980s." But if the United States acted, it could be in a position to reduce its demand for foreign oil by the mid-1980s, diminishing its present adversary relationship with its allies and its potential adversary relationship with its enemies. The post-1985 aspects of the National Energy Plan were left in rather vague terms. It was clear that the United States was still going to be dependent on fossil fuels in the 1980s but that the use of U.S. coal supplies would buy time to move to a long-term technology solution to the energy problem based on solar or geothermal means and perhaps fusion.[22]

20. On November 15, 1974, the OECD Council established the International Energy Agency as an autonomous body within the OECD framework. Sixteen OECD members entered into an agreement on an International Energy Program. The OECD countries not participating in the agreement were Australia, France, Finland, Iceland, and Portugal. Thus with a few notable exceptions, the industrialized democracies had established an institutional vehicle to make common policy in the energy area. The 1977 report by the secretary-general became an influential portion of the energy literature: Secretary-General, Organisation for Economic Co-operation and Development, *World Energy Outlook: A Reassessment of Long-Term Energy Developments and Related Policies* (Paris: OECD, 1977).

The Workshop on Alternative Energy Strategies, directed by Carroll L. Wilson, was sponsored by MIT and the MIT Energy Laboratory. Before the 1973 oil embargo Wilson had published a call for a "crash program" to avert energy disaster: "A Plan for Energy Independence," *Foreign Affairs,* vol. 51 (July 1973), pp. 657–75. Wilson's pessimism and proposed solutions were developed in Workshop on Alternative Energy Strategies, *Energy Demand Studies: Major Consuming Countries* (MIT Press, 1976). The MIT Energy Laboratory also helped produce a study indicating that it would not be in the interest of the United States to achieve energy independence by the 1980s: the premium paid for such national energy insurance would exceed the cost of the damages against which the insurance was supposed to protect the United States. See MIT Energy Laboratory Policy Study Group, *Energy Self-Sufficiency* (American Enterprise Institute for Public Policy Research, 1974).

21. "National Energy Program," *Weekly Compilation of Presidential Documents,* vol. 13 (April 25, 1977), pp. 573–83.

22. Executive Office of the President, *The National Energy Plan,* p. xiii.

Although the post-1985 goals of the National Energy Plan were somewhat vague, the goals for 1985 were extraordinarily concrete, perhaps to a fault. The Carter energy planners recognized that these goals were "ambitious" but feasible. The administration argued that the package of carrots and sticks making up the plan would achieve seven quantitative goals, with cooperation from the American public:

—reduce the annual growth of total energy demand to below 2 percent;
—reduce gasoline consumption 10 percent below its current level;
—reduce oil imports from a potential level of 16 million barrels per day to 6 million, roughly one-eighth of total energy consumption;
—establish a Strategic Petroleum Reserve of 1 billion barrels;
—increase coal production by two-thirds, to more than 1 billion tons per year;
—bring 90 percent of existing American homes and all new buildings up to minimum energy efficiency standards; and
—use solar energy in more than 2½ million homes.[23]

The Carter administration argued that a major test of the plan was whether it would make a significant improvement in trends of energy use. Based on the assumption that the U.S. population would increase from 216 million in early 1977 to 235 million by 1985 and that President Carter's economic goals would be achieved, the energy planners offered the plan/no plan outcomes displayed in tables 8-1 and 8-2. The Carter plan was to have a significant favorable effect on the U.S. energy situation, whether viewed from a demand, supply, or fuel sector viewpoint.

Several technical points should be made about these tables. First, the word "fuel" is used in the title of each table although the data refer to *total* utilization. For example, oil data include oil used as fuel plus oil used for other purposes such as petrochemical feedstock. (The Carter program was both an oil import plan and an energy plan.) Second, the demand data in the electricity portions of table 8-1 represent *all* primary fuels consumed at the point of electricity production. The data are *not* consumption levels on site, expressed in terms of millions of barrels of oil a day. (The amount of primary fuels required for the delivery of one unit of electricity is a small fraction of the oil equivalent of that unit of electricity. This fraction has declined historically owing to increasingly efficient fuel utilization in electricity production.) Third, table 8-1 indicates an expected oil import level of 11.5 million barrels a day in 1985 without the plan and 7 million barrels with the plan. Thus the Carter planners would often speak of the

23. Ibid.

Table 8-1. *Fuel Balances by Sector for 1976 and Projected to 1985,* *with and without the National Energy Plan*
Millions of barrels of oil equivalent per day

Item	1976	1985, without plan	1985, with plan	1985, plan plus additional conservation
		Demand		
Total	**37.0**	**48.3**	**46.4**	**45.2**
Total residential and commercial	13.8	16.1	15.2	...
Oil	3.5	3.2	2.7	...
Natural gas	3.9	3.8	4.1	...
Electricity	6.3	9.1	8.4	...
Coal	0.1	*	*	...
Total industry	13.7	21.4	20.6	...
Oil	3.2	7.0	4.0	...
Natural gas	4.4	4.5	4.5	...
Electricity	4.2	7.2	7.1	...
Coal	1.9	2.7	5.0	...
Total transportation	9.5	10.8	10.5	...
Oil	9.2	10.6	10.2	...
Natural gas	0.3	0.2	0.3	...
Total electricity[a]	10.5	16.3	15.5	...
Oil	1.6	2.0	1.3	...
Natural gas	1.5	0.9	0.5	...
Coal	4.9	8.2	8.3	...
Nuclear	1.0	3.6	3.8	...
Other	1.5	1.6	1.6	...
		Supply		
Total	**37.0**	**48.5**	**46.4**	**45.2**
Total domestic	30.0	37.1	40.0	...
Crude oil[b]	9.7	10.4	10.6	...
Natural gas	9.5	8.2	8.8	...
Coal	7.9	12.2	14.5	...
Nuclear	1.0	3.7	3.8	...
Other	1.5	1.7	1.7	...
Refinery gain	0.4	0.9	0.6	...
Net imports	7.0	11.5	6.4	5.2
Oil	7.3	11.5	7.0	5.8
Natural gas	0.5	1.2	0.6	...
Coal	−0.8	−1.2	−1.2	...

Source: Executive Office of the President, Office of Energy Policy and Planning, *The National Energy Plan* (Executive Office of the President, April 29, 1977), pp. 95–96. Figures are rounded.
* Less than 0.05 million barrels of oil equivalent per day.
a. Included in previous sector totals.
b. Includes natural gas liquids.

Table 8-2. *Supply and Demand Balances by Fuel*
Millions of barrels of oil equivalent per day

Item	1976	1985, without plan	1985, with plan	1985, plan plus additional conservation
Oil				
Consumption	17.4	22.8[a]	18.2	17.0
Domestic supply[b]	9.7	10.4	10.6	10.6
Refinery gain	0.4	0.9	0.6	0.6
Imports	7.3	11.5	7.0	5.8
Natural gas				
Consumption	10.0	9.4	9.4	...
Domestic supply	9.5	8.2	8.8	...
Imports	0.5	1.2	0.6	...
Coal				
Consumption	6.8	10.9	13.3	...
Domestic supply	7.9	12.2	14.5	...
Exports	0.8	1.2	1.2	...

Source: Executive Office of the President, Office of Energy Policy and Planning, *The National Energy Plan* (Executive Office of the President, April 29, 1976), p. 96. Figures are rounded.
a. Assuming compliance with automobile efficiency standards under current law and reduced driving as a result of higher gasoline prices. Without these assumptions, consumption would be 25 million barrels a day.
b. Includes natural gas liquids.

plan as "saving" 4.5 million barrels of imported oil in 1985.[24] But the third of the seven specific quantitative goals listed above was the reduction of "oil imports from a potential level of 16 million barrels per day to 6 million," a 1985 "savings" level of 10 million barrels a day. These alternative numbers were discussed in the National Energy Plan literature as a worst-case scenario: a vision of 1985 characterized by the absence of compliance with conservation programs already in place when Jimmy Carter took office (resulting in domestic consumption of 25 million barrels of oil a day) and a low estimate for 1985 domestic oil production (9 million barrels a day). Finally, table 8-1 includes an entry, "refinery gain," that is not defined. (It is the change in the Btu content of a given amount of crude oil resulting from cracking heavy hydrocarbons into lighter ones. It is possible, particularly given technical improvements in-

24. Although it is easy to overburden readers with energy minutiae, it might be useful to some if the peculiar 42-gallon barrel is explained. A barrel is generally 55 gallons, but according to Wallace N. Seward, measurements coordinator for the American Petroleum Institute, petroleum was first transported to market in wooden barrels by horse-drawn wagons. There was so much slopping around in transit that refiners came to be willing to pay only for 42 gallons, per barrel delivered.

troduced since the early 1970s, for the refinery output of a given amount of crude oil to have more Btu than the input, even after heat used and heat lost in cracking are taken into account.)

The basic point of the tables is that the lion's share of oil import reduction was to be achieved by cutting industrial use of oil, from 7 to 4 million barrels of oil a day. Thus nearly half of the overall 1985 reduction in oil imports was to come from one sector of the economy. The amount of reduction expected from the *major* oil-consuming sector, transportation, was by comparison quite modest.

The administration argued that the National Energy Plan would have a favorable macroeconomic impact on the United States. Of course, the plan would reduce oil imports and help ease U.S. balance-of-payments deficits. The administration estimated that the plan would stimulate about 100,000 jobs by 1985, increasing GNP by 0.7 percent in 1978 and about 0.4 percent in 1985. It was recognized, however, that the plan would be inflationary, but the inflationary effect was predicted to be modest, resulting in an increase in the GNP deflator of only about 0.4 percent a year through 1985. Immediately following a White House Rose Garden ceremony at which President Carter signed the 283 pages of National Energy Plan legislation for formal transmittal to Congress, James Schlesinger told reporters that the net cost of the plan to U.S. taxpayers through 1985 would be $7 billion, a relatively small loss. This was an estimate of the accumulated spread between taxes and rebates embodied in the plan. Later in the day Schlesinger's associates advised reporters that this number was "a preliminary figure."[25]

National Energy Plan Proposals

The Carter National Energy Plan of April 1977 included about one hundred interdependent proposals consisting of pricing policies and the creation of regulatory mechanisms and administrative actions. Some of these proposals could be implemented simply by Executive Office action, usually by placing appropriate language in the *Federal Register*. Nevertheless, a great deal of the Carter program required congressional action.

The National Energy Plan began with ten principles thought to provide a framework for the plan and for the development of future programs. These principles ranged from the belief that "healthy economic growth

25. Edward Cowan, *New York Times,* April 30, 1977.

must continue" to the belief that energy prices should generally "reflect true replacement costs."[26] Just as there were ten principles, the plan had ten major categories or component parts. What follows is based on the Carter administration's description of the plan.

Conservation

The first of the plan's ten components was conservation, defined as achieving the cleanest and cheapest source of new energy *supply*. (But "conservation" was really an anticipated *demand*-reducing reaction to a set of sticks, carrots, and moral suasion.) The first of eight subjects listed under conservation was "transportation." This was not by accident; the transportation industry was consuming over one-fourth of all U.S. energy, most of it in the form of petroleum, and automobiles were using about half the energy requirement of the transportation sector. So it is not surprising to see the Carter plan beginning with a gas-guzzler tax and rebate. The Carter administration proposed the imposition of a graduated excise tax on new automobiles and light-duty trucks when fuel economy standards failed to be met.

The 1975 Energy Policy and Conservation Act mandated automobile fuel efficiency standards, with a 1985 target of an average of 27.5 miles per gallon (mpg) on all new cars, penalizing manufacturers failing to meet the average. The Carter administration proposed putting more bite into these standards, fixing an excise tax schedule by statute beginning with model year 1978, to increase each year through 1985 and remain constant beyond 1985. The purpose of the tax-rebate scheme was to obtain a *fleet average* of 27.5 mpg by 1985. The notion of taxes and rebates directly relevant to consumers would help assure that the automobile industry would be able to sell fuel-efficient cars. Simply mandating that the industry had to meet certain fuel-economy standards by a certain year was considered to be less attractive than combining such rules with a package of sticks and carrots directed toward car buyers. In 1977, as the National Energy Plan was formulated, the fleet average fuel consumption in the United States was 14 mpg. The 1977-model automobiles were averaging 18 mpg. Even given rapid obsolescence, obtaining a 27.5 mpg fleet average by 1985 was a rather ambitious target.[27] But it was an important one,

26. Executive Office of the President, *The National Energy Plan*, pp. 26, 29.
27. In what appeared to be a surrender to the three-martini lunch the National Highway Traffic Safety Administration exempted Rolls-Royce (averaging about 11 mpg) from the rules.

given the extraordinarily large volume of imported energy used by automobiles.

The rebate schedule was to be adjusted in advance of each year by the Internal Revenue Service, to assure that total estimated rebate payments did not exceed estimated tax receipts. That is, ex ante adjustments in the energy plan were to make the gas-guzzler tax and rebate scheme a fiscal wash. A widely publicized tax and rebate schedule was provided with the fact sheet distribution on April 20, 1977. It was certainly something most Americans could relate to and certainly generated its fair share of controversy. It provided for a tax of $2,488 in 1985 on new automobiles getting less than 12.5 mpg. Rebates of approximately $500 were offered producers of automobiles getting fuel economy in the 35 mpg and up range. The Energy Policy and Planning Office document released on April 29, 1977, seemed to be directed to America's European allies as much as to the American public. It was noted that among foreigners "there is no greater symbol of American energy waste than the heavy, powerful, accessory-laden American automobile." This symbol, known abroad as the Yank-Tank, was to be eliminated from American society. The gas-guzzler and rebate scheme had a number of companion statutes to buttress the administration's attempts to curtail gasoline consumption.

Probably the most important of these was a rather interesting scheme of goals for limiting increases in gasoline consumption from 1978 through the mid-1980s. The general notion was to impose automatically a tax of 5 cents a gallon on January 15 of each year, beginning in 1979, when gasoline consumption during the previous calendar year exceeded targets set by the government. Each year the targets were missed the tax would be increased by an additional 5 cents a gallon for each percentage point that consumption in the prior year exceeded the target, with 5 cents a year being the maximum increase. The cumulative amount of tax applicable for any one year would not be permitted to exceed 50 cents a gallon. The proposal truly captured the spirit of the Carter National Energy Plan. It was a standby gasoline tax. If the aggregate behavior of the American public was inconsistent with national targets, the American public would be punished. The punishment would continue until the retail price of gas reached rather heady levels. The plan offered no solution for the potential equity problems associated with such a tax; it did not provide for a rationing scheme should the retail price of gas begin pricing low-income Americans out of the market.

Any funds collected from this gas tax would be rebated back to the

American people progressively through the federal income tax system; direct payments would be made to persons not paying income tax. These two pricing mechanisms represent the core of the transportation side of the President's conservation program. They were buttressed with several additional rules and suggestions, some of which could be executed simply by administrative action and some of which required legislative approval. Perhaps the one that has turned out to have affected Americans more than they might have expected was the Carter administration's decision to ask state and local governments to enforce more vigorously the national speed limit of 55 miles an hour. The secretary of transportation received administrative authority to withhold highway trust fund revenues from states and local governments judged not to be enforcing the limit. Moreover, the Carter administration asked Congress to eliminate federal excise tax preferences for general aviation and motorboat fuel. Americans were being asked to pay more for the pleasures of Beachcrafts and bass boats. Another proposal requiring congressional action caused a substantial reaction on the part of the Republican minority in Congress. The Carter administration proposed that the federal government initiate a van-pooling program by purchasing about 6,000 vans as part of a demonstration project, showing how commuter transportation could be facilitated by employer action.

The second conservation subject in the President's National Energy Plan was directed toward buildings; the most important of the various programs and policies was a national residential energy conservation program for existing structures. Homeowners were to be offered a tax credit of 25 percent of the first $800 and 15 percent of the next $1,400 spent on approved conservation measures. The administration noted that there were approximately 74 million residential units in the United States as well as 1.5 million nonresidential buildings. Almost 20 percent of U.S. energy was used to heat and cool these structures and it was estimated that about half this energy was wasted. "The hermetically sealed glass and steel skyscraper" was described as the "analogue of the gas-guzzling automobile."[28] Just as homeowners received tax credits, businesses would be entitled to a 10 percent tax credit, in addition to the investment tax credit, for investments made to improve the energy efficiency of buildings. One controversial provision was the requirement that state public utility commissions direct utilities under their jurisdiction to offer their customers

28. Executive Office of the President, *The National Energy Plan*, p. 41.

residential energy conservation services that would be performed by the utilities and financed by loans repaid through monthly utility bills. There were many other components of this portion of the plan, including mandatory efficiency standards for new buildings and solar hot water and space-heating demonstration programs in federal buildings, but the two major tax credits represent the core of the progam.

The six additional categories of conservation measures included strengthening certain home appliance energy efficiency standards and a package of incentives to increase the utilization of heat now wasted during the production of electric power. The Carter administration debated whether or not to use the word "cogeneration"—the multiple use of a given amount of steam for electricity, say, and industrial use—in the fact sheet. They did and it became part of the vocabulary of the American reading public. Congress was asked to enact legislation that would encourage cogeneration. The general thrust of the cogeneration proposals was to encourage cascading, that is, the multiple use of a given amount of steam as it cools and becomes appropriate for a varying range of tasks. The final two conservation measures—utility rate reform and oil and natural gas tax and pricing policies—were quite controversial. Utility rate reform was designed to remove the waste and inequity in conventional utility pricing. It was noted that utility customers consuming the least commonly paid the highest unit price. A variety of measures were suggested to eliminate this practice, including the prohibition of master metering for electricity in new structures. A set of oil and natural gas pricing and tax policies was designed to conserve natural gas and petroleum and was of sufficient importance to be discussed in a special section later in the document.

Management Information Systems

Anyone working on U.S. energy problems has been frustrated by the general lack of data. If the federal government in particular was going to move into the energy field in the substantial way detailed in the Carter National Energy Plan, it was obvious that more specific and reliable information on fossil fuel reserves, energy company operations, and energy supplies and demands were needed. In response to this need the Carter plan called for a three-part energy information program representing the beginning of a National Energy Information System, which would provide comprehensive and authoritative information. The Carter administration proposed that the Department of Energy, once it was established by Congress, would take over the audit and verification function being performed by the American Gas Association and the American Petroleum Institute.

The Carter administration acknowledged the need to provide some protection for proprietary information. A federal takeover of the data work of the association and the institute would produce a Petroleum Production and Reserves Information System. The system would be supplemented by a Petroleum Company Financial Data System requiring all large companies, and a sample of small ones engaged in crude oil or natural gas production, to submit detailed information on a uniform basis to the federal government. Finally, an Emergency Management Information System would be created to provide Washington with the requisite local supply and demand needs in case of emergencies such as an oil embargo or the natural gas shortage during the winter of 1977.

Industry Competition

The Carter energy planners acknowledged a substantial horizontal and vertical concentration in the energy industry and that horizontal diversification by oil and gas producers into all areas of energy had aroused fears that major firms would restrict the development of alternative fuel sources. The Carter plan called for increasing reliance on coal, uranium, and renewable energy sources; the movement of the major oil and gas producers into these fields represented a potential restriction on development. Yet the Carter administration chose not to urge either horizontal or vertical divestiture in the industry. The plan was based on the assumption that new laws mandating divestiture were not required to promote or maintain competition in the energy industries, although it was observed that this conclusion was subject to change. This was, of course, obvious to any student of the industry. In 1974 a Federal Trade Commission study, "Concentration Levels and Trends in the Energy Sector," noted that the top four energy companies controlled 23.4 percent of U.S. production of all fuels including oil, gas, coal, and uranium. The top eight companies controlled 34.8 percent, while the top twenty controlled 57.2 percent. This was a rather concentrated industry, but it would take a strong-willed administration and Congress to do anything about it.

State and Local Government Participation

The section of the fact sheet dealing with the participation of state and local governments simply provided some guarantee that President Carter was committed to ensuring that no state, local community, or Indian tribe would suffer as a result of energy development. Unfortunately the terseness of this section simply indicated the hopelessness of offering such a guarantee.

Assistance for Low-Income Persons

This section did not contain any direct proposals to protect low-income citizens from the energy crisis. Rather, it indicated how other components of the plan, such as the weatherization program, would protect low-income people.

Oil and Natural Gas

In the mid-1970s oil and natural gas represented the primary energy sources for the United States, providing approximately 75 percent of the country's energy needs. But they constituted less than 8 percent of the country's reserves. Both fuels were priced below their marginal replacement costs and therefore were overused.

The Nixon-Ford entitlements program was designed to equalize the price of foreign and domestic crude paid by U.S. refineries and hence to help small independent refiners. It had the effect of subsidizing imports, and it had become an administrative nightmare. The Carter administration's oil and natural gas program was designed to wean American households and businesses away from these two fossil fuels. Oil and natural gas were in short domestic supply, at least at the regulated prices currently in effect. The United States had to develop a pricing system compatible with the new world price, without allowing excessive windfall profits. At the same time, the Carter administration wanted to continue the Ford administration's program of creating a strategic reserve of crude oil to provide some short-term cushion against another possible embargo.

The administration's oil and natural gas proposals fell under four general categories: oil pricing, tax program, natural gas pricing, and "other measures." The first, oil pricing, required legislative action. Contrary to what some may have thought had been said during his campaign, President Carter made a commitment to retain domestic oil price controls for an indefinite period to prevent windfall profits to domestic oil producers. The Carter plan was a request to Congress to revise and extend the basic pricing mechanism adopted by the Energy Policy and Conservation Act signed by Gerald Ford on December 22, 1975. The EPCA codified a set of automobile fuel efficiency standards and called for a gradual phasing out of price controls on domestic oil plus the creation of a 1-billion-barrel strategic reserve of oil and petroleum products. This act was supplemented by the Energy Conservation and Production Act, which became law on August 14, 1976. The ECPA extended the life of the Federal Energy Administration through December 31, 1977, and provided some additional conservation measures.

The Carter strengthening of the pricing mechanism would work in the following way:

A new, long-range oil pricing system would be based on a threefold classification of domestically produced oil. First, the Carter plan would continue indefinitely to maintain the price ceiling of $5.25 a barrel for "old" or "first tier" oil (that is, oil from wells producing before 1975) and of $11.28 a barrel for "new," "second tier," or "upper tier" oil. Oil coming from so-called stripper wells (wells producing ten barrels a day or less) would be freed of all price controls and allowed to sell at approximately $13.50, the world price. Of course, the actual price of oil produced by a particular well would depend on a number of factors including location, sulfur content, pour point, and so forth. In this sense, the Carter plan extended the existing program. The price ceilings, however, would be subject to escalation at the general rate of inflation. "Newly discovered oil" (oil discovered since 1975) would be allowed to rise to the current world price (adjusted for the rate of inflation) over a three-year period. From then on newly discovered oil would continue to be priced at the 1977 world price with appropriate adjustments for general inflation.

This pricing scheme represented a way to decrease the pain of adjusting to the world price of oil. But the adjustment process, of course, would provide substantial additional revenues to oil producers and to owners of oil leases. So the equity side of the Carter oil program was designed to spread the benefit of the adjustment to world pricing around to the American public at large. This would be done through the second component of the Carter oil and natural gas program, the tax program.

The Carter plan was for all domestic oil to become subject to a crude oil equalization tax to be applied in three equal stages beginning January 1, 1978. When the three stages were complete the present barrel tax would close the gap between the controlled domestic price and the world price. The net revenues collected as a result of this tax would be passed along to the American people in the form of tax credits or direct payments for those Americans with no tax liability. Thus the crude oil equalization tax would have no net effect on the U.S. Treasury and no net loss to American consumers. It would permit the termination of the entitlements program and establish a more realistic energy pricing system. That is, oil would be priced more closely to marginal replacement costs. It would achieve the effects of free markets on the demand side but not the supply side.

The third proposal was a legislative program for natural gas pricing, a nettlesome issue. The Carter administration argued that U.S. pricing policy for natural gas had developed during the period after World War II when there were abundant supplies, even at the very low prices then prevailing. Moreover, the history of regulation of interstate natural gas involved the complex history of the Federal Power Commission's authority in this area as a result of the 1954 Supreme Court decision in the Phillips case. Natural gas pricing policies evolved at a time when gas was a surplus by-product of oil and, according to some observers, when the monopoly power of the pipelines was failing. By the 1970s it was the most underpriced and oversold fuel in the United States.

The Carter administration wanted to bring natural gas supply and demand back into balance as a *first step* toward deregulation. Candidate Carter had spoken only of natural gas price deregulation, not about first steps toward deregulation, and candidate Carter had carried the state of Texas. The National Energy Plan pricing proposal for natural gas would subject all new gas sold anywhere in the United States to a price ceiling defined by the average refiner acquisition cost (before tax) of domestic crude oil. It was estimated that this rather cumbersome price limitation would yield a price of $1.75 per thousand cubic feet (mcf) at the beginning of 1978. As in the case of crude oil, this price ceiling would be adjusted over the years for inflation. The inflation adjustment would be indirect, operating through the inflation adjustment on the ceiling price of crude oil. It was estimated that the wellhead price of $1.75 per mcf for new natural gas at the beginning of 1978 was equivalent to an $8.50-per-barrel price of oil. Between implementation of the plan and the middle-term target date of 1985, the wellhead price for new natural gas was expected to move to the neighborhood of $3 per mcf, with all prices measured in constant (1977) dollars. The 1985 price for new natural gas would result in a 20 percent increase in natural gas supply. As the Carter plan was formulated, the average retail price of natural gas, including both old and new gas and both the wellhead price plus transportation and marketing costs, was $1.90 per mcf. The wellhead price contributed about 60 cents to this average retail price. The Carter administration estimated that under existing regulations, without the plan, the price would be $2.60 by 1985. Under the assumption that the plan was enacted so that in 1985 roughly one-fifth of all gas consumed would be new gas, the Carter administration estimated that the average of old and new retail prices paid by consumers in 1985 would be $2.16. That is, American consumers of natural gas would be better off if the plan were enacted. "New natural gas" in the Carter plan was defined using the same approach as that used to define newly discovered oil; a well drilled more than two and one-half miles from an existing onshore well as of April 20, 1977, or more than 1,000 feet deeper than any well within any two and one-half mile radius. New offshore wells would be limited to oil and natural gas produced from lands leased after April 20, 1977.

The fourth and last category under the general heading "oil and natural gas" was "other measures" and consisted of ten general propositions. These ten measures ranged from expansion of the strategic petroleum reserve that would enable the United States to withstand a serious supply interruption for about ten months, to a replacement of the Nixon-Ford limitation on the importation of liquefied natural gas.

Coal, Nuclear, and Hydroelectric Power

Coal was the key to the Carter plan since it would serve as the bridge to fill the gap between even the modestly rising energy requirements of sustained economic growth and the relatively stable U.S. production of oil and natural gas. If the United States was to achieve economic growth and if the growth was to be fueled by something other than imported fossil fuels, coal would have to take up the slack. Coal was once the premier fuel in the United States, but by the late 1970s its use was reduced to just a handful of industrial processes such as generating electricity and making coke for the steel industry. Oil and natural gas were cleaner and weight-for-weight provided more energy. Conventional burning of coal produced soot, sulfur dioxide, and nitrogen oxides. Research on coal gasification and liquefaction had been proceeding for many decades but the processes used substantial amounts of water and "20 to 35 percent of the energy is lost in conversion."[29] Of course, the United States could attempt a "coal solution" to avoid a 1980s doomsday. Unlike other countries, the United States had substantial coal resources. In the mid-1970s, U.S. recoverable reserves of coal were estimated to be 218,400 million short tons (a short ton is 2,000 pounds, a metric ton is 2,200.46 pounds).[30] In comparison, the recoverable resources of coal in the USSR, the next richest country in coal, were only 91,400 million short tons. The United States had nearly double the recoverable reserves of coal of the USSR, which had been thought to have approximately 50 percent greater coal resources. In 1975 U.S. coal production was 626.2 million short tons, a production rate that could be maintained for approximately three and one-half centuries. The USSR's 1975 coal production was estimated to be 590.8 million short tons, a production rate sustainable for approximately a century and a half. Other countries, particularly other NATO members, were simply not in the game. Coal was not part of the answer for them.[31]

The first of four major components of the Carter plan for coal was an oil and natural gas users' tax designed to shift industry away from oil and natural gas as fuels. The users' tax was complicated by exceptions and by the fact that it represented an attempt to achieve several simultaneous goals. Essentially the plan called for most industrial users of natural gas to be taxed beginning in 1979 an amount equal to the difference between their average cost of natural gas and a price target keyed to the current price of distillate oil. The target level for the 1979 tax would be $1.05 below the Btu-equivalent price of distillate oil. The target price would rise to equal the distillate price in 1985 and beyond. For example, in 1979 an industrial user paying $1.65 per mcf for natural gas would be penalized and required to pay a tax of 30 cents per mcf to bring the internal cost of

29. Mason Willrich, *Energy and World Politics* (Free Press, 1975), p. 113.

30. The U.S. government defined "resources" in a theoretical sense. Resources included deposits merely surmised to exist on the basis of geological theory. Reserves are calculated more rigidly, and some concrete evidence of their actual existence is required. The phrase "recoverable reserves" was generally applied to coal and was synonymous with "proved reserves" used to discuss petroleum. Both phrases conveyed the meaning that the reserves were recoverable, given current technology and present economic conditions.

31. Ralph Stuart Smith, *The United States and World Energy* (U.S. Department of State, Bureau of Public Affairs, November 1977), p. 23.

using natural gas up to the target level of $1.95 per mcf, based on the assumption that the Btu equivalent of distillate oil in 1979 was $3. By 1985 the target level was expected to rise to approximately $3.30 per mcf.

The point is that the price of distillate oil would move freely and the actual cost to the industrial user of natural gas would move in tandem. But the higher prices paid by the industrial user would be captured by the federal government in the form of tax receipts. Utilities using natural gas as a boiler fuel would be taxed in a similar fashion beginning in 1983 in such a way that their cost of natural gas would be 50 cents per mcf below the Btu-equivalent price of distillate oil. The tax would rise so that by 1988 the cost of natural gas to utilities would finally be equal to the cost of an equivalent amount of distillate oil. Utilities were given a later starting date for the imposition of the tax since they required longer lead times for coal conversion. Both industrial and utility petroleum users would be taxed at a flat rate. Beginning in 1979 industrial users would be taxed 90 cents a barrel with the tax rising to $3 a barrel by 1985. Again, utilities would have more time to respond since their tax on petroleum use would begin only in 1983 at a constant rate of $1.50 a barrel. Industry would be eligible for either an additional 10 percent investment tax credit for capital expenses associated with coal conversion or a rebate of any natural gas or petroleum taxes paid, not to exceed the level of expenditures incurred for coal conversion. It should be noted that there were potential hardships in some sectors. There are major problems associated with using coal in some applications, such as textile drying, where a clean fuel is mandatory.

Thus the Carter plan was firmly grounded on incentives, both positive and negative, for industrial and utility users of oil and natural gas to convert to coal. In order to assure the greatest possible conversion from oil and natural gas, additional proposals were submitted under the general category of coal conversion regulatory policy. The conversion process would be stimulated by prohibiting the burning of natural gas or petroleum in new boilers. With limited temporary exceptions, no utility would be permitted to burn natural gas after 1990.

Another component of the administration's program for coal, nuclear, and hydroelectric power was an environmental policy for coal. While trying to get the United States to embrace coal, the administration feared that this was potentially a major step backward in environmental policy. To temper this potential backward step, the administration supported a strong environmental protection package to go along with the coal conversion incentives. For example, administration policy would require installation of the best available control technology in all new coal-fired plants, including those burning low-sulfur coal.

The fourth component of the industry's coal, nuclear, and hydroelectric power program was a major expansion of executive branch activity in coal research and development. Administrative action was taken to make sure that everything was being done to ease the substitution of coal for gas and petroleum products. These efforts included the search for more effective and more economical methods to meet air pollution control standards, including flue gas desulfurization systems (scrubbers), a technology of several varieties that has been around for many years, as well as extensive expansion of synthetic crude technology.

The administration made two basic points concerning the controversial subject of nuclear energy. Significantly, it asked Congress for very little action in the area of nuclear power, instead discussing the nuclear side of the plan in terms of administrative action. First, the Carter plan stated that it was the policy of the United States to defer indefinitely commercial reprocessing and recycling of spent fuels produced in U.S. civilian nuclear power plants. Specifically President Carter informed Congress that he had decided to defer indefinitely construction of the Clinch River Liquid Metal Fast Breeder Reactor demonstration project and to cancel all component construction, commercialization, and licensing efforts. Second, the Carter energy planners addressed the issue of domestic nuclear safety and storage and again they were negative. Light-water reactors, recognized as having good safety records, were also identified as not being a nuclear proliferation hazard. But the administration announced a number of expanded audit and inspection techniques ranging from unannounced inspections to asking the Nuclear Regulatory Commission to mandate currently voluntary reporting of minor mishaps.

Nonconventional Sources of Energy

The Carter plan considered the long-term economic growth of the United States beyond the year 2000 to be dependent on successful exploitation of the renewable sources of energy, including solar, geothermal, biomass, and other technologies. Explicit incentives were provided to both households and businesses to stimulate development and commercialization of solar hot water and space-heating technologies.

The administration recognized that controlled thermonuclear reactions, fusion, had been a major element in energy research and development over the years. It also recognized, however, that the projects to date had been engineering nightmares. In addition, if the engineering and metallurgical problems associated with the laser approach to fusion are solved and if the laser method is used, the facilities could be used as a shortcut for converting uranium into plutonium or thorium into U-233, another nuclear explosive. So fusion might have the same doomsday characteristics as the breeder reactor. When the Carter plan was released there was little basis for optimism about either the magnetic confinement or inertial confinement (laser or beam) approaches to fusion. Scientific feasibility for net production of power had not yet been demonstrated.

Decentralized Systems

As part of the administration's belief that a long-term solution to the energy problem rested on the more esoteric approaches, the administration proposed administrative action to encourage increased funding for a variety of projects that were not economically feasible, at least on a large scale, in the late 1970s. These projects ranged from the development of solar space cooling technologies to biomass demonstration projects.

Transportation Study

The last topic in the administration's National Energy Plan was a short paragraph noting that the United States urgently needed to reassess its energy transportation system. The Carter administration promised to establish a committee to study and make recommendations. Essentially the problem was that during the era of cheap energy following World War II the United States had developed a system for moving oil and natural gas from the South to the North and Northeast. Perhaps because of environmental and other legal problems, the private sector in the United States had not seemed to respond to the problems of transporting increased supplies of oil and gas from Alaska and from the outer continental shelf and of moving western coal in some form to the East.

The Energy Plan and the Congressional Obstacle Course

In an interview published in May 1977 President Carter gave October 1, 1977, as the deadline for congressional approval of his plan;[32] the

32. "Carter Up Close," Newsweek, May 2, 1977, p. 37.

Ninety-fifth Congress was given until the beginning of the new fiscal year to digest and pass his package. (This may have been a tactical error.) When the National Energy Plan was released it received some praise: a comprehensive plan had been developed. But as should have been expected, it also received a barrage of criticism from disparate sources within government and from the public at large. Transmission of the plan to Congress and to the American public on the deadline date of April 20, 1977, was accompanied by a media blitz led by the President. The administration had obviously approached the energy crisis as *the* major problem facing the country and had tried to capture the imagination of Congress and the public. President Carter and his associates felt that the people of the United States needed to recognize the energy crisis and to accept the administration's solution.

Different Approaches of House and Senate

The President was in a relatively enviable position. A Democratic President, he had Democratic majorities in both houses of Congress. On the House side he could rely on the leadership of Speaker Thomas P. O'Neill, Jr., who had committed himself to get the complete Carter energy plan passed in the House. He viewed the plan as a test of whether the Democratic party could provide responsible government when it controlled both the executive and legislative branches of government. O'Neill's first step was to handcraft a select committee under the chairmanship of Congressman Thomas Ashley of Ohio that was balanced in favor of Democrats generally sympathetic to the Carter plan. He set strict deadlines for consideration of appropriate components of the bill by the regular House standing committees. The standing committees finished their work in six weeks; the select committee did its job in three days. The Carter plan was then sent to the House Rules Committee, which not only acted favorably but attached rules to the bill designed to ease its passage on the House floor. Whenever emergencies arose O'Neill intervened to keep the plan moving through the House of Representatives. When a ground swell of anger arose in the House concerning the Carter natural gas policy, O'Neill broke the back of the uprising by appealing to party unity and congressional responsibility. On August 5, 1977, the House passed the Carter energy plan virtually intact. To the surprise of many people, including members of Congress, Carter's October 1 deadline had been met.

But the U.S. Senate was another story. There, President Carter had to rely on the leadership of Majority Leader Robert C. Byrd. Senator Byrd did clear all other bills from the Senate agenda so that senators could concentrate on the energy plan. Nevertheless, as the summer of 1977 wore on it became obvious that the Senate was going to deliberate and deliberate. By the time the Senate acted a number of critical changes had been made in its version of the energy bill, mostly in favor of markets over regulations. Beginning in October 1977 the House-Senate Conference Committee began the most difficult job of resolving the conflicts between the House–Carter energy plan and the variant of the plan that had passed the Senate. During the remaining weeks of the first session of the Ninety-fifth Congress the conferees remained bogged down in a variety of problems, including the perennial issue of natural gas price deregulation. The session adjourned on December 15 with the conferees deadlocked in intense disagreement.

As the members of Congress went home for the holidays, a great deal of speculation arose both in government and in the press about why President Carter's October 1977 deadline had been missed and about why the Carter plan appeared to be in serious trouble. Many basic problems plagued the plan from the viewpoint of Congress, including the fact that congressmen had not been consulted during the early days of the Carter administration when the plan was hammered out. The President had plopped this gigantic document on their desks on April 20 and had then told the press it would be passed by October 1. Many people on the Hill who had worked on U.S. energy policy intensively for years were irate about the way they were being treated. One could look at the Carter plan and find major elements of previous Democratic initiatives that had been around Congress for quite some time. Many elements of the National Energy Plan would create a sense of déjà vu among former Ford administration energy staffers as well. Little in the plan was original; virtually all components had been discussed in the protracted period of shadowboxing during both the Ninety-third and the Ninety-fourth Congress. The Carter administration gave Congress *one* program, packaged as a critically necessary national energy *conservation* policy.[33] But some people at the east end of Pennsylvania Avenue believed the President and his energy advisers had not given much recognition to the roots of the plan's compo-

33. For a brief comparison of some of the Carter plan components with the Ford policies on the same issues, see "Carter's Proposals: A More Unified Framework . . . But Many Familiar Elements from the Ford Years," *Congressional Quarterly Almanac: 1977*, vol. 33, pp. 716–17.

nents. Most congressmen and their aides also freely criticized the Carter administration's legislative liaison, arguing that the Carter people were not effectively selling the plan to Congress. They viewed success in the House as Speaker O'Neill's rather than anyone's in the executive branch.

There were more fundamental problems. Any comprehensive energy plan would contain something to offend everyone. The Carter plan became the object of intense lobbying activity on behalf of special interest groups affected by a particular component of the bill. The plan was designed to serve the national interest, to override the special interests. Everyone in some way would be hurt by enactment of the plan, but overall it was designed to be in the best interests of the United States as a whole. Unfortunately lobbyists concerned about some particular component were much more successful, particularly in the Senate, than the lobbyists for national interests, represented by the Carter administration.

Many states have substantial petroleum and natural gas reserves and were ably represented not only in the Senate in general but on critical committees. For example, the tax components of the plan had to be considered by the Senate Finance Committee, chaired by Russell B. Long of Louisiana, a major producing state. Senator Long had always been forthright in stating that he represented the oil and gas industry. In his mind the interests of the oil and gas industry were synonymous with the interests of Louisiana. Senator Long thus proved to be an extraordinary obstacle. No similar obstacle faced Speaker O'Neill in the House; the tax-writing House Ways and Means Committee was no longer chaired by Wilbur D. Mills. Under the chairmanship of Democratic Congressman Al Ullman of Oregon the Ways and Means Committee had become internally more democratic and more responsive to House leadership. Furthermore, Chairman Ullman was not from a producing or refining congressional district.

There were similar contrasts throughout the committee structure of Congress. All these committee problems were compounded because, unlike Speaker O'Neill, Senate Majority Leader Byrd had a deep commitment to the Senate rather than to the Democratic party. He was certainly unwilling and perhaps unable to run the Senate as Lyndon Johnson had done in the 1950s. Although several senators argued that no one could run the Senate in the 1970s as strong majority leaders had run it in the past, it is not clear that the present Senate is unique. An extremely strong personality might, if willing, have provided leadership in the Senate commensurate with that provided by O'Neill in the House. It is possible that the nature of Senate committees is an additional explanation for the difficulties the National Energy Plan had in the Senate. The House of Representatives has many members, each of whom serves on relatively few committees. Members are more inclined to specialize and therefore to listen to colleagues who have specialized in other areas. The Senate, however, spreads fewer members over a great deal of ground. Senator Byrd may have suffered from a confluence of difficulties, including, perhaps, the desire of the independent senators to maintain the freedoms they enjoyed under the relatively benign leadership of Majority Leader Mike Mansfield. Whatever the reason, the Senate balked. As 1977 drew to a close, a Conference Committee was charged with reconciling the House and Senate legislation. Both houses by then were in a state described as "the Moral Equivalent of Chaos."[34]

During December 1977 the House and Senate conferees engaged in three weeks of negotiations, with no real progress toward resolving the problems of natural gas pricing and the tax side of the Carter plan. There was a continuing battle over the critical Clinch River Nuclear Breeder Reactor. On November 5, 1977, Carter used his first presidential veto, rejecting the $6.7 billion Department of Energy Authorization Act of 1978 because Congress had included $80 million for Clinch River. The President described the project as unnecessarily expensive, technically obsolete, and economically unsound. The Clinch River project was first estimated to cost $450 million, but by the fall of 1977 the cost estimate was around $2.2 billion. It was clear, however, that Congress was going to press the issue; Clinch River would remain on the agenda for 1978.

Second Session Impediments

The second session of the Ninety-fifth Congress found congressmen returning to Washington on January 19, 1978, to face a variety of issues, including the energy problem. The Panama Canal Treaty diverted Senate attention just as the Korean influence-peddling scandal diverted the House. The chronic New York City financial crisis had to be addressed. The House-Senate conferees were continuing to try to resolve the differing versions of the energy bill but were stumbling over a number of problems, including the price of natural gas. An end-of-the-year series of polls had showed that the American public gave Congress poor marks for

34. Robert J. Samuelson, "Economic Focus: The Moral Equivalent of Chaos," *National Journal,* October 22, 1977, p. 1653.

handling the Carter energy initiative. Cambridge Reports, the public opinion service, found that while 35 percent of the American public favored Carter's original proposal only 2 percent rated congressional performance excellent. Differential comparisons of the "average congressman" and the "average senator" with President Carter, based on their relative "sincerity about solving energy problems," indicated that 73 percent of the American public considered President Carter to be sincere on the issue while Congress, on the average, was judged to be only about 30 percent sincere.[35]

Of course, the second session of the Ninety-fifth Congress had a substantial body of internally generated evidence that there were some major difficulties with the Carter plan. The job of the Carter administration was to press the congressional conferees to wade through this growing tide of criticism and pass the plan, faults and all. Any hint that the administration would compromise on some element of the plan was immediately slapped down by the White House Press Office.

At the same time, the press ran an unfortunate series of stories debunking the certainty of a world oil shortage in the 1980s. The Carter planners' assumption that the industrialized world faced a severe shortage of petroleum in the 1980s shaped the time profile of the Carter plan as well as the plan's component parts. In early January 1978 a number of experts in the field argued that oil supplies would be abundant through the 1970s and would remain adequate through the 1980s, causing the world oil market to soften with decreases in prices and U.S. imports. This would make the probability of OPEC price action rather remote, knocking out the foundation from the logic of the April 1977 plan. The bullishness about oil supply was the result of an increasingly wide expectation of an economic recession in the late 1970s and early 1980s, thus reducing the demand for oil. Moreover, oil experts were surprised by the degree to which the industrialized democracies were learning to use oil more efficiently.[36]

President Carter's fiscal year 1979 budget proposal contained no new major energy policy proposals. The energy content of the budget was in harmony with the April 1977 plan. Of course, the largest budgetary item was support for the Department of Energy, in operation since October 1, 1977. The Carter proposal was for a Department of Energy budget authority of $12.6 billion. The largest item in the department's budget was $4.3 billion for the Strategic Petroleum Reserve Program, designed to

35. Adam H. Clymer, *New York Times,* January 2, 1978.
36. Anthony J. Parisi, *New York Times,* January 18, 1978.

immunize the United States against a repetition of the catastrophic 1973–74 Arab oil embargo.[37] The Carter budget included a $150 million cutback for breeder reactor programs reflecting the administration's effort to scuttle the Clinch River program.[38]

On January 19, 1978, President Carter reminded Congress that the comprehensive National Energy Plan was still a major part of its unfinished agenda. In one section of his State of the Union Message entitled "Developing and Protecting Our Natural Resources" President Carter outlined the action that had already been taken during 1977 but noted that a "number of difficult, contentious issues remain to be settled."[39] In his economic message to Congress on January 20, 1978, President Carter reminded Congress that more than four years had passed since the U.S. economy had been buffeted by the Arab oil embargo and had suffered the aftermath of sharply higher oil prices. He reminded Congress that during 1977 the United States continued to be dependent on imported oil, paying about $45 billion for oil imports, compared with $8.5 billion in 1973.[40]

Throughout the spring and summer of 1978 the House and Senate searched for a compromise on natural gas pricing. In May 1978 after six months of negotiations the Senate and House energy conferees agreed to legislation on pricing natural gas. The compromise would immediately raise the price of newly discovered natural gas from $1.49 per mcf to $1.93 per mcf, 18 cents more than President Carter originally proposed. The price of new gas at the wellhead would increase annually by about 10 percent, assuming an expected inflation rate of 6 percent. Price controls on new gas would then expire at the end of 1984 but could be reimposed for one eighteen-month period by the President or Congress. If controls *were* reimposed, they could not be in effect beyond 1988. Following the conferees' resolution of the natural gas pricing issue, the major unresolved issue in the nontax part of the energy plan was the so-called gas-guzzler program. The Senate had voted to ban the production and sale of gas-guzzling cars, while the House had voted for a tax but no ban.

37. "Carter Energy Proposals Carry No Major Initiatives," *Congressional Quarterly Weekly Report,* January 28, 1978, pp. 177–79.

38. In July 1978 the Department of Energy announced an acceleration of the Strategic Petroleum Reserve Program. Four Gulf Coast salt dome sites had been acquired with a capacity of 275 billion barrels. The July 1978 fill rate was 150,000 barrels a day, with a 32.5 million barrel storage total. The department predicted 125 million barrels would be in storage by the end of the year. U.S. Department of Energy, *Energy Insider,* July 10, 1978.

39. *Congressional Quarterly Weekly Report,* January 28, 1978, p. 212.

40. Ibid., p. 217.

During 1978 the Clinch River Breeder Reactor remained a major problem. The House Science Committee on April 12, 1978, insisted on continuing the development of the project. It rejected an administration-backed compromise that would have required a thirty-month study of various breeder reactor options. As the second session wound down toward election time, the nuclear industry was buffeted by a bewildering variety of good and bad news. The Nuclear Regulatory Commission seemed to be placing high priority on environmental concerns, as indicated by their temporary halt of construction at the Seabrook, New Hampshire, nuclear plant. At the same time, the U.S. Supreme Court affirmed the constitutionality of the Price-Anderson Act (1957), which limited liability for any single nuclear accident to $560 million, reversing a lower federal court decision. During 1978 evidence mounted that light-water reactors, the great hope of the industry, were turning out to be much more costly than anticipated. They also were proving to be a magnet for disparate protest movements, raising such issues as general safety, waste disposal, and plutonium thefts.

Congressional Action at Last

After eighteen months of deliberation, about half the Carter administration program was approved by Congress, much of it during the hectic closing days before the 1978 elections. On November 9, one year, six months, and nineteen days after the package had been sent to Congress, President Carter signed the National Energy Act of 1978 before an East Room audience in the White House. The package, standing about eight inches high, had five components:

—The National Energy Conservation Policy Act
—The Powerplant and Industrial Fuel Use Act
—The Public Utilities Regulatory Policy Act
—The Energy Tax Act
—The Natural Gas Policy Act

The National Energy Conservation Policy Act provided for a utility conservation program for residences, weatherization grants for low-income families, solar energy and energy conservation loan programs, and a grant program for schools and hospitals. These conservation programs were not modest; the last one, for example, represented a commitment of $300 million annually for three years. The act also required the Department of Energy to set efficiency standards over the next two years for thirteen categories of home appliances and provided the department with $100 million for solar demonstration programs in federal buildings.

The Powerplant and Industrial Fuel Use Act prohibited the use of oil or gas as fuel in new electrical generating plants or in new industrial plants. The Department of Energy was authorized to restrict the use of oil or gas to fire large boilers having a coal capability. Recognizing diseconomies both in coal production and use, the act included support to reduce the negative effects of increased coal production and an $800 million pollution control loan program.

The Public Utilities Regulatory Policy Act provided eleven voluntary standards for rate design, including a ban on declining block rates (reducing unit prices as consumption increases). This act included many additional regulatory changes, from new Federal Energy Regulatory Commission rules favoring cogeneration to federal support for consumer interventions in utility rate proceedings.

The Energy Tax Act embraced many new taxes, tax credits, and exemptions from taxes, including a tax credit for homeowners who insulate their houses or install solar heating systems and a gas-guzzler tax milder than originally proposed by the Carter administration ($200 tax on a 1980 car that fails to get 15 mpg, increasing gradually to $3,850 on 1986-model cars failing to get 12.5 mpg).

The Natural Gas Policy Act was the most controversial of the five components passed by Congress. It came close to defeat at virtually every stage of its existence. Its effect on natural gas prices, reserves, and production as well as on other sectors of the economy, particularly oil imports, was bitterly debated. The act provided a series of maximum lawful prices for various categories of natural gas, including gas sold in both the interstate and intrastate markets. This eliminated the regulatory distinction between the two markets. The basic price of natural gas was set at $1.75 per mcf as of April 1977. Producers were permitted to charge above that ceiling by the rate of inflation since April 1977 plus 3.7 percent. After 1981 the ceiling price was to change at the rate of inflation plus 4 percent. Newly produced gas was to be "incrementally priced," that is, higher prices would be borne first by industrial users rather than home consumers. The administrative difficulties associated with implementation of the Natural Gas Policy Act were staggering. Before the act took effect (December 1, 1978) there were four basic prices of natural gas: the unregulated intrastate price as well as three interstate prices: gas from wells drilled after January 1975 ($1.52 per mcf), between January 1975 and

January 1973 ($0.92 per mcf), and before January 1973 ($0.295 per mcf). This pricing system was replaced with a much more complex one with over seventeen categories of natural gas based on distinctions such as offshore-onshore and gas committed to the interstate market before or after December 1, 1978. All these prices are for a homogenous product. The possibilities for mischief are great. The burdens of administration are awesome. Nevertheless, natural gas will continue to be an energy bargain: the Department of Energy has estimated that a thousand cubic feet of natural gas will cost the average homeowner $3.31 in 1985, while an equivalent amount of Btu from oil and electricity will cost $3.90 and $12.80, respectively.

The Carter administration and others analyzed the five parts of the National Energy Act of 1978 in terms of barrels of imported oil a day "saved" by 1985. As indicated at the bottom of table 8-1, the Carter National Energy Plan was expected to reduce oil imports by 4.5 million barrels a day by 1985, from an expected 11.5 million barrels to 7 million barrels. Little disagreement has arisen about the effect on 1985 oil imports of the first four parts of the National Energy Act of 1978. The conservation, industrial fuel, public utilities, and tax acts, were expected to reduce U.S. oil imports by about 1.5 million barrels a day by 1985. Although some disagreed about this number, independent estimates did not vary widely. The main dispute was over the effect of the Natural Gas Policy Act on 1985 oil imports. As indicated in table 8-2, the Carter plan for natural gas was expected to yield domestic supply increases equivalent to a reduction of oil imports of 700,000 barrels of oil a day in 1985. In August 1978 the Department of Energy was estimating that the natural gas bill would save up to 1 million barrels a day in 1985, while an October 1978 White House briefing paper raised this number to 1.4 million. The American Gas Association, which supported the bill, used a number roughly half of the department's. And critics of the bill estimated that its net effect on oil imports would be much lower than even the American Gas Association's estimate, ranging from a saving of 363,000 barrels a day to 1 million barrels a day *additional* oil imports. Thus according to the Carter administration, the Ninety-fifth Congress provided for about half the target reduction of U.S. oil imports of 4.5 million barrels a day in 1985. But the lion's share of this reduction was attributable to a bold executive branch estimate of the effect of the Natural Gas Policy Act.

What about the parts of the Carter plan that Congress chose not to pass? Congress rejected the centerpiece of the Carter program—the crude oil equalization tax and taxes on industrial users of oil and natural gas. The Carter administration had argued that these two programs would lower oil imports by 2.3 million and 230,000 barrels, respectively, of oil a day in 1985.

After Congress adjourned, about half of Carter's plan was legislative reality. A Department of Energy was busily engaged in pushing energy research and development in all areas from coal liquefaction to hydrogen fusion. Nevertheless, the basic problem surrounding the domestic price of oil was unresolved. And the United States continued to run substantial trade deficits, with a monthly oil import bill of over $3 billion, about 20 percent of total U.S. imports.

Categories of Criticism

Some critics of the Carter plan have argued that the delays in Congress and the deletions in the final program were not signs of weakness in the American political system but represented a remarkable political success. The political system was not "panicked by momentary energy jingoism."[41]

Quantitative Criticism

Regardless of legislative success or failure the National Energy Plan was subjected to detailed external scrutiny. (Some of the negative results may help explain the delays and deletions.) Virtually every congressional research organization with analytical capability was directed to investigate the National Energy Plan. And every report was critical. Reports were produced by the General Accounting Office and the Legislative Reference Service of the Library of Congress as well as by the staffs of appropriate permanent committees. The Office of Technology Assessment offered an early and thorough critique.[42]

41. David A. Stockman, "The Wrong War? The Case against a National Energy Policy," *Public Interest*, vol. 53 (Fall 1978), pp. 2–44. Stockman was a minority member of the House Energy and Power Subcommittee during the Ninety-fifth Congress. He was particularly critical of the world oil reserves doomsday mentality represented by the April 1977 CIA forecasts.

42. U.S. Congress, Office of Technology Assessment, *Analysis of the Proposed National Energy Plan* (GPO, August 1977). This report was prepared in response to requests from Chairman Olin E. Teague of the House Committee on Science and Technology and Chairman Morris K. Udall of the House Committee on Interior

Energy as a field of inquiry had been a minor cottage industry even before the 1973 Arab oil embargo. Successive administrations were increasingly sensitive to the absence of an integrated U.S. energy policy. Researchers spent less time analyzing specific fuels and concentrated increasingly on a broad spectrum of interrelated energy sources. This approach certainly characterized the efforts of the Office of Science and Technology in the last eighteen months of the Johnson administration as well as much of the research and policy during the Nixon-Ford years. Economists were no exception to the rush to move into energy as a field of technical and policy analysis. By the time the Carter plan was submitted to Congress a significant body of experts was prepared to offer criticism and advice. The surge in the employment of these experts in the executive branch did not exhaust the pool of available talent; many experts were available to Congress and many remained independent, prepared to offer criticism from the outside.

Much of the quantitative complaint about the National Energy Plan had to do with alleged internal inconsistencies. One of the earliest (June 1977) congressional reactions to the Carter proposals came from the Congressional Budget Office, directed by Alice M. Rivlin.[43] The CBO argued that while the Carter administration's analysis assumed that the National Energy Plan would reduce oil imports by 4.5 million barrels a day by target year 1985, the reduction would in fact be only 3.6 million barrels a day. Two-thirds of the difference of 0.9 million barrels a day was attributable to the CBO's less generous estimate of coal conversion potential, while one-third was due to lower estimates of the effectiveness of home insulation and solar equipment tax credits. The CBO report was relatively mild when compared with the General Accounting Office report published the next month. The GAO began its evaluation of the plan with a remarkable piece of understatement. Comptroller General Elmer B. Staats observed that the Carter plan had "one major flaw": on the basis of the administration's own numbers, the plan was "not strong enough to meet four

---

and Insular Affairs. The Office of Technology Assessment (OTA) currently operates with a distinguished energy advisory committee chaired by Milton Katz of the Harvard Law School. It has several ad hoc energy panels as well as a substantial external support staff, and its Congressional Board is chaired by Senator Edward M. Kennedy. There is a definite current need in the United States for institutions such as the OTA. This quasi-public forum provides a means for objective discussion of public policy questions that have substantive technical content.

43. Congressional Budget Office, "President Carter's Energy Proposals: A Perspective," Staff Working Paper (June 1977).

of the seven established goals."[44] The GAO had provided an internal preliminary report, developed at the request of the chairman of the House Subcommittee on Energy and Power, on July 8. Then GAO representatives met with administration officials on July 15 and received formal comments from them on July 21. The administration's defense was communicated to Staats by Schlesinger assistant Alvin L. Alm. Alm was "concerned that this report may be a major source of unintended confusion." His defense was not a very stout one; he argued that although the Carter plan was not optimal, it was better than nothing.[45]

There is some folklore about why the quantitative goals of Carter's National Energy Plan could not be achieved by the measures outlined in the plan. Several persons argue that the following happened: when Council of Economic Advisers Chairman Schultze and Treasury Secretary W. Michael Blumenthal learned about the contents of what Schlesinger's shop was producing, they demanded a meeting with Carter and Schlesinger. Just a few days before the April 20 deadline, Schultze and Blumenthal were able to talk Carter out of several critical supply and demand measures in the Schlesinger program. The National Energy Plan was left with the original 1985 targets, and the instruments to achieve those targets were reduced. During what is alleged to have been a stormy three and one-half hour meeting, Schultze and Blumenthal made a persuasive case to drop certain items. They won the battle but lost the war in the sense that their relationships with President Carter were never the same after this confrontation. The *New York Times* reported on April 24, 1977, that Schlesinger defended the National Energy Plan before the entire cabinet on April 6 and 7, meeting with a great deal of vehement criticism.[46]

Natural Gas

The Carter administration also ran into an unfortunate incident in the natural gas area during 1977 that gave opponents of the plan strong ammunition to make a case that the administration was not being honest. The issue concerned what the true reserves and true supply of natural gas

44. U.S. General Accounting Office, *An Evaluation of the National Energy Plan*, a Report to Congress by the Comptroller General (GAO, 1977), p. 1.

45. Letter, Alms to Staats, July 21, 1977, published as app. 2 of GAO, *An Evaluation of the National Energy Plan*, p. 10-6.

46. But—the *New York Times* obtained a copy of the Carter National Energy Plan dated April 9, 1977. The description published in the *Times* on April 13, 1977, and the plan as it was released on April 20 were the same.

would be over time and for various prices. It all began in January 1977 when a group of researchers from the Energy Research and Development Administration (ERDA) assembled to do a market orientation program planning study, known as MOPPS. Three substudies of natural gas "were oriented toward internal research issues, not toward policy decisions."[47] They were intended to assess the long-term supply situation beyond the 1985 Carter target date and to make recommendations concerning long-term research objectives. None of the findings of the MOPPS research were relevant to policy issues before 1985. MOPPS was done by "assigning two analytical groups the responsibility for essentially the same task. In a bureaucratic sense, the groups were in direct competition and felt this keenly."[48]

The first group, led by Christopher Knudsen (later to be fired from the Department of Energy by Phillip White), attempted to evaluate published U.S. Geological Survey reserve estimates. This group was concerned about the quantity of natural gas in existence in the United States and about supply over a thousand years, that being a sufficient period of time to find all the natural gas capable of being found under any circumstances. The Knudsen group included some very broad cost estimates but placed no great weight on them and certainly did not consider them to have anything to do with price. The group concluded that the Geological Survey estimates were too high and that thus it was futile to use them for policy affecting the next decade. The Knudsen group also produced some interesting material concerning emerging natural gas technologies.

The second ERDA group went about the problem quite differently. "To them, the resource estimates and their theoretical costs were relatively unimportant."[49] Members of this group decided to develop middle-term estimates of market shares for fuels. They used a linear programming model developed by the Stanford Research Institute and the Gulf Oil Corporation; estimation of this model's parameters was done in part using Gulf Oil Corporation data. (The two groups did not share data sources.) The second group tried to determine the natural gas prices required to support various alternative energy technologies and what the market share of various fuels would be under various technologies.

47. Larry Oppenheimer to Elizabeth Moler, "Evaluation of MOPPS," June 21, 1977, Congressional Budget Office, Internal Memorandum.
48. Ibid.
49. Ibid.

To do this kind of analysis supply curves for different technology regimes are necessary, and the Adams group apparently employed those being used by the Stanford Research Institute. A third set of estimates was produced by a task force of experts during a three-day workshop in late May 1977.

Unfortunately for the Carter administration, a reporter for the *Wall Street Journal* got a copy of the Knudsen group study, and although the study had not been publicly released, the *Journal* published an editorial, "1,001 Years of Natural Gas" on April 27, 1977. This editorial gave a large and important portion of the American reading public the impression that the natural gas shortage was phony; there was only a shortage of gas at the artificially controlled price. Public exposure of the Knudsen report, which was used by the *Journal* in a way incompatible with the logical foundations of the report, caused ERDA to release a less optimistic report about a week later. That is, using the MOPPS results, ERDA tried to deflect the *Wall Street Journal* piece by releasing different supply-price speculations. Unfortunately conventional wisdom was that "ERDA's management, under top administration pressure, sat down and rewrote the study in five days to make it look less optimistic."[50] An ERDA delegation headed by acting administrator Robert Fri called on the *Wall Street Journal* to explain what had happened. The *Journal* followed the visit with another editorial, "ERDAgate!" on May 20, 1977, and continued to hammer away at the theme that it was all a cover-up, contending that the government study had proved there was no natural gas problem and that the United States had sufficient natural gas reserves if only the government would get its hands out of the market and let supply and demand operate.

The MOPPS problem is interesting primarily because it reflects the quickness with which critics of the Carter plan pounced on any apparent discrepancy. The *Wall Street Journal* was critical of Exxon, for example, because the oil company had sent a delegation to the newspaper office to try to explain what was going on. The *Journal* viewed this visit as a result of Exxon having many ERDA contracts.

Even with the passage of the Natural Gas Policy Act of 1978 (and given the assumption that it can be successfully put into practice), unresolved problems remain with other fossil fuels as well as with generating electricity using nuclear power.

---

50. George Melloan and Joan Melloan, *The Carter Economy* (Wiley, 1978), p. 132.

Petroleum

Criticism of the way the Carter plan dealt with petroleum was directed
mainly at supply problems. The President's message to Congress on
April 20, 1977, and the White House release about it never referred to
OPEC. A number of clever plans for dealing with OPEC had been circulated around Washington and elsewhere for years, such as Morris
Adelman's auction scheme.[51] The Carter plan also was not integrated
with a national transportation plan, and transportation absorbed 25 percent of all energy consumption. The only direct reference to mass transit
in the Carter plan was a proposal to drop the federal excise tax on interstate bus tickets.

Another fundamental criticism was that the National Energy Plan
failed to provide adequate drilling incentives. The industry argued that
the Carter plan would result in the drilling of 1,800 million feet of new
wells through 1985, although the 1985 domestic production target required 2,500 million feet. There was also a substantial shortfall in incentives for overall petroleum industry research and development. The
Carter plan gave the industry insufficient notice about future policy concerning new offshore leases. In fact, the administrative mechanism for
releasing the outer continental shelf was not at all clear. Industry officials
were not sure when various new, promising tracts would be open for
bidding. Even in early 1977 there was major concern that the administration had not thought through the problem of what to do with the potential West Coast surplus of heavy, high-sulfur crude oil being sent down
from the Alaskan North Slope. Congress approved the Alaskan pipeline
only after mandating that the Alaskan oil could not be exported. But the
Alaskan North Slope was going to yield much more petroleum than was

51. Adelman suggested that the United States sell tickets at auction, anon-
ymously. The highest bidder would receive the right to import a barrel of oil. A resale market in tickets would be encouraged. OPEC would be encouraged to establish brokers, circumspectly if it chose, to bid for and purchase tickets. If a member
of the producing cartel wanted to undercut its rivals in the cartel, wanting to sell
crude oil at, say, $2 a barrel below the cartel price, the member could have its bro-
ker quietly bid for and, if successful, purchase tickets at $2 each. The tickets would
then be transferred to an importer in return for an agreement to buy oil from the
cartel member at the official posted cartel price. But the cartel member would, de
facto, be giving the U.S. government (the auction managers) a rebate of $2 a bar-
rel that could be transferred to the oil-using American public. See M. A. Adelman,
"Politics, Economics, and World Oil," *American Economic Review*, vol. 64 (May
1974, *Papers and Proceedings, 1974*), pp. 58–67.

needed on the West Coast. By putting the pipeline from Prudhoe Bay to the port of Valdez rather than through Canada to the American Midwest, the United States had committed itself to a buildup of petroleum inventories on the West Coast that eventually would become a political problem. During late 1978 the Carter administration found itself trying to figure out how to rid the United States of this embarrassing surplus without giving the American public the impression that the energy crisis no longer existed. The economics of the problem were straightforward. It was in the United States' interest to export this West Coast oil to Japan, particularly if a way could be found to circumvent the high maritime labor costs of full compliance with the Jones Act, giving preferential treatment to American ships. It was relatively inefficient to ship the West Coast crude to the Gulf of Mexico or to the East Coast of the United States. And it was not efficient to build a pipeline to transship oil that was going to be depleted very quickly.

As noted above, world oil supply and demand continued to be debated during the first two years of the Carter administration. And the Ninety-sixth Congress came to Washington in January 1979 facing the issue of what to do about the U.S. prices of domestically produced crude oil, just as the Ninety-fifth Congress had two years earlier.

Coal

From the vantage point of coal producers, two major sets of constraints prohibited the industry from enjoying the full benefits of the Carter coal plan. First, the Clean Air Act of 1977 was a source of delay and interference in siting, constructing, and operating facilities that either produced or consumed coal. The Environmental Protection Agency had substantial latitude in promulgating rules concerning the emission of sulfur oxides, requirements for stack gas scrubbing and coal cleaning, particulate limits, dust limits for surface mines, and nitrogen oxides standards for power plants. And in the late 1970s the various states were in the process of implementing various air quality standards. In general the coal industry as well as users of coal had no concrete idea of the environmental rules of the game. This uncertainty encouraged a tendency to delay decisions, to wait for government officials to set the rules. One might have expected the coal industry to be very happy about the Carter plan, but in fact it was not, particularly the portion represented by the National Coal Association. And of course that part of the industry operating west of the Mississippi was unhappy because its low-sulfur reserves might not be fully exploited.

Basically, this first set of constraints had to do with the uncertainty of government action. The industry was concerned about the failure of officials to settle the environmental rules of the game once and for all. At the same time, it worried about court challenges by environmentalists once the rules were established. The Carter plan gave the coal industry a major position in U.S. energy production, but the industry was reluctant to accept it. Coal industry equity prices dropped approximately 20 percent between the release of the National Energy Plan and the end of 1977. Certainly financial analysts were not bullish about the future of coal. The general attitude toward coal seemed to be reflected in the GAO report to Congress: "Coal is dirty. It is bulky. It seldom occurs where it's needed, and it varies widely in quality. At every stage in its development, coal has problems—in mining, transporting, storage, handling, and burning." In short, even the comptroller general's office was unexcited about a coal future. Moreover, the GAO believed that achieving the administration's proposal to double annual coal production and consumption to 1.2 billion tons a year by 1985 was highly unlikely.[52]

The second general set of constraints on the coal industry was that government regulation of natural gas and petroleum prices kept the coal industry from being an economically attractive substitute for the other two major fossil fuels. It was not clear to the coal industry that government would completely decontrol natural gas and petroleum prices, letting them find their true market levels. The coal industry also was keenly aware that most state public utility regulators favored oil and natural gas over coal for a variety of reasons ranging from the environment to the higher capital costs of coal-fired public utilities. In addition there are strong reliability incentives to have a varied fuel base.

Less than a month after the President transmitted the National Energy Plan to Congress, the University Council on Energy Resources of the University of Texas had completed a 400-page document extremely critical of the plan.[53] Walt Rostow, William Fisher, and their Texas colleagues were concerned about the inconsistency between the President's 1985 quantitative targets and the policy package supposed to

52. U.S. General Accounting Office, *U.S. Coal Development—Promises, Uncertainties,* a Report to Congress by the Comptroller General (GAO, 1977).

53. W. W. Rostow and others, "Preliminary Assessment of the President's National Energy Plan," Report of the University Council on Energy Resources of the University of Texas at Austin, May 11, 1977.

achieve these targets. They argued that the Carter plan was deficient in several ways, particularly by not providing producers with sufficient incentives to find reserves that would yield the 1985 production levels. They observed that the Carter plan goals would require 40 percent more drilling to meet the 1985 production goals. The Carter plan for coal was based on a compromise between production and environmental considerations. That is, coal was to play an increasing role as an energy source, but air pollution standards would not be relaxed. By maintaining the requirements for stack gas scrubbers to hold down sulfur dioxide pollution while at the same time requiring all new plants to be coal fired, the Carter plan provided a stimulus to the high- and medium-sulfur coal fields east of the Mississippi. It did not help development of the U.S. coal fields west of the Mississippi, generally characterized by low-sulfur content. (Thus the Carter plan failed to capture the benefits of the higher labor productivity of western coal fields. The latter compared favorably with the underground mines in the East, which were further hindered by difficulties with the United Mine Workers of America.)[54] Since users of coal had to meet stringent air pollution requirements by building safeguards into their capital structure, there was no incentive to search for low-sulfur coal.

To many unbiased observers the Carter coal plan favored the East. The biggest required shift to coal was by the Texas and Oklahoma electric utilities, still relying predominantly on gas-fired boilers. The favoritism coupled with federal strip-mining regulations made the development of western coal very uncertain. There were many additional technical arguments such as the fact that the United States simply would not be

---

54. All these difficulties with coal were exacerbated by the perennial labor problems in the coal fields. In October 1977 negotiations began between the United Mine Workers and the Bituminous Coal Operators Association. Joseph P. Brennan, President of the BCOA, argued that the producers wanted labor stability in the Appalachian coal fields. The UMW wanted full restoration of the health benefits that had been curtailed because of summer wildcat strikes. The union, led by President Arnold R. Miller, also wanted a limited right to strike over local issues and additional pay and vacation time. On December 6 the 1974 contract expired and 160,-000 miners went on strike, cutting U.S. coal production by 50 percent. Following stormy months of negotiations, the UMW rank and file rejected a proposed contract on March 5, 1978. The next day the Carter administration invoked the strike-halting provisions of the Taft-Hartley Act, rejecting the alternative of federal seizure. On March 24 a different contract proposal was accepted by the UMW members. This episode was a test of crisis management, and the Carter administration did not cover itself with glory. It also indicated that the UMW central leadership had at best a shaky hold on its membership and on its future.

able to produce and transmit the required volume of coal mandated by the 1985 target. Although the initial University of Texas Council report and its later reports did not say this, one was forced to think of the Carter plan not only in terms of environmental considerations but also in terms of the 1976 election, an election in which Carter failed to carry many states west of the Mississippi.

Electric and Nuclear Power and More Esoteric Sources

The major issue surrounding the generation of electricity in the 1970s concerned the issue of nuclear power. And the use of nuclear power was caught up in a variety of controversies. As the years go by it might turn out that the major effect of the Carter administration's energy plan will have been to get the United States off the road to the breeder reactor. President Carter fought the major breeder demonstration program, the Clinch River project, as strongly as possible. But the final U.S. breeder reactor decision may turn out to be an economic decision, based in part on the potential supply of uranium. There is a substantial amount of disagreement concerning the available world supply of uranium. If uranium is in fact abundant, within reasonable prices, the breeder reactor is unnecessary. But if uranium is in short supply, the by-product of a project like Clinch River may be an economic necessity.

From a policy point of view the running battle between proponents and opponents of the Clinch River breeder reactor is quite interesting. It is much like the supersonic transport debate. The debate takes place between technologists and environmentalists. But the real decision turns out to be based on economic feasibility. If breeder reactors are economically feasible—that is, if reliable pessimistic guesses can be made about the supply of uranium over the next twenty to thirty years—the United States will develop breeder reactors. The environmental argument will be muffled. In 1977–78 the United States watched its European rivals developing breeder reactors just as it watched the United Kingdom, France, and the Soviet Union develop the supersonic transport, which had been debated in terms of the ozone layer and so forth, but all that was somewhat irrelevant. The question was whether or not the supersonic transport was economically feasible.

One gets the impression from industry organizations, such as the Atomic Industrial Forum, that the Carter administration not only has gotten the United States off the road to the breeder reactor but also has (indirectly) said "no" to the light-water reactor. By 1979 it had been a very long time since any power company in the United States had ordered a new plant based on nuclear energy. Under present circumstances producers of electricity are gravely uncertain about getting a nuclear plant sited and licensed. Furthermore, the nuclear alternative does not offer a clear cost advantage over coal at current prices.[55] The industry appears to be very pessimistic about the Nuclear Regulatory Commission's stance on siting and licensing controversies.

All this activity is a holding action until the more esoteric energy sources can be economically brought into play. The administration appears to have made a decision that the United States, unlike Western and Eastern Europe, might just skip a nuclear age and move from fossil fuels to a long-term technology solution that does not involve nuclear power as it is known today. Whether this long-term technology fix involves solar energy, geothermal energy, extraction of hydrogen from water, or hydrogen fusion, the Carter administration appears confident that U.S. engineering and physical science capabilities are capable of permitting the United States to exploit its extraordinary coal reserves and avoid the dangers and potential terrors of reliance on conventional nuclear sources. (It is interesting that nuclear critics seem to ignore the fact that it would be much easier for terrorists to steal a nuclear warhead from the military than to steal plutonium and make a bomb.)

It is very possible that the United States will stand alone in attempting to try this particular solution to the energy problem. No other country has the combination of human and physical resources that make leaping a conventional nuclear age possible. This, however, may prove to be a difficult course of action to follow because of widespread environmental limitations on coal production and use; frustrating technical difficulties with coal synthesis, in situ conversion, and so forth; and fundamental questions left unresolved about outer continental shelf leasing as well as oil and natural gas price-tax-incentive issues. The American nuclear

---

55. Some evidence of the shifting balance against nuclear power, based on Commonwealth Edison (Chicago) experience with nuclear and coal-fired plants, is provided in A. D. Rossin and T. A. Rieck, "Economics of Nuclear Power," *Science,* vol. 201 (August 18, 1978), pp. 582–89. Rossin and Rieck noted that in 1977, twenty years after the first almost-commercial-size unit began operating (Shippingsport), nuclear power plants were producing about 12 percent of U.S. electricity. They are concerned about the future path of this percentage, noting that nuclear power's economic advantage has been eroded by unfavorable changes in regulations, construction costs, and fuel costs.

establishment looks with envy to the superior breeder reactors being developed in France and the Soviet Union. This establishment—unaccustomed to the United States not being in the forefront of all phases of nuclear research and development—correctly observes that the United States is lagging behind in the development of this technology. The Carter administration made this decision rather quickly. One can speculate about the logical grounds on which the decision was made. Certainly one would have expected former AEC Chairman Schlesinger and Admiral Rickover's protegé Carter to be as attracted to the nuclear road as anyone.

Conclusion

One of the major sources of difficulty for Carter administration energy policy was the decision to work on two components of the energy problem simultaneously—formulating the comprehensive National Energy Plan as well as constructing the Department of Energy. It was extremely difficult for the small core of Carter energy officials to do both. In September 1976, as a presidential candidate, Jimmy Carter had proposed the creation of a cabinet-level department to be responsible for all energy matters. (In January 1977 President Ford made a similar proposal.) Unfortunately the Schlesinger team had difficulty separating their work designed to meet the ninety-day deadline and that required to follow through on the Carter initiative to create a department. Congress, however, was generally amenable to the administration's desire and after some hesitation approved the creation of the Department of Energy, to begin with the 1978 fiscal year. Some people in Congress wanted to embed a December 31, 1982, sunset provision in the act. Carter and Schlesinger effectively eliminated this provision. Congress gave the Department of Energy the task of producing detailed five- and ten-year energy plans biannually. Congress created the semiautonomous Federal Energy Regulatory Commission, a lineal descendant of the Federal Power Commission, and placed it in the Department of Energy. Nuclear siting and licensing decisions remained in the hands of the Nuclear Regulatory Commission, created when the old AEC was broken up during the Ford administration.

People making significant contributions to the development of the Carter plan gained positions of leadership in the newly formed Department of Energy, as well as in the Nuclear Regulatory Commission, the TVA, and the Federal Energy Regulatory Commission. As vacancies occurred or were created in these executive branch agencies, Carter and his political lieutenants naturally gave major consideration to members of the team developing the energy plan.

As the first half of the Carter administration and the Ninety-fifth Congress came to an end, there was still widespread concern over U.S. energy policy. The flow of Alaskan oil coupled with offshore discoveries in Britain and optimism about the Baltimore Canyon made it difficult to keep the American public aware of the long-term difficulties facing the United States. The Alaskan crude and Baltimore Canyon natural gas were remissions; the disease was still there. By late 1978 conventional wisdom seemed to be that the Carter administration had an extraordinary opportunity in early 1977 to take the momentum of the Carter candidacy, couple it with the Democratic majorities in the House and Senate, and put the United States on track. The Carter people faced three issues.

First, they needed an acceptable pricing-tax system for fossil fuels that would encourage domestic production in an equitable fashion and at the same time reduce U.S. dependence on imported crude. The administration was unsuccessful in addressing or recognizing the *trade-offs* involved in the efficiency and equity sides of this issue. (On May 12, 1977, Schlesinger was asked if the decision to use $1.75 per mcf as the key natural gas price was a political decision. After drawing on his pipe, Schlesinger inadvertently entertained the House Energy and Power Subcommittee by responding that no, it was a "judgmental decision.")[56]

56. The following colloquy occurred between Schlesinger and Congressman W. Henson Moore (*National Energy Act,* Hearings before the Subcommittee on Energy and Power of the House Committee on Interstate and Foreign Commerce, 95 Cong. 1 sess. [GPO, 1977], pt. 2, p. 90):

"MR. MOORE. I would like to move to the Btu equivalency proposition. Why didn't your plan give us a Btu equivalency of new oil instead of the average price of oil?

"MR. SCHLESINGER. The figure chosen represents the Btu equivalency of the price of oil that is currently used in the United States, and was regarded as adequate to that purpose. As I have indicated earlier, it represents a figure that is higher than the price that existed in the Louisiana intrastate market until last December, and higher than the price that existed in the Texas intrastate market until roughly 18 months earlier.

It is a substantial price, and it reflects the present composition of the barrel of oil in the United States.

"MR. MOORE. It does not reflect a comparable barrel of oil on the world market,

The second issue facing the Carter administration was the pressing need to establish the rules of the energy game once and for all so that private sector decisionmakers could have a steady, dependable arena within which to operate. This applied to air pollution standards, the host of coal regulations, leasing policies, and nuclear siting and licensing procedures. In a world of uncertainty it was natural for decisionmakers to wait for the regulatory environment to become firmer before embarking on energy adventures.

The third category of issues the Carter administration faced and failed to resolve was the relationship between public and private participation in developing energy sources for the period beyond 1985. Even after two years of activity a philosophy had not emerged that would indicate how the public and private sectors would interact in what were currently defined as the more esoteric solutions to the energy situation. By late 1978 editorial opinion in the leading business publications had soured badly against the Department of Energy. The department was subjected to a steady barrage of ridicule: an average American family of four paid $200 a year for the department and, so the arguments were going, got little in return.

---

and doesn't reflect the comparable new barrel of oil under our then proposed regulations to free up the price of new discovered oil. Therefore, it's really an artificial figure, is it not, and not a true Btu equivalency of what the going price of new oil is?

"MR. SCHLESINGER. It is a true Btu equivalent of the price of a barrel of oil as used in the United States, reflecting the degree of imports into the United States.

"MR. MOORE. Didn't the administration consider a different figure than $1.75? Did it not consider a Btu equivalency of new oil?

"MR. SCHLESINGER. It considered a whole range of figures.

"MR. MOORE. Would you answer as candidly as you can be with us, was this really an economic decision or was it a political decision not to go to the equivalency of new oil?

"Could you get support of certain Senators to pass your plan if you had used the equivalency of new oil?

"MR. SCHLESINGER. It was a judgmental decision.

"MR. MOORE. Then I take it we have no econometric models to show we really have injured the economy and there are really problems if we go to a higher Btu equivalency.

"MR. SCHLESINGER. Yes, indeed we have that.

"MR. MOORE. After the fact.

"MR. DINGELL. The time of the gentleman has expired."

CHAPTER NINE

The Energy Battles of 1979

JOSEPH A. YAGER

AT THE BEGINNING of 1979 the Carter administration probably neither expected nor wanted energy problems to dominate another year of the President's term of office. Much of 1977 and 1978 had been spent in a grueling and only partly successful effort to get Congress to enact the comprehensive energy proposals the President had made in April 1977. It is reasonable to assume that insofar as energy policy was concerned 1979 was to be a year of consolidation, leaving the administration free to concentrate on other more pressing concerns, including the fight against inflation, ratification of the second strategic arms limitation treaty, and progress toward peace in the Middle East. A quiet year on the energy front could also have been used to good advantage by the new Department of Energy.

President Carter's State of the Union Address to the new Ninety-sixth Congress contained only two brief references to energy. Near the end of an extensive discussion of the inflation problem the President called on Congress "to take other anti-inflation action—to expand our exports to protect American jobs threatened by unfair trade, to *conserve energy,* to increase production and to speed development of solar power, and to reassess our Nation's technological superiority."[1]

Two days after delivering his address, President Carter sent Congress a longer State of the Union Message. Approximately three pages of this fifty-page document were devoted to energy and another page briefly treated the energy-related subject of nuclear weapons proliferation. The main theme of the energy part of the message was "building upon the framework of the National Energy Act," which the President had signed

THIS CHAPTER was prepared with the assistance of Elizabeth C. Davis.

1. "The State of the Union," Address Delivered before a Joint Session of the Congress, January 23, 1979, *Weekly Compilation of Presidential Documents,* vol. 15 (January 29, 1979), p. 105. (Hereinafter *Presidential Documents.*)

two months previously. Decontrol of domestically produced crude oil was not mentioned. The President only hinted at this action, stating that he would be making his "decisions and recommendations on domestic crude oil pricing and related issues" later in the year. Nothing was said about an all-out effort to build a synthetic fuel industry, which the President was to propose in July. Attention was drawn, however, to the fact that the budget for fiscal year 1980 provided "outlays of $3.7 billion for a wide range of programs to develop energy technologies for the future."[2]

The President devoted several paragraphs to both solar and nuclear energy, calling for "accelerating" the use of solar energy and declaring that "the time for solar energy has come." His statements on nuclear energy were more cautious, but he did somewhat obliquely endorse continued reliance on "current nuclear technologies to meet power needs." He also said that his administration would "maintain and strengthen the strong research and development program we now have for more advanced nuclear fission technologies such as the fast breeder reactor." He reiterated his opposition, however, to the Clinch River breeder reactor project, labeling it "premature" and "technically inadequate."[3]

The part of the message that dealt with the problem of nuclear weapons proliferation hailed the enactment of the Nuclear Non-Proliferation Act of 1978 as a "promising beginning" but did not note the problems that this act was causing between the United States and other countries. The President said that during 1979 the United States would work with other nations in the ongoing International Nuclear Fuel Cycle Evaluation to develop a consensus that "will adequately balance energy needs with non-proliferation concerns." He also said that "more substantial progress" would be sought "in the problem of managing nuclear waste and in attracting greater international support for the acceptance of nuclear safeguards."[4]

The budget message and the economic report that President Carter also sent the new Congress in January 1979 put less emphasis on energy problems than did his State of the Union Address and Message.

In his budget message the President stated that it was "essential that we continue to move forward with an effective national energy program that will decrease our demand for foreign oil and protect against disrup-

2. "The State of the Union," Annual Message to the Congress, January 25, 1979, ibid., pp. 147, 148, 149.

3. Ibid., p. 149.

4. Ibid., p. 159.

tion of foreign oil supplies." He noted that the fiscal year 1980 budget provided for "the continued buildup of the strategic petroleum reserve" and for continued assistance in "the development of technologies to tap our domestic energy resources more effectively." The President's proposal to spend $7.9 billion on energy in fiscal 1980, compared with $8.6 billion in fiscal 1979, was consistent, however, with his efforts to hold down government spending.[5]

The economic report gave greatest attention to the inflation problem and to the balance of payments deficit, as did the accompanying longer annual report of the Council of Economic Advisers. The President mentioned energy only twice. He applauded the passage of the National Energy Act in late 1978 as an important step to correct the balance of payments deficit. And he noted that at the Bonn meeting of the leaders of the major industrialized countries in July 1978, the United States had "committed itself to combat inflation and reduce oil imports."[6]

Trouble in Iran

In retrospect the low-key approach to energy problems taken in the President's messages to the new Congress was somewhat surprising. The political crisis in Iran, the second largest exporter of oil, had steadily worsened in the weeks before Congress convened. In late 1978 strikes and the departure of foreign technicians had caused Iran's oil production to fall sharply below its normal level of more than 5.5 million barrels a day. By mid-December production was only 1.5 million barrels a day. On December 27 it reached a twenty-seven-year low of 500,000 barrels a day and exports ceased.[7] On January 16 Shah Mohammed Riza Pahlevi left Iran on a "vacation" of indefinite length. The ability of the newly installed Bakhtiar government to ride out the rising political storm was at best uncertain, and prospects for the early resumption of oil exports appeared poor.

The early reactions of the Carter administration to the cessation of Iranian oil exports were cautiously optimistic. Thus immediately after the

5. *The Budget of the United States Government, Fiscal Year 1980*, pp. 5, 127.
6. *Economic Report of the President, January 1979*, pp. 13, 14.
7. For accounts of the effects of political disorders on Iran's oil production see Martin Quinlan, "Oil Cutoff Hits World Supplies," *Petroleum Economist*, vol. 46 (February 1979), pp. 54–57; and "Aftermath of a Revolution," ibid. (April 1979), pp. 138–39.

cutoff of Iranian oil, Secretary of Energy James R. Schlesinger expressed the hope that the United States would not experience shortages.[8] In mid-January, the situation was officially described as "serious but not critical."[9] By early February, however, Schlesinger took a more gloomy view. In testifying before the Senate Energy and Natural Resources Committee, he characterized the loss of Iranian oil exports as "prospectively more serious" than the Arab oil embargo of 1973–74."[10]

The fairly relaxed view that the Carter administration at first took of the cessation of Iranian oil exports was not without some justification. Iran had accounted for only 5 percent of U.S. oil supplies in the first half of 1978 when output was not depressed by political disorders.[11] Some of the loss from Iran was made up by increased exports from Saudi Arabia, Kuwait, Iraq, and Nigeria,[12] and in any case there was nothing the administration could do to restore production in Iran's oil fields.

The administration sought to deal with the loss of Iranian oil by calling for voluntary energy conservation and by working for a concerted approach by the members of the International Energy Agency (IEA). At a press conference on January 17 President Carter suggested that oil consumption might have to be cut by 5 percent and called for conservation measures.[13] At another press conference on February 12 the President put the shortfall at 2.5 percent and again called for voluntary conservation such as obeying speed limits and turning down thermostats.[14]

The IEA estimated the net shortfall of oil supplies for its members as a group at about 5 percent. Some IEA countries had imported more than 20 percent of their oil from Iran, but the oil companies spread the burden of the shortfall more evenly by shifting supplies from other sources. The IEA's emergency sharing plan could have been activated if any member experienced a shortfall of 7 percent, but no member made that claim

8. Steven Rattner, *New York Times,* December 29, 1978.

9. "Iran: Carter's Biggest Crisis," *U.S. News and World Report,* January 15, 1979, p. 24.

10. *Energy: Fiscal Year 1980 Budget Request,* Hearing before the Senate Committee on Energy and Natural Resources, pub. 96-9, 96 Cong. 1 sess. (Government Printing Office, 1979), p. 8.

11. Quinlan, "Oil Cutoff Hits World Supplies," p. 55.

12. Ibid., pp. 54–55.

13. "The President's News Conference of January 17, 1979," *Presidential Documents,* vol. 15 (January 22, 1979), p. 52.

14. "The President's News Conference of February 12, 1979," ibid. (February 16, 1979), p. 255.

formally.[15] The IEA therefore concentrated on achieving agreement on energy conservation targets.

At a meeting in Paris on March 1 and 2 the IEA Governing Board agreed that the members of IEA would reduce "their demand for oil on the world market by around 2 million barrels per day, or about 5 per cent of IEA consumption."[16] The language of this agreement was so imprecise that it would be difficult to determine whether individual countries had honored their obligations under it. It was generally understood, however, that the United States had undertaken to save "up to 1 million barrels of oil per day."[17]

President Carter proposed to reach this level of savings by the end of 1979 through the following measures:[18]

Source of saving	Amount (thousands of barrels a day)
Mandatory thermostat settings	195–390
Electricity transfers	100–200
Switching from oil to gas	200–400
New domestic oil production	80–250
Voluntary conservation	200–500
Other	39–49
Total	814–1,789

Mandatory thermostat settings required congressional action, and the savings from voluntary conservation were necessarily highly speculative. The President had the authority, however, to take the other measures on which he relied in seeking to meet the IEA commitment. The new domestic oil production, it might be noted, depended on the decontrol of the price of domestically produced crude oil that the President proposed to begin on June 1. (See discussion below of the energy address of April 5.) It would be difficult to determine whether the various measures listed

15. One IEA member explored privately the possibility of triggering the IEA emergency sharing plan but received a discouraging response.

16. International Energy Agency, Organisation for Economic Co-operation and Development, press release, IEA/PRESS (79)4, Paris, p. 1.

17. Office of the White House Press Secretary, "Fact Sheet on the President's Program," April 5, 1979, p. 5.

18. Ibid., pp. 1–6. "Electricity transfers" involved the transfer of electricity among utility companies in such a way as to maximize the use of nonoil-burning generating capacity. "Other" savings included 19,000 barrels a day in reduced consumption by federal agencies and 20,000–30,000 barrels a day from the deferral of stricter requirements on the lead content of gasoline.

above actually produced the savings attributed to them. Too many other variables were at work, and it is hard to say what oil consumption would have been in the absence of a given measure.

On March 5 Iran resumed oil exports, but production and exports did not recover their past levels. By summer, production had leveled off at about 3.6 million barrels a day, or approximately 2 million barrels a day below the average for 1977, the last normal year.[19] At this level of production Iran could export only about 3 million barrels a day—roughly 2 million barrels a day below the precrisis norm.

The principal effect of the temporary cessation of exports and the failure to recover past levels was on oil prices. (Only later did events in Iran contribute to a tight supply situation that showed itself in gasoline lines in the United States.) Spot prices reacted sharply. In the third quarter of 1978 the spot price of heavy fuel oil (1 percent sulfur), f.o.b. Rotterdam, averaged $11.83 a barrel. By the second quarter of 1979 the average price was $21.12.[20]

Events in Iran also affected the price policies of the Organization of Petroleum Exporting Countries. On December 17, 1978, the OPEC oil ministers meeting in Abu Dhabi had decided to raise oil prices a total of 14.5 percent during 1979 by quarterly steps. On March 26 in Geneva OPEC abandoned this schedule and made the full 14.5 percent increase effective on April 1.[21] The direct sales price of "marker" crude (Saudi Arabian light) rose from $12.70 a barrel in the third quarter of 1978 to $15.68 a barrel in the second quarter of 1979.[22]

The Standby Gasoline Rationing Plan

The Energy Policy and Conservation Act of 1975 requested the President to submit a gasoline rationing plan to Congress for approval. Neither President Ford nor President Carter had given priority to this project. The cessation of oil exports from Iran, however, caused members of Congress (especially members of the Senate Energy and Natural Re-

19. *International Energy Statistical Review,* October 31, 1979, p. 2.
20. Ibid., p. 19.
21. Quinlan, "Aftermath of a Revolution," p. 139.
22. *International Energy Statistical Review,* October 31, 1979, p. 21. The price increase over this period reflected varying premiums charged by different exporting countries, as well as the OPEC decision.

sources Committee) to press the White House for action. On March 1 President Carter sent a standby gasoline rationing plan to Congress.[23]

Under this plan rations would have been allocated primarily on the basis of motor vehicle registrations. Supplemental rations were to be provided for "a limited number of priority activities, such as police and fire protection." Farmers were to be assured "allotments sufficient to meet fully the national food and fiber production goals approved by the President." Rations were to be transferable, and a "white market" in ration rights was to have been permitted.[24]

The plan proved to be quite controversial. Supporters argued that gasoline rationing would not only distribute limited supplies efficiently but would also promote conservation by encouraging car-pooling and the purchase of small cars. Critics feared that gasoline rationing would be both inequitable and expensive to administer. They foresaw profiteering by interstate coupon sharks.[25]

Differences between rural and urban interests were important in determining the fate of the plan. On May 9 the Senate approved the plan by a vote of 58 to 39, after the administration had modified its proposal to provide extra coupons for rural residents. This concession backfired in the House, where urban constituencies are more heavily represented, and on May 10 the House voted down the plan 246 to 159.[26]

President Carter professed to be "shocked" and "embarrassed" by the House's action. He accused members of letting "political timidity prevent their taking action in the interest of our nation." After this defeat, the White House took the position that if there was to be a standby gasoline rationing plan, Congress must take the initiative.[27] Congress did so several months later. Its action, however, did not produce a plan but only a procedure for developing one. An amendment to the 1975 legislation, the Emergency Energy Conservation Act of 1979 approved (77 to 18) by the Senate on October 17 and by the House (301 to 112) on October

23. For text, see U.S. Department of Energy, "Standby Gasoline Rationing Regulations," *Federal Register,* vol. 44 (March 14, 1979), pt. 2, pp. 15567–97.

24. Ibid., p. 15568.

25. "House Debate on Standby Gasoline Rationing Plans," *Congressional Record,* daily edition (May 10, 1979), pp. H2971–3018; and "Gasoline Rationing Prospects Look Dim," *National Journal,* May 19, 1979, p. 834.

26. See "House Defeats Gasoline Rationing Plan," *Congressional Quarterly,* May 12, 1979, pp. 875–76.

27. "Standby Gasoline Rationing Plan: Remarks on the House of Representatives Disapproval of the Plan, May 11, 1979," *Presidential Documents,* vol. 15 (May 14, 1979), pp. 840–41.

23, called on the President to prepare a gasoline rationing plan and submit it to Congress. The act specified that the plan must ensure equal
treatment among states and provide extra coupons for farmers, energy
producers, health and safety agencies, and telephone and telecommuni-
cation services.

The plan would become available for use on a standby basis, unless
Congress rejected it within thirty days by a joint resolution. The President could veto such a resolution, and in that event Congress could make
its disapproval stick only by overriding the veto by a two-thirds vote of
each house.

Avoiding congressional disapproval of a standby plan would not give
the President a free hand, however. He could actually impose gasoline
rationing only if he first obtained the approval of both houses of Congress, or if a 20 percent shortage of gasoline had existed for thirty days.
In the latter case either house could block rationing by passing a resolution against it within fifteen days.

Three Mile Island

At 4:00 A.M. on March 28, 1979, several pumps supplying water to
the steam-generating system of the Unit 2 nuclear power plant on Three
Mile Island, Pennsylvania, stopped. A series of events was thus initiated
that became the most serious crisis yet experienced by the U.S. nuclear
power industry.

The story of what happened at Three Mile Island is quite complicated
and was not fully known until some months later.[28] Essentially a combination of mechanical malfunction and human error caused a loss of
coolant that seriously damaged the plant's reactor core. Some radioactive
gas escaped into the atmosphere, and for several days a catastrophic
emission of radioactive materials was feared. Evacuation of a large area
surrounding the plant was seriously considered. Schools were closed for
a time, and pregnant women and preschool children were advised to
keep out of an area within five miles of the plant.

In retrospect the main health effect of the accident was the mental
stress it imposed on nearby residents. The amount of radioactivity re-

28. For a day-by-day account see *Report of the President's Commission on the
Accident at Three Mile Island, The Need for Change: The Legacy of TMI* (GPO,
1979), pp. 81–149.

leased was so small that "the accident may result in *no* additional cancer deaths or, if there were any, they would be so few that they could not be detected."[29] The economic cost of the accident, however, will be quite large, even if the plant can be refurbished and put back into service, which is by no means certain. Cost estimates range from $1 billion to $1.9 billion, including the heavy expense of replacing the electric power lost by the plant shutdown.[30]

Because of the confusion surrounding the events at Three Mile Island and the fears that had been aroused, President Carter appointed a commission to investigate the accident and submit appropriate recommendations within six months.[31] The chairman of the commission was John G. Kemeny, president of Dartmouth College and a mathematician with experience in nuclear matters. Other members included a state governor, an industrialist, a labor leader, a journalist, a public health specialist, a sociologist, a lawyer, an environmentalist, a nuclear engineer, a physicist, and a resident of a town near the plant.

The commission submitted its report in October. Its principal conclusion was:

To prevent nuclear accidents as serious as Three Mile Island, fundamental changes will be necessary in the organization, procedures, and practices—and above all—in the attitudes of the Nuclear Regulatory Commission and, to the extent that the institutions that we investigated are typical, of the nuclear industry.[32]

The commission further observed that "unless portions of the industry and its regulatory agency undergo fundamental changes, they will over time totally destroy public confidence and, hence, *they* will be responsible for the elimination of nuclear power as a viable source of energy."[33]

The commission's most important recommendation was that the five-member Nuclear Regulatory Commission should be abolished and replaced by "a new independent agency in the executive branch." This new agency would be headed by a single administrator who would serve at the pleasure of the President. The President's commission also submitted detailed recommendations on the responsibilities of utility companies and their suppliers, the training of operating personnel, the technical

---

29. Ibid., p. 13.
30. Ibid., p. 32.
31. "President's Commission on the Accident at Three Mile Island," Executive Order 12130, April 11, 1979.
32. *Report of the President's Commission,* p. 7 (emphasis in the original).
33. Ibid., p. 25.

assessment of equipment, the health and safety of workers and the public, emergency planning and response, and the public's right to information.[34]

Reactions to the report of the President's commission varied.[35] The nuclear power industry, having feared even stronger criticism, interpreted the report as a mandate to proceed but with caution. Opponents of nuclear energy saw the report as a serious indictment of the industry but felt that it could have been tougher. Although the commission took no position on the issue, its report had the effect of sharpening controversy over whether there should be a moratorium on the construction of new nuclear power plants. In accepting the report President Carter thanked the commission for its work but gave no indication of how he would respond to its recommendations.[36]

The accident at Three Mile Island increased uncertainty concerning the contribution nuclear power would make to the solution of the nation's energy problems. The accident also had the immediate effect of making nuclear energy almost a taboo subject for the Carter administration. Discussion of nuclear energy within the upper levels of the administration appears virtually to have ceased. Requests of other governments for pronuclear statements were denied. Efforts by the French and Germans to include discussion of nuclear energy in plans for the economic summit meeting to be held in Tokyo in June 1979 failed (although it was in fact discussed briefly).

The April 5 Energy Address

On April 5, 1979, President Carter delivered his second major energy address to the nation over television and radio.[37] Unlike his first energy address in April 1977, this address was not made before a joint session of Congress, but it was comparable to the earlier address in scope and importance. As in April 1977, the White House issued a fact sheet spell-

34. Ibid., pp. 61, 68–79.
35. See Jeff Gerth, *New York Times*, November 1, 1979, for a summary of reactions to the report.
36. "President's Commission on the Accident at Three Mile Island, Remarks after Receiving the Commission's Final Report, October 30, 1979," *Presidential Documents*, vol. 15 (November 5, 1979), pp. 2061–62.
37. "Energy, Address to the Nation, April 5, 1979," ibid. (April 9, 1979), pp. 609–14.

ing out the President's energy proposals in greater detail.[38] In a coincidence that was surely unplanned, both the 1977 and the 1979 fact sheets were twenty-eight pages long.

The April 1979 speech was an outgrowth of work by an interagency group on what was known as the Iran response plan. The initial purpose of the group was to prepare recommendations concerning what should be done to cope with the disruption of oil exports from Iran. Early meetings of the group had a heavy foreign policy emphasis. Later, as Iranian oil exports partly recovered, the emphasis became more domestic, and the purpose shifted to planning an energy address by the President.

The interagency group that worked on the Iran response plan and the presidential address was chaired by the President's domestic policy adviser, Stuart E. Eizenstat, or (more frequently) by Katherine P. Schirmer, associate director of the Domestic Policy Staff for energy and natural resources. Representatives of the Office of Management and Budget; the National Security Council staff; and the Treasury, State, and Energy departments participated in all phases of the group's work. The Central Intelligence Agency took part in early meetings but dropped out as the group focused on domestic concerns. This shift in emphasis was also reflected in the increasingly active participation of the Environmental Protection Agency and the Council on Environmental Quality at later meetings.

Like the 1977 energy speech and the associated fact sheet, the April 1979 address and fact sheet contained an almost bewildering array of executive actions, legislative proposals, and appeals for voluntary cooperation. Its central theme was nevertheless quite clear. The President had been convinced by some of his advisers that controls on the price of domestically produced oil encouraged consumption and discouraged production.[39] He was therefore determined, as he had been two years earlier, to raise the domestic price of oil to the international level. He was also still determined not to allow the oil companies to retain the full benefit of the higher price.

The President's determination to end the period of artificially low oil

38. Office of the White House Press Secretary, "Fact Sheet on the President's Program."

39. Advocates of this position included Treasury Secretary W. Michael Blumenthal, Energy Secretary Schlesinger, Under Secretary of the Treasury Anthony M. Solomon, Under Secretary of State Richard N. Cooper, and Henry Owen, special assistant to the President for international economic affairs and summits.

prices was reinforced by the commitment he had made at the Bonn summit meeting in July 1978 to raise the prices paid for oil in the United States to the world level by the end of 1980. During preparation of the April 5 speech a dispute raged within the administration over how to honor this commitment. Should controls be removed? If so, should decontrol be immediate or gradual? If the latter, how gradually, and how should different categories of oil be treated?

In 1977 the President had proposed to push up the domestic price of oil by levying a crude oil equalization tax. Having failed to obtain congressional approval for this tax, the President now announced that he would use the authority of a law passed during the Ford administration to decontrol the price of domestically produced oil gradually. He asked Congress to enact a new tax on the additional revenues that the oil companies would receive as a result of decontrol. He further requested authority to put the proceeds of this tax in an Energy Security Trust Fund that would finance a variety of energy-related projects.

The law under which the President acted to decontrol the price of domestic oil was the Energy Policy and Conservation Act of 1975. As was explained in chapter 8, the EPCA set limits on increases in the price of domestically produced crude oil before June 1, 1979. Between that date and September 30, 1981, when the authority to control oil prices would end, the President was given the power to determine whether and how price controls would be applied.

In his April 5 speech President Carter announced: "phased decontrol of oil prices will begin on June 1 and continue at a fairly uniform rate over the next 28 months."[40] In part because the system of price controls was complex, the President's decontrol program was also not simple.

At the time the President announced his intention to lift controls about 3 million barrels a day of domestic oil production were classified as old oil that had been found and put into production before 1973. Another 3 million barrels a day were classified as new oil that had been put into production in 1973 or later. The remainder of domestic production or about 2.6 million barrels a day—oil from the Alaskan North Slope, the Naval Petroleum Reserve, and "stripper" wells (those producing ten or fewer barrels a day)—was uncontrolled. Old oil received the "lower tier" price of about $5.86 a barrel at the wellhead, new oil received the "upper tier" price of about $13.06 a barrel at the wellhead, and uncon-

40. "Energy, Address to the Nation," p. 610.

trolled oil was sold for about $18.50 a barrel at the refinery gate.[41] (The international price of marker crude was about $17.40 a barrel, f.o.b. the Persian Gulf.)

In essence the decontrol program would gradually classify more old oil as new oil and at the same time gradually raise the ceiling on the price of new oil to the world price. By October 1, 1981, when under the terms of the EPCA all controls would end, all domestically produced oil would sell at the international price. The main features of the decontrol program can be summarized as follows:[42]

—On June 1, 1979, newly discovered oil and incremental new production resulting from the use of certain enhanced recovery methods, could be sold at the world price.

—Also on June 1, 80 percent of production from marginal wells (wells producing less than specified amounts per day, depending on depth) could be sold at the upper tier price. The remaining 20 percent of production from marginal wells would be allowed to receive the upper tier price on January 1, 1980.

—Beginning on January 1, 1980, the amount of oil in the old oil category would be permitted to decline at an accelerated rate (that is, a growing proportion of production would be treated as new oil).

—Also beginning on January 1 the price of new oil would be permitted to rise in monthly increments until it would reach the world price on October 1, 1981.

The White House estimated that this phased decontrol program would reduce oil imports in 1980 by 180,000–200,000 barrels a day below what they would otherwise be. The estimated reductions in oil imports would rise in subsequent years, reaching 950–1,100 barrels a day in 1985. The White House conceded, however, that the decontrol program would have some inflationary effect. Assuming that international oil prices remained constant in real terms, the White House estimated that decontrol would increase the consumer price index by 0.75 percent in the period 1979–82.[43]

41. Congressional Budget Office, *The Decontrol of Domestic Oil Prices: An Overview,* Background Paper (GPO, 1979), pp. xi–xii.
42. "Windfall Profits Tax and Energy Security Trust Fund, Message to the Congress, April 26, 1979," *Presidential Documents,* vol. 15 (April 30, 1979), pp. 722–23.
43. Office of the White House Press Secretary, "Fact Sheet on the President's Program," p. 12.

President Carter did not make decontrol dependent on enactment of a tax on the resulting oil company profits as he in effect had done in April 1977. He did, however, place great emphasis on capturing part of these profits—which he labeled "huge and undeserved"—for the American people. He predicted that "as surely as the Sun will rise tomorrow, the oil companies can be expected to fight to keep the profits which they have not earned."[44]

The President proposed that a "windfall profits tax" of 50 percent (which was really an excise tax) be levied on producer revenues attributable to decontrol or to future price increases by OPEC. The White House estimated that such a tax on revenues attributable to decontrol would yield a total of $5 billion in the next three fiscal years. If the OPEC price increased by 3 percent annually in real terms, the tax would yield another $2.4 billion over the same period, or a total of $7.4 billion. Since OPEC increased its price by much more than the assumed amount in 1979 alone, this figure has turned out to be a gross underestimate.[45]

Decontrol and higher OPEC prices would also increase the yield of existing income taxes on the profits of oil companies. The White House estimated the former at $6.5 billion and the latter at $0.3 billion over fiscal years 1980, 1981, and 1982 for a three-year total of $6.8 billion. The increased tax revenues attributable to both decontrol and the assumed increase in OPEC prices were therefore estimated at a grand total of more than $14 billion for the three-year period.[46]

The President proposed that these revenues, and revenues from the same sources in subsequent years, be put in a new Energy Security Trust Fund. He further proposed that this fund be used for three purposes: low-income assistance, mass transit, and energy investments. In the initial three years (fiscal 1980–82) a total of $2.1 billion would be devoted to low-income assistance and $0.7 billion to mass transit. The remainder of $8.6 billion to $11.3 billion would go into energy investments.[47] (The exact amount available for energy investments would depend on the size of any tax revenues resulting from OPEC price increases.)

44. "Energy, Address to the Nation," pp. 610–12.

45. Office of the White House Press Secretary, "Fact Sheet on the President's Program," p. 11. The administration's legislative proposals used the market incentive base price of $16 a barrel for the fourth quarter of 1979 as the base price in assessing the windfall profits tax.

46. Ibid.

47. Ibid. The legislative proposal submitted to Congress eliminated the income tax as a source of contributions to the Energy Security Trust Fund after fiscal 1982.

Low-income assistance would be designed to ease the burden of higher oil prices on poor families. An assistance program was contemplated that would give a typical low-income household about $100 annually. The expenditures on mass transit would be in the form of increased grants for bus and rail rehabilitation under the Surface Transportation Assistance Act of 1978.[48]

The energy investments to be financed by the Energy Security Trust Fund would include tax credits and loan guarantees, as well as actual expenditures. Tax credits would be provided for shale oil development, agricultural and solar equipment, passive solar construction, and residential wood stoves. The fund would also provide loan guarantees for a variety of nonnuclear demonstration projects and would directly finance additional coal research and development, a second solvent refined coal demonstration plant, a development program for synthetic liquid fuels, and regional petroleum storage in Hawaii and the Northeast.[49]

The President's proposals produced widespread debate and analysis, but little immediate legislative action.[50] Some critics deplored the inflationary impact of decontrol and the burdens it placed on the poor. Others questioned the need for the windfall profits tax or argued that the tax rate should be higher or lower than the President had proposed. The oil companies predictably welcomed decontrol and generally opposed the windfall profits tax. Their public comment on the tax, however, was less strident than the White House appears to have expected.[51]

One of the strongest critics of the tax was the *Wall Street Journal*. The *Journal* argued that the tax would not produce the revenues its advocates claimed, that it would encourage the export of refining operations, and

48. Ibid., pp. 20–21.
49. Ibid., pp. 21–26.
50. Detailed analyses of the President's proposals included *Updated Analysis of the President's April 5, 1979 Crude Oil Pricing Plan,* Committee Print 96-IFC 15, Subcommittee on Energy and Power of the House Committee on Interstate and Foreign Commerce, 96 Cong. 1 sess. (GPO, 1979); Congressional Budget Office, *The Decontrol of Domestic Oil Prices*; and Comptroller General of the United States, *The Economic and Energy Effects of Alternative Oil Import Policies,* Report to the Congress (U.S. General Accounting Office, 1979).
51. See for example the statement of Charles J. DiBona, president of the American Petroleum Institute on April 9, 1979. DiBona praised President Carter for "moving toward sound, long-term solutions of our most serious energy problems." On the President's tax proposals, DiBona commented mildly that "more taxes aren't necessary—and they could shortchange the consumer on the full benefits of the President's pricing reform." American Petroleum Institute, news release, April 9, 1979, p. 1.

that it would lead to lower domestic production by reducing incentives for oil development and hastening the closing of existing wells.[52]

Both the House and the Senate began hearings on those of the President's proposals that required legislation, but no components of the President's program had been enacted by July 1979 when the energy problem entered still another phase marked by another presidential address in which he made additional major proposals. The decontrol program announced by the President in his April 5 speech, however, did begin on schedule on June 1.

Gasoline Lines

The spring of 1979 will be remembered for a gasoline shortage that the public and many members of the administration found inexplicable. There was an explanation, but it was complicated and slow in coming. In the meantime distrust of the oil companies grew, and President Carter's standing, as reflected in public opinion polls, continued to fall. The fact that despite controls the price of gasoline rose steadily during the period of shortage fed suspicions that the crisis was somehow the result of a conspiracy between the companies and the government.

The gasoline shortage first became acute in California in April. Long lines formed at gasoline stations as motorists competed for available supplies. Night after night the gasoline shortage in California was featured on news programs broadcast by the national television networks. In May and June the shortage spread to other areas, especially in the East. Washington, D.C., and its suburbs experienced particularly long gasoline lines.

By midsummer the problem had eased. Motorists cut their consumption enough to bring supply and demand into an uneasy balance. The adjustment was facilitated by two kinds of widely used local or state regulations. The practice of "tank-topping" that had contributed to the congestion of gasoline stations was discouraged by minimum purchase requirements. And the number of cars eligible for lining up at stations was

52. On January 22, 1980, the *Wall Street Journal* carried an editorial, "The Close-the-Wells Tax," and an article, "Further into the Arms of OPEC," by Stuart Sweet and Bruce Bartlett (identified as Senate staff members). Both the editorial and the article attacked the windfall profits tax on economic grounds.

halved by the "odd-even rule": cars with licenses ending with odd numbers could be served only on odd days of the month, and cars with even license numbers on even days.

Efforts were made by the government to explain the gasoline shortage while it was under way. On May 21 John F. O'Leary, deputy secretary of energy, made a long statement on the oil supply situation before the Senate Committee on Energy and Natural Resources.[53] He attributed the gasoline shortage principally to the delayed impact of curtailment of Iranian oil production and to the low inventories of U.S. refiners in early 1979. The data he was able to present, however, did not constitute a full quantitative explanation of what had happened.

The testimony of Alfred F. Dougherty, Jr., director of the Bureau of Competition of the Federal Trade Commission, before the House Subcommittee on Commerce, Consumer and Monetary Affairs on June 11 brought out some of the questions that were being raised about official explanations of the shortage. Dougherty noted that the United States had imported more crude oil in the first quarter of 1979 than in the same quarter of 1978, that the refinery utilization rate in early 1979 was below normal, and that available statistics did not account for the disposition of all the gasoline refined in the first quarter of 1979. He called for "a full, expeditious investigation by the Federal Government," preferably a "public investigation by a congressional committee," into the cause of the gasoline shortage.[54]

Because of confusion concerning the cause of the shortage and suspicions concerning the behavior of the oil companies, President Carter on May 25 asked the Department of Energy to investigate the activities of the companies affecting gasoline supplies. On July 24 the department submitted an interim report, which the White House promptly released to the press.[55]

This report attributed the gasoline shortage principally to a shortfall

53. *Shortages of Gasoline, Heating Oil and Diesel Fuel,* Hearings before the Subcommittee on Energy Regulation of the Senate Committee on Energy and Natural Resources, 96 Cong. 1 sess., pub. 96–40 (GPO, 1979), pp. 58–94.

54. *Progress of the Federal Trade Commission's Investigation into the Gasoline Supply Situation (Part 1),* Hearings before a Subcommittee of the House Committee on Government Operations, 96 Cong. 1 sess. (GPO, 1979), p. 9. See also Alfred F. Dougherty, Jr., "Is There a Gasoline Shortage? *Challenge,* vol. 22 (September-October 1979), pp. 51–54, which is based on the June 11 testimony.

55. U.S. Department of Energy, "Report to the President on the Activities of Oil Companies Affecting Gasoline Supplies," July 24, 1979.

of 800,000 barrels a day during February through May 1979 in the level
of oil imports needed to meet 1978 consumption levels. More imported
oil was needed in 1979 than in 1978 because stocks were at lower levels.
No evidence of hoarding of oil by refiners was found, "but some refiners
may have been conservative in the use of their stocks."[56] The public ac-
ceptability of this report was diminished by criticism concerning its use
of oil company data.[57] Its findings, however, were generally consistent
with those of a more comprehensive study issued on September 13 by
the General Accounting Office.[58]

The GAO found that because of events in Iran the United States experienced an average shortfall of 600,000–700,000 barrels a day during
the first four months of 1979. Compensating actions (increased supplies
from Saudi Arabia, Nigeria, and some other countries and decreased
sales to third parties) were largely canceled by reduced supplies from
certain other countries, reduced domestic production, and the way in
which oil companies allocated available supplies among their affiliates.[59]
The shortfall of crude oil imports had a disproportionate effect on gasoline supplies in some areas because of the Department of Energy's allocation and price regulations. The GAO found no evidence of hoarding of
crude oil or refined products.[60]

Solar Energy Proposals

On June 20 President Carter sent a message on solar energy to Congress.[61] Following the Carter administration practice, a detailed fact sheet
spelling out the President's proposals was released concurrently.[62] On

56. Ibid., p. 5.
57. Patrick Tyler and Jonathan Neumann, *Washington Post*, August 7, 1979.
58. Comptroller General of the United States, *Iranian Oil Cutoff: Reduced Petroleum Supplies and Inadequate U.S. Government Response,* Report to the Congress
(GAO, 1979).
59. Shortfalls were allocated proportionately to all affiliates, irrespective of their
actual dependence on Iranian oil.
60. For an analysis that is more critical of the role of the Department of Energy,
see Philip K. Verleger, Jr., "The U.S. Petroleum Crisis of 1979," *Brookings Papers
on Economic Activity, 2:1979,* pp. 463–76.
61. "Solar Energy, Message to the Congress, June 20, 1979," *Presidential Documents,* vol. 15 (June 25, 1979), pp. 1097–1107.
62. Office of the White House Press Secretary, "Fact Sheet: The President's Message on Solar Energy," June 20, 1979.

this occasion the President sought to draw further attention to his proposals by presiding over the dedication of a new solar system to do part
of the task of heating water for the White House.[63]

The President's message emphasized solar energy, but it also dealt
with renewable sources of energy: firewood, biomass, and low head hydropower. He proclaimed the social and environmental benefits of solar
and renewable energy technologies and proposed an intensified effort to
promote their development and use. He set the goal of obtaining 20 percent of the nation's needs from solar and renewable energy by the year
2000. A number of specific measures, many of them requiring congressional action, were proposed in order to reach this goal.

The President's program for solar and renewable energy was based on
a policy review of solar energy, which he had initiated in May 1978. This
review had concluded that "a maximum practical effort" could increase
the amount of energy derived from solar and renewable sources to 18.5
quads (quadrillion Btu's) by the year 2000, as contrasted with only
4.2 quads in 1977. (In more familiar energy units, the projected change
was from the equivalent of 2 million barrels of oil a day in 1977 to the
equivalent of 9 million barrels a day in 2000.) The review further estimated total U.S. energy consumption in 2000 at 95 quads.[64] This estimate, however, may be low. Another estimate by the Department of
Energy put U.S. energy consumption in the year 2000 at 125 quads.[65] In
that event the projected level of solar and renewable energy would be
only about 15 percent of the total, rather than 20 percent.

The major elements of the program proposed by the President were:

—Creation of a solar bank to provide interest subsidies for owners
and builders of residences and commercial structures who install solar
equipment.

—Tax credits to encourage the use of passive solar designs in new
homes, the adoption of solar technologies to provide process heat in
industry and agriculture, and the installation of woodburning stoves in
principal residences.

—The exemption of gasohol (a mixture of gasoline and alcohol) from
the federal gasoline tax of 4 cents a gallon.

63. "Solar Energy, Remarks Announcing Administration Proposals, June 20,
1979," *Presidential Documents*, vol. 15 (June 25, 1979), pp. 1095–96.
64. U.S. Department of Energy, *Domestic Policy Review of Solar Energy* (GPO,
1979).
65. U.S. Department of Energy, Energy Information Administration, *Annual
Report to the Congress, 1978*, vol. 3: *Forecasts*, p. 96.

—The expenditure of $646 million in fiscal 1980 on research and development in the field of solar and renewable energy.

The total cost of the President's solar program in fiscal 1980 in both budgetary expenditures and tax credits was estimated at over $1 billion, 29 percent greater than in fiscal 1979. The President proposed that the cost of the solar bank and the tax credits to encourage the use of solar and renewable energy be met from the Energy Security Trust Fund that he had called for in his April 5 energy address. The White House subsequently estimated the combined cost of the bank and the tax credits at $3.5 billion during the period 1980–90.[66]

Despite the broad scope of the solar and renewable energy proposals, it is probably fair to say that their enactment was not given high priority by the administration. In any event they received relatively little attention in Congress during 1979.

The July Crisis

April, May, and June 1979 were not happy months for the Carter administration. The President was doing badly in public opinion polls, and energy problems were seen as a major source of his difficulties and a threat to his prospects for reelection.

Iran's oil exports revived somewhat in the spring of 1979, but this favorable development was partly canceled by reports of cuts by other exporters. A gloomy view of the future was projected by studies circulated by the Department of Energy and the Central Intelligence Agency.[67] The effort to deal with the energy problem in the International Energy Agency was considered inadequate. The commitments to conserve energy that had been negotiated in the agency were imprecise and subject to different interpretations.

The administration's preparations for the next meeting of leaders of the major industrialized countries—scheduled to be held in Tokyo in late

66. Office of the White House Press Secretary, "Fact Sheet on the President's Import Reduction Program," July 16, 1979, p. 5.

67. See U.S. Department of Energy, Energy Information Administration, Midterm Analysis Division, *Energy Supply and Demand in the Midterm: 1985, 1990, and 1995* (GPO, 1979); and U.S. Central Intelligence Agency, Office of Economic Research, *The World Oil Market in the Years Ahead: A Research Paper* (Washington, D.C.: National Foreign Assessment Center, CIA, 1979). An earlier version of this study was circulated within the U.S. government in the spring of 1979.

June—emphasized the need to get specific national commitments to hold down oil imports.[68] Work also began before the summit meeting on yet another presidential energy address. This work was stimulated by the feeling that Congress was getting ahead of the administration in the area of synthetic fuels.

During this period some of the senior members of the White House staff, and possibly the President himself, were unhappy with the support they were receiving from within the administration on economic issues and on energy problems in particular. This unhappiness contributed to the cabinet shake-up later in the year. Some of the President's close advisers were also dissatisfied with the style of the administration and urged a new start to reverse the deterioration in its political standing.[69]

The Tokyo Summit and the Meeting of OPEC Oil Ministers

By chance the meeting of the leaders of the major industrialized countries in Tokyo and the meeting of OPEC oil ministers in Geneva overlapped. Whether this circumstance affected the outcome of the OPEC meeting is doubtful, but it may have caused the leaders meeting in Tokyo to issue a more concrete communiqué than they otherwise would have.

The OPEC oil ministers met in Geneva from June 26 to June 28, 1979. The disruption of oil production in Iran had created chaotic conditions in the international oil market that made reaching agreement on price policy more difficult than at previous OPEC meetings. Saudi Arabia, supported by some smaller Persian Gulf producers, wanted a more moderate price increase than did other OPEC members. A compromise was reached on a two-tier system: Saudi Arabia, Abu Dhabi, and Qatar agreed to raise the price of marker crude from $14.54 to $18 a barrel. Other countries accepted a ceiling of $23.50 a barrel. The result was to raise crude oil prices by an average of about 15 percent, effective July 1.[70]

Word of OPEC's action reached Tokyo very late on the first day of

68. Edward R. Fried, who was then U.S. executive director at the World Bank, played a key role in these preparations. Later in the year he left the bank and joined the White House staff as the U.S. member of the high-level group established to monitor the energy commitments made at the Tokyo summit.

69. For a detailed account of the unrest in the Carter administration during the spring and early summer of 1979, see Elizabeth Drew, "Phase: In Search of Definition," *New Yorker*, August 27, 1979, pp. 45–73.

70. Roger Vielvoye, "OPEC Crude Prices Take Another Jump," *Oil and Gas Journal*, July 2, 1979, pp. 60–61.

the two-day summit meeting. The participants were able to include in the declaration issued on the next day, June 29, a paragraph deploring the increase in oil prices and labeling it "unwarranted" and "bound to have very serious economic and social consequences."[71]

Energy had in fact been the principal topic of discussion at the Tokyo summit meeting. The participants agreed on the urgent need to reduce oil consumption and "expand alternative sources of energy."[72] Despite the political sensitivity of the subject in the aftermath of the accident at Three Mile Island, they identified nuclear power as one of the energy sources that must be developed.

The major, if limited, achievement of the Tokyo summit meeting was agreement on oil import ceilings for 1979 and 1980 and targets for 1985. The United States agreed to hold imports in 1979 and 1980 below 8.5 million barrels a day and to adopt the same figure as the goal for 1985.[73]

Events Leading to the July 15 Address

While President Carter was in Japan the mood in the White House approached despair. The worsening gasoline crisis was believed to be crippling the President politically and undermining his chances for re-election.[74] This mood was reflected in a long memorandum, dated June 28, that Stuart Eizenstat sent to him in Tokyo.[75] Eizenstat's memorandum began by describing how the domestic energy problem had continued to worsen. He declared that "nothing which has occurred in the administration to date . . . has so frustrated, confused, angered the American people—or so targeted their distress at you personally. . . ."

"In many respects," Eizenstat wrote, "this would appear to be the worst of times. But I honestly believe that we can change this to a time of opportunity. We have a better opportunity than ever before to assume

71. "Tokyo Economic Summit Conference, Declaration Issued at the Conclusion of the Conference, June 29, 1979," *Presidential Documents*, vol. 15 (July 9, 1979), p. 1199.

72. Ibid.

73. Ibid., pp. 1197–98. U.S. efforts to obtain specific country commitments from other participants were hampered because the members of the European Economic Community had met at Strasbourg immediately before the Tokyo summit and had agreed on a collective goal of limiting oil consumption to 10 million barrels a day in 1979. The European participants used this agreement to justify their unwillingness to accept specific country goals.

74. Martin Schram, *Washington Post*, July 1, 1979.

75. This memorandum was obtained by the *Washington Post* and was published in full on July 7, 1979.

leadership over an apparently insolvable problem, to shift the cause for inflation and energy problems to OPEC, to gain credibility with the American people, to offer hope of an eventual solution, to regain our political losses."

Eizenstat then enumerated a number of specific recommendations for the immediate future, including:

—Addressing "the enormous credibility and management problems" of the Department of Energy.

—Acting on proposals concerning how the proceeds of the windfall profits tax would be spent. (Eizenstat suggested that the President might then consider making a major address to the nation on energy problems.)

—Establishing a National Energy Mobilization Board to expedite selected energy projects.

Eizenstat concluded by repeating his main theme: "With strong steps we can mobilize the nation around a real crisis and with a clear enemy— OPEC."

After the Tokyo summit meeting President Carter paid a brief visit to Seoul. He had been scheduled to take a three-day vacation in Hawaii, but—as Eizenstat had urged—he flew directly back to Washington, arriving on the evening of July 1. The atmosphere in the White House was one of mounting crisis. Sporadic violence erupted in some gasoline lines. The independent truckers strike remained unsettled. Inflation was running at an annual rate of almost 13 percent, and a predicted decline of 3.3 percent in the real gross national product (later revised to 2.3 percent) seemed to indicate the onset of an economic recession. The President's approval rating in a public opinion poll on the day of his return was only 25 percent—lower than the lowest rating of President Nixon.[76]

Shortly after his return from East Asia, President Carter accepted the recommendation of Jody Powell, his press secretary, and Gerald Rafshoon, his media adviser, that he deliver an energy speech as soon as possible. The speech was to have been delivered on July 5 and would have contained a proposal for a large crash synthetic fuels program and renewal of the earlier request for standby gasoline rationing authority.[77]

Eizenstat had wanted the speech delayed until there was more to announce, especially about a synthetic fuels program on which he was working. Patrick Caddell, the President's public opinion specialist, be-

76. The account of events after the President's return to Washington draws heavily on Drew, "Phase: In Search of Definition."
77. Hedrick Smith, *New York Times*, July 4, 1979.

lieved that it would be disastrous for the President to deliver another speech devoted solely to energy. He wanted Carter also to address broader questions and gave him a 107-page memorandum spelling out what he had in mind.

On July 4 the President went to Camp David, taking Caddell's memorandum with him. After reading it he canceled the speech scheduled for the following evening. No public explanation for the cancellation was given.

For the next ten days the President engaged in a series of consultations that came to be known as the domestic summit. Over 100 persons —governors, mayors, members of Congress, labor leaders, business executives, and others—were invited to Camp David to give the President their views on the country's problems and his handling of them.[78] Concurrently his senior advisers held separate meetings at which they discussed "what sort of speech the President would give, how the nature of his Presidency should change, how the changes should be put into effect."[79]

The President returned to Washington on July 14. On the next day he delivered an address to the nation that contained important energy proposals but that by no means was purely an energy speech.

The July 15 Address

President Carter's July 15 address was in effect two speeches. The first was a gloomy sermon in which the President proclaimed his belief that the nation suffered from a crisis of confidence that threatened to destroy its social and political fabric. He called on the country to take "the path of common purpose and the restoration of American values," rather than "the path that leads to fragmentation and self-interest." The President saw the energy problem as "the immediate test of our ability to unite this Nation, and it can also be the standard around which we rally."[80]

In the second part of his speech, the President outlined his new energy proposals. He presented them in somewhat greater detail on the following day in a speech before the National Association of Counties meeting

78. A list of those who met with the President at Camp David is given in the *Congressional Quarterly Weekly Report*, July 14, 1979, p. 1393.

79. Drew, "Phase: In Search of Definition," p. 60.

80. "Energy and National Goals, Address to the Nation, July 15, 1979," *Presidential Documents*, vol. 15 (July 23, 1979), p. 1238.

in Kansas City, Missouri.[81] The proposals are set forth most fully, however, in the fact sheet (again twenty-eight pages) issued by the White House.[82]

The President's most important proposals were (1) to create an Energy Security Corporation "to direct the development of 2.5 MMB/D (million barrels a day) of oil substitutes from coal liquids and gases, oil shale, biomass, and unconventional gas by 1990," (2) to establish an Energy Mobilization Board "empowered to expedite permitting and construction of critical energy facilities," and (3) to impose a ceiling of 8.2 million barrels a day on oil imports, so the United States "will never use more foreign oil than we did in 1977." The President also made a number of other proposals including new incentives for the development of heavy oil, unconventional gas, and oil shale; mandatory reduction of oil consumption by electric utilities; a new residential and commercial conservation program; and additional expenditures on mass transportation and automobile efficiency.[83]

The Energy Security Corporation was described as "an independent, government-sponsored enterprise with a Congressional charter."[84] Its seven-person board of directors would consist of a chairman and three outside directors appointed by the President and confirmed by the Senate, plus the secretaries of energy and treasury and one other department head. In order to achieve the goal of producing 2.5 million barrels a day of substitutes for imported oil by 1990, it was estimated that the corporation would have to direct the investment of $88 billion. The corporation would use a variety of devices to stimulate the development of new energy-producing facilities: direct loans, loan guarantees, purchase agreements, and financing "a limited number" of government-owned and operated or government-owned, company-operated plants. The corporation would be financed largely by the windfall profits tax proposed by the President in his April 5 speech, although it would also receive the proceeds of up to $5 billion in special energy bonds.

81. "Kansas City, Missouri, Remarks at the Annual Convention of the National Association of Counties, July 16, 1979," ibid. (July 23, 1979), pp. 1241–47.

82. Office of the White House Press Secretary, "Fact Sheet on the President's Import Reduction Program."

83. Quotations in this paragraph are from ibid., p. 1, and "Energy Address to the Nation," p. 1239. The Energy Security Corporation was reminiscent of the ill-fated Energy Independence Authority proposed by Vice-President Nelson A. Rockefeller in 1975.

84. Office of the White House Press Secretary, "Fact Sheet on the President's Import Reduction Program," p. 7.

The Energy Mobilization Board would have three members, would be located in the Executive Office of the President, and would be authorized (1) "to designate certain non-nuclear facilities as critical to achieving the nation's import reduction goals," (2) "to establish binding schedules for federal, state, and local decision-making" with respect to designated projects, and (3) to act in the place of any agency failing to meet established schedules. The board would also be empowered to waive the procedural requirements of any law, in order to expedite critical energy projects.[85]

The oil import quota established by the President for 1979 was 300,000 barrels a day below the ceiling to which he had committed the United States at the recently concluded Tokyo summit meeting. The quota was also above the level of imports anticipated for 1979. The President indicated that the import quota for 1980 would also be below the Tokyo ceiling of 8.5 million barrels a day. He did not explain how the quota would be administered or what would be done if in some future year demand exceeded supply at the going price. Presumably it would then be necessary to allow the price to rise or to constrain consumption by some form of rationing.

The fact sheet issued by the White House after the President gave his July 15 address estimated that the following savings in U.S. oil imports in 1990 would be produced by the Carter administration's energy initiatives:[86]

Source of saving	Estimated oil import savings (millions of barrels per day)
National Energy Act of 1978	2.50
April 5 program and June solar energy message	1.50
July 16 initiatives	
Synthetic fuels and unconventional gas	2.50
Heavy oil	0.50
Utility reduction	0.75
Residential conservation	0.50
Mass transit and auto efficiency	0.25
Subtotal	4.50
Total estimated savings	8.50

85. Ibid., p. 9.
86. Ibid., p. 3.

The White House stated that "under a continuation of the 1977 status quo . . . import levels in the range of 13 million barrels per day would not have been improbable" in 1990.[87] The administration's energy initiatives could therefore reduce oil imports in 1990 to between 4 million and 5 million barrels a day.[88]

Events after the July 15 Address

The July 15 address was by no means the only consequence of the President's stay at Camp David. For reasons that are not altogether clear the members of the cabinet and the senior White House staff were told to offer their resignations.[89] Five cabinet resignations were accepted, including that of Secretary of Energy James R. Schlesinger. Deputy Secretary of Energy John F. O'Leary had resigned previously, effective September 30. President Carter nominated Charles W. Duncan, Jr., who had been deputy secretary of defense, to succeed Schlesinger. John C. Sawhill, president of New York University, was named to succeed O'Leary.

Before joining the Carter administration, Duncan, a native of Texas, had held senior executive positions in a family coffee firm and in the Coca Cola Company. His academic training was in chemical engineering and management. Sawhill was born in Cleveland, but he had grown up in Baltimore. An economist, he had headed the Federal Energy Administration during the Nixon and Ford administrations.

After Duncan took over the Department of Energy on August 24 the Energy Coordinating Committee, established by executive order in September 1978 to coordinate energy policy among executive agencies, became much more important. This committee, which met every Friday under Duncan's chairmanship, included Secretary of State Cyrus R. Vance, Secretary of the Treasury G. William Miller, and Assistant to the President for National Security Affairs Zbigniew Brzezinski. In practice Under Secretary of State Richard N. Cooper represented Vance, Henry Owen of the White House staff represented Brzezinski, and Under Secretary of the Treasury Anthony M. Solomon sometimes took the place of Miller.

87. Ibid., p. 4.
88. An irreverent comment circulated in the government that two more energy speeches would make the United States a net exporter of oil.
89. In some detail an account of the cabinet resignations is given in Drew, "Phase: In Search of Definition."

A staff energy committee of subordinates of the members of the Energy Coordinating Committee met twice a week under the chairmanship of Eliot R. Cutler of the White House staff (formerly with the Office of Management and Budget). Cutler coordinated the handling of energy problems between the White House and Duncan. Under this arrangement, the role of the domestic White House staff under Eizenstat was less important than it had been.

Congressional Actions

Energy was a major concern of Congress during most of 1979, but little new energy legislation was passed. Perhaps the most notable achievement was the establishment of procedures for creating a standby gasoline rationing plan.

Congress spent a great amount of time on President Carter's three major energy proposals: the windfall profits tax, the Energy Security Corporation, and the Energy Mobilization Board. Eventual enactment of all three in some form appeared likely when Congress adjourned for the year on December 21, but the resolution of remaining issues was deferred until after the legislators reconvened one month later.

The Windfall Profits Tax

Both politically and financially the windfall profits tax was an indispensable component of the President's energy program. Without a substantial tax on the increased earnings of the oil companies, the President's phased decontrol of the price of domestically produced crude oil would be vulnerable to attack from the liberal wing of his own party. Revenues from the tax were needed, moreover, to finance the development of a large synthetic fuel industry and a number of other energy measures proposed by the President. Remembering the fate of the crude oil equalization tax, the administration made a strong and sustained effort to induce Congress to enact an acceptable windfall profits tax.

As it had done in 1977 in the case of the proposed crude oil equalization tax, the House of Representatives voted fairly promptly in favor of a windfall profits tax that met the administration's requirements (House bill 3919). The Senate, where representatives of oil-producing states had greater influence, was again a more serious problem. After prolonged consideration in the Finance Committee (whose powerful chairman,

Senator Russell B. Long, had his own ideas) and a complicated floor debate the Senate finally passed a windfall profits tax on December 17 that was substantially different from the tax approved by the House.[90]

Over the next ten years the Senate version of the windfall profits tax was estimated to yield $178 billion and the House version $277 billion. About half the difference resulted from the Senate's exemption of the first 1,000 barrels a day of the output of independent producers. The other half was attributable to the Senate's taxing newly discovered oil, heavy oil, and incremental oil produced by tertiary recovery methods at lower rates than those approved by the House.

Under heavy White House pressure, a House-Senate conference committee tentatively agreed that the windfall profits tax should raise $227.3 billion over the next decade, thereby splitting the difference between the two versions. There was not time before adjournment, however, to determine how that revenue target would be achieved. Major issues put over to the new year included the division of the tax burden between major oil companies and independent producers. A decision on whether and how to provide for eventual termination of the tax was also deferred.[91]

After Congress adjourned, the White House announced an action that it presented as a means of inducing prompt action when the House-Senate conference committee on the windfall profits tax resumed work in the new year. Under the phased decontrol program, the price of 20 percent of the output from marginal (low-producing) wells was scheduled to rise from $6 to $13 a barrel on January 1, 1980. (The other 80 percent had moved up to the $13 price on June 1, 1979.) The President decided to hold the price of the oil in question at $6 a barrel for an unspecified period.[92]

This action affected only about 100,000 barrels of oil a day, or roughly 1 percent of domestic production. By itself, the President's decision could not have been expected to have much effect on Congress. It did, however, suggest that other steps in the decontrol process might be delayed until passage of an acceptable windfall profits tax. It was also at least a partial answer to critics who said that the President should not have decoupled decontrol and the tax on increased oil company earnings.

90. For a succinct comparison of the two versions see "Lawmakers Seek Excise Tax Compromise," *Oil and Gas Journal,* December 24, 1979, p. 24.

91. *New York Times,* December 21, 1979.

92. "Decontrol of Marginal Oil Wells, Executive Order 12187, December 29, 1979," *Presidential Documents,* vol. 15 (December 31, 1979), p. 2290. See also *Wall Street Journal,* December 26, 1979.

The Energy Security Corporation

The House also acted first on the creation of an energy security corporation to promote the development of a large synthetic fuel industry. The House bill (3930), which had been under consideration long before the President made his proposal, passed on June 26. This bill, however, sanctioned the expenditure of only $3 billion for this purpose—a small fraction of the $88 billion that the President had requested for a ten-year period.[93]

The Senate did not act until November 8, but its version (Senate bill 932) was much closer to the President's proposal insofar as synthetic fuels were concerned. The Senate approved the use of $20 billion over a five-year period to stimulate the production of synthetic fuels. If the technologies involved proved to be commercially feasible, a second phase $68 billion program would then begin. The Senate bill also included a $14 billion "conservation package" that had no counterpart in the House bill. The largest items in this package were funds to encourage the production of gasohol and the conservation of energy in homes.[94]

Formation of a House-Senate conference committee to resolve the considerable differences in the two bills was delayed by a jurisdictional dispute between the Senate Energy and Banking Committees. When the conference committee did begin work on December 7, it agreed to consider a compromise framed by House Majority Leader James Wright that was close to the provisions on synthetic fuels in the Senate bill.[95] Although Wright's proposal improved prospects for the enactment of a synthetic fuels program and the creation of a government corporation to administer it, the complex problem posed by the conservation package in the Senate bill remained to be solved.

The Energy Mobilization Board

The Senate passed a bill (1308) creating an Energy Mobilization Board on October 4, 1979. The House voted in favor of an EMB with somewhat greater powers on November 1 (House bill 4985). The prin-

93. The Interior Department and Energy Department appropriations bill for fiscal 1980 (H.R. 4930), passed by the House on July 30, actually provided funds for the synfuels program. See the *New York Times,* July 31, 1979.

94. For a comparison of the House and Senate bills see "U.S. Senate Approves Synfuels Program," *Oil and Gas Journal,* November 19, 1979, p. 74.

95. *Wall Street Journal,* December 10, 1979.

cipal difference between the two versions was in the authority of the EMB to override substantive, as opposed to procedural, provisions of Federal laws.[96] The Senate bill authorized the EMB to waive temporarily the requirements of laws coming into effect after a given priority energy project was begun. Such waivers, however, were subject under some circumstances to veto by the administrator of the Environmental Protection Agency or the secretary of the interior. The House bill authorized the EMB to recommend to the President that provisions of a broad range of laws be waived. If the President agrees with an EMB recommendation, he must obtain the approval of both Houses of Congress for a waiver to take effect.

Appointment of a conference committee to reconcile the differences in the Senate and House bills was delayed by a jurisdictional dispute between the House Commerce and Interior committees.[97] When the conference committee did finally meet on December 7, it got off to a bad start by arguing over the secondary questions of the number and pay of members of the EMB.[98] The conference committee did decide that the EMB should have three members before it suspended work on December 20. The major problem of the EMB's power to waive substantive provisions of law was put off to the new year.

International Developments

The final months of 1979 brought important international developments in the field of energy. The Iranian revolution entered a new and more threatening phase, the International Energy Agency agreed on tighter oil import quotas, and OPEC failed to agree on measures to restore order to the international oil market.

Iran Again

On October 22 the deposed shah of Iran flew from Mexico, where he had taken up residence some months previously, to New York for medical treatment for cancer and gallstones. On November 4 an armed group

96. For a critique of the board and a comparison of the Senate and House bills, see John Quarles, *Wall Street Journal,* November 13, 1979.
97. Warren Weaver, Jr., *New York Times,* December 4, 1979.
98. *Wall Street Journal,* December 10, 1979.

of young Iranian militants, sometimes described as students, occupied the U.S. Embassy in Tehran and made hostages of the embassy staff. The militants, supported by the Iranian Revolutionary Council and the top leader of the Islamic revolution, the Ayatollah Ruhollah Khomeini, declared that the hostages would not be released until the former shah was returned to Iran to stand trial for his alleged crimes against the Iranian people. The U.S. government refused to comply with this demand and pressed for the immediate unconditional release of the hostages. Non-U.S. citizens and most American women and blacks were subsequently released, but fifty Americans remained hostage at year-end.[99] The departure of the shah for Panama on December 15 did not cause the militants to relax their demands.

The crisis in U.S.-Iranian relations dominated all other concerns of the U.S. government, including the energy problem. The crisis did have an energy aspect, however. On November 12 President Carter ordered the cessation of purchases of Iranian oil for delivery to the United States.[100] On November 15 Iran canceled all contracts with U.S. oil companies, thereby preventing them from continuing to supply Iranian oil to non-U.S. markets.[101]

At the time these actions were taken the United States was importing about 750,000 barrels of oil a day from Iran (approximately 4 percent of total U.S. consumption), and U.S. companies were supplying another 700,000 barrels a day of Iranian oil to other countries (about 3.8 percent of the total oil imports of Western Europe and Japan in 1978).[102] From the Iranian point of view the oil affected by Iran's action and that of the United States was almost half of Iran's exports of roughly 3 million barrels a day.

None of this oil, of course, was withdrawn from the world market, although it was feared for a time that Iran would cut back its production and exports by the amount that it had formerly sent to the United States. The action on both sides was largely symbolic, but normal marketing arrangements were disrupted and new arrangements had to be improvised.

---

99. The U.S. chargé d'affaires and two other embassy officers continued to be held at the Foreign Ministry.

100. "Imports of Petroleum and Petroleum Products," Proclamation 4702, November 12, 1979, *Presidential Documents,* vol. 15 (November 19, 1979), pp. 2108–09.

101. *Wall Street Journal,* November 16, 1979.

102. Ibid.; ibid., November 13, 1979; and *International Energy Statistical Review,* December 12, 1979, p. 4.

The trend toward greater use of the volatile spot market was probably strengthened. The most important effect of the U.S. and Iranian actions was to increase uncertainty concerning the future reliability of oil supplies and to make it easier for oil-exporting countries to raise prices.

The IEA and OPEC Meetings

The energy ministers of the countries belonging to the International Energy Agency had been scheduled to meet in Paris in January 1980.[103] The meeting was advanced to December 10, one week before the oil ministers of OPEC were to meet in Caracas. The IEA hoped it would be able to display a determination to restrict oil imports that would encourage the moderate members of OPEC to resist a large increase in oil prices.[104]

The objectives of the United States at the Paris meeting were to obtain agreement on (1) individual country oil import quotas, (2) closer monitoring of oil imports, (3) sanctions against countries exceeding their quotas, and (4) a reduction of about 1 million barrels a day in the previously agreed upon collective IEA quota for 1980. The United States achieved only the first two of these objectives.[105]

Individual country quotas (which the United States had unsuccessfully sought at the Tokyo summit meeting in June) were made possible by a decision on December 5 by the members of the European Economic Community on how to divide their joint quota. This prior consultation among the nine members of the community was, however, a major reason for the failure of the United States to obtain agreement on a lower total IEA quota for 1980.

The total IEA oil import quota for 1980 remained 23.1 million barrels a day (not including 1.4 million barrels a day for ship bunkers), which was slightly below estimated imports of 24.2 million barrels a day. The IEA target for 1985, however, was set at 24.6 million barrels a day (excluding bunkers) rather than the previously agreed upon 26 million barrels a day.[106]

It is unlikely that the OPEC oil ministers, who met in Caracas from

103. The IEA consists of the members of the Organisation for Economic Cooperation and Development, except France, which participates indirectly through the European Economic Community.

104. Joseph Fitchett, *International Herald Tribune,* December 11, 1979.

105. Paul Lewis, *New York Times,* December 11, 1979.

106. Ibid., and Felix Kessler, *Wall Street Journal,* December 11, 1979.

December 17 to 20, were greatly influenced by the results of the IEA meeting. They were too preoccupied by their internal disagreements. In early December the price of crude oil sold outside the spot market ranged from $18 a barrel for Saudi Arabian light to $26.27 a barrel for Algerian oil. The ceiling of $23.50 that had been established at the June OPEC meeting was being widely violated, and possibly 20 percent of all internationally traded oil was being sold on the spot market at $40 a barrel or more.[107]

On December 13, only four days before the Caracas meeting was to open, Saudi Arabia raised the price of its marker crude to $24 a barrel. Venezuela, the United Arab Emirates, and Qatar announced comparable price increases.[108] The Saudis and their supporters clearly hoped that at Caracas the other members of OPEC could be induced to return to the traditional arrangement under which the prices of all other crudes would be aligned around the price of Saudi Arabian light, the so-called marker crude. Differences in price would then reflect quality differences or varying distances from market, rather than the estimates of individual exporting countries of what the market would bear.

The Saudi strategy failed at Caracas. Libya and Iran announced large price increases during the meeting that were inconsistent with alignment around a $24-a-barrel price for marker crude. Similar price increases by several other oil-exporting countries appeared likely. The Saudis, however, did not abandon their effort to restore a unified OPEC price structure. They indicated that they would maintain their own production at 9.5 million barrels a day during the first three months of 1980 (1 million barrels a day above their usual ceiling) in a deliberate effort to create a modest glut of oil on the international market. They clearly hoped in this way to bring about a softening of prices and to improve their bargaining position within OPEC. An extraordinary OPEC meeting was scheduled to meet at Taif, Saudi Arabia, at the end of the first quarter of 1980.

The oil-importing countries derived no benefits from the continued turmoil within OPEC. The weighted average price of internationally traded crude oil was $13.80 a barrel on January 1, 1979. Because of chaotic market conditions, a weighted average price for December 31 cannot be calculated, but it was clearly more than twice the January 1 figure.

107. The summary of events immediately before the Caracas OPEC meeting presented here draws heavily on the account in Roger Vielvoye, "Action by OPEC Further Disarrays Crude Prices," *Oil and Gas Journal*, December 24, 1979, pp. 19–22.
108. Steven Rattner, *New York Times*, December 14, 1979.

The Unfinished Story

As the 1970s drew to an end the future of U.S. energy policy was obscured by major uncertainties. No one could say how the confrontation with Iran would end or whether it would lead to a further reduction in Iranian oil exports. Disorders affecting oil production in other exporting countries also could not be ruled out. Even if oil supplies were not subjected to further disruption, the chaotic conditions in the international oil market might well persist. And in any event the prospect that supply might not keep pace with demand in future years meant that already high oil prices might go still higher.

If additional measures to check energy consumption appeared to be needed, agreement among the major industrialized countries on how cuts were to be allocated would not be reached easily. It was also not clear how the United States would go about achieving lower energy consumption targets. In the final weeks of 1979 the administration considered imposing either an import fee on oil or an increased excise tax on gasoline.[109] President Carter, however, decided against taking either of these actions at that time.[110] Nonetheless, the administration did complete a standby gasoline rationing plan that was to be submitted to Congress after being revised to take account of public comments.[111]

Nuclear energy was subject to its own special uncertainties. The impact of the accident at Three Mile Island had still not worked its way fully through the political system. The Nuclear Regulatory Commission's suspension of issuing operating licenses for new nuclear power plants remained in effect, and the President awaited the report of an interagency review group before acting on most of the recommendations of the Kemeny commission.[112] The President did indicate that he would not ask Congress to replace the five-member Nuclear Regulatory Commission with an agency headed by a single executive, as the Kemeny commission had proposed. Instead, he fired Joseph M. Hendrie as chairman of the NRC and made Commissioner John F. Ahearne acting chairman.

109. Richard J. Levine and Rich Jaroslovsky, *Wall Street Journal,* December 18, 1979; and Steven Rattner, *New York Times,* December 7, 1979.

110. Steven Rattner, *New York Times,* December 21, 1979.

111. U.S. Department of Energy, Economic Regulatory Administration, "Standby Gasoline Rationing Plan," *Federal Register,* vol. 44 (December 10, 1979), pp. 70799–858.

112. "Will Carter Call a Referendum on Nuclear?" *Nuclear Engineering International,* vol. 24 (December 1979), p. 11.

At the same time the President made the strongest statement in favor of nuclear energy in many months, declaring that the country did not "have the luxury of abandoning nuclear power or imposing a lengthy moratorium on its future use."[113]

Energy promised to be an important issue in presidential politics in 1980. How important seemed to depend on the outcome of the Iranian crisis. In the summer and early fall of 1979 Senator Edward M. Kennedy, President Carter's principal rival for the Democratic nomination, made energy policy one of his main lines of attack on the President's performance. He particularly criticized the President's decontrol of the price of domestic crude oil. Senator Kennedy did not drop his criticism of President Carter's energy policy after the occupation of the U.S. Embassy in Tehran on November 4,[114] but the crisis that ensued overwhelmed all other issues and placed a premium on national unity.

The Iranian crisis had the effect of dramatically improving President Carter's standing with the U.S. public. A Harris survey of likely Democratic voters conducted between December 14 and 16 gave the President a 58–38 percent lead over Senator Kennedy for the nomination.[115] This kind of political strength—if it lasted—would clearly improve the President's chances of obtaining congressional approval for his major energy proposals. If the Iranian crisis ended badly, however, prospects would be much different. The President might then be hard-pressed to defend many aspects of his performance, including energy policy, from critics in and out of his party.

113. "President's Commission on the Accident at Three Mile Island, Remarks Announcing Actions in Response to the Commission's Report, December 7, 1979," *Presidential Documents,* vol. 15 (December 10, 1979), pp. 2202–03.

114. On December 20 in an address to the Chamber of Commerce of Rochester, New Hampshire, Senator Kennedy sharply attacked the administration for allegedly encouraging OPEC to raise oil prices. See B. Drummond Ayres, Jr., *New York Times,* December 21, 1979.

115. Louis Harris, "Carter-Kennedy Contest Narrowing," *ABC News–Harris Survey,* vol. 2 (January 10, 1980).

CHAPTER TEN

Energy in America's Future: The Difficult Transition

JOSEPH A. YAGER

THE UNITED STATES has experienced two major changes in the way it has satisfied its energy needs. In the nineteenth century, wood—long the dominant fuel—was largely replaced by coal, and in this century coal has lost its leading role to oil and natural gas. Today the United States is in the early stages of a third energy transition that may prove to be more difficult than those of the past.

The years covered in this book saw the end of U.S. energy self-sufficiency and growing dependence on imported oil. The Arab oil embargo of 1973–74 and the associated fourfold increase in the international price of oil demonstrated that this dependence involves substantial political and economic costs. This fact was again underlined in 1979 when the Organization of Petroleum Exporting Countries took advantage of the disruption of oil production in Iran to impose another large increase in the price of oil.

Even if the United States were comfortable with its increasing dependence on foreign oil, this trend could not continue indefinitely. World oil production may peak before the end of the century. Other forms of energy must then take over oil's role as the major incremental source of supply. None of the available substitutes for oil, however, is free of serious problems.

A return to coal as the mainstay of the U.S. energy economy would involve heavy environmental costs. Nuclear power is perceived by many as unsafe, and domestic policy toward its development is complicated by the U.S. effort to check the spread of nuclear weapons internationally. The potential contribution of some other sources of energy is limited in

THE AUTHOR is grateful for comments on an earlier draft by Derriel Cato, Joy Dunkerley, and William Ramsay.

the near-term by high costs and the need for further technological development.

Choosing the right energy path for the United States has been further complicated because energy policy affects the achievement of other domestic and international goals, including economic growth, price stabilization, and peace in the Middle East. An additional difficulty is the lack of a clear view of the long-term future in the field of energy itself. The most readily available substitutes for oil are seen, not as permanent solutions, but as means of making the transition to some still undetermined energy economy of the future, possibly a combination of solar energy, fast breeder reactors, and nuclear fusion, but no one can be sure. The energy policymaker of today in effect is asked to build a bridge to a distant shore that he cannot see.

Trends in Energy Production and Consumption

Before examining U.S. energy choices and problems in greater detail, it is useful to consider briefly the prospects for energy production and consumption, both globally and in the United States itself.

The Global Context

For many years U.S. energy policy was concerned largely with domestic problems, such as helping an ailing coal industry or regulating the interstate transportation of natural gas. As U.S. dependence on foreign oil has grown, so has the need to make energy policy in an international context. The desire of the United States to limit its oil imports is shared by other oil-importing nations, and the American move away from oil and toward other sources of energy is part of a global process.

Table 10-1 presents recent projections of primary energy consumption in non-Communist areas in 1985, 1990, and 1995, broken down by energy source. Actual figures for 1974 are also given as a basis for comparison. The assumptions on which the estimates of future consumption are based are spelled out in some detail in the Department of Energy's annual report to Congress for 1979.[1] Key assumptions deal with the world price

1. U.S. Department of Energy, Energy Information Administration, *Annual Report to Congress, 1979,* vol. 3: *Projections* (Government Printing Office, 1980). Estimates for all areas except the United States are from the department's "low-mid"

of oil, the rates of economic growth in various parts of the world, and the relationship between economic growth and energy consumption.

The world price of oil (defined as the average landed price of crude oil on the East Coast of the United States) is assumed to remain constant at $27 a barrel in real terms.[2] Since other energy prices tend to follow the price of oil, this assumption has the effect of holding the prices of all forms of energy constant. In this way it is possible to examine separately the effects of nonprice variables on future energy consumption.

The estimates of energy consumption in table 10-1 rest on the assumption that the gross domestic products (GDP) of non-Communist countries will grow at an average annual rate of 3.6 percent during 1975–95. The economies of the oil-importing developing countries are assumed to grow at an average annual rate of 5.1 percent, but those of the industrialized countries are assumed to grow much less rapidly. Thus the rate assumed for the United States is 2.7 percent and for OECD Europe, 2.5 percent.[3]

Since energy consumption in non-Communist areas as a whole is projected to increase at an average annual rate of 2.7 percent, a 1 percent increase in GDP is associated with a 0.7 percent increase in energy consumption. In the developing countries the relationship between energy consumption and economic growth is close to one-to-one. In the United States a 1 percent increase in GDP is associated with only a 0.65 percent increase in energy consumption and in OECD Europe with only a 0.60 percent increase. (The comparable figure in the 1960s and early 1970s was about 0.9.)

These energy-GDP relationships have no independent validity but are the result of more detailed assumptions concerning the effect of a variety

---

projection series (unpublished, April 1980). Except for the assumption that the world price of crude oil remains constant, this projection is based on the assumptions used in the department's middle-growth projection series (see *Annual Report, 1979*, pp. 8–10). Estimates for future U.S. consumption are DOE's low oil price projection series (see ibid., chap. 4). Estimates for all areas assume that the world price of oil remains constant at $27 a barrel in 1979 dollars.

2. This price approximates the landed cost of Saudi Arabian light, the "marker" crude, at the end of 1979. Until recently the prices of other crude oils were aligned above and below the marker crude on the basis of differences in quality and distance from major markets.

3. The "other" category in the stub of table 10-1 consists almost entirely of non-oil-exporting developing countries. Almost all industrialized countries belong to the OECD: the United States, the Western European countries (OECD Europe), Japan, Canada, Australia, and New Zealand.

Table 10-1. *Estimated Primary Energy Consumption in Non-Communist Areas, by Source, 1974, 1985, 1990, and 1995*[a]

Millions of barrels of oil per day equivalent

Area and year	Oil	Natural gas	Coal	Nuclear	Other	Total
United States[b]						
1974	15.6	10.4	6.5	0.6	1.5	34.6
1985	15.9	9.2	11.0	2.7	1.6	40.4
1990	17.0	9.8	12.5	3.9	1.8	45.0
1995	18.3	9.4	14.9	4.7	2.0	49.3
OECD Europe						
1974	14.1	2.8	5.1	0.4	1.6	24.0
1985	13.2	3.9	6.0	2.0	2.3	27.4
1990	14.2	4.1	6.0	2.6	2.5	29.4
1995	16.3	4.4	6.2	3.3	2.5	32.7
Japan						
1974	5.1	0.2	1.3	0.1	0.4	7.1
1985	6.7	1.1	1.0	0.5	0.6	9.9
1990	7.2	1.9	1.4	0.7	0.7	11.9
1995	8.8	3.0	1.9	1.0	1.0	15.7
Other OECD (Canada, Australia, New Zealand)						
1974	2.4	0.8	0.8	0.1	1.2	5.3
1985	2.5	1.2	1.2	0.3	1.6	6.8
1990	2.9	1.4	1.0	0.4	1.9	7.6
1995	3.4	1.5	1.1	0.5	2.3	8.8
OPEC countries						
1974	2.0	0.9	...	...	0.1	3.0
1985	3.8	1.7	...	0.1	...	5.6
1990	5.2	2.5	...	0.1	...	7.8
1995	6.9	3.4	...	0.1	...	10.4
Other						
1974	6.4	0.7	2.6	...	1.0	10.7
1985	8.9	1.2	4.6	0.4	1.9	17.0
1990	11.4	1.6	6.0	0.7	2.6	22.3
1995	14.7	2.1	8.1	1.2	2.6	28.7
Total						
1974	45.6	15.8	16.3	1.2	5.8	84.7
1985	51.0	18.3	23.8	6.0	8.0	107.1
1990	57.9	21.3	26.9	8.4	9.5	124.0
1995	68.4	23.8	32.2	10.8	10.4	145.6

Sources: Actual consumption figures for 1974 are from Organisation for Economic Co-operation and Development, *World Energy Outlook* (Paris: OECD, 1977), pp. 90–99. Estimates of future consumption in all areas except the United States are the "low-mid" forecast of the U.S. Department of Energy, Energy Information Administration, unpublished data, April 1980. These estimates are based on DOE's "middle growth" projection series, with the exception that world oil prices are held constant; see DOE, EIA, *Annual Report to Congress, 1979*, vol. 3: *Projections* (Government Printing Office, 1980), pp. 8–10. U.S. estimates are from ibid., p. 118. Figures are rounded.

a. The world oil price (the average landed price of imported crude oil on the U.S. East Coast) is assumed to remain constant at $27 a barrel in 1979 dollars. The following conversion ratios are used: 1 cubic foot of natural gas = 1,000 Btu; 1 short ton of coal = 22.2 million Btu; 1 terawatt of electricity a year = 0.01 quadrillion Btu a year; and 1 million barrels of oil a day = 0.485 quadrillion Btu a year. Net energy trade between Communist and non-Communist countries is assumed to be zero.

b. Estimates of U.S. oil consumption include additions to the Strategic Petroleum Reserve.

of developments on energy consumption. The developments include changes in the structures of the economies in question, the continued effect of past increases in energy prices, and government conservation measures such as fuel efficiency standards for automobiles and tax credits for energy-saving investments.

The breakdown of energy consumption by source shown in table 10-1 illustrates only possible future developments. Thus the large increase forecast for coal consumption may not occur if major mining, transportation, and environmental problems are not overcome, and if demand for coal by electric utility companies does not rise markedly. On the other hand the more modest increase projected for consumption of natural gas could prove to be too low if international trade in that fuel expands and if higher energy prices bring more gas into domestic markets. The estimates for nuclear power could be either too high or too low: too high if antinuclear forces have their way in a number of industrialized countries; too low if nuclear power gains greater acceptance as a means of reducing dependence on oil imports.

In the present period oil is the fuel that makes up the difference between total energy requirements and available supplies of other sources of energy. Therefore, if the estimates of total energy consumption in table 10-1 are too low, or if the estimates of consumption of other sources of energy are too high, requirements for oil must be increased. Errors in the opposite direction would reduce requirements for oil.[4]

A number of estimates of future energy consumption have been published in recent years that differ somewhat from those presented in table 10-1 because of differences in the underlying assumptions used.[5] All such estimates can do no more than provide a quantitative framework for thinking about possible future developments. The estimates in table 10-1, however, have the advantages of being both comprehensive and recent.

If these estimates are accepted for purposes of the present discussion, they suggest that several significant developments may take place between now and the mid-1980s. First, even if energy prices do not continue to

4. The changes in oil requirements would not exactly equal the errors in the other estimates, however. In the real world, energy prices would change, total energy consumption would move above or below projected levels, and other fuels would absorb some of the required adjustment.

5. Several estimates of future energy consumption are compared in *Energy: An Uncertain Future: An Analysis of U.S. and World Energy Projections through 1990*, Senate Committee on Energy and Natural Resources, Pub. 95-157, 95 Cong. 2 sess. (GPO, 1978), especially pp. 37–56. See also James Just and Lester Lave, "Review of Scenarios of Future U.S. Energy Use," *Annual Review of Energy*, vol. 4 (1979), pp. 501–36 (Brookings Reprint T-021).

rise, total energy consumption will grow much more slowly than it did in the recent past.[6] Second, the share of oil in total energy consumption will be lower in the period 1985–95 than it was in the mid-1970s. Third, the absolute volume of oil consumption will nevertheless increase over the long run.

In the short run the estimates used here indicate that the rise in oil consumption may slow down, and demand for oil from the Organization of Petroleum Exporting Countries may actually decline slightly. Oil consumption will then resume a more rapid rise. Oil production in non-OPEC areas will not keep pace. By 1995 import requirements for OPEC oil will be about 30 percent greater than in 1978 and half again as large as the estimate for 1985 (see table 10-2).

Because of rising consumption and declining domestic production, the oil import requirements of the OECD nations are projected to increase substantially in the period 1985–95. Despite a relatively steep increase in consumption, expanded oil production is expected to hold the growth of oil import requirements of the other non-OPEC countries (most of which are in the developing category) to a relatively small amount. All the estimates of oil consumption and production presented in table 10-2 are necessarily subject to error, but the projected increase in oil production in the non-OPEC developing countries must be regarded as especially speculative. Of the 12 million barrels a day attributed to this group of countries in 1995, 5 million barrels are to be produced by Mexico, which would require that country's output almost to quadruple over 1978 levels.

Table 10-2 assumes that net oil exports of the Communist countries will fall to zero in the early 1980s and that those countries as a group will be neither exporters nor importers of oil in the period 1985–95. This in effect means that the oil exports of China would be counterbalanced by the oil imports of the Soviet Union and Eastern Europe. Other outcomes are possible. Some observers believe that in the 1980s the net oil imports of the Soviet Union and Eastern Europe will exceed China's oil exports by a significant margin.[7] If so, the demand for OPEC oil would be correspondingly increased.

6. From 1960 to 1976 energy consumption in non-Communist areas grew at an average annual rate of 4.3 percent. U.S. Department of Energy, Energy Information Administration, *International Energy Assessment,* Analysis Report DOE/EIA-0184/1 (GPO, 1979), p. 16.

7. See U.S. Central Intelligence Agency, National Foreign Assessment Center, *The World Oil Market in the Years Ahead,* ER 79-10327U (CIA, 1979), pp. 37–42. (Available from National Technical Information Service.)

Table 10-2. *Demand for OPEC Oil, 1978, 1985, 1990, and 1995*

Millions of barrels per day

Item	1978	1985	1990	1995
United States[a]				
Consumption	18.3	15.9	17.0	18.3
Production	10.3	9.0	8.8	8.0
Import requirements	8.0	6.9	8.2	10.3
OECD Europe				
Consumption	13.9	13.2	14.2	16.3
Production	1.8	3.5	3.3	3.3
Import requirements	12.1	9.7	10.9	13.0
Japan				
Consumption	5.1	6.7	7.1	8.8
Production	*	*	*	*
Import requirements	5.1	6.7	7.1	8.8
Other OECD (Canada, Australia, New Zealand)				
Consumption	2.6	2.5	2.8	3.4
Production	2.1	2.1	2.2	2.0
Import requirements	0.5	0.4	0.6	1.4
Other non-OPEC				
Consumption	7.9	8.8	11.4	14.7
Production	4.6	8.8	10.3	12.0
Import requirements	3.3	0.0	1.1	2.7
Total non-OPEC, non-Communist				
Consumption	47.8	47.1	52.5	61.5
Production	18.8	23.4	24.6	25.3
Import requirements	29.0	23.7	27.9	36.2
Net Communist exports[b]	1.0	0.0	0.0	0.0
Demand for OPEC oil				
Net import requirements	28.0	23.7	27.9	36.2
OPEC consumption	2.5	3.8	5.2	6.9
Total	30.5	27.5	33.1	43.1

Sources: For the United States, 1978 figures and projections are from low oil price projection series, U.S. Department of Energy, Energy Information Administration, *Annual Report, 1979*, vol. 3: *Projections* (Government Printing Office, 1980), pp. 22, 83; all other projections are from the low-mid series, DOE, EIA, unpublished data, April 1980. The world price of crude oil is assumed to remain constant at $27 a barrel in 1979 dollars. Figures are rounded and include natural gas liquids.

* Less than 0.05 million barrels a day.

a. U.S. consumption includes purchases for the Strategic Petroleum Reserve.

b. Communist countries are assumed to be neither net importers nor net exporters in 1985, 1990, and 1995.

Table 10-3. *Crude Oil and Natural Gas Liquids Production Potential of
OPEC Countries, 1980, 1985, 1990, and 1995*

Millions of barrels per day

Item	Available production capacity 1980	Estimated production capacity			
		1980[a]	1985	1990	1995
Crude oil					
Iran	3.5	5.5	4.0	4.0	4.0
Iraq	3.5	3.5	3.8	4.0	4.5
Kuwait[b]	1.8	2.8	2.5	2.5	2.5
United Arab Emirates	1.8	2.4	2.5	2.5	2.5
Libya	2.2	2.2	2.0	2.0	1.7
Nigeria	2.2	2.2	2.1	2.0	2.0
Venezuela	2.2	2.4	2.0	2.0	2.3[c]
Indonesia	1.6	1.6	1.5	1.6	1.3
Algeria	1.1	1.1	0.8	0.7	0.6
Other OPEC[d]	1.0	1.0	0.9	0.8	0.7
Natural gas liquids	0.8	0.8	1.5	1.5	1.7
Subtotal	21.7	25.5	23.6	23.6	23.8
Saudi Arabia[b]	9.8	9.8	10.5	11.0	11.0
Total	31.5	35.3	34.1	34.6	34.8

Sources: Figures for both available and estimated maximum sustainable capacity for crude oil production in 1980 are from *International Energy Statistical Review*, June 24, 1980, p. 3. Estimates of natural
gas liquids in 1980 and estimated capacity for both crude oil and natural gas liquids in 1985, 1990, and
1995 are from the middle projection series of the U.S. Department of Energy, Energy Information Administration, *Annual Report to Congress, 1979*, vol. 3: *Projections* (Government Printing Office, 1980),
p. 19.
a. Maximum sustainable capacity.
b. Includes 50 percent of Neutral Zone capacity.
c. Includes 0.3 million–0.5 million barrels a day of heavy oil.
d. Ecuador, Gabon, and Qatar.

Table 10-2 does not present forecasts of OPEC production, because
several members have in the past restricted output as a matter of policy,
and what their policy will be in the future is unpredictable. It is somewhat
more feasible to arrive at estimates of OPEC's production potential. One
set of such estimates is presented in table 10-3.

The estimates of production capacity in table 10-3 are subject to the
usual uncertainty concerning the size of oil resources. In a few cases—
most notably Saudi Arabia and Iran—uncertainty also exists with respect to governmental policies toward the exploitation of resources. The
capacity figures shown for these two major producers are in fact estimates of what their governments will permit rather than of what may be
physically possible. Table 10-3 is organized in a way that brings out the

key role of Saudi Arabia. Perhaps the most striking feature of this table is the nearly constant level of OPEC's total productive capacity.

It is instructive to compare estimates of the production capacity of the OPEC nations with the estimated demand for OPEC oil:[8]

	Millions of barrels per day		
	1985	1990	1995
Production capacity	34.1	34.6	34.8
Demand for OPEC oil	27.6	33.2	43.1
Balance	6.5	1.4	−8.3

These figures should not be taken too literally. The shortage shown in 1995 could not in fact occur. The price of oil in real terms would rise, rather than remain constant, as was assumed in projecting the future demand for OPEC oil. At the higher price, supply and demand would be brought into balance.

It is virtually certain that not all of OPEC's productive capacity will be continuously available. Capacity can be kept idle as a matter of government policy or its use can be disrupted by war or domestic turmoil. Supply may lag behind demand and cause further increases in the price of oil long before 1995.

What price increase may be needed to clear the market (and whether there will be price increases at all) will depend on (1) the validity of the estimates of demand for OPEC oil (at the assumed price) and of OPEC's sustainable production capacity, (2) how much of that capacity would actually be made available by governments, and (3) the responsiveness of supply and demand in the non-OPEC countries to increases in the price of oil. Developments that would moderate any price increase include a slower growth of energy consumption than is projected in table 10-1 and a decision by the government of Saudi Arabia to expand production capacity beyond the 11 million barrels a day shown in table 10-3.[9] Developments with the opposite effect include a more rapid increase in energy consumption than projected and a failure of supplies of energy other than OPEC oil to expand as much as projected.

8. Capacity figures are from table 10-3, demand figures from table 10-2.
9. A lower rate of growth of energy consumption could result from a slower rate of economic expansion or a stronger reaction to past increases in energy prices than was assumed. Saudi Arabia could decide to increase production capacity to prevent a sharp increase in the price of oil that would damage the international economy— and Saudi Arabia has an increasing stake in that economy—or it could do so in the belief that higher prices would result in less than optimal revenues from its oil resources over the long run.

A major uncertainty affecting the future price of oil is the responsiveness of demand to changes in price. In the short run, demand for energy appears to be relatively inelastic (that is, to effect a 1 percent change in the quantity demanded, price would have to move by much more than 1 percent in the opposite direction). In the long run, demand is probably much more elastic.

Any effort to predict the future price of oil would be foolhardy. For present purposes, it is sufficient to conclude that further substantial increases in the international price of oil are quite possible and may even be probable. U.S. energy policy will undoubtedly be made in that context.

U.S. Prospects

Table 10-4 presents estimated energy balances for the United States for 1985, 1990, and 1995 and the actual balance for 1978. The projections of future production, consumption, and imports shown in this table are subject to the various problems and qualifications discussed in the preceding section. They do provide a useful starting point, however, for a discussion of U.S. energy prospects.

The most striking feature of the estimates of future energy production in the United States is the large role assigned to coal. Total domestic energy production is projected to increase 33 percent from 1978 to 1995, but coal is projected to increase 127 percent. About 95 percent of the estimated increase in energy production from 1978 to 1995 is to be in the form of coal. This return to coal has of course been a major objective of U.S. energy policy ever since the Arab embargo and the large jump in international oil prices in 1973–74.

The projected rise in coal production (and consumption) in effect assumes that the measures adopted to achieve this objective will succeed. In particular, oil-fired electric power plants must be retired and replaced by coal-burning plants when it is economically feasible to do so, and the prohibition on new oil-fired power plants in the Powerplant and Industrial Fuel Use Act of 1978 must be enforced. Potentially serious conflicts between environmental goals and the program of shifting from oil to coal in the generation of electricity must also be resolved.

The projected increase in coal production depends on a substantial growth in the use of electricity. Except in certain industrial processes, little coal is used directly today. Most coal is used to make electricity. This situation may change someday if large amounts of coal are converted to liquid and gaseous fuels.

Table 10-4. *U.S. Energy Supply and Demand, 1978, 1985, 1990, and 1995*
Millions of barrels of oil per day equivalent

Item	1978	1985	1990	1995
Domestic production				
Oil	10.0	9.0	8.8	8.0
Gas	9.4	8.8	8.9	8.2
Coal	7.3	12.1	13.8	16.6
Nuclear	1.5	2.7	3.9	4.7
Other	1.5	1.6	1.8	2.0
Total production	29.7	34.2	37.2	39.5
Imports				
Oil	8.3	6.9	8.2	10.3
Gas	0.4	0.4	0.9	1.2
Coal (exports)	(0.4)	(1.1)	(1.3)	(1.7)
Total net imports	8.3	6.2	7.8	9.7
Total supply	38.0	40.4	45.0	49.3
Consumption				
Residential	5.4	5.4	5.4	5.3
Commercial	3.7	3.5	3.6	3.8
Industrial[a]	10.7	11.6	13.6	15.2
Transportation	10.1	9.7	10.2	11.3
Total consumption	29.8	30.4	32.9	35.7
Conversion losses[b]	8.0	10.0	12.0	13.5
Total disposition	37.8	40.4	45.0	49.3

Source: Low oil price projection series, U.S. Department of Energy, Energy Information Administration, *Annual Report, 1979*, vol. 3: *Projections* (Government Printing Office, 1980), pp. 83, 93, 95, 103. The world price of crude oil is assumed to remain constant at $27 a barrel in 1979 dollars. The gross national product is assumed to increase at an annual rate of 2.7 percent in the period 1975–95. Figures are rounded.

a. Includes refinery consumption of refined petroleum products and natural gas.

b. Includes losses or gains from electricity generation, synthetics production, and petroleum refining.

The domestic production of both oil and natural gas is projected to decrease from 1978 to 1995. Substantial reductions in output from known reserves will not be fully matched by production from newly discovered reserves in the lower forty-eight states (both onshore and offshore), production from Alaska's North Slope, and the use of enhanced recovery techniques at known fields. Whether these projections will prove to be correct depends on a variety of factors, including the domestic prices of oil and gas; the prices of competing fuels; the costs of exploration, production, and transportation; and the degree of success achieved in the search for new reserves. The possibility of error in any attempt to forecast the future production of oil and gas is obviously great.

The estimates of future production of nuclear and other[10] kinds of energy are also subject to substantial margins of error. The nuclear estimates are based on conservative assumptions concerning licensing and regulatory delays and construction costs. They may prove to be too low, but it is also possible that public fears concerning the safety of nuclear energy could further retard its development. Environmental problems may interfere with the development of energy from new technologies, such as coal conversion, and whether energy from these new sources will be able to compete economically with more conventional fuels is uncertain.

The estimates of energy from other sources presented in table 10-4 include only small amounts of synthetic fuels. No shale oil has been included, and no effort has been made to project the possible effects of the massive synthetic fuel program that President Carter proposed in July 1979.

Total energy consumption is estimated to increase by the equivalent of 5.9 million barrels of oil a day from 1978 to 1995, but three-quarters of that increase, or 4.5 million barrels a day, is to be in the industrial sector, whose consumption is to increase 42 percent. By contrast, consumption in the transportation sector is projected to rise only 12 percent. Estimated consumption in the commercial and residential sectors is almost the same in 1995 as actual consumption in 1978. Projected consumption in all four sectors is substantially below historical trends and assumes both continued strong responses to past increases in energy prices and the success of various governmental policies designed to encourage energy conservation.

Sectoral consumption is measured in terms of end-use and does not account for all the primary energy used by the U.S. economy. The difference is the energy lost in the generation and distribution of electricity. In 1978 these conversion and distribution losses were about one-fifth of the total consumption of primary energy; by 1995 they are projected to rise to more than one-fourth. This trend is the inevitable consequence of the increased electrification of the U.S. economy, which is in turn associated with the greater emphasis on coal in U.S. energy policy.

Import requirements are of course the difference between total consumption of primary energy and domestic energy supplies (production

10. "Other" energy includes hydropower and new technologies, including synthetic liquid and gaseous fuels from coal, geothermal energy, and the production of energy from renewable resources (solar, wind, ocean, thermal, and biomass).

minus exports). The United States will continue to satisfy a fraction of its import requirements by bringing in gas by pipeline from Canada (and probably also Mexico) and by ship in liquefied form from overseas. Principal reliance must, however, be placed on oil to fill the gap between energy needs and domestic supplies.

Imported oil is in effect the residual item in the energy balance. If domestic energy production is lower than has been estimated, or if consumption is higher, oil imports will be larger than projected. Errors in the opposite direction would of course cause oil imports to be smaller than anticipated.

It is difficult to judge the validity of the particular projections of oil imports presented in table 10-4. Circumstances can easily be imagined in which they would prove to be either too high or too low. The underlying estimates that appear most likely to be off the mark, however, are those calling for a very large increase in the production of coal and a marked reduction in the rates of growth of energy consumption, especially in the residential and commercial sectors. If the optimism concerning the success of governmental policies that these estimates reflect proves to be unwarranted, oil imports could be significantly higher than projected.

In any event it seems prudent to assume that U.S. oil imports will remain in the range of 7–8 million barrels a day or could go higher unless additional measures are taken to increase domestic energy production and hold down the increase in energy consumption. Reducing oil imports is desirable for several reasons. First, the vulnerability of the U.S. economy to sharp increases in the international price of oil would be decreased. Second, the U.S. balance on current international account would be improved, which would facilitate efforts to stabilize the value of the dollar. And third, the effectiveness of any future Arab oil embargo would be reduced.

U.S. Policy Choices

The past three U.S. administrations have made the reduction of oil imports the principal goal of their energy policies. Unless U.S. energy prospects improve drastically, this goal is not likely to be abandoned soon. In concentrating on reducing oil imports, future administrations can be expected also to set goals for energy consumption and production and to break them down by consuming sectors and energy sources, respectively.

Since the policy horizons of governments are limited, it is unlikely that meaningful long-range goals for energy consumption and production will be set. Shorter-range goals, however, can have lasting consequences. Whether intentionally or not, the energy goals of successive future administrations will do much to shape the transition from the age of oil to the energy economy of the future through which the United States and other nations are now passing.

With respect to means, the fundamental problem is how much to rely on market forces as opposed to various kinds of government intervention. Setting clear energy goals may seem to prejudge this issue in favor of intervention, but this need not be the case. Market forces, left to themselves, may in some circumstances be the most effective means of restraining consumption, stimulating production, and thereby reducing imports.

If the free market approach is regarded as undesirable or is not feasible politically, a formidable array of means of government intervention is available, most of which have been tried by past administrations and are described in the earlier chapters of this book.

The government can forbid some actions (for example, the burning of oil in new power plants). It can set standards (for example, speed limits on highways) that are designed to influence energy consumption. It can also engage directly in the production of energy materials (for example, the enrichment of uranium).

Taxes can also be used to discourage undesired behavior, such as the manufacture of heavy automobiles, and tax credits can be granted to encourage such desired behavior as the insulation of dwellings. Use of the tax system to achieve energy goals, it might be noted, is a hybrid approach, in that its success depends on a correct appraisal of market forces.

Some government intervention in the name of energy policy is designed to counter the effect of other actions by government itself. Thus price controls on energy materials tend to create artificial shortages that the government may attempt to deal with by allocation among distributors or rationing among consumers.

The choice of means to achieve energy goals should be strongly influenced by a comparison of costs and benefits. In practice this is often quite difficult. Some costs, such as the economic distortions caused by government intervention in energy markets, are hidden and not easily measured. Opinions may also differ on the weight to be given to some costs and benefits. Thus how much air pollution should be accepted in order to facilitate the substitution of coal for oil in generating electricity is a subjective question on which diverging views are to be expected.

The setting of goals and the selection of means are of course not done in isolation from one another. In the real world, debates will always concern alternative policies, each of which will be an amalgam of means and ends. Moreover, no future administration can expect to enjoy the luxury of a really fresh start. New initiatives in the field of energy policy must always contend with the inertia of past policies.

Problems of Energy Policy

The problems that past administrations faced in making and executing energy policy have been described in earlier chapters. Many of these problems will undoubtedly persist in the future. Some of them appear to have grown more acute as energy has become a more prominent subject of concern, both domestically and internationally. These problems fall under five headings: conflicting domestic priorities, competing interests, the roles of government and business, foreign policy, and decisionmaking.

Conflicting Domestic Priorities

The years covered by this book have seen energy policy move from the wings to the center of the national stage. Energy policy has become more politicized, and awareness of the ways in which it affects other domestic concerns has grown. Reconciling energy, environmental, and economic goals has often been especially difficult.

The conflict among domestic priorities may well be sharpened by the continuing effort to check the rise of oil imports. Shifting from oil to other sources of energy will create both environmental and economic problems.[11] Reducing the rate of increase in total energy consumption will yield some environmental benefits, but it can also interfere with the achievement of important economic objectives.

The most readily available substitutes for oil in the near term are coal and nuclear energy. Both involve environmental problems. Mining coal damages terrain (especially strip mining) and causes water pollution. Using coal causes air pollution. Requiring mining and power companies to abate or remedy some of these effects is clearly justifiable from the environmental point of view. It is also justifiable on broad economic grounds if one accepts the proposition that every economic activity should bear its

11. For estimates of the environmental consequences of increasing energy consumption and shifting patterns of use, 1975–2000, see U.S. Department of Energy, Office of the Assistant Secretary for Environment, *National Energy Plan II*, Appendix: *Environmental Trends and Impacts* (DOE, 1979), especially chap. 1.

full costs. One consequence of these environmental requirements, however, may be to retard the desired shift from oil to coal.

Public concerns over the safety of nuclear power plants have produced a somewhat similar result. Prolonged litigation over the siting of such plants and strict safety requirements have increased the cost of nuclear power and narrowed its competitive advantage over electricity from plants burning conventional fuels.

In the midterm, efforts to produce so-called synthetic fuels from coal and oil-bearing shale may create additional conflicts between energy and environmental goals. To the extent that the coal and shale are strip-mined, an existing problem will be aggravated. Plants to convert coal to gaseous and liquid fuels and to extract oil from shale will be major new sources of air pollution and solid waste. Measures may be taken to abate these and other forms of pollution, but they will unavoidably add to energy costs.

Some easing of the conflict between energy and the environment may occur in the longer run, but great optimism on this score is not warranted. Systems that capture solar energy directly are environmentally benign, but some indirect systems have environmental costs. (For example, biomass systems can create both air and water pollution.) Fast breeder reactors, which would both generate and use plutonium, would have much less environmental impact than today's reactors at the mining and milling stage of the nuclear fuel cycle. Their relative impact at other stages is less clear. Pure nuclear fusion might pose fewer environmental problems than any system based on nuclear fission; however, problems with neutron fluxes and tritium effluents could complicate the comparison. In any case, pure fusion may not prove to be commercially viable, and adoption of a hybrid fusion-fission technology would not provide an escape from the problems of nuclear fission.[12]

The shift from oil to other sources of energy could cause economic distortions if it is carried out under forced draft. Heavy investments in energy projects—by government directly or by private firms subsidized by government—could drive up prices and interest rates and create temporary shortages of some items. These effects would be especially unwelcome in a period, like the present one, in which price stability, increased productivity, and reduced unemployment were major objectives of economic policy.

Energy policy and general economic policy also come into conflict if

12. In the hybrid technology, neutrons produced by fusion would be captured by atoms of the most common isotope of uranium (U-238), thereby creating plutonium (PU-239) that would be used as fuel in fission reactors.

energy prices are increased in order to discourage energy consumption and check the rise in oil imports. If energy prices had been subject to controls, they could simply be permitted to rise to levels determined by market forces. Otherwise they could be increased by levying new or additional excise taxes. In either case higher energy prices will be seen as contributing to inflation and imposing unfair burdens on persons with low incomes.

No clear resolution to the conflict among energy, environmental, and economic priorities is to be expected. Instead, compromises will continue to be made on issues as they arise. The consequence—which is certainly not surprising—will be an evolving energy policy that will always fall short of theoretical perfection.

Competing Interests

The conflict among priorities described above is of course not an abstract intellectual exercise but is conducted on the level of practical politics by groups with different interests. Such competition is also a major determinant of the content of energy policy itself.

The interest groups that seek to influence energy policy cannot be neatly classified. They overlap and regroup to deal with different specific issues. The major interest groups and forms of competition are clear, however:

—Organized consumer groups contend with organized producer groups, principally on questions of energy prices.

—Business and labor groups in the different energy industries (for example, coal, oil, gas, nuclear) compete for preferential treatment by governments.

—The federal and state governments differ from time to time over the division of authority in energy questions.

—Geographic regions seek to influence energy policy in ways favorable to their situations as energy producers or consumers.

There can be little doubt that competition among these and other narrower interest groups will continue. It will in fact probably intensify.

Price will more and more be seen as the key component of energy policy, both as a means of adjusting supply and demand and as a means of encouraging desired shifts among sources of energy. The focus on questions of price will inevitably lead to political controversy involving consumer and producer groups, energy industries, and regional interests.

If, as appears likely, the federal government vigorously pursues the goal of increasing domestic energy production, conflict with state and regional interests will be virtually unavoidable. A strong, centrally managed effort would leave less scope for state initiatives, and decisions made from the national point of view can easily appear to threaten regional interests.

Competition among interests must be accepted as an integral part of the policy process. The critical question in the years ahead is whether such competition will yield workable energy policies or create impasses, as it sometimes has in the past.

Roles of Government and Business

Many problems in energy policy involve the question of the appropriate roles of government and business. In its most general form this question concerns the degree of reliance to be placed on market forces that was discussed earlier in this chapter. The question arises, however, in numerous narrower contexts.

Several examples from the recent past can be cited. Can oil companies be relied on to distribute supplies of gasoline fairly in a period of shortage, or should the government impose a system of allocations? Should private firms be permitted to build uranium enrichment plants? Should natural gas produced and marketed in the same state be subjected to federal price controls?

The tradition of government intervention in the energy sector of the U.S. economy is strong. Plants that generate electricity have been closely regulated as public utilities, if they are not actually government-owned. Governments of major oil-producing states have long set production quotas, and for many years oil imports were regulated by federal quotas. Large amounts of public money are spent every year for research and development in the field of energy.

The list of examples could go on. The important point for present purposes is that over the years government intervention in the energy sector has come to seem increasingly natural. Energy has not only become more politicized, but it has also acquired a special public status that makes it appear to be a particularly appropriate object of governmental concern.

Whether this trend will continue, and if so, how far it will go cannot be foreseen. In terms of the balance between business and government, the Carter administration appears to be headed in two directions simultaneously. On the one hand it favors gradual decontrol of the prices of oil and natural gas. But on the other hand it has proposed massive governmental expenditures to create a synthetic fuel industry.

Foreign Policy

For a very good reason the earlier chapters of this book devote relatively little space to the international aspects of energy policy. Until quite recently energy was not given high priority in U.S. foreign policy. Occasional overseas developments, such as the nationalization of foreign oil properties by Iran in 1951, required the attention of senior U.S. officials, but energy was usually a secondary item on the foreign policy agenda.

All this was changed in 1973–74 by the Arab embargo and the related huge increase in oil prices. The importance of energy questions in U.S. foreign policy was further increased in 1976–77 when first the Ford administration and then the Carter administration adopted a harder line against the spread of sensitive nuclear technology. For the indefinite future the United States will probably be concerned with (1) the international political aspects of energy policies, (2) the threat of further large increases in the price of oil, and (3) the fear that the growth of the civil nuclear energy industry will facilitate the spread of nuclear weapons.

ENERGY AND INTERNATIONAL POLITICS. Energy materials have affected U.S. relations with other countries in much the same way other major imported commodities have done. In this sense oil and gas have the same kind of political importance as, say, bauxite or tin. U.S. investment in foreign energy resources and U.S. imports of energy materials will continue to influence U.S. relations with other countries. Thus oil and gas will be increasingly important in U.S. relations with Mexico. And if the United States becomes a net importer of uranium, trade in that commodity may affect U.S. relations with Australia, Canada, and several African countries. In periods of tight supplies and rising prices, competition for oil can affect U.S. relations with Japan, Germany, France, and other major oil-importing countries.

The political importance of energy—in this case oil—is by far the greatest in the Middle East, which contains about two-thirds of the oil reserves outside Communist countries.[13] In 1973–74 the Arab oil-exporting countries used oil as a political weapon with telling effect. More recently the failure of Iran to regain the level of oil exports that prevailed before the overthrow of the Shah is at least in part attributable to political causes.

Other oil-exporting countries could experience the same kind of politi-

13. "Worldwide Issue," *Oil and Gas Journal,* December 31, 1979, pp. 100–01.

cal turmoil as Iran and with similar consequences for oil exports.[14] A more serious threat, however, is the possibility of another Arab embargo. This threat could of course be removed by a lasting settlement of the Arab-Israeli dispute. Pending such a development, the United States must do what it can to prevent further use of the oil weapon and limit the economic damage if preventive measures fail.

Under the heading of prevention, diplomatic efforts to mediate the Arab-Israeli dispute are obviously useful, as are policies that increase the interdependence of the Arab and industrialized nations. Damage-limiting measures include building up oil stocks and maintaining the emergency allocation system of the International Energy Agency.[15]

The most effective damage-limiting measure would be to reduce the dependence of the United States and its major trading partners on Arab oil. Reducing U.S. dependence alone would not be enough, since if the economies of Western Europe or Japan were damaged by a reduction in oil supplies, the U.S. economy would also suffer.

Shifting to non-Arab sources of oil is not a feasible way for the major oil-importing countries to reduce their vulnerability to an Arab embargo. There is very little excess capacity outside Arab countries today. Moreover, the Arabs now control almost two-thirds of OPEC's total sustainabie oil-producing capacity, and their share may approach 70 percent by 1995. (See table 10-3.) As a practical matter, the only way to reduce dependence on Arab oil is to reduce the overall level of oil imports.

THE PRICE PROBLEM. The United States and the other oil-importing countries have two good reasons to want to avoid further increases in the international price of oil. First, higher oil prices mean larger transfers of real resources to the oil-exporting countries. And, second, large upward movements in oil prices can have seriously disruptive effects on the economies of the oil-importing countries and impose strains on the international financial system.[16]

Several solutions to the oil price problem have been advanced since the problem burst on the world in 1973–74. Most proposed solutions

14. The revolution in Iran may not have run its course, and further disorders adversely affecting oil production cannot be ruled out.

15. Some oil-exporting countries, it should be noted, oppose the stock-building program and could seek to frustrate it by reducing exports to the United States.

16. Somewhat surprisingly, public discussion of the problem of higher oil prices has generally ignored the first effect, which has lasting importance, and has concentrated on the second, which is transitory and can to a considerable extent be countered by means at the disposal of the oil-importing countries.

would not work, but that does not mean that they will not be revived from time to time.

Economic sanctions against the oil-exporting countries would be virtually impossible to organize and might in any case produce a devastating response in the form of a suspension of oil shipments. The political and financial costs of military sanctions would be prohibitive. "Breaking up OPEC" appeals to many, but how this is to be done is not clear.[17]

Exhortation and diplomatic persuasion, directed particularly at Saudi Arabia, have been tried, but with only limited results. It is true that Saudi Arabia's public stand has been more moderate than that of many oil-exporting countries, but this position is consistent with its long-term economic interests. It does not have to be explained as the result of U.S. diplomacy. In any event the Saudi ability to restrain OPEC's price hawks will be undermined if and when it no longer has excess productive capacity.

The only solution to the oil price problem that has had much chance of success is a concerted effort by the oil-importing countries to reduce their purchases of OPEC oil. There was a time when such an effort might have caused some members of OPEC to cut prices in order to maintain sales.[18] The shrinking of excess capacity, however, has reduced the incentives of OPEC members to break market discipline.[19]

Actions by the oil-importing countries to reduce their dependence on foreign oil will nevertheless continue to be desirable if only to moderate the rate of increase in oil prices. In the absence of such actions oil supplies may lag behind rising demand, and steep price increases are quite possible. The rate at which the price of oil would increase would depend on a variety of factors, including the availability (and substitutability)

17. The proposal of M. A. Adelman that OPEC members be drawn into competition against one another by a system of secret bidding for import licenses might conceivably have worked when substantial excess productive capacity existed. Little excess capacity exists today, however, and even less will probably exist in future years. For a full description of this proposal, see Adelman, "Oil Import Quota Auctions," *Challenge*, vol. 18 (January-February 1976), pp. 17–22.

18. A good opportunity to test this thesis may have been missed during the recession of 1974–75 when reduced economic activity dampened the demand for energy.

19. In mid-1979 the maximum sustainable capacity of OPEC exceeded current output by only 3.1 million barrels a day (less than a tenth of total capacity). Because of government policies and the turmoil in Iran only 0.4 million barrels of excess capacity were in fact available. *International Energy Statistical Review*, October 31, 1979, p. 3.

of other sources of energy and the ability of consumers to substitute capital (for example, insulation) for energy. If supply and demand moved in a fairly predictable manner, the rise in the price of oil would be relatively smooth. Sudden discontinuities in supply, however, would cause sharp fluctuations in price because the demand for oil is quite unresponsive to price in the short run.

The prospect of steadily rising oil prices and the danger of unexpected sharp price increases make it highly likely that the need to reduce oil imports will continue to be high on the agenda of consultations among the industrialized nations. As the largest oil importer, the United States will be expected to take the lead in this effort. This will be relatively easy in the near term as the effects of past increases in energy prices continue to be felt and as various conservation measures take hold. It will become more difficult later if—as appears quite possible (see table 10-2)—oil consumption resumes its upward trend and domestic oil production declines.

U.S. relations with the oil-exporting nations could worsen as oil prices rise. Oil-exporting countries that do not produce at capacity may be accused of waging economic warfare against the United States and other oil-importing countries. Saudi Arabia may be subjected to similar criticism if it fails to increase productive capacity to meet growing demand. The result could be to make oil an even more political commodity than it is today.

INTERNATIONAL NUCLEAR ENERGY ISSUES. Only a few years ago it was generally assumed that the safeguards administered by the International Atomic Energy Agency could effectively deter the diversion of fissile materials from peaceful to military uses. It was thought that the agency, by its system of inspections and materials accountancy, would detect any diversion in time for the international community to prevent the use of the diverted material in nuclear weapons. This doctrine of timely warning is valid in the case of nuclear reactors. It breaks down when applied to enrichment and reprocessing plants, which can produce the essential explosive component of nuclear weapons. The agency would have little chance of detecting the diversion of enriched uranium from an enrichment plant or plutonium from a reprocessing plant in time for effective preventive action to be taken. These sensitive facilities give their possessors a near-nuclear weapons capability. In recent years the U.S. government and a few other like-minded governments have devoted increased attention to keeping such a capability from spreading to more nations.

In part, this effort has involved national controls over the export of sensitive nuclear components and technology. Some coordination of national policies has been achieved through the Nuclear Suppliers' Group,[20] but full agreement on a system of international controls has thus far not been reached. The limited effectiveness of existing controls was demonstrated by Pakistan's recent acquisition of the means of building a centrifuge enrichment plant.

Another approach to checking the spread of sensitive nuclear energy facilities is to reduce the incentives for their acquisition. This was the underlying purpose of the United States in organizing the International Nuclear Fuel Cycle Evaluation, which completed its work in February 1980.[21] At its outset in the fall of 1977 some hoped that the INFCE would produce a consensus on technological measures that would channel the development of the civil nuclear energy industry in a more proliferation-resistant direction. This hope was not realized. The INFCE, however, may lead to largely institutional initiatives to (1) increase the assurance of nuclear fuel supplies, (2) deal with the problem of managing spent nuclear fuel, and (3) control the plutonium extracted from spent fuel by reprocessing.

Increasing the assurance of nuclear fuel supplies is obviously desirable from the economic point of view. It is also a means of reducing the incentives to acquire enrichment and reprocessing facilities. The United States has proposed the establishment of a nuclear fuel bank to provide natural or enriched uranium to countries whose normal sources of supply have been interrupted. This proposal has received little support outside the United States, however. Other possibilities that may be considered include cross guarantees among fuel suppliers, fuel stockpiles, and a system of international consultation on problems of nuclear fuel supplies.

At the present time spent nuclear fuel is accumulating in water-filled ponds at reactors. More storage space at or away from reactors will soon be needed, pending either reprocessing or final disposal. Existing and planned reprocessing capacity is insufficient to handle spent fuel arisings, and no non-Communist government has yet approved a means of final

20. The Nuclear Suppliers' Group, also known as the London Suppliers' Group, consists of Belgium, Canada, Czechoslovakia, France, East Germany, West Germany, Italy, Japan, the Netherlands, Poland, the Soviet Union, Sweden, Switzerland, the United Kingdom, and the United States.

21. See International Nuclear Fuel Cycle Evaluation, *INFCE Summary Volume,* INFCE/PC/2/9 (Vienna: International Atomic Energy Agency, 1980), and reports by the eight working groups.

disposal of spent fuel (or of the high-level wastes from reprocessing plants). The possibility of building storage facilities under international auspices has been discussed by the INFCE and elsewhere. Reducing national inventories of spent fuel would both ease an economic problem and reduce the risk that those inventories would be used as a source of plutonium for nuclear weapons.

Despite U.S. efforts to obtain international agreement to defer reprocessing, some reprocessing has occurred, and more will take place in the future. Consideration is therefore being given to the means of controlling the plutonium that results from reprocessing. One possibility that was studied in the INFCE is to establish plutonium depositories under the control of the International Atomic Energy Agency. All newly produced plutonium would be put in the depositories and released only in conformity with agreed upon international rules.

It is too early to say which of these or other institutional proposals will become the subject of active negotiations. The probability that some of them will be taken up seriously appears high, however. As a result, nuclear energy issues may play an increasingly prominent role in U.S. foreign policy.

Making and Administering Energy Policy

Future changes in the U.S. energy economy will impose sevei strains on the government machinery charged with making and administering energy policy. Resolving conflicts among energy and other domestic goals, such as economic stability and protection of the environment, may be even more difficult than in the recent past. Energy problems can also be expected to complicate U.S. relations with both energy-importing and energy-exporting countries.

The creation of the Department of Energy in 1977 reflected the increasingly prominent place of energy in the overall concerns of the U.S. government. In organizational terms energy now has the same standing and can claim the same attention as other major problems such as defense, housing, transportation, and welfare. And at least in theory energy policy need no longer be the sum of decisions made in various corners of the bureaucracy but can be an integrated whole, representing conscious choices among alternatives.

The extent to which the Department of Energy will realize its theoretical potentialities cannot be foreseen, but even under the best of circumstances this department cannot by itself ensure the smooth and effective handling of energy problems. In a period of change and instability the role of Congress will be crucial. Moreover, no sharp lines separate energy from other areas of public policy, and resolving conflicting priorities will be a continuing challenge to both the executive and legislative branches of government.

The organization of Congress has not yet been fully adjusted to the increased importance of energy policy, and a disparity exists between its arrangements in this field and the more centralized structure of the executive branch. The Senate has a standing energy and natural resources committee, but the House (after a brief experiment with an ad hoc energy committee) shares its energy business among several subcommittees. Consideration of the possible merits of a joint Senate-House energy committee presumably lies some distance in the future.

The coordination of energy policy with other policy areas could in principle be centered in the White House or in one of the cabinet departments, or it could be entrusted to an interdepartmental committee. Each of these approaches has been tried in the past. The Carter administration has followed the third approach, coupled with a strong role for the White House staff and for the Office of Management and Budget in particular.

Future administrations will have to decide whether to keep this arrangement or to adopt one of the other two possibilities. As a practical matter, the choice is likely to be between an interdepartmental committee and direct White House control. The day when a single strong department chief could dominate both energy policy and its ramifications in other areas of policy is probably past.

If coordination of energy and related problems is again centered in the White House, decisions will be required concerning the organization of the White House staff. One possibility would be to create an office of energy policy, but to do so might undermine the authority of the secretary of energy and create problems with other components of the White House staff, such as the staff of the National Security Council and the Office of Management and Budget. Centralizing the problem of interdepartmental coordination might merely leave the President with the task of coordinating the coordinators.

Whatever the system of internal coordination, the United States will face the continuing need to adjust to—and, if possible, influence—the energy policies of other countries. The annual economic summit meetings of the leaders of the major industrialized countries can continue to provide a useful forum for seeking a common approach on energy questions. These meetings and lower-level consultations, however, may not prove to be enough to achieve the desired degree of policy coordination. In that event an increased role might be given to the International Energy Agency. Some special consultative arrangement will probably also be necessary in the field of nuclear energy as a sequel to the INFCE.

Relations with the oil-exporting countries pose procedural as well as substantive problems. The fundamental question is whether to continue to rely exclusively on bilateral diplomacy or to supplement such diplomacy with a regular system of multilateral consultations among oil exporters and oil importers. Multilateral consultations would clearly be useful if they helped to stabilize the international oil market. Reaching a consensus on oil production, consumption, and prices would be difficult, however, and the consultations could also bog down in disputes over North-South issues.

Quite apart from the domestic and international coordination problems discussed above, the technical difficulty of planning energy policy may increase. The transition on which the United States and other countries have embarked will confront energy policymakers with a series of complex choices. Reliable projections of energy supply and demand will be essential guides. The difficulty of making such projections was brought out earlier in this chapter. Important technical judgments must also be made, sometimes on the basis of inadequate information.[22]

In brief, the making and administering of energy policy does not promise to be a quiet occupation. The stormy events of the past few years may well be an accurate indication of the future.

Conclusions

The United States is in the early stages of a transition from the age of oil to a new energy economy whose nature is not yet clear. This transition has been forced at this time because of the political and economic problems caused by dependence on imported oil. It would probably have been

22. For example, the size and content of research and development expenditures on fast breeder reactors should reflect an estimate of when these reactors are likely to be deployed commercially. Such an estimate must be based in part on judgments concerning the competitiveness of these reactors with other sources of energy and the availability of fuel for the present generation of reactors. Opinions differ on both these questions.

necessary in any event later in the century as world production of oil peaked and then slowly declined.

Reducing dependence on imported oil will continue to be the principal goal of U.S. energy policy for many years. Achieving this goal will require both slowing the rise in total energy consumption and shifting from oil to other sources of energy. In seeking these changes a choice must be made between reliance on market forces and various forms of government intervention.

A number of problems that affected the making and administration of energy policy in recent decades may become more acute in the future. These problems include resolving conflicting priorities among energy, environmental, and economic policies; dealing with the competing economic and political interests that seek to influence energy policy; and adjusting the roles of government and business in the field of energy.

The international dimension of energy policy may become more important and more troublesome. The involvement of energy in politics, especially in the Middle East, could grow. Further increases in the price of oil, and the attendant economic and political problems, will be inevitable if demand continues to grow more rapidly than productive capacity. And efforts to channel the development of the civil nuclear energy industry in directions that do not increase the risk of a further spread of nuclear weapons will be an important part of U.S. foreign policy in coming years.

CHAPTER ELEVEN

The Lessons of History

CRAUFURD D. GOODWIN

THE UNITED STATES emerged from World War II with a heightened appreciation of the importance of energy for the economy. This had been the first fully mechanized war in history, and energy supplies were crucial to both sides. It became clear very soon that energy would be equally important to the peace. Moreover, some sophisticated observers could see that unless decisive action were taken, the nation's long-standing independence of foreign energy sources would come to an end. For America's allies the level of foreign dependence would become even greater.

An economist has little difficulty explaining how in theory a free market economy may arrange for the production and distribution of energy as for any other good. The preferences of consumers for final goods and services that require energy for their production will be expressed in their demands for these goods. Producers, taking account of the prices of inputs and outputs, as of known technology, will continue to use additional increments of energy as long as marginal product exceeds marginal cost. Owners of depleting energy sources make them available as long as the expected rate of increase in price over time is below the market rate of interest. When the marginal cost of one energy source rises to the level of that of a competitor, the second source begins either to complement or to replace the first. Society, acting for all producers and consumers collectively, may conclude that for reasons of security, a special concern for future generations, or other reasons the market is not yielding optimum results; therefore government should act to modify price signals to take account of social costs and benefits through taxes, subsidies, or other devices. If parts of the energy markets fall under the sway of "natural" monopolies, the public may regulate these parts and try to make them act as if they were competitive. And of course government has the obligation to penalize and thereby to prevent the creation of artificial monopolies and monopsonies that would generate incorrect price signals of all kinds.

Abandonment of the Free Market

The story of energy policy in the United States is largely an account of the failure of genuinely free markets to appear and of the unwillingness of most market participants—buyers, sellers, and government—to allow a free market structure to develop. Despite much rhetoric from all parties on behalf of free enterprise, far more effort was devoted to destroying market freedom if it began to emerge than to perfecting it. For quite different reasons these generalizations hold for all major energy sources.

Economists have a conception of how the two extremes of economic systems, free markets and central planning, may work. Both can be designed or modified from time to time to achieve specified objectives. In the case of energy neither system was allowed to prevail and the particular hybrid institutional structure that emerged was both a puzzle to observers and, as events may prove, a tragedy for the nation.

By the end of World War II it was evident that petroleum would be the most important energy source for well into the future. But petroleum illustrated very forcibly the weakness of free market forces. On the supply side the industry came into the postwar world with remnants of its share in New Deal antidepression programs intact. A complex structure of legislation and control mechanisms permitted the industry, in cooperation with government, to limit supply so as to conform to demand at arbitrary prices. Some government policies, in a contradictory fashion, also served to stimulate domestic petroleum production artificially— notably, favored tax treatment through percentage depletion and other devices. As the years went on it became necessary to supplement domestic monopolistic devices with restrictions on oil imports, first on a voluntary and then a mandatory basis. All these interferences with the petroleum market were designed to cope with a situation of relative plenty, with abundant supplies discovered first at home and then abroad. A case can be made that much of the market interference was justified at particular times for various reasons ranging from the welfare of oil-producing states to national security. But two effects all the same were the constraint of market forces and the destruction of confidence in the market as an allocator of resources. These effects resulted in creating a climate of uncertainty for investors, because so much turned on government action, and making it worthwhile for the industry to lobby for the kind of action it wanted. In addition the experience of constantly coping with excess supply generated by prices above market-clearing levels undoubtedly made it difficult for the nation to focus on the upcoming problems of scarcity. Many of the restrictive devices were not dismantled until the 1970s when shortage replaced plenty and upward pressure on prices prevailed. By this time, however, a half-century of market intervention was a fact of life, and it was simple now for consumers to use well-known interventionist arguments, perfected by the producers, to insist on grounds of "equity" and other considerations that prices should be restrained from moving upward as well as downward. Moreover, the large oil companies, long the target of trustbusters, remained an agreeable scapegoat for those who sought a conspiratorial theory of upward price pressure.

In the electric power field, intervention on the supply side consisted, not of price supports through the creation of artificial monopoly, but rather of control of natural monopolies by the Federal Power Commission and state regulatory authorities, as well as subsidies to public power projects to keep rates below what they might have been. Subsidies went to hydroelectric construction, rural electrification, and to research on and development of nuclear reactors. The depth of attachment by the American people to major participation of the federal government in the electric power market transcended party ideology. It continued in Republican and Democratic administrations alike with only differences in place and terminology—for example, with President Eisenhower emphasizing a public-private "partnership," instead of the New Deal and Fair Deal rhetoric of "democracy on the march." The large government role in electricity seems not to have been carried over in full magnitude to nuclear generation during the early decades covered by this study simply because this mode was not yet needed in volume. When that need came in the 1970s concerns for safety and for the environment overwhelmed the earlier doctrine, and later administrations trod cautiously.

It was revealing and in no small degree poignant that coal, the energy industry with by far the most problems and sufferings, was also the most unorganized and competitive. Mine owners and workers did not fail to note the correspondence between the relative freedom of the market for their product and their economic difficulties. They loudly bemoaned their position with respect to concentrations of power on all sides. Widespread and continuing unemployment and stagnation in the coal fields led to a disproportionate number of public inquiries into the "coal problem." In fact, as early as the 1950s the very notion of a "national energy policy" was perceived by other energy sectors as mainly the concoction of intellectuals and bureaucrats to penalize them in favor of coal. Certainly "coal studies" were the trigger for much of the earliest attention to energy problems in general. Nevertheless the failure to pursue the vigorous development of synthetic fuels after the administration of President Truman and until the 1970s reflects in part the relative weakness of coal interests that synthetics were seen to benefit.

Consumers were no less vigorous than suppliers in advocating interference with energy markets to keep prices different from market-clearing levels. In general, consumers of energy have believed that a large portion of payments to energy producers consists of "economic rent," that is, that changes in price either up or down will not substantially change the amount supplied. In consequence they have pressed either for price control to capture some of the rents for themselves or for a profits tax to transfer the rents to the public purse. Suppliers understandably sought to counter these pressures by claiming significant elasticity of supply, that is, that price declines would cause a relatively large decrease and price rises a relatively large increase in amounts offered for sale. The main instrument for the expression of consumer pressures was Congress, where concerns were fragmented, sometimes conflicting, and represented by changing coalitions on behalf of geographical regions or particular groups. Such is the complexity of energy markets that petroleum refiners came to be considered "consumers." Repeatedly in the struggles over particular pieces of energy policy the conflict was between organized producers, such as the Southwest oil states, and equally effective consumer groups in the Northeast cities and states. A major success for mobilized consumers occurred in the 1950s when the Federal Power Commission received authority to fix rates paid by pipelines to suppliers of natural gas in interstate commerce. Subsequently the FPC employed this power to keep rates artificially low. Seldom could anything be seen in controversies of this kind that might be called the broad long-term *national* interest. Usually the most eloquent statements in defense of the free market as an efficient allocator of energy resources and as a mechanism by which to preserve a free society came not as might have been expected from professional economists or business people but rather from lawyers in the antitrust division of the Justice Department, the Federal Trade Commission, and other places in government.

One of the most prevalent market infringements in the energy area has been the government regulatory commission. A familiar feature of all regulatory programs is that they tend to generate the basis for their own immortality. They "vest" benefits in the so-called iron triangle of protected buyers or sellers, regulators, and supervisory legislative committees. This phenomenon was certainly the curse of many energy markets.

When the energy "crisis" struck in the 1970s many of the proposals to deal with it, both the plans for individual fuels and the comprehensive schemes of Presidents Ford and Carter, counted on "market solutions," meaning an increase in prices to ration demand and stimulate production. By this time, however, the conception of free markets in the energy field had been abandoned so completely by almost everyone involved that the notion could not simply be put to work anew at the stroke of a pen. Many of the market mechanisms for price competition had atrophied and could not immediately be reinvigorated. Moreover, market participants and the public at large could not be made suddenly to believe in the competitiveness of market institutions they had long understood to be agents of market restraint. Secretary of the Treasury William Simon might plead eloquently for invigoration of the institution of the free market in the solution of energy problems, but many Americans were surprised even at reports that it still lived. Consumers in the 1970s had for decades perceived price increases of energy sources to be the result of the machinations of suppliers, often with good reason. Moreover, low prices had been presented to them as a matter of democratic right. Therefore it was not persuasive to consumers to be told suddenly that increases were both desirable and the result of *real* forces. Suppliers, on the other hand, had seen government succumb repeatedly to pressures for artificially low energy prices, for gas and electric power at least, and they too could not be expected to believe that market signals of higher prices were necessarily there to stay. The decision taken during the Ford administration to achieve conservation of petroleum by mandatory mileage standards of automobiles rather than through an increase in the price of gasoline was one manifestation of the low repute in which market solutions were held.

Perhaps the greatest obstacles to the use of market solutions for the energy problems of the 1970s were the innumerable well-mobilized and securely entrenched special-interest groups that over the years had benefited from favored treatment under regimes of administered prices. Virtually all the suppliers of energy arrived at the postwar period with sophisticated spokesmen and effective organizations to defend their interests. Lobbies on behalf of petroleum, coal, gas, and all forms of electrical energy made the wider public interest difficult to specify and even harder to pursue. Moreover, bureaucratic special interests in such government units as the Atomic Energy Commission, the Corps of Engineers, the Bureau of Reclamation, and the large public power authorities were every bit as vigorous as those in the private sector. Organizations on behalf of each energy source normally maintained a complex network of relationships among private bodies, units in the executive branch, and Congress. On the demand side of the energy markets consumers were organized generally behind their elected representatives at the municipal, state, and federal levels. Individual demanders or suppliers in energy markets who might talk in general terms of the need for a "national energy policy," when marshaled behind their leaders could usually be found observing tight discipline on behalf of particular higher prices, lower quotas, larger public subsidies, or other self-interested objectives. Ironically the well-known existence of supplier organizations may have stood in the way of rapid price rises for fuels called for in the 1970s because politicians when authorizing price increases had come to fear charges of manipulation by special interests and political corruption.

One of the reasons why the discrediting of the free market as far as energy was concerned was so unfortunate for national policy was that few tools other than market forces seemed to have any impact on problems. Virtually every president at one time or another during his administration either engaged in exhortation of producers and consumers or presided over some administrative apparatus designed to achieve greater production, less consumption, or another specific goal. Invariably it turned out that price adjustments, if they had been tolerated, would have done the job more quickly, easily, and in many cases more fairly. In some instances nonprice solutions to problems, such as quotas on imported oil, turned out to generate a nightmare of side effects and unanticipated results.

The Alternative of a National Plan

But if the markets for energy were no longer free and therefore were not efficient allocators of resources, what could be put in their place? Some sort of national plan was clearly an alternative. Except in wartime, deep depression, or other comparable emergency, however, the United States has always had a strong ideological aversion to "planning" and has been consciously slow to create institutions with planning as their task. Indeed, the very notion of planning has to many American ears a dangerous "intellectual" ring; it appears as the product of systematic academic minds and to be inconsistent with rugged American democracy. Critics have had little difficulty in gathering opposition to it. By and large private firms in energy markets feared that the consequences of planning would be nationalization, prosecution for antitrust violations, or enforced divestiture of some operations. Consequently they were quick to give strength and muscle to the critics of planning. In any event what was seldom made clear was that where free markets were prevented from operating there was really no alternative to planning of some sort, even if it was only by one market participant in its own interest. The great virtue of free competitive markets is that they permit prices and allocation of resources to be determined by a complex of impersonal forces. When free markets are supplanted there is simply no alternative to individual persons making these decisions. The questions then become which persons and on what criteria. The story told in the chapters of this book is largely of rival parties jockeying for the authority to make those decisions about the production of energy goods and the distribution of income not left to the market.

Yet even if effective national energy planning had occurred at an early date and had been tolerated by the innumerable special interests that would have been threatened thereby, it would still have been extraordinarily complex and difficult for a variety of reasons.

First of all, in order to identify the goals of an energy plan it is necessary to estimate and to specify public preferences for a large set of alternative and often conflicting objectives: for example, the immediate production of the largest number of goods and services, a high rate of economic growth, conservation of resources for future generations, and a high degree of national security. Inevitably when trade-offs are fixed among goals that please one group they anger another. Second, the formulation of public policy in the energy field requires detailed understanding of market forces and projections of the progress of technology in a variety of very complicated areas. For example, answers must be provided to the following questions: what can be expected to happen to reactor safety, rates of petroleum recovery, gas discovery, or the development of competitive synthetic fuels? Assumptions of constancy or linear progress in these variables may be selected as seemingly safe options, but such assumptions in fact constitute predictions.

The strength of Keynesian macroeconomics and the overwhelming concern after World War II with the need to prevent another great depression and long-run stagnation affected energy policy in many, often quite subtle, ways. First of all, the dominant emphasis in Keynesian policy on demand management shifted attention away from supply considerations, including the long-standing worry of economists about resource constraints and bottlenecks to production. Even the policymaking apparatus implied by the Keynesian doctrine left little room for attention to energy issues. Before the 1970s at least, neither the Council of Economic Advisers nor the Joint Economic Committee of Congress were directed or motivated to cope with a complicated microeconomic topic such as energy policy. Moreover, some of the economic policies associated with energy planning, such as regional favoritism and massive public works construction unresponsive to the state of the business cycle, were actually perceived to be inimical to wise macroeconomic management.

The problem of obtaining adequate data about energy sources has been exceptionally exasperating for policymakers from the earliest postwar years. By tradition, most data were provided voluntarily by a multitude of firms and units of government, usually with a substantial time lag, a consciousness of the importance of "image" in the lobbying process, and without inclusion of such privileged information as rates of profitability on particular corporate units such as refineries or power plants. The weakness of the data base may explain the strikingly small amount of modeling of energy markets attempted in government between the pioneer work of Barnett in the late 1940s and the projections of Zausner under President Nixon. It was not until the 1970s that the collection of energy data became the direct responsibility of government.

One of the most difficult technological judgments for energy planners to make has been about the transitions among fuels that most serious observers agreed were bound to occur. As early as the 1930s it was widely believed that because of limited supplies heavy dependence on petroleum would only be a relatively brief interlude, perhaps a few decades. A return to coal quite soon for direct provision of energy and as the base for synthetics was thought to be inevitable. After coal, which might last a century or more, nuclear power seemed a likely possibility. At issue was whether society had an obligation to prepare collectively in various ways for these transitions, through stimulation (or preservation, in the case of coal) of the new fuel industry, or through research and development (for example, for synthetics and nuclear reactors). In general the petroleum industry answered "no" to this question on the ground that when a transition was near, private enterprise would make all the necessary preparations on its own. Arguments in favor of the government role, from the coal industry in particular, were dismissed as special pleading. But a nod in the direction of coal was made usually in the form of limited funds for coal research. Nuclear power obtained encouragement largely under the guise of security. It is not at all clear, even with the benefit of hindsight, just what the nation should have done to prepare for the energy transitions that lay ahead. What is striking, however, is that with very few exceptions persons taking part in the discussion seldom had any broad national interest at heart. Moreover, an observer gains the strong impression that in conflicts among energy sources, new or unconventional modes, which were by definition without any corps of supporters and defenders, were bound to lose out to entrenched interests. In addition comparisons typically were made between current costs of existing energy sources and projected future costs of new sources, and these biased decisions against the new sources. For proponents of solar or geothermal energy, or even synthetic fuels, to face the oil majors or public power authorities was like David facing Goliath with only a hypothetical stone.

Energy planning as a substitute for the free market had two dimensions. The long run brought serious uncertainties and difficulties of implementation. As presidents discovered in the 1970s, however, the short run could yield near-chaos. The task facing government of coming to grips with innumerable economic, technological, and political complexities and ramifications seemed still to be nearly insuperable. One observer compared energy policy formation in a crisis to pounding a pillow— when you push in one place it pops out in another. To get the pillow under control was a challenge awaiting the 1980s.

The Complication of Foreign Dependency

The formulation of energy policy was already complex before World War II when considerations were largely domestic in character. But after the war a wide range of new international complications was added, growing out of both sides of energy markets. On the demand side the United States had to face up to its new worldwide obligations and interests and to worry about the need for energy for its free world allies and trading partners as well as for itself. On the supply side the crucial change was the end of domestic energy independence. The most important dependency questions were raised by petroleum, but international complications arose with other energy sources as well, notably natural gas and hydroelectricity coming from Canada and uranium coming from various parts of the world. A number of exceedingly difficult issues of national policy were posed by the new international dimensions of energy markets. For example, would the enormous new supplies of petroleum in the Middle East overwhelm domestic producers and the delicate restrictionist mechanisms they had set up through the Interstate Oil Compact and other devices?

Economists agree that allocative efficiency will be achieved only when the price of energy, like the prices of other inputs to production, reflects full social costs. It was clear by the late 1940s that unrestrained worldwide competition would yield costs and prices that would dictate a massive shift away from domestic production of petroleum. It was necessary then for the nation to decide whether social, political, security, or other costs external to the world market justified the establishment of administered prices different from what they would have been under competition. Related to this large issue was a variety of smaller questions. For example, was it safe and sensible for U.S. interests to be represented in world energy markets by private U.S. corporations alone? If so, should these corporations be permitted to engage in practices abroad, such as monopsonistic and monopolistic activity, which would not be tolerated under antitrust laws at home? What should be the relationship between the U.S. government and these corporations abroad? If supportive, how much so? Should favored treatment be given to such hemispheric neighbors as Canada and Venezuela? And above all, what was a tolerable level of dependence on foreign energy? How much should the American people be willing to pay for a measure of independence? In the case of petroleum would independence in fact come from buying as much as possible abroad during normal periods and saving domestic reserves for emergencies (in which case, it was argued, the domestic industry would decay), or would it come from forswearing foreign sources and developing domestic sources as rapidly as possible? What real security could come from strategic reserves such as Elk Hills? The old military planner President Eisenhower professed confidence in the value of reserve pools underground, but few agreed with him. Virtually every administration was attracted to the concept of petroleum stockpiling, but before Presidents Ford and Carter none were willing to face the technical problems, the cost, and the adamant opposition from the industry.

The Pratt report during the Truman administration set forth a fairly clear rationale and a set of recommendations for a tolerable level of foreign dependence.[1] But such a prescription was not attempted again until President Nixon's Project Independence. In the interim the inherent complexity of the dependence problem and the political pressures it engendered caused other presidents to grope toward some ill-defined but sensible trade-off between dependence and cost. Ironically, in light of what happened in 1973–74, when considering the hazards of dependence attention was seldom given to the possibility of an oil embargo in circumstances other than total war.

A profound change occurred in America's attitudes toward its proper place in world energy markets in the 1970s. Replacing concerns about free world supplies and the trade-off between cost and domestic independence was an overwhelming worry simply about U.S. access to sufficient foreign supplies at affordable prices. One important result of this change was a new worldwide perception of the United States and a new domestic self-image. Others came to see the United States, and it saw itself, as simply one competitor among many whose self-interest must remain dominant, in contrast to the earlier conception of the nation as benevolent leader of the free world expected to make sacrifices for the greater good. One vestige of the old concern for international welfare was the controversial Carter administration policy regarding nuclear energy and nonproliferation. Here a host of new questions were raised about the efficacy of constraints on the transfer of sensitive nuclear technology, the legitimacy of America imposing its will on other nations in this respect, and other related issues.

It was necessary for the American people to provide answers to questions such as these. It was essential, for example, to decide whether to proceed with the subsidized development of synthetic fuels to gain energy independence, whether to prosecute U.S. oil companies for cartel practices abroad, and whether and at what level to have restraints on oil imports. One of the most striking features of the evolution of American responses to these and similar questions was the place of ideology in policy formation. Despite the prevalence of monopolistic elements almost everywhere, policymakers clung to the ideal of preserving or recreating competition. This ideology explains the imposition of restraints on the behavior of large international oil companies in contrast to the

1. National Security Resources Board, "A National Liquid Fuels Policy: A Preliminary Staff Study of Liquid Fuels for National Security" (August 1948). This study, prepared by Wallace E. Pratt, is discussed in chapter 2.

freedom experienced by those of other nations, and the artificial encouragement given to small inefficient producers and refiners.

It is striking that despite their fundamental character most answers to these policy questions were in fact provided without serious and well-informed national debate. Perhaps it was their structural, almost constitutional, quality that caused them to be submerged. Or perhaps it was the need usually for prompt action. Some parts of government engaged in discussion, and the special interests involved presented their arguments. A question such as how much residual fuel oil to import was discussed vigorously by Northeast politicians and by coal interests who feared increased competition. But these and other issues seldom received attention against a background of broader considerations. What debate there was within government was often complicated by interdepartmental conflict among such principal actors as the State, Defense, and Interior departments. In particular, the social costs and the implications for aggregate income distribution of such policies as oil imports or synthetic fuels were seldom raised. In the absence of clear-cut conclusions about the best paths to follow on various issues a rather bland middle ground was often chosen (some oil imports but not too many; some research on synthetics but not too much, and so on). This approach was termed "balance" by President Eisenhower. If there was balance there was continuity as well. A striking feature of the history of American energy policy is the extent to which foreign policy issues and problems refused to go away. For example, it is depressing to see the period bracketed by Iranian oil crises under Presidents Truman and Carter.

The Emergence of Energy Planners

Related to the complexities of forming energy policies while under pressure from strong special interests and facing uncertainties about goals and technical change was the question of who should advise on and indeed formulate energy policy. For other kinds of economic policy this question seemed easier to answer. For macroeconomic policy it was possible to put together a Council of Economic Advisers and a Joint Economic Committee of Congress staffed by professionals who had no obvious links to special interests. The Keynesian Revolution had attracted a substantial number of bright and committed young people to the new field of macroeconomics, and many of them were willing or eager to accept short- and long-term government service. Similarly, for antitrust work there was a cadre of lawyers and economists in the mold of Thurman Arnold and Louis Brandeis who saw themselves as guardians of democracy and the free market system. But the field of energy lacked a comparable group with sufficient skill, impartiality, and access to data to provide authoritative and unbiased guidance to government. The Interior Department came closest to developing a corps of well-rounded energy advisers, especially during the Truman administration and as part of the continuing pressure for a Department of Natural Resources. The strong industry and production orientation of the department, however, as well as the jealousy of other parts of government prevented this development from proceeding very far. A number of congressional committees devoted substantial attention to energy policy over the years, but they too failed to develop an effective complement of skilled staff. It appears now that a centralized unit of broad-based energy advisers could have developed and thrived within the federal structure only with the support of a strong national constituency. Before energy problems were perceived as vital national ones this constituency simply did not exist. The substantial increase of the environmental movement during the Nixon administration provided one of the first bases for the growth of such a constituency. Before the mid-1970s, however, dispersion of responsibility for energy and special pleading remained the rule, making for an extremely unsatisfactory situation when crisis struck.

Instead of independent advisers, then, the representatives of special interests inside and outside government often became by default the dominant intellectual force in energy policy formation. They not only filled many of the senior positions in the Departments of the Interior, State, and Energy; the regulatory bodies; and other parts of the executive branch but also found seats on key congressional committees and in other places of power. If you wanted advice on petroleum, you received it usually from someone with deep roots in the industry; electric power guidance came from those who had spent a lifetime with the utilities or, more likely, in public power. One of the fundamental problems with advisers from the energy industries was their seeming manic-depressive attitude toward many policy issues. Experience trained these advisers, consciously or not, to take a very optimistic, upbeat attitude toward energy markets in normal times; this often undermined arguments both for government constraints of all kinds and for support of actual or potential competitors. In emergencies, however, when favors were being distributed by government, the incentives were present for these advisers to picture the situation in much darker tones. When accelerated depreciation, access to scarce materials, or direct subsidies were at stake it was only natural for an industry to describe its circumstances as suddenly critical. For government planners dependent on accurate information and balanced interpretation from its advisers, this situation of fluctuating mood was far from satisfactory, and it raised difficult wider questions about the appropriate relationship between government and the private sector in a market economy.

One important body of nonindustry advisers on energy policy by the 1960s, at least, were physical scientists ensconced in the White House in the office of the science adviser. In general the scientists seem to have joined the industrial advisers in stressing optimism about the capacity of science and inventiveness to conquer all obstacles: the discovery of ever more natural resources, the production of safe and cheap nuclear power and synthetic liquid fuels, and smooth transitions between fuels when the right time came. At the same time it should be remembered that it was S. David Freeman, a lawyer located in the science adviser's office in the late 1960s and early 1970s, who began the campaign for conservation as a component of energy policy.

Failure to develop in America a sizable and capable body of disinterested and broad-gauged specialists competent to deal with complex issues of energy policy and lodged in powerful administrative units helps to explain in part the quality and form of the public policy that emerged.

The need for effective energy planning existed in good times and in bad, but it became critical in an emergency. From 1945 to 1978 there were literally dozens of suggestions, and some serious efforts, to create an effective administrative structure that would be ready when needed in an energy emergency. But the suggestions and warnings were seldom heeded. Ironically, in light of the continuing and pervasive nature of energy problems, at least when viewed ex post, the problems were often assigned to the various ephemeral "emergency" offices periodically created and destroyed in Washington over the years: the National Security Resources Board under Truman, the successor Office of Emergency Preparedness, and others. An obstacle to all emergency planning is that most people simply refuse to take it seriously before the emergency is at hand. In consequence some of the relatively little serious reflection on energy issues that did take place in government was regularly interrupted as the structure in which it occurred was dismantled.

Failure to establish a single government unit with overall responsibility for energy policy until the Carter administration created the Energy Department explains the remarkably long series of commissions, special committees, and task forces to explore the problem listed in these chapters. It helps also to explain the need for a very large and seemingly ineffective bureaucracy when government action became essential in the 1970s.

A Preference for Inaction

In general this account of energy policy formulation imparts the sense that circumstances were stacked heavily in favor of a policy status quo. There were several reasons. First, unless a genuine crisis occurred, such as that in 1973, it was almost impossible to attract the attention of the White House and of the American people to the subject. There were always just too many other matters of seemingly greater urgency. Even then the public memory was extraordinarily short, as candidate Carter discovered when he found that energy was no longer a major issue as soon as three years after the Arab oil embargo. Moreover, as issues that in their own right were usually not at the top of the national policy agenda, energy questions often became inextricably bound up in and submerged by other disputes. For example, both the question of public power and the issue of developing synthetic fuels became involved with the ideological dispute over the place of government in the economy. To some extent energy activities, and these two programs in particular, grew under President Truman as much because they were part of the role of government envisioned under the New Deal and successor Fair Deal as because of a perception of their exceptional importance for the future of the country. For a similar reason in reverse these activities languished under President Eisenhower. Exploitation of the offshore oil and gas resources, the tidelands, was another example of an energy issue ensnared in wider questions, in this case states' rights versus the authority of the federal government. One of the explanations given for the relatively high cost of most synthetic fuel experiments was the need to take account of pork barrel politics in the siting of plants and other decisions. Gas policy was involved with regional tensions, nuclear power with security and safety, oil imports with multilateral trade negotiations, producer-consumer state rivalries, and so on. The oil import program in its early days was one rare case where a protectionist energy policy over-whelmed other national goals—in that instance restraint of inflation and an increase in international free trade. Ultimately, however, when world prices of petroleum moved dramatically ahead of American ones, anxiety over inflation was the explanation used publicly for the slowness in allow-ing domestic petroleum prices to rise to their effective marginal replace-ment cost. Perhaps, finally, the high premium placed on other economic problems in the postwar world, problems such as employment, inflation, and balance-of-payments stability, simply did not leave time for "energy."

Public positions on most energy issues—natural gas pricing, oil im-port quotas, synfuel development, reactor licensing, or whatever—were achieved only after complicated bargaining among interested parties; and after a conclusion had been reached, even if the public welfare could be shown to benefit from some added adjustment, the prospect of com-plex renegotiation tended to inhibit reopening the question again. In many cases, of course, the immensity of the challenge in finding agree-ment among producers, consumers, bureaucrats, legislators, and en-vironmentalists was enough even to discourage the formation of any policy at all. Unlike some areas of macroeconomic policy—for example, programs to achieve full employment in the days before stagflation—where it could be argued that almost everyone would gain from success, in the field of energy when one person gained another often lost. The need to sort out schemes of compensation was a continuing excuse for policy paralysis. Occasions abound in these chapters where advisers on energy issues, even though conscious of imperfect circumstances, recom-mended against change on the ground that the process of negotiation might generate greater ills than those it sought to eliminate. Two ex-amples are the recommendation of the Paley Commission not to reduce percentage depletion and the conclusion of the special study committee of President Kennedy not to make drastic changes in energy policy of any kind. A costly feature of this proclivity toward the status quo was a slowness in dismantling some emergency measures, designed for the short run, after the emergency had passed. The persistence into the late 1970s of devices such as an oil import program created to cope with the abundance of an earlier era is one example.

There are numerous cases in this history where a policy adopted to deal with one problem generated unforeseen difficulties of its own; for example, supposed equity considerations in administration of the oil import pro-gram led to the use of quotas rather than tariffs and thereby to both innu-merable requests for exceptions and, ironically, dependence on the program of economically weak but politically strong independent refiners who had then to be dealt with whenever a change in policy was contemplated thereafter. In addition implementation of the protectionist oil import program at a time when many of the supplying nations were anxious for more income may have contributed to the birth of OPEC, the nemesis of policymakers at a later time. The two-tiered oil price program introduced under President Nixon perpetuated the favored treatment of smaller refiners by engendering a need (in equity) for subsidies called entitlements comparable to those of the import quotas.

Implications for the Future

It is dangerous to attempt generalizations from one area such as energy to the broad subject of economic policy formulation. The American experience with energy policy over the past forty years, however, must give one cause for concern about the capacity of government to deal intelligently and effectively with such a series of challenges. What we witness above all is a Congress dominated by relatively narrow special interests, both regional and industrial, an executive branch riven by bureaucratic conflicts of all kinds, and a presidency distracted constantly by "larger" issues and with a time horizon normally extending not beyond the next election and often much less. Moreover, there is little evidence that until the subject was firmly forced upon President Nixon any chief executive really attempted to grapple with the whole subject of energy rather than with occasional problems related to individual fuels. If it takes a real crisis to get the attention of presidents, this did not come until the 1970s. Certainly Iran, oil imports, dam construction, the agony of Appalachia, the great Northeast blackout, did briefly catch a presidential eye. But the underlying pressure of domestic energy demand growing ever more quickly than domestic supplies did not attract attention until the explosion of 1973–74. One conclusion that may be drawn from this record is that if the American people wish such topics to be dealt with more satisfactorily in the future, this may require fundamental government reorganization to create the requisite efficient and responsible institutions. That this need for reorganization still existed in 1980, for the nuclear energy industry at least, was suggested by the Kemeny report on the accident at Three Mile Island.[2]

2. See *Report of the President's Commission on the Accident at Three Mile Island, the Need for Change: The Legacy of TMI* (Government Printing Office, 1979). The commission and its chairman, John G. Kemeny, are discussed in chapter 9.

Many strands of conflict run through the history of American energy policy, but one of the most striking is that between what might be called the "diminishing returns pessimists" and the "technology optimists." The notion of resource constraints limiting economic growth and causing a redistribution of income in favor of resource owners was enshrined for economists in David Ricardo's famous Corn Model. It was reinterpreted and applied directly to energy by William Stanley Jevons in *The Coal Question* (1865). The suspicion that resource problems lurked not far over the horizon and could be the ultimate supply constraint on a modern economy found a prominent place in energy discussions throughout the postwar period. It received particular attention in the work of the Paley Commission, the Interdepartmental Energy Study Group of President Kennedy, and of course in reactions to the oil embargo of 1973.

But the notion that technology could effectively counteract, or at least alleviate, resource scarcity also ran strong throughout the discussion. This grew out of the sense that American technology had contributed substantially to victory in World War II, not only through the Manhattan Project, but by an extraordinary degree of economic mobilization for the production of sophisticated munitions of all kinds. The high point of optimism about technology seems to have occurred in the 1960s as a consequence of the challenge laid down by sputnik and the reorganization of government to deal with it, especially locating a science adviser in the White House. Presidents Kennedy and Johnson probably received the strongest doses of optimism from those around them. The optimism was most influential on four subjects: the capacity to keep finding and improving techniques for recovering petroleum, the development of competitive and safe nuclear energy, the availability of synthetic fuels if the need arose, and the unlikelihood of protracted wars in the future in which energy stockpiles might be crucial.

A notable manifestation of the optimism was the interdepartmental study prepared for President Johnson in 1966 that predicted a smooth transition to nuclear and synthetic fuels a comfortable distance ahead.[3] The dispute between pessimists and optimists came to the fore directly in estimates of the responsiveness of energy supplies to price. Optimists, usually including industry spokesmen, projected that moderate price increases would easily stimulate virtually any increases in output needed to

3. *Energy R&D and National Progress,* Prepared for the Interdepartmental Energy Study Group under the direction of Ali Bulent Cambel (GPO, 1966). This study is discussed in chapter 5.

restore market equilibrium. Pessimists, on the other hand, argued that after a short interlude of a few years, at most, energy supplies would become substantially unresponsive to price. In consequence market equilibrium would have to be achieved through repeated upward price adjustments that would constrain demand simply by making consumption much more expensive for energy consumers. One conclusion often reached by "elasticity pessimists" was that a confiscatory tax should be placed on the "unearned" economic rents received by energy suppliers—very much on the model of Henry George's single tax on the unearned rent of land so popular in the last century. It may well be that the blows delivered to technology optimism on all four fronts during the late 1960s and early 1970s were so decisive that the pendulum swung too far in the other direction. Certainly by the late 1970s resource pessimism was sharply on the ascendant once again.

Behind the controversy between technology optimists and pessimists lay the question of whether economic growth was related linearly to energy production. Some of the earliest projections carried out for energy markets during the Truman administration assumed this was the case; the implication of this assumption, of course, was very serious. In an absolute sense energy shortages might then place a constraint on growth and contribute to the "secular stagnation" that in the postwar world was still an American nightmare. Not until the early 1970s, under the urging of David Freeman in particular, did attention shift to the possibility that systematic "conservation" by both producers and consumers might change the consumption of energy per unit of output and permit the production of goods and services to grow more rapidly than energy consumption. Perhaps the slowness of others to accept this notion reflects their reluctance to concede the significance it had for the character of future capital stock and direction of growth.

In general, concerns for the safety and quality of the environment did not affect debates over energy policy substantially until the mid-1960s. Ironically, the location of government units mainly responsible for the various fuels—petroleum, coal, and gas—in the Interior Department next to such agencies as National Parks and the Fish and Wildlife Service might have made for an early integration of energy and environmental interests. But it seems to have taken the public outcry growing out of the movement epitomized by Rachel Carson's *Silent Spring,* as well as such dramatic incidents as the oil well blowout in the Santa Barbara channel, to link the two subjects inextricably together. Environmental concerns did not begin to impose significant constraints on energy policy—for example, by discouraging the use of coal and high-sulfur oil—until just before the crisis struck in the early 1970s. And then, with the mood of crisis all around, it began to seem that the cost of protecting the environment might be too high.

The American model of a political system with decentralized democracy and an economic system of markets approximating competition is perceived by many within and without the country to provide the conditions necessary both for maximum personal liberty and for economic efficiency. In this structure the interests of particular individuals and groups are maintained in some sort of balance and the great decisions facing society are made in a cooperative fashion under sets of rules rather than in response to centralized authority. The energy "crisis" of the 1970s as well as a host of other problems that plagued the decade, such as inflation and declining productivity, have caused the nation to reexamine these perceptions of the system and to ask whether the structure really behaves as the theory predicts and whether improvements in it cannot be devised.

This history of energy policy formulation does not answer any of the structural questions definitely, nor does it attempt to provide prescriptions for systemic change. It does, however, describe almost half a century of inadequate policy response to problems that were growing in magnitude and complexity all the time. It is the hope of the authors that increased public awareness of the weakness and ineffectiveness of policy formulation in the past may set the stage for improvement in the future.

U.S. Energy: A Quantitative Review of the Past Three Decades

JAMES L. COCHRANE *and* GARY L. GRIEPENTROG

THE PURPOSE of this appendix is to give readers of the administrative histories in this book an appreciation of the changing nature of U.S. energy markets. Some readers may find it helpful to have a quantitative overview of U.S. energy, with special attention to such things as changing industrial structure as well as changing market shares of various energy sources.

Energy Balances by Sector

The energy balances in table A-1 provide a brief summary of the change in energy use over the past three decades. In the table energy loss in conversion to electricity has not been distributed to the various consuming sectors. In each consuming sector, except electricity generation, total primary energy can be thought of as total fossil fuel consumption. In the electricity sector total primary energy also includes hydro and nuclear power. The miscellaneous consumption category includes relatively negligible consumption such as hydropower use in the industrial sector.

"Gross primary energy consumption" is the sum of total primary energy from the residential and commercial, industrial, transportation, and electric utility sectors. The miscellaneous amount is included in both gross consumption and net consumption. "Net primary energy consumption" is the sum of total energy consumed from the residential and commercial, industrial, and transportation sectors. The difference between gross and net is the energy loss in the generation of electricity. (The ratio of net to gross is called the "conversion efficiency," as shown in table A-2.)

Table A-1. *U.S. Energy Balances by Sector and Source, Selected Years, 1947–76*
Trillions of Btu

Sector and source	1947	1950	1955	1960	1965	1970	1976
				Consumption			
Gross primary energy consumption[a]	**33,035**	**33,992**	**39,703**	**44,569**	**53,343**	**67,444**	**73,705**
Net primary energy consumption	**29,632**	**30,140**	**34,989**	**38,892**	**45,868**	**56,206**	**59,307**
Total residential and commercial	7,148	8,139	9,449	11,436	13,778	16,988	18,412
Total primary energy	6,775	7,593	8,595	10,174	11,830	13,988	14,262
Oil	2,251	3,038	4,001	4,923	5,635	6,453	6,270
Natural gas	1,125	1,642	2,849	4,268	5,517	7,108	7,770
Coal	3,399	2,913	1,745	983	678	427	222
Utility electricity	391	546	854	1,262	1,948	3,000	4,150
Total industrial	13,254	12,884	14,999	15,948	18,810	22,643	21,412
Total primary energy	12,795	12,325	13,991	14,642	17,176	20,433	18,602
Oil	2,490	2,641	3,330	3,682	4,139	5,267	6,200
Natural gas	3,007	3,727	4,935	6,287	7,671	10,162	8,760
Coal	7,298	5,957	5,726	4,673	5,366	5,004	3,642
Utility electricity	459	559	1,008	1,306	1,634	2,210	2,810
Total transportation	8,820	8,640	9,845	10,836	12,732	16,361	19,450
Total primary energy	8,791	8,616	9,826	10,818	12,714	16,345	19,434
Oil	5,761	6,785	9,109	10,372	12,179	15,592	18,900
Natural gas	0	130	253	359	517	745	534
Coal	3,030	1,701	464	87	18	8	0
Utility electricity	29	24	19	18	18	16	16
Electric utilities							
Total primary energy	4,264	4,981	6,595	8,263	11,075	16,464	21,374
Oil	468	662	512	564	744	2,087	3,450

Natural gas	386	651	1,194	1,785	2,392	4,015	3,140
Coal	2,084	2,228	3,482	4,251	5,843	7,483	9,714
Hydropower	1,326	1,440	1,407	1,657	2,058	2,650	3,030
Nuclear	...	...	...	6	38	229	2,040
Total electricity distributed	879	1,129	1,881	2,586	3,600	5,226	6,976
Total miscellaneous	410	477	696	672	548	214	33
Supply							
Gross supply	**33,035**	**33,992**	**39,703**	**44,569**	**53,343**	**67,444**	**73,705**
Total domestic	35,052	33,552	39,252	41,913	49,341	61,819	59,247
Oil	10,960	11,903	14,996	15,997	17,726	22,558	19,672
Natural gas	4,537	6,177	9,252	12,550	15,653	21,256	19,287
Coal	17,818	13,555	12,901	11,031	13,318	14,912	15,185
Nuclear	0	0	0	6	38	229	2,040
Hydropower	1,326	1,440	1,407	1,657	2,058	2,650	3,030
Miscellaneous	410	477	696	672	548	214	33
Total imports	962	1,872	2,748	4,123	5,825	8,235	16,623
Oil	954	1,862	2,728	3,955	5,349	7,388	15,613
Natural gas	0	0	11	161	471	846	983
Coal	8	10	9	7	5	1	27
Addenda							
Total exports	2,978	1,432	2,297	1,467	1,823	2,610	2,165
Oil	944	639	772	411	378	547	465
Natural gas	19	27	32	12	27	72	66
Coal	2,015	766	1,493	1,044	1,418	1,991	1,634

Sources: Walter G. Dupree, Jr. and James A. West, *United States Energy through the Year 2000* (U.S. Department of the Interior, 1972), app. B; and U.S. Department of the Interior, Bureau of Mines, *Minerals Yearbook 1976*, vol. 1: *Metals, Minerals, and Fuels* (Government Printing Office, 1978), pp. 44–47.
a. Sector totals may not sum to gross consumption total due to stock changes, losses, gains, and independent rounding.

Table A-2. Selected U.S. Economic, Demographic, and Energy Indicators, 1947–78

Year	Gross energy input[a] (quadrillions of Btu)	Net energy input[b] (quadrillions of Btu)	Population (millions)	Gross energy input per GNP (thousands of Btu)	GNP (billions of 1972 dollars)	Gross energy input per capita (millions of Btu)	Net energy input per capita (millions of Btu)	Conversion efficiency (percent)[e]
1947	33.0	29.2	144.1	70.5	468.3	229.0	202.8	88.5
1948	33.9	29.1	146.6	69.5	487.7	231.2	198.6	85.8
1949	31.5	27.3	149.2	64.2	490.7	211.1	182.7	86.5
1950	34.0	29.7	152.3	63.7	533.5	223.2	194.8	87.3
1951	36.8	32.1	154.9	63.8	576.5	237.6	206.9	87.1
1952	36.5	31.6	157.6	61.0	598.5	231.7	200.6	86.6
1953	37.6	32.6	160.2	60.5	621.8	234.7	201.1	85.7
1954	36.3	31.2	163.0	59.1	613.7	222.7	191.5	86.0
1955	39.7	34.3	165.9	60.6	654.8	239.3	206.7	86.4
1956	41.7	35.8	168.9	62.4	668.8	246.9	211.7	85.7
1957	41.7	35.6	172.0	61.2	680.9	242.2	206.9	85.4
1958	41.7	35.5	174.9	61.4	679.5	238.4	202.8	85.1
1959	43.1	36.4	177.8	59.8	720.4	242.4	205.0	84.6
1960	44.6	38.2	180.7	60.5	736.8	246.8	211.5	85.7
1961	45.3	38.7	183.8	60.0	755.3	246.5	210.6	85.8
1962	47.4	40.5	186.5	59.3	799.1	254.1	217.2	85.5
1963	49.3	42.0	189.2	59.3	830.7	260.5	222.0	85.2
1964	51.2	43.6	191.8	58.6	874.4	266.9	227.3	85.5

Year								
1965	53.3	45.3	194.3	57.6	925.9	274.3	233.1	85.0
1966	56.4	47.6	196.6	57.5	981.0	286.9	242.1	84.4
1967	58.3	49.4	198.7	57.9	1,007.7	293.4	248.6	84.7
1968	61.7	52.2	200.7	58.7	1,051.8	307.4	260.1	84.6
1969	65.0	54.4	202.7	60.3	1,078.8	320.7	268.4	83.7
1970	67.1	56.0	204.9	62.4	1,075.3	327.5	273.3	83.6
1971	68.7	57.0	207.0	62.0	1,107.5	331.9	275.4	83.0
1972	72.1	59.5	208.8	61.6	1,171.1	345.3	285.0	82.6
1973	74.7	61.3	210.4	60.5	1,235.0	355.0	291.3	82.1
1974	73.1	59.9	211.9	60.0	1,217.8	345.0	282.7	81.9
1975	70.7	56.3	212.7	58.8	1,202.3	332.4	264.7	79.6
1976	74.5	59.3	214.4	58.5	1,273.0	347.5	276.6	79.6
1977	76.5	60.5	216.1	57.1	1,340.5	354.0	280.0	79.1
1978	78.2	61.2	217.9	55.9	1,399.2	358.9	280.9	78.3

Sources: Data for 1947–74 are from Walter G. Dupree, Jr., and John S. Corsentino, *United States Energy through the Year 2000 (Revised)* (U.S. Department of the Interior, Bureau of Mines, 1975), p. 16; and *The National Income and Product Accounts of the United States, 1929–74, Statistical Tables,* Supplement to the *Survey of Current Business* (Government Printing Office, 1977), pp. 6–9. Data for 1975–78 are from *Survey of Current Business,* vol. 57 (July 1977), p. 18; ibid., vol. 59 (July 1979), p. 26; *Monthly Energy Review,* October 1979, pp. 2, 24–26; and U.S. Bureau of the Census, *Current Population Reports,* series P-20, no. 350, "Population Profile of the United States, 1979" (GPO, 1980), p. 4.

a. Gross energy is the total of inputs into the economy of the primary fuels (petroleum, natural gas, and coal, including imports) or their derivatives, plus the generation of hydro and nuclear power converted to equivalent energy inputs.

b. Net energy is the sector inputs (household and commercial, transportation, and industrial), and consists of direct fuels and purchased electricity.

c. The conversion efficiency factor is the percentage of total gross energy going into the final consuming sector.

Import and export data combined with the consumption data can be used to derive a consistent set of values for domestic supply of fossil fuels. The relationship is consumption plus exports minus imports equals domestic supply. Thus gross energy supply equals gross primary energy consumption.

One of the major trends perceived in the table is the absolute decline of coal in the three consuming sectors and the relative decline of coal in recent years in electricity generation. Recent changes include the tripling of oil imports from 1965 to 1976 and the rapid growth of nuclear power.

U.S. Energy Consumption

An overall view of U.S. energy consumption between 1947 and 1978 can be obtained from table A-2. The main factors of energy demand, population growth, and economic activity are presented in relation to consumption. Since 1947 energy consumption has increased or remained the same every year over the previous year in all but five years. Four of the declines corresponded to diminished economic activity in 1949, 1952, 1954, and 1974–75.

Gross energy consumption increased from 33.0 quadrillion Btu in 1947 to 78.2 quadrillion Btu in 1978, a 2.8 percent average annual rate of growth. For five-year periods, 1950–75, and for 1975–78, the following growth rates can be calculated:

Year	Gross energy inputs (quadrillion Btu)	Average annual growth rate (percent)
1950	34.0	. . .
1955	39.7	3.1
1960	44.6	2.3
1965	53.3	3.6
1970	67.1	4.6
1975	70.7	1.0
1978	78.2	3.4

The large growth from 1960 to 1970 coincided with the long business cycle from 1960–69. The period also was characterized by declining real prices of energy and rising real income per capita.

The average annual growth rate for net energy inputs (which increased from 29.2 quadrillion Btu in 1947 to 61.2 quadrillion Btu in 1978) is 2.4 percent. This rate is below the rate of gross energy consumption because an increasing amount of primary energy has been consumed through the secondary source of electricity. This determinant of net energy consumption also explains the decline in conversion efficiency.

Gross energy use per capita is another measure of increasing energy use. Overall, its movements are similar to those of gross energy consumption. For the following five-year periods, 1950–75, and for 1975–78, the outstanding feature is growth during the 1960s:

Year	Gross energy per capita (million Btu)	Average annual growth rate (percent)
1950	223.2	. . .
1955	239.3	1.4
1960	246.8	0.6
1965	274.3	2.1
1970	327.5	3.5
1975	332.4	0.3
1978	358.9	2.6

Another indicator of the trend in energy consumption is energy consumed per constant dollar of GNP. This may be due to both increasingly efficient use of energy and the changing composition of the GNP. There have been some reversals in the trend in the mid-fifties and early seventies.

The import-export picture also changed drastically over the three decades. In 1947 the United States exported 2,978 trillion Btu of energy while importing 962 trillion. The exports were 2,015 trillion Btu of coal, 944 trillion Btu of petroleum, and 19 trillion Btu of natural gas. Imports consisted basically of 954 trillion Btu of petroleum. By 1978 U.S. exports were a little less, but imports had increased by a factor of twenty to 19,262 trillion Btu. Of the 17,311 trillion Btu of net imports, 17,057 trillion Btu were crude oil and petroleum products (44.9 percent of U.S. petroleum consumption) and 941 trillion Btu were natural gas. U.S. exports were still mainly coal. Overall, in 1978 imports represented 22 percent of U.S. consumption.[1]

1. Table A-1 and *Monthly Energy Review,* April 1980, pp. 2, 8.

Petroleum

The annual production of petroleum increased by over 60 percent in the thirty-one-year span from 1947 to 1978, while additions to reserves were relatively constant until 1974. The major addition was the Alaskan find in 1970. Recently, as shown in table A-3, there has been a slight decline in the reserve-production ratio. An indication of the distribution of reserves can be obtained by finding those states with at least 500 million barrels of crude oil reserves at the end of 1971: Alaska, 10,116 million barrels; California, 3,706 million; Kansas, 502 million; Louisiana, 5,399 million; New Mexico, 657 million; Oklahoma, 1,405 million; Texas, 13,024 million; and Wyoming, 998 million. Colorado and Mississippi had approximately 300 million barrels of reserves at that time.[2]

Consumption and imports of petroleum for 1947–78 are displayed in table A-4. Imports during this period increased at 9.5 percent a year, more than triple the gross energy consumption rate. Annual consumption of oil increased at a rate of 4.0 percent a year, while annual production increased at 1.6 percent a year. During the 1960s imports were a relatively constant fraction of consumption. That fraction increased rapidly in the 1970s. Distillate imports increased rapidly following 1968 until substantial price increases resulted in a reduction in 1975. Changes in residual imports were larger during the same period. As shown in table A-5, the production of both distillate and residual petroleum products rose steadily during the period.

The nominal price of crude oil is expressed as the average value of a barrel at the well. The price was relatively constant until 1970, as shown in table A-6. The average value of imported crude can be computed from Census Bureau data on import value before customs. In 1966, 1972, 1973, and 1974 the average import value of crude was $2.75, $3.04, $3.71, and $12.52 a barrel, respectively.[3] The degree to which price controls held U.S. oil prices down during the post-1973 embargo period is

2. *Energy Facts,* Committee Print, prepared for the Subcommittee on Energy of the House Committee on Science and Astronautics by the Science Policy Research Division, Congressional Research Service, Library of Congress, 93 Cong. 1 sess. (Government Printing Office, 1973), p. 339.

3. Authors' calculations based on data in U.S. Bureau of the Census, *U.S. General Imports: World Area by Commodity Groupings,* Report FT 155, annual issues for years shown.

Table A-3. *Discoveries, Production, and Proved Reserves of Crude Petroleum in the United States, 1947–78*

Millions of barrels

Year	Gross additions to proved reserves	Production	Proved reserves, end of year	Ratio of reserves to production
1947	2,465	1,850	21,488	11.62
1948	3,795	2,002	23,280	11.63
1949	3,188	1,819	24,649	13.55
1950	2,563	1,944	25,268	13.00
1951	4,414	2,214	27,468	12.41
1952	2,749	2,257	27,961	12.39
1953	3,296	2,312	28,945	12.52
1954	2,873	2,257	29,561	13.10
1955	2,871	2,419	30,012	12.41
1956	2,974	2,552	30,435	11.93
1957	2,425	2,559	30,300	11.84
1958	2,608	2,373	30,536	12.87
1959	3,667	2,483	31,719	12.77
1960	2,365	2,471	31,613	12.79
1961	2,658	2,512	31,759	12.64
1962	2,181	2,550	31,389	12.31
1963	2,174	2,593	30,970	11.94
1964	2,665	2,644	30,991	11.72
1965	3,048	2,686	31,352	11.67
1966	2,964	2,864	31,452	10.98
1967	2,962	3,038	31,377	10.33
1968	2,455	3,124	30,707	9.83
1969	2,120	3,195	29,632	9.27
1970	12,689	3,319	39,001	11.75
1971	2,318	3,256	38,063	11.69
1972	1,558	3,281	36,339	11.08
1973	2,146	3,185	35,300	11.08
1974	1,994	3,043	34,250	11.26
1975	1,318	2,886	32,682	11.32
1976	1,085	2,825	30,942	10.95
1977	1,404	2,860	29,486	10.31
1978	1,347	3,030	27,804	9.18

Source: American Petroleum Institute, American Gas Association, and the Canadian Petroleum Association, *Reserves of Crude Oil, Natural Gas Liquids, and Natural Gas in the United States and Canada as of December 31, 1978*, vol. 33 (June 1979), p. 24.

Table A-4. *Consumption and Imports of Petroleum, 1947–78*

Millions of barrels

Year	Consumption[a]	Crude imports	Refined imports	Total imports	Imports as percent of consumption
1947	1,960.5	97.5	61.9	159.4	8.1
1948	2,085.8	129.1	59.1	188.2	9.0
1949	2,103.5	153.7	81.9	235.6	11.2
1950	2,357.1	177.7	132.5	310.2	13.2
1951	2,560.9	179.1	129.1	308.2	12.0
1952	2,660.7	209.6	138.9	348.5	13.1
1953	2,773.9	236.5	141.0	377.5	13.6
1954	2,831.0	239.5	144.5	384.0	13.6
1955	3,086.2	285.4	170.1	455.5	14.8
1956	3,211.7	341.8	183.8	525.6	16.4
1957	3,215.3	373.3	201.3	574.6	17.9
1958	3,328.0	348.0	272.6	620.6	18.6
1959	3,477.2	352.3	297.2	649.5	18.7
1960	3,585.8	371.6	292.5	664.1	18.5
1961	3,641.3	381.5	318.1	699.6	19.2
1962	3,796.0	411.0	348.8	759.8	20.0
1963	3,921.4	412.7	362.1	774.8	19.8
1964	4,034.2	438.6	388.1	826.7	20.5
1965	4,202.0	452.0	448.7	900.7	21.4
1966	4,410.8	447.1	492.0	939.1	21.3
1967	4,584.5	411.6	514.3	925.9	20.2
1968	4,901.8	501.7	537.7	1,039.4	21.2
1969	5,159.9	552.9	602.7	1,155.6	22.4
1970	5,364.5	522.6	725.5	1,248.1	23.3
1971	5,552.6	658.6	774.3	1,432.9	25.8
1972	5,990.3	856.8	878.5	1,735.3	29.0
1973	6,317.3	1,234.2	1,049.3	2,283.5	36.1
1974	6,078.2	1,313.4	917.6	2,231.0	36.7
1975	5,957.5	1,511.2	699.2	2,210.4	37.1
1976	6,384.1	1,946.9	723.1	2,670.0	41.8
1977	6,727.5	2,425.6	789.1	3,214.7	47.8
1978	6,879.0	2,329.7	722.9	3,052.6	44.4

Sources: *Business Statistics, 1977*, Supplement to the *Survey of Current Business* (Government Printing Office, 1978), p. 159; and *Survey of Current Business*, vol. 59 (December 1979), p. S-31.
a. Includes both fuel and nonfuel uses.

Table A-5. *Production, Imports and Price Index of Distillate and Residual Fuel Oil, 1947–78*

Millions of barrels

	Distillate			Residual		
Year	Domestic production	Imports	Price index (1967 = 100)	Domestic production	Imports	Price index (1967 = 100)
1947	312.2	4.2	65.2	447.8	54.2	94.1
1948	380.7	2.5	90.3	466.3	53.3	125.6
1949	340.8	1.8	76.8	424.9	73.2	74.5
1950	398.9	2.6	80.1	425.2	120.0	86.8
1951	475.8	1.8	86.5	469.4	119.2	97.3
1952	520.4	2.7	87.1	453.9	128.5	87.2
1953	528.1	3.4	90.0	450.0	131.5	85.7
1954	542.3	3.2	91.2	416.8	129.1	91.6
1955	602.5	4.4	93.5	420.3	152.0	102.8
1956	665.7	5.2	97.8	426.7	162.9	117.0
1957	668.6	8.6	103.2	415.7	173.3	138.8
1958	631.4	14.9	94.6	363.4	182.0	109.6
1959	678.9	17.7	96.1	347.9	222.6	102.9
1960	667.0	12.8	90.5	332.1	233.2	109.7
1961	696.6	17.4	94.9	315.6	243.3	113.3
1962	720.1	11.8	93.6	295.7	264.3	111.5
1963	765.1	9.1	93.9	275.9	272.8	107.6
1964	742.4	11.8	86.5	266.8	295.8	104.8
1965	765.4	13.0	91.9	268.6	345.2	107.7
1966	785.8	13.8	93.7	264.0	376.8	105.0
1967	804.8	18.5	100.0	276.0	395.9	100.0
1968	840.7	48.1	101.9	275.8	409.9	95.7
1969	848.4	50.9	102.4	265.9	461.6	93.3
1970	897.1	53.8	106.5	257.5	557.8	125.5
1971	912.1	55.8	110.0	274.7	577.7	166.0
1972	963.6	66.4	111.3	292.5	637.4	158.8
1973	1,030.2	143.1	139.7	354.6	676.2	190.4
1974	974.0	105.6	272.0	390.5	579.2	485.4
1975	968.6	56.7	309.4	451.0	446.5	495.5
1976	1,070.2	52.5	337.0	504.0	511.7	452.9
1977	1,196.3	91.3	384.1	640.1	496.1	522.5
1978	1,156.1	63.3	398.0	608.6	494.6	498.0

Source: *Business Statistics, 1977*, Supplement to the *Survey of Current Business* (Government Printing Office, 1978), p. 161; and *Survey of Current Business*, vol. 59 (December 1979), p. S-31.

Table A-6. *U.S. Average Wellhead Price of Crude Oil, Selected Years, 1950–78*

Year	Dollars per barrel
1950	2.51
1955	2.77
1960	2.88
1965	2.86
1970	3.18
1971	3.39
1972	3.39
1973	3.89
1974	6.87
1975	7.67
1976	8.19
1977	8.57
1978	9.00

Sources: American Petroleum Institute, *Basic Petroleum Data Book* (Washington, D.C.: API, 1979) sec. 6, table 1; *Monthly Energy Review*, October 1977, p. 72; and ibid., October 1979, p. 76.

Table A-7. *Acquisition Cost of Crude Oil, U.S. Refineries, 1974–79*
Dollars per barrel

Year	Domestic	Imported	Composite
1974	7.18	12.52	9.07
1975	8.39	13.93	10.38
1976	8.84	13.48	10.89
1977	9.55	14.53	11.96
1978	10.61	14.57	12.46
1979	14.27	21.67	17.72

Source: *Monthly Energy Review*, October 1977, p. 75; and ibid., June 1980, p. 70.

shown in table A-7. Even though domestic prices steadily rose between 1974 and the end of 1979, the spread between the price of domestically produced oil and imported oil increased.

Natural Gas

As shown in table A-8, the production of natural gas has steadily increased since 1947. Until 1974 the average annual growth rate was 5.4

Table A-8. *U.S. Natural Gas Production and Reserves, 1947–78*
Trillions of cubic feet at 60° F and 14.73 pounds per square inch absolute

Year	Gross additions to proved reserves	Production	Proved reserves, end of year	Ratio of reserves to production
1947	10.92	5.60	165.03	29.5
1948	13.82	5.98	172.93	28.9
1949	12.61	6.21	179.40	28.9
1950	11.99	6.86	184.58	26.9
1951	15.97	7.92	192.76	24.3
1952	14.27	8.59	198.63	23.1
1953	20.34	9.19	210.30	22.9
1954	9.55	9.38	210.56	22.4
1955	21.90	10.06	222.48	22.1
1956	24.72	10.85	236.48	21.8
1957	20.01	11.44	245.23	21.4
1958	18.90	11.42	252.76	22.1
1959	20.62	12.37	261.17	21.1
1960	13.89	13.02	262.33	20.1
1961	17.17	13.38	266.27	19.9
1962	19.48	13.64	272.28	20.0
1963	18.16	14.55	276.15	19.0
1964	20.25	15.35	281.25	18.3
1965	21.32	16.25	286.47	17.6
1966	20.22	17.49	289.33	16.5
1967	21.80	18.38	292.91	15.9
1968	13.70	19.37	287.35	14.8
1969	8.38	20.72	275.11	13.3
1970	37.20	21.96	290.75	13.2
1971	9.83	22.08	278.80	12.6
1972	9.63	22.51	266.08	11.8
1973	6.83	22.61	249.95	11.1
1974	8.68	21.32	237.13	11.1
1975	10.48	19.72	228.20	11.6
1976	7.56	19.54	216.03	11.1
1977	11.85	19.45	208.88	10.7
1978	10.59	19.31	200.30	10.4

Source: American Petroleum Institute, American Gas Association, and the Canadian Petroleum Association, *Reserves of Crude Oil, Natural Gas Liquids, and Natural Gas in the United States and Canada as of December 31, 1978*, vol. 33 (June 1979), pp. 116–17.

percent. Since 1973 production has decreased. Unfortunately the average growth rate of proved net reserves over the 1947–73 period was under 2 percent, thus the continuously declining ratio. Moreover, production is currently exceeding additions to reserves and proved reserves have actually declined since 1970.

Table A-9. *U.S. Price of Natural Gas, Selected Years, 1955–78*

Year	Average wellhead price (cents per thousand cubic feet)	Wholesale price index, gas fuels (1967 = 100)
1955	10.4	61.6
1960	14.0	87.2
1965	15.6	92.8
1970	17.1	103.6
1975	44.5	216.7
1976	58.0	286.8
1977	79.0	387.8
1978	91.9	428.7

Sources: American Gas Association, *Gas Facts, 1977 Data* (Arlington, Va.: AGA, 1978), pp. 113, 124; *Monthly Energy Review*, October 1979, p. 92; *Business Statistics, 1977*, Supplement to the *Survey of Current Business* (Government Printing Office, 1978), p. 48; and *Survey of Current Business*, vol. 59 (December 1979), p. S-7.

Nominal natural gas prices for marketed production are measured by average wellhead price in cents per thousand cubic feet (mcf). This price increased from 4.9 cents per mcf in 1945 to 17.1 in 1970. (Table A-9 shows the price for selected years, 1955–78.) The price stayed at about 15 cents in the 1960's.[4] The average price hides a large interstate variation in price that can be as much as 20 cents.

The price rose rapidly in the 1970s. For comparison, the compound annual average growth rates from 1955–77 for the consumer price index, natural gas, fuel oil, and electricity prices were 3.8, 4.4, 5.3, and 1.6 percent, respectively.[5]

Imports of natural gas are mainly from Canada. In 1955, 11 billion cubic feet were imported from Canada and by 1977, 1 trillion cubic feet. In the 1960s annual imports from Mexico were approximately 50 million cubic feet. Since 1970 small quantities have been imported from Algeria, reaching 11 billion cubic feet in 1977. Natural gas has been exported to Mexico and Canada, but the amounts are small and decreasing. Exports to Japan from Alaska, starting in 1970, surpassed 50 billion cubic feet in 1977.[6]

4. *Energy Facts,* p. 239.
5. Based on average residential costs; fuel oil is for no. 2 fuel oil. American Gas Association, *Gas Facts, 1977 Data* (Arlington, Va.: AGA, 1978), pp. 119–20.
6. Ibid., p. 31.

Coal

From right after World War II until the early 1960s, total consumption of coal declined as did employment.[7] With the expansion of the electric utility market, consumption increased until it is currently back at World War II levels. Employment in the coal industry, however, is now half of the World War II level. Table A-10 shows the history of bituminous coal mining in the United States. There is a rapid decline in employment in the early 1950s followed by a more moderate decline in the 1960s. In 1970 the trend turns and employment begins to increase.

The turn in employment has caused problems in productivity, as indicated in table A-10. Some of the decline in productivity is attributable to the mine safety acts and the environmental constraints on strip mining. During the 1970s the demand for labor required the entry of new workers into the mining force, and shortages of skilled workers and supervisory personnel developed. Training programs were strained and training requirements were increased due to the safety acts. As a result, absenteeism and wildcat strikes increased. Productivity in underground mines decreased by almost 40 percent from its peak in 1969, but it is still double its level in 1940.

Unstable labor conditions and an increasing demand for labor altered the basic relationship between earnings in bituminous coal mining and earnings in all manufacturing. As table A-10 shows, through the 1960s there was a premium of approximately 30 percent for working in coal mining over all manufacturing. By the late 1970s this had increased to 50 percent. Earnings in coal mining approximately doubled between 1969 and 1977.

Another interesting aspect is the source of bituminous coal. Strip mine production was relatively constant until 1960. After that it started increasing so rapidly that strip mine production tripled between 1960 and 1977, surpassing underground production in 1974. Underground production has been basically stable. Reserves of anthracite and bituminous are east of the Mississippi, while reserves of subbituminous and lignite are west of the Mississippi. The demonstrated coal reserve base of the United States was estimated by the Bureau of Mines to be 438 billion

7. The text of this section is based on material from Charles River Associates, Inc., *Coal Price Formation*, Final Report EPRI EA-497 prepared for Electric Power Research Institute, Palo Alto, Calif. (Cambridge, Mass.: CRA, 1977).

Table A-10. *Employment, Production, and Earnings in the U.S.*
Bituminous Coal Mining Industry, 1940–77

Year	Number of employees (thousands)	Average short tons per man-day, all mines	Average hourly earnings, production workers[a] (dollars)	Average hourly earnings, all manufacturing
1940	435.0	5.19	0.85	0.66
1941	431.4	5.20	0.96	0.73
1942	474.7	5.12	1.03	0.85
1943	437.2	5.38	1.10	0.96
1944	419.2	5.67	1.15	1.01
1945	383.7	5.78	1.20	1.02
1946	372.7	6.30	1.36	1.08
1947	425.6	6.42	1.58	1.22
1948	436.1	6.26	1.84	1.33
1949	393.3	6.43	1.88	1.39
1950	367.9	6.77	1.94	1.44
1951	372.0	7.04	2.14	1.56
1952	327.8	7.47	2.22	1.65
1953	288.9	8.17	2.40	1.74
1954	228.5	9.47	2.40	1.78
1955	218.7	9.84	2.47	1.86
1956	228.6	10.28	2.72	1.95
1957	229.8	10.59	2.92	2.05
1958	193.0	11.33	2.93	2.11
1959	178.5	12.22	3.11	2.19
1960	168.5	12.83	3.14	2.26
1961	147.1	13.87	3.12	2.32
1962	140.0	14.72	3.12	2.39
1963	137.7	15.83	3.15	2.46
1964	136.1	16.84	3.30	2.53
1965	131.8	17.52	3.49	2.61
1966	129.6	18.52	3.66	2.72
1967	132.0	19.17	3.75	2.83
1968	126.4	19.37	3.86	3.01
1969	129.6	19.90	4.24	3.19
1970	139.6	18.84	4.58	3.36
1971	140.4	18.02	4.83	3.57
1972	157.1	17.74	5.32	3.81
1973	158.0	17.58	5.75	4.08
1974	176.0	17.58	6.26	4.41
1975	209.3	14.74	7.25	4.81
1976	221.4	14.46	7.78	5.19
1977	219.8	14.84	8.29	5.63

Sources: U.S. Department of Labor, Bureau of Labor Statistics, *Employment and Earnings, United States, 1909–78*, Bulletin 1312-11 (Government Printing Office, 1979), pp. 19–20; Bureau of Labor Statistics, *Handbook of Labor Statistics, 1978*, Bulletin 2000 (GPO, 1979), p. 313; U.S. Department of Energy, Energy Information Administration, *Annual Report to Congress, 1979*, vol. 2: *Data*, p. 119; and Charles River Associates, Inc., *Coal Price Formation*, Final Report EPRI EA-497 prepared for Electric Power Research Institute, Palo Alto, Calif. (Cambridge, Mass.: CRA, 1977), p. 4-27.

a. For 1962 through 1977, figures given are eleven-month averages.

short tons in 1976; about half of this amount is estimated to be recoverable.[8]

Nuclear Energy

The growth of the nuclear power industry is summarized in table A-11.[9] From 1961 to 1978 there seem to have been two cycles in the number of nuclear steam supply system orders. The rate of growth in installed capacity was sufficient to result in, roughly, a doubling every two years from 1966 to 1976. By 1978, when 71 units were operating, another 122 units were in the construction licensing phase, and these could be expected to quadruple capacity in the next ten years to approximately 200,000 megawatts. However, twelve units of 13,274 megawatts were canceled in 1978, and this trend has continued.[10]

Whether the volume of orders will rise in the future depends on delays in licensing and construction and on demand and costs. Environmental concerns have caused a change in the length of time to obtain a construction permit by a multiplicative factor ranging from 3 to 4, now close to a four-year delay. Construction costs of a nuclear power plant have changed rapidly, showing an average increase of approximately 30 percent a year in the price of a kilowatt of installed capacity since the mid-1960s. Historical capital-cost data for coal and nuclear power plants through 1971 indicate that nuclear nonturnkey plants were approximately 70 percent more costly than coal. By 1973–74 this cost disadvantage had dropped to 50 percent.[11]

The nuclear fuel, uranium, goes through a process called the nuclear fuel cycle: exploration, mining, milling, conversion, enrichment, fabrication into fuel rods, power production, and reprocessing of spent fuel. The impact of the former Atomic Energy Commission on this process

8. U.S. Department of Energy, Energy Information Administration, *Annual Report to Congress, 1979*, vol. 2: *Data*, p. 123.

9. The text of this section is based on material from Charles River Associates, Inc., *Uranium Price Formation*, Final Report EPRI EA-498 prepared for Electric Power Research Institute, Palo Alto, Calif. (Cambridge, Mass.: CRA, 1977); and W. David Montgomery and James P. Quirk, "Cost Escalation in Nuclear Power," in Lon C. Ruedisili and Morris W. Firebaugh, eds., *Perspectives on Energy: Issues, Ideas, and Environmental Dilemmas*, 2d ed. (New York: Oxford University Press, 1978), pp. 339–58.

10. Gordon D. Friedlander, "1979 Nuclear Plant Survey," *Electrical World*, January 15, 1979, p. 71.

11. Montgomery and Quirk, "Cost Escalation in Nuclear Power," pp. 349–55.

Table A-11. *U.S. Nuclear Power Reactor Orders and Capacity, 1955–78*

	Orders		Year-end operating reactors	Year-end gross capacity (millions of kilowatts)
Year	Number	Megawatts		
1955	5	776	...	...
1956	2	33	...	...
1957	2	76	1	0.1
1958	3	122	1	0.1
1959	1	72	1	0.1
1960	0	0	2	0.3
1961	1	50	3	0.4
1962	1	575	4	0.7
1963	4	2,560	7	0.7
1964	0	0	9	0.9
1965	7	4,624	10	0.9
1966	20	16,603	11	1.9
1967	30	25,633	10	2.9
1968	14	12,903	10	2.8
1969	7	7,203	13	4.0
1970	14	14,266	19	6.5
1971	16	15,122	21	8.7
1972	30	34,322	29	15.3
1973	35	39,862	40	21.0
1974	20	27,058	53	31.6
1975	4	4,100	56	39.8
1976	3	3,440	62	42.9
1977	4	5,100	67	49.9
1978	2	2,300	71	53.5

Sources: W. David Montgomery and James P. Quirk, "Cost Escalation in Nuclear Power," in Lon C. Ruedisili and Morris W. Firebaugh, eds., *Perspectives on Energy: Issues, Ideas, and Environmental Dilemmas*, 2d ed. (New York: Oxford University Press, 1978), p. 341; Gordon D. Friedlander, "1979 Nuclear Plant Survey," *Electrical World*, January 15, 1979, p. 71; and U.S. Department of Energy, Energy Information Administration, *Annual Report to Congress*, 1979, vol. 2: *Data*, p. 157.

cannot be overestimated. In May 1956 the AEC announced that starting in April 1962 it would pay a flat rate of $8 a pound for uranium ore concentrate. Thus the quantity of reserves has been defined for quite some time in terms of a price of $8 a pound. AEC purchases of ore from both foreign and domestic sources increased following the May 1956 annnouncement, reaching a peak in the early 1960s. Purchases ended in 1970. In the late 1960s the $8 price of uranium ore was dominant. The price in the 1970s increased rapidly, especially on the spot market. Discovery of $8 reserves per foot of drilling is declining and drilling costs per foot are increasing. The rapid increase in market prices in 1974 and

1975 did not result in an immediate supply response. The factors accounting for this have been summarized by J. Fred Facer, an official of the Energy Research and Development Agency:

Many people do not understand why uranium production has fallen during the last 18 months when spot prices for uranium were rising rapidly. Few realize that producers during that period were receiving an average price of about $8 per pound U_3O_8 in filling contracts made several years earlier. Although producers could have sold excess concentrate on the spot market, their mines were not geared to obtain additional ore on short notice. Instead, to supplement mill-feed the mines decreased their average mining cut-off grades and also started milling low-grade material (0.02 to 0.07 percent U_3O_8) set aside during the previous 15 to 20 years of mining. This resulted in a 10 percent increase in the tons of ore processed in 1974 over that processed in 1973, but a 10 percent decrease in the total amount of U_3O_8 produced. The mill production situation was further complicated in some areas because a few independent miners held ore in stockpile in anticipation of higher prices.[12]

Electric Power

The changing shares of the sources for electric power generation during 1946, 1959, 1971, and 1978 are shown in table A-12. The decline of the hydroelectric and coal shares was offset by the rapid increase through 1971 of oil and gas. Since 1971 the dominant changes have been the decline of the share of gas and the large increase in the nuclear share. Oil's share, however, has continued to increase and has the largest average annual increase of any fossil fuel. Another view of oil's role can be seen in the rapid increase of imports of residual and distillate fuel oil in the late 1960s (table A-5). Given the dramatic fossil fuel price changes, it is not surprising to see that the average retail electricity price increased from 1.96 cents per kilowatt-hour in 1973 to 3.97 cents per kilowatt-hour in 1979.[13]

A more detailed look at nuclear power's growing importance is shown in table A-13. The increases in share in electricity generation have slowed after 1977. The dramatic decline in April through June of 1979 reflects national concern about reactor safety following the Three Mile Island incident.

12. J. Fred Facer, Jr., "Production Statistics," in Energy Research and Development Administration, *Uranium Industry Seminar, Grand Junction, Colorado, 1975* (ERDA, 1976), p. 156.
13. *Monthly Energy Review,* April 1980, p. 90.

Table A-12. *Distribution of Electric Power Generation by Energy Source, Selected Years, 1946–78*

Energy source	Electric power output											
	Kilowatt-hours (millions)				Percent of total				Average annual percent increase			
	1946	1959	1971	1978	1946	1959	1971	1978	1946–59	1959–71	1971–78	1946–78
Hydroelectric	78,404	137,782	266,320	280,579	35.1	19.4	16.5	12.7	4.7	5.7	0.7	4.1
Coa¹	111,654	378,424	714,756	975,749	50.0	53.3	44.3	44.3	10.2	6.0	4.5	7.0
Oil	14,082	46,840	218,162	365,088	6.3	6.6	13.5	16.6	8.2	14.2	7.6	10.7
Gas	18,820	146,619	375,939	305,380	8.4	20.6	23.3	13.9	16.5	8.5	−2.9	9.1
Nuclear	...	188	37,899	276,403	...	*	2.3	12.5	...	44.0	32.8	...
Total	222,960	709,853	1,613,076	2,203,199	100.0	100.0	100.0	100.0	9.4	7.4	4.5	7.4

Sources: Richard L. Gordon, *U.S. Coal and the Electric Power Industry* (Johns Hopkins University Press for Resources for the Future, 1975), p. 21; and *Monthly Energy Review*, October 1979, p. 62.
* Less than 0.05 percent.

Table A-13. *Share of Nuclear Power in Total Electricity Generation, United States, 1972–79*

Percent

Year	Share
1972	3.1
1973	4.5
1974	6.1
1975	9.0
1976	9.4
1977	11.8
1978	12.5
1979 (January)	13.3
1979 (February)	13.9
1979 (March)	13.3
1979 (April)	10.8
1979 (May)	8.4
1979 (June)	8.6
1979 (July)	10.3

Sources: *Monthly Energy Review*, October 1979, p. 70; and ibid., October 1977, p. 42.

Index

707

dents, 612, 613; automobile efficiency standards, 571; data-collecting authority under, 515; and gasoline rationing, 606; and IEA, 511; and oil price decontrol, 612, 613; pricing provisions, 503–05
Energy Reorganization Act of *1974*, 480
Energy Research and Development Administration (ERDA), 435, 460, 480, 542, 550; conflict within, 541; MOPPS and, 590–91
Energy resources: CEA and planning of, 21–24; Interior Department studies of, *1947–49*, 36–40; interaction among, 337–38; National Resources Committee recommendations for, 6–8; nonconventional, 576–77; substitutability of, 49; TNEC study of monopoly in, 4–6, 8. *See also* Conservation, energy
Energy Resources Board, 480
Energy Resources Council, 480–81, 532, 533, 537, 541, 542
Energy Resources Finance Corporation (ERFCO), 518, 519
Energy Security Corporation, 625, 630
Energy Security Trust Fund, 614, 620
Energy storage, 487, 674, 682. *See also* Naval Petroleum Reserves
Energy Supply and Environmental Coordination Act of *1974*, 515, 534n, 538
Energy Tax Act, 585
Entitlements program, 454, 469–74, 498, 570
Environmental Protection Agency, 487; and coal, 593; and independent petroleum refineries, 430; and Iran response plan, 611
Environmental quality: coal and 396; costs of, 538, 539; energy policy implementation and, 651–53, 683–84; mandatory oil allocations and, 439; standards for, 404; trade-off between energy development and exploration and, 480; trade-off between energy requirements and, 558; utility interests and, 480
Enzer, Hermann, 477n, 479n
EPCA. *See* Energy Policy and Conservation Act
Eppen, Gary D., 425n
ERDA. *See* Energy Research and Development Administration
ERFCO. *See* Energy Resources Finance Corporation
Essley, Phillip L., Jr., 422n, 424, 429n, 430n, 431, 432, 465

Ettinger, Karl, 122–23
European Economic Community, 301
Evans, John K., 381
Evans, Rowland, Jr., 405n, 530n
Evins, Joe L., 361
Export-Import Bank, 225

Falck, Edward, 136n, 141, 179
FEA. *See* Federal Energy Administration
Federal Council for Science and Technology, 340, 341
Federal Energy Administration (FEA), 426n, 454, 509, 525, 542–43, 571; on aid to utilities, 521–22; conflicts within, 481–82, 541; energy policy contexts, 483; and entitlements program, 469–74; and EPCA, 504–05, 541; proposals, *1974*, 486, 492–93; regional town meetings on energy, 555
Federal Energy Administration Act of *1974*, 465, 469
Federal Energy Office (FEO), 454, 457, 458; and gasoline allocations, 455–56; price controls, 498; responsibilities, 451–52. *See also* Federal Energy Administration
Federal Energy Regulatory Commission, 598, 599
Federal government: demand stimulants by, *1954*, 217–18; and energy policy responsibilities, 398–400, 654; intervention in private energy markets, 63–64, 207, 221–22; Nixon reorganization plan for, 416–17; and power development responsibility, 269–70; role in atomic energy development, 274–77; as sponsor of energy production, 517–20
Federal Inter-Agency River Basin Committee, *1943*, 174, 185
Federal Power Commission (FPC), 2, 4, 174, 365, 400, 411; and electric power, 172, 184, 218; investigation of interstate natural gas regulation, 132; jurisdiction over private oil companies, 134; National Power Survey, *1962*, 327, 333, 335; natural gas regulation, 224, 261–62, 265, 320–23, 364, 509, 668; and PAD, 136; petroleum field price regulation, 221
Federal Trade Commission (FTC), 27, 65, 127, 400, 668; electric power regulation, 171; investigation of concentration in energy industry, *1973*, 443–44, 516–17, 569